yong-m

The Political Influence of the Military

The Political Influence
of the Military

A COMPARATIVE READER

Amos Perlmutter & Valerie Plave Bennett

NEW HAVEN AND LONDON
YALE UNIVERSITY PRESS *1980*

Published with assistance from
the Louis Stern Memorial Fund.

Designed by Thos. Whitridge
and set in Monotype Baskerville
Printed in the United States of America by
The Vail-Ballou Press, Binghamton, N. Y.
Published in Great Britain, Europe, Africa, and
Asia (except Japan) by Yale University Press,
Ltd., London. Distributed in Australia and
New Zealand by Book & Film Services, Artarmon,
N.S.W., Australia; and in Japan by Harper & Row,
Publishers, Tokyo Office.

Library of Congress Cataloging in Publication Data

Main entry under title:

The Political influence of the military.

   1. Sociology, Military. 2. Armed Forces.
3. Military government. 4. Despotism. I. Perlmutter,
Amos. II. Bennett, Valerie Plave.
U21.5.P63   322'.5   78-26154
ISBN 0-300-02230-1

Contents

Preface

After teaching and researching in the field of the military and politics for over two decades, we were surprised that no comprehensive reader on the subject existed. In all the 1,400 works written on the military (see Kurt Lang's bibliography, *Military Institutions and the Sociology of War*, compiled in 1972) there are only a few compendium readers, most of them symposia collections limited to particular aspects of the military (for example, revolutionary war) or to a single geographic area (for example, Latin America). We saw a clear need for an integrated reader to serve as an introduction to the study of the military in politics.

Most significantly, we knew of no compendium or reader that is organized around a major, all-inclusive theme that spans the spectrum of the field, covering, in addition to the military and politics, military sociology, the study of conflict, international relations, comparative politics, the politics of modernization, and developing countries.

Therefore, to fill the void, we offer this reader as a companion to Amos Perlmutter's *The Military and Politics in Modern Times*, published by Yale in 1977. Our aim was to select from the extensive literature (books, articles, monographs, and documents) pieces which integrally parallel the themes developed in *The Military and Politics*.

We hope we have compiled a reader that is theme oriented, comprehensive, relevant to a variety of disciplines, and of some lasting value. Particular care has been taken to balance landmark works in the literature with works that are less well known but maybe of significant interest.

The footnotes that appeared in the original publications of these essays have, with a few exceptions, been deleted.

Without the support, concern, and dedication of Marian Neal Ash, senior editor at Yale University Press, this reader would not have been published. We are most grateful for her patience and sagacity. Lawrence Kenney of Yale Press did an excellent job of editing, carefully weeding out errors and improving the flow of the reader.

Codelle Rosenberg of American University, who typed the messy manuscript we presented her, merits our thanks and recognition.

Michel Ross and Christianna Nicols, Perlmutter's students, managed splendidly the tedious work of seeking publishers' permission to reprint from the articles.

To the School of Government of the American University and especially to Dean Lee Fritschler and Dean Glynn Wood we are grateful for financial aid to complete the various stages of the typing of the manuscript.

To all our deepest thanks. Needless to mention, the responsibility for the vigor and the rigor of this enterprise is ours alone.

AMOS PERLMUTTER
Washington, D.C.

VALERIE PLAVE BENNETT
Waban, Massachusetts

Introduction

R EGARDLESS of the nature of the political culture in which he lives, the modern military officer is oriented toward maximizing his influence in politics and/or policy. In nations with highly institutionalized political systems, the military attempts to exert its influence over the making of national security policy. In nations with poorly institutionalized political structures, the government itself is the prize sought by the military; third-world officers turn to the political system as the arena in which to maximize their influence. Politicians in third-world countries fear the activism of officers, but lack the power to prevent the military from replacing them.

The professional soldiers of the Western powers and of the Soviet Union, lacking interventionist ambitions, have restricted their influence demands to those aspects of the political process which directly impinge on the military role. Although seeking to maximize his influence in policy making, the professional soldier allows institutional constraints on his demands. After having fought for policy and suffered defeat, the professional soldier accepts the limits imposed by the institutional policy process. Officers in poorly institutionalized polities, on the other hand, need not be restrained by the rebuffs of civilian leaders. When they are convinced that military rule would be far more salutary for society than civilian government, they can seek to exercise their authority over the entire political process, rather than limiting themselves to a single (though significant) aspect of policy making.

Today, the United States, the Soviet Union, the nations of Western Europe, the former British dominions (Canada, Australia, New Zealand), and Japan all enjoy civil-military relations notable for the primacy of the civilian over the military. But this was not always the case in Western Europe, where centuries were required for the emergence of the professional soldier and the pattern of relations between civil and military authority that has developed in the latter part of the twentieth century. However, in many less developed nations, ineffective governments frequently find that they are unable to control their military establishments, which come to exercise independent political power. We refer to such armies as *praetorian* (the term is borrowed from the Roman guard that made and unmade emperors).* Praetorianism is most readily observable in four parts of the world: the Middle East, Africa, Latin America, and Asia. In these areas military intervention frequently outweighs the electoral process as a means of regime change.

Finally, we identify the professional revolutionary soldier. He is neither a bureaucratic agent of the regime (as is the professional soldier) nor is he the menacing praetorian guard; he is rather an independent and coequal part of the government. Successful revolutionary movements foster the growth of the professional revolutionary soldier.

We will first examine the efforts of professional soldiers in industrial states to influence national security policy, turn then to the praetorian soldier and his approach to the political process, and, finally, examine the relationship between army, party, and state in postrevolutionary regimes.

THE PROFESSIONAL SOLDIER IN HISTORIC PERSPECTIVE

The classical professional soldier, prevalent in stable political systems, emerges when civilian authority establishes political control over the military. The professional military, controlled by civilians, rarely intervenes in politics; when interventions do occur, they are usually of short duration. The professional military is managerial, organizational, technical, and subordinate to higher political authority. Modern professionalism is also corporate; that is, it inspires a group consciousness and a tendency to form corporate professional associations. These associations have two purposes: to maintain the integrity of the profession's expertise and to defend its exclusivity. Military exclusivity includes military, rather than civilian, control over selection and promotion of officers and over such associations as veterans' groups. While modern professionalism is corporate, historically corporatism has been seen to undermine professionalism.

Military corporatism is, therefore, Janus-faced. Studies of Prussia and England can be used to illustrate the first Janus face of military corporatism —the way in which it hindered the development of the political order and undermined the integrity of military professionalism. France is an example of the other Janus face—corporate docility. In France, corporatism has enhanced professional docility and aloofness. In the USSR, a ruthless regime has hindered professionalism, and the military, lacking corporate protection, has suffered heavily in men, skill, and performance.

The history of the Prussian state has been closely linked with the emer-

*Frederick Watkins in *Encyclopedia of the Social Sciences*, s.v. "praetorianism."

gence of the modern Prussian army, which played an extraordinary role in a monarchy historically disposed to favor the military—a role that was strengthened by the reforms of 1807, which created the first modern, efficient, professional army in Europe. The military became the most favored client of the Prussian warlord. The reforms opened the ranks of the army to nonaristocrats and non-Prussians, resulting in a widening of the scope of military recruitment. Mutual reinforcement of status and court clientship made the military politically more powerful than any other party or group within the state.

The structure of the bureaucratized Prussian state and the nature of the monarchy's autocracy gave the military still greater privilege and power. The influence of the *Kriegsakademie* ("military college") was disproportionate to that of the liberal university. Political asymmetry between the military and the civil society and its political groups became more pronounced after the reforms when the powers of the general staff, the most effective instrument of the Prussian autocracy (far stronger than the bureaucracy), were broadened. Almost a century of protracted but steady military ascendancy (1807–90) and of monarchial and bureaucratic rule, contrasted with the retarded development of democratic, liberal, and associational institutions, left the military the undisputed power in the realm of defense and foreign policy.

Even after the Prussian army's imperialist orientations were tamed by Bismarck, the role of the military in Prussian-German nation-building was disproportionate to that of the civil authority. From 1890 to 1914, there were conspicuous weltpolitik (global) interests championed by both the kaiser and his politician-bureaucrats, and the military reached its zenith of power and influence. The middle classes were militarized under a regime dedicated to conquest or militarism, but militarism collapsed in 1919. But, again, the army "saved" the *Vernunftrepublik* of Weimar (the professor's republic) from the Communists.

Only Hitler's powerful, Nazi-dominated, civilian regime, outclassing the military in intrigue and violence, could have tamed this privileged group. Hitler used the modern instruments of power—propaganda, mob violence, and the Brown and the Black Shirts of the SA and the SS—to overwhelm the military establishment. He destroyed the Reichswehr's exclusive position and oriented its corporate identity toward a new warlord, this time a civilian, who led the military to war and to the annihilation of the proudest army in Europe.

The British army avoided both corporatism and professionalism longer than any of the European forces. Until the Napoleonic Wars, Britain had maintained a large naval fleet and a small army; but after 1804, she began recruiting a more substantial land force. Two years earlier, the Royal Military College had been established at Sandhurst. The officers were gentlemen who had purchased their commissions, and many were members of Parliament. The ranks were composed of long-serving volunteers, initially lured by the promise of bounty money. Conditions were ghastly and discipline harsh; only the desperate enlisted.

The only qualification required for a commission was the money to purchase it; promotions were similarly for sale, and officers were not obligated to attend Sandhurst. Michael Howard has written that

for the majority of officers, the regiment was an agreeable club, a uniformed extension of Bucks' or Boodles', and a campaign was equally an extension of the foxhunting with which they normally passed the winter. It was not a system which lent itself either to professional efficiency or to hierarchical subordination.

But there was scant civilian enthusiasm to reform the army. English politicians believed that an inefficient army which was inexorably linked to the ruling class was the best guarantee of constitutional rule. Wellington, who commanded the British army during and after the Napoleonic Wars, supported this viewpoint. An officer corps composed of gentlemen, Wellington argued, "prevented the growth of that most dangerous of all elements in society—a group of professional officers of humble birth with no fortune save their wits and their swords." Wellington resisted many of the efforts to professionalize and reform the army; so it was that the British army entered the Crimean War unprepared for the changes in the standards of performance that had taken place in her opponent's forces. As a result, in 1857 the staff course at the Royal Military College was separated and formed into a staff college; but, as Huntington has noted, this staff was concerned with administration and supply, not strategy and tactics. For the rest of the nineteenth century, the British army was split between those who wished to professionalize the military and those who believed in the gentlemanly ethos of Wellington.

The further disasters experienced in the Boer War led directly to the creation of the Army Council and to the establishment of the position of Chief of the General Staff in 1904. Two years later, Lord Haldane, the Secretary of State for War, in imitation of the German pattern, separated the functions of administration from those of training and command. The War Office was given responsibility for command and training, while administrative authority was placed in the territorial forces.

The continuance of the aristocratic tradition in the officer corps, while the government passed into the hands of the liberals, had similar (although milder) results to the events in Weimar Germany. In Ireland in 1913, the upper-class officers mutinied rather than carry out the policy of the liberal government.

Not until Kitchener took control of the War Office during World War I were British forces controlled by a civilian leader who believed in the Prussian concept of professionalism, rather than in Wellington's vision of the gentleman soldier.

The French military establishment, on the other hand, which managed to outlive several regimes it opposed, adopted the apolitical corporate attitude of being "above the battle" of politics. In actuality, it held the view, sometimes subterranean but often open, that republicanism was essentially a depraved form of government, and that only the military could preserve and protect the noble values of eternal France: duty, community, and familial integrity. The French version of corporatism claimed that the army represented the unity and continuity of historic France. The principle of exclusivity was regarded as noble, historically French, and an integral part of the military elite. The army's special duty was to guide France in those terrible areas of republicanism, democracy, and egalitarianism, and to protect France from politics—politics being foreign orientation.

The French army, like eternal France, was a community of solidarity where the clientship principle uniting junior and senior officers was personal, not structural—not an artificial, "modern" type of organization. The military was a source of human pride and French integrity. Its ideology remained that of the early nineteenth-century philosopher de Maistre: "Man's characteristic privilege is that the bond he accepts is not physical, but moral; that is, social. . . ." As Richard Griffith wrote, "The Vichy motto, *Travail, Famille, Patrie* . . . was to replace the Republic's *Liberté! Egalité! Fraternité!*"* While French corporatism enhanced military docility, it also revealed a bit of the first face of Janus—by conspiring against political orders which did not conform to the French military's concept of Frenchmen and France. In the words of Griffith,

A claim to be non-political often denotes a political interest. A dislike for "politics" and "politicking" may just mean that one disapproves of the democratic process. It is, in fact, one of the characteristics of a certain kind of right to make such protestations. The comments are usually sincere; nevertheless, they are usually *political*, without those who make them fully realizing it. Politics, in its narrower sense (which is the sense such people are using), is the *business* of politics, the wheeling-dealing, the deceit, the agreements, the alliances. Politics, in

*Richard Griffith, *Pétain* (New York: Doubleday, 1972), p. 160. (Italics added)

its wider sense, is the consideration of what is best for a community, and the means to achieve it. Most of those who disapprove of politics do so because they have strong ideas in the second area.*

The historic development of the Soviet armed forces diverged substantially from the Western European pattern. The Red Army, built on the ruins of the Imperial Russian Army after World War I, never acquired the autonomy of the French or German forces. New, politically motivated officers, imbued with the ethos of the revolution, acquired more influence than the prewar traditionally motivated officers who chose to remain in the army. Conflict raged between the "revolutionary" and the "professionally" minded for several decades. The Bolshevik party tried to ensure the primacy of the revolutionary over the professional by recruiting proletarian officers who would identify more with the Communist party than with the professional officers. Political officers (military commissars) were introduced into the army in 1918 in an effort to control the professional officers.

The rise of Stalin meant the destruction of the Soviet officer corps built up under Lenin and Trotsky, for Stalin, fearing that the military could threaten his own authority, systematically destroyed the autonomy of the Red Army. In Stalin's day, the military of the USSR was a frustrated professional group with little identity of its own. But, since the Second World War and the rise of the Soviet Union as a super power, the Russian government has had little choice but to uplift the status of the military, expand its role, and identify it with their own global plans. The modernization, rejuvenation, and technocratization of the military that began in 1965 had resulted by 1977 in military ascendance. The military did not rule the USSR, but it could influence defense and even foreign policy, which had formerly been the exclusive domains of the party and the government. Even if the military elites were as divided as other Russian political elites over global and imperial policies, military ascendance was nonetheless likely to have far-reaching consequences and to increase the newly acquired corporate satisfaction of the Red Army.

In all these nations, civilians rule while the military exercises influence in defense and foreign policy, and attends to its corporate interests. But in nations where the civilian government is neither effective nor institutionalized, the executive is unable to control the military.

THE PRAETORIAN SOLDIER

The collapse of executive power is a major precondition for praetorianism,

*Ibid.

defined as "a situation where the military class of a given society exercises independent power by virtue of an actual or threatened use of force."* In modern praetorian states, the military challenges civilian legitimacy while offering a new type of political authority.

In the twentieth century, a developing country is considered to be ripe for praetorianism when the civilian government comes to a standstill in its efforts to achieve such goals as unification, order, modernization, and urbanization. In a praetorian state, the motivation of the army to intervene is, therefore, clearly political. A state may be praetorian before its army is praetorian. An army becomes praetorian only when a small group of officers, a few key activists, succeed in propelling the military into politics. Praetorian armies may be of two ideal types: arbitrator armies, which have no political organization, but which have a status quo ideology; and ruler armies, which are politically organized, ideological, and eager to take a more permanent place in politics.†

In Africa and the Middle East, and in Latin America, praetorianism manifests itself in different forms. In the Arab Middle East, North Africa, and sub-Saharan Africa, the absence of stable and sustaining political institutions, structures, and procedures, and the bureaucratization of the military, have led to the rise of modern military praetorianism since the Second World War. In these areas, the successor to imperial control has not been parliamentary government, but rather the "man on horseback."

Egypt is the home of the first ruler-type military regime. Before the 1952 coup d'etat of Nasser and the Free Officers, military intervention usually resulted in the replacement of one group of civilian rulers by another group considered friendly to the military. The Egyptian coup heralded the arrival of the military to stay in politics, replete with political organization, ideological commitment, and disdain for civilian government. But the Egyptian pattern was not replicated in Africa. With rare exception, the military takeovers in Africa in the early 1960s were of the arbitrator type— intervention followed by a short period of military rule during which there was a moratorium on politics, followed in turn by a return to civilian rule.

Unlike the Middle East and Africa, Latin America has a long tradition of military involvement in politics. Because the Latin American armies participated actively in the wars for independence, the military did not immediately reject the state or the regime as the African and Arab military

*Amos Perlmutter, *The Military and Politics in Modern Times* (New Haven: Yale University Press, 1977), p. 89.

†Amos Perlmutter, "The Praetorian Army and the Praetorian State," *Comparative Politics* (April 1969): 392–94.

did. The early independence period was one of arbitrator-praetorianism. In the postrevolutionary era, the liberating armies decayed into lawless, violent brigands and bandits, leading to efforts at the end of the nineteenth century to professionalize the military. This professionalization came through a conscious political effort to maximize order; thus, the Latin American military was aware from the outset of the twentieth century that it was designed to achieve and to maintain political order. After 1950, military interventions in Latin America ceased to be of the arbitrator type, and came to be of the ruler type. In fact, by 1976 the classical liberator army could no longer be found in the intense mobilization politics of Latin America.

Unlike Latin American armies, which helped their nations gain independence, most Asian armies were created by colonial occupying powers. As a rule, Asian armies reflect both the multiethnic nature and the communal fragmentation of their respective societies. In the colonial era the imperial powers favored recruitment of certain ethnic groups—either for their supposed martial values or for their political docility. In the post-independence era national leaders manipulated recruitment and promotion patterns to favor the continuation in power of the existing governments. In several countries obvious efforts to ensure the tractability of the armed forces have led civilian governments to intervene actively in military recruitment and promotion patterns. These civilian forays into military affairs, if not accomplished with speed and finesse, only serve to exacerbate the illness they were meant to cure.

At least four Asian states exhibit the pattern by which colonial governments built armies along one ethnic bias and independent government sought to remake that pattern to serve its own interests. The Dutch raised colonial military forces in Indonesia with particular emphasis on recruitment from the outer island. Sumatra and Malaya were jointly administered by the Japanese army during World War II, with few ties to the army units in Java. The result of the Japanese military conquest was two armies, one Javanese and one Sumatran. And East Indonesia was completely ignored in this competition, being administered by the Japanese navy. These splits widened until they ripped apart in 1958, with a full-scale rebellion in Sumatra and the Celebes. At the height of the civil war "at least 30 rebel battalions were operating in guerrilla formations in Sumatra and 17 in the Celebes."* The revolt came to an end in 1961 and the rebel forces were reintegrated into the Indonesian army. After the peace settlement the

*Guy J. Pauker, "The Role of the Military in Indonesia," in *The Role of the Military in Underdeveloped Countries*, ed. John J. Johnson (Princeton, N. J.: Princeton University Press, 1962), p. 222.

Indonesian army was more divided by ideology than ethnicity. The growing role of the Communist party between 1959 and 1966 polarized the Indonesian army, although the officer corps was predominantly Javanese.

Imperial intervention took a different guise in Burma. According to Lucian Pye, it was the Karens, Chins, and Kachins who were assumed to be the martial tribes in British Burma. Immediately after World War II, when the Karens accounted for most of the officers and nearly half the soldiers, they revolted and mobilized to try to gain a separate Karen state. "Those Karen officers who did not join the insurrection were relieved of their commands and returned."* The Burman majority found it difficult to stem the tide of the communal demands put forward by the Karens, Shans, and Arakanese, but rather easy to alter the ethnic recruitment pattern after independence.

India is probably the best example of the colonial pattern of ethnic recruitment, both because the theory of recruitment was more highly refined on the subcontinent and because Indian soil was so receptive to these theories. India's caste-based culture recognized a warrior caste—the Kshatriya. In addition to the Kshatriya caste in all ethnic groups, entire ethnic groups were considered "martial races" who fought for and with the British Raj. Thus it was that entire ethnic groups, such as the Pathans, Dogras, Gurkhas, Sikhs, and Juts, became soldiers while the Bengalis and Kashmires were ignored until the intense manpower demands of World War I. But the first soldiers to be demobilized were those belonging to the nonmartial classes. The same expansion pattern was repeated in World War II, and for many years after independence little was done to alter the ethnic composition of the officer corps. But after 1965 there was a rethinking of recruitment criteria and the Minister of Defense was able to declare that "we are all Kshatriyas now."†

The tensions generated within the army itself and between the army and the civilian leaders in Asia are a reflection of the multiethnic nature of these societies. But patterns of civil-military relations and the primacy of soldiers or politicians are not a result of these conflicts. Patterns of civil-military relations grow out of the wider political culture. Indonesia and Burma have military governments. Ceylon and India are unique in the postcolonial world, having an unbroken record of competitive elections and civilian leadership. But in none of these nations has the military been im-

---

*Lucian Pye in *The Role of the Military in Underdeveloped Countries*, ed. John J. Johnson (Princeton, N. J.: Princeton University Press, 1962), p. 236.

†Stephen P. Cohen, *The Indian Army: Its Contribution to the Development of a Nation* (Berkeley: University of California Press, 1971), p. 190.

mune from the ethnic conflicts that have rent the society at large. In Asia, armies have been neither more modern nor more national than the civil society, but neither have they let ethnic tensions permanently disrupt the cohesiveness of the army.

One of the few developing countries whose army is clearly *not* praetorian is that of the People's Republic of China; the soldiers of the People's Liberation Army may best be described as professional revolutionaries.

THE PROFESSIONAL REVOLUTIONARY SOLDIER AND THE PRINCIPLE OF EXCLUSIVITY

The most distinguishing characteristic of the revolutionary soldier is that he will not defend the principle of exclusivity, as will the historical professional and praetorian soldiers. He is anticorporate or noncorporate. Whereas the motivation of the corporate professional is often defensive, the political motivation of the revolutionary soldier is integrated with a revolutionary movement. The revolutionary soldier is dedicated to mass military mobilization; he represents no social class. Successful revolutionary soldiers are not necessarily those trained to be professional soldiers; lateral integration of other professional skills into the military can introduce valuable innovations in military organizational format, strategy, and tactics.

The main type of revolutionary soldier is found in the Maoist Chinese People's Liberation Army (PLA). In China, the PLA has remained the instrument of the ideological movement, the home of the revolution. The PLA is professional, but not concerned with historical corporate professionalism. Because the PLA is as much an embodiment of the revolution as the Chinese Communist party (CCP) and the Maoists, it needs no corporate shield against a "revolutionary" China. Even in the Great Proletarian Cultural Revolution (GPCR) of 1966–69, the PLA did not intervene in politics against the wishes of the political leadership, but rather was brought into the political arena by the civilian rulers. Seen in this perspective, the chances for praetorianism appear slim in China.

The Israeli Defense Force (IDF) is another type of professional revolutionary army. In contrast to other states in the Middle East, Israel is not a praetorian state. It developed as a nation-in-arms to meet an external threat, and even though citizenship in Israel is attainable only through service in the military, the military is not a career, but rather a system of permanent reserve. The Israeli professional soldier is also a revolutionary in the sense that his professionalism is untainted by corporatism. Civilian control over the military persists, but the IDF is not a political partner of the regime as is the PLA in China.

THE PROFESSIONAL SOLDIER TODAY

In nonpraetorian states, the military organization is motivated not to replace the civilian regime but to play a key role (even to supersede other groups) in the making of national security policy. The concept that professionalism removes the military from politics is derived from the classical tradition of administrative theory, among others, which is built on the premise that politics can be separated from administration; i.e., that policy making (the responsibility of politically elected officials) is distinguished from policy implementation (the responsibility of appointed officials).* This conceptual distinction was once advanced to explain the separation of bureaucrats from politics, but the theory no longer holds. The new administrative theory is fusionist; i.e., it recognizes that bureaucracy and politics, government and administration experts, and politicians are all symbiotically connected. This inherently pluralistic notion of politics argues that power in society is diffuse and that advanced societies are characterized by highly complex and highly differentiated organizations that hyphenate experts and nonexperts, policy makers and policy implementers.

Richard Betts advances an interesting division between two types of administrative values: classical administrative values whose priorities are efficiency, whose administrative style is command-obedience, and whose political orientation is supposed to be neutral; and revisionist values whose aim is political control, whose administrative process is negotiations, and whose involvement in politics is deep.†

The authorities of the modern industrial state have imbued the professional military organization in recent times with a sense of belonging. The military professional in the industrialized state is highly skilled in the sciences of management. He understands that he *shares* with the authorities not only the conception of strategy and the maintenance of the bureaucratic hierarchical orientation, but also participation in the making of national security policy. Thus, antagonism between the military professionals and the civilian bureaucrats is partially mitigated. In fact, the nineteenth-century distinction between professionals and bureaucrats has almost disappeared. Concomitantly, the virtues of bravery and discipline have now been replaced by the skills of management and strategy.

In the post–World War II era military regimes were established only in weak states; the coup zone is composed totally of Latin American, African,

*Dwight Waldo, *The Administrative State* (Ronald Press, 1946).
†Richard Betts, *Soldiers, Statesmen and the Decision to Go to War: 1945–1975* (Cambridge: Harvard University Press, forthcoming).

Asian, and Islamic independent states. There are only three European states in the *successful* coup zone: Greece, Spain, and Portugal. And none of the super and major world powers are dominated by military regimes. What is remarkable is that in all the super powers and the major powers (China, Western Europe, and Japan) the function of the military was integrated into a system of national security.

Samuel P. Huntington first drew attention to the fusionist theory of military and national security policy makers, and to the emergence of the military as an influential political group in the making of national security policy.* Thus, in the changed political conditions after World War II, the strategy of deterrence changed both the external and domestic environments of states. The strategy of deterrence propelled the creation of the national security state. Strategic decisions brought about structural changes in both the military organization and the organization of security, according to Huntington. National security policy had been previously made by diplomats, but in the postwar world it became primarily a matter of negotiations conducted among the different executive agencies—both civilian and military.

In the Soviet Union, despite three decades of Stalinist suppression, the military has become very influential in the making and implementing of national security policy. The present role played by the Soviet military in national security affairs is closely linked to their trials attendant to maintaining the integrity of their professionalism. The Soviet military was able to achieve professional autonomy only through its participation in the making of defense policy, and by conceiving the doctrine of deterrence. Nevertheless, although the Soviet military appears to hold a predominant position vis-à-vis civilians in the national security arena (especially in weapon system procurement policy), they are not the *single* or decisive voice—as cases such as the invasion of Czechoslovakia in 1968 demonstrate. The Soviet military feared the consequences of intervention in Czechoslovakia, while the civilian national security policy makers placed long-range foreign policy goals above the corporate interest of the army.† While striving for high professional standards for the Soviet army, the party insists on maintaining political control.

Whether or not they are in total agreement with the policy outcomes, high-ranking officers in postindustrial society regard the making of national security policy as more important than the protection of corporate interests and exclusivity. This is a dramatic change in the orientation of the professional soldier.

*Samuel P. Huntington, *The Common Defense: Strategic Programs in National Politics* (New York: Columbia University Press, 1961).

†John R. Thomas, "Soviet Foreign Policy and the Military," *Survey*, 17, 80, 1971, pp. 129–31.

THE PRAETORIAN SOLDIER IN POLITICS

The military's motivation to intervene is primarily political. Students of the coup d'etat have advanced several hypotheses and causal inferences purporting to "explain" coups and regime replacement. The dominant explanation, according to William Thompson, is the weakness of the system. "Much of the indirect theorizing on military coups," writes Thompson, "is concerned with the question of regime vulnerability. It is by far the dominant concern in the 'military politics' literature."* Although this is a valid generalization, it is an insufficient explanation for the pull-down of regimes by military coups.

THE DECLINE OF AUTHORITY

There is practically no student of the military in politics who has failed to propose the decline of authority as an explanation or a cause for military coups. Although the literature is replete with empirical and other "proofs," the fact remains that not *all* declining authorities are pulled down by military coups; and some are removed by alternative civilian elites, rather than by the military. All the great revolutions since 1789 have resulted in the overthrow of civilian regimes without accompanying military coups. In some political systems, coups may be the only way to replace regimes, but they are merely one of several means of removing an ineffective civilian government. Numerous changes of regimes are not designed or propelled by the military. But the military has played a key role in the formation of most African and Asian military regimes since 1945, and in Latin American regimes since the turn of the century. Nonetheless, the cases of Portugal, Spain after the death of Franco, and the Russian and Chinese revolutions serve to illustrate situations in which the decline of authority did not result in the army alone overthrowing the system. In these instances when the army did act, it served as an *instrument* of the civilian revolutionaries (as in the cases of China and the USSR), or in *coalition* with an *established* political party or group, as in Portugal. In the period between the wars, all the Eastern European regimes (with the exception of Czechoslovakia and, to some extent, Yugoslavia) were pulled down by military coups; and the resulting weak regimes were later overthrown by Communist parties with the assistance of the USSR after 1945. Even though numerous weak regimes have been overthrown by military coups, the decline-of-authority explanation for military intervention is insufficient. It explains only the praetorian

*William Thompson, "Explanation of the Military Coups" (Diss., University of Washington, 1972), pp. 82–97.

nature of the political system; i.e., regime vulnerability may be exploited by any organized political force, one of which might be the military.

Authority, the argument goes, is linked to social cohesion, and the military tends to intervene in its absence. The world depression did not bring about the rise of praetorianism in the capitalist world, but it did help weaken the authority in low-institutionalized regimes, which were eventually replaced by military regimes in Latin America and Eastern Europe. But the military regimes emerged only because the military was now relatively more powerful and possessed a tradition of political activism, not because of socio-economic dislocations. But the explanation of why the *military* and *not another group* replaces a "declining authority" does not stem so much from the political motivation of the military (which, indeed, exists) as it does from the *relative* power of the military in regimes whose authority has declined.

Let us now turn to the dynamics of military coups themselves. It can be posited that the military replaces a civilian regime when the military is the most cohesive and *politically* the best organized group at a given time in a political system; the military intervenes and succeeds in the *absence* of relatively more powerful opposition. The existence of a countervailing force is likely to delay or deter military intervention. The presence of French troops in several francophone West African countries in the years following independence helped stave off military intervention in those areas. And for more than a decade, the Egyptian Free Officers hesitated to intervene, afraid of a combined Court-British retaliation. Only after the Free Officers no longer feared the British, realizing that the Court and the Wafd Party were weak, did they dare to intervene.

Military coups and military intervention in politics are conducted by political activists in the military organization who are frequently members of political clubs and conspiratorial cabals within the military organization. These officers do not consider the military as their life's only career and harbor present or future political ambitions. Political ambition seems a more powerful explanation for intervention than age, rank, seniority, and corporatism.

The politicization of a significant segment of the officer corps may derive from three sources: (1) a few politically or ideologically committed officers, or civilians who infiltrate the military in search of army collaborators for a "civilianistic" coup; (2) a new weltanschauung, such as fascism, socialism, or communism; and (3) dramatic events that tend to politicize entire generations, such as anticolonial struggles, independence movements, or economic disasters. In turn, military coups can run the gamut organizationally from a conspiracy of a small group of officers who consult no outsiders to a loose coalition of the political activists within the army and their civilian allies. But regardless of the organizational style, military coups are political actions connected with the political designs of the activists, the conspiratorial clubs, and the politically ambitious officers.

The decision to intervene, i.e., to *execute* the coup, is both political and tactical, depending on factors internal and external to the coup group. Internal factors include the maturity of the cabal, the degree of its political cohesiveness and commitment, and the nature of its leadership; factors external to the conspirators may include the strength of the authority to be replaced, the status of other groups plotting against the government, and political events such as elections.

For every conspiracy that becomes a coup d'etat, dozens may actually be plotted; most conspiracies never reach fruition because the plotters are discovered or fail to carry through their plans. Occasionally there are several conspiracies under way at the same time within a single military establishment. In the Greek coup of 1967, the conspirators were galvanized into action by their discovery that other officers were also planning to intervene.

Immediately after intervening successfully, the conspirators must attempt to consolidate their authority. The process of coup legitimization, which begins as soon as regimes are replaced, depends upon the nature of the conspiratorial organization. If the intervention was carried out without civilian support, the military begins to search for political allies and kindred souls among the opposition, and occasionally ·among the disgruntled or the opportunists of the recent fallen regime. If, however, the coup group was a civil-military coalition, a political struggle between the military activists and their civilian allies is likely to ensue because of the efforts of the former to replace or dominate the latter.

The institutions through which the military governs are frequently different from those that existed under the preceding civilian regime. The political institutions and structures that military regimes have a propensity to squash at the onset of their rule include the legislative, the electoral, and the judicial. On the other hand, the favorite institutions which the military advances, cultivates, and reforms are usually the executive and the single political party. The negative attitude toward electoral politics, parliamentary and legislative systems, and the judiciary characteristic of the military stems from a variety of sources; nevertheless, the outcome is inevitably authoritarian government.

Military regimes emulate authoritarian executive systems, single-party states, or nonparty systems. The classical explanation for this authoritarian style is that the military regimes are established in ex-colonial countries

American and Middle Eastern pattern. Nationalism predated military intervention by at least a decade and the military ousted the nationalists, who actually had inherited the colonial state, the liberals having been defeated at the polls during the transfer of power.

With the passage of time and the accumulated failures of civilian politicians, the military has gained confidence at the game of rulership. Today, even if the military has failed to form a political party or lacks an ideology, military governors rarely think of themselves as actors with "walk-on" parts on the political stage. They intervene to govern and stay; frequently, they proclaim deep ideological commitments. After a decade, their ideological motivation has dissipated and their political organization survived, merely because they are the best organized interest group in weak societies. The view of the corporate praetorian as an armed trade unionist is not entirely inappropriate.

The attitude of the soldiers in mufti toward the political process is extremely ambivalent. While desiring to maximize political support, most, if not all, military regimes suffer from an inability to tolerate political participation. In the final analysis, military regimes are authoritarian and therefore incapable of efficient mass mobilization and sustained political institutionalization.

Almost without exception military regimes restrict acts of participation, primarily out of fear of losing control of the resulting political conflict. As a result, those institutions that articulated and aggregated interest during the previous civilian regime tend to atrophy; and the process of interest aggregation is incomplete. In praetorian states the only "representative" institution often permitted is the military party, but the party's function is not to represent interests but rather to *restrict* electoral participation and political representation.

Regardless of the aspirations of the praetorian soldier, he inevitably finds himself unable to build regime support without endangering the control of the military over government and society. Although the praetorian attempts to replace the political process with political rhetoric, he is unlikely to be successful in the long run. Since this rhetoric may have a revolutionary flavor, most Latin American and Middle Eastern, and some African militaries appear revolutionary on the surface. Their *pronunciamientos* approximate the language of modern revolutions, of nationalism, of socialism, and of modernization. But in reality praetorians are *abortive* revolutionaries. Operating in a praetorian environment, they merely reflect the authority of their weapons. If they genuinely hold revolutionary aspirations, their aspirations frequently clash with their corporate orientation, which overwhelms all other beliefs. And if corporatism does not diminish the commitment to progressive ideals, then the pressing problems of day-to-day government will, and over time only the rhetoric remains. Social mobilization comes to be viewed as a threat rather than a blessing to the praetorian soldier. A comprehensive social and political revolution is considered a danger to the military organization, for it might annihilate the corporate soldier.

CHARACTERISTICS OF THE PROFESSIONAL REVOLUTIONARY SOLDIER

The only type of soldier that has achieved professional proficiency and pride, as well as a high status in his society and state, is the professional revolutionary soldier. The existence of the revolutionary soldier demonstrates that professionalism and corporatism are not necessarily linked, and that one is not needed to advance the other. A professional stance does not necessarily prevent intervention; nor does a corporate orientation (as the case of Nazi Germany illustrates) necessarily bring about intervention. High professional performance and corporate pride have been enhanced by the least corporate-oriented of all soldiers—the revolutionaries. The autonomy of the military organization in Israel and China has guaranteed both its high professionalism and its political subordination.

The revolutionary soldier is more ideological than the professional or the praetorian. His ability to cope with the revolutionary environment and his influential role in the realm of foreign and defense policy are partial explanations of his failure to intervene. He is subordinate to a movement, party, or regime that is certainly more resilient than the military, even if the latter is a major factor in the making of the revolution, as was true in China and North Vietnam. The PLA has been as much a nation-building institution as the Chinese Communist party. The IDF has been not only an instrument of Zionism, but a Zionist-oriented military. The military in China, Israel, and Cuba, however different one from the other, have participated in the full life of the revolution, the nation, and the society.

While the historical professional soldier in the West has been declining, the revolutionary soldier has been on the rise elsewhere. The classical professional, losing his prestige in a complex society, has not inspired the best of the nation to join the military. Neither the West European nor the American society-at-large has served as a reservoir for future military leadership; the more industrious and talented have joined the civic society, but in China, and especially Israel, the opposite has been true.

In Israel, the army has drawn on the entire society for manpower. Universal military obligation has required every man to serve in the armed forces for at least three years. The high prestige of the Israeli army has meant that the officers have been the flower of the country. As a "nation-in-arms," the whole society has been in uniform during crises, as in May-June 1967, and again in October 1973. The professional army has been small, with fewer than 100,000 members, but it has been constantly revitalized by the inclusion of well-motivated soldiers who are not planning life-term military careers. The army's professionalism, as high among veterans as among junior regulars, has combined with a close identification between people and army to produce a military force whose influence on society and politics has been considerable. In the case of China, the military as a revolutionary leadership institution and the officer as a model personality have propelled the nation toward the goal aspired to by the CCP, China's guiding movement. In a certain sense, the military has been even more autonomous in China than in Israel, but it has not rejuvenated itself.

Because the Chinese Communist party was almost destroyed in the 1920s and survived only because the army survived, the party has treated the army as coequal partners in the revolution. The revolutionary generation of leaders (both party and army) still holds power in China. The Chinese officer corps is a bastion of the gerontocracy, while Israeli officers of the revolution have long since retired.

The archetypical political revolution of modern times is a revolution conducted by socialist political parties. Struggling against an imperial power or a traditional regime can be very dangerous. To accumulate political power and eventually to win complete power, the Socialist party in Israel and the Communist party in China created military forces closely tied to and highly controlled by the party. In Israel, the socialists' best organized Zionist political party established the first Jewish self-defense groups—the Haganah. In China, after the defeat of the CCP in 1927, the party leaders retreated to the countryside and organized the PLA. It was at the bosom of the PLA that the CCP was revived; the link between army and party was never broken and remains intact yet. The growth of the Jewish community in Palestine resulted in the eventual nationalization of the military after the failure of the challenge from the revisionist and center Zionist political parties; the Haganah became the basis of the future Israeli Defense Force. In Israel, the Haganah tradition, spearheaded by the Palmach, its officer corps (which mainly consisted of the kibbutz-socialist oriented officers), united the legacy of professionalism with a revolutionary and nationalist ideology.

The PLA, however, became a Chinese Communist party instrument. This turn of events might have been predicted on the basis that in Bolshevik theory, the *Parteistaat* should dominate other institutions, including the military.* Although the later development of the PLA and Haganah-Palmach took radically different courses, the commitment of Haganah Socialist and Communist nationalist officers left its impact both on the type of professional soldier nurtured and on the nature of civil-military relations in the two nations. The revolutionary soldier did not need to become corporate or interventionist in either revolutionary China or Jewish Palestine, where the soldier's participation in politics was extensive and tolerated by the civilian leadership. The function of the revolutionary is to participate in and to serve the party and the regime, simultaneously. Thus, participation of the military in the political process is tolerated more in revolutionary societies than in stable political orders.

While the military in postrevolutionary society is more highly politicized than the professional soldiers in the West, the revolutionaries' insistence that they be equal partners in the making of national security policy is not perceived by civilian bureaucrats as illegitimate. The diffuseness of the boundaries between the civil and the military is acknowledged by both soldiers and politicians.

However, the dilemma of the military in postrevolutionary times is that the revolutionary soldiers must be politically disarmed and professionally re-armed. The transition for revolutionary soldiers is difficult, especially for those officers who become romantic and nostalgic for the heady revolutionary days. Soldiers, like party ideologists who find themselves bored and impatient with the mundane chores of government, become political liabilities for the regime. On the whole, the government finds alternative roles for them; but if they insist on continued military service, they must submit to the professionalization and routinization process that engulfs the military in the postrevolutionary period. Ideally, the postrevolutionary army should become routinized, depoliticized, and professionalized. Postindependence Israel has succeeded in this more than China. Even after the GPCR and the turmoil surrounding the death of Mao Tsetung and the struggle for succession between Mao's heirs, the radicals, and their pragmatic antagonists, the army-party symbiosis appears to be still intact, the PLA continues to play a key mediator role.† But the lingering appeal of the revolutionary ethos for some officers means that the final chapter in the post-Maoist political struggle has not yet been written. Yet we have seen and we expect to see further proof of the routinization of the

*Leonard Shapiro, The Origin of Communist Autocracy (Cambridge: Harvard University Press, 1966).

†Ellis Joffe, "The Chinese Army after the Cultural Revolution: The Effects of Intervention," The China Quarterly (July/September 1973): 410–77.

Chinese revolutionary soldier and the eventual incorporation of the Chinese military into a more stable, pragmatic, and less revolutionary China. In Israel, the revolutionary soldier achieved his peak in 1948–49. In the last quarter century, while the prestige of the Israeli soldier in his society has remained high, the training and military functions of the IDF have become more professional and routinized. The Revolution is *not* permanent.

PART I

The Professional Soldier

PROFESSIONALISM AND CORPORATISM

OFFICERSHIP is an occupation which requires advanced and specialized training. Professional training calls for the maintenance of reasonable standards according to the rules of the profession, exercised either by the concerted opinion of its peers or by the organization that patronizes the profession. On the whole, the maintenance of standards is the preoccupation of the professionals themselves; in addition to control over training, a profession demands control over performance. Internal control is exercised by professionals, who by virtue of their specialized training exert considerable authority in relations with their clients. But in some cases, control may also be externally exercised by the profession's clients. In the case of the modern military organization, external control is conducted by the state, its client. (Although, as we shall find in the cases of praetorian and revolutionary soldiers, the professionals could also serve clients other than the state—e.g., the party, the ethnic group, the tribe, or the military organization itself.)

The two key internal qualitative variables of military professionalism are control and skill.

CONTROL

The military is controlled on two organizational levels. From within there is a colleague group which oversees internal cohesion of the officer corps as professionals and as a social group. The colleague group sets standards for the personal behavior and professional conduct of the officer corps. The external source of control and of discipline is the hierarchy of authority. Success in professional skills and conduct is judged by the standard of how well directives from above are followed. Professional status and advancement are derived from the officer's behavior on the two levels at which his conduct is judged, as a professional and a bureaucrat.

SKILLS

Historically, the most valued attributes of the professional soldier were

bravery and discipline. But today's professional must be as much a bureaucrat as a hero, and he must have acquired the modern skills of management
and of strategy. Whatever damage it may have done to the romantic image
of the soldier, corporate professionalism has widened the social and political
horizons of the military. As a professional group it must preserve group
standards and values, which are, on the whole, conservative, protectionist,
and exclusive.

As bureaucrats, the military professionals are closely linked to the modern
nation-state, which is oriented toward the employment of modern technology in both the fields of management and strategy. The potential clash is,
therefore, between the self-imposed standards of the peer group, who on
the whole are conservative and exclusivist, and the bureaucratic managerial orientation of the modern nation-state, which is technological and
scientific. Integrating new skills is a challenge to the corporate identity of
military professionals, who espouse continuity and tradition, and abhor
innovation. Nevertheless, the technological revolution in management and
strategy has led to the adoption of new skills by the military. A more subtle
change brought on by this revolution has been the politicization of the
military.

The propensity of the military professional to intervene (in politics and
in policy formation) is linked to his corporate (internal) and bureaucratic
(external) roles and orientations; as a corporate body the military organization strives for internal control of the profession and for the protection of
the military establishment from external political manipulation. In order
to achieve corporate goals the military must try to influence the political
process which hurls the military into the political arena. In addition, as a
bureaucratic profession the military is in politics in the sense that it is a key
partner with civilian politicians and bureaucrats in the formation and implementation of national security policy.

In the case of the military establishment professional and bureaucratic
responsibilities converge. As a professional the soldier is responsible to his
client, the state (the sense of professional "calling"), while as a bureaucrat
he is responsible to the *government*. In both cases the modern soldier is corporate (exclusive), bureaucratic (hierarchical), and professional (mission-
oriented).

The managerial and organizational revolution in modern officers' skills
encourages the professional military to strive for autonomy and therefore
to establish a unique corporate identity in order to triumph in the bureau-
cratic-political struggle so characteristic of modern organizations.

In national security systems where some functions of the military have
been taken over by political leaders, professional academics, and business

and industrial managers, the challenge to corporatism is particularly acute. In view of the fact that the category "professionalism" will be extensively used in this reader, it is imperative that a clear and concise definition of the concept of a profession be firmly established. After all, the conduct, method, character, status, and standards of the modern military are judged by their professional claims. N. Elias's entry, "Professions," in *A Dictionary of the Social Sciences* (1964), argues that true professionals possess considerable authority in relations to "clients." Talcott Parsons, for instance, writes that the professions, a structural and cultural innovation of the modern West, are systems of learning and of status. "Professional men are neither 'capitalists' nor 'workers,' nor are they typically governmental administrators or 'bureaucrats.'" The military profession belongs to the category of "applied" professionals, which Parsons says are represented by law and medicine. Parsons, a social theorist, was not entirely aware of the importance of the military as both a modern corporate profession and a political bureaucracy; he did not even identify the military as a modern profession and ignored the bureaucratic nature of the military profession.

TALCOTT PARSONS

Professions

The development and increasing strategic importance of the professions probably constitute the most important change that has occurred in the occupational system of modern societies. The growth of the professions has brought to prominence a set of occupations which never figured permanently in the ideological thinking that, after having crystallized in the late nineteenth century, has tended to dominate public discussion in the twentieth. Professional men are neither "capitalists" nor "workers," nor are

From Talcott Parsons, International Encyclopedia of the Social Sciences, vol. 12 (New York: Macmillan and Free Press, 1968), s.v. "professions," by permission of the publishers.

they typically governmental administrators or "bureaucrats." They certainly are not independent peasant proprietors or members of the small urban proprietary groups.

As for so many categories of social status, the boundaries of the group system we generally call the professions are fluid and indistinct. There are some borderline groups whose professional status is, for one reason or another, equivocal. However, the core criteria within the more general category of occupational role seem to be relatively clear. First among these criteria is the requirement of formal technical training accompanied by some institutionalized mode of validating both the adequacy of the training and the competence of trained individuals. Among other things, the training must lead to some order of mastery of a generalized cultural tradition, and do so in a manner giving prominence to an *intellectual* component—that is, it must give primacy to the valuation of cognitive rationality as applied to a particular field. The second criterion is that not only must the cultural tradition be mastered in the sense of being understood, but skills in some form of its use must also be developed. The third and final core criterion is that a fully fledged profession must have some institutional means of making sure that such competence will be put to socially responsible uses. The most obvious uses are in the sphere of practical affairs, such as the application of medical science to the cure of disease. However, the skills of teaching and of research in the "pure" intellectual disciplines are also cases of such use. . . .

Another sociologist, Bernard Barber, did identify the military as a profession, but assigned it a rather inferior position in the hierarchy of modern professions. Professional behavior, according to Barber, is defined in terms of: (1) high degree of generalized and systematic knowledge, (2) primary orientation toward community interest, (3) high degree of self-control and internalized ethic, and (4) a system of rewards. Barber does not consider concepts of life style, corporate solidarity, and socialization structures and processes as the professions' *differentia specifica*.

BERNARD BARBER

Toward a Definition of the Professions

Theoretical and methodological consensus is not yet so great among sociologists that there is any absolute agreement on the definition of "the professions." And of course among the public at large the debate over the boundary between "professional" and "nonprofessional" continues, a debate which is kept going by the fact

From Bernard Barber, Daedalus 92 (Fall 1963): 670–73, by permission of the editors.

that these terms carry an important assignment of differential occupational prestige. Still, considerable progress toward a definition has been made, and this section of the paper seeks to summarize that progress.

A sociological definition of the professions should limit itself, so far as possible, to the *differentia specifica* of professional behavior. For example, concepts like style of life, corporate solidarity and socialization structures and processes, which apply to all other groups as well as to professional ones, are not the *differentia specifica*.

There is no absolute difference between professional and other kinds of occupational behavior, but only relative differences with respect to certain attributes common to all occupational behavior. Some occupational behavior, seen in the light of these attributes, which we discuss below, is fully professional; other behavior is partly professional; and some can be thought of as barely or not at all professional. On this view, for example, there may be some professional elements in some kinds of business behavior. Similarly, on the same view, the medical profession is more professional than the nursing profession, and the medical doctor who does university research is more professional than the medical doctor who provides minor medical services in a steel plant. Professionalism is a matter of degree.

Professional behavior may be defined in terms of four essential attributes: a high degree of generalized and systematic knowledge; primary orientation to the community interest rather than to individual self-interest; a high degree of self-control of behavior through codes of ethics internalized in the process of work socialization and through voluntary associations organized and operated by the work specialists themselves; and a system of rewards (monetary and honorary) that is primarily a set of symbols of work achievement and thus ends in themselves, not means to some end of individual self-interest. Some amplification of these four attri-

butes will be useful.

All occupational behavior has some degree of knowledge as one of its attributes. As the phrase "the learned professions" vividly signifies, a high degree of generalized and systematic knowledge early became one of the commonly used defining characteristics of professional behavior.

Its relation to individual and community interest is another attribute of all occupational performance. Since generalized and systematic knowledge provides powerful control over nature and society, it is important to society that such knowledge be used primarily in the community interest. Where such knowledge exists, orientation primarily to community rather than individual interest is an essential attribute of professional behavior. Individual self-interest is, of course, not utterly neglected in professional behavior, but is subserved *indirectly*.

Social control depends in part, obviously, upon substantive understanding of the behavior to be controlled. In the case of behavior characterized by a high degree of knowledge, the requisite understanding is available in full measure only to those who have themselves been trained in and apply that knowledge. It follows that some kind of self-control, by means of internalized codes of ethics and voluntary in-groups, is necessary. In the realms of professional behavior, such codes and such associations for the setting and maintaining of standards proliferate. Further controls on professional behavior exist, of course, in the informal agencies of public opinion and in governmental-legal agencies. But these other forms of social control are less important than in nonprofessional areas.

Money income, general prestige and specific honors or symbols of achievement are among the different forms of social reward for occupational performance. Since money income is a more appropriate reward for individual self-interest, and since prestige and honors are more appropriate for community interest, these latter types of reward are relatively more important in professional than in nonprofessional behavior. The actual reward system in the professions tends to consist, therefore, in a combination of prestige and titles, medals, prizes, offices in professional societies, and so forth, together with sufficient monetary income for the style of life appropriate to the honor bestowed. Although the professions are not so well paid, on the whole, as equal-ranking business roles in American society, all studies show that the public ranks the pro-

fessions at the top of the occupational prestige hierarchy and that professionals themselves are more satisfied with their work-rewards than are other occupational groups.

These four essential attributes define a scale of professionalism, a way of measuring the extent to which it is present in different forms of occupational performance. The most professional behavior would be that which realizes all four attributes in the fullest possible manner. Justice of the United States Supreme Court, or professor of physics and Nobel Prize winner in a distinguished university, would be defined as very highly professional roles. A $100,000-a-year vice president in charge of legal affairs for a middle-size business corporation would be clearly less professional in these terms. And a $6000-a-year school teacher would be ranked as less professional still. . . .

We identified the military as a formal modern organizational structure; modern man acts within organizational constraints. Organizations are of various kinds, have diverse aims, vary in size and complexity, and display different characteristics. The military is a social and formal organization, according to Blau and Scott, *Formal Organizations*. The military is also a complex organization with several social objects. One could classify formal organizations into several basic models of organization found in modern society where the military model is one that emphasizes a fixed hierarchy of authority and status. Blau and Scott typologize the military organization as a commonweal organization, i.e., one whose prime beneficiary is the public-at-large.

PETER BLAU AND W. RICHARD SCOTT

The Military as Commonweal Organization

It is not always meaningful to speak of the clients of an organization, since this term refers to both the segment of the public in direct contact with the organization and the segment that benefits from its services. In service organizations, the two are identical; hence, only when referring to these is it appropriate to speak of clients. But who would be the clients of, say, an army? Surely not the enemy it fights; neither would it be the citizens who benefit from its operations, since they are not in direct contact. An army has no clients in the above sense.

The distinctive characteristic of commonweal organizations is that the public-at-large is their prime beneficiary, often, although not necessarily, to the exclusion of the very people who are the object of the organization's endeavor. Examples of this type are the State Department, the Bureau of Internal Revenue, military services, police and fire departments, and also the research function as distinguished from the teaching function in universities. Most of these organizations either perform protective services for the community or serve as its administrative arm. The public could be considered the owners as well as the prime beneficiaries, and this type could then have been subsumed under

From Peter Blau and W. Richard Scott, Formal Organizations (New York: Harper & Row, Chandler Publishers, 1962), pp. 54–56, by permission of the authors.

our second category: organizations serving the interests of their owners. However, it seems preferable to separate these types since great differences in the nature and function of an organization depend on whether the community at large or a select number of owners are the prime beneficiaries.

The issue posed by commonweal organizations is that of external democratic control—the public must possess the means of controlling the ends served by these organizations. While external democratic control is essential, the internal structure of these organizations is expected to be bureaucratic, governed by the criterion of efficiency, and not democratic. The challenge facing these organizations, then, is the maintenance of efficient bureaucratic mechanisms that effectively implement the objectives of the community, which are ideally decided upon, at least in our society, by democratic methods. (*Internal* democratic control by the membership might well be at the expense of efficiency and thus lessen the organization's ability to effect the democratic will of the community.)

Three problems of commonweal organizations will be briefly discussed: the problem of power, the problem of promoting extraordinary performances, and the problem of dealing with outcasts.

The problem of power is perhaps best exemplified by the military service. In the interests of national security, most countries maintain military organizations of considerable strength. The existence of such a force creates the danger that it can be used to dominate the society that produced it, thus destroying democratic control or other forms of civilian government. This situation is illustrated by the army coups which have occurred in South American countries and the Algerian adventures of the French generals in 1961. . . .

A second problem confronting some commonweal organizations is that of promoting such extraordinary performance as bravery or creativity. Military organizations must find ways of eliciting bravery from their members under combat circumstances; police and fire work also frequently call for individual heroism. Of course, bravery by itself may be insufficient for guaranteeing military success. . . . Nevertheless, it would seem to remain

true that military success depends on fielding soldiers who are brave, not cowardly. And if there is less need for great heroes in today's battles, even "routine" action in combat requires much courage. Another form of extraordinary behavior is required in research organizations, namely, scientific creativity. This elusive quality is considered by many to be inborn and thus, by definition, outside the sphere of organizational influence. Actually, however, organizations do influence research creativity. If extraordinary qualities are required of individuals to insure the successful operations of an organization, it is important to learn how an organization can select personnel that possess such qualities, can stimulate their further development among its staff, and can motivate and help its members to apply their relevant talents to the pursuit of organizational objectives. . . .

Blau and Scott elaborate on the structure of the military profession, which is essentially bureaucratic in orientation. Its decisions, actions, specificity of expertness, client-relationship, and decisional procedures are collegial, hierarchical, and directed by self-imposed standards and peer-group surveillance.

PETER BLAU AND W. RICHARD SCOTT

Professional and Bureaucratic Orientation

SIMILARITIES AND CONTRASTS

The professional form of occupational

From Peter Blau and W. Richard Scott, Formal Organizations *(New York: Harper & Row, Chandler Publishers, 1962), pp. 60–63, by permission of the authors.*

life and the bureaucratic form of organizational administration are two institutional patterns that are prevalent today and that in many ways typify modern societies. Professional principles share many elements with bureaucratic ones, but include some that are not common. Let us briefly survey the underlying characteristics of professionalism and compare them to those of bureaucratic organization, focusing on principles rather than on specific practices.

First, professional decisions and actions are governed by universalistic standards; that is, they are based on certain objective criteria which are independent of the particular case under consideration. These principles rest upon and are derived from a body of specialized knowledge, such as the science of medicine, and practice consists of applying these principles with appropriate skill to particular cases. The mastering of this body of knowledge and the acquiring of appropriate skills requires a period of specialized training. The character of bureaucratic administration does not differ greatly in this respect. Bureaucratic operations are also governed by abstract principles and consist of the application of these principles to particular cases. Although the period of training for professionals is generally longer than that required of bureaucrats and contains some unique features, to be discussed presently, bureaucrats too undergo a period of technical training and indoctrination to qualify for their positions.

A second characteristic of professionalism is the specificity of professional expertness. The trained professional is a specialized expert qualified to deal with problems in a strictly limited area; he makes no claim to generalized wisdom—he is neither sage nor wise man. The practitioner's authority over his clients rests on their confidence in his expertness in some specific area; he enjoys no authority outside that sphere. In the interests of good health, for instance, the physician can tell his patient what he should eat, but he cannot tell him with authority what friends to chose. Contrast the limited authority exercised by the professional over his clients with the diffuse authority exercised by the parent over his children. The principle of specificity applies with equal force to the bureaucrat; in his case, too, specialization is the key to expertness, and the essence of bureaucracy is circumscribed authority.

Third, the professional's relations with clients are characterized by affective neutrality. Professional codes of ethics condemn emotional involvement with the client. These norms protect the client from being emotionally exploited and the practitioner from being torn apart by sympathy for his troubled clients. In addition, detachment insulates the professional so that he may exercise reasoned judgment. The relations between bureaucrats and clients are also marked by such impersonal detachment, with similar ends being served.

Fourth, professional status is achieved by an individual's performance, not ascribed to him because of some qualities he cannot change, such as sex or birth order. The professional's success rests upon outstanding performance in accordance with the principles laid down by his colleague group. In a similar manner, the bureaucrat is appointed to a position because of his technical qualifications rather than because of who he is or what connections he has, and his career advancement is governed by objective and explicit official criteria.

A fifth element in professionalism, essential to protect the welfare of dependent and vulnerable clients, is that professional decisions must not be based on the practitioner's self-interest, whereas in business life self-interests are expected to govern decisions. This difference does not mean that professionals are less selfish than businessmen, or less interested in economic advancement. It means that while each party to a business transaction is assumed, by the other and by the community, to act strictly in terms of his own interests, it is not legitimate for a professional to let his decisions as to what services to render be influenced by self-interest. If he does, the condemnation and the sanctions of his colleagues and of the community will hurt his interests in the long run. Thus, the structure of a profession tends to make the practitioner's own interests dependent on his serving the interests of his clients to the best of his abilities. . . .

In contrast to the first four principles, this fifth one is not characteristic of all formal organizations but only of certain types. Lack of self-interest is not expected to govern the operations of business concerns or of mutual-benefit associations, but it is expected of commonweal organizations and, particularly, of service organizations. As a matter of fact, the conditions for realizing this principle are probably more favorable for professionals working in service organizations than for professionals working outside this organizational context. The traditional practitioner in the free professions is

not only a professional but also a businessman who makes a living by collecting fees from clients. . . . The salaried professional in the service organization is free of this pressure, and the organization supported by community or philanthropic funds is not dependent on fees from clients either. These conditions would seem to be more conducive to promoting disinterested service.

A final characteristic of the professions is their distinctive control structure, which is fundamentally different from the hierarchical control exercised in bureaucratic organizations. Professionals typically organize themselves into voluntary associations for the purpose of self-control. As Goode explains, "the larger society has obtained an *indirect* social control by yielding *direct* social control to the professional community, which thus can make judgments according to its own norms." Professional control appears to have two sources. First, as a result of the long period of training undergone by the practitioner, he is expected to have acquired a body of expert knowledge and to have internalized a code of ethics which governs his professional conduct. Second, this self-control is supported by the external surveillance of his conduct by peers, who are in a position to see his work, who have the skills to judge his performance, and who, since they have a personal stake in the reputation of their profession, are motivated to exercise the necessary sanctions. Professionals in a given field constitute a colleague group of equals. Every member of the group, but nobody else, is assumed to be qualified to make professional judgments. To implement these values, professional organizations usually seek to have them enacted into laws establishing the exclusive jurisdiction of the organized colleague group in a given area of competence and granting it the right to license practitioners. The medical profession, for example, enjoys such a mandate in the area of healing; psychologists are now seeking legislation to obtain the right to license psychological counselors and testers, and even other practices in which their expertise is more questionable.

It is clear that this type of control structure differs greatly from that employed in bureaucratic organiza-tions. The source of discipline within a bureaucracy is not the colleague group but the hierarchy of authority. Performance is controlled by directives received from one's superiors rather than by self-imposed standards and peer-group surveillance, as is the case among professionals. This difference in social control . . . constitutes the basic distinguishing feature between professional and bureaucratic institutions, which have otherwise many similar characteristics. The significance of this difference is brought into sharp relief if one examines people who are subject to both forms of social control; that is, professionals in a bureaucracy.

Samuel P. Huntington, a pioneer social and political scientist in the field of civil-military relations, has integrated the concept of the profession with the military occupation. In his classic, *The Soldier and the State* (1957), Huntington introduces the concept of modern officership as a profession.

Samuel P. Huntington

Officership as a Profession

PROFESSIONALISM AND THE MILITARY

The modern officer corps is a professional body and the modern military officer a professional man. This is, perhaps, the most fundamental thesis of this book. . . . Professionalism distinguishes the military officer of today

From Samuel P. Huntington, The Soldier and the State *(Cambridge, Mass.: Harvard University Press, Belknap Press, 1957), pp. 7–18, by permission of Harvard University Press.*

from the warriors of previous ages. The existence of the officer corps as a professional body gives a unique cast to the modern problem of civil-military relations.

The nature and history of other professions as professions have been thoroughly discussed. Yet the professional character of the modern officer corps has been neglected. In our society, the businessman may command more income; the politician may command more power; but the professional man commands more respect. Yet the public, as well as the scholar, hardly conceives of the officer in the same way that it does the lawyer or doctor, and it certainly does not accord to the officer the deference which it gives to the civilian professionals. Even the military themselves are influenced by their image in the public mind and at times have refused to accept the implications of their own professional status. When the term "professional" has been used in connection with the military, it normally has been in the sense of "professional" as contrasted with "amateur" rather than in the sense of "profession" as contrasted with "trade" or "craft." The phrases "professional army" and "professional soldier" have obscured the difference between the career enlisted man who is professional in the sense of one who works for monetary gain and the career officer who is professional in the very different sense of one who pursues a "higher calling" in the service of society.

THE CONCEPT OF PROFESSION

The first step in analyzing the professional character of the modern officer corps is to define professionalism. The distinguishing characteristics of a profession as a special type of vocation are its expertise, responsibility, and corporateness.

EXPERTISE

The professional man is an expert with specialized knowledge and skill in a significant field of human endeavor. His expertise is acquired only by prolonged education and experience. It is the basis of objective standards of professional competence for separating the profession from laymen and measuring the relative competence of members of the profession. Such standards are universal. They inhere in the knowledge and skill and are capable of general application irrespective of time and place. The ordinary skill or craft exists only in the present and is mastered by learning an existing technique without reference to what has gone before. Professional knowledge, however, is intellectual in nature and capable of preservation in writing. Professional knowledge has a history, and some knowledge of that history is essential to professional competence. Institutions of research and education are required for the extension and transmission of professional knowledge and skill. Contact is maintained between the academic and practical sides of a profession through journals, conferences, and the circulation of personnel between practice and teaching. . . .

RESPONSIBILITY

The professional man is a practicing expert, working in a social context, and performing a service, such as the promotion of health, education, or justice, which is essential to the functioning of society. The client of every profession is society, individually or collectively. A research chemist, for instance, is not a professional man because the service he renders, while beneficial to society, is not essential to its immediate existence and functioning: only Du Pont and the Bureau of Standards have a direct and immediate interest in what he has to offer. The essential and general character of his service and his monopoly of his skill impose upon the professional man the responsibility to perform the service when required by society. This social responsibility distinguishes the professional man from other experts with only intellectual skills. The research chemist, for instance, is still a research chemist if he uses his skills in a manner harmful to society. But the professional man can no longer practice if he refuses to accept his social responsibility: a physician ceases to be a physician if he uses his skills for antisocial purposes. The responsibility to serve and devotion to his skill furnish the professional motive. Financial remuneration cannot be the primary aim of the professional man *qua* professional man. Consequently, professional compensation normally is only partly determined by bargaining on the open market and is regulated by professional custom and law.

The performance of an essential service not regulated by the normal expectation of financial rewards requires some statement governing the relations of the profession to the rest of society. Conflicts between the professional man and his clients, or among members of the profession, normally furnish the immediate impetus to the formulation of such a statement. The profession thus becomes a moral unit positing certain values and ideals which guide its members in their dealings with laymen. This guide may

be a set of unwritten norms transmitted through the professional educational system or it may be codified into written canons of professional ethics.

CORPORATENESS

The members of a profession share a sense of organic unity and consciousness of themselves as a group apart from laymen. This collective sense has its origins in the lengthy discipline and training necessary for professional competence, the common bond of work, and the sharing of a unique social responsibility. The sense of unity manifests itself in a professional organization which formalizes and applies the standards of professional competence and establishes and enforces the standards of professional responsibility. Membership in the professional organization, along with the possession of special expertise and the acceptance of special responsibility, thus becomes a criterion of professional status, publicly distinguishing the professional man from the layman. The interest of the profession requires it to bar its members from capitalizing upon professional competence in areas where that competence has no relevance and likewise to protect itself against outsiders who would claim professional competence because of achievements or attributes in other fields. Professional organizations are generally either associations or bureaucracies. In the associational professions such as medicine and law, the practitioner typically functions independently and has a direct personal relationship with his client. The bureaucratic professions, such as the diplomatic service, possess a high degree of specialization of labor and responsibilities within the profession, and the profession as a whole renders a collective service to society as a whole. These two categories are not mutually exclusive: bureaucratic elements exist in most associational professions, and associations frequently supplement the formal structure of bureaucratic professions. The associational professions usually possess written codes of ethics since each practitioner is individually confronted with the problem of proper conduct toward clients and colleagues. The bureaucratic professions, on the other hand, tend to develop a more general sense of collective professional responsibility and the proper role of the profession in society.

THE MILITARY PROFESSION

The vocation of officership meets the principal criteria of professionalism. In practice, no vocation, not even medicine or law, has all the characteristics of the ideal professional type. Officership probably falls somewhat further short of the ideal than either of these. Yet its fundamental character as a profession is undeniable. In practice, officership is strongest and most effective when it most closely approaches the professional ideal; it is weakest and most defective when it falls short of that ideal.

THE EXPERTISE OF OFFICERSHIP

What is the specialized expertise of the military officer? Is there any skill common to all military officers and yet not shared with any civilian groups? At first glance this hardly seems to be the case. The officer corps appears to contain many varieties of specialists, including large numbers which have their counterparts in civilian life. Engineers, doctors, pilots, ordnance experts, personnel experts, intelligence experts, communications experts—all these are found both within and without the modern officer corps. Even ignoring these technical specialists, each absorbed in his own branch of knowledge, just the broad division of the corps into land, sea, and air officers appears to create vast differences in the functions performed and the skills required. The captain of a cruiser and the commander of an infantry division appear to be faced with highly different problems requiring highly different abilities.

Yet a distinct sphere of military competence does exist which is common to all, or almost all, officers and which distinguishes them from all, or almost all, civilians. This central skill is perhaps best summed up in Harold Lasswell's phrase "the management of violence." The function of a military force is successful armed combat. The duties of the military officer include: (1) the organizing, equipping, and training of this force; (2) the planning of its activities; and (3) the direction of its operation in and out of combat. The direction, operation, and control of a human organization whose primary function is the application of violence is the peculiar skill of the officer. It is common to the activities of the air, land, and sea officers. It distinguishes the military officer *qua* military officer from the other specialists which exist in the modern armed services. the skills of these experts may be necessary to the achievement of the objectives of the military force. But they are basically auxiliary vocations, having the same relation to the expertise of the officer as the skills of the nurse, chemist, laboratory technician, dietician, pharmacist, and X-ray technician have to the expertise of the doctor. None of the auxiliary specialists contained within or serving the military profession is capable of the "management of violence," just as none of the specialists aiding the medical profession is capable of the diagnosis and treatment of illness. The essence of officership is embodied in the traditional admonition to Annapolis men that their duty will be to "fight the fleet." Individuals, such as doctors, who are not competent to manage violence but who are members of the officer corps are normally distinguished by special titles and insignia and are excluded from positions of military command. They belong to the officer corps in its capacity as an administrative organization of the state, but not in its capacity as a professional body.

Within the profession itself there are specialists in the management of violence on sea, on land, and in the air, just as there are heart, stomach, and eye specialists within medicine. A military specialist is an officer who is peculiarly expert at directing the application of violence under certain prescribed conditions. The variety of conditions under which violence may be employed and the different forms in which it may be applied form the basis for subprofessional specialization. They also form the basis for evaluating relative technical competence. The larger and more complex the organizations of violence which an officer is capable of directing, and the greater the number of situations and conditions under which he can be employed, the higher is his professional competence. A man who is capable of directing only the activities of an infantry squad has such a low level of professional ability as to be almost on the border line. A man who can manage the operations of an airborne division or a carrier task force is a highly competent professional. The officer who can direct the complex activities of a combined operation involving large-scale sea, air, and land forces is at the top of his vocation.

It is readily apparent that the military function requires a high order of expertise. No individual, whatever his inherent intellectual ability and qualities of character and leadership, could perform these functions efficiently without considerable training and experience. In emergencies an untrained civilian may be capable of acting as a military officer at a low level for a brief period of time, just as in emergencies the intelligent layman may fill in until the doctor arrives. Before the management of violence became the extremely complex task that it is in modern civilization, it was possible for someone without specialized training to practice officership. Now, however, only the person who completely devotes his working hours to this task can hope to develop a reasonable level of professional competence. The skill of the officer is neither a craft (which is primarily mechanical) nor an art (which requires unique and nontransferable talent). It is instead an extraordinarily complex intellectual skill requiring comprehensive study and training. It must be remembered that the peculiar skill of the officer is the management of violence not the act of violence itself. Firing a rifle, for instance, is basically a mechanical craft; directing the operations of a rifle company requires an entirely different type of ability which may in part be learned from books and in part from practice and experience. The intellectual content of the military profession requires the modern officer to devote about one-third of his professional life to formal schooling, probably a higher ratio of educational time to practice time than in any other profession. In part this reflects the limited opportunities of the officer to acquire practical experience at the most important elements of his vocation. But to a large degree it also reflects the extreme complexity of the military expertise.

The peculiar skill of the military officer is universal in the sense that its essence is not affected by changes in time or location. Just as the qualifications of a good surgeon are the same in Zurich as they are in New York, the same standards of professional military competence apply in Russia as in America and in the nineteenth century as in the twentieth. The posses-

sion of a common professional skill is a bond among military officers cutting across other differences. The vocation of the officer also possesses a history. The management of violence is not a skill which can be mastered simply by learning existing techniques. It is in a continuous process of development, and it is necessary for the officer to understand this development and to be aware of its main tendencies and trends. Only if he is aware of the historical development of the techniques of organizing and directing military forces can the officer expect to stay on top of his profession. The importance of the history of war and military affairs receives sustained emphasis throughout military writings and military education. . . .

THE RESPONSIBILITY OF OFFICERSHIP

The expertise of the officer imposes upon him a special social responsibility. The employment of his expertise promiscuously for his own advantage would wreck the fabric of society. As with the practice of medicine, society insists that the management of violence be utilized only for socially approved purposes. Society has a direct, continuing, and general interest in the employment of this skill for the enhancement of its own military security. While all professions are to some extent regulated by the state, the military profession is monopolized by the state. The skill of the physician is diagnosis and treatment; his responsibility is the health of his clients. The skill of the officer is the management of violence; his responsibility is the military security of his client, society. The discharge of the responsibility requires mastery of the skill; mastery of the skill entails acceptance of the responsibility. Both responsibility and skill distinguish the officer from other social types. All members of society have an interest in its security; the state has a direct concern for the achievement of this along with other social values; but the officer corps alone is responsible for military security to the exclusion of all other ends.

Does the officer have a professional motivation? Clearly he does not act primarily from economic incentives. In western society the vocation of officership is not well rewarded monetarily. Nor is his behavior within his profession governed by economic rewards and punishments. The officer is not a mercenary who transfers his services wherever they are best rewarded, nor is he the temporary citizen-soldier inspired by intense momentary patriotism and duty but with no steadying and permanent desire to perfect himself in the management of violence. The motivations of the officer are a technical love for his craft and the sense of social obligation to utilize this craft for the benefit of society. The combination of these drives constitutes professional motivation. Society, on the other hand, can only assure this motivation if it offers its officers continuing and sufficient pay both while on active duty and when retired.

The officer possesses intellectualized skill, mastery of which requires intense study. But like the lawyer and doctor he is not primarily a man of the closet; he deals continuously with people. The test of his professional ability is the application of technical knowledge in a human context. Since this application is not regulated by economic means, however, the officer requires positive guides spelling out his responsibilities to his fellow officers, his subordinates, his superiors, and the state which he serves. His behavior within the military structure is governed by a complex mass of regulations, customs, and traditions. His behavior in relation to society is guided by an awareness that his skill can only be utilized for purposes approved by society through its political agent, the state. While the primary responsibility of the physician is to his patient, and the lawyer to his client, the principal responsibility of the military officer is to the state. His responsibility to the state is the responsibility of the expert adviser. Like the lawyer and physician, he is concerned with only one segment of the activities of his client. Consequently, he cannot impose decisions upon his client which have implications beyond his field of special competence. He can only explain to his client his needs in this area, advise him as to how to meet these needs, and then, when the client has made his decisions, aid him in implementing them. To some extent the officer's behavior towards the state is guided by an explicit code expressed in law and comparable to the canons of professional ethics of the physician and lawyer. To a larger extent, the officer's code is expressed in custom, tradition, and the continuing spirit of the profession.

THE CORPORATE CHARACTER OF OFFICERSHIP

Officership is a public bureaucratized profession. The legal right to practice the profession is limited to members of a carefully defined body. His commission is to the officer what his license is to a doctor. Organically, however, the officer corps is much more than simply a creature of the state. The functional imperatives of security give rise to complex vocational institutions which mold the officer corps into an autonomous social unit. Entrance into this unit is restricted to those with the requisite education and training and is usually permitted only at the lowest level of professional competence. The corporate structure of the officer corps includes not just the official bureaucracy but also societies, associations, schools, journals, customs, and traditions. The professional world of the officer tends to encompass an unusually high proportion of his activities. He normally lives and works apart from the rest of society; physically and socially he probably has fewer nonprofessional contacts than most other professional men. The line between him and the layman or civilian is publicly symbolized by uniforms and insignia of rank.

The officer corps is both a bureaucratic profession and a bureaucratic organization. Within the profession, levels of competence are distinguished by a hierarchy of ranks; within the organization, duties are distinguished by a hierarchy of office. Rank inheres in the individual and reflects his professional achievement measured in terms of experience, seniority, education, and ability. Appointments to rank are normally made by the officer corps itself applying general principles established by the state. Assignments to office are normally somewhat more subject to outside influence. In all bureaucracies authority derives from office; in a professional bureaucracy eligibility for office derives from rank. An officer is permitted to perform certain types of duties and functions by virtue of his rank; he does not receive rank because he has been assigned to an office. Although in practice there are exceptions to this principle, the professional character of the officer corps rests upon the priority of the hierarchy of rank over the hierarchy of office.

The officer corps normally includes a number of nonprofessional "reservists." This is due to the fluctuating need for officers and the impossibility of the state maintaining continuously an officer corps of the size required in emergencies. The reservists are a temporary supplement to the officer corps and qualify for military rank by education and training. While members of the corps, they normally possess all the prerogatives and responsibilities of the professional in the same rank. The legal distinction between them and the professional is preserved, however, and entrance into the permanent corps of officers is much more restricted than entrance into the reserve corps. The reservists seldom achieve the level of professional skill open to the career officers; consequently, the bulk of the reservists are in the lower ranks of the professional bureaucracy while the higher ranks are monopolized by the career professionals. The latter, as the continuing element in the military structure and because of their superior professional competence as a body, are normally charged with the education and indoctrination of the reservists in the skills and the traditions of the vocation. The reservist only temporarily assumes professional responsibility. His principal functions in society lie elsewhere. As a result, his motivations, values, and behavior frequently differ greatly from those of the career professional.

The enlisted men subordinate to the officer corps are a part of the organizational bureaucracy but not of the professional bureaucracy. The enlisted personnel have neither the intellectual skills nor the professional responsibility of the officer. They are specialists in the application of violence not the management of violence. Their vocation is a trade not a profession. This fundamental difference between the officer corps and the enlisted corps is reflected in the sharp line which is universally drawn between the two in all the military forces of the world. If there were not this cleavage, there could be a single military hierarchy extending from the lowest enlisted man to the highest officer. But the differing character of the two vocations makes the organizational hierarchy discontinuous. The ranks which exist in the enlisted corps do not constitute a professional hierarchy. They reflect varying aptitudes, abilities, and offices within the trade of soldier, and movement up and down them is much more fluid than in the officer corps. The difference between the officer and enlisted vocations precludes any general progression from one to the other. Individual enlisted men do become officers but this is the exception rather than the rule. The education and training necessary for officership are normally incompatible with prolonged service as an enlisted man.

THE CLASSICAL PROFESSIONAL SOLDIER

According to Huntington, the modern military, unlike the pre-1789 military, is distinguished by being a professional corporate group. The professional officer of modern times is a new social type and shows the following basic characteristics: (1) expertise ("the management of violence"); (2) clientship (responsibility to its client, society or the state); (3) corporateness (group consciousness and bureaucratic organization); and (4) ideology (the "military mind"). These characteristics are found in all modern military establishments in developed and developing politics. For a study of civil-military relations, two of the variables—corporatism and ideology—are more important than the others.

SAMUEL P. HUNTINGTON

The Rise of the Military Profession in Western Society

A NEW SOCIAL TYPE

The art of fighting is an old accomplishment of mankind. The military profession, however, is a recent creation of modern society. Historically, professionalism has been a distinguishing characteristic of western culture. The great civil professions originated in the late Middle Ages and existed in highly developed form by the beginning of the eighteenth century. The profession of officership, however, was essentially a product of the nineteenth century. It was, indeed, one of the most significant institutional creations of that century. Only in the Napoleonic Wars did officers begin to acquire a specialized technique to distinguish themselves from laymen and begin to develop the standards, values, and organization inherent in that technique. The professional officer as a social type is as uniquely characteristic of modern society as is the industrial entrepreneur. The emergence of the officer corps as an autonomous professional body cannot, of course, be given any precise dates. It was gradual

From Samuel P. Huntington, The Soldier and the State *(Cambridge, Mass.: Harvard University Press, Belknap Press, 1957), pp. 19–20, by permission of Harvard University Press.*

and faltering. Two facts, however, stand out. Prior to 1800 there was no such thing as a professional officer corps. In 1900 such bodies existed in virtually all major countries.

The emergence of a professional officer corps created the modern problem of civil-military relations in Europe and North America. It is possible to speak of the issues of civilian control, militarism, and the military mind as existing prior to 1800, but the fundamental transformation in the first part of the nineteenth century makes it relatively profitless to go back before that time in search of light on modern problems. Knowledge of the manners and outlook of that aristocratic, individualistic amateur, the medieval knight, is of little help in understanding the professional values and attitudes which constitute the contemporary military mind. The activities of the Praetorian Guard offer few useful lessons for civilian control: the problem in the modern state is not armed revolt but the relation of the expert to the politician. The cleavage between the military and civilian spheres and the resulting tension between the two are phenomena of distinctly recent origin.

Huntington elaborates on the special attributes of the modern military professional. The military professional is a conservative realist concerned with national security policy; his attitude toward the state, his client, is positive. Above all, what distinguishes the military professional from others is his sense of mission, of history, and of nation.

SAMUEL P. HUNTINGTON

The Professional Military Ethic

THE PROFESSIONAL MILITARY ETHIC: MAN, SOCIETY, AND HISTORY

The existence of the military profession presupposes conflicting human interests and the use of violence to further those interests. Consequently, the military ethic views conflict as a universal pattern throughout nature and sees violence rooted in the permanent biological and psychological nature of men. As between the good and evil in man, the military ethic emphasizes the evil. Man is selfish. He is motivated by drives for power, wealth, and security. "The human mind is by nature one-sided and limited." As between the strength and weakness in man, the military ethic emphasizes the weakness. Man's selfishness leads to struggle but man's weakness makes successful conflict dependent upon organization, discipline, and leadership. As Clausewitz said, "All war presupposes human weakness, and against that it is directed." No one is more aware than the professional soldier that the normal man is no hero. The military pro-

From Samuel P. Huntington, The Soldier and the State (Cambridge, Mass.: Harvard University Press, Belknap Press, 1957), pp. 62–64, 70–73, 79, by permission of Harvard University Press.

fession organizes men so as to overcome their inherent fears and failings. The uncertainty and chance involved in the conduct of war and the difficulty of anticipating the actions of an opponent make the military man skeptical of the range of human foresight and control. As between reason and irrationality in man, the military ethic emphasizes the limits of reason. The best schemes of men are frustrated by the "friction" existing in reality. "War is the province of uncertainty," Clausewitz said; "three-fourths of the things on which action in war is based lie hidden in the fog of greater or less uncertainty." Human nature, moreover, is universal and unchanging. Men in all places and at all times are basically the same. The military view of man is thus decidedly pessimistic. Man has elements of goodness, strength, and reason, but he is also evil, weak, and irrational. The man of the military ethic is essentially the man of Hobbes.

The existence of the military profession depends upon the existence of competing nation-states. The responsibility of the profession is to enhance the military security of the state. The discharge of this responsibility requires cooperation, organization, discipline. Both because it is his duty to serve society as a whole and because of the nature of the means which he employs to carry out this duty, the military man emphasizes the importance of the group as against the individual. Success in any activity requires the subordination of the will of the individual to the will of the group. Tradition, *esprit*, unity, community—these rate high in the military value system. The officer submerges his personal interests and desires to what is necessary for the good of the service. As a nineteenth-century German officer put it, the military man must "forego personal advantage, lucre, and prosperity . . . Egotism is beyond all doubt the most bitter enemy of the qualities essential to the officer-corps." Man is preëminently a social animal. He exists only in groups. He defends himself only in groups. Most importantly, he realizes himself only in groups. The "weak, mediocre, transient individual" can only achieve emotional satisfaction and moral fulfillment by participating in "the power, the greatness, the permanence and the splendour" of a continuing organic body. The military ethic is basically corporative in spirit. It is fundamentally anti-individualistic.

The military vocation is a profession because it has accumulated experiences which make up a body of professional knowledge. In the military view, man learns only from experience. If he has little opportunity to learn from his own experience, he must learn from the experience of others. Hence, the military officer studies history. For history is, in Liddell Hart's phrase, "universal experience," and military history, as

Moltke said, is the "most effective means of teaching war during peace." The military ethic thus places unusual value upon the ordered, purposive study of history. History is valuable to the military man only when it is used to develop principles which may be capable of future application. The military student of history constantly tries to draw generalizations from his study. Yet the military ethic is not bound to any specific theory of history. While it rejects monistic interpretations, it also emphasizes the importance of force as contrasted with ideological and economic factors. The permanence of human nature makes impossible any theory of progress. "Change is inevitable. Progress is not inevitable." Insofar as there is a pattern in history, it is cyclical in nature. Civilizations rise and fall. War and peace alternate, and so also does the supremacy of offensive and defensive warfare. . . .

THE MILITARY AND THE STATE

The military profession is expert and limited. Its members have specialized competence within their field and lack that competence outside their field. The relation of the profession to the state is based upon this natural division of labor. The essence of this relationship concerns the relative scope of competence of the military expert and political expert or statesman. Before the professionalization of military science in the nineteenth century, the same person could be simultaneously qualified in both fields. Now this is impossible. Napoleon embodied the old unity of military science and politics. He was replaced by Bismarck and Moltke who symbolized the new dichotomy. The exact character of the relationship which should exist between statesman and military officer cannot be defined precisely. But it is possible to state some of the principles which should govern that relationship.

Military science is an area in which specialized competence acquired by professional training and experience is necessary for decision and action. This field, which concerns the implementation of state policy by armed force, is divided into constant and variable components. This division was recognized only after the emergence of the military profession. The constant element reflects the permanency of human nature and physical geography. This may be called strategy, and so distinguished from the variable elements, tactics and logistics, or it may be formulated into a set of "fundamental," "immutable," "eternal," "unchanging and unchangeable" principles of war. Military historians differ as to the number and content of these principles but they do not question their existence as the fundamental core of military science. Their application, however, is constantly changing with changes in technology and social organization. The ideal military man is thus conservative in strategy, but open-minded and progressive with respect to new weapons and new tactical forms. He is equally expert in both the constant and variable aspects of military science. The essence of his art may indeed be defined as the relation between the two: "the unchangeable fundamental conditions of good generalship in their relation to changeable tactical forms · · ·" It is this area within which the statesman must accept the judgments of the military professional.

Politics deals with the goals of state policy. Competence in this field consists in having a broad awareness of the elements and interests entering into a decision and in possessing the legitimate authority to make such a decision. Politics is beyond the scope of military competence, and the participation of military officers in politics undermines their professionalism, curtailing their professional competence, dividing the profession against itself, and substituting extraneous values for professional values. The military officer must remain neutral politically. "The military commander must never allow his military judgment to be warped by political expediency." The area of military science is subordinate to, and yet independent of, the area of politics. Just as war serves the ends of politics, the military profession serves the ends of the state. Yet the statesman must recognize the integrity of the profession and its subject matter. The military man has the right to expect political guidance from the statesman. Civilian control exists when there is this proper subordination of an autonomous profession to the ends of policy. . . .

The statesmen set the goal and allocate to [the military man] the resources to be used in attaining that goal. It is then up to him to do the best he can. This is indeed the meaning of military strategy in relation to policy: "the practical adaptation of the means placed at a general's disposal to the attainment of the object in view."

Obviously a considerable area exists where strategy and policy overlap. In this realm the supreme military commander may make a decision on purely military grounds only to discover that it has political implications unknown to him. When this turns out to be the case, considerations of strategy must then give way to considerations of policy. The military man must recognize that a wide number of conceivably purely military decisions, such as the selection of a theater of war, also involve politics, and he must be guided accordingly. As Clausewitz said, "the art of war in its highest point of view becomes policy, but, of course, a policy which fights battles instead of writing notes." The top military leaders of the state inevitably operate in this intermingled world of strategy and policy. They must always be alert to the political implications of their military attitudes and be willing to accept the final decisions of the statesmen. When required in his executive capacity to make decisions involving both military and political elements, the military man ideally should formulate his military solution first and then alter it as needs be on the advice of his political advisers.

The military profession exists to serve the state. To render the highest possible service the entire profession and the military force which it leads must be constituted as an effective instrument of state policy. Since political direction comes only from the top, this means that the profession has to be organized into a hierarchy of obedience. For the profession to perform its function, each level within it must be able to command the instantaneous and loyal obedience of subordinate levels. Without these relationships military professionalism is impossible. Consequently, loyalty and obedience are the highest military virtues: "the rule of obedience is simply the expression of that one among the military virtues upon which all the others depend . . ." When the military man receives a legal order from an authorized superior, he does not argue, he does not hesitate, he does not substitute his own views; he obeys instantly. . . .

CONSERVATIVE REALISM

The military ethic emphasizes the permanence, irrationality, weakness, and evil in human nature. It stresses the supremacy of society over the individual and the importance of order, hierarchy, and division of function. It stresses the continuity and value of history. It accepts the nation state as the highest form of political organization and recognizes the continuing likelihood of wars among nation-states. It emphasizes the importance of power in international relations and warns of the dangers to state security. It holds that the security of the state depends upon the creation and maintenance of strong military forces. It urges the limitation of state action to the direct interests of the state, the restriction of extensive commitments, and the undesirability of bellicose or adventurous policies. It holds that war is the instrument of politics, that the military are the servants of the statesman, and that civilian control is essential to military professionalism. It exalts obedience as the highest virtue of military men. The military ethic is thus pessimistic, collectivist, historically inclined, power-oriented, nationalistic, militaristic, pacifist, and instrumentalist in its view of the military profession. It is, in brief, realistic and conservative.

The major contribution of Huntington to a theory of civil-military relations is his belief that the rise of military professionalism is inversely related to military intervention, that is, that the modern professional sense of mission, military mind, and corporate autonomy inclined the military against political intervention. Huntington's theory that high professionalism and corporate orientation incline the military professional toward a low military political posture has been challenged by several authors.

Professor W. H. Morris Jones, in a review article, "Armed Forces and the State" (1957), argues that Huntington is not content simply to offer a model but ends by falling in love with it. He contends that, in fact, it is the very professionalization of the modern military officer that makes him an interventionist, e.g., de Gaulle, MacArthur, Eisenhower, and Ludendorff.

W. H. MORRIS JONES

Armed Forces and the State

Everyone knows that American isolationism was sunk at Pearl Harbour. After World War II, there could be no withdrawal, no return to as-you-were "normalcy." Many people knew further that under the leadership of Morgenthau and Kennan there has been an attempt to re-think the fundamentals of foreign policy and international relations in realist terms of interests and power, an effort to get rid of utopianism and ideology in America's view of her place in the world. Less known, but equally deserv-

From W. H. Morris Jones, "Armed Forces and the State," Public Administration 35 (Winter 1957): 411–16, by permission of the editors.

ing of recognition, is the allied examination which has been taking place in the States of the problem of civil-military relations. A bibliography of the post-war contribution to this subject already made a tidy volume in 1952; by now the literature is enormous and the participants in the discussion include journalists, academics, politicians, and service leaders. Mr. Huntington writes: "The basic issue raised was: How can a liberal society provide for its military security when this requires the maintenance of professional military forces and institutions fundamentally at odds with liberalism?" His book is the latest but by no means the least contribution to this debate. It merits widespread attention for its subject matter and treatment alike. It is a work of considerable scholarship, at once thorough and provocative. Even so, it is less than wholly convincing.

"Nothing," said de Tocqueville (whose chapter "Warfare among democratic peoples" is one of the classic discussions of this subject), "is so dangerous as an army amid an unwarlike nation." He thought that America was simply fortunate in that her geographical security enabled her to be content with an army of a few thousand soldiers, but, in general, he envisaged all kinds of troubles for democracies obliged to have armies, and some of his fears have stuck. In aristocracies, armies reflect and harmonise with the society: the military spirit is esteemed throughout—"the nobleman enters the army to find an honorable employment for the idle years of his youth"—and accepted inequality is the rule—"the officer is noble, the soldier is a serf." As soon as egalitarian and democratic ideas take hold, complications set in. While war remains "an occurrence to which all nations are subject," the pursuit of wealth and welfare now causes "the spirit of military glory to be weakened." One consequence is that "the profession of arms ceases to be held in honour, and military men fall to the lowest rank of public servants: they are little esteemed, and no longer understood. . . . The best part of the nation shuns the military professions. . . . Military ambition is only indulged in when no other is possible." Moreover, whereas in aristoc-

racies rank in the army is no more than "an appendage" to rank in society, in democracies an army officer often "has no property but his pay and no distinction but that of military honours"; "his rank in society almost always depends on his rank in the army"; in fact, he is a social nobody except in so far as military rank helps to make him somebody. But this means that rank is very important to the military man. And since social status no longer indicates firmly the army rank to which one can decently aspire, "the bounds of military ambition" come to be "immeasurably extended." "In democratic armies the desire of advancement is almost universal: it is ardent, tenacious, perpetual; it is strengthened by all other desires, and only extinguished with life itself." This might not be particularly awkward were it not for the fact that in normal times of peace, promotion opportunities are really very limited. The military man is not so dull that he cannot see where's the rub: in times of peace. The great thing about war is that it "makes vacancies and warrants the violation of that law of seniority which is the sole privilege natural to democracy." "We thus arrive," de Tocqueville concluded, "at this singular consequence, that of all armies those most ardently desirous of war are democratic armies, and of all nations those most fond of peace are democratic nations." And there, more or less, de Tocqueville left it, the largely insoluble problem of an unassimilated group in the community, forming "a small nation by itself, where the mind is less enlarged and habits more rude than in the nation at large." The only faint ray of hope was to be seen in the direction of "infusing into the spirit peculiar to the army the general spirit of the nation." In this way, with luck, this "turbulent, restless, ill-tempered and dissatisfied" group might have its opinions and desires "tempered."

In place of these shrewd, anticipatory guesses, Mr. Huntington gives us an elaborate theoretical analysis and a widely-ranging historical account. Instead of de Tocqueville's vivid writing, we have here a solemn, measured style. Mr. Huntington's earnestness is understandable but it is a pity that it drives away so much of the fun and drama which belongs to this subject. He also finds de Tocqueville wrong in some of his guesses and quite mistaken in his hopes. The main theme of Mr. Huntington's book is that military professionalism has been misunderstood and that the solution of the problem of civil-military relations depends not on the modification and tempering of the military mind but on its preservation, purification and cultivation. Now this is evidently a piece of dynamite worth closer examination.

Quite a lot depends on the concept of military professionalism which Mr. Huntington works hard. No doubt de Tocqueville himself used the phrase "military profession" and we, too, would not normally regard it as something to be avoided. Nevertheless, more usually, we would continue to make a distinction between "the services" and "the professions," intending by this to point perhaps to the "public" nature of the former and the

"private" and "learned" character of the latter. Mr. Huntington will have none of this casualness nor of its implications. The principal criteria of professionalism are expertise, social responsibility and corporateness, and "the vocation of officership" meets all three. Accepting as quite justified in this context the exclusion from consideration of all noncommissioned ranks, we may readily grant the corporateness of the officer corps, reinforced as it so obviously is by uniforms, jargon and ranks. The other two criteria are more slippery and difficult to grasp. The present reader was unable to allow himself to be carried away by the author's persuasive pages on military expertise. There exists, we are told, "a distinct sphere of military competence which is common to all, or almost all officers, and which distinguishes them from all, or almost all, civilians." "This central skill is perhaps best summed up in Lasswell's phrase, 'the management of violence'," and it is "an extraordinarily complex intellectual skill requiring comprehensive study and training"— so much so that "the intellectual content of the military profession requires the modern officer to devote about one-third of his professional life to formal schooling, probably a higher ratio of educational time to practise time than in any other profession." With all respect, it looks as if West Point has been shooting a line; Harvard should have known better than to swallow it. Similarly, in social responsibility: when the author says that "the motivations of the officer are a technical love for his craft and the sense of social obligation to realise this craft for the benefit of society," we can only have a feeling of embarrassment if this is meant to be a generalisation from the body of facts.

But at times the author seems to disclaim such an intention and to be, rather, seeking a statement of the "idea" or model of the profession. Unfortunately, it requires great skill to play the Plato game and keep what ought to be distinct from what is.

The delicate operation of model construction is again seen when the book moves on to describe "the military mind" or "the military ethic." For the author's method is not to generalise from a survey of actual attitudes held by a variety of military men, but instead to build up the "ideal type" of military mind as a deduction from the nature of the professional military function as already defined. The attitudes of mind which the author finds to be logically attached to the profession of arms include views of human nature, society and history as well as distinct approaches to national security and war. There are here some well-expressed passages of great interest and penetration such as: "The military man will always argue that the danger of war requires increased armaments; he will seldom argue that increased armaments make war practical or desirable. He always favours preparedness, but he never feels prepared. He rarely favours war . . . he contributes a cautious, conservative, restraining voice to the formulation of State policy. He is afraid of war. He wants to prepare for war. But he is never ready to fight a war." This is a brilliant correction of de Tocqueville,

but strictly speaking, of course, the author is indifferent as to whether he is giving an account of actual military attitudes; this is only abstract model-construction. But models are—or become, as one plays with them—standards. What must logically be becomes what ought to be, and what it is judged thereby.

Some of the consequences of Mr. Huntington's theory can be noted at once. His marked emphasis on the distinctness of the military profession and its ethic inclines him to neglect or pay too little attention to other aspects of armies. Thus, while he admits that an army is a bureaucracy, this for him is a "secondary, not essential characteristic." But a large number of military professionals are for a lot of their time engaged in administration. Granted, the way they administer will owe something to their "military ethic," but will not involvement in administration have its independent influence on their ways? Again, while military professionalism surely colours civil-military relations, it would seem unreal to treat these as wholly *sui generis*. Is there nothing to be learnt from the relations between career civil servants or career diplomats and their political masters? The attempt to abstract "profession" from everything else leads equally to a dismissal of other factors such as social composition. . . .

Beyond these questions, there is another. Is it part of the attitude of the military mind to despise the politician? Most people would agree that the records show that such an attitude is at least very common. Whether it forms part of the "essential" military view is not quite clear from this book. But in any event, in so far as it exists it must always make it difficult for the military officer group to act as a perfectly passive obedient neutral instrument in the hands of the policymakers. And what evidence is there that an enhancement of the position of the military would of itself serve to make them respect "the frocks"? Further, is it not likely that encouragement of pure professionalism would tend to make mutual understanding between soldier and politician still more difficult? . . .

It is difficult not to feel that the immense good there is in this book comes in spite of the author's theory.

We have concentrated attention on the theory and we return to it in conclusion partly because the author himself attaches importance to it, partly because it colours so strongly the final impression which the book leaves on the reader. The fact is that Mr. Huntington is not content to offer a model: he falls in love with it. His immersion in "the military ethic" has made him quite sentimentally attached to it. In the end he is pleading not only for *lebensraum* for military professionalism, but for a reshaping of the whole of society's values to make a cosy home for the "managers of violence."

The classical professional soldier is thus a product of the modern nation-state and has been inspired by the modern military organization just as much as the modern nation-state's administrative apparatus. In fact, their relationships are symbiotic. The great Italian political theorist, Gaetano Mosca, in his classic, *The Ruling Class,* clearly distinguishes the modern from the nomadic, barbaric, feudal, and aristocratic military. "As society advances," writes Mosca, "economic production absorbs larger and larger numbers of hands and brains, and civilized peoples come to regard the arts of peace as their customary occupations"; Mosca argues further that the modern standing army is, in fact, a severe custodian of the law and is obedient to established authority.

GAETANO MOSCA

Standing Armies

1. We have already discussed the predominance of military classes and

we have seen that in some cases warriors have come exclusively from dominant classes, though in other cases those classes supply only generals, officers and picked corps, while a certain number of the rank and file in less esteemed divisions are recruited from lower classes.

In savage or barbarous countries, where economic production is very rudimentary, all adult males are soldiers in the rather frequent event of war. In such societies, assuming that pastoral nomadism or even an embryonic agriculture and industry exist, they are never so highly developed as to absorb human activity entirely. Sufficient time and energy are always left for adventurous raids and forays. These furnish an occupation that is not only agreeable in itself but is almost always lucrative. Among such peoples the arts of peace are regularly left to women or to slaves. The men devote themselves by preference to the chase and to warfare. . . .

One factor favorable to the permanence of such a state of affairs is the existence of very small political organisms—a de facto autonomy on the part of each little tribe or village, which can make war a daily routine and thefts and reprisals between neighbors unending. In the long run, when even very barbarous tribes become subject to a regular government that prevents internal strife, they become peaceful. . . .

But as soon as great political organisms, however rudimentary and imperfect, come to be set up and, more especially, as soon as economic development has advanced somewhat and war ceases to be the most lucrative occupation, we find a special class devoting itself to the bearing of arms and making its living not so much by plundering its adversaries as by levying tribute in some form or other on the

peaceful toilers of the country which it polices and defends. As we have many times remarked, production is almost exclusively agricultural when civilization and culture are at a low level, and warriors either are the owners of the land, which they force others to cultivate, or else extort heavy tribute from those who do own the land. This was the situation in the early period of Greco-Roman antiquity, when the dominant military element in the city was made up exclusively of landed proprietors, and the same phenomenon recurs more markedly still in all countries that are feudally organized. . . . In short, we find it in all societies that have not yet issued from the early period of crude culture that appears in the history of every great nation; and we find it also in the periods of deterioration or decline, whether due to internal or external causes, by which countries that have attained a high level of civilization change and perish as social types (the Roman Empire would be an example).

2. However, as feudal states advance in civilization, a trend toward centralization, toward bureaucratic organization, sets in, since the central power is constantly trying to free itself of dependence upon the good will of the minute political organisms that make up the state—a good will that is not always prompt and freely offered. With that in view, and incidentally for the purpose of keeping the small organisms more obedient and better disciplined, the central power tries to obtain direct control of the agencies that will enable it effectively

to enforce its will upon other men—control of money, in other words, and soldiers. So corps of mercenaries, directly in the service of the head of the state, come into being, and that development is so natural and so regularly recurrent that we find it, in embryo at least, in all countries that are feudally organized. . . .

Under the early republic the Romans had a citizen army that was recruited from the dominant and well-to-do classes and was made up of individuals who took to arms only in case of need. Nothing less than the Roman genius for organization was required to bring that system to such perfection as to make it possible for the citizen army to develop without shock and almost imperceptibly into a real standing army made up of professional soldiers. That evolution, as is well known, began in the last century of the republic and was already complete when the empire was founded. As a rule, standing armies have originated in units of native or foreign mercenaries hired by the central power to support it against other military forces that have been feudally organized.

As regards the practice of hiring mercenaries, it is interesting to note that it was especially characteristic of countries that not only were rich but derived their wealth from commerce and industry rather than from agriculture. In such countries the ruling classes grew unaccustomed to life in the open, which was the best preparation for the career in arms, and found it more to their advantage to superintend banks and factories than to go off to wars. That was the case in

Carthage, in Venice and quite generally in the wealthier Italian communes, where the mercantile and industrial burghers soon lost the habit of fighting their wars in person, and became more and more inclined to entrust them to mercenaries. In Florence citizens were still fighting in the battles on the Arbia and at Campaldino, but the latest record of a campaign conducted wholly by citizens belongs to the year 1325. The nationality of the mercenaries themselves may sometimes be determined by political considerations, and perhaps by the traditional habits and aptitudes of certain peoples; but the consideration that most commonly prevails is the plain economic consideration of the largest results from the smallest expenditure—in other words, the desire to have the greatest possible number of soldiers for the least possible outlay. Therefore countries relatively poor in capital and rich in population, in which time and lives can be bought on very favorable terms, have always been the ones to furnish the largest number of hired troops.

When the soldier's outfit was expensive and the style of fighting required a long apprenticeship, as was the case with the medieval knight and the Greek hoplite, the mercenary career was ordinarily adopted by younger sons, or unplaced members of good families, who by choice or of necessity went seeking their fortunes outside their native lands. Xenophon's Ten Thousand originated in that way. When equipment was cheap and no very long period of training was required, mercenaries were preferably sought in poor countries where man power was plentiful and industry and capital were scarce. Down to very recently the volunteer English army was largely recruited from the poorer counties of Ireland. Machiavelli in his day noted how hard it was to raise mercenaries in the manufacturing cities in Germany. Two centuries later Voltaire remarked that of all the Germans the Saxons were least given to enlisting as soldiers, Saxony being the most industrious region in Germany. In our day, even if the Swiss federal government were to allow it, very few Swiss, probably, would be available as mercenaries, since Switzerland has become a fairly wealthy country. For their part, the European governments that once depended on Switzerland for hired guards could now probably spend their money to greater advantage right at home.

3. Native or foreign, once regularly organized mercenaries have become the preponderant force in a country, they have normally tried to force their rule upon the rest of society. Like their feudal predecessors, they have regularly taken advantage of their monopoly in the bearing of arms to levy blackmail, to live as fatly as possible at the expense of the producing population and, especially, to reduce the supreme political power to dependence on their will. The more perfect their organization and the more complete the military disorganization of the rest of the country, the more far-reaching has the influence of mercenaries been.

Pertinent examples suggest themselves. One thinks at once of the praetorian guards and the legions that toyed as they saw fit with the Roman Empire. But in general, whenever and wherever governments have built up standing armies in order to deal with feudal unruliness, or for other reasons, they have almost always found themselves at the mercy of those armies. In order to govern with greater absolutism and not be wholly dependent upon the contingents that were supplied by the boyars, Ivan IV of Russia organized the Strelitzes, a regularly paid force directly responsible to the sovereign. Very soon the Strelitzes were making and unmaking czars. They became virtually omnipotent in Russia, and Peter the Great was able to free himself of them only by shooting them down with grapeshot, or beheading them by the thousand. At Constantinople, again, the sultans decided to have a thoroughly loyal militia made up of men who had no countries and no families and could therefore be brought up in wholehearted devotion to Islam and the Padishah. Such a force, they thought, would march without scruple and as need required, not only against the infidel but against the sheiks in Arabia and Kurdistan, the begs in Albania and Bosnia, and the khans of Turkistan and Tartary. So they filled their corps of Janizaries with young boys of Circassian, Greek and other Christian stocks, whom they bought or kidnaped from their families. But very soon the Janizaries became the real authority in the Osmanli empire and were creating and deposing sultans. They strangled the unfortunate Selim III, who made a first move to curb their omnipotence, and in order to get the better of them the sultan Mahmud II had to exterminate them almost to the last man.

The sultans of Constantinople might have profited by the experience of the Abbassids of Bagdad, their predecessors in the caliphate. The Abbassids, as far back as the ninth century, and perhaps earlier, had organized their Turkish guard in order to have a loyal militia that would not be raising the standard of the Fatimids or the Ommiads every other day, as their Arab troops had been in the habit of doing. By the time of Motasim, who was caliph between the years 833 and 842, the Turkish guard had become omnipotent. Turkish mercenaries were doing very much as they pleased in Bagdad and committing all sorts of outrages. Motasim's successor, Watthik by name, was deposed by the Turks and replaced by his brother Motawakkil. Then in the space of four years, 866–870, the Turkish guard made and unmade three other caliphs. The caliph Motamid took advantage of the death of their general, one Musa, to break up their power somewhat. He scattered them along the frontiers of Khurasan and Dzungaria, and counted every defeat they suffered there as a victory for himself.

In a word, history teaches that the class that bears the lance or holds the musket regularly forces its rule upon the class that handles the spade or pushes the shuttle. As society advances economic production absorbs larger and larger numbers of hands and brains, and civilized peoples come to regard the arts of peace as their customary occupations. Under these circumstances, to declare in principle that all citizens are soldiers, without providing for a sound military organization with a nucleus of generals and officers who are specialists in matters of war, means in practice that in the moment of peril there will be no soldiers at all, and that a populous country will be in danger of falling prey to a small army, national or foreign, if that army happens to be well trained and well organized. On the other hand, to entrust the bearing of arms exclusively to elements in a society that are temperamentally best suited to the military trade and voluntarily assume it—an altogether rational and obvious system which many peoples have in the past adopted—also has its numerous and serious drawbacks. If the society is unorganized or loosely organized, that system means that every village and town will have its band of armed men. The band will comprise those who feel the greatest repugnance to regular work and the greatest inclination toward adventure and violence, and sooner or later the band, or its leader, will begin to tyrannize over peaceful producers quite ignoring any rule or law. If the society is somewhat better organized, the bands taken as a whole will constitute a ruling class, which will be lords and masters of all wealth and all political influence—that was the case with medieval feudalism in western Europe and with the Polish nobility down to a century and a half ago. In a bureaucratic state, which represents the most complicated type of social organization, the standing army will absorb all the more belligerent elements, and, being readily capable of prompt obedience to a single impulse, it will have no difficulty in dictating to the rest of society.

The great modern fact is the huge standing army that is a severe custodian of the law, is obedient to the orders of a civil authority and has very little political influence, exercising indirectly at best such influence as it has. Virtually invariable as that situation is in countries of European civilization, it represents a most fortunate exception, if it is not absolutely without parallel, in human history. Only a habit of a few generations' standing, along with ignorance or forgetfulness of the past, can make such a situation seem normal to those of us who have lived at the end of the nineteenth and the beginning of the twentieth century, and so find it strange when we chance upon exceptions.

Exceptions have occurred on rare occasions in France, and more often in Spain. In Spain the standing army has at times overthrown the men in supreme power and even changed the form of government. One should remember, however, that this has happened at moments of crisis and social disorganization, and that once changing governments by violent means has become a practice, each party or social class uses the means most congenial to it and within easiest reach in order to gain the upper hand.

As a matter of fact, it has been possible to subordinate the standing army to the civil authority only through an intense and widespread development of the sentiments on which juridical defense is based, and especially through an exceptionally favorable sequence of historical circumstances.

Perhaps we had better touch on these circumstances at some length at this point, but we might note at once that it is not at all impossible that different historical circumstances that are now maturing may end by weakening, or even undoing, the complex, delicate and sagely elaborated mechanism of the modern army. If that actually takes place, we may find ourselves back with a type of military organization perhaps simpler and more natural but certainly more barbarous and less suited to a high level of juridical defense.

4. The historical process by which the modern standing army developed goes back to the end of the Middle Ages. During the fifteenth century, first in France and then in other regions of Europe, centralized monarchy, parent of the modern bureaucratic state, gradually replaced feudal militias with standing armies. Even in those days Europe suffered relatively little from military insurrections and military tyranny. This was due largely to the fact that the substitution came about slowly and gradually. Even toward the end of the Middle Ages European armies were becoming so complicated in structure that many different social elements were represented in them and served to balance one another. At the opening of that historical period, the cavalry was in general made up of men-at-arms, who were of gentle birth and were profoundly imbued with the aristocratic and feudal spirit, but who nevertheless were in the king's pay. The infantry was a motley collection of adventurers hailing from any number of countries. Little by little a

system came to prevail whereby the command of infantry regiments, and eventually of infantry companies, was entrusted to gentlemen, who differed in birth, temperament and background from their soldiers. Besides, down to the time of Louis XIV, and even after that, an old practice lingered on whereby a nobleman organized at his own expense a squadron of cavalry or a regiment or company of infantry from among the men who lived on his lands, and then hired himself out to some sovereign with his troop ready-made. It was always taken for granted that in case of need the king could call the whole nobility of the realm to arms.

The practice of leasing and hiring private regiments lasted down to the end of the eighteenth century. The traffic flourished especially in Switzerland and Germany. The La Marck regiment of German infantry was usually in service in France. Recruited preferably in the county of that name, it was always commanded by a member of the La Marck family, and the officers were appointed by the colonel. It passed on from generation to generation by inheritance. All that down to the French Revolution! The last general call of the whole nobility to arms took place in France early in the reign of Louis XIV. It became apparent at that time that an assemblage of twelve or fifteen thousand knights, all with different sorts of equipment, some too young and some too old, all personally courageous but untrained to fight in concerted movements, had very little value in actual practice. For much the same reasons the Polish cavalry lost most of its

military importance in the eighteenth century. The Magyar nobility was called to arms for the last time in 1809, when the French invaded Hungary. The body so formed was composed of horsemen who were individually brilliant but it showed little effectiveness in the battle at Raab, which was fought in connection with Napoleon's Wagram campaign.

Though the mixing of different social elements and different nationalities prevented the armies of the sixteenth and the first half of the seventeenth century from becoming masters of the countries they served, it was no easy matter to maintain tolerable discipline among troops made up of adventurers from everywhere and largely from the worst elements in society. The outrages committed by the German landsknechts and the Spanish miquelets became proverbial, but we have no reason to assume that the French, Swiss, Italian, Croat or Walloon regiments behaved very much better. The letters of Don Juan of Austria show what hard work, what shrewdness, what energy, that general and his officers were called upon to display in order to maintain a very relative discipline among the troops that put down the Moorish revolt in the Alpujarras, embarked on the galleys that won at Lepanto and then served in the war in Flanders. There is the story, from early in the sixteenth century, that on hearing that a Spanish army, which had gone overseas to conquer Algiers, had been defeated and all but destroyed, Cardinal Ximénez exclaimed: "God be praised! Spain is free of that many blackguards at least!" At the end of the same century, among the unattainable desires that Cervantes ascribes to the priest and the apothecary in the village where the Caballero de la Mancha was born was a hope that the soldiers who were marching from the interior to the seaboard to embark for foreign lands would not sack the homes of the peasants, their countrymen, along the road. Well known are the feats of the troops of all the countries that fought in the famous Thirty Years' War. One of the chief reasons for the aversion to standing armies that persisted so long in England was dread of the licentious ways of professional soldiers. In the reign of James II an English regiment under Colonel Kirke returned home after some years of service in Tangiers. It became notorious for its rapes and robberies. The regimental banner bore a lamb as its device, and British humor dubbed the soldiers who belonged to it "Kirke's Lambs."

In parts of Europe where medieval immunities and privileges survived down to modern times, the inhabitants of towns clung jealously to their right to man the walls and fortifications of their cities with local militiamen. Under the Spanish domination at Palermo, for instance, though the inhabitants, apart from some few lapses, remained loyal subjects to His Catholic Majesty, only a very small number of foreign soldiers were allowed to enter the town to guard the royal palace and the castle. The ramparts with their artillery remained in the control of the city militia made up of "the worthy guilds." At times when a question of strengthening the royal guard in the city came up, the guilds, loud-voiced in their professions

of devotion and loyalty to the king, nonetheless barricaded the streets and trained the guns of the ramparts upon the royal palace. The revolt at Messina in 1676 was brought on in part by an attempt by Don Luis del Hoyo, the strategos, to capture by surprise the forts that were manned by the town militia. The licentious conduct which could be taken for granted in soldiers was commonly alleged as the reason for such suspicions of the soldiery.

No better discipline was obtained until well toward the end of the seventeenth, or rather till the eighteenth century. Then feudal and town militias disappear almost everywhere, and the era of real standing armies in the modern sense begins. During those periods the necessity of keeping many men in arms and the difficulty of paying wages large enough to attract volunteers brought on conscription in most countries on the European continent. That system meant that common soldiers no longer came from the adventurous and criminal classes but were recruited from among peasants and workingmen, who never thought of devoting their whole lives to military service but returned, after the few years required of them, to their ordinary occupations. The officers continued to belong to a totally different class. They more and more became a sort of bureaucratized nobility, combining the orderliness and conscientiousness of the civil service employee with the chivalrous spirit and the high sense of honor that were traditional in the wellborn.

Frederick II of Prussia in his time

apologized for having been obliged during the Seven Years' War to make army officers of many men who were not of noble birth. He felt a certain dislike for this new type of officer because, he said, the man who was a gentleman by birth could offer greater moral and material guarantees. If he dishonored himself as an officer, he could not turn to some other pursuit, whereas the plebeian could always find some way to get along and was therefore less interested in scrupulously living up to the standards of his rank. The founder of Prussian power was an altogether unprejudiced individual. Such reasoning on his part shows that in Germany, as elsewhere, the growth of a class of people of superior education, yet not belonging to the nobility, is a relatively recent phenomenon.

Only in England and the United States has the old system of recruiting volunteers, preferably from among the unemployable elements of the poorer classes of society, hung on, conscription being resorted to only in great crises, such as the American Civil War or the World War. In those two countries, however, and especially in the United States, standing armies have always been relatively small. In view of their geographical situation, defense against foreign foes can in large part be entrusted to a navy, while internal order is maintained partly by local militias and in larger part by strong and well-organized police forces. Class distinctions between officers and privates in the regular armies are, furthermore, much more rigorously stressed than is the case in armies on the continent of Europe. The result

is that, in virtue of family connections and education, army officers retain close ties with the minority which by birth, culture and wealth stands at the peak of the social pyramid.

The corps of English officers has always maintained a highly aristocratic character. The system of purchasing rankings held on in the English army down to 1870. In his *English Constitution*, Fischel justly notes that it is not the Mutiny Act that has kept the English army from becoming a tool for coups d'état, but the fact that English officers belong by birth and sentiment to the classes that down to a few years ago were most largely represented in Parliament. The United States has followed the English tradition in all this matter. In the federal army there is a great difference in class, as well as in rank, between the commissioned officer of lowest rank and the noncommissioned officer of highest rank. In fact, between them lies an abyss that may well be compared to the gulf that separates the Negro from the white in the United States, a country where distinctions of color are of far greater moment than elsewhere.

5. The American nonprofessional militia has so far proved to be of very mediocre practical value. Washington himself remarked that if he were compelled to declare under oath whether he considered the militia useful or the reverse, he would have no hesitation in replying that it was useless. American foreign wars have been fought almost exclusively by federal armies augmented by volunteer enlistments, and that was also the

case in the Civil War. As regards internal disorders, one may at least wonder whether the American militia is more effective in quieting than in aggravating them. It has not been able to prevent the lynchings that are still frequent in the United States, and in dealing with strikes it has often dispersed or else come to terms. In any event, the American militia set the pattern for the European national guard, and was in a sense the parent of it. Great importance was attached to civilian militias down to a century or more ago, mainly on account of the political role which they were supposedly destined to play. The idea underlying the national guard was that it would provide an armed force free of blind, unreasoning military discipline and partisanship, which would serve to protect parliamentary institutions from encroachments by an executive power supported by a standing army.

As far back as the French Revolution, Mirabeau pointed very soundly to the drawbacks of such a military body. It would, he thought, be likely to favor or suppress a revolt according to the mood it happened to be in at the moment, and so in a way come to function as an armed arbiter between constituted authority and revolution. In spite of that, when the French Charter was revised in 1830, a special article provided that "the Charter and all the rights which it sanctifies shall continue to be entrusted to the patriotism and courage of the National Guard." When Garibaldi entered Naples to save the Sant' Elmo castle, whence the royal troops had theretofore held the city under their guns,

he had to promise that it would always be garrisoned by the Neapolitan national guard. As regards France, to tell the truth, the national guard did not always prove ineffective. In 1832 and 1834, and again in June 1848, fear of socialism inspired the peace-loving Parisian burghers with spurts of courage, and the national guard helped the army to put down the rioting. But in February 1848, dissatisfied with the Guizot ministry, and not realizing that a revolution was going on, it was at first hostile to the army, then puzzled, then finally inert, and its conduct was the main cause of the fall of the July Monarchy. It failed to prevent the coup d'état of December 2, 1851. In 1870–1871 socialist workers had been allowed to serve in its ranks. The elements of disorder therefore prevailed over the elements of order, and the citizen militia of Paris became the praetorian guard of the Commune. In our day, partly because the low efficiency and unsoundness of the institution are too well realized, and partly because by now every tradesman and shopkeeper has served for a time in the regular army and so has lost his enthusiasm for parades and uniforms, the national guard has been abolished in all the great countries of Europe. The fact that the national guard has lasted longest in Belgium, where the introduction of universal compulsory military service was also longest delayed, would lead one to suspect that the second of the reasons mentioned may not have been the less influential of the two.

6. On this matter of modern military

organization in Europe and its relation to juridical defense, two further remarks will be in point.

As we have seen, our modern armed forces comprise two classes of people, a class of officers, usually recruited from the politically dominant ranks of society, having a special education and training and beginning service at a fairly high rank, and another class made up of privates and petty officers, who find it hard to make their way into the higher ranks. Now absurdly conventional and arbitrary as this distinction may seem to be at first glance, it has always been more or less definitely present in all great and well-organized standing armies, whatever the period or country. It prevailed at certain periods in ancient Egypt. Papyri dating back to the dynasties that won greatest glory in arms speak of chariot officers and infantry officers who were educated in special military academies where they were introduced to all the hardships of army life. To enter such colleges one had to pay not money, which did not then exist, but slaves and horses. The same distinction was enforced to a certain extent in modern China, where the status of the military mandarin was somewhat similar to that of the modern army officer in the West. The military mandarin had to pass an examination before the military authorities of his province. He then entered the militia of one of the eighteen Chinese provinces with a relatively high rank. The examination was usually taken before the Tchang-kun, or chief, of the Tatar garrison, which was to be found, down to a few years ago, in all the strategic cities of China. After the civil wars of the middle of the nineteenth century, the various ranks of the military mandarinate came to have little importance, because they were often conferred so arbitrarily that a man who was discharged with a rather high rank in one province was often enrolled as a plain soldier in the next province, and vice versa. All the same, command of large bodies of soldiers was entrusted to governors of provinces and other civil mandarins of high rank, who won advancement only after a series of hard and thoroughgoing examinations. In China, it should be noted, as in ancient Rome, the higher civil posts were combined with high military posts.

But the distinction in question was unusually strict in the Roman legions during the last centuries of the republic and the first centuries of the empire. There a line was sharply drawn between the ordinary and the so-called equestrian militias. A militiaman of the equestrian class began service as a *contubernalis*—today we would say "aide-de-camp"—to the consul, or to the commander of a legion. This cadetship opened the way to the rank of military tribune and to the other higher ranks. For long centuries, on the other hand, the man who began his career as a private in the ordinary militia could at the most become a senior centurion, or "first spear," a grade that was the marshal's baton, as it were, of the Roman rank and file. This organization assured the tenure of high ranks in the army to the same social class that held the high civil magistracies and which, since it possessed both wealth and political power, made up the aristocracy of ancient Rome. The distinction between the *militia equestris* and the ordinary militia was based on a law that made the nomination of military tribunes and higher officers the prerogative of the comitia. Now popular elections in ancient Rome, as today in many countries which are not in a state of latent revolution and where the elective system has been long established, almost always gave preference to the rich, or to persons whose families already enjoyed great prestige and occupied prominent positions. In the early centuries of the empire the same organization held on. Tribunes and other higher army officers were still chosen from the more conspicuous Roman families. Little by little, however, the emperors began to excuse, first senators and then knights, from military service, fearing them as potential rivals. During the period of military anarchy that supervened in the third century A.D.—the so-called era of the Thirty Tyrants—privates could become generals and even emperors.

7. Our other observation relates to one of the most widespread conceptions, or misconceptions, in the world —that military qualities are very unequally distributed among peoples, some being naturally timorous and cowardly, other daring and courageous. Of course it could never be proved that there is no truth whatever in such notions. But beyond question the more or less warlike habits of a people and the type and soundness of its military organization are the elements that contribute most, on the whole, to increasing its military prestige.

In war, as in all dangerous occupations, a certain amount of experience is required if one is to face danger calmly and coolly. When that experience is lacking it can be made up for only by those moments of frenzy that occur at rare intervals in the life of every people or by a high sense of duty and honor that can be created and kept alive in a limited class of superior individuals by a special training. In civilized countries, where the great majority of people cannot devote themselves to bloody conflicts as a regular profession, one of the goals of military organization should be to keep distributed through the masses a small minority of individuals who are familiar with such conflicts and have been so prepared by the special training mentioned that they can dominate the plain soldier, exercise a decisive influence over him and lead him to face dangers from which he would otherwise recoil. The World War showed that the soundness of an army depends very largely on the strength of the patriotic sentiments that have been instilled by long and careful education, both intellectual and moral, in individuals belonging to the ruling classes and in the masses.

The organization in question may be more or less perfect, or even completely absent, and a ruling class may be familiar with the business of arms or, for one reason or another, completely shy of it. As one scans the history of civilized peoples, therefore, it is apparent that almost all of them have had their moments of military glory and their periods of material weakness. The Hindus were conquered and despoiled time after time by Turks, Mongols, Afghans and Persians, and they submitted to a few thousand Englishmen in the eighteenth century; yet of all the Asiatic peoples they were the ones who offered the stoutest resistance to the Macedonians. The natives of Egypt have for centuries had the reputation of being cowardly fighters, yet the troops of Amasis and Thutmosis, in their day the best armies in the world, were recruited among the inhabitants of the lower valley of the Nile. From the day of Leonidas down to Alexander the Great, the Greeks were considered very valiant soldiers, and in Xenophon's time they spoke with the greatest scorn of the Syrians and the Mesopotamians. But when Islam rose, the Semitic peoples of Asia took the lead again and literally massacred the unwarlike populations that gave their obedience to Byzantium. Amari seems inclined to ascribe the submissiveness that the Greeks displayed under Byzantine rule to the influence of Christianity. Now in the first place the Byzantine Empire lasted for ten centuries, and during that time it had not a few moments of extraordinary military energy. Then again, Christianity did not have any such effect on the Germans or the Slavs, and it is to be noted that the warlike spirit also revived among the Latin peoples of the West, once Roman administration had actually been obliterated and a feudal organization had emerged from anarchy. The real fact is that imperial efficiency and the Pax Romana had unaccustomed the citizens of the empire to arms, so that once the regular army was disposed of they fell a ready prey to any invader.

The Italians of the Renaissance made wretched soldiers, being unused to anything like real warfare. However, the Roman legionaries had been recruited among their ancestors. They had shown not a little valor in the day of the communes, and not so many generations after Machiavelli's time, the Italian regiments rivaled the Spanish in steadiness at the famous affair at Rocroi. The Neapolitans owed the very special reputation for cowardice that they enjoyed in a day not long past rather to a lack of cohesion and moral unity, which they displayed on a number of occasions, than to any deficiency in personal courage. In Spain and Russia under Napoleon I, and on other occasions as well, Neapolitan troops gave a fairly good account of themselves. Preeminence in some special branch of warfare and in certain definite military qualities is a very ephemeral thing among the nations, everything depending on the civil and military organization of the country in question. Machiavelli judged the French cavalry the best in Europe, since, he said, the French nobility were wholly devoted to the military calling. The infantry of that same nation he considered very poor, "because it was made up of the lowest rabble, and of artisans who were so overridden by the barons in everything they did that they could only be craven cowards." But, lo, the social and military organization changes, and the infantry becomes the backbone of the military power of modern France!

Muza ben Noseir, the Arab general who conquered Spain, said, in one of his reports to his caliph, Walid I, that the Goths (by which he meant all the Spanish) were "eagles on horseback, lions in their castles, weak women afoot." During the Peninsular War Wellington deplored the unsteadiness of the Spanish infantry in the open field, whereas behind the battlements of Saragossa, Tarragona and other cities, the same infantry showed extraordinary valor and stubbornness. Now we must assume that at the time of the Arab invasion the cavalry was composed of nobles, who were well trained in arms. As was the case later on, in the day of Napoleon, the infantry was probably thrown together by mass conscription and could show its native courage only behind battlements or in fortresses, not having acquired as yet the courage that comes from long habituation to military life and from a well-selected personnel. That, beyond any doubt, was the main asset of the Spanish infantry of the late Renaissance, from the day of Ferdinand the Catholic down to the day of Philip IV. During that period the Spanish army was regarded as the best fighting force in all Europe.

8. In our day a reaction against large standing armies has set in. They are blamed for withdrawing hands from factory and field, for instilling vices in the young and for occasioning almost unbearable expenditures of public treasure. Such plaints come in the main, it is true, from social elements that have at all times most conspicuously exhibited an inclination to assert themselves and to impose their will on the rest of society by force—from those who spontaneously and by nature have the greatest taste for the bearing of arms, and who, perhaps unconsciously, find an obstacle to the full expression of their instincts in the present military organization of the peace-loving, producing masses. We allude to the subversive revolutionary elements of our time, who count among their number the boldest, most adventurous and most violent elements in modern societies. But it is nonetheless true that the very pressures that have led the different European nations to create the prevailing organization of standing armies are now tending so to broaden and extend the application of the principles on which modern armies are founded as to alter and denature their structure.

First in the Napoleonic wars and then, and more particularly, in the Franco-Prussian war of 1870, victory went to the nations that had equipped and mobilized the largest armies. Those experiences brought the system of compulsory military service to exaggerated extremes in almost all the continental countries of Europe, and we have now come to the point where people think that in case of need they can turn the whole able-bodied populations of states of thirty, forty, seventy millions of inhabitants into armies. But to bring such an undertaking within range of the possible, it has been necessary to curtail terms of preliminary service, and that makes it doubtful whether conscripted recruits have time to acquire the habits and the special frame of mind which should distinguish the soldier from the rest of society, and which for technical and especially for political reasons must not be weakened beyond a certain point. Military expenditures for men, officers and armaments, which have to be renewed constantly, have enormously increased. It is becoming harder and harder to keep up with them, and public debts have piled up monstrously. This is one of the most serious afflictions of many modern countries, and under it some of the economically weaker nations are in danger eventually of succumbing.

In the introduction to the 1884 edition of *Das Volk in Waffen*, the late General von der Goltz expresses a favorite idea of his, that in the military history of the nations one may detect the conflict and alternating triumph of two opposite military tendencies. A first tendency is to increase masses of combatants more and more, to conquer by sheer weight of numbers. That process goes on and on until huge masses of men are led to war. Such masses are hard to handle and are always inadequately drilled, so that they come to be conquered by small armies of well-drilled professional soldiers. So specialization in the military function becomes the second tendency, which in turn leads to a renewal of mass armings.

General von der Goltz believed in the eighties that in Europe the trend toward increasing numbers of combatants had not yet reached its limit, and his prophecy was certainly valid for the World War. But the historical phenomenon which he stressed does not always unfold in regular rhythm. It at least undergoes exceptions and fluctuations, however clearly it may manifest itself in some few special cases. The Medo-Persians, according to the accounts of the Greek historians, succeeded in conquering all southwestern Asia by mobilizing enormous masses of men. The fact that Cyrus was able to keep a huge army under

the colors for more than one season was the cause of the rapid decline of the kingdom of Lydia. Great units of armed men held the field for long periods of time, also, during the two sieges of Babylon that took place under Cyrus and under Darius, son of Hystaspes. Other great masses were mobilized in the expedition against the Scyths and in the campaign of Xerxes. It was during the latter that the Persian military machine began to betray its defects. Because of the very fact that they belonged to a wide-rambling state the contingents from the various peoples who made up the Persian empire came to lack the training required for unending wars. Gradually their military abilities declined. The army became a mere assemblage of disorganized mobs which could not withstand the onrush of the Greek hoplites. These were few in number but they were thoroughly trained, heavily armed and skilled in fighting in mass formations.

Certainly in its process of expansion the modern military machine has become more and more complicated, more and more delicately adjusted. To direct its functioning in time of mobilization and war has become a task that bristles with greater and greater difficulties. We may even ask ourselves whether war itself will be possible when each passing day of hostilities, what with economic losses to the country and expenditures from the exchequer, will cost every nation tens and tens of millions, and when a declaration of war will harm the interests and shock the emotions of every single family in a whole civilized population. If the moral aversions and the economic interests that are opposed to war among civilized nations are able to stave such conflicts off for as few as sixty or seventy successive years, it is doubtful whether the military and patriotic spirit upon which modern armies are based, and which alone makes possible the enormous material sacrifices that wars require, can be passed on to the rising generations.

When the decline of that spirit and prolonged peace have abolished standing armies, or reduced them to "semblances vain and subjectless," a danger will again arise that the military predominance of the West may revert to other races, other civilizations, that have had, or will have had, different developments from the European, and will meantime have appropriated European methods and instruments of destruction. If that danger seems too remote and too fanciful to some of us, no one can deny that, within the structure of European nations themselves, there will always be violent characters and timid characters—there will always be conflicts of interest, and the will to have one's own way by brute force. Now the modern organization of the standing army has so far stripped the class of persons who have natural tastes and capacities for violence of their monopoly of the military function. When that organization has been dissolved or weakened, what is to prevent small organizations of the strong, the bold, the violent, from again coming to life to oppress the weak and the peaceful? When war has ended on a large scale, will it not be revived on a small scale in quarrels between families, classes or villages?

Indeed, from the doubts we have been voicing, a conclusion which we hardly have the courage to put into words may be drawn. It is that war itself—in its present forms the root of so many evils, the parent of so many barbarities—becomes necessary every now and again if what is best in the functioning of our western societies today is not to decline and retrogress to lower types of juridical defense. Grave and terrible as this conclusion is, it is, after all, only one more consequence of our complex and contradictory human nature. In the history of the nations, good and evil are inevitably linked. The juridical and moral improvement of society goes hand in hand with expressions of the basest and most selfish passions and the most brutish instincts.

The modern organization of armies, it will be noted, runs counter to the economic principle of the division of labor and to the physiological law of the adaptability of the various bodily organs to given purposes. That shows once again how hazardous it is to set up analogies between the phenomena of the human body and the phenomena of the social body, and once again calls attention to the reservations that have to be made in regard to certain economic laws when they are applied in the field of politics. If the principle of the division of labor were to be too rigorously followed in the political field it would easily upset all juridical balance, for the whole of a society would become subject to the group that exercises not the highest function from the intellectual or moral standpoint but the most indispensable function—the function that most readily enables some men to force their will upon others—the military function, in other words.

Modern nation-states tend to monopolize the normative use of force. In fact, this trait is an essential characteristic. At the same time, bureaucratic and corporate autonomy is also the chief characteristic of the modern military organization. The linkage between the two is high.

"The development of modern forms of organization in all fields is nothing less than identical with the development and continual spread of bureaucratic administration. This is true of church and state, or *armies*, political parties, economic enterprises, interest groups, endowments, clubs, and many others. Its development is, to take the most striking case, at the root of the modern Western state."*

The modern army is a bureaucratic army, as the modern nation-state is a bureaucratic state. The major characteristics of modern bureaucracy have been established by Weber's classic formula: (1) rationality in decision-making: a style of behavior that is appropriate to the achievement of given goals within limits imposed by given constraints; (2) impersonality in social relations: operation through impersonal application of rules; (3) centralization of authority: superordination/subordination relationship subject to impersonal rules; and (4) routinization of tasks through rules, roles, and files. "Only the bureaucratic army structure allows for the development of the professional standing armies which are necessary for the constant pacification of large territories as well as for warfare against distant enemies, especially enemies overseas. Further, military discipline and technical military training can normally be fully developed, at least to its modern high level, only in the bureaucratic army."† On the whole, the two salient components of the modern nation-state—mass armies and parties—have both developed complex and rational bureaucracies. "In most cases, the bureaucratic tendency has been promoted by needs arising from the creation of standing armies . . . "‡

Weber makes no distinction between bureaucracy and organization. (In fact, what we today call bureaucracy Weber called administration, or the technical quality of bureaucratic organization.) Because both the nation-state and the modern military organization are organization-bureaucracy types, both represent the legal-rational form of domination,

*Max Weber, *Economy and Society: An Outline of Interpretive Sociology*, 3 vols., 4th ed., eds. Guenther Roth and Claus Wittich, trans. E. Fischoff (Totowa, N. J.: Bedminster Press, 1968), 3:1006.
†Ibid., p. 946.
‡Ibid., p. 952.

and both are professional (that is, both have professional expertise or authority). "Bureaucratic administration means fundamentally domination through knowledge. This is a feature of it which makes it specifically rational."* The military and the modern nation-state are also hierarchical, rational, and legal in orientation. A profession of office (role) and a pursuit of exclusive and specialistic careers—in other words, *corporate* professionalism—are the fundamental characteristics of both the modern bureaucracy and the modern army. The modern official, according to Weber, always strives for a salary attainment and for a distinctly elevated social status. Here the aspirations of the modern bureaucrat and the modern military professional converge; both are searching for social esteem and corporate endowment.

Like Janus, the God of Gates, the military professional has two faces looking in opposite directions. He is both an expert and a bureaucrat. As a professional he must be dedicated to the universal standards of expertise which are acquired within the organization and set by the collegial community. In their dedication to protecting the organization, officers develop corporate orientations. As a client of authority, his corporate orientations are further institutionalized as a bureaucrat. But the military organization is not a simple elite of the state; it is also the state's major defender. Thus, the professional permanently guards the stability and well-being of the state, the military's client. Any perceived inefficiency, corruption, instability, or radical tendencies will immediately reflect on the professional corporate and organizational integrity, and the military will feel obliged to intervene. Thus, the propensity to intervene stems from the *same* corporate orientations of the professional, who under normal conditions, i.e., a stable, efficient, and nonradical (left and right) regime, is a loyal noninterventionist and, in most cases, is a subservient to the regime in power.

The balance between the professional and the bureaucrat, to reiterate, is the dependent variable that explains military interventionism or noninterventionism. Military corporatism is the key to explaining modern civil-military relations. The emphasis on either professionalism or on a bureaucrat orientation is the one that will be used here to explain the relationship between authority, regimes, and the military organization, the types of civil-military relations that emerge from these types of relationships: which can result in either professional, praetorian, or revolutionary military orientations. In sum, on one hand, emphasis will be on one face of Janus, i.e., military corporatism which acts as a bulwark against nonintervention, and the other face of Janus in different times and regimes, corporatism which stimulates interventionism.

*Ibid.,

The military establishment, like any other instrument of the state, has no autonomous reason to exist. It can exist only if its client defines its functions, expectations, and behavior. When the soldier delves into politics, he, unlike laborers, farmers, and industrialists, undermines the very reason for his corporate existence, becoming a political master instead of a political instrument. Nevertheless, when the corporate role and conception of the military establishment is challenged, the military will contemplate political intervention. In the absence of a stable, legitimate political authority, the military establishment will move into politics as surrogate, to fulfill its raison d'être as defender against domestic and external violence and to protect its own corporate body.

In summary, the professional and the bureaucrat in the modern military organization are symbiotic. Thus their convergence satisfies military corporate orientations. A conflict between the professional-bureaucrat and his client—the state—creates disaffection, distrust, and apprehension on the part of the corporate professional, which, on the whole, ends with military interventionism.

THE PROFESSIONAL SOLDIER IN PRUSSIA-GERMANY, FRANCE, BRITAIN, AND THE USSR

We focus on four examples of modern civil-military relations in Europe—three autocracies and one democracy. The first nation, Prussia-Germany, moved along a continuum from aristocratic autocracy to popular tyranny. The second, France, swung from revolutionary Jacobinism and democratic-republicanism to Vichy etatism. The third, Britain, evolved from aristocracy, amateurism, and corruption to professionalism. The last, the USSR, changed from monarchical to Stalinist tyranny; in the middle 1970s it still follows the one-party Bolshevik style. These four nations were among the great powers of Europe (with the exception of the USSR, until the 1930s), and their military establishments were among the most professionally skilled, obedient, powerful, and sizable of all times.

Analysis of the four different political systems points to the following general conclusions: (1) The military behaves like a corporate group, as do all other modern, rational, bureaucratic groups. (2) Professional proficiency is not necessarily correlated with, nor does it guarantee, a regime's objective control. (3) It is not ideology, but corporate integrity, which accounts for the officer corps' loyalty to the principle of clientship. (4) Like other organized groups in society, different officer groups espouse different ideologies. (5) Although a few prominent officers may prefer one type of regime, at different times they may uphold conflicting types of regimes.

(6) Although the officer group as a corporate entity is politically conservative, with most officers preferring a traditional regime, it can adjust to radical regimes in order to protect its corporate integrity. (7) Military corporatism is Janus-faced: instability invites the military to abandon its clientship responsibility and intervene. Intervention bolsters the solidarity of the military as a corporate group. The officer is always responsible to the state (the threatened client), but not to the regimes. (8) If the military becomes interventionist under an unstable regime, it will ultimately lose its autonomy, its corporate integrity, and perhaps even its client—the nation.

PRUSSIA-GERMANY: THE SWORD ON HORSEBACK, 1807–1945

More has been written on the Prussian-German than on any other modern military. Theorists of modern civil-military relations agree that the Prussian model is analytically the most fertile. The history of nineteenth- and twentieth-century Prussia, from Scharnhorst to Hitler, demonstrates the whole range of military behavior examined in this reader.

The most comprehensive history of the politics of Prussia-Germany and of civil-military relations in Prussia-Germany is Gordon Craig's classic, *The Politics of the Prussian Army, 1640–1945*. Craig is at his best in analyzing the role of the Prussian army (section I), its creation (section II), its institutionalization into a state within a state (section III), and the relationship between the military, statecraft, and foreign policy (section IV).

GORDON CRAIG

The Army and the State: 1640-1807

In his *Deutsche Geschichte* Franz Schnabel has written that the foundation of the Prussian state is the greatest political accomplishment in German history, the more so because the favourable geographical conditions which helped in the formation of other national units were totally lack-

From Gordon Craig, The Politics of the Prussian Army, 1640–1945 *(London, 1956)*, pp. 1–14, by permission of Oxford University Press.

ing in the case of the Hohenzollern domains. The lands which formed the nucleus of modern Prussia were in the seventeenth century scattered in a haphazard fashion across the five parallel streams which flow through northern Germany. . . . That the disparate fragments of territory were forged, not only into a viable political union, but into one which was recognized as a Great European Power, was the result of two things: the political will and sagacity of the Hohenzollern rulers after 1640 and the effectiveness of the army which they created.

When Frederick William, later called the Great Elector, assumed the throne of Brandenburg in 1640, he was confronted with conditions that might well have made him despair. The religious wars that had ravaged the German lands since 1618 had reduced the Elector's authority over his realm to the lowest possible point. In an age of war, Frederick William's father had made the fatal mistake of relying for safety upon diplomatic adroitness. . . . As a result his reign had ended with his Rhineland holdings ringed round by Dutch and Spanish armies, the province of East Prussia in open disaffection, and even Brandenburg itself, with the exception of Berlin and a few fortresses, under foreign occupation.

The new ruler . . . [was] convinced that the time had come to make a clean break with the policy of the past. The Hohenzollerns could not protect their heritage, he felt, by continuing to depend upon diplomatic manœuvre and shifting alliances. . . . The key to safety lay in military force, and the Elector set out deliberately to create a reliable military establishment.

From the very beginning, the military problem was closely intertwined with the whole question of state administration and local politics. The military weakness of the Elector at the beginning of his reign was largely caused by the desire of the hardnecked notables of his separate provinces to protect the privileges which they had extorted from previous rulers. Chief among these was their control of taxation. The Elector was dependent upon the Estates of Brandenburg, Cleves, Mark, and East Prussia for the funds with which to support his administration and pay his troops; and, despite the extraordinary expenses incurred by the war, the Estates had been unwilling to weaken the advantage they held over the ruler by unwise generosity. So niggardly had they been in their grants that, in 1640, the only troops at the disposal of the Elector were a few thousand mercenaries and refugees from other armies—*Landsknechte* of the lowest type, who were incapable of operations against organized forces and who terrorized the provinces they were supposed to defend. To replace these with a reliable army would require the assent of the Estates, and it was doubtful, in view of their past conduct, that this could be obtained.

It was this task, however, which the Elector set himself and which, in the end, he accomplished, with revolutionary political consequences. . . . In the first years of his reign, the undesirable and the unfit were purged; the rebellious colonels who had blackmailed the citizens of the fortress towns were arrested or driven into exile; and the most incompetent of the foreign mercenaries were discharged. What was left was a tiny force of 2,500 men, but this was the nucleus of the standing army of the future. The Estates, grateful for the relief from military anarchy, proved willing to supply the funds necessary to keep this force equipped and even to increase its numbers, and the

Elector took advantage of this mood to build up his army rapidly in the last years of the Thirty Years War. . . .

Once the war was over, the Estates reverted to the suspicion which had characterized their relations with the ruler in the past, and they made frequent demands in the course of the next thirty years for a substantial reduction of the army. By a mixture of timely concessions, studied evasions, and careful economy, however, the Elector was able to continue his policy of military expansion without serious interference until he was strong enough to defy his critics and destroy their centres of resistance. The key to his success in this regard was the famous arrangement which he made with his Brandenburg Estates in 1653. Here, in return for a grant of 530,000 talers, payable in instalments over a period of six years, the Elector made a sweeping grant of power to the great landholders who had been the most intransigent of his antagonists. The estates of these so-called Junkers he transformed from fiefs held in compensation for military and other services into alodial estates held in absolute ownership. Eliminating the legal restrictions which had bound the Junkers in the past, he recognized them as the only class authorized to acquire estates, he specifically exempted them from payment of taxes, and he gave them the right of absolute control over their peasants. Finally, he recognized the authority of the Junkers in local affairs, while simultaneously commissioning them as his agents in all matters that concerned Brandenburg as a whole. . . .

The immediately significant result of the compromise of 1653 was that it provided the Elector with the army he desired. It is true that the funds granted in 1653 were sufficient to maintain only a modest force, one which was probably not in excess of 5,000 men; but this was a foundation on which to build, and how quickly and efficiently the Elector could build when given an opportunity, he demonstrated when war broke out between Sweden and Poland in 1655. Pointing to the manifest dangers inherent in this conflict Frederick William ordered his agents to begin recruiting additional forces in both Brandenburg and the principalities on the lower Rhine and called out the East Prussian militia. The protests of the Brandenburg Estates, who had no inclination to contribute funds for the defence of provinces other than their own he brushed aside unceremoniously and proceeded to impose a variety of extraordinary taxes to support the new recruits. With this encouragement, his army grew rapidly. . . .

Prussia's standing army was born during the war of 1655–60. There were reductions in its size after 1660, but they were never as extensive as previous reductions had been; and the Elector and his successors were never again forced to build a military establishment virtually from the ground up when an emergency faced the state. Between 1660 and 1672 the Elector was able to keep between 7,000 and 12,000 men with the colours. . . . After 1672, when the expansionist aims of Louis XIV involved the European Powers in a long series of wars, Frederick William's army began to expand again and, thanks to the Elector's ability to exact sizeable subsidies from those who wished his alliance, at a faster rate than before. Nor was the Elector inclined any longer to make concessions to provincial authorities who resisted the rapid increase of his forces. . . .

When the Elector died in 1688 he left an army whose strength has been estimated at about 30,000 men. It was a force whose organization had undergone radical change since 1640. The old mercenary system in which the colonels contracted to supply the ruler with regiments of a stipulated size but brooked no interference on his part with the administration and command of their troops, was gradually modified in the course of the Great Elector's reign. The first steps were taken toward the modern system of centralized army administration. In 1655 the Elector gave Freiherr von Sparr general command over all troops in the Hohenzollern lands, a step which, theoretically at least, unified the hitherto unco-ordinated provincial forces; and under Sparr's direction a kind of General Staff came into existence which gave some practical meaning, in matters of command, to this concept of unification. Simultaneously the activities of Claus Ernst von Platen, who was appointed as *Generalkriegskommissar* during the Swedish war and was charged with overall supervision of such things as the assembling, remounting, provisioning, and billeting of the army, its payment, stores, and magazines, and the imposition of contributions at

home and abroad, also rapidly promoted uniformity within the Elector's army. As a result of these measures the authority of the colonels inevitably declined. Increasingly, the Elector sought to avoid specific contracts (*Kapitulationen*) with individual commanders; progressively he curtailed the colonels' right to commission junior officers and laid the basis for a system in which all officers owed complete allegiance to the ruler as commander-in-chief of the army. Finally, he tried . . . to alter the mental outlook of his officers and to persuade them to think of themselves less as speculators and business men than as servants of the state.

Incomplete as they were, these efforts in the direction of centralization were reflected in increased efficiency in the field. During the reign of the Great Elector the army of Brandenburg-Prussia not only demonstrated that it was capable of defending the territories of its ruling house but, by its victories at Warsaw and Fehrbellin, won the consideration and respect of the Great Powers of Europe, a fact adequately demonstrated by the eagerness with which its aid was solicited in the Elector's last years. . . .

The lesson was not lost upon his successors. The Great Elector's son is generally considered to have been a weak ruler. . . . But this first Prussian King nevertheless respected the realities, as well as the trappings, of power; he recognized the army as the bulwark of his authority; and he gradually increased its strength until it stood at a level of 40,000 men. And when his son, the remarkable Frederick William I, came to the throne in 1713, the growth of the army was made the first objective of his policy.

Like the Great Elector, Frederick William I believed that the international position of a prince was determined entirely by the number of troops he could maintain. . . .

Acting upon his own precepts, Frederick William, from the outset of his reign, bent all his energies to the task of increasing the size and efficiency of the army and, at the same time, of freeing it from that dependence upon foreign subsidies which had, in previous reigns, involved the Hohenzollerns in wars which did not always advance their own interests. By a policy of the most rigid economy, in which the Prussian state spent four and five times as much annually on its army as it did on all other obligations, Frederick William increased the size of his military establishment from 40,000 to 83,000 men, a figure which made Prussia's army the fourth largest in Europe although the state ranked only tenth from the standpoint of territory and thirteenth in population.

This remarkable increase was accompanied by fundamental changes in the composition and personnel of the army and its leaders. The king's greatest source of concern in the early years of his reign was man-power. The fantastic severity which characterized Prussian discipline encouraged desertion. . . . More important sources of attrition were age and sickness which led annually to the discharge of 20 per cent. of the effective force. The king soon found that he could not hope to replace these losses by relying upon volunteers. During his early years,

therefore, he resorted increasingly to the impressment of his own subjects and to recruiting—and recruiting which was at times indistinguishable from kidnapping—in neighbouring states. The results of this, however, were scarcely satisfactory. Not only was the king involved continually in disputes with other rulers, who resented the infringement of their rights, but he was confronted in his own lands with mounting public indignation and—and this was probably more troubling to his frugal nature—with an increase in emigration which had deleterious effects upon the economy of the state.

Frederick William I sought to escape these difficulties by making service in the standing army legally binding upon all his subjects. The obligation to defend the country in time of emergency by service in local militias had been assumed ever since the Thirty Years War and had been given legal weight by a regulation of 1701. The militia system had never, however, been systematically applied; the temporary formations were ineffective as reserves for the standing army; and enrolment in the militia had all too often been used as an excuse to escape service in the regular military establishment. Frederick William, then, in the first year of his reign, abolished the existing militia organizations and simultaneously decreed that anyone who left the kingdom in order to escape service in the regular army would be treated as a deserter. By implication this decree established the principle of universal liability to military service.

Over the next twenty years other

declarations regularized recruiting procedure, culminating in the decrees of 1732-3 which established the basic features of what came to be called the Prussian canton system. Every regiment in the army was assigned a specific recruiting district; all young males in the district were enrolled upon the regimental recruiting list; and, when the quotas could not be filled by voluntary enlistment, the difference was made up from the eligibles on the rolls. . . . In practice liberal exemptions were made in the interest of trade, industry, and the public service; the whole upper stratum of society, including the more prosperous artisans and workers in industries which were of interest to the state, were freed of the duty of service; and the burden fell almost exclusively upon the agricultural workers and the less prosperous peasantry. Moreover, even these conscripts were granted very liberal furloughs. In order to safeguard the interests of the large landholders, the peasant conscripts were released from active duty after a two months' drill period every spring and thus, in time of peace, the army was at full strength only in April and May.

Even with this limited application, the canton system was a notable innovation. It assured the army of what was in effect a large trained reserve which could be mobilized quickly in time of emergency. It also wrought an important change in the very character of the military establishment, for, despite the large number of foreign mercenaries in the service, the army would now, at least in time of war, be predominantly national in composi-

tion. Finally—and not least important —the accepted convention of a universal obligation to render military service was to supply the necessary basis for the thorough-going reorganization of the Prussian army which was to be effected in the Napoleonic period.

Fully as important as the canton system, was the king's successful effort to persuade his nobility to take service in the army. In the proud and truculent barons of his marches he recognized the military virtues of which the state stood in need, and he clearly discerned that these rural lords were the natural leaders of the peasant boys who were now subject to military service. . . . In order to integrate the rural masses into his military establishment, Frederick William relied upon his Junkers, whose service in the officer corps would effectively introduce into the army a relationship between officer and soldier similar to the traditional relationships of rural society.

The reconciliation of the nobility with the Crown had begun under the Great Elector, the way having been opened by the compromise of 1653. Despite the personal prestige of the Elector, however, and despite the advantages he had been willing to offer the nobles who entered his service, resistance had continued, especially in East Prussia. Frederick William I determined to overcome this as much for political as for military reasons. . . . At the beginning of his reign he made it illegal for members of the nobility to enter foreign service. At the same time he ordered lists prepared of all young noblemen between the ages of 12 and 18 years and, on the basis of these, personally chose those who were to be admitted to the cadet corps in Berlin, which was the gateway to the officer corps. For a time this practice met with spirited opposition, especially in East Prussia. . . . But the king had little patience with such evasions and was not above sending police agents or detachments of troops to round up his prospective officers and to march them to Berlin in gangs.

By 1724 there was scarcely a noble family in the Hohenzollern domains that did not have a son in the officer corps, and by 1740 the king's private battle had been won. This was probably the result, less of his willingness to use force, than of the solid advantages which he held out to his nobility. To the sons of families which often possessed more pride than economic means, he offered an education, a standard of living higher than they could otherwise expect, an opportunity to rise to positions of great military and political authority, and a social position second to none in the state. They were offered also the less tangible, but certainly no less attractive, advantages of association with the king in an honourable calling on terms of complete social equality. In the new officer corps Frederick William wore the same coat as did his captains and lieutenants; with the sole exception of the generals no officer bore any designation of rank, and the ruler and his nobles comprised a closed society governed by the laws of professional competence and feudal honour. It is not surprising that the nobility should find this atmosphere congenial and should come to regard the service, which it entered with initial reluctance, as its natural profession.

While the canton system and the mobilization of the nobility for military purposes gave his army a national basis which it had not had before, Frederick William continued along the lines so shrewdly plotted by the Great Elector and advanced the uniformity and centralization of his armed force. Dress and weapons were carefully prescribed by the king and his advisers. In 1714 Frederick William himself wrote the first comprehensive Infantry Regulations ever to be issued to the army, a set of instructions which henceforth governed every phase of the soldier's life in the garrison and the field. The manual exercises and tactical evolutions laid down here, and the endless drilling with which they were impressed upon the troops, gave to Frederick William's infantry a flexibility and precision in manœuvre which had hitherto been unknown in continental armies, while at the same time they produced the rapidity and accuracy of fire which was to make Prussian armies famous throughout all Europe under Frederick William's successor.

For all the importance which he attributed to the possession of an army, Frederick William was very reluctant to use it, and he carefully avoided adventures which might jeopardize the safety of his beloved grenadiers. Not so his son. Even before his accession to the throne the prince, who was to be remembered as Frederick the Great, had chafed at Prussia's inactivity and had been ashamed that, despite her strength, she should be reckoned as a mere pawn on the European chessboard. . . . In her present state Prussia was still a her-maphrodite, more electorate than kingdom; her sprawling provinces offered an open invitation to foreign aggression; consolidation was necessary but could be effected only by new acquisitions; and new acquisitions would necessarily involve resort to force. This being so, Prussia must grasp the first opportunity that presented itself, and Frederick found it in the accession of Maria Theresa to the throne of Austria in 1740. As he prepared what can only be called a war of aggression against this ruler, Frederick paid no heed to the legal objections of his ministers or the doubts of his military advisers. . . . When he threw his troops across the frontiers of Silesia in 1740, inaugurating a generation of devastating conflict, Frederick risked nothing less than the utter destruction of his state. But, by winning Silesia, and proving his ability to retain it, he destroyed the old German constitution and

raised Prussia to a position of virtual equality with Austria.

The wars of Frederick the Great completed the constructive work of the Great Elector and Frederick William I, at once testing the perfected weapon and achieving the purpose for which it had been forged. . . . In the fire of the Seven Years War the reconciliation between the king and his nobles was finally completed, and the officer corps became the embodiment of the spirit of devotion to the Crown and the state, while the common foot-soldier gained a consciousness of his own ability which, handed on to his successors, was to make Prussian troops the finest soldiers in Europe. Finally, the achievements of the army crowned with success the process begun in 1640, effected a fundamental change in the European balance of power and established beyond question Prussia's title to Great Power status.

GORDON CRAIG

Stein, Scharnhorst, and Reforms

[The era of reform (1807–9) represents one of the most significant events in the history of Europe, Prussia, and its army. Napoleon's challenge to Europe was also a turn of events in the history of Prussia. Prussia was the first German state after 1806 to be subjected and the first to be reconstructed. The

From Gordon Craig, The Politics of the Prussian Army, 1640–1945 (London, 1956), pp. 38–52, by permission of Oxford University Press.

subjection occurred in the war of the Third Coalition (1805–6) of Austria, Russia, Sweden, and England against France and Spain. After Napoleon's Victory at Austerlitz (2 December 1805) Prussia concluded a treaty with France. But the treaty didn't last long. The Prussian army, declining under the command of the vain and incompetent Duke of Brunswick, brought about the greatest Prussian disaster of the 1806–7 battles of Jena and Auerstädt, when, on 14 October 1806, the main Prussian armies were completely routed and quickly fell to pieces. By October 27, Napoleon occupied Berlin.

The shock to the Prussians was severe. Government disorganization and a rotten army caused the disaster. A team of brilliant civilian and military reformers emerged to save Prussia, led by Hardenberg and Baron vom Stein. Generals Scharnhorst, Gneisenau, and Boyen formed a military commission which totally reformed the Prussian army and which, in fact, helped lead to the victory against Napoleon in the battles of 1813–15. This successful campaign brought about the liberation of Prussia. Thus began an uninterrupted growth of German nationalism and militarism and the rise of one of the most brilliant and successful armies of all times—the Prussian army—whose impact upon the history of Prussia-Germany and of Europe in general was most significant. In military terms, the work of the reformers was successful; the Prussian army played a significant role in the defeat of Napoleon.]

The period of the reforms may be said to have begun in July 1807 when King Frederick William III appointed a Military Reorganization Commission and instructed it to investigate the recent campaign, to cashier and punish those officers whose conduct had been improper, and to propose changes in army organization, supply, service regulations, selection of officers and education and training. The establishment of such commissions was not new, and, after a major defeat like Jena, some sort of investigation was to be expected. There was less immediate expectation that the commission would propose any startling changes in the existing system. In the eyes of many senior officers—including Count Lottum, one of the original members of the commission, and generals York and Knesebeck—the defeat of 1806 had been caused by no fundamental defects in the military or political system but rather by a combination of incompetent leadership and bad luck. Consequently, although they believed that the more patent abuses should be corrected, they saw no necessity for anything in the nature of basic reorganization and reform.

From this kind of superficial patchwork, the Prussian state was saved by two circumstances. The first was the fact that the Military Reorganization Commission, after some initial internal disharmony, came to be dominated by Scharnhorst and his disciples Gneisenau, Boyen, and Grolman. The second was Napoleon's insistence in July 1807 on the dismissal of Hardenberg, the king's chief minister, an event which led Frederick William to recall the Baron vom Stein to his service and to intrust him with the direction of all internal and external affairs. The ascendancy of Scharnhorst and Stein gave the post-war reorganization its distinctive character and made the years 1807–15 one of the most promising periods of reform in German history.

Temperamentally, Stein and Scharnhorst were poles apart. . . . In their political and social philosophy, however, and in their attitude toward the recent defeat, their attitudes were remarkably similar. Both realized that Jena and Auerstädt represented more than a military misfortune, that they were, in fact, a terrible judgement against the political and military system of the past. Both felt, moreover, that the most shameful aspect of the recent débâcle was the fact that the Prussian people had so openly disassociated themselves from the fate of their government and their army. This deplorable absence of a popular sense of duty and sacrifice in extremity was clear proof, they believed, that the mass of the population regarded the state as a mere instrument of oppression and the army as an alien establishment serving the king rather than the land. If Prussia was to survive, the interest of the masses in their state must be awakened and they must be persuaded to serve it willingly. . . .

The reformers were unanimous in their belief, however, that this regeneration was unlikely, if not impossible, under existing conditions. How could a peasant in the Mark be expected to act like a responsible citizen as long as he continued to be held in hereditary bondage to the local landholder? How could the middle classes of the towns be expected to recognize their duties to the state as long as they were barred from any participation in local government? And how, above all, could Prussian subjects who were called to the colours be expected to fight loyally and bravely in an army which showed no respect for their individual moral worth, which allowed them no opportunity for advancement during their service, and which regarded them as cannon fodder rather than as citizens? Certainly an amelioration of the burdens of the past and a grant of basic social and political privileges to all Prussian subjects were the prerequisites of the revival needed to free Prussia from French domination. And because they believed this to be true, the reformers could not be satisfied with the kind of superficial reform which the more conservative members of the ruling class considered adequate. Stein embarked on the programme which was to bring the abolition of hereditary serfdom in October 1807 and the institution of local government in the cities in November 1808. . . . The reform party in general were of the opinion that the best way of [improving the quality of the officers] was to put an end to the aristocratic monopoly of the officer corps. . . . Certainly it was not the Junker class who would rescue Prussia from her present extremity. 'What can we expect', [Grolman] wrote, 'from the inhabitants of these sandy steppes— these artful, heartless, wooden, half-educated men—who are really capable only of becoming corporals or book-keepers?' The time had come, he and the other reformers argued, to open the officer corps to talented members of the middle class and to make educational qualification the decisive fact in securing a commission.

Despite his natural antipathy to daring innovations, the king placed no immediate obstacles in the way of the reformers in this matter. It is probably true that his bitterness at the conduct of the aristocracy, and the officer corps in particular, led him to regard the middle classes with more affection than might have been expected. . . . The order of 6 August 1808 declared that:

A claim to the position of officer shall from now on be warranted, in peace-time by knowledge and education, in time of war by exceptional bravery and quickness of perception. From the whole nation, therefore, all individuals who possess these qualities can lay title to the highest positions of honour in the military establishment. All social preference which has hitherto existed is herewith terminated in the military establishment, and everyone, without regard for his background, has the same duties and the same rights.

To implement this sweeping statement, regulations were issued putting an end to the system whereby Junkers of 12 and 13 years were permitted to serve as corporals until they could be commissioned. From now on, any young man who had reached the age of 17 years and had served three months in the ranks could take regimental examinations for admission to the rank of cornet (*Portepéefähnrich*), fourteen of whom were authorized for each infantry regiment and eight for each cavalry regiment. The new examination system was applied also to promotions to the higher grades. Before the cornets were admitted to the grade of lieutenant, they were forced to undergo a second examination before a board in Berlin; and it was intended—at least originally—that all officers should pass examinations before promotion to a higher grade.

These innovations were regarded with horror by the officers of the old school. The admission of the *bourgeoisie* to the officer corps they regarded as an attack upon their own class and an unjust deprivation of prerogatives which belonged to them. . . . The conservatives . . . felt that the emphasis on book-learning was ill-advised, since 'too much learning kills character', and they did not hesitate to intimate to the king that the elaborate system of examining boards would destroy the intimate relationship which had always existed between the sovereign and his officers. These arguments were not without effect and, even at the very inception of the new system, important reservations were made. In the instructions to the examining commissions it was pointed out that 'knowledge and scholarship are not the only qualifications which mark a useful officer— presence of mind, ready perception, precision, correctness in his duty and propriety in his deportment are essential qualities which every officer must possess'. This was doubtless a reasonable safeguard against excessive emphasis upon book-knowledge, but it was certainly open to abuse by prejudiced examiners. In addition, a royal order of March 1809 reaffirmed the king's right to appoint commanding officers at his own discretion—a reminder to the reformers that he did not intend to allow his royal rights to disappear.

These reservations could not alter the fact, however, that the reformers had effected a serious breach in the old system. The opening of the officer corps to the middle classes and the new emphasis upon educational qualifications, supplemented the reforms inaugurated by Stein to lower class barriers and to remove social inequalities. The conservatives were at this time powerless to introduce more than minor modifications in the new regulations, since the memory of Jena was still sharp and the need for intelligent officers apparent. Thus Scharnhorst was able to go on his way and to supplement the order of August 1808 with a thorough-going reorganization of the military schools. By the middle of 1810 all of the old basic schools, except the *Kadettenhaüser* in Berlin and Potsdam, had been dissolved. In their place new schools of war were established in Berlin, Königsberg, and Breslau, offering nine-month courses to give candidates for commissions 'whatever is required by those who desire to be officers'. For the 'spiritual advancement' of officers in general a superior military academy—the germ of the later *Kriegsakademie*—was founded in Berlin, where small groups of selected officers were given a three-years' course in military specialties, including mathematics, tactics, strategy, artillery, military geography, French and German, physics, chemistry, horse care, and mess administration. The upper class of this academy, the so-called *Selekta*, became the chief recruiting ground for the General Staff, and it was in the training of future staff officers that Scharnhorst's disciples, Clausewitz and Tiedemann, first won renown throughout the army. The effect of these changes was not immediate, but it was important. The proper relationship between book-learning and soldierly qualities was to be a matter of heated controversy until late in the century; but there can be no doubt that the number of well educated and culti-vated officers was greatly increased by Scharnhorst's reforms.

The reform of the officer corps was perhaps the most successful aspect of the work of the Military Reorganization Commission. Their progress in reorganizing the army as a whole into an effective fighting force was slower, and their achievement less spectacular. There was, of course, good reason for this. The structure of the army and the machinery for conscription had to be overhauled completely in view of Napoleon's virtual control of the Continent, which made foreign recruiting impossible and forced Prussia, with greatly reduced territory, to rely entirely on native forces. It was, moreover, difficult to set a limit to the size of the standing army without knowing what Napoleon would permit and what the shattered finances of the state would stand. . . .

The Treaty of Paris [1808] not only imposed restrictions upon the size of the standing army but forbade extraordinary measures for national defence or the formation of a civil guard. The latter condition was an even more serious blow to the reformers than the former, and Scharnhorst, Gneisenau, and Grolman tried in vain to induce the king to refuse to accept it, since it threatened to make impossible the fulfilment of their plans for complete reform of the conscription system and the establishment of a truly national army. Gneisenau in particular feared that the treaty would encourage the natural timidity of the king and persuade him to be content with a mere reorganization of the old style standing army, the kind of army which, he wrote scornfully, 'had contributed more than anything else to the enervation and degeneration of peoples, which destroyed the warlike spirit of the nation and its sense of community by relieving the other sections of society from the duty of directly defending the State'. Although some members of the commission had, during the early months of its labours, talked in terms of perpetuating the old canton system with all of its exemptions, the reform party—both those on the commission and those, like Stein and Oberpräsident Schön, who were active in civil affairs—were determined that the principle of universal liability must be firmly applied and that all young men who were not called into the standing army must be made liable for service in some kind of national militia. In a memorandum to the king on 15 March 1808 the commission unanimously recommended the application of the principle of universal service; and in December of the same year they elaborated this demand by recommending universal conscription for all men between 20 and 35. They recommended further that no exemptions of any kind should be allowed; that the selection for the regular army should be by lot; and that plans for a reserve militia, working in conjunction with the regular army, should be made.

It is impossible to over-estimate the importance which the reformers attributed to this aspect of their work. . . .

In December 1808, when the commission, as has already been mentioned, recommended the establish-ment of universal conscription, the king took no action. Frederick William had no desire to see the professional army replaced by a more popular one, and he was encouraged in his resistance by his financial advisers, who told him it would ruin the state; by men like Niebuhr who opposed it out of religious conviction and by provincial authorities who regarded it as a dangerous French idea. As for the plans for a national militia, the king regarded them with disfavour from the very first. What he knew of the history of England and France convinced him that militias were inimical to royal authority, and he feared, moreover, that the creation of a second force would lower the prestige, and eventually the efficiency, of the standing army. The Treaty of Paris was a blow to the reformers because it gave the king an additional reason for refusing to follow their programme; and their cause was even more seriously injured in November 1808 when Napoleon once more asserted his influence in Prussian affairs and forced the dismissal of Stein from office. The fall of this indomitable fighter for basic reform rejoiced the hearts of conservatives like York, who wrote: 'One mad head is already severed; the remaining rabble of serpents will die in its own poison.' This prophecy was premature, but it nevertheless seemed true that the influence of the reformers was on the wane. Certainly they made no immediate progress with their plans for universal conscription or for a national militia. Until 1813 the old canton system, with all the customary exemptions, remained in force, and no steps were taken to erect supplementary popular formations.

Retention of the canton system not only blocked the basic objectives of the reformers but made impossible any appreciable increase in the size of the army. Attempts were made after 1807, and especially after 1809, to build up the strength of the forces, primarily by means of the so-called *Krümper* system, whereby each company or squadron annually gave leave to a prescribed number of trained men and replaced them with raw recruits. . . . The *Krümper* system, first suggested by Scharnhorst in July 1807, was designed . . . to train replacements for war; it was not applied to the whole army until 1809 and was interrupted in 1811; and it was far less effective than has been imagined. At the outbreak of war in 1813 the Prussian army and its trained reserves numbered only 65,675 officers and men.

It need not be concluded from all this, however, that the accomplishments of the reformers were trifling. While it is true that they had been checked in their desire to form a truly national military establishment, they had at least laid the foundations upon which such a force could be established at some later date. Moreover, such reforms as the opening of the officer corps to the middle classes and the revision of military justice, which were animated by the same philosophy as Stein's reforms of the civil government, were received with favour by the general public and helped to reduce the popular bitterness against

state and army which had been so strong after Jena. The reformers were realistic enough to understand that they must now wait upon events, in the hope that the growing arrogance of Napoleon and the increasing popular irritation at French exactions would compel the king to abandon his cautious course and take up arms again. When he did this, they were determined to persuade him to complete the work begun so well in 1807 and 1808 and to create the citizen army from which they expected so much.

Quite apart from this Scharnhorst and his colleagues had good reason for satisfaction, for, in the field of technical efficiency, they had effected decided improvements in the existing armed force. The basic equipment of the army, from uniforms to ordnance, was studied with a critical eye. Diligent attempts were made to improve the supply and efficiency of small arms and artillery, and new foundries were established for the manufacture of arms, although the rate of output was always severely limited by the shaky finances of the state. In the field of tactics serious efforts were made to benefit from French practice, and new training manuals were written which emphasized the use of light troops, the columnar battle formation, and the cooperation of all arms in the field. With respect to the last of these, the brigade organization which was introduced after the French treaty of 1808 enabled infantry and cavalry units to train together and to become accustomed to the kind of collaboration in the field that had been so conspicuously absent in 1806. It made possible also a complete overhauling of the supply services, and distribution and accounting of supplies were now centralized under the authority of a newly established War Commissariat with representatives in each of the six brigades.

By all odds the most important of these technical innovations was the establishment of the new Ministry of War in March 1809. . . .

The new ministry would have authority 'over everything which pertained to the military and to its constitution, its establishment and its maintenance and . . . everything which hitherto lay within the jurisdiction of the *Oberkriegskollegium*, the *Militärdepartement* of the General Directory, the Provincial Magazine Departments of Silesia and Prussia as well as the *Generalintendantur*. . . .' The new ministry was divided into two departments, a General Department of War *Allgemeine Kriegsdepartement* and a Military Economy Department (*Militär Ökonomiedepartement*). The first of these, which was to deal with all matters of administration and command, comprised three divisions, the first handling questions of personnel, including promotions, pay, decorations, justice, and dismissal, the second dealing with training, educa-

tion, war plans, and mobilization, and the third having supervision over artillery, engineering, fortifications, ordnance, and the testing of inventions. The Military Economy Department, with four divisions, was to concern itself with all matters of finance and supply.

Having granted this much the king, characteristically, baulked at the final step needed to complete the reform. Doubtless fearing to give too much power in military affairs to any single individual he refused to appoint a Minister of War. Instead, Scharnhorst was made head of the General Department of War, with the additional title Chief of the General Staff, while Graf Lottum, a conservative, was made Chief of the Military Economy Department. . . .

Although the Ministry of War was not united under a single minister until 1814, the king's caution was not productive of very great harm. After the ministry began to function, in March 1809, it was dominated by the personality of Scharnhorst, and the two departments seem to have worked together amicably. . . . The competing agencies whose strife had contributed so directly to the confusion at Jena now disappeared or were subordinated to the new ministry. . . .

The Prussian experience, according to historian Hans Rosenberg in his opus *Bureaucracy, Aristocracy and Autocracy* (1966), is a classic model of the convergence of monarchial conservatism and bureaucratic aristocracy (civilian and military) that produced an authoritarian civilian control system, the opposite of the Huntingtonian model, which was essentially based on democratic regimes' relations with the military.

The union of the military and the regime in Prussia took place at the expense of the growth of a civil society. The monarch, as chief warlord, reigned supreme over his bureaucratic clients, the bureaucracy and the military. The client of the Prussian officer class was not the state, but the Hohenzollern warlord.

Rosenberg's fascinating analysis of the emergence of dynastic absolutism clearly demonstrates the other route (other than the Huntingtonian) by which the modern state marshalled the military. He presents a picture of a Junker aristocracy apparatus recruited from the Junker classes, while at the same time showing the creation of *étatisme* by the Junker-directed Regierungen, based on a coalition of territorial *Stände* (estates) and of military office.

The new bureaucratic elite and the formation of large administrative and military bureaucracies and the recruitment of new classes, lifted former restrictions on the social mobility of non-Junker classes. "Common intruders entered the exalted bureaucratic elite."*

Yet, as Theodore Hamerow, a leading social and intellectual historian of nineteenth-century Prussia, writes, "Service in the armed forces was part of an educational process which tended to make the lower classes politically submissive."†

Corporate exclusivity, military anti-Semitism, and antiliberalism were products of the military's isolation from society and of the arrogance of the Junkers—those favorite sons of the warlord. All three of these phenomena were multiplied in the era of the Prussian army's professionalization and institutionalization when the professional quintessence of the Prussian military general staff was created. Military corporatism, the other side of the Janus face, also challenged professionalism by putting forward General von der Goltz's dictum that officers should be selected more for their heart and character than for their intellect and scientific attainment. This was designed to discourage the bourgeoisie from entering the military and to defend the army from Jewish aspiration to enter the exalted Junker estate— the Prussian officer corps.

The army was expected to function as a laboratory for national integration. According to General von der Goltz, it was to be a system protecting heart and character from the onslaught of science, industry, intellectualism, and populism. Both he and General Bernhardi, a chief propagandist of the theory of preventive war, espoused a militant pan-Germanism as the proper kind of *virtu* to inculcate into society. Bernhardi spoke of the Prussian historical mission as a racial crusade against Slavs, an antiliberal weltpolitik, and von der Goltz echoed him. The officer's professional responsibility to the state and its ideals was identified by von der Goltz with devotion to

*Hans Rosenberg, *Bureaucracy, Aristocracy and Autocracy* (Cambridge, Mass.: Harvard University Press, 1966), pp. 11–14, 23–25.

†*The Social Foundation of German Unification*, 1858–1871 (Princeton: Princeton University Press, 1967), p. 276.

absolutist Prussian patriotism, while liberal republicanism was considered anti-Prussian and antihistorical in spirit. Von der Goltz identified dynastic and patriotic Germany with the mind of the professional officer corps. Thus, the special bond between the officer corps and the legitimate source of authority in Germany created a particularist military professionalism, despite the generally accepted view of the Prussian army as the very model of modern military professionalism. As military and political institutions became inseparable, they acted in society as mutually dependent variables, a change in the character of one producing a corresponding change in the other.

"The Officer Corps regarded its code of honor and the right to defend it in a duel," writes Martin Kitchen, "as an essential condition of its continued existence as a special caste." In fact, as Kitchen writes further,

the rigorous code of honor and the duels formed part of an attempt by the army to preserve its exclusive position in the state by underlining the differences between the military and the civilian population, by claiming for itself a higher sense of values, and by binding the members of the Officer Corps closer together in a corporate attitude to life that remained distinct from, and in many ways opposed to, the generally accepted ideas of the day.

The strength of the Officer Corps lies in its homogeneous composition and in its exclusiveness. Neither a title nor riches give one the right to hope to become an officer, but an innate feeling for duty, education and the aristocracy of character. The more exclusively we concentrate on that section of the community from which we wish to draw out recruits, the more certain we are to be able to protect our profession from alien elements, in spite of the general mania for equality. . . . the duel must not be thought of as an act of revenge, but as a confession of faith . . . an act that shows fidelity to one's beliefs and also an act of justice, the necessity and moral justification of which lies deep in noble human feelings.

MARTIN KITCHEN

The Army and the Civilians

The re-unification of the Reich by blood and iron gave the army an

From Martin Kitchen, The German Officer Corps, 1890–1914 (London, 1968), pp. 115–21, 131–35, by permission of Oxford University Press.

immense popularity; amongst patriotic Germans, who regarded the foundation of the second Reich as something approaching a miracle, admiration for the army was unbounded.

At the same time the army, flattered by this praise, was only too willing to return some of the attention lavished upon it. An American friend of the Kaiser, who knew Germany well, wrote, 'in the halcyon days which succeeded 1870 there was the most cordial fellowship between soldiers and civilians. Officers in uniform were a familiar sight at the hotel tables of small garrison towns'. These halcyon days were however numbered. As memories of Königgrätz and Sedan faded, and the Reich seemed to be less of a miracle and more of a commonplace, the army lost its popularity and retired from the hotel tables to the exclusiveness of the mess. Within a few years the cordial relations between the army and civilians became increasingly strained until they virtually ceased to exist. . . .

The army tended to pay very scant regard to the problems of civilian life, and this was particularly true of its attitude to reserve officers. The Ministry of Justice, for example, sent frequent complaints to the War Ministry that lawyers were being called up for service in the reserve too frequently and without sufficient notice, thus often causing considerable difficulties to the Ministry. The army also frequently disregarded the regulations and called up reservists without informing their superiors. This naturally enough led to complaints against such a high-handed attitude. Civil servants also complained that the time they spent on manoeuvres was subtracted from their holidays, and the War Minister was prepared to support their claim that reserve training should not be treated as a holiday. Although many ministries asked their employees to co-operate as far as possible, many still resented the somewhat inconsiderate attitude of the army.

The distinction between the army and civilians was nowhere more striking than in their respective legal positions. Throughout the period there was a strong movement demanding that soldiers be tried for civilian offences in civil courts. This encountered the steadfast opposition of the War Ministry. Military courts almost inevitably gave milder punishments to soldiers who were on trial for civil offences. Thus after one fight in a restaurant between soldiers and civilians the soldiers were all acquitted, but the civilians involved had also to be acquitted because all the witnesses declared that they had been acting in self-defence. . . . These and other examples of the army enjoying a particularly favoured position in the eyes of the law did not help the establishment of good relations between the army and civilians.

The fact that the army had a privileged position in society was not of its own enough to cause the degree of animosity that existed. Even more important were the encroachments the army made on the basic rights of civilians, usually when the army was called in to act as a police force. . . . In 1892 there were a number of cases of sentries firing on civilians. In order to show his active support for the army the Kaiser sent a personal note of congratulation to a soldier involved in one such case, along with a signed photograph. The man was promptly promoted.

The army's activities were not

confined to police actions, it also interfered directly in purely civil matters. In 1912 a group of citizens of Rastatt decided to erect a statue to Carl Schurz who had come from their town. Schurz had been a *Freischärler* in 1849 and had shortly afterwards emigrated to America where he became a general and a statesman. The army command in Karlsruhe objected strongly to the plan, saying that the statue would serve as a bad example to the troops, and that the whole idea came ominously from a group of 'democrats'. General Huene, who had heard of the plans to erect the statue, went to see the Minister for the Interior of Baden, and expressed his horror at the idea. The Minister agreed with the General that the statue was a monument to revolution and *Umsturz*, and that it was clearly an attempt to make the troops break their oath of allegiance to the Grand Duke of Baden. The Minister's colleagues in the Baden government did not share his anxiety and were unwilling to undertake anything against the 'Monument to Revolution'. Enraged at the government's failure to take any action, Huene wrote a frantic letter to the War Ministry in Berlin about the dangers of allowing the statue to be erected. The army was fortunate in that the new mayor of Rastatt, elected at this time, agreed with its views and was opposed to the building of the monument. In America the members of the 'Deutsch-Amerika Club' protested to the German Ambassador. The army remained adamant in its view that the monument would be 'a serious insult to the Prussian and Baden troops stationed in Rastatt, and a grave danger to the discipline of the same'. The War Minister endorsed this attitude in a letter to the Chancellor of 21–8–1913. The monument was never built.

These incidents, some comic, some tragic, could only occur in a state where the army had excessive influence, and the influence of the army could only be maintained with the active support of a wide section of the *bourgeoisie*. The army was prepared to make some concessions to the *bourgeoisie*, partly out of the need for a larger army, but more important as a means of building up a bloc of influential supporters for its reactionary views. The essential role the army played in the state made the task easier. The *bourgeois* was only too anxious to share something of the glamour and glory of the army, and a lieutenant's epaulettes or an invitation to the mess was a low price for the army to pay for loyal support against liberalism and democracy. The civilian thus profited in that his social status was enhanced and he was brought closer to the seats of power; and the army gained in that military rank and attainments were taken, in civilian life, as absolute standards for judging a man. Entry to the officers' mess was essential if a young man wished to have a successful career in any part of the public service. . . .

There were other aspects of the army which made it popular in some sections of the community. It was estimated that an average infantry regiment brought a garrison town 900,000 marks a year, money which did not all go to those who could hope to entertain military ambitions. . . .

The army remained exclusive and found a ready and obsequious ally in the *bourgeoisie*. Secure in its position, unfettered by any form of liberal democracy, it paid little regard to the rights of civilians who remained outside its orbit. As this situation increasingly failed to correspond with the fundamental changes in German society, tension was bound to increase. Bebel wrote, 'the numerous professional soldiers who, through lack of any serious work to do, concentrate on the outward trappings, and in particular the attempt to make an artificial rift between the army and the people and to create a certain antagonism between the two, have made the army what it is.'

The system of reserve officers was an effective and popular way of assimilating the *bourgeoisie* into an aristocratic and monarchical state. The army was able to thrust its ideology on to a considerable and influential section of the civilian middle-classes, in return for the glamour and privilege of wearing the 'King's jacket'. Being a reserve officer brought with it social advantages, giving one access to the upper stratum of society and a sense of belonging to an army which had done so much to form the Reich. For the State it had the considerable advantage of ensuring the sound conservative support of an important section of society, and it further enhanced the prestige and influence of the army.

The reserve officer was immensely proud of his rank, and was a passionate defender of the army to which he had the privilege of belonging. This feeling was almost universal, and by no means confined to a small section of social-climbers or ambitious go-getters. An influential majority of the *bourgeoisie* wished to become reserve officers, and those who counted themselves lucky enough to have reached this goal were often more proud of their military rank than they were of their often considerable attainments in civilian life. . . .

The close co-operation between the state and the *Kriegerverein* [the veterans' organization that functioned as a right-wing military trade union] had only recently been established. The War Ministry had been worried that the *Verein* might wish to follow an independent policy, and also that socialists and anarchists might work their way into the organization. In 1887 the Prussian War Minister ordered the local army commanders to put trusty men into the *Kriegerverein* to make certain that they toed the line. This appeal did not meet with complete success, for the Minister had to repeat it two years later, urging officers to play a more active part in the *Kriegerverein*. In many places the local area commander (*Bezirkskommandeur*) became the honorary chairman of the local *Kriegerverein*. The question of regular officers being members of the *Kriegerverein* is an interesting example of the 'politics' of the army. Since the *Kriegerverein* was generally considered to be a political organization officers were forbidden to join it, but since the *Kriegerverein* was essential to the army, and since the army wished to keep the closest possible control over its activities, officers could become honorary members. Thus the War Ministry was in the curious position of saying that officers should not be members of the *Kriegerverein*, and at the same time encouraging them to join. The emphasis for and against did, however, change under different War Ministers. General von Heeringen, who was War Minister from 1909 to 1913, was particularly anxious that officers should co-operate with the *Kriegervereine*, and encouraged reserve officers to join. . . .

As time passed the political activities of the *Kriegerverein* became increasingly pronounced. In 1903, when the membership had increased to 2,097,527 the *Verein* again expressed its determination to fight the Social Democrats in its official programme. It stressed the necessity of educating members so as to combat the evil forces of socialism, and of turning the organization into an active conservative political force. This development was welcomed by the government. The Ministry of the Interior stressed, in a note to the Ministry of Justice, that the *Kriegerverein* should be given every possible support, for it had proved itself to be a stronghold of 'monarchical and patriotic sentiment.'

By 1909 there were 16,533 *Kriegervereine* in Prussia alone with a membership of 1,439,145. The *deutscher Kriegerbund* had 19,625 *Kriegervereine* with 1,687,990 members. The *Kyffhäuser Bund*, which included all the *Kriegerverbände* of the various states, had increased its membership to 2,528,667. By now the Prussian War Minister had no doubts as to the loyalty of the *Kriegerverein;* he agreed to give the *Verein* the names and addresses of soldiers as they were demobilized, so that the *Verein* might more easily gain new members.

One of the weaknesses of the *Kriegerverein* was that, in spite of the encouragement given to officers to join as honorary members, they were loath to do so. Officers feared that they would lose caste if they joined the *Verein,* for they were called upon to treat ex-soldiers as their equals. . . . Class-consciousness was not so easily forgotten, however, and it remained a problem for the *Kriegerverein* that officers and the more influential members of the *bourgeoisie* showed no little reluctance to join the *Verein*. In an attempt to convince the *bourgeoisie* of the importance of joining the *Verein* it appealed to the various ministries to call upon their members to co-operate with the *Kriegerverein*. In 1903 a propaganda offensive was launched to gain the support of this influential section of society. One hundred thousand pamphlets were printed and distributed among officers and civil servants stressing the vital work which the *Kriegerverein* had done to strengthen monarchical and patriotic feeling. The Minister of Justice was particularly forthcoming and sent out a circular calling upon members of his ministry to co-operate with the *Kriegerverein*, adding that trained lawyers could make an important contribution to its work. . . .

In spite of the inadequate financial resources of the *Kriegerverein,* and in spite of the reluctance of officers, civil servants and members of the upper *bourgeoisie* to join it, it played an important part in German society of the time. Particularly in local politics it exercised considerable influence, being one of the most important centres of conservative opinion. . . .

On the national level the *Krieger-verein* concentrated on its mission as a stronghold against Social Democracy and the *Umsturz*. . . . The *Krieger-verein* also tried to increase its effectiveness by drawing members not only from ex-soldiers who had been through the 'school of the nation' and who were therefore considered on the whole to be more reliable, but also from young men who had not yet served so that they might be brought up as good patriots. . . .

If the *Kriegerverein* worked closely with the government, after an initial period of distrust, the government took some time before it finally made up its mind about the activities of the Army League (*Wehrverein*). The *Wehr-verein* was founded in 1912 by General Keim and was the army equivalent to the Navy League (*Flot-tenverein*), which had been founded in 1898 as a propaganda organization to support the construction of the large fleet which was so dear to the Kaiser's heart. With an immense membership and powerful contacts with the navy and with the captains of industry the *Flottenverein* played an important political role which, with the exception of minor ups and downs, was encouraged by the government. . . . Keim was a good example of the new type of German officer, the 'pure soldiers', highly professional men who were neither landowners nor Prussians, who called for fundamental reforms in the organization and equipment of the army, and who demanded above all a large army; this they regarded as an essential condition of winning the two-front war for which they longed. . . .

The army's attitude toward civilians was based on an unbounded self-admiration and an unflattering attitude toward civilians. The army became the means to mobilize and control civic society.

The twentieth century became the twilight of the Prussian officer corps. The German war cabinet dictatorship (1916–18), led by the wooden-headed Hindenburg and the conniving captain of the German industrial-military complex, Ludendorff, ended in a debacle; the glorious general staff was routed. Nevertheless, the German army, as Reichswehr and Wehrmacht, enjoyed another quarter century of notoriety and glory between 1921 and 1945.

The renaissance of the German military after the 1918 disaster is due to three individuals—two officers and one politician: General Hans von Seeckt, the enigmatic Prussian officer-intellectual; General Wilhelm Groener, the Schwabian military politician; and Adolf Hitler, the Nazi führer. Each in his different way restored the Prussian army to its past glory and led it to its disastrous end in 1945.

Hans von Seeckt, the illustrious Junker officer of the twentieth century, is a controversial figure, and, obviously, opinion on his role will vary. A sympathetic portrait of the general is painted by the historian, intellectual, and personal friend of the leading German politicians—mainly center and right statesmen and conservatives—John W. Wheeler-Bennett, the doyen of modern German military politics. Wheeler-Bennett was impressed by a single interview he conducted with von Seeckt. We choose first two excerpts on von Seeckt from Wheeler-Bennett's interview, and find how much it influenced the latter's historical judgment several years later.

John W. Wheeler-Bennett

The Seeckt Period: 1920-1926

The name of Hans von Seeckt is written with those of von Moltke, von Roon, and von Schlieffen in the annals of German military fame. Like von Moltke, he fashioned anew the pattern and the mould of the military machine, starting from very small beginnings; like von Schlieffen, he looked forward and planned and contrived for a day, the exact time of which he could not foresee, when his master plans would be put into effect for the greater glory of Germany. Like both his predecessors, he left the German Army stronger and more efficient than he found it. But, whereas both von Moltke and von Schlieffen based their calculations on the security born of victory and well-being, von Seeckt, like Scharnhorst and Gneisenau, was compelled to build upon the ashes of defeat, yet withal finding them no unsubstantial a foundation for achievement. His genius lay, not in the formation of large

From John W. Wheeler-Bennett, The Nemesis of Power: The German Army in Politics (London, 1953), pp. 83–87, by permission of Macmillan, London and Basingstoke.

armies but in the creation of a military microcosm, complete within itself in every detail, yet capable at the given moment of limitless expansion.

Hans von Seeckt was born in Schleswig on April 22, 1866. His family were of ancient and noble Pomeranian lineage; they had given to Prussia sons who had found distinction both as soldiers and as civil servants. His father, also a General, had been awarded by Wilhelm I the highest Prussian honour, the collar of a Knight of the Order of the Black Eagle. Von Seeckt himself entered the First (Emperor Alexander's) Regiment of Foot Guards as a subaltern at the age of nineteen and almost immediately became marked for rapid preferment. Not only did he display an ability to handle troops, but, to that lynx-eyed group who were continually on the watch for promising material, he disclosed himself as a born staff officer. As a result, in 1899, at the age of thirty-three, and as a mere lieutenant, he was transferred to the élite of the General Staff Corps. In the intervals of an exceptionally rapid career, he found time to travel widely in Europe and even to Africa and India, where, at Delhi, he established friendly relations with Lord Kitchener.

Von Seeckt's record showed him to be an outstandingly successful example of that item of German military organism, to which such great importance was attached, a Chief of Staff, and it was in this capacity that he began the War. As Chief of Staff to the Third Corps, he greatly distinguished himself in the planning of the local break-through at Soissons, and his perfection of this technique caused him to be appointed Chief of Staff to Mackensen's newly formed Eleventh Army on the Eastern Front. Here, in May 1915, he achieved one of the most spectacular victories of the War, the break-through at Gorlice which crushed the Russian front and penetrated it to a tremendous depth. Whole provinces were yielded up to the German advance, and the fortresses of Przemysl, Ivangorod. Lemberg, Warsaw and Brest-Litovsk fell into their hands.

The victory of Gorlice earned for von Seeckt the coveted order *Pour le Mérite*; it also singled him out as the perfect Chief of Staff. As such he served many commanders and on numerous fronts in the ensuing years. The end of the war found him in Turkey, whence he made his way home to Germany via the Black Sea, the Ukraine and Poland.

The collapse of November 1918 came as an appalling shock to von Seeckt. He has left it on record that he wept, but he never lost faith or hope. He followed the lead of Hin-

denburg and of Gröner, and in January 1919 he was sent by them to organize the retreat of the German armies from White Russia and the Ukraine and the protection of the frontiers of the Reich against the incursions of both Poles and Bolsheviks. On the theory—which he was later to develop on a greater scale—that attack is the best means of defence, von Seeckt launched an offensive which in May resulted in the recapture of Riga. Though of minor and ephemeral importance this success had an important psychological effect upon both commander and troops. It confirmed von Seeckt in his belief in the military future of Germany, and it taught the men that they could still win battles. Of this new confidence were born the *Freikorps* of the Eastern Marches.

Summoned home from his last victory, he was despatched by Gröner and Noske to Versailles as the military member of the German Peace Commission. His reports forewarned his Chiefs of the bitter draught which was being prepared for them in the disarmament clauses of the treaty; they, in their turn, recognized that the one man who could carry out, and, if possible, circumvent, these conditions was von Seeckt himself, and they therefore appointed him Chairman of the Preparatory Commission of the Peace Army.

Such was the career of Hans von Seeckt, but what of his personality?

Seeckt's is not an easy character to analyse, for he combined the best traditions of the Prussian military caste with a breadth of outlook and a political flair unusual in these circles.

His travels abroad had rendered him a man of the world in the best sense of the term, shrewd in judgment and adroit in the handling of men and affairs; his *savoir-faire* gave him a particular charm; he was well and widely read and his keen appreciation of beauty in every form—music, art, women and nature—afforded an ampler vision than could ever have been achieved by, for example, Ludendorff. To dine with him was always a pleasurable experience, for, apart from excellent food and wine, the host, himself an excellent conversationalist, so assorted his company that talk ranged from horsebreeding and military history to politics and the arts. Von Seeckt, himself, in later years declared that vanity, a sense of beauty and the cavalier's instinct were the three outstanding traits in his character, but this was an understatement. Lord D'Abernon wrote of him as having 'a broader mind than is expected in so tight a uniform, a wider outlook than seems appropriate to so precise, so correct, so neat an exterior', and this was nearer to the mark.

A strange man, Hans von Seeckt; at first glance a typical Prussian officer, with his thin, red turkey-neck, his inscrutable face and its inevitable monocle. Just another General, one thought, as he entered a room, but that impression only remained until he took his hands from behind his back, and one was amazed at their beauty. Long, thin, sensitive, they might have belonged to Cellini or to Chopin, and, indeed, in his military genius von Seeckt combined the precision and accuracy of the soldier with the vision and imagination of the creative artist. For such he was, an artist in making bricks without straw, in beating ploughshares into swords, in fashioning a military machine which, though nominally within the restrictions of the Peace Treaty, struck admiration and awe into the heart of every General Staff in Europe.

Like many soldiers von Seeckt had an attitude of ambivalence towards war. 'The soldier, having experience of war, fears it more than the doctrinaire, who being ignorant of war talks only of peace', he wrote on one occasion before Hitler came to power. 'The figure of the sabre-rattling fire-eating general is an invention of poisoned and unscrupulous political strife.' Yet after the rearmament of Germany— the foundations for which he had so ably laid—had been publicly proclaimed, he gave vent to sentiments similar to those of the elder Moltke: 'War is the highest summit of human achievement; it is the natural, the final stage in the historical development of humanity.' It is not impossible that the fierce and savage beauty of war, as well as the professional pride of the soldier, may have been present in his mind, for he was artist as well as warrior.

Never fundamentally converted to belief or confidence in a republican Germany, von Seeckt was prepared, unlike many of his caste, to use the Republic for his own ends; and to co-operate with it as the existing constituted authority to restore the strength and power of those two institutions to which his devotion and loyalty were deep and unswerving, the German Reich and the German Army. 'The Reich!' he wrote in ecstasy. 'There is something supernatural in this word. It embraces far more and connotes something other than the conception of a State. It does not stand for the State institutions of to-day. . . . It is an organic living entity (*Lebewesen*) subject to the laws of evolution.' As such it must neither become rigid nor tyrannical; it must contain, not dominate the individual. 'The starting point is the individual with his natural right to Freedom, not the State conception with its right to Might. In the same way, the ultimate end is the individual, not the State.'

But within this 'living entity' von Seeckt had no doubt as to what should be the place of the Army. 'The Army should become a State within the State, but it should be merged in the State through service; in fact it should itself become the purest image of the State.'

With these as his basic principles von Seeckt set himself two great objectives: first, so to organize the new *Reichswehr* within the restrictions imposed by the treaty that in due course it could be expanded into a national army, and, secondly, to preserve intact the German military traditions despite these same treaty restrictions. In later years he himself avowed that his consistent policy had been 'to neutralize the poison (*das Gift*)' contained in the disarmament clauses of the Treaty of Versailles', and that in consummating this ambition he 'owed everything to the German Officer Corps'. Von Seeckt recognized, above all, the vital and essential truth that the spiritual disarmament of Germany was more important to the Allies—and consequently more dangerous to Germany —than her physical disarmament; it was his mission to prevent this, and he succeeded.

F. L. Carsten is not as charitable about von Seeckt as Wheeler-Bennett. He has this to say on the general.

F. L. CARSTEN

Seeckt's Personality

. . . Lord d'Abernon, the British ambassador to Berlin, in 1923 gave this

From F. L. Carsten, The Reichswehr and Politics, 1918–1933 *(London, 1966), pp. 103–07, by permission of Oxford University Press.*

description of Seeckt: 'In appearance he is emaciated and severe. His face reminds one of a death's-head, or, as somebody has said, of "General into Fox"; but he has few of the fox characteristics, being an honourable and even punctilious gentleman. Those who criticise him say that his principal fault is that he is too intelligent to be a general. Some of his subordinates who aim at a military régime complain that he has insufficient political ambition. . . .' But on this point Lord d'Abernon was misinformed, for Seeckt had a burning political ambition and aimed at playing a prominent political part.

His close collaborator during many years, Colonel Hasse, saw Seeckt much more correctly when he wrote in his diary in 1922: 'Seeckt criticizes again the narrow-mindedness of the Foreign Office which does not want the generals to be active in politics. . . .' In this respect Seeckt agreed with Groener. Like Groener he was disinclined to conduct his policy openly and was always active behind the scenes. He was rightly considered 'the sphinx' who kept his most secret plans and decisions to himself. One of his closest collaborators, Joachim von Stülpnagel, then a major and later a general, wrote of Seeckt: 'His reticence and disinclination to talk made him appear sinister in the eyes of outsiders, president Ebert, defence minister Dr. Gessler, politicians, and foreign diplomats. They never knew what he really thought and distrusted him often, but they respected his personality. He entered office with the clear intention of forming an army, loyal to the constitution, well disciplined, faithful to the Prussian tradition, and devoted to himself. . . .' These three components—Prussian tradition, strict discipline, and loyalty to himself—were indeed the three basic principles

of Seeckt's work. A critical British observer stated that Seeckt 'combined the best traditions of the Prussian military caste with a breadth of outlook and a political flair unusual in these circles. . . .'

Hans von Seeckt was born in 1866, the son of a Prussian general, his family belonging to the Pomeranian nobility. But in contrast with Ludendorff, Groener, Reinhardt, and the majority of the other generals, he was not educated in a cadet school, but attended, until his finishing examination in 1885, a secondary school at Strasbourg, and only then became an ensign in the Emperor Alexander Guards Grenadier Regiment. Perhaps the width of his interests and vision was connected with the fact that during his education he got to know a world entirely different from that of Pomerania and the typical officers' mess. Perhaps too his pro-Russian attitude had something to do with the fact that his regiment was that of a Czar in which any anti-Russian feeling can hardly have existed prior to 1914. In any case, even during the war years, Seeckt was friendlier towards Russia than many other Germans. Thus he wrote in 1915: 'You know that my wishes go in the direction of a conciliation with Russia which opens up further possibilities and prepares them. Only we must not try to make Russia too strong. . . .' And in the same year—while the most far-reaching plans of annexation were discussed in Germany—he wrote to his wife: 'It seems that in Berlin very many people are busy with conditions of peace, including some who should not do so.

There is evidence of an enormous lack of knowledge and responsibility. To us . . . it seems a little stupid and frivolous to act as if we had the choice between annexing half of France or half of Russia. . . .' Even after the outbreak of the Russian revolution and the clear military defeat of Russia Seeckt retained this sober approach: 'The difficulty lies in our wish to retain Courland and Lithuania. I have never been convinced of this necessity; on the contrary I consider it a worsening of our geographical position. . . .'

In the field of home policy, on the other hand, Seeckt sharply opposed any concessions to democracy, any reform of the Prussian three-class franchise. In 1916 he wrote about the plan of such a reform: 'The Prussian diet has not an ideal composition . . . but has done useful work; in spite of this it will be necessary to preserve the [general] franchise for the *Reichstag* and to change the franchise for the diet. I most sincerely regret the announcement of such a change. It is merely a concession to the supposed popular will. . . .' Only two months before the military collapse Seeckt wrote in good Prussian manner to his wife: 'You recently mentioned a speech of [Chancellor] Hertling to the students. Quite nice, but the one in the *Herrenhaus* [House of Lords] is very, very bad. This is the worst we have ever heard. So the dynasty is in danger if we do not introduce the idiotic equal franchise, against better conviction? And no Prussian gives him a reply? That is worse than the whole Bethmann and much worse than anything that happens or can happen

at the front. . . .' An open mind in questions of foreign policy and a negative attitude towards democracy and the republic at home remained characteristic of Seeckt throughout his life. He was and remained a Prussian aristocrat, and had no understanding of the time of the masses and of mass movements.

His officers found Seeckt 'unapproachable, but his whole demeanour strongly impressed all soldiers. He talked little, his words were highly polished; he used short sentences to laud and to reprove. His criticisms showed an excellent military vision and always included great ideas. . . .' In all military questions there existed only one opinion, his own. When the commanding officer of the Second Cavalry Division added a mounted battery to each cavalry brigade, Seeckt refused his consent. Even Hasse had to state that in questions of troop formation there was for Seeckt 'only his own view; everything else he declines harshly. . . .' When another division desired more fire power, Seeckt refused brusquely, and Hasse noted: 'In such a situation Seeckt has a frightfully wounding manner which he [Hasse] himself also has to experience frequently. . . .' The same is reported by the chief of the training department (*Heeresausbildungsabteilung*) of the *Truppenamt*, Colonel von Blomberg. When he suggested to Seeckt that he should abolish the lances of the cavalry so as to give it greater fire power, the latter replied: 'For the same reason I proposed the removal of the lances during the war. This was refused. Now the cavalry can retain

the lances as far as I am concerned.'
When the same officer wanted to equip
the companies of bicyclists with motor
cycles, Seeckt answered: 'Dear Blomberg, if we want to remain friends,
then you must refrain from such
proposals.'

Entirely unacceptable to Seeckt was
anything that smacked of criticism of
his own measures. When the *Wehr-
keiskommando* v, which was under
Reinhardt's command, wrote to the
army's administrative office that too
many telegrams were sent, even for the
merest trifles, above all by the defence
ministry and the *Gruppenkommando* at
Cassel, Seeckt wrote in the margin:
'a threatening, inadmissible criticism
which I cannot tolerate. This is to be
communicated to the *Wehrkreiskom-
mando.*' And a letter was sent to Lieutenant-General Reinhardt which pronounced the criticism 'inadmissible in
form and content'. Twelve months
later Colonel Hasse wrote in his diary:
'S. difficult as a leader, creates easily
the impression of being ill-tempered,
and lets one know, each time he is
listening to a suggestion, however
cautiously it is made, that he is not
willing to take any advice. It is rather
difficult to get along. I am doing my
best to overlook every whim and
touchiness. . . . '

It is perhaps strange that Seeckt, in
spite of these traits, was able to gain
the confidence and the veneration of
so many subordinate officers—although there were many officers who
remained critical of him. The cause
seems to have been his great military
knowledge, the width of his vision, his
striking personality, and, last not least,
his emphasis on Prussian traditions,
which influenced the north-German
officers. What they had so often criticized in Reinhardt now worked in
favour of Seeckt. Many hoped that—
after the failure of the Kapp Putsch—
he would find a way to promote the
conservative cause, to terminate political unrest and strikes, and to secure
to the traditional forces in Germany
their proper place. After all the insecurity brought about by the revolution and the reduction of the army, the
officer corps again had a 'head' in
which it could put its complete trust.
Thus Seeckt, in the opinion of a junior
officer of the time, became 'a substitute for the monarch' who filled
'the void' created by the abdication
of the Emperor. Soon the officers
recognized him as their political head,
as a substitute for the 'royal shield'
which they had lost on 9 November
1918.

In *Germany Since 1918* David Childs argues that if von Seeckt had not been
indecisive and Hitler not impetuous, the course of Germany—and for that
matter, of the world—would have been different. In fact, a benevolent con-
servative-praetorian German regime would have certainly destroyed both
right and left German extremists; this, of course, would have included
Hitler's petit party, the NSDAP.

David Childs

Hitler's Putsch

. . . On 26 September 1923 Gustav Stresemann, who had become Chancellor in August, announced, no doubt to the surprise of those who remembered him as a hardline nationalist during the war, the end of resistance to the French in the Ruhr. He had taken the precaution of getting President Ebert to declare a state of emergency under Article 48 of the Constitution, tantamount to turning the country over to the army under General Seeckt. Seeckt saw his task as maintaining the unity of the Reich and of 'law and order'. However, he had greater ambitions too. He planned to take over as Chancellor and actually drew up a 'government programme' along authoritarian lines. Germany might well have got a military regime at that time had not some Right-wing officers, and later Hitler, jumped the gun. Led by former Major Ernst Buckrucker Right-wing rebels attempted to seize Berlin. Seeckt put down this rebellion. He continued to be pressed by his own officers to take over and in the end it appears to have been a combination of lack of unity on the Right, Hitler's impetuosity and Seeckt's indecisiveness, which saved Germany from military dictatorship in 1923.

Bavaria, which since the fall of the Kaiser had been operating almost as

From David Childs, Germany Since 1918 (New York, 1970), pp. 27–29, by permission of Harper & Row.

an independent state, was run by an extremely reactionary clique headed by Dr Gustav Ritter von Kahr. After a personal attack on General Seeckt in the Völkischer Beobachter, the Nazi newspaper, he ordered its prohibition. The Reichswehr commander General Lossow refused to execute the order and was backed by von Kahr. The situation gradually deteriorated and open secession broke out with officers taking a new oath to Bavaria replacing the one they had taken to the Reich. Hitler hoped to exploit this situation and tried to force the hand of von Kahr, Lossow and police chief Col. Hans von Seisser. He hoped to get them to launch a complete takeover in Munich leading to a march on Berlin. Using the s A he arrested them as they attended a businessmen's meeting in a Munich beer hall. At first reluctant to cooperate with him, they agreed when threatened with a revolver and when they heard that Ludendorff was behind the Nazi leader. Hitler now made a fatal mistake of leaving them in the custody of his subordinates. The three Bavarians slipped away and being enraged by their treatment they ordered troops and police to deal with the Nazis. The putsch of 8–9 November ended in bloodshed with 16 sA and three police killed and many others wounded.

There was bloodshed in other parts of Germany that autumn. In Hamburg the Communists revolted from

23 to 26 October. Ernst Thälmann was in charge and it was hoped that the rising would spread throughout the country. In fact it was put down without too much difficulty. In Saxony and Thuringia Left-Socialist and Communist coalition governments had been established. Seeckt acted with much more decisiveness than he had shown in dealing with Bavaria. These governments were perfectly legal though the Communist partners foolishly called for the setting up of the dictatorship of the proletariat throughout Germany. Workers' militias were formed. Seeckt ordered the Reichswehr in, disbanded the armed workers' organisations and arrested the governments. This action led to the break-up of the coalition government in Berlin due to the withdrawal of the Social Democrats. Stresemann fell on 30 November and was replaced by the Centre Party politician Marx who ruled with the help of an enabling act until February of the next year. Stresemann was included in the government as Foreign Minister, a post he occupied until his death in 1929. General Seeckt gradually relinquished control of things after the crushing of the revolts. Why he did so is not clear though he may have felt by so doing he could legally get power by becoming next President. As it turned out his fellow officer Hindenburg was elected to that position after the death of Ebert in 1925. In the autumn of 1926 the politicians felt the position of the Republic had been so stabilised that they could dismiss Seeckt, officially for introducing a member of the old royal family in uniform to a regimental exercise, without any fear of a military coup. They were over-optimistic. The officers had merely changed their loyalty from Seeckt to Hindenburg and he was to lead them and the country into Hitler's lap. . . .

The battle between Hitler and the military began in 1934 during the high days of Roehm's SA and ended in February 1938 when Hitler purged both General Field Marshal Werner von Blomberg, the Reichswehrminister (Reich Defense Minister), and General Oberst (General) Werner von Fritsch, Commander-in-Chief of the Army. Hitler, a petit bourgeois Austrian expatriot, was personally and intellectually contemptuous of the Prussian officer class. Inferior by rank and social status, Hitler showed a contempt of the aristocratic warlords that paralleled that of other lower middle- and working-class "intellectuals." Nevertheless, to advance Germany's war it was necessary for Hitler and the Nazis to create the world's greatest war machine and to make sure the Prussian officers were tamed to the Nazi state. The struggle, however, started between Hitler's chief rival, ex-Captain Ernst Roehm, and the Reichswehr. It ended in 1934 with Hitler's annihilation of Roehm with the help of Himmler's SS. Amos Perlmutter explains the struggle.

Amos Perlmutter

The Romantic Revolutionary: The Storm Troopers and the Waffen SS

Between 1918 and 1945 Germany spawned the most remarkable paramilitary movements in modern history. These organizations, which combined worship of youth, idealism, nationalism, and violence, were motivated by zealotry and buttressed by elitist practices. Marching, plundering, and killing were widespread. Between the Free Corps (1918) and the Waffen SS (1941) the paramilitary organizations in Germany were so numerous that they cannot be listed here. The SA, the Waffen SS, the Allegemeine SS, the Steinwerke, Himmler's system RSHA, the Gestapo, the Schutzpolitzei, and others shared a common dedication to rightist revolutionary activities, political violence, political assassination, and paramilitary action undertaken to police and silence liberalism, socialism, and democracy. Even before the Nazis rose to power, several paramilitary groups had become autonomous. They represented a movement as well as an instrument of violence, and the instrument of violence served also as a political movement. Hitler's most remarkable achievement was to harness and subjugate paramilitary organizations to the Nazi state and military apparatus by professionalizing the nationalist

From Amos Perlmutter, The Military and Politics in Modern Times (New Haven, 1977), pp. 211–15, by permission of Yale University Press.

romantic revolutionaries.

A movement involving this type of revolutionary soldier exhibits definite ideological and organizational characteristics. Ideologically, it resembles a *jugendtkultur* (youth culture). It is antibourgeois, antidemocratic-liberal, and fascist; it is chauvinist and extremist, nostalgic, romantic, and past-oriented. Dedication to war is a personal and group aspiration. "War," writes Ernst Junger, "the Father of all things, is also our father." "What we wanted . . . was war and adventure, excitement and destruction." Violence is considered an act of personal and national liberation. To crush the left, especially leftist revolts, is an overwhelming need. Activism and nihilism are the proper attitudes toward established order. As Junger expressed it: "What do we believe in? you ask. Nothing besides the possibility of action." Organizationally, there is a well-trained and cohesive elite. Superlative fighting abilities are developed and maintained, including cloak and dagger skills. There is strict discipline, or "discipline to the death" (*Kadaver* discipline). Though it is hierarchical, the society is egalitarian and classless. It is an organization of captains and lieutenants. (The familiar "du" is used, and there are a large number of noncommissioned officers, who may even serve as battalion commanders.)

The society is celibate and Spartan, and emphasizes excellent physical condition for its members. Its membership is secret and its operations clandestine. Recruitment is strictly voluntary.

Roehm's Storm Troopers were the ultimate political soldiers and revolutionaries. They were an anticorporate and antiprofessional (that is, not classical professional) elite of fanatics composed mainly of noncommissioned junior officers contemptuous of both the political and military orders of the "bourgeois state." They were antiprofessional in the sense that they never accepted subservience to the capitalist nation-state. (They even staged an unsuccessful revolt against Hitler in 1934.) They denied classical military discipline and organization. Impressive warriors and believers in action, they were no ordinary professional soldiers. They did not make the military a lifetime career, but were dedicated to violence as a political way of life and an instrument of the revolution against the bourgeois and liberal political orders. They rejected the professional soldier's code and coat of arms as well as his historical responsibility to the established order.

The emergence of the Waffen SS signaled the change from anarchy to Nazi order. The SS, the private army of Hitler and the Nazi party, was distinguished from the pre-Nazi Storm Troopers in that it was subservient to Hitler. It eventually became a highly disciplined army of romantic revolutionaries, a professional, elitist, military group. It was Hitler's praetorian guard and military pride in wartime. By 1936 the armed SS had been divided into two clearly defined services: the SS Verfugungstruppe, Hitler's bodyguard, which eventually became a military SS or Waffen SS; and the SS Totenkopfverbande, heir to the Storm Troopers, an organization of bullies and sadists in charge of concentration camps and the "final solution" for the Jews and others. The SS Verfugungstruppe became Hitler's own military organization; the second performed police and extermination functions. Both SS revolutionary armies were legitimized as "organizations in the service of the state" only because they served the dictator himself. But their functions, roles, and behavior were clearly differentiated.

If the Nazi party aspired to the role of vanguard of the "German race," the armed professional SS sought the revolutionary role in leading the German military establishment. Although the Waffen SS fought valiantly and won a considerable military reputation on the eastern front, it was never accepted by the Wehrmacht as a legitimate military organization. Beginning as an instrument of terror, the revolutionary soldier organization became an appendage of the state war machine. However, failing to achieve legitimacy through its professional merits, it never became institutionalized as a regular bureaucratic-military establishment. Its function was revolutionary action, and, being imbued with the Nazi *geist*, it served as the vanguard of the revolutionary party. It was never an instrument of the state as much as it was an instrument of the dictator. Nor could it become part of military corporatism since its functions were not strictly military even when it acted as a military combat group, as it did after 1941.

The more important provisions separating the armed SS from the Wehrmacht stated that the SS Verfugungstruppe was a special formation unconditionally at Hitler's personal disposal; that it was part neither of the Wehrmacht nor of the Police; that during peacetime its command was vested in the Reichsführer SS and Chief of the German Police; that regardless of its employment it remained "politically" (but not juridically) a formation of the NSDAP; and that its financial support was to continue to come from the police budget of the Ministry of the Interior.

Included among the provisions linking the armed SS to the Wehrmacht were those which decreed that duty in the SS Verfugungstruppe counted as military service (*Wehrdienst*); that its weapons and equipment were to be provided by the Army; that its officers were to attend Army training courses; that its personnel were to receive their pay and allotments according to Wehrmacht regulations; and that in the event of mobilization it might (with Hitler's approval) serve within the framework of the Wehrmacht and under the tactical command of the Army.*

"Indeed," writes Stein, "it was the SS, not the National Socialist Party, that proved to be the dynamic core of the Nazi system." The Waffen SS took the following oath to Hitler: "I swear to you, Adolf Hitler, as Führer and Reichschancellor, loyalty and bravery. I vow to you, and those you

have named to command me, obedience unto death, so help me God." Like all revolutionary armies it was task- or project-oriented. It was to serve as Hitler's elite guard in the period of transition, probably until the great war ended. It was designed to protect the führer and his regime by acting as a militarized police force. Hitler (unlike Himmler) never intended it to become the established military institution.

Hitler's decision to allow the armed SS to take an active part in the war was based on his conviction that it would not be able to retain the respect of Germans unless it did its share at the front. Hitler regarded the Waffen SS in its military role as a Guard formation, in the eighteenth- and nineteenth-century meaning of the term. As the military apotheosis of National Socialism, its task was to set an example for the Army. But Hitler assured the generals in 1940 that after the war the Waffen SS would become the "militarized state police" of the Third Reich and would not exceed 5 to 10 percent of the Army's peacetime strength.†

Hitler clearly distinguished between the functions of the revolutionary and the professional soldier. He had no intention of creating a fourth branch of the Wehrmacht, which was the prime instrument of Nazi militarism, the spearhead of Nazi aggression. The Waffen SS was an heir to the Free Corps. "Few of the men in the Waffen SS were old enough to have had any personal contact with the post-World War I Freikorps movement; yet it was

*George H. Stein, *The Waffen SS: 1939–1945* (Ithaca, N.Y.: Cornell University Press, 1966), p. 294.

†Ibid., p. 282.

the spirit of their movement, its nihilism and elitism, which perhaps comes closest to that of the Waffen SS." The Waffen SS, like the Freikorps before it, was distinguished from the established military by its emphasis on toughness, recklessness, and savagery instead of skill, training, order, and military education. The heroes of the SS troops were not the brutal police, the *alte Kampfer* type of Hitler's early days, but regular army officers who had commanded the SS Verfugungstruppen. From these officers they acquired their ruthlessness. The early officers' group egalitarianism and cohesion were emulated, even down to the military uniform. The Waffen SS shared the egalitarianism, as well as the high political commitment, of the modern revolutionary soldier. Nostalgic for the strict feudal values of the medieval northern German forests, the Storm Troops and the Waffen SS were two of the most notorious groups of anticorporate revolutionary professionals of modern times. . . .

Thus, the quintessence of the Prussian state, the Prussian officer class, became an instrument of the führer and the Nazi state. The corporate pride of the aristocratic and professional officers was continuously compromised by Hitler. The Reichswehr meekly and unsuccessfully revolted as late as 1944, and this only under the leadership of a few aristocratic and conservative officers.

Among several excellent monographs on the German army since 1918 (Wheeler-Bennett, *The Nemesis of Power,* 1953; Harold Gordon, *The Reichswehr and the German Republic, 1919–1926,* 1957; F. L. Carsten, *The Reichswehr and Politics, 1918–1933,* 1966; Robert O'Neill, *The German Army and the Nazi Party, 1933–1939,* 1966), the O'Neill work is, in our view, the most authoritative analysis of the relationship between Hitler and the German officer corps. O'Neill is not as critical of the Prussian warlords as are Wheeler-Bennett, F. Carsten, and Amos Perlmutter.

The successors to the ambitious Ludendorff and the politically naive von Hindenburg were two generals, Groener and von Seeckt, who not only determined the rules of behavior for the military and the general staff between 1919 and 1933, but also helped to lay the foundations of the short-lived, trouble-prone Weimar Republic. Although the war had clearly been lost by the army, the high command was shrewd enough to lie low, passing the onus of defeat on to civilians. Thus, a Catholic politician, Matthais Erzberger, conducted the humiliating negotiations for the armistice in Paris. Groener reminisces: "The High Command deliberately adopted the position of refuting the responsibility for the armistice and all the later steps. Strictly legally seen, it did so without justification, but to me and my associates it was vital to keep the armor shining (*die Waffe blank*) and the General Staff free of burdens for the future." Thus was launched the Reichswehr, the last phase in the glorious history of the Prussian army and its venerable general staff.

The corporate orientation of the German military converged naturally with the Versailles idea of a limited Reichswehr. Not unlike the reformers of 1808, von Seeckt was unwilling to be a surrogate for the kaiser or to "surrender" the army to the new legitimacy, Weimar—at best, a *Vernunft-republik* ("Republic of Convenience"). The general philosophy of the *Herresleitung* (army command), he felt, should be to maintain a reliable, efficient, strong army, and for this, corporate autonomy was necessary. "The Reichswehr must obey the orders given to it by the duly constituted authority, but General von Seeckt and the Heeresleitung bitterly resented any attempt by these authorities to interfere with the internal functioning of the Reichswehr." Thus, the correlation between corporatism and professionalism—between the need to maintain group consciousness and exclusivity, as well as the sense of professional responsibility—was high when the military became politically involved.

With military defeat and the Weimar revolution of 1918 came a general movement to the political left in Germany. In the officer corps, where corporate feeling was threatened by the disintegration of the empire, apprehension of the Bolshevik menace spread from the high command to the lowest subaltern. Hoping to stem the tide of socialism, the leaders of the new Reichswehr plunged into politics.

Both generals Groener and von Seeckt had faith that military corporatism could be protected by their own political intervention, and they insisted that "politics" (in the words of General Groener) "must be conducted by a few only—tenaciously and silently." At best, they could only tolerate Weimar, which they considered a paper wall incapable of protecting corporatism and legitimacy from leftist insurrections. The very weakness of the civilian authority, in fact, led the military to conceive the role of the Reichswehr to be that of an independent suprapolitical national organization. In 1918–19 von Seeckt and Groener allied with Ebert's right socialists in order to defend not the Republic but the military organizations from a threatened Communist takeover. During the 1920s, von Seeckt inculcated into the army command its praetorian role, which at the time contributed to republican stability even though it proved unable to buttress the dwindling Republic permanently.

Now comes Hitler, exploiting von Seeckt's achievement and taming the Reichswehr for Nazi goals.

Amos Perlmutter

Hitler and the Army

Ultimately, the Reichswehr fell victim to its own stubborn corporatism and its principles of organizational autonomy.

A Reichswehr which in the hour of peril would have cooperated with the Prussian police and the republican organizations, instead of intriguing against them, could have been the rock on which the waves broke. But the policy of the army command prevented such a cooperation and led to a weakening of the Republic and of the organizations willing to defend it. In so doing, however, the army command also undermined the foundations of its own power. The position it had acquired could only be held while the government remained weak. If a really strong government supplanted it, the autonomy of the Reichswehr would come to an end, and with it the strong influence which it wielded in the political sphere.*

In fairness to some of the leaders of the Reichswehr, the members of Hitler's general staff were not necessarily political simpletons or arrogant professionals or subservient corporatists. In fact, the revisionist study of party-army relationships by Robert O'Neill clearly demonstrates that the

From Amos Perlmutter, The Military and Politics in Modern Times (New Haven, 1977), pp. 55–59, by permission of Yale University Press.

*F.L. Carsten, The Reichswehr and Politics, 1918–1933 (Oxford: Clarendon Press, 1966), p. 405.

high command was not monolithic. General von Hammerstein-Equord—a man of great courage and initiative, chief of the high command—had labored hard to keep the Reichswehr's neutrality in 1933 and to protect the army from the Nazi party.

The high command after Hitler's first reorganization (1934–35) continued to seek the goal of the classical professionals—separation of military from politics. Nevertheless, the four most important positions within the German high command between 1934 and 1938 were occupied by four individuals who represented two schools of thought. The traditionalists were led by von Fritsch, chief of the high command, and von Beck, his chief of staff. They aspired to continue in the spirit of von Hammerstein-Equord. The second school, representing the New Era, was led by General von Blomberg, the new Reichswehr minister and the head of the Wehrmachtamt (Armed Forces Office), and General von Reichenau. The first group wanted "to increase greatly the size and standard of efficiency of the army." The second group "were concerned with the adaptation of the Reichswehr to the Nazi government, the Nazi party, and Nazi ideology; so that political-military relations ran as smoothly as possible."

Disputes within the high command, the army's failure to oppose Hitler's militaristic policies, and the von

Fritsch crisis led to the second reorganization of the Reichswehr in 1938. Now Hitler took direct command. He appointed himself supreme commander, purged the most senior officers—von Blomberg and von Fritsch—and appointed his creature General Keitel head of the Oberkommando der Wehrmacht (OKW), the new Armed Forces High Command, which replaced the 1934 Armed Forces Office with functions of a military staff under the führer as supreme commander. Hitler then appointed General von Brauchitsch, of the old school (his inclinations were those of a pre-Nazi Prussian officer), as head of a new office, the Oberkommando des Heers (OKH), the Army High Command, the functional-professional chief officer of the Reichswehr. Thus the führer gradually assumed personal control of the army and purged the professional officers who opposed him. O'Neill's revisionist analysis does not refute my argument that professionalism is neither a buttress against the army's politicization nor a buffer against its domination by authoritarian politicians and parties. In fact, O'Neill's study clearly demonstrates that many factors—the army's role in formulating military policies, its anxiety to attain military goals, its desire to compromise with the party for the sake of national security, its exploitation of the new atmosphere of rearmament, induced by the führer to further Nazi military aims—created exactly the opposite situation from the neutrality to which the traditional-professional officers aspired. Their disunity reduced their ability to oppose Hitler, but so, to reiterate

O'Neill, did "their lack of political consciousness' and overabundant concern for the "defense" of Germany. "The majority of officers averse to Nazism were like rudderless ships amidst swift currents."

Corporatism is certainly Janus-faced. "Their education and traditions had kept them apart from politics, and so their realization of the significance of events taking place around them was, at best, slow." What was their "education"? Subservience to Prussian warlords. What were their traditions? Those of the spoiled elite culture of the Hohenzollerns. What kept them apart from "politics" and "events"? Their cognition that "politics" is managed by their warlord, that "events" will be handled by the state, that is, the traditional Prussian system. Thus, their professional commitment under Hitler, their lack of activity in anti-Nazi politics, cost them their lives and reputations and eventually their cherished Prussian general staff. The Hitler officers were remarkably different from their Weimar seniors, von Seeckt, Groener, and von Schleicher, who were interventionists. The Hitler officers made, in the end (1944), merely a fragile and futile coup. Certainly the reasons why von Seeckt and his colleagues could assert political influences lay in the nature of the politically precarious Weimar regime. Under the Hitler regime, von Blomberg and the traditionalists could not intervene politically. Von Blomberg's efforts to ensure the Reichswehr's integrity through faith in Hitler and his dedication in bringing the army and the party into intimate union produced totally contrary results. The army became subservient to Hitler.

This subservience was not, as O'Neill contends, the result of the military's "lack of political consciousness." More accurate is Bracher's argument that it resulted from "political ineptitude and unpolitical arrogance." O'Neill himself argues that "when this outlook [man's honor and his pledged loyalty to Hitler] has combined with the strict code of military obedience which inhibits protest against orders, the Nazi Party was given a degree of control over the German army quite unknown to the armies of Western democracies." The Prussian officer corps from Moltke to von Blomberg (although it always contained dissenters) contributed (as the interventionist von Schleicher and the "neutral" von Hindenburg in Hitler's time certainly did) to the demise of democracy in Germany. This is not true of other Western countries, including France.

In fact, O'Neill admits that "the greater availability, compared with the days of the Weimar Republic, of materials, men, and finance, the improved conditions of service, the modernization of the Army, the fascination of new work and the emphasis on professional proficiency were associated in the minds of many soldiers, and with considerable justification, with the National-Socialist government. Apart from local friction with minor Party officials which was often rationalized in terms of the Führer's ignorance of the misconduct of his juniors, there was much about the Third Reich in its pre-war years which seemed to the German Army at large

to be wholly right and proper. The overall system had provided the good things—it only remained for Hitler to clean up the defects on the lower levels, when he had time, for Germany to be put back on her feet again as a healthy and vigorious nation which had cast off the gloom and shame of the 'twenties. It was only too easy for the Party propaganda machine to impress this sort of thinking upon the receptive minds of many soldiers and to make others, who were less credulous, more hesitant in criticizing the Party.

"Thus the German Army came to be dominated by Hitler. The forces acting on the Nazi Party enabled it to pursue its own policy with little need for compromise with the Army, while the Army was subject to an overwhelming number of influences which combined on many levels to make it subservient to its political master."

The high command moved from wavering cooperation with the Weimar Republic between 1918 and 1926 to surrender to the totalitarian state after 1938. All the while the corporate entity of the military remained its chief concern. But "politics" caught up with the Reichswehr. A century of silence, of monarchical subordination, and of equality at the royal court had blinded the gray-uniformed elite to the reality of politics under any other regime than a benevolent dynasty. In the long run, even the most politically minded officer of Weimar, General Kurt von Schleicher, who was highly skilled in political deception, proved to be no match for Adolf Hitler. By manipulating the conservative and nationalist politicians, parties, and groups, von Schleicher rose meteorically to become the éminence grise of the aging, politically inept "wooden titan," Field Marshal von Hindenburg. Von Schleicher made himself head of the war ministry, and as a result of his intrigues von Groener was appointed to the ministry of defense in 1928.

Von Schleicher's appeasement policy was based on the hope that he "could guide the German ship of State into safety . . . by means of clever and devious maneuvers calculated either to beguile or to divide the enemy." But he was outflanked by Hitler in 1933 and assassinated by Nazi henchmen in 1934, leaving the republic, the military, and the conservative nationalists at the mercy of a mercurial déclassé corporal.

It is one of the most curious paradoxes of modern history that a political man like Hitler was able to subdue the independent corporate spirit of the German officer corps and that he also succeeded in "civilizing" the German state and providing for po-

litical legitimacy, even though it was not a legitimacy supported by the officer corps. The military never saw in Hitler a real replacement for monarchical legitimacy, but in the king's absence, it preferred the legitimacy of the state and favored the ideals of the Right over those of the Left. Supporting the moderate and conservative parties in the hope that they could defend historical legitimacy, under Hitler the army as an autonomous corporate group slowly disintegrated. Hitler returned the army to its strictly "professional" role as an instrument of violence. The Nazi party, a tremendous political machine, acted as a counterbalance to the military, and Hitler's paramilitary structures inherited its political-ideological functions. Above all, Hitler took advantage of the weakness, naivete, and timidity of members of the high command. He used his own Reichswehr appointments to bring about the end of one of the most successful professional officer systems of modern times.
. . .

FRANCE: LA GRANDE MUETTE

If the Prussian army in the nineteenth century represents the archetype of modern military professionalism as a subservient instrument of the state, the French military during almost a century and a half exhibits modern military corporatism. David Ralston writes: "To protect the army against the perils of French political life in the nineteenth century required that the soldiers themselves revise, consciously or unconsciously, certain of their fundamental assumptions with regard to such matters as discipline, obedience, loyalty, and military honor."*

The French military did undergo several cycles in its evolution. From a monarchial-aristocratic army, it turned Bonapartist and revolutionary;

---

*David Ralston, ed., *Soldiers and States* (Boston: D. C. Heath, 1966), p. 11.

from *levée en masse*, peoples' revolutionary style in 1793, to rigid professionalism by 1815; from a highly politicized army into one of the tamest of European professionals; from the nation-in-arms citizens' army, led by monarchists
and Bonapartists, to exclusionary conservatism, led by Republican soldiers;
from a mobilizable force to the army of *La Grande Muette*, preparing for
La Revanche in 1918, it became once more tame—only to revolt again, this
time led by a conservative-Maurasist soldier, Charles de Gaulle. The
Jacobin Army of the Revolution became the Army of Vichy in 1940. The
silent army of the nineteenth century harbored more revolts: de Gaulle in
1940, this time led by former *maquisards* and anti-Nazis who sought to
perpetuate French colonialism in Indochina and Algeria. These lost soldiers
were purged not by the Vichyists but by their "own" de Gaulle. The
Republican Army of 1939 became the Army of Vichy in 1940. The Army
of Vichy, some of whose officer corps were tried for treason, while others
were ousted, returned to dominate the French army by 1947. A direct line
of descent from the Armistice Army to the post–World War II army could
be established. All 139 generals in the active army after 1945 were Armistice
Army veterans. Several Armistice Army veterans became chief of staff.
After the war, every chief of staff of the army and of national defense had
served in the Armistice Army (Ely, De Lattre, Zeller, Guillaume, etc.).

   We have selected some of the most brilliant analyses of this army to
explain its trials, tribulations, and orientations, and its spirit. We begin
with Richard Challener's concept of the nation in arms.

RICHARD CHALLENER

The Nation in Arms

The concept of the nation in arms, like
so many of the theories and institutions
on which modern France has been
built, originated in the war-torn years
of the Revolution. Universal and compulsory military service—a more accurate if prosaic equivalent for the
revolutionary phrase "the nation in

   From Richard Challener, French Theory of the
Nation in Arms (New York: Russell & Russell,
1965; reprint of 1952 edition), pp. 3–9, by permission of Russell & Russell.

arms"—was, to be sure, an unexpected
and unwanted consequence of the
events which followed from the meeting of the Estates General in 1789.
Many of the *cahiers de doléances* compiled in preparation for this meeting
had in fact called for the abolition of
the royal practice of recruiting provincial militias, and many a revolutionary bourgeois had fondly imagined
that the creation of a constitutional
regime would usher in an era of per-

manent peace. Yet within a few short years conscript soldiers formed the rank and file of the French forces defending *la patrie* from the armies of the First Coalition, and the National Convention had, with a patriotic flourish, decreed that "the battalion organized in each district shall be united under a banner bearing the inscription: The French people risen against tyranny." This same assembly had, in August of 1793, laid down both the theory and practice of what the twentieth century was to call "total war": the young men were to go forth to battle, the married men would forge arms, the women were to make tents and clothing, and the aged were "to preach hatred of kings and the unity of the Republic."

Many events and forces united to kill the hopes of 1789 and create the realities of 1793. National guard units, arising spontaneously, had seemed to prove that an armed citizenry could safeguard the bourgeoisie from both the real and the assumed threats of counterrevolutionary action. At the same time the "old army," in which the purchase of commissions was a zealously guarded prerogative of the rich and well-born, appeared as a legitimate object for the reforming ardor of the Third Estate. French liberal thought of the prerevolutionary years had itself foreshadowed the coming of conscription. Had not Rousseau advised the Poles as early as 1772 that only a well-trained militia, in which it was the duty of every citizen to serve as a soldier, would assure the defense of a free nation? But above all the harsh realities of military necessity demanded the creation of armies far

greater in size than the professional forces employed in the dynastic warfare of the earlier part of the eighteenth century. Both patriotism and egalitarianism, vital attributes of the revolutionary ideology, affected this development; patriotism demanded that all the sons of France be enrolled in her defense, and egalitarianism insisted that the burden of sacrifice must be equally shared. The result was the nation in arms.

The citizen turned soldier—indeed, conscript service as both the badge and moral consequence of citizenship—was one of the major results of the French Revolution. It was by no means the least important legacy bequeathed by the revolutionary age to the generations of the modern world.

Since the decade of revolution the concept of the nation in arms has been an integral part of the French military heritage and has served as a focus around which the French have elaborated theories for military organization as well as for the conduct of warfare. Yet however interesting and important the concept was in the years of the First Republic and the First Empire, it has played an even greater role in the more recent military history of the French nation. Especially since the closing years of the Second Empire and throughout the entire life-span of the Third Republic— roughly, from 1866 to 1940—the theory has been of major importance in the determination of French military policies. . . .

The fact that army leaders had no faith in the conscript soldier and that the French people were unwilling to accept the rigors of compulsory military service is a significant aspect of the defeat of 1870. Likewise, the prevailing interpretations of the concept of the nation in arms in 1914 and in 1939 led the French to expect and plan for a particular type of warfare which never materialized, and thus had a marked effect upon the military outcome.

There are several problems concerning the evolution of the nation in arms. . . .

The first of these is the question of definition. For while the Jacobin origin of the theory is both clear and well established, it is a difficult task to give precise meaning to the phrase "the nation in arms." For this there are two main reasons. The first is simply that the political outlook of an individual has always affected his definition of the nation in arms; a Socialist follower of Jaurès, for instance, would describe the concept in words that no marshal of the Second Empire could ever have used. The second reason is that the concept of the nation in arms has itself changed in the course of time; no Frenchman writing in 1939, whether a left-wing politician or a hidebound military officer, would have defined it in the same way as he would have twenty-five years earlier.

At the level of basic meaning—a sort of lowest common denominator of accepted belief—"the nation in arms" implies perhaps nothing more than the principle of universal and compulsory military service. Yet even this definition carries with it the important corollary that one of the primary moral obligations of the French citizen is to fulfill his conscript duties.

But the range of individual definitions is great. Republican heirs of the Revolution, devoted to egalitarian principles, have consistently made the concept of the nation in arms into a moral touchstone with which to judge the virtue of all succeeding French military institutions; conservative enemies of that Revolution, no less devoted to principle, defined it as an open invitation to anarchy and the social disorders produced by undisciplined armed mobs. A generation of French military officers after 1870, impressed by both the quantity and the quality of the German army, thought of the nation in arms in purely military terms; for them it was the most rational principle on which to build the mass armies demanded by mass warfare. On the other hand, the militia-minded political reformers of the Dreyfus era, desiring to weaken the influence of the military hierarchy in French society, emphasized the role of the citizen-soldier in their definitions. In their view, a young Frenchman should be a citizen first, a soldier second, so that, through the mysterious workings of patriotic devotion, he would be a better guardian of the nation.

The passage of time has had an even greater effect upon definitions of the nation in arms. Prior to the war of 1914 French thought on the nation in arms concerned itself only with the military relationship between the state and its male citizens; it dealt with the human resources of the nation and not at all with the economic or industrial potential of France. But after four years of relentless struggle had revealed the expanded and altered character of modern war, the concept of the nation in arms became a body of ideas which dealt with the organization of every phase and every aspect of French life in time of war. Before 1914 the concept was political in content; thereafter it became a theory of total war.

In addition to the problem of changing definition there is a second aspect of the history of the nation in arms which must be noted in advance. This is the fact that much of the story is narrowly political and can be explained only by reference to the complicated and often exasperating network of French party politics. This orientation arises from the fact that the army has played a vital role in French domestic affairs ever since 1789. National guards, popular militia, and disgruntled regulars were in large measure responsible for the success of revolutionary and insurrectionary movements from the storming of the Bastille to the creation of the short-lived Commune of 1871; on the other hand, the two most famous crises of the young Third Republic—the "affairs" of Boulanger and Dreyfus—seemed to many to be manifestations of a plot by reactionary military officers to dominate if not destroy parliamentary institutions.

Because of the importance of the army in the life of the nation French political parties have always held strong, even violent opinions on military affairs. The Right, fearful that conscription would put guns into the hands of the politically unreliable, long maintained that only a large regular army would guarantee social stability and the preservation of law and order; the republicans and their allies, afraid lest "the military" achieve an undue influence over civil institutions, were equally insistent that only an army of citizen-soldiers satisfied the needs of a democratic nation. The concept of the nation in arms has thus always been an issue of political life in France—in fact, as early as 1789 the Revolutionary leader Dubois-Crancé indicated the political overtones lurking behind the theory when he told the Constituent Assembly that "each citizen should be a soldier, and each soldier a citizen, or we shall never have a constitution." As a result, the concept of the nation in arms, involving as it does such fundamental questions as the recruitment, organization, effectiveness, and loyalty of the army, cannot be discussed outside the framework of French political life.

The third and final preliminary consideration is of the nature of a paradox. Although the French, as has been said, originated the concept of the nation in arms during the Revolution, there was a gap in both theory and practice which stretched from the Bourbon restoration to the latter days of the Second Empire. Furthermore, it was an event in the history of Central Europe—the crushing victory over Austria of the Prussian conscript army at Sadowa in 1866—which produced a revival of French thought on the nation in arms. The impetus to reconsider the problems of military structure and organization was the result of foreign rather than domestic events, and it came after many long years in which both theory and practice had been neglected. The reasons for this . . . are perhaps less important than the fact. Consequently, despite the fact that the nation in arms was born in the years immediately after 1789, [implementation awaited 1866 when the unexpectedly decisive victory of the Prussian war machine forced the France of Napoleon III to begin re-examination of its military institutions and the theories on which they were founded.

The isolation of the French army, which led a professional existence of its own, is well summarized from the literature by David Ralston, historian of modern France.

David Ralston

The Army and the State: 1815–1870

The military force of the Third Republic was a "national" army consisting chiefly of conscripts called to the colors for a comparatively short period of time. The army of the constitutional monarchies and the Second Empire had been a corps of long-term professionals. Yet, even with this significant change in the shape of French military institutions, there was an underlying continuity between the old and the new. Having inherited the defeated and battered army of Napoleon III, the Third Republic altered the method of recruitment for the men in the ranks and by stages introduced a system of universal conscription. The new regime could not so easily replace the personnel or transform the spirit of the professionals who constituted the real nucleus of the army. Because the officer corps had survived the Franco-Prussian War more or less intact, the army of

Reprinted from The Army of the Republic *by David Ralston by permission of The M.I.T. Press, Cambridge, Massachusetts.* © *1967 by The M.I.T. Press.*

the Third Republic was from the beginning commanded by men molded in outlook and attitude by the old army. They gave a decisive imprint to the army of the Republic.

In the years from 1815 to 1870, the French army as a whole led an existence completely apart from the rest of the nation. In contrast to the exhilarating years of the Revolutionary and Napoleonic wars, with their unceasing saga of military glory, and in contrast to the period after 1870, when the French people "cherished their army with a love that was slightly childish . . . ," during the middle years of the nineteenth century the army was something unknown, something outside the main currents of national life. The great majority of the French people, possibly worn-out by the martial clamor of the Napoleonic era, simply seemed to have no interest in military affairs. The middle classes grew accustomed "like the Chinese . . . to look on soldiering as the lowest of human occupations." The pay of an officer was low, life in a series of dreary garrison towns was monotonous, and, in time of peace, promotion for all but the very gifted or the very lucky was slow. It was difficult for an officer to marry or to establish any kind of reasonable home when each regiment changed garrison on the average of every twelve or eighteen months. Under these circumstances, a military career was not a very attractive one.

The men in the ranks were recruited from those too poor to buy their way out. The annual contingent of conscripts generally numbered about 30,000 out of the 300,000 who each year became eligible for military service. Conscription was regulated by drawing lots. Men who drew "good" numbers were exempt from all but the most nominal and unlikely reserve obligation, but the ones with "bad" numbers were liable for induction. Even so, the possessor of a "bad" number was not automatically obliged to serve, for if he could find a substitute and pay him an adequate premium, he could still escape the army. Companies were set up to ensure people against drawing a "bad" number and to procure substitutes for those who did. Naturally enough, the sons of even the moderately well-to-do never experienced military life as conscripts. For those who were inducted, the term of service was at first eight and later seven years. So long a period of time was usually sufficient to break a young man of all binding attachments to civilian life. In seven years a recruit could develop a taste for military life, could grow to think of himself as having no other home than the army. He

could also expect to be made a noncommissioned officer, a further inducement for him to remain in uniform.

There was a remarkable homogeneity in the army of the constitutional monarchies and of the Second Empire. Between the officers and the troops, there was much less class distinction than was to be found in either the Prussian or the British armies of the time. More than half the officer corps was recruited from the men in the ranks, for there were never enough young men from the educated classes, who entered the army via the great military schools, Saint-Cyr and Polytechnique, to fill the available billets.

If the majority of the French people systematically scorned or ignored the army, the military in turn were glad to segregate themselves from what they considered to be the corrupt and enervating influences of civilian life. The conditions of a soldier's existence —the distinctive uniform, the low scale of pay, the constant changes of garrison, the special code of justice and discipline—all conspired to keep him on the margin of French society in the nineteenth century. The great stirrings in French intellectual and scientific life passed him by, as did also the political developments of the era. The latter is particularly significant because in the period just ended the army had come to be an accepted path to political preferment, the outstanding example here being Napoleon Bonaparte. Despite the actions of a few ambitious officers in the *coup d'état* of December 2, 1851, the army was behind none of the changes of regime in the nineteenth century. To the degree that the soldiers found themselves involved in the political turmoil, it was as involuntary participants, drawn in against their better judgment.

Prior to 1870 every soldier was bound by his oath of fidelity to the sovereign. This oath was a remnant of the old personal feudal contract between lord and vassal, and for most officers and enlisted men it committed their honor, in itself an effective brake on any seditious sentiments that one might harbor toward the powers that be. But a problem arose for a soldier as to how far he was bound by his oath when his sovereign was deposed and replaced by another. This had taken place with great frequency during the years of revolution, from 1789 to 1814, and was to continue to do so down until 1870. Under the circumstances, where the nation periodically repudiated the sovereign whom the soldiers had sworn to uphold, a new concept of military honor had to come into existence. The revolution of July 1830 supplied a particular impetus to this evolution.

Under the restored Bourbons, the officer corps had consisted of an uneasy amalgam of Napoleonic veterans and members of the old privileged classes, many of them émigrés. Never absolutely certain of the sentiments of the men from the Grande Armée, and with some justification, considering their behavior during the One Hundred Days, the government had systematically sought to assure the devotion of the army to the regime by reserving the more important posts for former émigrés, although many were lacking in military experience. Though the oath of fidelity was sufficient to prevent any overt reaction to this policy so long as the regime lasted, its collapse in July 1830 appeared to release the pent-up discontent of many soldiers. As a result the morale of the officer corps was profoundly shaken. . . . On the other hand, some officers adhering to traditional values interpreted their oath of loyalty to the legitimate sovereign in the most literal fashion and resigned their commissions. In all, about two thousand officers quit the army in the wake of the Revolution of 1830.

Those officers who remained in the army might well ask themselves how their oath of personal fealty to Charles X could be reconciled with the fact that there was now a new king on the throne, placed there by a band of revolutionaries. In due course, the military were obliged to swear allegiance to Louis Philippe, and this could be taken as superseding any former oath. Still a malaise persisted among the officers. An individual oath of personal fidelity to the sovereign could not alone provide adequate assurance for the solidity or the moral cohesiveness of the officer corps. Though it did guarantee to the government that in normal times its orders would be obeyed throughout the military hierarchy, it did not guarantee to the soldiers themselves that the necessary bonds of mutual trust and camaraderie would not again be subjected to a terrible strain.

To meet this problem, there evolved the ideal of passive obedience to orders from above. Military honor was to be based not merely on the concept of personal fealty to the sovereign but also on the principle of absolute obedience pure and simple to whomever should be in a position of supreme power. If it is a truism that no army can function effectively or even exist without discipline, it is a necessary corollary that discipline is seriously endangered when political events force the soldier periodically to question the legitimacy of the ultimate authority in the state and therefore the validity of the orders that he is told to obey. The instinctive need of the soldier to have a clearer and more binding concept of obedience was enshrined in military regulations three years after the advent of the July Monarchy. . . .

Before the Revolution of 1830, the principle of subordination had been defined as follows: "Discipline being the principal basis of military strength . . . the right of protest is permitted to the one who has obeyed." Apparently the military authorities sensed some degree of ambiguity here, for by the ordinance of November 2, 1833, the regulations were amended to read: "The right to protest is permitted to a subordinate only after he has obeyed." Henceforth a soldier was allowed no doubts concerning orders no matter how legitimate or well-founded these doubts might be. We may surmise that the military were happy to have their initiative so circumscribed. The situation of the officer vis-à-vis the state was further defined by a number of measures enacted at a relatively early date in the July Monarchy. The chief sin of the Bourbon dynasty as far as the army was concerned had been its unjust and

heavy-handed efforts to put in place a military personnel specifically devoted to its cause. To protect soldiers against the arbitrary, politically motivated policies of any future government and also against their own inclination to profit by such policies, Marshal Soult, one of the abler lieutenants of Napoleon and twice Minister of War under Louis Philippe, sponsored two laws, one stating the conditions under which an officer was to be promoted and another defining and giving legal protection to his professional status.

By the promotion law of April 14, 1832, the government sought to reconcile the larger needs of the army with the vital interests of each individual officer. Every officer was guaranteed his rights to promotion by strict seniority up to the rank of *commandant* or major, but the law also enabled a fixed percentage of evidently gifted men to be advanced more rapidly, after having served a specified minimum of time in each rank. This last provision was meant to permit the men capable of commanding a division or an army to reach the higher ranks at a reasonably young age, while they still had their mental and physical vigor, rather than spending their best years vegetating as captains or majors. The 1832 law was to remain in effect until World War I.

Even more significant in terms of the place of the army within the French state was the law of May 19, 1834, on the status of the officer. By this law, a fundamental distinction was made between the rank of an officer and his assignment or post. Rank, since it was conferred on an officer by governmental decree, became his property, something of which he could be deprived only under exceptional circumstances and in accordance with legal forms. His military assignment, on the other hand, depended on the needs of the moment as understood by the government. Such legal protection against the vagaries of politics gave the officer unusual security and even moral independence, compared to the other servants of the French state, and he was to be much envied by the other functionaries. All of the afore-mentioned measures and the point of view they reflected within the army meant that the abstract concept of the state was replacing the more specific, personal idea of the sovereign as the focus of military loyalties and as the guarantor of a soldier's honor. The obligations of an officer toward a particular regime could last only as long as the regime did, but his obligations with regard to the state, and his rights as a servant of the state, endured as long as he was an officer. The consequences of such an attitude were to be seen as early as the Revolution of February 1848.

The military were distressed by the fall of the Orléans dynasty, and they regarded the advent of the Republic of 1848 with real distaste. The troops of the Paris garrison did their best to uphold the regime against the mob in the streets, but once the abdication of Louis Philippe had made the situation hopeless, no one in the army thought to raise a hand on his behalf. . . .

The new regime lasted less than four years, its existence cut short by the brilliantly planned *coup d'état* of the President of the Republic, Louis Napoleon Bonaparte. With this act of violence, carried out by the troops of the Paris garrison, he broke a three-year-long constitutional deadlock between the legislative and the executive branches. . . . Rather than seeking to impose their own solution in the conflict between the Prince-President and the conservative Assembly, the soldiers were drawn into the conflict in spite of themselves. "Solicited by both parties, the army, in the very name of the obedience it owed the constituted authorities, could not refuse to take sides."

In his contest with the Assembly, Louis Napoleon possessed one important trump: by the terms of the Constitution he was the Commander in Chief of the armed forces. Even so, the majority of the more eminent generals owed their careers to the House of Orléans and were thus in some degree opposed to the ambitions of the present Bonapartist pretender. Knowing that he had little support within the highest ranks, Louis Napoleon had to replace the overscrupulous commanders of the Paris garrison with younger, more ambitious officers, recruited mainly in Algeria. For all the careful sounding of opinions carried out by Major Fleury, aide-de-camp to the Prince-President, only one man could be found to assume responsibility for the military end of the *coup d'état,* Saint-Arnaud. At the time an obscure brigadier general, he was hardly typical in spirit or outlook of the French officer of the period. Other generals . . . obviously favored the enterprise and declared themselves willing to carry out orders, but no one except Saint-Arnaud would take the necessary initiative. Even after he was placed in command of one of the divisions of the Paris garrison, Saint-Arnaud in a moment of fainthearted-ness wanted to back out of the under-taking. It was only when his meteoric rise was climaxed by his nomination as Minister of War, that is, as chief of the French army, that he was able to overcome his scruples, thus permitting the operation to be launched.

Once the *coup d'état* was successful, the army rallied to Louis Napoleon with enthusiasm and obvious joy. A new Bonapartist regime implied gov-ernmental attention to the needs and desires of the army, as well as partic-ular favors to those who had early given witness to their belief in Louis Napoleon's "star." The new Emperor went to great lengths to show that even if he lacked the military genius of his uncle, he was nevertheless a Bon-aparte with a profound affection for the army and a great concern for its well-being. He raised the pay of the soldiers and increased their pensions; he created the Military Medal for the men in the ranks; he reinstituted the Imperial Guard. Napoleon III wore a uniform and staged frequent reviews and parades, all meant to restore to the army its splendor and its éclat and to give a military aura to the regime. "These were acts to which no one could remain indifferent. They won the almost unanimous adhesion of the officer corps to the Empire as long as it was brilliant and successful."

To the degree that the soldiers had any coherent political convictions, they were Bonapartists. This did not, however, preclude the existence of a number of Legitimists, Orleanists, and even a few discreet republicans among the higher-ranking officers. That there was always a current of opposition to the regime within the officer corps could be seen from the various plebi-scites held during the eighteen years the Empire lasted. In the plebiscite of 1870, approximately one sixth of the military voted "no," despite pressure from above and to the great discontent of the government. Though this op-position was statistically of some note, politically it was of little importance.

Despite all that he owed to the army, Napoleon III gave it no sig-nificant part to play in the actual governing of France. "Of military origin, the government of the Second Empire was in no way the government of the military." Once the *coup d'état* had been accomplished, the army deserted the political arena and again assumed its accustomed role as the passive agent for the policies of the government, evidently content to be a recipient of imperial solicitude but to have no influence at all on the great decisions of state. The events of 1870 were to reveal that the soldiers of Napoleon III, like their predecessors in 1848, could accept with equanim-ity almost any political development.

When the catastrophe of Sedan brought down the dynasty, those officers who had escaped captivity or the encirclement at Metz rallied with-out hesitation to the orders of the revolutionary Government of Nation-al Defense. The Emperor had known how to win a greater degree of loyalty and affection from the French soldiers than any other sovereign since 1815. Every one of them had sworn an oath of personal fidelity to him, yet when he was captured and his regime overthrown, all tacitly considered themselves no longer to be bound. . . .

The years from 1815 to 1870 were a period of intellectual stagnation for the French army. In contrast to the vigor and excitement to be found in other sectors of nineteenth-century French intellectual life, one may speak of ossification, even sterility, in the realm of military theory and practice. This was possibly both a manifestation and a consequence of the cult of passive obedience. Rather than learning to use his own initiative and common sense, the typical officer came to look no further than the orders given by his immediate superior or the appropriate military regulations. In many officers this reverence for regulations was carried to the point of learning them by heart, and a few even prided themselves on their ability to recite them word for word, but backwards. In the end, the attitude of the French army could be characterized by a general fear of responsibility at every echelon of the military hierarchy.

That there was a tremendous reservoir of intellect and ability within the officer corps cannot be doubted. The military renaissance of the two or three decades after 1870 is witness to its existence. Unfortunately the system in honor before 1870 gave the first-rate men in the army no opportunity to apply their intellectual talents fruitfully. The man who studied or who showed any interest in scientific matters or in any questions outside the day-to-day life of the army was not likely to gain much by it. Promotion was based on other criteria.

"A fine physique, good health, and an impeccable appearance, these were sufficient, with some luck and a little backing, for a man to make a career."

During the first half of the nineteenth century, France was at war far more often than any other European power. The French soldiers were thus afforded abundant occasions to display their warlike qualities, particularly during the conquest and pacification of Algeria. The best of them won rapid promotion, with the result that the army of Napoleon III was led by a group of dashing and courageous soldiers. Their laurels had been won at the head of small units in pell-mell encounters with the Arabs, and they had an ill-disguised contempt for any graduate of the Staff School who really thought that there might be another dimension to warfare. Nothing in the Crimean or Italian war disturbed their confidence that they knew more about the realities of war than any other soldiers in the world. Of the three armies involved in the Crimea, the French turned out to be considerably less incompetent and poorly organized than either the British or the Russians. In 1859, the indolence of the Austrians prevented them from taking advantage of the blunders of the French high command prior to Magenta and Solferino. French soldiers, and not the French generals, won the two bloody victories of 1859.

The rapid Prussian victory in the 1866 war against Austria revealed to the more prescient of the French officers that there might be more to warfare than the "Africans" cared to admit. A few tentative steps were taken to remedy the obvious insufficiency in advanced military planning. In 1867, at the initiative of the Emperor, the most eminent officers of the army were called together at the Châlons encampment to undertake a *Kriegspiel* on the Prussian model. No one there was capable of evolving a general theme for the exercise. No one knew how to analyze a military situation or how to give the necessary orders. . . .

A far more significant response to the rising Prussian menace than this belated attempt to teach his generals about warfare on a grand scale was the plan of reform sponsored by Napoleon III which called for a general broadening of military service. The project involved an increase in the size of the active army and the effective organization of the reserves much in the manner of the Prussians. The Emperor found no real support for his ideas either within the army or in the country at large. The soldiers were frankly doubtful that short-term conscripts, such as those in the Prussian army, were of any real military value at all. A conscript began to be worth something only after he had served a few years and regimental life had broken him of all civilian ways. Marshal Randon declared: "These proposals will give us only recruits. It is soldiers we need." The bourgeois did not want their sons wasting their time in the army, while the peasants still preferred to take their chances on drawing a "good" rather than a "bad" number. In the end, Marshal Niel, the Minister of War and the author of the law, was able to do no more than have the term of service reduced to five

years, thereby giving military training to a slightly larger percentage of the population than formerly. Elaborate provisions were also made for the organization of the reserves, but these were still a dead letter in 1870 when war broke out. The Niel law of 1868 was a pale reflection of what Napoleon III and his more farsighted advisers demanded. It did little to improve the state of the army on the eve of the Franco-Prussian War.

A simple narrative account of the French performance in the War of 1870 makes it difficult to believe that France had been the preeminent military power on the European continent for the past fifty years. The confusion of mobilization was probably no worse than it had been in 1859, as described by General Trochu in his work *L'armée française en 1867*, or at the time of the Crimean War. The enemy, however, was of a caliber different from the Russians or the Austrians. The causes of the French defeat in 1870 are numerous. In numbers of men mobilized, the French with 250,000 soldiers could not match the 400,000 in the army of Prussia and her allies, not to mention the 100,000-man reserve and a large force of militia. The French artillery was inferior in quantity to that of the Prussians and shorter in range. The French army had no plan of campaign, other than to rush the troops headlong to the frontier, in the vague hope of invading South Germany. The Prussian war plan was carefully worked out in advance, with due allowances made for unforeseen contingencies. Since no unit in the French army larger than a regiment had an organized peacetime existence, brigades, divisions, army corps, and armies had to be created at the time of mobilization, their components drawn from the farthest parts of France and their command structures improvised in haste. In the Prussian army all such things had been carefully worked out in advance and tested in numerous *Kriegspielen*.

Despite all its organizational and material deficiencies, the French army might yet have made a respectable showing in the war but for one irremediable defect. The army had no leadership. There was no general in unquestioned command of the armies in the field who was able to impose his will on his higher-ranking subordinates or on the government, as Pélissier had done in the Crimea. The command of the main French field army changed hands three times in the course of six weeks. None of the subordinate commanders displayed any initiative, possibly because absolute obedience had become so ingrained in their mentality that very few of them dared to make a move without first receiving a specific order. The French generals were profoundly ignorant of war on a grand scale; thus the years of careful peacetime planning necessary to mobilize an army and to launch a campaign were completely lacking as was also the training required to manage the movements of an army in the field. The confusion caused by the intellectual deficiencies of the generals in command was heightened by the personal enmity many of them felt toward each other.

The French chiefs were all mutually jealous and ready to abandon one another at the moment of danger. A sovereign, sick and lacking in prestige, could not through fear suppress their rivalries. Opposed to them were to be seen the chiefs of the German army, possessing not only the most brilliant qualities, but also a perfect sense of solidarity, which led them to rush to the help of each other and to move spontaneously, without orders, toward the sound of cannon fire in order to render mutual support. . . .

Bravery was not lacking in the French army, either among the generals or the men in the ranks. Badly provisioned through the incompetence of the military commissariat, suffering terrible losses in battle, and then subjected to the crushing fatigue of marches and countermarches as the generals tried to evolve or improvise a plan of campaign, the soldiers fought with traditional verve and courage. On occasion, by their fierceness and their tenacity, they would win a temporary local advantage, only to have their generals throw it away. In the recent past, the French soldier had been able to win his own battles while his chiefs did little more than stand aside observing the slaughter, but it was to no avail against the superior numbers and the methodical maneuvers of the Prussian armies.

To climax the list of mistakes committed by the French in the war, Napoleon III insisted on accompanying the armies, although he was in such pain that he often seemed hardly aware of what was taking place around him. He could do little to impose any order on the quarreling generals, while the Regency Council under the incompetent direction of the Empress tried to run the war from Paris. Napoleon III was not a soldier as his uncle had been. The sight of the slaughter at Solferino and Magenta had sickened him. His presence with the armies added nothing, while his absence from Paris was a disaster. After the opening defeats the only salvation for the French army lay in a retreat to Paris. Here it could dig in and regroup its forces, but for political reasons the Empress vetoed even the return of Napoleon III to Paris, let alone the army. The hastily formed Army of Châlons, accompanied by the Emperor, thus wandered into the encirclement of Sedan. Had Napoleon III remained in Paris, he would perhaps have taken the political risk of withdrawing his army back on the capital.

Napoleon III had come to power because he had known how to exploit the ambitions and the sentimental Bonapartism of certain officers to his own political advantage. Once the Empire was reestablished, he showered favors on the military in an effort to keep any current antipathetic to himself from gaining strength. In the matter of choosing the men to lead the armies, much depended on how well the general in question stood with the imperial couple. "Gallantry in the field and an agreeable personality were the passports to court favour and court favour was the passport to high command." Public opinion also had to be heeded in the choice of generals. . . . After the fact, few would deny that the Emperor's constant interference in the affairs of the army, be it for personal reasons or motives of state policy, had contributed greatly to the disasters of 1870.

The more prescient soldiers asked of the emerging Republic that they be given the greatest possible latitude in the management of their own affairs. In making such a request, they were not acting out of any desire to resist the general policies of the government, or because of their supposedly innate antirepublicanism. Rather their experiences under the Second Empire had indicated that too much politically motivated interference was incompatible with the primary function of an army in time of peace: preparing for war. Republican politicians could never overcome completely their distrust of the army, but most of them over the years came to see the soundness of the military argument and to allow the soldiers to make the institutional arrangements necessary to profit by the increased autonomy of the army within the state. This was to be one of the constant themes in the evolution of the relationship between the Third Republic and the French army.

Robert Paxton has written a classic study of military corporatism. His seminal *Parades and Politics at Vichy* (1966) is the story of how the French army continued to live on as the Armistice Army between 1940 and 1942; of how Jaurès's concept of a socialistic *armée nouvelle* became Europe's and France's most corporate and conservative Pétainiste instrument. How the Army of the Republic avenged the Republic, and how the old guard became the new regime, is a remarkable study of military corporatism and exclusivity.

Robert Paxton

June 1940: The French Army Lives On

FRENCH DUNKIRK

During the first days of June 1940, ten divisions of the British Expeditionary Force in France were snatched from annihilation on the beaches at Dunkirk to fight again another day. Three weeks later, under conditions less starkly dramatic but no less fateful, the French Army faced a Dunkirk of its own: a political Dunkirk. When the government of Marshal Pétain sued for armistice from its temporary retreat at Bordeaux on June 17, it was in Hitler's power virtually to abolish the French Army as an institution. For the first time since France had been a nation, there might be no French Army on the face of the earth.

When General Charles-Léon Huntziger set out from Bordeaux on June 20 to represent France in the armistice negotiations, he could anticipate harsh terms. Marshal Pétain's ill-timed public declaration on June 17 that "the fighting must be stopped" had spread quickly to the remotest battalion, reducing French defenses to pockets of individual resistance. General Erwin Rommel, pushing his Seventh Panzer Division toward Brest and the

From Robert O. Paxton, Parades and Politics at Vichy: The French Officer Corps Under Marshal Pétain *(Princeton, N. J., 1966), pp. 3–11, by permission of Princeton University Press.*

tip of Brittany that day found French units standing along the road, their officers anticipating an immediate cease-fire. Rommel covered 150 miles on June 17, the longest day's advance ever made until then by an entire division.

The Commander in Chief of French Armed Forces, General Maxime Weygand, had briefed Huntziger on the potential German demands which France must reject. If Germany sought major concessions in the French Fleet or the Empire, the last two French trump cards still unplayed, there could be no armistice. Of course, the French were hardly in a position to bargain, and the conditions of Huntziger's trip northward from Bordeaux showed it. Huntziger did not even know where the parleys would be held.

Setting out from Bordeaux in the afternoon of June 20, Huntziger and his party traveled for seventeen hours without food or rest, along roads choked with frightened refugees and idle soldiers, hardly a scene to stiffen negotiators' backs. Charles-Léon Huntziger was filling an unenviable role for a career officer. A *marsouin*, or colonial infantry officer, descended from an Alsace family which had moved after 1870 in order to remain French, Huntziger had spent much of a brilliant career in the Near East.

At the close of World War I, he was aide to Marshal Franchet d'Esperey at Constantinople, and in 1933 commander of French forces in the Levant. By 1940 he had been promoted and was the youngest French *général d'armée*.

In mid-June 1940, despite the fact that the initial German breakthrough at Sedan had occurred on the fissure between General Corap's Ninth Army and Huntziger's Second Army, Huntziger stood out as the officer most likely to reach supreme command. Prime Minister Paul Reynaud considered that among army commanders only Generals Billotte, Giraud, and Huntziger had sufficient personal ascendancy and prestige to make future commanders in chief; by the time Pétain replaced Reynaud on June 17, Billotte had been killed in an automobile accident and Giraud was a prisoner of war. Huntziger remained, almost by default, the preeminent French general after Georges, commander of the northeast front, and Weygand. General Huntziger's eminence was more a commentary on the officer generation of 1940 than on his personal qualities. A slender man, still young and briskly military in his bearing, he was supple rather than strong. Foreign observers commented on his amiability and his skill in debate rather than on any elemental force of character. He was to be, in Hitler's words, "one of the wiliest and cleverest of French representatives," but he had neither the *panache* of a De Lattre de Tassigny nor the dogged straightforwardness of a Giraud.

Everything in Huntziger's career prompted him to swallow his dismay and accept this repugnant assignment in a spirit of abnegation. Moreover, an instinctive sympathy with Marshal Pétain's views made him all the more ready to serve the new government, even in its ultimate gesture of national humiliation. Before June 1940, Huntziger's fellow officers considered him "apolitical," which meant that he did not frequent governmental anterooms for the sake of his career, as *politiquard* officers did, and that he obeyed orders in the spirit of serving eternal France rather than the Third Republic. His handpicked press officer during the battle of France was Henri Massis, the prominent *Action Française* pamphleteer. Huntziger and the Marshal were to develop warm relations as kindred spirits, both preoccupied with questions of morale and education. When the *Francisque* order was created as a mark of the Marshal's special esteem, Madame Huntziger was awarded the first emblem. With mixed feelings then, appalled at the role he was called˙ upon to play, yet eager to serve the Marshal loyally, General Huntziger set out from Bordeaux not knowing where he was to confront the German conquerors.

Only at Paris did Huntziger and his team discover their destination. Arriving at the little railroad station of Rethondes, in the forest of Compiègne, on June 21, Huntziger could recognize the statue of Marshal Foch, now draped in a swastika. The railroad car in which Weygand himself, as Foch's aide, had once read the Allied armistice terms to the defeated German high command stood on a siding. The ceremonies of 11 November 1918 were to be replayed in reverse, according to stage directions heavy with ironic symbols. Once installed in the railroad car where Hitler formally presented Huntziger with a copy of the armistice, the weary French delegates learned that they could hear the armistice terms but not discuss them. The armistice was to be a German *diktat*.

In the mood of exhausted foreboding in which Huntziger and his party prepared to learn the German terms, the fate of France and of the French Army appeared a dark one indeed. No wonder the provisions as read to them seemed a concession.

On the first evening at Rethondes, June 21, a telephone connection with Bordeaux was arranged for General Huntziger, and, as the German interpreter Paul Schmidt listened from an adjoining railroad car, the French delegate relayed his first impressions to General Weygand. The armistice terms, though harsh, contained nothing against French honor. "In particular, one point, which he had discussed with Weygand before his departure, was not included in the terms. In this respect, things were quite different from what Weygand and he had assumed." The fleet could remain in French hands.

There was good news, too, about the army. The German authorities, Huntziger reported over the telephone, "had orally and provisionally conceded [*sic*] a 100,000-man army." The verb is a revealing one. For Huntziger and Weygand, a French Army to keep order in the Unoccupied Zone was a precious concession to French interests rather than a German device to free more German troops for the invasion of Britain.

It was no accident that Hitler's terms seemed lenient. Hitler had carefully planned their effect to avoid provoking the French into further resistance. As early as June 16, Hitler had instructed that proposed armistice terms be drawn up, and the next day—the day Marshal Pétain asked for negotiations—he outlined to Colonel Böhme of the *Wehrmachtführungsstab* a formula designed to lull France into acquiescence. France would remain sovereign, faced with no territorial demands "for the present"; only part of France would be occupied, that part necessary for pursuing the invasion of England; the French Fleet would be neutralized rather than taken over by Germany, and France would retain some armed forces. Hitler's armistice strategy presumed, of course, that after Britain's surrender the velvet gloves could be removed for the final peace conference. . . .

That France should continue to have an organized armed force during the armistice period was thus an integral part of Hitler's French policy, calculated to serve German interests during the weeks before the final peace conference. An Armistice Army would help the Germans keep order in their rear during the final assault on Britain, and a France with all the trappings of sovereignty would spare Germany the chores of total occupation and would prevent British exploitation of the remaining assets of French world power: the fleet and the empire. The Armistice Army was part of the German *diktat*.

To many French officers, however, the provisional 100,000-man army seemed the precious "concession" which General Huntziger had announced over the telephone to Weygand the night of June 21. General Emile Laure, for example, a former Pétain aide who was released from Königstein prison in October to resume his duties with the Marshal, discovered that "the military clauses of the armistice were better than he had imagined." German idea or not, the Armistice Army might well serve French interests, particularly as the armistice period began to drag on beyond Hitler's first expectations.

Hitler's need for an interim French Army coincided very neatly with two preoccupations nagging the minds of many a French officer. Beyond the immediate bread-and-butter worries of good assignments and promotion, the prospect of the French Army's dissolution, even for a brief armistice period, made French officers smell the smoke of social revolution, like nervous householders awakened in the night. . . . Clearly the dread of a Paris Soviet, which had helped

persuade General Weygand to insist on an armistice in the first place, continued to influence officers after the armistice. "The Armistice Army exists above all for the preservation of order," wrote General Huntziger in his General Order No. 2 of 25 November 1940. It was an order of priorities upon which German and Vichy authorities could agree.

Neither the natural concern for job security nor the uneasy state of public order, however, fully explains the relief with which many French officers learned that a French Army would continue to exist during the armistice period. French officers had been taught to believe that a root-and-branch domestic opposition was threatening the very existence of a professional army in France. For one black moment, it had seemed that the German *diktat* might accomplish what a century of French antimilitarism had tried but failed to do: to abolish the institution of professional soldiery altogether in France. . . .

ROBERT PAXTON

The Gaullist Resistance Movement

. . . One officer [who could follow his personal inclinations] was Charles de Gaulle. Colonel de Gaulle had commanded the Fourth Armored Division in its desperate effort to halt the German drive to the sea, from

From Robert O. Paxton, Parades and Politics at Vichy: The French Officer Corps Under Marshal Pétain *(Princeton, N. J., 1966), pp. 28–38, by permission of Princeton University Press.*

May 15 to June 6, and had he retained a field command, De Gaulle would no doubt have found it very hard to leave his men and go abroad. On June 7, however, his friend and sponsor Paul Reynaud promoted him and called him into the cabinet as Under Secretary of War. On June 8 he made the first of a series of flying trips to England to seek additional air cover and additional shipping to permit building a fresh force in North Africa. In London, deeply impressed by Churchill's determination, he became an active sponsor of Churchill's dramatic stroke of psychological warfare, the offer to merge France and Britain into a single country to carry on the war against Hitler.

When he learned in the night of June 16–17 that his sponsor had resigned as Prime Minister, Brigadier General Charles de Gaulle could hardly have looked forward to a brilliant career as ex-Under Secretary of War. Not only was his morale intact, but he was free of official responsibilities. Having prepared a means of escape for his family, therefore, De Gaulle managed to slip aboard the plane carrying General Spears from Bordeaux to London on the morning of June 17, where the next night he broadcast his famous appeal for continued resistance abroad.

Charles de Gaulle did not create the overseas opposition to the armistice. During his first week in London, he tried to put himself at the disposal of the far more important leaders of that opposition in positions of command, Generals Noguès and Mittelhauser. Before June 25, indeed, the relatively obscure brigadier general in London hardly presented as yet a clear alternative to the far more important commanding generals in Algiers and Beirut. Indeed, many French officers were in no position to hear the eloquent appeal of June 18. An officer who had been trying to hold one of the Loire bridges that day could well comment to an interviewer twenty years later with some acerbity

that he had not been at his fireside "in slippers" to tune in the B.B.C. Certainly there were would-be resisters who reached England in those days without having heard of De Gaulle. The future General Leclerc only heard of the London movement on June 25. The name De Gaulle begins to appear in the minutes of German staff meetings only on July 7. Through June 1940, to go by General Halder's diary, Algiers and Beirut were far more nervously watched than London as a center for resurgent French resistance.

After June 25, however, by a process of elimination which shocked and surprised De Gaulle, the young brigadier general was left as the one figure around whom the remaining elements of resistance could crystallize. From all accounts, those elements were still very vigorous at the end of June. United States consuls reported from Algiers, Casablanca, Lagos, and Leopoldville on the "strong movement" among French officers to reject the armistice and go on with the war. In Beirut, the American consul was confident that whole units would cross into British Palestine with their commanding officers; he knew "a number of officers" who were making such plans. In the months to come, however, only a comparative handful of career officers were to join De Gaulle, and the Armistice Army was to be left the sole and undisputed heir of the French Army. The failure of even officers who bitterly resented the armistice to join Fighting France is baffling in retrospect. At the time, however, De Gaulle's movement had only a limited field of recruitment.

Unlike Generals Noguès and Mittelhauser, General de Gaulle had not pleaded privately for continuing the war from abroad. He had made a ringing public rejection of the armistice. As in 1935 when he broadcast his strategic concepts by having his friend Paul Reynaud promote them in the Chamber of Deputies, De Gaulle had short-circuited the established network of military decision-making. More seriously, his action threatened the forthcoming armistice negotiations in the most direct way. Since it was essential for favorable armistice terms that the French government and high command appear to be acting in good faith and in control of the forces in whose name they claimed to speak, General Weygand ordered De Gaulle to return to France at once. On June 20, De Gaulle rather curtly rejected the order. From the very first, therefore, his movement bore the brand of public disobedience.

After the armistice had been signed, Marshal Pétain and the high command needed more than ever to demonstrate their ability to enforce Article 10, a promise to prevent Frenchmen from continuing the war abroad. Violation of that promise could well jeopardize the whole armistice policy and cause the Germans to cancel their "concessions." General Weygand took vigorous action to demonstrate French compliance with Article 10. General Mittelhauser put his chief of staff, Colonel de Larminat, under arrest for having openly prepared the movement of French army units from Syria into British Palestine. In early July, General Germain was sent out to Djibouti

first to persuade and then to replace his old best man, General Legentilhomme, about whose refusal to lay down arms the Italians had been complaining. Even with the loyalty of senior officers overseas assured, however, there remained the discontent of the rank and file which had so impressed American observers. In the Levant command, Weygand's own high prestige remaining from the months in the spring of 1940 when he had been French Commander in the Eastern Mediterranean, helped reassure doubtful spirits. In Africa, Vice-Admiral Charles Platon spent much of July touring French West and Equatorial African garrisons. As Minister of Colonies, he urgently explained the necessity of keeping the French Empire intact under a single French authority; as a senior officer, he could informally help guide his fellow officers along the path of least resistance, which was also the path of obedience. Platon was evidently persuasive. Governor-General Brunot in the Cameroons, for example, whom an American diplomat had found staunchly pro-British shortly before, now became "disappointingly sour and frightened." The beginnings of disarmament and doubts about British survival began to corrode the bellicose feelings of junior officers in Africa, according to the same American observers who had been impressed by their morale in June.

Even if an officer were still determined to sacrifice career, family, and security to join De Gaulle, the refusal of Generals Noguès and Mittelhauser to launch a resistance movement meant that he had to reach British territory. The physical problems of transportation were formidable. The dramatic escape across the Pyrenees into Spain or across the channel by trawler could never be a mass travel route. It was no accident that fully one-third of the Free French force at Christmas 1941 were seafaring Bretons. By and large, the most fertile recruiting grounds were those French officers and men who were already on British soil, or with easy access to it. There were the disgruntled forces in Syria, who were expected to cross in great numbers into Palestine. In the end, however, after the arrest of Colonel de Larminat and growing doubts about British intentions in Syria, only some four to five hundred officers and men ever actually crossed the frontier, out of an army of 100,000. There were the crews of French ships of the Eastern Mediterranean squadron at Alexandria. But after the Franco-British naval clashes at Oran and Dakar, only about 100 officers and sailors out of 2,000 walked down the gangplank to join the little nucleus of Fighting French in Egypt.

There were, finally, three kinds of French units in England at the signature of the armistice: the crews of French ships in British ports, the forces evacuated with the British Expeditionary Force from Dunkirk on June 3 and still unrepatriated, and veterans of the Anglo-French force which had failed to hold Norway in April 1940. General Weygand ordered these units home in compliance with Article 10. And official agencies in Britain were stringently forbidden to give any assistance to the dissident general. Another barrier had been set in the way of overseas resistance.

In addition to the barriers of physical geography, there was a geography of the mind which made it difficult for a good officer to abandon his station and tear free from the web of responsibility which command placed upon him. It was almost impossible for General de Gaulle, standing outside the chain of command, to "break the charm," as he put it, to shatter the links which bound an officer to his seniors and his subordinates. Consider the example of General Maurice-Émile Béthouart, De Gaulle's classmate at Saint-Cyr and in July 1940 commander of the French detachment which had fought in Norway and had been brought back to Britain. General Béthouart's personal determination to rid France of the German occupation can not be doubted. In 1941, as liaison officer with the German Control Commission in Morocco, he hindered German freedom of movement sufficiently to provoke a crisis in the Armistice Commission. In 1942, he played a leading part among the pro-Allied conspirators who helped prepare the way for the American landing of November 1942. In July 1940, however, he saw no reason to question the validity of orders from the high command. The French Army still existed, and General Béthouart intended to serve France within it. Deciding on his own part to return to France, he left his junior officers free to take the decision which seemed proper to them. Nine officers joined De Gaulle, including such central figures in the Gaullist movement as Captain Dewavrin, better known as "Colonel Passy,"

Lieutenant Colonel Magrin-Vernery, later better known as "General Monclar," and Captain Pierre Koenig.

Among even those whom geography permitted to join De Gaulle, therefore, the career officers who joined the movement at its beginning were largely restricted to men already detached from the close hierarchy of command functions, like De Gaulle himself, men for whom the chain of command had been broken. Captain Philippe de Hautecloque, for example, the only northeastern front veteran among prominent Free French career officers, heard about De Gaulle on June 25 after he had escaped to Paris from a military hospital taken over by the Germans. His biographer doubts that he would have abandoned an active assignment. General Georges Catroux had retired from active duty in 1939, only to be named Governor-General of Indochina when war was declared. After being replaced in that job by Admiral Decoux on July 14, he went to Singapore where he set out on August 25 for London. General Legentilhomme, who refused to cease fire in French Somalia, was joint Allied Commander in Chief at Djibouti; he did not move to British territory until August 2, after he had been removed from French command and had failed to rally his former officers to continued resistance. Colonel de Larminat, imprisoned in Syria for too openly preparing to move French units into Palestine, had already burned his boats when he escaped to join De Gaulle. Admiral Muselier, the only naval officer of flag rank to join De Gaulle, had been retired in 1939 after

an ancient feud with Admiral Darlan reached the point of complete rupture. Navy Captain Philippe Auboyneau was already in Egypt as a liaison officer with the British Navy.

There was also a group of military attachés from Latin American capitals who felt freer to follow their inclinations than officers with troop commands, men like Air Force Colonel Martial Valin from Brazil and Army Colonels Petit, Angenot, Brosset, and Dassonville. The adventures of Colonel Angenot, who was detailed to the Paraguayan army as a cavalry instructor in 1940, suggest how hard it was for even an officer off French soil to tear free from the web of routine responsibilities. Colonel Angenot cabled his allegiance to De Gaulle in June 1940, and received orders to work for the good cause in his current assignment. Thereupon the entire French military mission in Paraguay followed suit, only to receive a revised order from General de Gaulle summoning the whole group to London. After much indecision, Colonel Angenot left Asunción alone in early September.

Another category of Gaullist recruits were officers who escaped from German prisoner-of-war camps, such as Edward Corniglion-Molinier and Pierre Billotte. Captain Billotte, who escaped into the Soviet Union and was interned there until Russia was brought into the war on the Allied side, reached London in the summer of 1941 at the head of a little band of kindred spirits, 15 officers and 200 men. By contrast with all these officers set apart in one way or another from the chain of command, the vast majority of staff officers and troop commanders in metropolitan France and the Empire simply remained in place in the routine operation of the continuing French Army.

To make matters worse, Prime Minister Churchill took a step in the first days of July which slowed even this small flow of officer recruits to a trickle, and which gave a new impetus to Weygand's efforts to assure loyal obedience overseas to the armistice policy. Churchill regarded the eventual disposition of the French Fleet as a matter of life and death for Britain. In early July, he saw nothing to prevent the world's second most powerful fleet from falling into German clutches. Article 8 of the armistice required not only that French ships be disarmed under German and Italian supervision, but also that they return to home ports, Toulon or Brest. Despite the German promise in Article 8 not to use these ships for war purposes during the armistice period, and despite repeated private assurances given by Admiral Darlan, the return of French warships to home ports put them uncomfortably close to German power in case the armistice should be denounced or violated. Churchill decided to prevent the return of French warships in Britain and in North Africa to metropolitan ports. On July 3, British troops seized the French ships in British ports, and on the same day off Mers-el-Kébir, the naval base at Oran, a British squadron presented the French Commander, Admiral Gensoul, with three choices: to join the British forces against Germany, to sail to some remote French area such as Martinique, or to scuttle his ships. Admiral Gensoul having rejected this ultimatum, the British squadron shelled the French ships at anchor, causing 1,269 casualties.

The reaction of Frenchmen to this news was a spasm of anger, humiliation, and hatred. Opinions were "violent in the extreme," Ambassador Bullitt told Washington, and moderation was not assisted by the fact that Admiral Gensoul neglected to mention the Martinique option in his reports of the British ultimatum. Marshal Pétain wrote President Roosevelt on July 4 that "nothing could justify this odious aggression." Twenty years later officers could describe the incident to an interviewer as "those British murders." For General de Gaulle, this "lamentable incident" meant the end of hope for any official resistance in North Africa. In Syria and Lebanon, numerous officers who had planned to cross to Palestine changed their minds. In French Africa, a wave of animosity to London swept over circles which only recently had longed for a way to keep up the war alongside Britain. That "terrible axeblow," as De Gaulle called it, virtually cut off the slender stream of voluntary exiles reaching London.

By the end of July, the Gaullist movement had leveled off to about seven thousand persons, officers and men, only a fraction of whom were career officers. Senior officers consisted of two generals who had been dismissed from remote overseas posts, one disgruntled admiral and one Navy captain who was already in London, and seven colonels and lieutenant-colonels, five of them attachés from

Latin America. Only by acquiring new territory in French Equatorial Africa in August and September was the Gaullist movement able to enroll whole units in the normal exercise of their functions. By October 1940, the Gaullist force had risen to the modest total of 35,000 men, which remained its size up to November 1942.

By the end of July 1940, then, two questions vital to the future of the French officer corps had been decided. There would continue to be a French Army in spite of the defeat. And the Gaullist movement, failing to break into the chain of command at any decisive point, was never to represent more than a minor fraction of French officers. The Armistice Army was to be the mainstream of social continuity in the French officer corps.

BRITAIN: THE EBBING OF AMATEURISM

Correlli Barnett in his study, *Britain and Her Army, 1509–1970: A Military, Political and Social Survey*, argues that Britain suffers from a "blue water" myth. The British, who are reluctant to accept the need for a strong army, have come to believe that the island nation is protected by sea power. Barnett argues that five centuries of British involvement in continental wars do not support the myth.

The Napoleonic Wars pointed up the importance of the army and made a national hero of Wellington. The Iron Duke's officers had only one qualification—enough money to purchase a commission. Wellington supported this practice, arguing that the excellence of the British army was mainly due to "the circumstance that its officers were gentlemen in the true sense of the word." This attitude lasted until the British army was forced to fight in the Crimea. In *Studies in War and Peace*, Michael Howard quotes a French observer of British troops in the Crimea as saying that England was utterly devoid of military talent, as much in administration as in fighting.

MICHAEL HOWARD

Wellington and the British Army

In 1814 the Duke of Wellington enjoyed among the victorious Powers in Europe a prestige which in this coun-

From Studies in War and Peace, *Michael Howard (New York, 1971), pp. 51–64. Copyright © 1970 by Michael Howard. All rights reserved. Reprinted by permission of Viking Penguin Inc.*

try is taken very much as a matter of course. Yet to her continental allies the part which Britain had played in the downfall of Napoleon was not altogether evident. The destruction of French fleets and the acquisition of lucrative French colonies seemed marginal if not irrelevant activities to

Germans, Austrians and Russians who had had to face the *Grande Armée*. The recurrent failure of British forces to establish themselves in the Low Countries or the Mediterranean could arouse nothing but scorn. But the successes of the Army in the Peninsula, limited as they were and secondary as was the front on which they were achieved, could not be ignored. Wellington's little Army was like a terrier with its teeth firmly sunk in a boar's hind leg: doing no serious damage, but maddening and impossible to shake off. When in 1813 he secured at Vitoria a victory such as no allied force had achieved over a major Napoleonic Army since the Austrian defensive triumph at Aspern in 1809, Britain could again hold up her head, and Wellington entered France with as much right as his allies to a conqueror's laurel crown. He went to Vienna, moreover, as the representative of a Power tainted with no suspicion of duplicity, as was Austria, nor of revolutionary infection, as was Prussia, nor, as was Russia, of territorial ambitions in Europe. At Waterloo he gave the revived monster a dramatic and final *coup de grâce*. Thus it was at his feet that the princes of Europe poured, in enthusiastic token of their gratitude, that treasury of orders, marshals' batons, plate, dinner services, pictures and *objets d'art* which now lies, all too little visited, at Apsley House.

The Duke, to the Powers at Vienna, represented a country which, untouched by invasion and firmly controlling its own civil strife, seems to enshrine all the massive certainties of the eighteenth century. Courteous,

immaculate, humorous and shrewd, Wellington himself was their very embodiment. And the army which he led belonged quite as surely to that age. Napoleon's continental adversaries had been able to make head against him only by adapting themselves to the military revolution which the French armies had set on foot. They also had to adopt measures of conscription, abandoning, with far-reaching political consequences, the small and expert professional armies of the eighteenth century with their noble officers and their ranks recruited from the social misfits of their lands. But the British Army of 1815, though purged of its greatest abuses by the herculean efforts of its Commander-in-Chief, the Duke of York, was still in essence that of 1793. There was no question of it representing a cross-section of the population in which the sons of the literate, professional and mercantile classes served side by side with those of gentry, craftsmen and common labourers. The ranks were still made up of long-serving volunteers who had said goodbye virtually for ever to civil life. They were tempted in by the immediate lure of bounty money; and once in they endured appalling hardships, not so much on active service—which must at times have come as a blessed relief—as in disease-ridden tropical garrisons where they might languish for twenty years or more, and in the fœtid squalor of overcrowded barracks at home. Drink was their only solace and escape, and discipline could be enforced only by plentiful application of the lash. Service under such conditions—and they were the normal conditions of the eighteenth century—attracted only the desperate. The Army was regarded as a midden fit only for outcasts, and the red coat was a badge less of honour than of shame.

The officers who commanded these men were neither skilled professionals nor dedicated idealists. The only qualification required for a commission was the money to buy it and the approval of the colonel of the regiment; and promotion went entirely by the ability to purchase higher rank. There was some professional improvement as the war proceeded; but for the majority of officers the regiment was an agreeable club, a uniformed extension of Bucks' or Boodles', and a campaign was equally an extension of the fox-hunting with which they normally passed the winter. It was not a system which lent itself either to professional efficiency or to hierarchical subordination. 'Nobody in the British Army,' complained Wellington in the Peninsula, 'ever reads a regulation or an order as if it were to be a guide for his conduct or in other manner than an amusing novel; and the consequence is that when complicated arrangements are to be carried into execution . . . every *gentleman* proceeds according to his fancy.'

This agreeable Whig anarchy applied not only to the officers but to the regiments in which they served. The colonel owned his regiment, much as the officer owned his commission; and his control of it was all the more absolute in that he was responsible, not to one hierarchical superior, but to a multiplicity of authorities, each of whom dealt with a different aspect

of its activities. Questions of discipline and promotion in cavalry and infantry came under the Commander-in-Chief. In the artillery and the engineers they were the business of the Master-General of the Ordnance, whose further responsibilities for the provision of weapons and ammunition to both services were much the same as those, in the Second World War, of the Ministry of Supply. Questions of expenditure were the responsibility of the Secretary at War. Transport and supply—the continental *intendance*—came under the control of the Treasury. Once troops left the United Kingdom they became the responsibility of the Secretary of State for War and the Colonies; while the Home Secretary supervised the auxiliary forces at home —the Militia, the Yeomanry and the Volunteers. The delay and inefficiency which resulted from this chaos of overlapping jurisdictions finds its monument in the melancholy succession of humiliations which the British Army suffered, from the early disasters of the American War of Independence to the notorious expedition to Walcheren. It was a sombre background against which the genius of Wellington was to shine all the more bright.

Yet unsatisfactory as was this force, there was little call, save on grounds of economy, to reform it. Its inefficiency was held to be a better guarantee of British liberties than its strength. English politicians, partly haunted by confused legends of the paid force which James II had accumulated to overawe his subjects, and more immediately fearful of any increase in the patronage at the disposal of the Crown, clung stubbornly to the belief that the country did not need a standing Army. It was a view which Wellington himself shared and repeatedly expressed. The Navy, he once declared to the House of Commons, was 'the Characteristic and Constitutional force of Britain, but the Army was a new force arising out of the extraordinary exigencies of modern times.' Any improvement in the administration and efficiency of the Army was seen by the House of Commons as a further addition to that power of the Executive which had, as Mr Dunning put it, increased, was increasing and ought to be diminished. Nor would that be the only danger. Any simplification must work to the advantage either of the civil element in military administration or of the Commander-in-Chief. The principal civil officer was the Secretary at War, who in 1783 had obtained sole responsibility for military expenditure. The office of Commander-in-Chief was held, from 1798 until his death in 1827, by the Duke of York. To pose so brutally the issue of who should control the Army, Crown or Parliament, would be to open wounds which even after 150 years were not totally healed. The very confusion of military administration enabled the British to evade a decision, and so long as the Navy held the seas, no urgent military necessity forced them to make one.

Such was the Army in which the Duke of Wellington was to pass his life, and he had no illusions about it. When asked how he learned his profession he replied, 'I learned more by seeing our own faults, and the defects of our system in the campaign of Holland, than anywhere else. . . .

The infantry regiments, taken individually, were in as good and proper hands as they are now but the system was wretched.' But he did not repine. He worked within the limitations set him, and made such limited improvements as he could. In the Peninsula, where he was able to gather the many threads of 'the system' into his own hands, he made it work with unprecedented efficiency. He accepted the strategic limitations of a pre-revolutionary army, with its need for the most scrupulous attention to supply; an attention which had slowed the campaigns of the eighteenth century to snail's pace, and from which the rough and ready methods of the French had broken triumphantly loose. Wellington, trained in his Indian campaigns to be meticulous about these details, did not attempt to copy his enemies. The French Army starved and Wellington's did not; and 'it is very singular,' commented the Duke acidly, 'that in relating Napoleon's campaigns this has never been clearly shown in anything like its full extent.'

So long as the Army was fed it remained an adequate weapon in Wellington's hands, for all the indisciplined insolence of its officers and the drunken barbarism of its men. The defects of both maddened him. Despatch after despatch from the Peninsula complained of the quarrels, the insubordination and the inefficiency of his officers. 'The croaking which already prevails in the Army,' he wrote in September 1810, 'and particularly about headquarters, is disgraceful to us as a nation and does infinite mischief to the cause'; and he confessed bitterly 'that a part of my business, and not the most easy, is to prevent discussion and disputes between the officers under my command.' The insubordination, reminiscent of the quarrelsome tenants-in-chief of some medieval array, led, as insubordination must, to military ineffectiveness. The British Army, he wrote, after his victory at Vitoria, 'is an unrivalled Army for fighting, if the soldiers can only be kept in their ranks during the battle; but it wants some of the qualities indispensable to enable a general to bring them into the field in the order fit to meet an enemy, or to take an advantage from a victory: the cause of their defects is want of habits of obedience and attention to orders by the inferior officers, and indeed by all. They never attend to an order with an intention to obey it, and therefore never understand it or obey it when obedience becomes troublesome or difficult.' Repeatedly he castigated 'the habitual inattention of the officers of the regiments to their duty' and 'the utter incapacity of some officers at the head of regiments to perform the duties of their situation.'

Yet on reflection he would not have them otherwise. Inefficient amateurs many of them may have been, but they had the virtues of their defects. 'The excellence of our own Army,' he later declared, 'mainly derives from the circumstance that its officers were gentlemen in the true sense of the word.' Here was a frank espousal of the classic view, that officers should be drawn from a distinct class of society, which had been commonplace in eighteenth-century military organi-

sation and which the ideals and practice of the Revolution had so remorselessly broken down. Such a caste system, believed Wellington, not only made for military harmony: it provided constitutional security as well. It prevented the growth of that most dangerous of all elements in society—a group of professional officers of humble birth, with no fortune save their wits and their swords. On these grounds Wellington, until the end of his days, defended the purchase of commissions, no matter what military disadvantages this brought in its train. 'It brings into the services men of fortune and character,' he commented, 'men who have some connection with the interests and fortunes of the country, besides the Commissions they hold from His Majesty. It is this circumstance which exempts the British Army from the character of being a "mercenary army" and has rendered its employment for nearly a century and a half not only not inconsistent with the constitutional privileges of the country, but safe and beneficial.' It was better that quarrelsome but reliable amateurs rather than efficient but rootless professionals should be in charge of the armed forces of the Crown.

As for the men, the Duke accepted them with all their drawbacks, and saw no chance of getting any better. He never believed, according to his friend and biographer, the Reverend G. R. Gleig, that the ranks could be filled with 'persons of what is called a respectable position in life. He still looked to want of other employment, and to idle habits, as the readiest source of recruitment.' With an army thus constituted any relaxation of discipline, and in particular any abatement of flogging, would be fatal. As it was, even with the savage powers of punishment at his disposal, it was all that he could do to keep them in fighting shape. 'They are a rabble,' he wrote home from the Peninsula, 'who cannot bear success any more than Sir John Moore's Army could bear failure'; and indeed the victories of the Army in the Peninsula did it almost as much harm as all the counterstrokes of the French. The troops after the Salamanca campaign were, 'he complained, 'little better than a band of robbers'; and their behaviour at Badajoz need hardly be recalled. Yet Wellington's final verdict, on his troops as on his officers, was more kindly. 'I will venture to say, 'he told Croker in 1826, 'that in our later campaigns and especially when we crossed the Pyrenees there never was an Army in the world in better spirits, better order or better discipline. We had mended in discipline every campaign until at last I hope we were pretty near perfect.'

Though he had little hopes of their personal improvement, Wellington was too good a commander to underestimate the importance of the welfare of his troops. 'I know of no [point] more important,' he declared, 'than closely to attend to the comfort of the soldier: let him be well clothed, sheltered, and fed. How should he fight, poor fellow! if he has, besides risking his life, to struggle with unnecessary hardships . . . one ought to look sharp after the young officers and be very indulgent to the soldier.' Within the framework which he regarded as

unalterable, the Duke did what he could. In war time he laboured to see the troops properly fed, and in peace he worked equally hard to get them decently housed. Under his governance the squalor of English barrack-room life was mitigated. The troops, who had previously slept four to a crib, obtained a bed apiece. He tried to obtain recreational facilities for them and to improve standards of ventilation and cleanliness in the barracks. But he expressed the fear, typically, 'that there was some danger both of overtaxing the liberality of Parliament and of spoiling the soldier, by first creating for him, and then supplying, wants which before enlistment he had never felt.'

Perhaps it was this fear which restrained him from taking up and developing the reforms with which Sir John Moore had been experimenting before his tragically early death. Moore, had he lived, might have done for the Army what Elizabeth Fry did for the prison system and Jeremy Bentham and his disciples for the law: dispelling the brutality and inefficiency of the eighteenth century with a combination of kindly Evangelical morality and brisk utilitarian competence. Moore had made his young officers train and drill with their recruits. He had held them personally responsible for the welfare of their men. He had introduced new forms of recreation and exercise into military training; and he had insisted on an entirely new standard of sobriety, courtesy and cleanliness throughout his command. But Moore was a Victorian born before his time: Wellington was a man of the eighteenth century who remained till the end of his life unsoftened by the arguments either of the Evangelicals or of Benthamites. If the Army remained one of the last uncleared sections of the great jungle of British institutions which the disciples of Bentham laboured so heroically to level, the Duke cannot rest entirely free from blame.

In 1818 Wellington relinquished his command in France and returned to England as Master-General of the Ordnance, with a seat in Lord Liverpool's cabinet. It was as much a political as a military appointment. Wellington was by now widely regarded as the wisest living Englishman; he was, as he always had been, closely in touch with political life and personalities; and the worried Government, in dealing with the country in the throes of near revolution, needed all the advice, both civil and military, that it could get. But Wellington's military influence was still limited. At the Horse Guards the Duke of York remained Commander-in-Chief and relations between him and Wellington were, and always had been, cool.

I can't say that I owe my success to any favour or confidence from the Horse Guards [Wellington confided to John Wilson Croker in 1826]. They never showed me any, from the day I had a command to this hour. In the first place they thought very little of anyone who had served in India . . . then because I was in Parliament, and connected with people in office, I was a politician, and a politician can never be a soldier. Moreover they looked upon me with a kind of jealousy, because I was a lord's son, 'a sprig of nobility', who came into the Army more for

ornament than use. They could not believe that I was a tolerable regimental officer. I have proof that they thought I could not be trusted alone with a division, and I suspect that they still have their doubts whether I know anything about the command of an Army, for I dare say you will be surprised to hear that in all the changes made since the war in the regulations of the Army, I have never been in the most trifling or distant degree consulted on any point.

But in the January of the following year the Duke of York died and Wellington himself became Commander-in-Chief. 'I am in my proper place,' he declared with open satisfaction, 'the place to which I was destined by my trade.' It was not a place to which he succeeded as a matter of course, nor one which on this occasion he held for very long. For a few days it seemed that King George IV might insist on taking over the command of the Army in person. Liverpool stigmatised the idea as 'preposterous', and Wellington himself threatened to 'protest against it in the most formal manner and with all the earnestness in my power.' The moment passed. Ministers and courtiers combined to persuade their eccentric sovereign to confine his military influence to the sartorial—where he certainly did damage enough—and Wellington assumed the office, temporarily combining it with the Master-Generalship of the Ordnance as well. Within four months, however, rather than serve with the odious George Canning, he had resigned both appointments. But the lure of the Horse Guards was too strong for him to absent himself for long. In August he returned; and when, the following spring, he accepted the King's commission to form a government, he was openly aggrieved to learn on becoming Prime Minister that he could not be Commander-in-Chief as well. 'I certainly did not contemplate this necessity [of resigning] as being paramount,' he admitted. That it *was* paramount was quickly pointed out both by his colleagues and by the opposition, and with rather an ill grace the Duke stood down. To facilitate his resumption of the office his successor, Lord Hill, assumed the title, not of Commander-in-Chief but, more cumbrously, of 'Senior General Officer upon the Staff in Great Britain and Ireland, etc. to perform the duties of Command-in-Chief.' But with or without the title, Hill remained at the Horse Guards for fourteen years, and it was only in 1842 that the septuagenarian Wellington was able to succeed his old subordinate, and enjoy the office for the last ten years of his life.

But whether officially in charge of the Horse Guards or not, the Duke was the most influential soldier in the United Kingdom during the quarter of a century which elapsed between his first assuming the command in 1827 and his death. The principal military officers—Lord Hill, Lord Anglesey, Sir George Murray, Lord Raglan—were his old subordinates of the Peninsula and Waterloo. He was necessarily the principal witness before the various commissions which were set up to investigate Army organisation and discipline as the century wore on. Had he been in favour of radical reform, much would have been achieved: but he was not. He was held back not simply by an innate scepticism and caution; even more influential was his realisation how very little in the way of military improvement the country and the House of Commons was prepared to stand. He was under no illusions about the anti-militarism of the British people: indeed to a great extent he shared it. If he did not participate in the popular mistrust of the military colleges and military clubs, he was profoundly sceptical about their value. No more than the most violent Radical did he approve of the proliferation of uniform in the London streets at the end of the war. No man was more anxious that the Army should not overstep its due constitutional and social limits; and 'he retained to the last a persuasion that the less the Army in its expenditure and general management is brought into public notice, the better.' When in 1828 a proposal was brought forward to increase Army pay, he set his face against it. Any increase in military expenditure, he foresaw, would be declared burdensome to the people; any increase in pay would have to be atoned for by a decrease in numbers; and the numbers of the Army, for the work it had to do, were already ludicrously small.

That work was considerable. First of all there was the obligation to garrison the posts overseas which Britain had been so casually accumulating during the past two centuries. 'The Empire is immense,' commented the Duke in August 1827, 'and includes nearly every important post in the world, whether naval, military or commercial. None of these posts are occupied even for defence, much less to be able to assist each other, even if they were within distance. Every service must be provided in, and proceed from, Great Britain.' So few were the troops available for garrison service that four regiments that returned to England in 1829 after twenty-four years' service overseas found themselves posted abroad again within five years. With such overseas posts we may include the garrison in Ireland; and when in 1816 the cry had been raised to reduce its strength, Sir Robert Peel pointed out all too truly that 'the gentry in Ireland could not reside on their estates unless they were secure.'

Secondly, troops had to be found to conduct operations overseas; and those who think of the period 1815–52 as being one of undisturbed peace should remember that during these years the United Kingdom was engaged in nearly a dozen conflicts in all parts of the world: Nepal, India, Afghanistan, South Africa, West Africa, Burma, and Canada. They were usually conducted only by a few battalions, but they imposed a severe drain on the man-power of an Army whose establishment had fallen between 1814 and 1816 from over 250,000 men to less than 80,500. In 1817 Castlereagh had declared that there were only 16,000 men available for duty in England; and the England of Peterloo and the Six Acts was itself virtually a theatre of war. On returning to the Horse Guards in August 1827, Wellington received from Sir John Byng, commander of the forces in the north of England, a

warning that 'the present tranquillity is not to be too much relied on, for the worst feeling exists between master and man; and the information given me from all the towns in Lancashire was, that if the troops were removed, I must expect in a short time urgent application for their return. The formation of the Metropolitan Police two years later an innovation for which Wellington, no less than Peel, deserves credit— relieved the Army of a considerable and unwelcome responsibility. When next serious public disorder threatened in London, during the Chartist demonstrations of April 1848, the old Duke prudently collected a military force of 7,000 infantry and a dozen guns to deal with it, but he equally prudently kept that force out of sight. On 10th April, the day of the great meeting at Kennington Common, not a soldier was to be seen in the streets. The Duke made all his preparations to deal with an emergency; yet only the police, plentifully stiffened by special constables, were in evidence, and such staff officers as had to appear in public wore civilian clothes. There was no horsed yeomanry to lose their heads and provoke another Peterloo; and the incipient revolt melted harmlessly away.

By discretion, by rigorous economies, Wellington thus kept the Army in being. He believed it impossible to do more. To increase its numbers, improve its conditions, renovate its weapons, all meant money; and money meant Parliamentary debate, Royal commissions, an unwelcome glare of hostile publicity which, with Whig and Radical strength swelling in the House of Commons, might be fatal to the military forces of the Crown. But even these motives do not entirely explain the Duke's persistent and successful opposition to the reform of that military administration of which Sir James Graham, on investigating it after the Duke's death, said, 'there is only one word to describe it—Chaos.' If Wellington was guided by an old Whig desire not to infringe the constitutional liberties of the British people, he was no less careful to uphold the proper prerogatives of the Crown; and his care to do so increased as, to his ageing and pessimistic eye, the forces of Radicalism and revolution grew ever stronger in the land. If the House of Commons had feared Army reform in the eighteenth century because it would increase the influence of the Crown, Wellington feared it no less in the nineteenth because it would increase the influence of the House of Commons. So long as the Army remained unreformed, it could be used as a tool neither of Royal despotism nor of political jobbery. When the possibility was mooted of the Secretary at War assuming control of the Army, he commented grimly, 'Let Her Majesty's Government try the experiment whether they can find an officer *whom the Army would respect and under whose control and command the officers and soldiers would cheerfully submit*, who will consent to be placed in this subordinate situation, under the superior direction of a political officer. . . . ' Sir John Fortescue wrote of Wellington that 'He considered that to place [the Army]

under the absolute control of a civilian responsible only to the House of Commons would be injurious to its discipline. Therein,' he added angrily, 'he was probably right.'

Right or wrong, Wellington opposed every project for the major reform of military administration that came up during his lifetime. He opposed the abolition of the Master-Generalship of the Ordnance, partly because of the value of having a dispassionate military specialist advising the Cabinet, who could 'not be supposed to have any political influence as a bias upon his mind.' He opposed equally the abolition of the Board of Ordnance, whose work, if combined with that of any other department, would constitute, he thought, an intolerably heavy burden for any office; and when, in 1837, a commission was set up to investigate the possibility of creating a War Office in which all the scattered branches of military administration would be combined, the Duke's comment was:

It has astonished me. I have always understood that it was a principle of the Government of this country, that he who exercised the Military Command over the Army should have nothing to say to its Payment, its Equipment, or even the Quartering thereof. . . . The Secretaries of State were considered, and were, responsible upon all the larger Political questions arising out of the existence of the Army, while the Commander in Chief exercised the Military Command, and, under their superintendence, administered the Patronage; as well for the benefit and encouragement of the Army itself, as upon

Constitutional grounds, in order to keep this Patronage out of the usual course of Parliamentary and Ministerial management.

The reforms proposed, he commented, would take

the Military power of the state totally and entirely out of the hands of the Person exercising the Royal Authority, and places it in the hands of one Member of the House of Commons and of the Cabinet. . . . The change cannot be made in this form without injury to the power of the Crown.

One cannot contemplate without nostalgia an age when military questions could be settled entirely on broad grounds of constitutional desirability, not modified in the slightest degree by any fears for the safety of the realm. It was not that the Duke did not feel such fears. In the 1840s, when French chauvinism was reviving and the development of steam navigation posed an entirely new threat to the security of the British coasts, the possibility of invasion 'haunted him like a nightmare.' 'Excepting immediately under the fire of Dover Castle,' he wrote in 1847, 'there is not a spot on the coast on which infantry might not be thrown on shore at any time of tide, with any wind, in any weather.' But he relied on the militia for the defence of the land. 'I should,' he confessed, 'infinitely prefer, and should have more confidence in, an Army of regular troops. But I *know* that I shall not have these'; and he complained, as have so many soldiers since, of 'the difficulty under which all governments in this country labour, in prevailing

upon Parliament, in time of peace, to take into consideration measures necessary for the safety of the country in time of war.'

An almost religious respect for the balance of the constitution thus combined with a practical statesman's appreciation of what was politically possible to strengthen the Duke's natural conservatism in things military. And why should he abandon it? With the British Army, imperfect as it was, he had beaten the greatest captain the world had seen for nearly two thousand years. Little wonder that he was reluctant to change even the armament and uniform of so triumphant a force. Seldom has the truism been so amply illustrated, that victory is more harmful to a nation's military prowess than the most shattering of defeats. Wellington could not see that a system which he himself had mastered might produce, in the hands of less talented successors, humiliations and failures as depressing as those which had been so characteristic of British military activity before his arrival in the Peninsula. After the British Army had been seen in action in the Crimea, a sympathetic Frenchman wrote to an English friend, 'The heroic courage of your soldiers was everywhere and unreservedly praised, but I found also a general belief that the importance of England as a military Power had been greatly exaggerated; that she is utterly devoid of military talent, which is shown as much in administration as in fighting; and that even in the most pressing circumstances she cannot raise a large army.'

These conclusions were shared by an appalled British public which discovered, as it watched the progress of operations in the Crimea, that the Army of Queen Victoria was still in all essentials the Army of George III. The reforms against which the Duke had fought could not be long delayed after the terrible winter of 1854-5. When they came, the Duke's fears were belied. The civil servants of the late nineteenth century had developed administrative techniques unimaginable to those of Wellington's day. The importance of political and royal patronage had disappeared; so had the significance of the Commander-in-Chief's direct responsibility to the sovereign—except, of course, in the eyes of the sovereign and of the Commander-in-Chief. This change in the spirit of the constitution was well under way during the Duke's lifetime, but it could have been detected only by younger eyes than his. In the 1820's and 1830's the dangers which he foresaw were still real, and he was well past seventy before they began to abate. The lessons of the Crimea opened all eyes; but by then the eyes of the Great Duke were for ever closed.

Numerous reforms followed the Crimean War: the secretaryship of state for war was separated from that of the colonies to give Britain a full-time war secretary, control over the militia was transferred from the Home Office to the War Department, and supply of armaments, a function previously exercised by an independent master-general of the ordnance, was turned over to the secretary of war. Further changes came in 1857, after a commission of reform visited the European military powers. A staff college was established at Camberley from the senior department of the Royal Military College at Sandhurst. Britain was following the continental practice of providing officers with professional training in peacetime.

But there was still a split within the administration of the military between the war secretary, who controlled supply and finance, and the commander-in-chief, who was responsible for the internal administration of the army. This split endured until the "Cardwell Reforms."

In 1868 Gladstone's reform government came to power. The new secretary, Edward Cardwell, an upper-class Victorian intellectual, was determined to save money by improving the efficiency of the army. His most notable reform was the abolition of purchased commissions. Barnett reminds us that Cardwell was not against purchase on principle, but because it stood in the way of his desire to amalgamate some of the existing regiments. But the abolition of purchase had little impact on the class-bound nature of the officer corps; "the need for private income was an excellent substitute to purchase as a social filter." Officers were poorly paid and could not, out of their salaries, support the constant rounds of polo, hunting, and entertaining which was the life of the officers' mess.

CORRELLI BARNETT

Cardwell and the Late Victorian Army

. . . Cardwell faced two major and inter-related problems: one was recruitment, and the other was Britain's dual strategic roles as both a European and a world-imperial power. Possible intervention in Europe required a nucleus organization of a field army backed by ample and quickly mobilizeable reserves: the Prussian system, although on a much smaller scale because Britain was an island. However, the Prussian system was founded on the sure base of an annual intake of conscripts, while any reformed British system would have to depend on voluntary recruitment. Cardwell abolished bounties as an incentive to enlist in 1869 as now ineffective, but Gladstone and the British taxpayer were unlikely to sanction such costly improvements in pay and conditions as to make the army a competitive occupation. In any case, a short-service army, even with steam-navigation, could not garrison India and the empire, for which long-service troops were needed. It was the kind of problem that had troubled the French before 1870, and the resulting unhappy compromise between European and colonial demands had contributed to the French army's defeat by the Purssians. Cardwell tried to find an answer

Reprinted by permission of William Morrow and Company, Inc. from Britain and Her Army, 1509–1970: A Military, Political and Social Survey. *Copyright © 1970 by Correlli Barnett.*

with his Army Enlistment Act of 1870. Enlistment was henceforth to be for twelve years: six with the colours and six in the reserve. However, while men in India would serve the full six years with the colours, men in Britain could pass into the reserve after three years. Cardwell hoped that eventually this Act would produce a reserve of 80,000 men. Under another Act of Cardwell's, men of bad character could be discharged from the army. It was hoped that the two Acts together would improve the quality of the rank-and-file without actually spending more money on them.

Cardwell's reforms are often, though wrongly, said to revolve round the 'linked-battalion' system, by which one battalion served abroad, while its pair was at home in the depot as a training and reinforcement unit. In fact two-fifths of the pre-Cardwell regiments already possessed two battalions, and since 1825 all battalions had been so divided as to provide a number of companies for duty abroad (the service companies) and one or more for duty at home (the depot companies). The key to Cardwell's reforms of the regimental system was in fact recruitment; and the best hope for recruitment at a time of dearth of Irish lay in the militia, composed of volunteers already partially accustomed to a military life. Thus 'localization' of the military system in territorial areas, where line regiments could be linked to militia regiments, was the essential frame of the Cardwell reforms. Although the model was Prussia, in Britain the place of army-corps districts was taken by districts of an administrative (not a field) brigade. There were sixty-six of these districts, fitted so far as possible into the British county map. The district and its brigade, under a lieutenant-colonel and a depot staff, welded together regular army, militia and volunteers into one system. The district comprised two regular battalions (one, and quite often both, away from the depot), two militia battalions and the volunteers. For the first time, regiments of the line were to be given fixed, permanent homes. Once new barracks had been built, it was hoped that through local pride the gulf between the army and the nation might be bridged, and recruitment stimulated by the close local association of militia and regulars. Thus Cardwell's 'localization' of the army was only made possible by the revival of the militia itself by the re-organization of 1852–3. For the district depots to be of adequate size and for ease of reinforcement, it was necessary to have two-battalion regiments. As Field-Marshal Lord Hardinge wrote at the end of the Crimean War:

The experience of the last two years affords a practical proof of the inefficiency and danger of relying on small regimental depots as a reserve for the field battalions, when the country may be suddenly involved in war.

Since the British regiment was self-contained and 'independent', single-battalion regiments well under strength could not be combined to make full-strength battalions. By contrast, the Royal Artillery, whose regiments had never been self-contained, could post men freely where needed. However, because of the strength of sentiment about the infantry regiments, with their individual customs and history, it was out of the question to form a Corps of Infantry on the lines of the Royal Artillery. Cardwell hoped instead to find some kind of answer by linking single-battalion regiments in pairs, one to be at home as a drafting and training unit, the other abroad, in alternation. However, his linkings demanded that very different kinds of regiment should work in double harness. Cardwell, by reforming too little, demanded too much. In 1881 another Secretary for War, Hugh Childers, took the final step of fusing the linked units permanently into new two-battalion regiments, with territorial designations of the style Cardwell had already applied to much of the remainder of the army. The cherished post-1881 county names often replaced sometimes very different county titles given to the numbered regiments of the line during the American War of Independence. In Cardwell's own time territorialization existed mainly on paper. For troubles in Ireland meant that the 'home' as well as the 'overseas' battalion of a linked-pair would sometimes be away from the depot. Depot buildings had to be constructed throughout the country before the regulars and the militia could really share a common local home and loyalty. And, in the event, an unexpected bonus to recruitment was provided by the agricultural depression of the 1870s.

Before Cardwell's master-plan for 'localization' could be carried through, two obstacles had to be removed. The first was the control of the militia (extending to the issue of commissions) by the Lords-Lieutenant. The second was the institution of purchase. Both were dealt with in the Regulation of the Forces Bill of 1871.

Because of the bitter and prolonged fight over the abolition of purchase, it has excited more notice than its importance in Cardwell's reforms merits. It was not so much for its own inherent evils that Cardwell wanted to abolish purchase, but because it stood squarely in the way of all his other reforms. Purchase blocked regimental re-organization and led to rigidity in the army's structure, because it made each regiment not simply a unit in an army but a colonel's private property. Two colonels' private properties could not be amalgamated or linked because of the possibility of financial loss. As Cardwell himself told the Commons:

Do you wish to increase the number of double battalions with a view to the Indian branch of the army, and to short terms of service—a point of the greatest possible importance? If you do so wish, you will be met immediately by difficulties arising from the purchase question. . . . Do you wish to unite closely the militia and the regular forces? If you do, one of the first things you will have to do will be to give subaltern officers of the militia, commissions in the line without purchase,

and how can this be done if there remain any conditions in reference to the purchase system?

The effects of purchase on the professional quality of officers was a lesser question than that of organization. Nevertheless there was wide agreement (except among the diehards) with the view expressed by the 1856 Royal Commission that purchase was

. . . vicious in principle, repugnant to the public sentiment of the present day, equally inconsistent with the honour of the military profession and the policy of the British Empire, and irreconcilable with justice.

Although Cardwell persuaded a thrifty government to pay over-regulation (black market) prices instead of the official tariff in buying out owners of commissions (which involved, for example, paying up £14,000 to buy out the owner of a cavalry regiment instead of £6,175), he failed to win over the opposition. A violent parliamentary struggle ended with the House of Lords throwing out the Regulation of the Forces Bill. To the diehards' fury, Cardwell turned their flank by inducing the Queen to end purchase by royal warrant, on the grounds that purchase had officially existed only by virtue of regulations established under earlier royal warrants. The Lords now passed the Bill, which, as well as abolishing purchase, transferred control over the militia and volunteers from the Lords-Lieutenant back to the Crown (and hence to the Secretary for War and the Commander-in-Chief). At last regular army and militia had been brought into one military system and the Lords-Lieutenant were deprived of their Tudor *raison d'être*. The Regulation of the Forces Act also gave the government powers of control over the national railway system in time of threatened invasion.

Cardwell's three great reforms (the Army Enlistment Act of 1870, the Regulation of the Forces Act of 1871, and the localization and linked-battalion scheme of 1872) provided the blue-print of the late Victorian army: short service, a reserve, a comprehensive military system based on the local depot. Cardwell was also responsible for other reforms, such as the abolition of flogging except in time of war, an increase in privates' pay to 1s. a day on top of free meat and bread, and some improvement in living conditions. In 1871 the first large-scale manoeuvres ever to be held in Britain were organized and repeated annually for several years before petering out again.

The War Office and Horse Guards also received the benefits of Cardwell's intellect and energy. By the War Office Act of 1870 and subsequent Orders-in-Council, Cardwell tried to complete the piecemeal reforms since 1854, and re-organize army administration on clear principles. The subordination of the Commander-in-Chief to the Secretary for War was placed beyond doubt by the new Act, which on behalf of Parliament and the Crown vested direct responsibility for every branch of the army in the Secretary of State. The army was no longer even residually under the royal prerogative, and the

constitutional ghosts of the seventeenth and eighteenth centuries had at last been laid. The Horse Guards and the War Office were now to constitute a single department, although they remained physically separated. The work of the combined department was divided between three executive officers: the 'Officer Commanding-in-Chief' (the strictly military aspects of all regular and irregular forces); the Surveyor-General of the Ordnance (all aspects of supply and equipment); and thirdly a financial secretary, responsible to the Secretary for War for pay, for all estimates and accounting, and for checking expenditure.

Cardwell's new consolidated War Office was marred by the hesitancy and compromise of all his schemes. There was only a partial approach to a general staff on the Prussian model (without the name). In practice, the Commander-in-Chief still ran the army independently of the Secretary for War. The forming of a general staff and the abolition of the personal power of the Commander-in-Chief were measures that went together, but there was an immovable obstacle in their way in the person of His Royal Highness the Duke of Cambridge, the Commander-in-Chief. Although Cambridge had given tepid support to Cardwell's other reforms, his taste for improvement did not extend to the abolition of his own unchallenged control over the army, or the loss of his job. Behind Cambridge stood his cousin, the Queen, and the court. Cardwell did not even attempt the impossible, and so instead of a general staff Britain continued to have Cambridge for another quarter of a century.

When Cardwell left office in 1874 his work remained unfinished in some respects, and half-baked in others. Even a double first at Balliol had found British institutions intractable material for the application of clear fundamental principles. His work does not therefore stand alone as a great turning-point of reform; it marks only one important stage in a continual, if spasmodic, process. . . .

The officer corps . . . failed to reflect the great changes in British society. Despite the abolition of purchase, the life of a regimental mess still reflected the life of the country's upper classes. After the 1880s the Victorian public schools began to infect the officer corps with their own very narrow snobbery and rigid sense of form. Such sons of the rich middle class as reached the army did so by courtesy of their private income and a public-school conditioning. The need for private income was an excellent substitute to purchase as a social filter. A life of racing, polo, hunting, balls and parties required an income much greater than an officer's pay, which was in any case not competitive with those of other professions. The control of the army remained in the hands of men out of touch with, and out of sympathy with, the social and technical changes of the age. Secondly, since both officers and men were recruited from unrepresentative social groups, the nation as a whole had little directly to do with the army. The human cost of imperial responsibility did not fall on the audiences who sang so patriotically in the music-halls, or damned lesser breeds at suburban tennis parties. What cheaper or less troublesome way of running a great empire could there be than a professional army whose officers all had private incomes, and whose rank-and-file were all paupers?

Many traditional institutions of the British way of life trace their present character no further back than the late Victorian period: organized cricket and football, mass tea-drinking, the popularity of the monarchy, the Labour movement—and the army. The army's principal homes today—like Aldershot—were then being built. The intense regimental spirit that has been so jealously defended in the face of amalgamations since 1945 owes more to Cardwell and Childers than to the era before the Crimea. The familiar full-dress uniforms of the Foot Guards and Household Cavalry in their present form are late Victorian. In Rudyard Kipling the army found a poet to express its own private values and record its way of life in India, the country that marked it so deeply. . . .

The Boer War disasters were dissected in the *Report of His Majesty's Commissioners on the War in South Africa* in 1903. The report indicted every aspect of the army from the commander-in-chief on down. The officers were heavily criticized for their lack of professionalism. Barnett notes that this lack of professionalism derived "from recruiting the officers from a leisured class to whom professionalism too often appeared as vulgar careerism."

CORRELLI BARNETT

Stagnation in an Age of Change

. . . The *Report of His Majesty's Commissioners on the War in South Africa,* published in 1903, stated that 'the whole military system as it stood at that date [1899] was tested by the war in South Africa'. It went on to indict almost every aspect of the army and its organization, from Wolseley, the then Commander-in-Chief, down to the private soldier. Only the Director of Military Intelligence and his fund-starved department received commendation, for as early as 1896 the D.M.I. had warned that the Boer war plan would probably be to invade Natal. In 1897 the D.M.I. had warned that in the event of war, two months would elapse before British reinforcements could reach South Africa; that in the meantime a Boer offensive would fall on the troops already there; and that therefore the British ought now to be raising their strength in South Africa. In 1898 the D.M.I. repeated his warnings and recommendations. However, the Intelligence Department was not a general staff. Wolseley, as Commander-in-Chief, was supposed to be a one-man general staff. The Royal Commission observed of Wolseley's performance:

. . . the general impression to be derived from the whole circumstances must be

Reprinted by permission of William Morrow and Company, Inc. from Britain and Her Army, 1509–1970: A Military, Political and Social Survey. *Copyright © 1970 by Correlli Barnett.*

that the special function of the Commander-in-Chief, under the Order in Council of 1896, viz: 'The preparation of schemes of offensive and defensive operations', was not exercised on this occasion in any systematic fashion.

And the Report also stated that it was 'not altogether remarkable under the circumstances described above that no plan of campaign ever existed for operations in South Africa'.

According to the Report, organized land transport (other than the railway), suitable maps, stores and equipment of all kinds were all lacking.

The Report noted that in 1899, out of a paper strength of 249,466 regulars and a reserve of 90,000, only two corps and a cavalry division (70,000 men) were available for overseas service—yet these also formed an integral part of home defence. India swallowed nearly 70,000 men, Egypt and the rest of the Empire nearly 60,000. It was an indication of how limited in scope and result Cardwell's reserve scheme and his attempted reduction of colonial garrisons had proved.

Witnesses before the Commission sharply criticized the standard of staff efficiency despite the fitful reforms in the Staff College and its syllabus since 1856. In Lord Roberts's opinion

. . . the absence of a definite system of staff duties, leading sometimes to an overlapping of responsibilities, sometimes to waste of time, and sometimes to a neglect of indispensable precautions, was undoubtedly prejudicial to the smooth running of the military machine . . . staff officers cannot be improvised.

The British field artillery, in Roberts's opinion, was inferior to European in range and rapidity of fire. There were muddles over small-arms and ammunition. Sixty million rounds manufactured at Dum-dum in India had to be withdrawn because they stripped in the rifle barrel. Over 200,000 Lee-Enfield rifles were found to have faulty sighting, firing eighteen inches to the right at 500 yards. Peacetime provision and planning for remounts and transport animals proved inadequate. The Royal Commission recorded that while the medical department did its best to care for an army three or four times larger than allowed for in the medical establishment, nevertheless pettifogging redtape and untrained orderlies caused needless suffering. The hospital equipment was, according to the Commission, 'old-fashioned', and, although campaigning in country where water supply was a crucial question, the British army had nothing equivalent to the German system for testing the purity of new water supplies. Sanitation in the British army was also inferior to the German. The Commission saw, however, some bright spots—in the excellent performance in its first war of the new Army Service Corps, despite the size of its task and shortage of personnel. This corps originated in the 'Military Train', kept in being after the Crimean War. In 1888 the old civilian commissariat system for the supply of food and other necessaries had at last been abolished, and both supply and transport vested in the Army Service Corps.

Of the unfortunate rank-and-file of the infantry, the evidence of witnesses and the final Report of the Commission had gloomy things to say. Reservists were fitter physically than regulars already with the colours. Too many British soldiers were industrial townsmen. Most witnesses thought the British rank-and-file was inferior in intelligence (partly owing to lack of education) both to the Boers and to British colonials who joined the war later. One witness believed that

. . . his [the British soldier's] mental qualifications are not up to the general run of European soldiers, and the reason of it is, that we get them mostly from a class where education is not looked to as much as it is in Germany and in France.

The Royal Commission in its final Report drew the conclusion:

If the terms offered are attractive only to men whose intelligence is underdeveloped, it is impossible to make them soldiers of the class required in modern warfare, with the same amount of training that will be sufficient for men whose mental calibre is higher at the time when they enter the army.

Roberts and Kitchener both agreed that the British soldier lacked resourcefulness and the ability to look after himself in the field; Kitchener said that 'he was usually too dependent on his officers and lacked individuality'.

However, the officers and non-commissioned officers themselves were heavily criticized by witnesses and by the Commission. There was a shunning of responsibility from the corporal all the way up the hierarchy. Of the officer, Kitchener observed: 'There appears to be too often a want of serious study of their profession by officers who are, I think, rather inclined to deal lightly with military questions of moment.' This opinion was completely endorsed by the *Report of the Committee appointed to consider the Education and Training of the Officers of the Army* (the Akers-Douglas Committee) in 1902. The Committee were impressed 'by the widespread dissatisfaction—a feeling expressed by practically all the witnesses—with the present state of education, both military and general, among the officers of the Army as a class'.

Both the Royal Military Academy, Woolwich (gunners and engineers) and the Royal Military College, Sandhurst (cavalry and infantry) came in for detailed criticism. Of Sandhurst the Committee observed that 'the cadets cannot be expected to derive much benefit from their instruction . . . when it is clearly established that they have absolutely no incentive to work'. The passing-out standard was low enough, and yet 'there is too much reason to fear that even those cadets who fail to attain this standard have been commissioned none the less'.

The training of young officers with their units was called by the Committee 'most unsatisfactory'.

By no part of the evidence laid before them have the Committee been more impressed than by that which shows in the clearest manner the prevalence among the junior commissioned ranks of a lack of professional knowledge and skill, and of any wish to study the science and master the art of their profession.

The Committee was informed that 'keenness is out of fashion . . . it is not the correct form'.

Even the minority of keen officers that did exist found it difficult to train themselves or their men in Britain, because

Under the existing system the officer rarely sees the men for whose military efficiency he is responsible. They are largely employed in non-military duties, such as waiting in the canteens and regimental institutes, the charge of cricket and tennis grounds . . . in addition to the large number constantly required for . . . fatigues . . .

Promotion examinations too were a farce.

All these aspects of lack of professionalism derived, as for two centuries, from recruiting the officers from a leisured class to whom professionalism too often appeared as vulgar careerism. The need for a private income to support the lavishness of military life was just as efficient a means as purchase in barring the poor but meritorious. As one witness told the Akers-Douglas Committee: 'I am sorry to say that the officer wanted in the Army is only one who can command from £150 to £1500 a year.'

It was noteworthy that in the cavalry, where living expenses were highest, professional standards were said by the Report to be lowest.

In 1903 yet another Committee specially investigated this question of expenses and private incomes*: its final conclusion was that:

The whole of the evidence before the Committee proves incontestably in their opinion, that the expenses of the Army form a very serious deterrent to parents in selecting a profession for their sons, and that many otherwise entirely suitable candidates are precluded from entering the Service by no other consideration than the insufficiency of their private incomes.

These expenses were almost entirely unprofessional—a dandy's wardrobe of uniforms, entertaining, sporting and social life.

Thus almost all aspects of the British military system had been found wanting in a war against 50,000 farmers. The deficiencies had historical roots going back probably as far as the Tudor militia. However, they were less forgivable in 1900 than they had

*'The Committee Appointed by the Secretary of State for War to Enquire into the Nature of the Expenses Incurred by Officers of the Army and to Suggest Measures for bringing Commissions within reach of Men of moderate means', or Lord Stanley's Committee, 1903.

been in 1800 or 1700. The army was no longer conceivably a threat to the constitution, and no longer 'belonged' even residually to the monarch. The army's poor quality could not therefore be attributed any longer to the earlier national desire to keep it feeble. On the contrary, late Victorians had wanted it to be efficient and economical. Nor could the state of the army in 1900 be blamed entirely or even largely on the army's own leaders, for the British army was not a self-regulating state-within-a-state like the German army. Its size, organization and efficiency were the responsibility of a civilian minister, and beyond him of a government responsible to the House of Commons, and beyond the House of Commons of an electorate ever more representative of the people as a whole. The army's obsolescence and the survival of its traditional weaknesses were ultimately the responsibility of civilian governments and of public opinion in general. In fact, neither government nor nation was very much interested in the army, except to cheer a victory. The British people did not wish to be conscious of the cost and pains of being an imperial power. Britain, as always, had got the army it deserved. . . .

As we have seen, the Boer War, in Barnett's words, "demonstrated the feebleness of the land forces of the British Empire." But it took a War Office committee (under Lord Esher) until 1904 to recommend the changes that would reform the British forces. The major changes suggested by the Esher report were an army council (modeled on the Board of Admiralty), a general staff, and a division of departmental responsibilities within the War Office. Administration was divided between the chief of the general staff (the post of commander-in-chief was abolished); the adjutant-general, who was responsible for the welfare of the troops; the quartermaster-general, whose responsibility was materiel supply; and, finally, a master-general of the ordnance. But it took a change of government in 1906 to bring Lord Haldane to the War Office and to bring these plans to fruition. Barnett concludes that the creation of the general staff gave the army a sense of professionalism it had not previously enjoyed in peacetime.

CORRELLI BARNETT

Radical Reform: 1902–14

The Boer War had shattered the Victorian complacency of the British ruling classes, if not of British public opinion. It had demonstrated the feebleness of the land forces of the British Empire before a gloating world: it had revealed how alone Britain stood in that gloating world. For the first time since 1815 there was an awareness that Britain needed strong friends. And there was now, ever more evidently, a new challenger to British world power—Germany. Since Bismarck had unified Germany in 1871, German industrial growth had swiftly eaten up the lead Britain had enjoyed since the beginning of the Industrial Revolution. The new Germany, restless, ambitious, conscious that she was too late to grab the richest of colonies, looked on Britain with envy and with resolution to overtake her. In 1900 Germany began to build a battle-fleet. Before the alarm caused by the Boer War could fade in Britain, Germany had emerged not

Reprinted by permission of William Morrow and Company, Inc. from Britain and Her Army, 1509–1970: A Military, Political and Social Survey. *Copyright © 1970 by Correlli Barnett.*

merely as a rival, but as a possible enemy. Edwardian Englishmen found themselves in the novel situation of facing the kind of problems their Georgian and Tudor ancestors had known so well. But it was hard to adjust quickly after half a lifetime under the Victorian peace. As recently as 1891, for example, the then Secretary of State for War, Edward Stanhope, in an important memorandum, had stated the tasks of the British army as (in order):

(a) The effective support of the civil power in all parts of the United Kingdom.

(b) To find the number of men for India, which has been fixed by agreement with the Government of India.

(c) To find garrisons for all our fortresses and coaling stations, at home or abroad . . .

(d) After providing for these requirements, to be able to organise rapidly for home defence two army Corps of Regular troops and one partly composed of Regulars and partly of Militia . . .

(e) Subject to the foregoing . . . to

aim at being able, in case of necessity, to send abroad two complete Army Corps . . .

However, the Stanhope memorandum had confidently added:

But it will be distinctly understood that the probability of the employment of an Army Corps in the field in any European war is sufficiently improbable to make it the primary duty of the military authorities to organise our forces for the defences of this country.

In hardly more than ten years the basking warmth of Victorian security displayed by this memorandum had been blown away.

It was not only a question of Germany. Other nations too had become great powers during the nineteenth century and, whether unfriendly, friendly or neutral, they were factors British policy had to take account of. America had burst out of her long isolation in 1898 in a war against Spain which won her a colonial empire in Cuba, Puerto Rico and the Philippines; she was now a considerable naval power. Italy was now united into a nation state, and since she was allied to Germany and Austria, her fleet was a potential menace to British control of the Mediterranean. Russia still seemed to pose a threat to the north-west frontier of India. And in the Far East, where forty years before nothing had stood in the way of European domination, a great Asiatic power based on western technology had emerged in Japan. In two decades the Japanese had pulled their society out of the Middle Ages into the modern world, with industries and an army

based on German exemplars and a navy based on the British model. In 1894 Japan had smashingly defeated China; in 1904–5 she was to stagger world opinion by inflicting an equally smashing defeat on Russia, a first-class European power. Thus after 1900 Britain's relative power was sharply diminished right across the globe. However, it was the direct threat in Europe from Germany—a threat to British command of the waters round the British Isles—that appeared most serious. Although in the wars of the eighteenth century the French navy might have inflicted serious damage on British seaborne trade, it could not have starved the British at home, because they were fed by their own agriculture. Now, thanks to the industrial revolution and free trade, Britain could neither work nor eat if seaborne supplies were cut off.

British foreign and defence policy after 1900 therefore attempted to put an end to British diplomatic isolation, to reduce the number of potential threats, and to re-build and modernize the army and navy. In 1902 Britain concluded an alliance with Japan, which left her free to concentrate on European affairs. In 1904 she concluded the *Entente Cordiale* with France, an ancient enemy with whom war had seemed possible as recently as 1898. The *Entente* was not, however, a formal alliance, laying down reciprocal obligations, but a settlement of various contested questions between the countries. In 1905–6 Germany tried to split the new *Entente* by truculent diplomacy in a manufactured crisis over French influence in

Morocco. The attempt failed, but war between the great European powers had for a time seemed to grow near.

This thickening European atmosphere was the background and the stimulus of a fresh period of military reform in Britain.

In autumn 1900 St John Brodrick became Secretary for War in the Conservative government. Brodrick, like all incumbents of his office, had to face the fundamental strategic problem posed by the British overseas empire. While the United Kingdom itself required troops for its own garrison and as an expeditionary force in the event of European war, the empire (especially India) also needed garrisons and (as the Boer War had shown) substantial ready field forces as well. The Boer War had been won only by leaving Britain herself absolutely defenceless on land. In 1901 Brodrick produced his answer to the problem:

. . . my proposition is that besides Home Defence we ought to be ready at any moment to send abroad three Army Corps with the proper Cavalry Division, in fact a force of 120,000 men.

Brodrick's own suggestion for creating such an expeditionary force was ambitious, logical, and copied from the German system.

The proposals I have to make to the House are as follows: I propose to re-organise the Army on a new system of which the bedrock will be that the whole country will be divided into six Army Corps by districts, that each district in times of peace will have the same relative proportions to the various arms that are necessary

to make up the corps, and that they will be under the commanders who will lead them in war.

. . . There was merit in Brodrick's attempt to unite regulars and auxiliary forces in one military organization based on readiness to take the field. However, in a country of voluntary and flagging recruitment (and bearing in mind India, which swallowed on average about half the regular army), Brodrick was hopelessly over-ambitious in planning for six army corps. Critics saw that these could only be achieved by a large increase in the army; a proposal that no British government could present to the voters. In 1903 the six army corps still remained merely imposing titles without reality. . . .

Although Brodrick's plans remained only a blue-print, his term at the War Office saw one great reform and many detailed reforms and developments. Britain had always lacked effective central machinery for planning imperial defence, although for many years there had been a Colonial Defence Committee concerned with local matters of detail. There was also a Defence Committee of the Cabinet, but this lacked a permanent organization and continuous life. As a later Committee on War Office reform was to report in 1904:

The scientific study of Imperial resources, the co-ordination of the ever-varying facts upon which Imperial rule rests, the calculation of forces required, and the broad plans necessary to sustain the burden of Empire, have, until quite recently, found no place in our system of government.

In 1902, therefore, after the Boer War, Brodrick in conjunction with Lord Selborne, the First Lord of the Admiralty, recommended to the Cabinet that this lack should be repaired. As a result, a Committee of Imperial Defence was set up. Balfour, the Prime Minister, thus described the new Committee to the House of Commons in March 1903: 'The idea the Government had in establishing it is . . . to make it its duty to survey as a whole the strategical military needs of the Empire.' The Committee was to consist of the Prime Minister, the Lord President, the First Lord, the War Minister, the Commander-in-Chief, the First Sea Lord and the heads of naval and military intelligence. . . .

In October 1903 Brodrick was replaced by Arnold-Forster, another man with a cut-and-dried scheme of army re-organization not closely enough related to the real situation. Nor had Arnold-Forster himself, a cold personality, the temperament of the successful reformer. Instead of biding his time, disarming opposition with dinners and reason, and above all listening in order to learn, Arnold-Forster plunged in with fixed ideas. He felt that the international situation made haste necessary, and in 1904 he expounded his own scheme for a new army to the House of Commons; or rather, for *two* new armies, a General Service Army and a Home Service Army:

The General Service Army will serve both abroad and at home in time of peace and in time of war.
The Home Service Army will serve at home in peace, and abroad, if necessary, in time of important wars.

Here was another simple, logical answer to the conflicting demands of imperial and European security, of garrisons and field forces.

The General Service Army would be long-service—nine years with the colours, three with the reserve. Instead of Cardwell's linked-battalion depot system, Arnold-Forster proposed that the General Service Army should have large depots, like those of the Guards and the Royal Artillery. The few General Service battalions to be kept in England would be allotted to a striking force at Aldershot. This striking force was a new incarnation of the first of Brodrick's six corps.

The Home Service Army on the other hand was to be short-service—two years with the colours and six with the reserve, approximating to European conscript service armies, though without the conscription itself. The Home Service Army was to be recruited and organized on an entirely territorial basis. Arnold-Forster had little constructive to say about the militia (declining in numbers and efficiency) and the volunteers. He thus ducked the problem of how to combine the various regular and auxiliary land forces into one system. His 'striking force' was to be composed of mature and trained regulars. It was an attempt to cure the present weakness of the First Class Reserve, which instead of supplementing the number of men with the colours on recall, merely replaced regulars too young to be sent abroad on active service. Instead of Brodrick's army corps districts, there would be administrative districts, as recommended by the Esher Committee.

Arnold-Forster's schemes were violently criticized as impracticable, and as once again turning the army upside down. However, their capital point—two kinds of service for two kinds of army—had to be abandoned not to the critics but to circumstance. The need for long service men for the empire (and above all, India) was so pressing that the existing three-year term of engagement had to be suspended in favour of nine years. Before any other of Arnold-Forster's plans came to fruition, Balfour's administration fell.

However, Arnold-Forster's tenure of the War Office was remarkable for major reforms of the War Office itself and the higher army command structure. These reforms did not emanate from Arnold-Forster himself, but it was he as War Minister and his colleagues in the government who backed them. The reforms stemmed from the three parts of the Report of the War Office (Reconstitution) Committee (the Esher Committee), which were published successively in February and March 1904. The Chairman of the Committee, Lord Esher, was a kind of middle-man in politics—a middle-man in ideas and also in people. He always refused the commitment and drudgery of office, preferring rather to use his connexions, influence and political flair independently. He was a confidant of King Edward VII. The Committee took no public evidence, and its report was crisp, brief and decisive. Its main recommendations were implemented by the government even as the parts of the Report were in turn appearing.

The importance of the Esher Report and its consequences can hardly be exaggerated. It coolly analysed the confusions and ineffectiveness of a military administration that had never been designed, but which had grown piecemeal, with piecemeal demolitions and re-building, ever since 1660. It laid the foundations of the War Office organization and general staff system that has endured in essentials to the present time. Without the Esher Report, and its acceptance by the government of the day, it is inconceivable that the mammoth British military efforts in the two world wars could have been possible, let alone so generally successful. It was the reconstruction of the 'brain' of the army on clear functional lines that followed the Report that made possible the successful reorganization of the body of the army. Unquestionably both Brodrick and Arnold-Forster were ill-judged in trying to reshape the body while the War Office itself remained unreformed.

The three essential recommendations of the Report were: an Army Council on the model of the Board of Admiralty; a general staff; and the division of departmental responsibilities inside the War Office on defined and logical principles.

The Army Council was to provide a single collective body to consider and decide questions of policy in place of the present ill-defined responsibilities of War Secretary, Commander-in-Chief, Adjutant-General and Quartermaster-General. The Secretary of State for War was to be placed in all respects on the same footing as the First Lord of the Admiralty. All submissions to the Crown on military topics were to be made through him: the final consummation of civilian and parliamentary control of the army. The Army Council was to consist of seven members: the War Secretary; the First Military Member (operations and military policy); the Second Military Member (recruitment and discipline); the Third Military Member (supply and transport); the Fourth Military Member (armaments and fortifications); a Civil Member (the Parliamentary Under-Secretary: civil business other than finance); and another Civil Member (the Financial Secretary). The Council was to meet frequently, and its decisions were to be collective. Dissenters might either accept the majority opinion or resign.

It was essential to the creation of both the Army Council and a general staff that the post of Commander-in-Chief be abolished. In 1904 therefore, Lord Roberts, the last incumbent, was evicted. Responsibility for preparation of the army for war was vested in the new post of Chief of the General Staff (C.G.S.).

The Esher Committee divided administration inside the War Office between the Chief the General Staff, the Adjutant-General, the Quartermaster-General and the Master-General of the Ordnance. The duties of the General Staff itself were divided between a Director of Military Operations (D.M.O.), Director of Staff Duties (D.S.D.), and a Director of Military Training (D.M.T.). The Adjutant-General was made broadly responsible for all that related to the maintenance and welfare of the troops. Under him were the Director of Recruiting and Organization, the Director of Personal Services, the Director-General of Medical Services and (to take care of the militia and volunteers) a Director of Auxiliary Services. The old post of Judge-Advocate-General was replaced by a Judge-Advocate, with more limited responsibilities. All aspects of material supply other than actual manufacture were grouped under the Quartermaster-General. His departmental heads were a Director of Transport and Remounts, a Director of Movements and Quartering, a Director of Supplies and Clothing, and a Director of Equipment and Ordnance Stores. The Master-General of the Ordnance's subordinates included a Director of Artillery, a Naval Adviser and a Director of Fortification and Works.

The clear logical division of responsibility was to be carried right down through the strata of the army. In the Esher Committee's own words:

The line of cleavage between the duties of the several staff officers should be . . . rigorously preserved. It is essential to prevent the confusion of staff arrangements which has hitherto prevailed.

Equally:

The principle of the division of training from administration, which we have sought to apply throughout our scheme, appears to us to be fundamental.

Thus the Esher Report re-made the core of the British military system on first principles.

It also re-organized the whole body of the army in the United Kingdom. Administration and policy had become concentrated in the War Office, to the detriment of efficiency and initiative. The Esher Committee was convinced that

. . . if the Army is to be trained to exercise the initiative and the independence of judgement which are essential in the field, its peace administration must be effectively decentralized. The object should be to encourage the assumption of responsibility as far as possible.

Instead of the existing paper army-corps districts, the Esher Committee recommended administrative districts to which many War Office functions should be delegated. The districts would look after organization and administration and thus leave commanders of field units free for their proper function of training for war. These recommendations too were in principle accepted by the government and formed the basis of army organization at home for the next sixty years.

When the Liberal government took office therefore in 1906, radical reconstruction of the military system had already begun on the lines of the Report of the Esher Committee, while the Committee of Imperial Defence had existed since 1903. The new Liberal War Secretary was also able to profit from the trials and errors of Brodrick and Arnold-Forster, whose proposals had at least pointed the way to the essential requirements of an ever-ready expeditionary force, and of an effective reserve system to back it.

The new minister, however, brought to office all-round personal talents far exceeding those of his predecessors. Richard Burdon Haldane was a Lowland Scot, whose first-class intellect had been trained in philosophy at the University of Edinburgh and, for a

brief stay, at Göttingen. From philosophy (in which he retained a deep interest) he passed to law. As a barrister he displayed remarkable capacity for intensive and continuous work, and for 'gutting' the essentials swiftly and accurately out of complicated briefs. He was keenly aware of modern developments abroad in technology, management and education. It was more owing to Haldane than any other single person that new teaching universities other than Oxford and Cambridge were at last being created in England and Wales. His table, cellar and cigar box were renowned, and his social world included many of the interlocking circles that made up the British ruling class. He was deft at handling men and human situations.

Haldane brought no prior military knowledge and no set scheme of reform into office. He was ready to spend months asking questions and listening. As he told his generals,

I was as a young and blushing virgin just united to a bronzed warrior, and that it was not expected by the public that any result of the union should appear until at least nine months had passed.

It was Haldane's great task to implement the Esher Report.

The year 1906 was spent in intensive study and planning. The reforms followed between 1906 and 1909. Haldane gathered about him a younger generation of professionally-minded soldiers. Ellison (the Secretary of the Esher Committee) and Douglas Haig were outstanding among them. Haldane said of his military collaborators:

The men one comes across, the new school of young officers—entitled to the appellation of men of science just as much as engineers or chemists—were to me a revelation. . . . A new school of officers has arisen since the South African War, a thinking school of officers who desire to see the full efficiency which comes from new organisation and no surplus energy running to waste.

For the first time in its history the British army was provided with official manuals laying down in detail staff responsibilities and procedures: *Field Service Regulations Part I—Operations—1909; Part II—Organization and Administration—1909.* When in 1907 the Imperial Conference agreed to common military forms and methods throughout the empire, the General Staff became 'the Imperial General Staff', and the new manuals later became the basis of standard staff procedures for all imperial forces. Without these manuals (for which Haig as, successively, Director of Military Training and Director of Staff Duties, was mainly responsible) the colossal expansion of the British and dominion armies during the Great War must have resulted in military chaos.

It was during the same three years 1906–9 that the new War Office and General Staff were transformed from a blue-print into an efficient machine.

However, the most difficult of Haldane's tasks (it had defeated his predecessors) lay in re-organization of the home field army and reserve system. Here he met the fiercest opposition from entrenched interests (such as those who feared a reduction in the number of generals); here in the end

he carried out what are generally remembered as 'the Haldane Reforms'.

European events gave an immediate impulse to the creation of an expeditionary force that his predecessors had not enjoyed. There was a crisis over Morocco, and during the General Election of 1906 Grey, the Foreign Secretary, asked Haldane what help Britain could offer the French, if, as persistent rumours suggested, Germany attacked her in the spring. As a result, unofficial and then official contacts were made with the French general staff, with special reference to both powers' treaty obligations to protect the neutrality of Belgium. When the Moroccan crisis died down, the staff talks continued.

Haldane saw the implications of the talks—British military commitment on the continent of Europe. He wrote:

We had therefore to provide for an Expeditionary Force which we reckoned at six great [i.e. with three instead of two brigades] divisions, fully equipped, and at least one cavalry division. We had also to make certain that this force could be mobilised and sent to the place where it might be required as rapidly as any German force could be.

'As rapidly' meant fifteen days, instead of the two months needed at that time to put only 80,000 men into Europe. All Haldane's reforms followed from the need to create this expeditionary force.

Haldane and his advisers decided that the expeditionary force would have to be formed out of the regular troops available in the United Kingdom under Cardwell's two-battalion regimental system, although non-combatant services might be partially manned by the auxiliary forces. Thus they avoided increasing either the size or the cost of the whole regular army or embarking on a fancy new organization such as Arnold-Forster's General Service Army. The new expeditionary force was to be expanded from the far-from-ready field force already stationed at Aldershot under Sir John French (Brodrick's 'First Corps' and Arnold-Forster's 'striking force'). A special Army Order of 1 January 1907 gave details of the new organization.

Re-organization of the two auxiliary forces was a much larger and more ticklish question that involved legislation. The militia had declined from its ancient and proud independence as the 'constitutional' land force of the kingdom. It had become a not always efficient adjunct to the regular army; an avenue to a professional military career for both officers and other ranks. Nor was it any longer filling its nineteenth-century role of a reservoir of mature and partly trained men for the regular army, for the Militia Reserve had been abolished. It had, however, garrisoned the United Kingdom and some overseas bases in both the Crimean and Boer Wars. The other auxiliary force, the volunteers, was not in much better shape, nor linked to the regular army in one coherent system. As Haldane wrote in a memorandum published in February 1907:

At present the numbers and organisation of the Military Forces in the United Kingdom are based on no scientific standard, and these forces have been raised on no definite plan.

Haldane's answer was to reduce the three echelons of the forces (regulars, militia and volunteers) to two:

. . . the National Army will, in future, consist of a Field Force and a Territorial or Home Force. The Field Force is to be so completley organised as to be ready in all respects for mobilisation immediately on the outbreak of a great war. In that event the Territorial or Home Force would be mobilised also, but mobilised with a view to its undertaking, in the first instance, systematic training for war. The effect of such training, given a period of at least six months, would be, in the opinion of all military experts, to add very materially to the efficiency of the force. The Territorial Force will, therefore, be one of support and expansion, to be at once embodied when danger threatens, but not likely to be called for till after the expiration of the preliminary period of six months.

Both militia and volunteers were to be abolished in favour of the Territorials. However, men and even units of the volunteers were to be incorporated in the new Territorials. It was hoped that men from the abolished militia would join the new special reserve of the regular army, for which men might volunteer without having first served with the colours. Even during the Great War the special reserve was often referred to as 'the Militia'. It also included a technical reserve, for the lack of technicians to run railways, telegraphs etc. had been sharply felt during the Boer War.

Haldane hoped to make these great changes by agreement with the commanders of the militia and the volunteers. A 'Territorial Force Committee' of some forty-five prominent men was formed under Esher. However, in the face of the bitter opposition of the militia colonels and the militia's political friends, Haldane was forced to fall back on compulsion by legislation. His Territorial Reserve Forces Bill was savagely attacked during its passage through both Houses of Parliament. Critics of Haldane's bill talked of the militia of 1907 as if it were still the proud institution of the eighteenth century. However, Haldane's success in reducing the army estimates by some two million pounds gave him political leverage. The Bill was eventually passed. It contained three main provisions: one, the territorial force was to be administered (but not commanded) by county associations headed by the Lords-Lieutenant; two, the force was to be liable for service anywhere within the United Kingdom but not abroad, and its numbers were to be voted by Parliament; and three, the creation of the new special reserve.

Unlike the old auxiliary forces, the Territorials were to be organized into field divisions, and equipped with all ancillary services such as transport and artillery. The climate of political and public opinion caused the government, however, to reduce Haldane's target of twenty-eight divisions to fourteen, together with fourteen cavalry brigades and corps troops. Many volunteer units were embodied as a whole in the Territorials, while seventy militia battalions amalgamated with regular regimental depots to form part of the new special reserve. The historic rivalry of standing army and militia had finally ended in a merger.

Haldane enjoyed the powerful assistance of royal backing, and in October 1907, Edward VII personally asked a meeting of all Lords-Lieutenant to support the Territorials. On 1 April 1908 the force came officially into being, and that year the first annual fortnight's training camp was held. By the beginning of 1910 the Territorials numbered 276,618 officers and men—88.5 per cent of establishment. It was a complete vindication of Haldane's hopes.

By 1909 the Haldane reforms were largely completed—new staff methods, new training, new men; an expeditionary force capable of taking the field in Europe within fifteen days, a simple and effective organization of regulars and auxiliaries.

Yet it was powerfully argued that all this was not enough—that compulsory service was essential because the Territorials could not possibly defend the island against the masses of the German army. Lord Roberts spoke for the National Service League on this topic. Three points need to be noted about the unsuccessful campaign for conscription, or, as its proponents preferred to call it, universal military service, or national service. Firstly, its proponents thought only of conscription for home defence, not for a mass army for deployment in Europe. Secondly, their case rested on the proposition that the navy could not prevent a German invasion—hence their nickname of the 'blue funk' school in contrast to the 'blue water' school of the Royal Navy, which believed that a serious invasion was not possible in the face of the British battle-fleet. Thirdly, and decisively, politicians of both parties were agreed that public opinion would not stomach conscription; exemption from responsibility for his own defence having come to seem an Englishman's constitutional birthright. Conscription in peacetime was never a runner.

After the Haldane reforms, there remained the re-training of the whole army, not only in tactics but in staff work and administration. However, the revolution in British tactics had begun even before the advent of Haldane and Haig, for the old drill-books had been replaced by modern tactical manuals in 1904–5. A foreign military observer had noted as early as 1904:

In their manoeuvres the British infantry showed great skill in the use of ground. Their thin lines of khaki-clad skirmishers were scarcely visible. No detachment was ever seen in close order within three thousand yards. Frontal attacks were entirely avoided . . .

With the creation of the General Staff, the Staff College at Camberley acquired a sense of purpose it had never enjoyed before. The remaining traces of the old arid curriculum were swept away in favour of practical training in different staff duties in the field. The war game, complete with full dummy orders and schedules, was introduced. Not since the days of the Commonwealth had the British army been so generally gripped with a sense of professional purpose in peacetime. . . .

This was the army that entered the First World War, although later filled out under Kitchener by many middle-class men holding commissions and enjoying the prestige of being "temporary gentlemen." Not only were there class divisions in the officer corps, but, as the Liberals soon discovered, there were also ethnic differences. The Irish crisis broke in the summer of 1914, due to the Home Rule Bill which would have placed Protestant Ulster under Catholic rule from Dublin. Many officers were Protestant Anglo-Irish and were so unwilling to coerce Ulster that they resigned their commissions at the Curragh army camp in June 1914. But all this was the last domestic quarrel before the guns of August.

RUSSIA: AUTHORITARIANISM AND THE SUPPRESSION OF PROFESSIONALISM

Russia, as Richard Pipes, the leading modern historian of Russia, demonstrates, became a police state toward the third quarter of the nineteenth century. Before that, the military organization was necessary, "for without it, Russian colonization, so essential to its economic survival, could not have been carried out."* Czarist patrimonial despotism was supported by a military instrument whose purpose was internal, i.e., the suppression and "integration" of nationalities and ethnic groups that were continuously being conquered to make the Russian empire. "Peter thought of himself, first and foremost, as a soldier,"† and he created the modern professional and military might of Russia. In a population of twelve million, Peter recruited 210,000 regular and 110,000 supplementary troops, a norm that, according to Pipes, "exceeded almost three times the proportion regarded in eighteenth-century Western Europe as a norm of what a country could support—namely, one soldier for each one hundred inhabitants."‡ The Russian historian V. O. Kluchevsky in *A History of Russia* (volume 4) tells us that Peter's military reforms were a reaction to the Northern Wars (1700–21), i.e., the war with Charles XII of Sweden. Peter at first was no match for Charles, who defeated him at Narva. But after the military and financial reform and the building of St. Petersburg (1703), Peter won a resounding victory in Poltava (1709). Kluchevsky tells of the effect of the Northern Wars and military reforms.

*Richard Pipes, *Russia Under the Old Regime* (New York: Scribner, 1975), p. 20.
†Ibid., p. 119.
‡Ibid., p. 120.

V. O. KLUCHEVSKY

The Northern Wars and Military Reforms

. . . "A History of the Swedish War" begins by remarking that upon the celebration of the victory of Poltava there must follow amendments of the State in respect of its civil affairs; whilst further evidence of Peter's post-Poltavan legislative activity may be gleaned from the highly incomplete digest of Russian legislative memorials which we know as *A Complete Collection of the Laws of the Russian Empire*

From V. O. Kluchevsky, A History of Russia, 5 vols., trans. C. J. Hogarth (1911–31; reprint ed., New York: Russell & Russell, 1960), 4:59–69, by permission of Russell & Russell.

(1830). Even in this "Complete Collection" there are included between the year 1700 (which for some reason or another Peter chose to regard as the opening year of the century) and the year 1709 as many as 500 legislative Acts, and during the next decade (to the close of 1719) 1238 more, and, during the next *half*-decade (for Peter died on 28 January, 1725) nearly as many again. And with that we see that the whole of this mass of Ordinances and Regulations and Statutes and Instructions and International Treaties marched strictly hand in hand with war; and that right up to the time of Poltava Peter used no other method of coping either with military demands or with administrative shortcomings and abuses than the method of issuing *ad hoc* letters and *ukazi* for such corrective measures as he deemed immediately necessary, and that in every province of his administrative activity until he attained both sufficient leisure and sufficient familiarity with State management to develop his temporary measures and amendments into regular laws and ordinances and institutions (though, even then, most of these regular laws and ordinances and new institutions were made to refer to one or two departments only, as well as were initiated on no definite system), the foregoing remained his only way of doing State business. At all events, his capital legislative Acts belong exclusively to the post-Poltavan period, and therefore war must have been the factor that converted his administrative legislation into institutional, and himself, originally only a builder of ships and a military organiser, into an all-round purveyor of reforms.

Hence there now lies clear to our view the connection between the reforms and Peter's conduct of military affairs. At first sight his reforming activity seems to have had no definite plan, no system of consecutiveness, and, though eventually covering the structure of State throughout, and affecting many sides of the national life, to have revised no sphere of government homogeneously, or integrally, or at a stroke, but always to have progressed by fits and starts, to have

modified departments piecemeal, or intermittently, or merely as necessity and current requirements demanded. Yet also we see from study of Peter's measures of reform that at least they had before them a general object of a sort, though no regular order of sequence, and no fixed plan or programme. We shall best understand their ordering if first we take them in connection with their warlike setting, and with the consequences of that setting. For just as war dictated their order, so war gave them their *tempo* and scope, and military necessities determined the system under which they developed into, and became established as, legislative enactments. First of all, requirements of campaigning gave rise to reforms of the country's military forces; and from those reforms sprang a double series of legislative measures for maintenance of naval and military establishments on a regular footing, and for consolidation of the necessary pertinent means. Next, those measures gave rise to changes in relative positions and mutual relations of social classes, and at the same time augmented, yet strained unduly, the State's main source of revenue as represented by the people's labour. And finally, all this being so, and Peter's military, social, and economic innovations being what they were, his administrative staff had to follow suit with a corresponding augmentation and acceleration of its performance of State business, and to grapple with new and complex problems which would altogether have baffled it on the basis of its old organisation and composition. And just as an indispensable condition to further reforms was a process of preceding and accompanying current innovations with a step-by-step overhauling, so Peter's workers of State and the popular mentality alike had to be given a certain course of preparation for those reforms' acceptance—success in present accomplishment of and future conduct of administrative changes could come only of anticipatory provision of trained, efficient executive officials, and of such a preliminary education of the people as should lead the people to support reform because the masses had become aware of reform's nature and significance. Wherefore, taking these factors together, we can understand why Peter began to display an ever-increasing solicitude for popular education, and to establish an ever-increasing number of popular training-schools based alike upon general-reformative and upon purely professional-technical principles.

Hence the general plan, rather, the general sequence, of the Petrine reforms was not one born of any thought-out programme, but one due to the fact that the goad of circumstances played upon the course of affairs. And since the driving-power of Peter's activity was always war, and the initial field of operations of that activity was military reform, and its ultimate goal was financial re-organisation, Peter began his work by reforming the State's defensive resources, and only when that had been done went on to reforms of the State's internal system. All of which, and other such, measures flowed inevitably from the main task, or were steps inevitable before that main task could be finally achieved.

Peter himself traces this link between war and his reforming efforts. . . . That is to say, it was Peter's idea that his *History of the Swedish War*, his account of all matters connected with the conflict, should cite not only measures accomplished for Russia's military re-organisation, but also measures accomplished for her territorial and ecclesiastical revision. We too, therefore, as we study his reforms, might do worse than follow a plan comprising (1) Peter's military reforms, (2) his measures for maintaining his naval and military establishments—in particular, his measures for so altering the State position of the *dvorianstvo* as to increase that class's service efficiency, (3) his measures for augmenting the State's revenue, for enlarging the aggregate of taxpaying labour, and for improving the quality of that labour, (4) his financial innovations, and (5) his measures for assuring successful execution of his military and popular-industrial reforms, and especially of his administrative reforms, through the establishment of schools and colleges. . . .

The first reforms to which Peter laid his hand were military reforms; and they constituted at once the heaviest and the most protracted task that fell to his and the nation's lot. And they are the more important in the story of Russia in that they involved not only State defence, but also something profoundly affecting, in equal measure, the adjustment of the Petrine community and the course of subsequent events.

From a roster of 1681 we see that by that year a sufficiently large portion of the Muscovite, or Home Service,

Section of the military forces had been transferred to the Foreign Service Contingent to raise the total of the latter from 89,000 to 164,000, exclusive of the Cossacks of Little Russia. . . . Peter had to muster his armies for the Swedish War in face of the circumstance that he would have no reserves to fall back upon if ever such reserves should become necessary, and that the existing regiments of the Foreign Service Contingent must be supplemented through the expedients alternatively (1) of "calling unto willing men to be soldiers" (that is to say, appealing for volunteers), (2) of collecting *datochnie,* or "ceded men," from seignorial estates in proportion to local numbers of peasant homesteads, and (3) of enrolling service-fit freed *kholopi* and *krestiané,* and allowing bonded *kholopi* to enter infantry corps without losing their right to return, after service, to their old employ. Yet whilst the system resulted in a raising only of hastily formed and German-trained conscript forces, and in their dispatch merely as what Korb, Secretary to the Austrian Embassy, a man resident in Moscow between 1689 and 1699, calls "a concourse of unworthy soldiers, mostly from the lower people," and as what another foreigner, Weber, Russian Resident for Brunswick between 1714 and 1719, dubs "an exceeding sorry multitude," Peter at least formed an army of twenty-nine regiments of freedmen and *datochnie* 29,000 strong, added to the four veteran corps represented by the two corps of Guards and the two cadral formations, and dispatched the whole to Narva. Moreover, lamentable as was this army's display of military

incapacity at Narva, it yet befell that in time the very course which the war assumed converted Peter's original rabble of freedmen and "ceded men" into a regular army in the true sense of the term, since, owing to the number and the length of the spells of campaigning, a new corps frequently was retained on service for several years at a time, until it had changed practically into a permanent unit. On the other hand, there set in, from Narva onwards, an enormous wastage of man power, an enormous melting away of Peter's improvised regiments under the stress of battle, of famine, of disease, of wholesale desertion, and of forced marches from the Neva to Poltava and Azov and Astrakhan and Riga and Kalisch and Vismar, whilst ever the theatre of operations kept extending, and calling for an increased army strength. And the method by which this shrinkage was made good, and the military complement reinforced, was a method of percentage enrolments of volunteers and "ceded men" from every class without exception—even to sons of *boyaré,* and to *posadskie, dvorovie,* sons of *Strieltzi,* and unbeneficed clergy: the year 1703 alone seeing 30,000 men thus recruited. On the other hand, the very fact that the army became an army drawn from the people as a whole infused into the forces an alloy of raw material which, if not absolutely non-military, was at all events inferior: and this gave rise to a need for such a system of filling up gaps as should serve not only to furnish a really trained reserve, but also to send that reserve to the front more regularly and quickly than had hitherto been the case. Hence to

Peter's first fortuitous and ill-organised enrolments of volunteers and "ceded men" there succeeded a system of regular and periodical and all-round conscriptions in which we see his heretofore conditions of recruitment only partially repeated. For under the new system all single men between the ages of fifteen and twenty (and, later, all married men between the ages of twenty and thirty) were sent to *stantzii* or muster-points (mostly these coincided with the towns nearest to the recruits' places of origin), and there divided into detachments of from 500 to 1000, billeted in cantonments, and entrusted, for their daily inspection and supervision, to corporals and *efreitori* (squad commanders) from among their own number, and, for their purely military instruction, to officers and men who had been retired for wounds or sickness, "so that all our warlike companies may be taught regularly, and according unto due ordinance." Later, when trained, and as the need might arise, these recruits were dispatched to "places of default," and used either for supplementing existing corps or for forming new ones. Wherefore, Peter's new military training-schools, as a whole, had for their purpose the purpose "that whensoever requests shall be made for a fresh filling of the army there shall be in readiness a sufficiency of men for all places of default." Also, these conscripts gradually came to be known as *bezs-mertnie*,* since an *ukaz* ordained that, in the event of a conscript dying at a

*Literally, "deathless men," but used in the sense of men in reserve against vacancies caused by casualties.

training-centre, or on ordinary service, or in action, or deserting, his place was at once to be taken by a conscript from the same district, "to the end that always there be soldiers in full, and ready to serve the State." The first general conscription Peter carried out in 1705; and thenceforth the process was repeated every year up to the close of 1709. As a rule the prescribed ratio was one recruit per twenty taxpaying homesteads; but though, at this rate, each of the first five conscriptions should have provided a total of a little over 30,000 men, and the warrants for them called for, provisionally, and in all, 168,000, we do not know what total actually was obtained, since with enrolments went defaultings—we know merely that between the opening of the Swedish War and the first general conscription the number of freedmen and "ceded men" commanded to be enrolled was 150,000, and that on the basis of that figure there were absorbed into the army, during the first ten years of the contest, 300,000 males out of an approximate population of both sexes of 14,000,000.

Thus, then, did Peter create his second, or Poltavan army: and, by the close of the year 1708, a series of three conscriptions had raised the complement of that army to 113,000. And during the next few years the army was filled up and augmented in the same way, whilst incidentally we find Weber, a foreign observer who made a careful study of Russia's then military establishment, writing in his curious *Notes on Reformed Russia* (*Das veränderte Russland*) that, though, ordinarily, 20,000 State recruits were enrolled per year, the number taken into service nevertheless varied according to whether the ratio of collection was one recuit per fifty homesteads, or one per seventy-five, or one per eighty-nine, so that the total might be variously, 10,000, 14,000, or 23,000, apart from naval service recruits: to which he adds that especially during the year 1724, although warfare on every front had then come to an end, the forces had impressed into them for completion of establishment of field and garrison regiments, artillery, and fleet, 35,000 fresh recruits. Such a swollen enrolment can be explained only by the fact that, in addition to the usual necessity of reinforcing units, heavy shrinkages had taken place, through desertion, sickness, and death, in the regiments specially assigned to fatigue duties by Peter's new military scheme, and that grave deficits of man-power had accumulated from past recruit-musters. At all events, we know that in 1712 the number of defaulters, of men who had failed to "join up" when called upon during their respective years, had reached the huge total of 45,000, and, of deserters, a total of 30,000. In which connection Weber remarks that, owing to bad organisation of maintenance, far more recruits died of hunger and cold before their training had come to an end than ever fell in subsequent battle. In sum, Peter's regular cavalry and infantry (exclusive of aliens) were estimated to be standing, towards the close of his reign, at a total of between 196,000 and 212,000, apart from his force of 110,000 Cossacks and other irregular details.

At the same period there came into being an altogether new armed force, an armed force never before known to Russia: which force was a Russian fleet. We have seen that when the Northern War began, Peter had to lay up his Azov squadron, and that, later, the battle on the Pruth lost him the whole of that marine region; and it was these circumstances that first led to his so thinking of creating a fleet on the Baltic that in 1701 he could dream of coming to have eighty large vessels afloat there . . . and by 1703 launching six frigates from the Lodeinopolsk Wharf, the first Russian squadron to take the Baltic's waters, and by the close of his reign beholding Russia in possession of forty-eight ships of the line, of 800 galleys and minor vessels, and of a man-power afloat of 28,000. Also, since the controlling, reinforcing, training, feeding, and clothing of the men of the fleet and the army called for a corresponding amount of military-administrative machinery, there came into being a War Office and an Admiralty, with, later, an Artillery Office under a Field-Marshal-in-Chief, an Office of Commissariat under a Director-General of Victualling, and a Chief Office of Supply under a *General-Kriegs-Kommissar*, an official so varied in his functions as to have under his charge the distribution of pay to the forces, their provision with uniforms, weapons, and horses, the reception of recruits at training-centres, and those recruits' corps-allotment. Also there materialised a General Staff consisting of, according to a roster of 1712, two field-marshals (Menshikov and Sheremetev) and thirty-one generals, with fourteen of the latter foreigners. And, lastly, there was issued to the land forces a standard dress, and if we look at illustrated works bearing upon our military history we shall see Peter's Guardsmen manipulating their muskets, and locking their "baginets," in a costume consisting of (in addition to other things) a *kaftan* of German cut and a three-cornered hat.

Thus Peter based his system of establishment of regular warlike forces upon the technical changes (1) that to enrolments of volunteers for the filling up of gaps there succeeded general recruit-enrolments, (2) that the old peace cadres of "chosen men" were developed until they became permanent corps, (3) that by degrees infantry were given a considerable predominance over cavalry in the correlation of military arms, and (4) that the State's armed forces all became transferred, for costs of maintenance, to the Treasury. Of which changes, and especially of the last, the net result was that the cost of military upkeep grew until in 1712 the General Staff alone was found to be absorbing 111,000 (900,000) roubles per year, as against a sum of 10,000,000 for the cost of the whole of the army put together about thirty years earlier, and that the land forces increased both in numbers and in costliness until by 1725 the military budget stood multiplied by five, if not more, and had reached 5,000,000 (Petrine) roubles for the army, and 1,500,000 roubles for the fleet, or a total which, if reckoned in modern currency, means, in all, a sum of from 52,000,000 to 58,000,000 roubles, or two-thirds of the General Budget designed for the State's every purpose! . . .

Next let us review Peter's measures for the attempted upkeep of his army and his fleet. . . .

Even if Peter's military reforms had not made the deep and lasting impression upon the social and moral adjustment of the community which they did, and also upon the course of political events, they would still have remained an outstanding feature in Russia's military history. For one thing, they inevitably gave rise to a need for some method of providing for the upkeep of Peter's reformed, but exceedingly costly, armed forces, and therefore to a series of measures for placing those forces' establishment upon a regular and permanent basis. And in proportion as Peter extended the obligation to perform military service to classes which had hitherto stood exempt from that liability, until the army had become an army drawn from the nation at large, there resulted an alteration also in social correlations, and, above all, an alteration in the service position of the *dvorianstvo*. Hitherto the *dvorianstvo*, as a class, had constituted the bulk of the army, but when conscriptions began to sweep even the *dvorianstvo's*, *kholopi* and bonded *krestiané* into Peter's reformed military corps, and to hold them there in the capacity, not merely of their masters' menials and henchmen whilst on service, but in that of full men-at-arms serving on an identical service footing with that held by their masters at the beginning of those masters' service, the *dvorianstvo* ceased to be the principal constituent in the country's armed forces. . . .

Czars, like kaisers, were military and patrimonial rulers. The military, to another great czar and tyrant, Nicholas I, was a model of political order, of legitimacy, of obedience, and of authoritarian rule. Nicholas Riasanovsky, the American historian of Nicholas I, writes on the convergence of official nationality, military order, and czarist patrimonial autocracy.

NICHOLAS RIASANOVSKY

Nicholas I, the Supreme Commander

Here [in the army] there is order, there is a strict unconditional legality, no impertinent claims to know all the answers, no contradiction, all things flow logically one from the other; no one commands before he has himself learned to obey; no one steps in front of anybody else without lawful reason; everything is subordinated to one definite goal, everything has its purpose. That is why I feel so well among these people, and why I shall always hold in honor the calling of a soldier. I consider the entire human life to be merely service, because everybody serves.—Nicholas I

. . . The heavy burden of an empire lay all the heavier on the shoulders of Nicholas because of his deep emotional involvement in his task and, in fact, in everything around him. The detachment and the superior calm of an autocrat, which Nicholas I tried so often and so hard to display, were merely a false front, and frequently they failed to perform even that function. In reality, the emperor was

From Nicholas V. Riasanovsky, Nicholas I and Official Nationality in Russia, 1825–1855 (Berkeley, 1959), pp. 5–9. Copyright © 1959 by The Regents of the University of California; reprinted by permission of the University of California Press.

usually seething with passions, especially with rage and with fear, but also with a kind of exultation when he felt that he was striking telling blows against the enemy. He was given to sentimentality and to tears which coursed down his cheeks, for example, when he was preparing his strange 1848 manifesto. Nicholas's violent hatred concentrated apparently with equal ease on an individual, such as the French king Louis-Philippe, a group, such as the Decembrists, a people, such as the Poles, or a concept, such as Revolution. Much has been written about the emperor's tremendous emotional involvement in the Decembrist affair, an involvement which ceased only with his death. But Nicholas I had the same general attitude in all his other relations as well, assailing with equal vehemence "the King of the French," a corrupt minor official, or a delinquent sergeant in one of his regiments. His impulse was always to strike and keep striking until the object of his wrath was destroyed.

Aggressiveness, however, was not the emperor's only method of coping with the problems of life. Another was regimentation, orderliness, neatness, precision, an enomous effort to have everything at all times in its proper place. Nicholas I was by nature a drill master and an inspector general. The army became his love, almost an obsession, from childhood to the end of his life. Toy soldiers and military games constituted the devouring passion of Nicholas's boyhood, as well as of that of his younger brother Michael. Attempts to turn his attention in other directions proved singularly unsuccessful. Typical is the story of one assignment. In 1810 the fourteen-year-old boy was told to write a theme on the subject that military service was only one of the careers open to a nobleman, and that he could also enter other occupations which were equally useful and honorable. The future emperor failed to produce any essay at all, and his teacher finally dictated one to him.

As he grew older, Nicholas's enchantment with the army retained its full force, while his activity in that field increased greatly. He became a most devoted and enthusiastic officer and a lifelong expert in such things as the field manual, drill of every sort, and playing the drum. When Emperor Alexander I put Nicholas in charge of the army engineers, the younger brother finally obtained a large military establishment which he could drill, inspect, and supervise continuously. Then, in 1825, he became the supreme commander of all the Russian armed forces, and of all of Russia besides. The new emperor eagerly took up his vastly expanded military functions, but he remained a junior officer at heart. His great attachment remained the minutiae of army life: the physical appearance of his troops,

small unit drill, uniforms with their buttons, ribbons, and colors which he proceeded to rearrange with a most painstaking devotion to duty. As emperor, Nicholas continued to participate personally in as many military reviews and exercises as possible. Indeed this kind of army life represented "as he himself admitted, his one true delight." It was also observed that the Russian emperor could not restrain his joy when he received honorary ranks and appointments in Prussian or Austrian regiments, and that he insisted on having appropriate uniforms made immediately and on drilling his new troops. Time and again he surprised Prussian and Austrian officers by his perfect knowledge of their field manuals.

It was especially at large-scale military reviews that Nicholas I experienced rapture, almost ecstasy, that he felt a violent swelling of his emotions and sensed the proximity of God. For instance, his letter to the empress describing the great military celebration arranged in 1839 on the field of Borodino is a remarkable combination of precise technical information about the ceremony and of powerful religious feeling. "From the depth of my soul I prayed to God for you, for our children, for the well-being of our entire great Russian family." At another huge military review, with the Austrian ambassador in attendance, the emperor, his eyes filled with tears, placed his hand over his heart, lifted his gaze to heaven and prayed loudly: "God, I thank Thee for making me so mighty, and I beg Thee to give me the strength never to abuse this power.". . . .

Like the Russian state machinery, the military became corrupt, venal, inefficient, and highly expensive for a primitive peasant economy. The patrimonial state became in the 1880s a police state, while the military command became a wooden-headed generalship. The epic of Alexander Solzhenitsyn, *August 1914,* is one of the finest military historical writings. His description of the senior Russian officers, and especially of the corporate professionals, is classic. Here are some excerpts from Solzhenitsyn.

ALEXANDER SOLZHENITSYN

The Russian Army's Seniority System

The ruin of the Russian army was the system of seniority: the supreme, indisputable factor was length of service and promotion by seniority. As long as you did not make a *faux pas* or arouse the ire of the powers that be, the mere passage of time would in due course elevate you to the coveted senior rank, and with the rank went a suitable command. Thus, every officer accepted it as the natural order of things, as inevitable as the stately progress of the heavenly bodies, that the first question one colonel or general should ask another was not what active service he had seen but what was the year, month, and date of his seniority in the rank—in other words, what stage had he reached in the due progression toward senior command. If a Yanushkevich were appointed chief of the General Staff, then a Postovsky would be made chief of staff of an army. In a system like this, what chance was there that such

From **August** 1914 *by Alexander Solzhenitsyn, translation by Michael Glenny, English translation Copyright* © *1972 by Michael Glenny. Reprinted by permission of Farrar, Straus & Giroux, Inc.*

men could grasp the lightning speed of modern warfare, or the need for efficient, sensitive, two-way communication? . . . There is no innate gift that brings unalloyed reward: it is always a source of affliction too. But for an officer it is particularly galling to be endowed with exceptional talent. The army will gladly pay tribute to a brilliantly gifted man— but only when his hand is already grasping a field marshal's baton. Till then, while he is still reaching for it, the army's system will subject his outstretched arm to a rain of blows. Discipline, which holds an army together, is inevitably hostile to a man of thrusting ability, and everything that is dynamic and heretical in his talent is bound to be shackled, suppressed, and made to conform. Those in authority find it intolerable to have a subordinate who has a mind of his own; for that reason, an officer of outstanding ability will always be promoted more slowly, not faster, than the mediocrities.

In 1903 General von François went to East Prussia as chief of staff of an army corps. Ten years later, when he was nearly sixty, he was sent there again—as a mere corps commander.

It was in 1903 that Count von Schlieffen held the General Staff war game in East Prussia, and von François was nominated to command one of the "Russian" armies. His happened to be the army on which von Schlieffen demonstrated his tactic of the double encircling movement. The official account of the exercise contained the remark: "Under threat of encircle- ment from the flank and from the rear, the Russian army laid down its arms." To this von François objected provocatively: "*Exzellenz!* As long as I command an army, it will not lay down its arms!" Von Schlieffen smiled and substituted the words: "Realizing the hopelessness of his army's position, *its commander sought death in the front line—and found it there.*" In real war, of course, such things do not happen.

The Bolshevik leadership aspired to change this army. The leading military theoreticians of the Bolsheviks were Lenin and Trotsky. Trotsky's philosophy of the new army of Bolsheviks is well summarized by his apologist-biographer, Isaac Deutscher.

ISAAC DEUTSCHER

Note on Trotsky's Military Writings

. . . A summary of Trotsky's military activities cannot be concluded without a reference to his military writings. As founder and leader of an army, he remained a man of letters with the urge to give form and expression to his experiences and ideas, even in the smoke of battle. The many volumes of his military essays, speeches, and orders are distinguished by such contrasting qualities as romantic *élan*, and practical realism and at times by an almost philosophical depth.

Radek relates that Trotsky, when he became Commissar of War, had read

From Isaac Deutscher, The Prophet Armed: Trotsky, 1879–1921 *(London, 1954), pp. 477–84, by permission of Oxford University Press.*

only a few books on military affairs. . . . During the Balkan wars and in the first years of the World War Trotsky had studied current military literature. He was certainly familiar, as Lenin was, with the work of Clausewitz, whom he quoted and in whose spirit he often approached his own problems. But Radek is right in holding that Trotsky was most strongly impressed by Jaurès's L'Armée Nouvelle, the work of a great historian and democratic Socialist, not a military expert.

Jaurès tried to reconcile two aspects of his own policy: his struggle against the reactionary French officers' corps, whose influence on domestic politics had shown itself in the Dreyfus affair;

and his patriotic desire to see the French Republic armed and ready for defence. He conceived a reform of the army which, he hoped, would fit in with the economic and political reforms which were to transform bourgeois France into a a 'social republic'. He advocated the replacement of the standing army by militias. The standing army, confined and trained within the rigid framework of the barracks, in artificial isolation from and latent opposition to civilian society, had been the officers' corps' main source of political strength. Militias were to be set up on the basis of productive units, factories, and village communities; the militiamen were to receive their training locally and were to continue to live and work as normal citizens, devoting themselves part-time or intermittently to the art and craft of war. The militias should therefore be so organically integrated into the civilian community that no ambitious general or military clique could use them as a political instrument.

Trotsky borrowed Jaurès's idea but put it in a different context. Jaurès believed that it would be possible to democratize the army into a militia system even under the capitalist system. To Trotsky this belief was a reformist illusion. The virtual or actual opposition of a standing army to civilian society reflected, in his view, the clash between the interests of the propertied classes, which that army defended in the last instance, and those of the working classes. Only after the interest of the working classes had become paramount, he argued, could the army become submerged in the people and identified with it. The abolition of the standing army fitted the state which was to wither away gradually, as the proletarian state was expected to do.

Nevertheless, Trotsky built the Red Army as a standing army. The militia system, he argued, could be fully effective only against the background of a highly industrialized, organized, and civilized society. The Russian environment dictated to the Red Army the principles of its organization, which were very much the same as those that had underlain the structure of the Tsarist army. The difference between the two armies lay in their political and social outlook, not in their strictly military features.

Trotsky excused this as a temporary necessity and insisted that party and government should commit themselves to the militia system as their ultimate objective. He argued the case in the 'Theses' which he submitted to the eighth party congress in March 1919 and which, in his absence, Sokolnikov defended before the congress. He looked forward to the time when men would receive their military training not in barracks but in conditions closely approximating to the workaday life of workers and peasants. The transition could not begin in earnest before a revival of industry; but even now, Trotsky insisted, a barracks must be made to resemble a military and general school, not a mere drilling-place. In the Red Army the commanding staffs were appointed, not elected; but Trotsky envisaged a return to the elective principle in the future. The eighth congress adopted Trotsky's 'Theses', and the ninth endorsed them again.

The programme aroused considerable criticism towards the end of the civil war, when Trotsky made the first attempt to put it into effect. The old professional officers were surprised that he, who had so severely centralized the army and extirpated the guerrilla spirit, should advocate a military organization which in their eyes looked suspiciously like the old Red Guards. They could not seriously entertain the idea that an army could be trained, disciplined, and inured to collective action otherwise than in the barracks. One of Trotsky's critics was General Svechin, the author of a standard work on strategy and professor at the Military Academy. Against this critic Trotsky defended 'the dreamer Jaurès':

If Professor Svechin thinks that the Communist Party has taken power in order to replace the three-coloured [Tsarist] barracks by a red one, he is gravely mistaken. . . . The objection that under a militia system the command would not enjoy proper authority strikes one with its political blindness. Has perhaps the authority of the present leadership of the Red Army been established in the barracks? . . . That authority is based not on the salutary hypnosis of the barracks but on the appeal of the Soviet régime and of the Communist Party. Professor Svechin has simply overlooked the revolution and the enormous spiritual upheaval it has brought about. . . . To him the ignorant, drunken mercenary, syphilis-ridden and numbed by Catholicism, who served in Wallenstein's camp, the artisan-apprentice of Paris, who, led by journalists and lawyers, destroyed the Bastille, the Saxon worker and member of the Social Democratic Party of 1914–18, and the Russian proletarian who first in world history took power—all these are to him approximately the same cannon fodder

to be delicately processed in the barracks. Is this not a mockery of history?

. . . The problem of military doctrine occupies an important place in Trotsky's writings. He himself claimed no originality in this field. But he brought to the discussion of the issues a broad view of history and a freshness of approach which, if they were not enough to make a new philosophy of war, did much to guard the Red Army from pitfalls of one-sided doctrines. He had to contend against the old generals on the one hand, and against young revolutionary officers on the other. To the former he spoke as an innovator, attacking their conservative habits of thought. To the latter he appeared almost as an advocate of military orthodoxy.

He was the presiding spirit of Moscow's Military Academy, where the old generals were professors and lecturers. He strove to modernize the Academy's curriculum, to free it from pedantry, and to bring it close to the fresh experiences of warfare. Once, for instance, he expostulated with the writers of the Academy for their lifeless pseudo-historical style and urged them to emulate French military writers who, he said, knew how to combine historical research with an interest in contemporary warfare and in its sociological background. The academicians viewed the civil war rather contemptuously, as a bastard of grand strategy. Trotsky retorted irritably:

It is said among you that in the present civil or small war . . . military science has no role, in any case. I am telling you, Messieurs the military specialists, that this is an altogether ignorant statement. . . . Civil war, with its highly mobile and elastic fronts, affords enormous scope to genuine initiative and military art. The task is just the same here as elsewhere: To obtain the maximum result through a minimum expenditure of strength. . . . It was precisely the last [world] war . . . that offered relatively little scope to strategic art. After the gigantic front from the Belgian coast to Switzerland had become fixed, the war became automatic. Strategic art was reduced to a minimum; everything was staked on mutual attrition. Our war, on the contrary, has been full of mobility and manœuvre which allowed the greatest talents to reveal themselves. . . .

While the old generals refused to learn the lessons of the civil war, the young ones were often reluctant to learn anything else. Their ambition was to construct a brand-new 'proletarian military doctrine'. That doctrine, they held, should meet the needs of the revolutionary class and suit its mentality: It must disdain defence and static warfare and favour mobility and the offensive. Only decaying classes, retreating in all fields, favoured the defensive attitude. The 'proletarian style of warfare' appealed to commanders who had risen from the ranks. Its most gifted expounders were Tukhachevsky and Frunze, while Voroshilov and Budienny also counted among its adherents. With Tukhachevsky the offensive doctrine logically supplemented 'revolution from without'; and in advocating both he remained within the Napoleonic tradition. But being of a more modern outlook than his colleagues, he saw the future offensive warfare as conducted by means

of mass formations of tanks and armoured vehicles co-operating with air forces. (He was also the originator of parachute troops, whom he intended to use far behind the enemy lines, in areas engulfed by civil war.)

Trotsky's polemic against this school of thought is perhaps the most instructive part of his military writings. He dismissed 'proletarian strategy', just as in another field he disavowed 'proletarian culture' and 'proletarian literature'. 'War bases itself on many sciences', he wrote, 'but war itself is no science—it is a practical art, a skill . . . a savage and bloody art. . . . To try to formulate a new military doctrine with the help of Marxism is like trying to create with the help of Marxism a new theory of architecture or a new veterinary text-book.' He protested, often with biting derision, against the treatment of Marxist dialectics as the philosopher's stone; and he demanded respect for a certain continuity of experience and cultural tradition. He saw in the 'proletarian' innovations a cover for intellectual crudity and conceit. He constantly drew the attention of his military audiences to the barbarous poverty, uncouthness, and dirt of the Red Army, to be mitigated only by hard work and attention to detail, from which the Russian only too frequently sought to escape into the realm of abstract doctrine.

The adherents of the 'proletarian doctrine of the offensive' theorized from their own experience in the civil war, in which rapid manœuvre predominated. Trotsky replied that the Red Army had learned manœuvrability, allegedly the exclusive virtue of a rising social class, from the White

Guards, just as the latter had borrowed methods of propaganda from the Red Army. Whites and Reds had become mutually assimilated in military matters: 'Fighting one another over a long time, enemies come to learn from one another.' Trotsky himself had issued his famous order 'Proletarians, to horse!', the signal for the formation of Budienny's cavalry corps, only at the height of Denikin's offensive when the White cavalry, led by Mamontov, threatened to disrupt the Bolshevik interior by its deep and swift raids behind Bolshevik lines.

But the high mobility peculiar to the civil war reflected (according to Trotsky) the primitive conditions in which the war was fought over vast, sparsely populated areas. He drew an analogy between the American Civil War and the Russian. In both, the opposed forces operated over thinly populated continents, with extremely poor lines of communication and means of transport. In both, cavalry had exceptionally wide scope. In both, the Whites were the traditional horsemen; and the armies both of the Northern States and of the Soviet shad to wrest the initiative and form their own cavalries. It did not follow that high mobility was the 'style' of civil war at large. On the Scheldte, the Seine, or the Thames civil war would be fought much more statically than in steppes or prairies.

The civil war had been fought in Russia in quasi-Napoleonic style, because of the country's low level of civilization. But it was foolish and unhistorical, Trotsky argued, to try to adopt the Napoleonic offensive doctrine for the Red Army, as Tukhachevsky tried to do. Trotsky sharply contrasted the position of revolutionary France in Europe with that of revolutionary Russia. At the beginning of the nineteenth century France was the most civilized and technically advanced nation on the Continent— this enabled Napoleon to pursue the offensive strategy. Russia was technically one of the most backward nations in Europe; Napoleonic strategy would bear no relation whatever to her social and military potentialities. He pointed out that the French General Staff, especially Foch, had in vain cultivated the Napoleonic strategy—France's position in Europe could not and did not allow for its application in 1914–18. And Trotsky poked fun at the brand-new 'proletarian doctrine' which on a closer view was merely a plagiarism of French pre-1914 text-books.

Attempts to define the 'essence' of warfare in general and of proletarian warfare in particular were, according to Trotsky, metaphysical doctrine-mongering. He himself argued the need for a certain eclecticism in military theory. 'In practical arts', he approvingly quoted Clausewitz, 'one should not drive the flowers and the foliage of theory too high—one should rather keep them close to the soil of experience.' He spoke with qualified respect about the empirical methods of the English imperialists, 'who think in centuries and continents' and slightingly about the German epigones of Clausewitz. None of the 'national' doctrines of war offered or could offer any 'final truth' about war. Each school of thought merely reflected temporary conditions of national existence. The English doctrine of balance of power and naval supremacy; the cautious military thought of Bismarck's Germany, which went hand in hand with diplomatic aggressiveness; the exclusively offensive doctrine of latter-day German imperialism, which, carried away by its own momentum, threw all caution to the winds; the Bonapartist offensive doctrine of pre-1914 France (and, one might add, the reaction from it in the form of the Maginot mood before 1940); all these doctrines merely isolate and exaggerate certain moments and aspects of military experience. The Marxist way of thinking is averse to military doctrinairism of any sort. 'Only the traitor renounces attack; only the simpleton reduces all strategy to attack.' . . .

The Soviet case represents an extreme, and therefore very obvious, example of subjective civilian control (as described by Samuel Huntington), in which the military participate in politics. "Subjective civilian control achieves its end by civilianizing the military, making them the mirror of the state. . . . the essence of subjective civilian control is the *denial* of an independent military sphere."*

The army of the USSR is a model of Bolshevik civil-military relations, the Communist party claiming hegemony over state, society, and groups. Unquestionably, the Soviet party-army relationship is a continuous struggle. The subordination of the military was costly between 1930 and 1942. One-third of its officers' corps was annihilated by Stalin.

The dynamics of party-military relations and the resulting strains have been conclusively demonstrated by political scientist and Sovietologist Roman Kolkowicz.

*Samuel P. Huntington, *The Soldier and the State* (Cambridge, Mass.: Harvard University Press, Belknap Press, 1957).

Roman Kolkowicz

The Dynamics of Party-Military Relations

CHANGES IN THE ROLE OF THE MILITARY

Ever since the Revolution, the Communist Party has relied on a profes-

From Roman Kolkowicz, The Soviet Military and the Communist Party *(Princeton, N. J., 1967), pp. 19–32, by permission of Princeton University Press.*

sional standing army for the defense of the socialist state. During the 1920's, when the ebbing revolutionary zeal of Communists in the rest of Europe and the rise of fascist movements combined to isolate the Soviet Union and confirm its fear of a "capitalist encirclement," Stalin's desire for a modern military establishment led to a series of far-reaching changes in the socio-economic structure in the Soviet Union. Through a policy of collectivization and industrialization, large sums of investment capital were to be extracted from the agricultural sector and invested in a large-scale heavy industry that would furnish the basis for a military organization well-enough equipped for defensive and political purposes.

Though Trotsky is correctly described as the creator of the Red Army, it was Stalin, during his long rule of the Soviet state, who shaped its characteristics, defined its internal role, and set the limits to its freedom of action. After the establishment of the Soviet state in the aftermath of the Revolution, Trotsky had been willing to sacrifice some of the Red Army's professionalism and military viability for the sake of ideological continuity and legitimacy. Stalin, who was less concerned with ideology than with pragmatic problems of statecraft, saw the necessity of maintaining a professional military establishment and, having prevailed over Trotsky in the intra-Party struggle, proceeded to mold the Red Army to fit his needs. His advocacy of a standing army did not bespeak the militarist or martinet in him. If anything, Stalin was even more distrustful of professional military establishments than Trotsky, as evidenced by his introduction of strong political controls from the very beginning, by his denial of full authority (*edinonachalie*) to the commanders, and by his strengthening the security organs' authority in the military establishment. The military did win concessions and privileges from Stalin, but these were intended to keep the

army loyal to the regime and to make it proficient; they were outweighed by negative measures and practices which resulted in severe curtailment of professional freedom, authority, and institutional self-esteem. Although the military emerged from the early intra-Party struggles with several gains, it found itself the captive of the Party elite, living in an "atmosphere of an armed camp surrounded by enemies." Its official role in the Soviet state, as it evolved in the early years, was unquestioningly to execute the policies and directives of the Communist Party elite; to protect the state and the regime and to put down challengers to the Party's hegemony within and without; to accept and tolerate the presence of Party functionaries in its midst even at the expense of interference with military efficiency and authority; and to be a citizen army, permeated with egalitarian virtues while performing in a disciplined, effective manner.

The major test of the Red Army came during World War II, when it dramatically proved its crucial role by successfully defending the state against German aggression despite the handicaps under which it suffered as a result of the 1937 purges and Stalin's handling of mobilization and other organizational problems on the eve of the hostilities. Since the war, Soviet foreign policy has become a grand strategic design with many commitments in various areas of the globe, a policy based on the viability of the Soviet army as well as on the political exploitation of this military capability. As long as the Party leaders adhere to the present dynamic, expansionistic foreign policy—and there is little reason to believe that the policy will change in the foreseeable future—the military will continue to have a vital role in the Party's scheme.

As a result of these postwar developments, the position of the military, once strictly subordinate to that of the Party and closely integrated with the Party's interests in the state, has become progressively less subordinate and more self-assertive. Since the death of Stalin, in particular, the role of the military, and its relations with the Party, have undergone a discernible change. Among the many factors which have contributed to this change, the most important have been the modification of the terror machine, the effects of de-Stalinization, the more moderate political and social climate in the Soviet Union, and the growing complexity of warfare. . . .

a. *Conflicts of Ideology and Organization.* A perennial source of tensions is the Party's antimilitary ideology, which clashes with the military's own institutional beliefs. As we look at the relations between Party and military, we see two institutions, with distinct ideologies and conflicting institutional interests, in a state of uneasy coexistence, both striving for exclusiveness, elitism, and detachment from the rest of the society; both subscribing to similar formalized codes of beliefs and behavior; both cultivating an almost messianic self-image. How can these exclusive ideologies accommodate themselves to each other in view of the Party's claim to hegemony? . . .

Some Western students of military affairs have compared the ideology of the military to that of the Church.

Other scholars have drawn the parallel between Church and Party, among them Zbigniew Brzezinski, who states that "both movements see themselves as the exclusive standard-bearers of an absolutely correct and normatively all-embracing vision of reality." It follows, then, that there are certain similarities also between the Party and the military. Indeed, to the extent that the Party may be described as a dedicated, exclusive elite, which deals with and serves society but stands apart, and which owes its cohesion to the institutional values upheld by a dogma, these characteristics can be transferred almost without qualification to the officer corps of most military establishments. . . .

The theme which is common to most of these views is that the profession of the officer is strongly motivated by selfless devotion to spiritual and patriotic values, making it more of a "calling" than a job. . . .

Communist Party experts on military affairs, well aware of this idealized image and self-image of military professionals, deny that it exists in the Soviet army. One of them, in a major work on militarism, has accused militarists of employing "the doctrines of the ruling church and various religious movements." (He is obviously referring to Western militarists, since, according to Party dogma, there can be no militarism in a classless society or in a society whose classes are in a "nonantagonistic relationship.") The author, V. I. Skopin, strongly attacks this "ideology of militarism," which he accuses of embodying an "idealistic philosophy." Methodically he uncovers and condemns these "idealistic" views which strive "to show the 'beauty' and 'wisdom' [of military life] and the 'benefits derived from war for the welfare of mankind.'"

However, while Communist Party ideologues express themselves in these contemptuous terms, Soviet military leaders and publicists, concerned about the deteriorating morale of their officers, speak proudly of the beauty of the military profession. . . .

A conflict of ideologies is inevitable in view of the Party's attempt to neutralize, equalize, and "depersonalize" all institutions and groups and claim exclusive features only for itself, and, at the same time, of the inherent tendency of all professional-institutional groupings to develop characteristics and personalities of their own.

b. Substantive Disagreements. Since the very beginnings of the Soviet state and the Red Army, the Party has maintained in the military establishment a multiple control network whose purpose it is to secure information, to indoctrinate and manipulate the military, to supervise and control the professional and private activities of officers and men, and, finally, to coerce the recalcitrant or anti-Party elements.

The military has seldom opposed or even questioned the principle of having some measure of political indoctrination or supervision. It does, however, resent and oppose any excessive pressure from the control machinery that substantially interferes with the performance of professional duties.

Disagreements have centered also around issues of strategy. Before World War II, the Soviets had no distinct, indigenous strategic doctrine, although there was some cross-fertilization from the German army in the pre-Hitler era. During the war, Stalin launched several new strategic concepts. These were subsequently formalized in a "scientific military doctrine," whose basic features were a set of "permanent factors," or immutable laws of warfare, and several "temporary factors," which were changeable with conditions.

Stalin's death and the ensuing struggles for power within the Party freed the military from a long silence. One by one, the Stalinist formulas were exposed to discussion, their failings and merits were analyzed publicly, and most of them were rejected. The introduction of thermonuclear strategic missiles and other advanced weapons and equipment led to a drastic change in Soviet strategy. But not all parts of the military welcomed this change. While the rejection of the obsolete Stalinist formulas had met with general approval, some aspects of the new Soviet strategic doctrine encountered strong opposition from the theater forces, which were most severely affected by the change, and some of whose spokesmen questioned its wisdom. The result was a continuous debate between the Party and the "traditionalists" (the theater forces) as well as between the "traditionalists" and the "radicals" (the military supporters of the new, Khrushchevian strategic doctrine).

Another source of tensions has been the Party leadership's divide-and-rule policy, by which it accords preferential treatment to favored factions within the military, and excludes other, politically unaligned officers from the highest Party councils and military positions.

While Stalin tended to reserve the highest military positions for "political generals," Khrushchev entrusted these vital positions to professional officers who had shown courage and ability during the war. These officers, who owe much of their career and thrust to prominence to Khrushchev (they are here called the Stalingrad Group, because the origins of their special relationship with Khrushchev go back to the battle of Stalingrad in 1942–1943), constitute the present Soviet High Command. They represent a strong beachhead of the Party in the military, because many of them, although capable professionals, tend to give primary weight to political considerations.

In the various substantive disagreements between the Party and the military, the Stalingrad Group, until recently, faithfully followed the lead of Khrushchev. In the doctrinal-strategic debate, many of its members advocate greater reliance on strategic missile-nuclear forces and a reduced role for the theater forces; on the role of the political control organs, they tend to support the Party line. . . .

THE PARTY'S METHODS OF CONTROLLING THE MILITARY

The measures by which the Party deals with the military range from the positive (the granting of socio-economic privileges, political cooptation, and acquiescence in military de-

mands), through the "prophylactic" (indoctrination and supervision), to the negative (intimidation and coercion). The objective of all these measures is to maintain high levels of effectiveness, discipline, and morale in the military and at the same time to prevent or eradicate any elitist, "Bonapartist," anti-Party sentiments or movements in its ranks.

a. Positive Measures. The Party grants the professional officer impressive privileges and allowances, which in the past placed the officer almost automatically among the socio-economic elite. This has been somewhat less true in recent years, not so much through deliberate action on the part of the government as because of the rising standard of living in the larger society and the greater availability of goods and services. But the higher officer and his family still continue to enjoy a privileged existence. . . .

The Party also coopts a certain number of prominent military leaders into the highest Party councils, such as the Central Committee and the Central Auditing Commission, thereby bringing them close to the decision-making centers where, theoretically, they may present the military's point of view and look out for the military's interests. In practice, however, most of those chosen for such representation are ideologically close to the Party's point of view and tend to give priority to political considerations over the purely institutional military interests.

b. "Prophylactic" Measures. The Party elite tends to view the citizenry with suspicion and distrust. By and large, it subscribes to the view that the individual in Soviet society must be made to feel that he has no alternative but to fulfill the role assigned to him, and must be placed under strict controls that limit his freedom to make unorthodox judgments. With respect to the military, this idea is being put into practice in a variety of ways: through an elaborate system of indoctrination, supervision, and manipulation, and through the deliberate creation of unease and distrust, by having different ranks mix with one another at Party meetings and encouraging the low-ranking officers publicly to criticize their superiors.

These measures are designed to keep the officer committed and loyal, to give him a set of objectives and values similar to those of the Party, and to imbue him with a negative view of the external world and an idealized image of Soviet reality, making him thereby into the "new Soviet man."

c. Negative Measures. Although "prophylaxis" is the preferred method for keeping the military loyal as well as strong, the Party also resorts at times to the harsher measures of intimidation, blackmail, and coercion, and Soviet officers well recall the notorious purges (*chistki*) of the Stalinist era. In the post-Stalin period, with its more moderate methods, the Party has used a most effective means of ridding itself of undersirables in the military: the periodic massive reductions of the armed forces and the dismissal of individual officers. Furthermore, it maintains provocateurs and informers within the military units,

who report the private and professional activities of their personnel to the political organs, providing the latter with dossiers that can be used for blackmail. The political control organs also play a major role during the yearly attestations of the officers, and their approval is indispensable to the officers' careers.

THE RESOURCES OF THE MILITARY

Given the Party's initiative and controlling power in the relationship with the military, what, we must now ask, are the military's resources and methods for questioning, neutralizing, challenging, or opposing the Party's dominance?

a. Professional Expertise. The age of atomic and nuclear warfare has transformed most large military establishments from tradition-ridden organizations, whose leadership was predicated chiefly on its ability to lead men in combat and maintain discipline, into vast bureaucracies based on complex equipment and weapons. The new elite in these establishments consists to an ever greater extent of technocrats in uniform; their officers must understand technology, economics, and logistics, and must be able to manage large projects which overlap with the civilian economy. . . .

With officer training increasingly complex, time-consuming, expensive, and exacting, any wholesale purges or massive replacements would seriously weaken the Soviet military, which even now suffers from a shortage of technically trained officers. The knowledge of their indispensability has caused officers in the technical and elite services to assert themselves more freely and often *vis-à-vis* the Party *apparatchiks*. The Party's attempts to place political officers in commanding positions and commanders in Party positions, so as to prevent situations where professional officers insist on greater independence and immunity, have not been very successful. By and large, therefore, the Party recognizes the importance of the military professional and interferes in his functions with greater circumspection than in the past.

b. Institutional Resilience. The Soviet officer corps retains many of the characteristics of guild-like institutions in all societies, despite the Party's constant efforts to eradicate them. Officers "cover up" for one another, further each other's careers, protect and favor their former comrades, and in other ways cultivate a sense of solidarity, in alliance against hostile surroundings. This cohesiveness and camaraderie is summed up in a sentence from the military's central organ, *Krasnaia zvezda*: "In a society where each man is a brother to his fellow-man, even an unknown soldier is best friend to each of us." The corporateness of the officer corps is strengthened by tradition, by pride in the craft, and by a patriotic sense of serving the fatherland.

These qualities have given the military establishment the resilience that has enabled it to raise effective obstacles to the Party's almost obsessive endeavor to break down the military's natural independence. They

are the mark of the military's institutional identity and strength. Though Stalin gained temporary mastery in this struggle by brutally cutting down the dissidents in the officer corps, his heirs in the Kremlin are no longer able, and are probably unwilling, to risk such a showdown.

c. Political Alliances. The inherent instability of power arrangements in the Soviet state has forced contenders for power to seek alliances with the major social groupings (the governmental bureaucracy, the Party professionals, the military, the terror machine, among others), either to protect a monopoly of power or to ensure against the possibility of a showdown in a future crisis. During periods of firm leadership and internal stability, the Party unequivocally dominates the state and is able to keep those institutions sufficiently divided and rigidly controlled. However, when the Party's hold is weakened—by internecine power struggles, succession crises, or external military threats— the groups that have formerly been kept submissive and politically impotent tend to gain in stature and influence.

The military establishment, being a well-integrated organization with a cohesive structure and powerful weapons and logistic facilities, is in an excellent position to exploit those occasions of division and other weaknesses in the Party and to fill the partial void of authority that they create. Stalin used to anticipate any danger of the military's political assertion in such situations, whether real or imaginary, by striking out at the military with preemptive measures designed to induce a state of near-shock. His successors do not exercise or enjoy the same freedom of action. Like Stalin, however, they have tried to bind the military to themselves through political alliances and personal ties intended to keep the military elite committed to the regime; to ensure cooperation and responsiveness in the High Command; and to divide the military leadership by favoring some segments and excluding others from such a preferential relationship with the Party rulers.

This last attempt, however, does not always succeed as intended. There have been times when military leaders in political alliance with the Party elite have found opportunity to exploit the military's implicit political weight and indispensability in the event of a crisis to their personal benefit as well as to the advantage of the military in general. . . .

Roman Kolkowicz

The Dialogue on Professional Autonomy: Military Independence vs. Political Integration

A remarkable feature of the communist state is the ruthless subordination of the interests and objectives of all social institutions to those of the Communist Party. Ironically, therefore, in a system that has so many characteristics of the authoritarian garrison state, the instruments of violence play a relatively minor role, for they must submit to the bureaucratic elite in the Party hierarchy, whose avowed aim is the integration of all social institutions into a homogeneous, monolithic whole. However, the military's institutional interests, objectives, and values, and the range of external factors and circumstances supporting them, tend to favor its resistance to the total subordination

From Roman Kolkowicz, The Soviet Military and the Communist Party (Princeton, N. J., 1967), pp. 103–05, by permission of Princeton University Press.

desired by the Party elite. In the following, we shall examine more closely this essential incompatibility between the Party's ideal model of the fully integrated military establishment, and the military's continuous efforts to free itself from the subordinate role that this demands and from the oppressive controls and intrusions of the Party. Although the relations between Party and military are analyzed here from the point of view of their antagonisms, the two protagonists do, of course, have a large number of mutually complementary objectives and common interests. Yet, despite these strong ties, the relationship between the two most powerful institutions in the Soviet state is often strained and at times hostile, and it occasionally borders on the critical.

The present chapter examines the tensions and conflicts that have afflicted the relations between the military and the Party (viewed here as distinct institutional entities) during the post-Stalin period, particularly those conflicts arising from the military's efforts to assert its claim to professional autonomy and the Party's constant attempts to deprive the military of the full exercise of that prerogative. The two main issues under analysis are (1) the Party's efforts to impose very rigid political controls at all levels of the military hierarchy and the military's strong resistance to such pressures, and (2) the Party's usurpation of the function of military planner and strategic innovator and the military's opposition to measures which it regards as injurious not only to its own institutional interests but also to the defensive capabilities of the country.

The conflicts described in this chapter are central to our understanding of the relation between Party and military, since they go back to deeply rooted sources of mistrust and antagonism. In seeking to politicize and control the officer corps, the Party is revealing its fears of the elitism that it believes will develop among a group of professionals who possess vast means of violence. It knows, moreover, that an officer corps allowed to become a closed institution could grow into a dangerous rival for power in the state. In an effort to break down the protective walls that the military seeks to erect, the Party divides and subdivides authority horizontally, vertically, and diagonally, hoping thereby to prevent the coalescence of power and authority at focal points; and it gathers the commanders together in collective bodies

in which they are open to scrutiny and criticism.

While controls and political indoctrination serve to prevent disloyalty in the military and to eliminate conditions that lead to elitism, the Party has still other concerns. Since the death of Stalin, and with the growing complexity of warfare, the military has sought to obtain a larger role in high-level planning and the formulation of strategic doctrine and military policy. The Party leadership, on the other hand, trying to prevent the military from gaining greater professional autonomy, has made major military decisions and launched innovations against overwhelming military opposition. While the military leaders' overt concern is about the possible harm to the defensive capabilities of the nation that may come of military policies created by civilians, their implicit fears center on the damage to the military's institutional interests that is inherent in the usurpation of their prerogatives by civilian amateurs. The Party elite and its spokesmen, on the other hand, regard military policy and the evolution of a strategic doctrine as the exclusive domain of the political decision-makers.

The military's objection to excessive political controls and its opposition to the Party's invasion of the strategic-doctrinal domain are aspects of the central struggle for influence between the two institutions. At stake in this larger conflict are the military's professional autonomy and the Party's political hegemony. Although, objectively speaking, these are not mutually exclusive ends, the Party apparently sees them as such; as in zero-sum games, where any advantage of one adversary is at the expense of the other adversary, so the Party elite regards any increment in the military's prerogatives and authority as its own loss and therefore as a challenge. . . .

Professionalism and technocratic-managerial skills became the instruments for military autonomy from party domination and for the dialogue on professional autonomy.

The technological-managerial revolution, indeed, bore its fruits; the Red Army, after Stalin's death, Khrushchev's reform, and its new adopted weltpolitik, became a junior but most significant partner of the party.

The leading contemporary analyst of the Soviet military and Soviet military history in the West is Professor John Erickson of the University of Edinburgh. Erickson writes on the creation of the new Soviet army.

JOHN ERICKSON

The Reshaping of the Soviet Military Command 1965–1970

It was 'not by accident', to use a familiar Bolshevik phrase, that the effort to 'rejuvenate' and to reorganise the Soviet military command entered a new phase once Khrushchev was removed from the scene in October 1964. For a number of reasons, not least Khrushchev's own waywardness with the officer corps, the problem was becoming increasingly urgent and by the end of 1965 a general survey of the efficiency of all Soviet officers (up to the ranks of general and admiral) was completed, with every *fourth* officer recommended for promotion by the

From *John Erickson*, The Soviet High Command, 1918–1941 *(London, 1962), pp. 13–16, by permission of Macmillan, London and Basingstoke.*

relevant reviewing boards. Prosaic and bureaucratic though this may sound, the result was far from some routine change and its implications raise questions of major importance for the future of the entire Soviet military establishment. It is the purpose of this section to examine some of these implications—the process of 'rejuvenation' and restructuring in the officer corps as a whole, personnel changes in the operational commands, the General Staff, arms and services, the connection between particular appointments and shifts in operational concepts—while at the same time approaching the more fundamental question of who 'runs' the Soviet armed forces, or, to put it another way, which are the 'key' appointments, to whom and in what manner are they distributed, and finally in what sense can 'military influence' on Soviet policies be understood? If nothing else, such a line of enquiry can be used to guard against glib insertions about 'the Marshals', 'policy', the military 'role' and a military 'take-over'. In short, it is a particular manner of looking at the Soviet military system and an attempt to evaluate it on its own terms. The Soviet officer corps is demonstrably a subject in itself, requiring its own institutional and sociological explanation, but there is little point in delineating the scope and outcome of the 'debate' on military policy without some subsequent attempt to prescribe the position and influence of the men entrusted to implement these decisions.

Khrushchev had tackled both the 'rejuvenation' and restructuring of the Soviet command in his own way and after his own particular requirements. His 'demobilisation' of the elderly and unacceptable among Soviet officers in 1958–60 forced out 250,000 officers and his 'planned promotions' brought in 454 new generals in 1960. The new strategic missile command imposed a radical alteration on the structure of the Soviet forces, bringing engineer officers into greater prominence and contributing to the steady diversification of skills within the Soviet officer corps. Indeed, Khrushchev regarded the consolidation of a 'new' officer corps as a deliberate form of social engineering, designed among other things to promote political compliance and military utility in one swoop. The result (as with so many other of Khrushchev's schemes) was latterly

both demoralisation and disorganisation; the pressure on the Soviet military cadres was very uneven and at the lower levels the speed of the turnover in men was dizzying, causing Marshal Malinovskii to complain at this cult of the 'new' when 'not even regimental commanders are assured of remaining in their positions', while at the higher levels the effect operated in reverse, inducing an unyielding conservatism. In short, the 'new men' did not match the 'new look' in the organisation of Soviet strategic forces. The 'old guard' gave ground only slowly and reacted with predictable hostility to the massive military redundancies which made such inroads on the privileged and protected social position of the military in Soviet society.

Nor did the infusion of engineers and technicians into the Soviet armed forces, in particular into the élite arms of the strategic missile forces, the air defence command and the submarine branch of the navy, prove to be a totally unmixed blessing. These soldier-technicians with their special skills and higher education represented at once a challenge to the dominance of the 'traditional' officers and a break with the accepted image of the military commander; it was, therefore, but a short step to question the nature of 'command' in modern war and thus to jeopardise the authority of the commander, who in an age of computers and nuclear weapons could no longer rely upon the simple military values of courage and 'selfless dedication'— even intuition was no substitute for technical skill and competence. On the other hand, the traditionalists were not slow to mount their own counter-attack against the encroachments of the technocrats; they pointed out that undue stress on 'theoretical training' could simply turn officers into *shkolasty*—bookworms—and that the technocrats showed a marked indifference to the political educational work conducted in the Soviet armed forces, insisting that their job was confined to 'the technological element' and ended with ensuring 'combat readiness'. As for the argument that the older and less competent barred the way to the young and the highly educated, this was also denied with some vehemence: on the contrary, there seemed to be a cult of youth and an excessive cultivation of educational qualification, which accounted for that rapid turnover about which Malinovskii complained in no uncertain terms. This initial eruption within the officer corps gradually subsided, though the flow of technical officers has not ceased as modernisation continues; if anything, the technocrat has tempered his criticism of the 'traditionalist' and has also come to want recognition as a 'commander' (a practical demonstration that an 'engineering philosophy' alone will not suffice to satisfy the needs of the armed forces). The officer-technocrat has similarly confined his pressure upon his traditionalist fellows to promoting modern techniques and technology, without seeking to re-interpret the *whole* system in terms of this self-same technology.

It will be seen at once that the structural and the actuarial aspects of the Soviet military command are closely connected. Of all the privileges enjoyed by the Soviet military, perhaps none was greater than that of simply serving on in the armed forces, thus continuing those social and economic benefits which were of such account in a tightly constricted society; behind much of the hostility on the part of the traditionalists towards the technocrats lay the very real fear that they were becoming or might speedily become redundant, misgivings only deepened by Khrushchev's 'one-sidedness' which stressed the role of the strategic arms at the expense of the conventional forces. The debate over 'doctrines', therefore, must also be viewed in the light of these attitudes and commitments. Yet this vested interest worked both ways, producing pressures at the upper and lower levels of the command. Military conservatism, the immobilism of 1948–52 and even Khrushchev's own personnel policy had all combined to give the Soviet officer corps a singular profile by the mid-60s: in 1945 this was the youngest officer corps in the world (particularly in its leading echelons), while in 1965 it had become indubitably the oldest. The Marshals and senior commanders in 1945 fell predominantly within the 41–48 age-bracket; in 1965 the senior officers represented on the 'Supreme Military Council' (composed of *Politburo* members, together with senior officers down to Military District/Fleet command level and including the Military Council members of such echelons) were almost to a man aged over 60, an 'old boy net' in the literal sense.

Though 'rejuvenation' might be taken to mean simply lowering the average collective age of the command, the problem is considerably more complex than mere actuarial adjustment. In the first place, there is the problem of numbers as well as of categories. This can be approached by taking the figure for Party membership in the armed forces as an approximate for officer strength (Party membership or candidate membership and officer status being virtually synonymous): this would give a figure of some 20 per cent for officer strength out of a total manpower strength in the region of $3\frac{1}{4}$ million men (not including the para-military formations). Such an assumption to a $1:5$ ratio does not run counter to the figures given by Khrushchev in 1960 about Soviet demobilisations, when 250,000 of the 1.2 million men released were identified as officers. There is, of course, the special problem of the configuration of the Soviet officer, the inflation of his role and functions—the absence of a large civilian component within the Soviet military establishment, the additives of the 'political officers', the performance of duties assigned in western armies to NCOs, all of which bears out this enlargement of the officer ratio. . . .

One of the more significant of the post-Khrushchev innovations has been the appointment of senior officers— Ogarkov, Alekseyev—to managerial and weapons programme co-ordination posts, even though such activity has not been given an institutional framework: it is this, among other things, which gives the present General Staff its singular prominence and importance, thus suffusing the influence of the technologists and engineers on an even wider scale and at the highest levels. In sum, an inspection of command changes provides some safeguard against sweeping conclusions drawn only from reviewing the abstractions of 'doctrinal debate' or simple contents analysis of Soviet pronouncements. Essentially the Soviet military system has eschewed the method of making either frequent or substantial institutional changes. It is not, therefore, institutional change but shifts in personnel—'key' officers who redefine the role and function of their positions—which must of necessity command close attention in order to make better sense of what is loosely called 'policy'. . . .

PART II

The Praetorian Army and the Praetorian State

THE study of the military in politics should not be restricted to an examination of the relationship between civil authority and the military as an institution or an elite group. Since World War II, the substantial number of governments controlled by military elites has caused attention to be focused on the role of the army in politics and government. The nations in Latin America, the Middle East, Africa, and Asia that have experienced a *perpetuum mobile* of coups, military governments, counter coups, civilian regimes, and further coups are usually referred to under the rubric of "praetorian states."

PRAETORIANISM IN HISTORICAL PERSPECTIVE

Praetorianism is a word frequently used to characterize a situation where the military class of a given society exercises independent political power within it by virtue of an actual or threatened use of military force. Like so many of the terms current among political scientists, this word represents a generalization from the ever suggestive field of classical history. The concept of praetorianism was developed with reference to the history of the praetorian guards of ancient Rome. The declining days of Rome saw a progressive assumption of political power by the soldiery. By the third century the imperial office had become a prize for the contending ambitions of the legions, which made and unmade emperors in order to secure special donatives and privileges for themselves. Although all the legions participated with varying fortunes in the profitable struggle for political power, the praetorian guards became notorious as the most strikingly successful. Established from the time of Augustus as the sole military force within the city of Rome, their proximity to the capital frequently enabled them to play a dominating role in imperial politics. Their most celebrated exploit was the murder of Pertinax and the sale of the empire at public auction to Didius Julianus. This and other striking acts of military usurpation have led posterity to look upon them as the typical representatives of their age, although they were only the most consistently successful of many contemporary military groups which were competing for political power.*

*Frederick Watkins in *Encyclopedia of the Social Sciences*, s.v. "praetorianism."

The influence of the Roman Praetorian Guard was based on three factors: the Guard's monopoly on local military power, the absence of definitive rules of succession, and the prestige of the Roman Senate. In other words, though there was no hard and fast rule as to how the *princeps* was to be chosen, the Senate's decree made him a legitimate ruler. The provincial armies would accept that decision. As the sole resident military force, the Praetorian Guards were able to impose their candidate upon the Senate. They were thus able to manipulate a widely subscribed *concept of legitimacy* and to attain a degree of political influence and power far beyond their actual numerical and military resources. When, however, the provincial armies stumbled upon the secret that emperors need not be made in Rome, the legitimizing powers of the Senate disappeared, and with them the strength of the Praetorians.

Here is the link between historical and modern praetorianism. A modern praetorian state is one in which the military tends to intervene and *potentially* could dominate the political system. The political processes of this state *favor* the development of the military as the core group and the growth of its expectations as a ruling class; its political leadership (as distinguished from bureaucratic, administrative, and managerial leadership) is chiefly recruited from the military, or from groups sympathetic, or at least not antagonistic, to the military. Constitutional changes are effected and sustained by the military, and the army frequently intervenes in the government. In a praetorian state, therefore, the military plays a dominant role in political structures and institutions.*

Praetorianism is not, however, a phenomenon that appeared in the Roman Empire and then vanished, not to reappear again until the second half of the twentieth century. Praetorianism has been identified in advanced agricultural societies such as the Ottoman Empire and in the colonial empires built by the major European powers in the nineteenth century.

The most primitive types of traditional authority are the cases where a personal administrative staff of the chief is absent. These are "gerontocracy" and "patriarchalism."

With the development of a purely personal administrative staff, especially a military force under the control of the chief, traditional authority tends to develop into "patrimonialism." Where absolute authority is maximized, it may be called "Sultanism."

Where governing powers are appropriated by members of an independent group, the costs of administration are met from the incumbent's own means, which are not distinguishable from his personal property. Persons exercising mili-

*Amos Perlmutter, "The Praetorian State and the Praetorian Army," *Comparative Politics* (April 1969): 383.

tary command or members of this type of army provide their own equipment and may even recruit units of the army on their own responsibility.

In patrimonial systems generally . . . all governmental authority and the corresponding economic rights tend to be treated as privately appropriated economic advantages.

. . . Furthermore, the appropriation of judicial and military powers tends to be treated as a legal basis for a privileged class position of those appropriating them, as compared to the appropriation of purely economic advantages having to do with the income from domains, from taxes, or other sources.*

Patrimonial power was particularly susceptible to military domination in those bureaucratic empires with large mercenary armies. In the Ottoman Empire the ruling institution became identical with the army during and after the reign of Suleiman the Magnificent in the sixteenth century; and the Janissaries, the praetorian guard of the empire, remained the chief instrument of the sultan until 1827.

Inasmuch as Ottoman armies were massive organizations constantly refurbished by new recruits from less vigorous Moslem lands, the necessary exhaustive assessment of military merit after each campaign could not be made without the early development of a large, well-trained, and wholly devoted administrative staff. And since the Koran limited the sultan's disciplinary powers over free-born Moslems but gave him almost unlimited authority over slaves, the government of Turkey in a short time was composed almost entirely of slaves.

By virtue of these extraordinary circumstances, the Turks were able to create one of the most remarkable, efficient, and pliant ruling classes ever known. The sultan had a free hand to select, educate, promote and punish his human tools according to their competence and loyalty. He could begin training them at an early age, shutting them off from all outside influences, until they were deemed fit to assume responsibilities. . . .

War and government were the central concern of the vast slave corps, and each slave was normally involved in both activities.

On the military side, this (slave) institution carried on war abroad, repressed revolt at home, kept itself in power, and preserved sufficient order in the empire to allow a busy and varied economic and social activity. . . . The high official of the government held high command in war. The generals of the army had extensive administrative duties. . . . War carried practically all the whole government into the field.†

*Max Weber, *The Theory of Social and Economic Organization* (New York: The Free Press, 1944), pp. 346–53.

†David C. Rapaport, "A Comparative Theory of Military and Political Types," in Samuel P. Huntington, ed., *Changing Patterns of Military Politics* (New York: The Free Press, 1962), p. 83.

Another example of the symbiotic relationship between military and bureaucratic elites in controlling governments was seen in imperial territories.

In military terms, the self-image of civilization is transformed into the policy role of aggrandizement. . . . The details of government do not, however, fall within the province of the imperial military elite. Members of this group, while they may consider themselves equal to the task of formulating the broad outlines of social policy, are not numerous enough to immerse themselves in the particulars of its execution. The near total absorption in and dedication to military life which an external dominant organization demands of its leaders renders an autonomous administrative apparatus necessary.

An external dominant organization must, therefore, create an auxiliary class, a stratum of administrators and middle-men, between itself and the conquered. These can be either lower caste members of the military organization's home society, local collaborators, or migrant adventurers; the sole requirement being non-membership in the military elite. The three classes created represent three worlds, authority at the top, privilege in the middle and subservience below.*

The imperial officer was expected to be a model for his colonial subordinate, whose capacity for leadership might win him the reward of political domination. The model of the imperial officer, slavishly emulated by his subordinates, had considerable influence on modern Arab and African praetorians.

MODERN PRAETORIANISM

In developing polities the military functions as it did in the patrimonial states, serving as a center for political turmoil, political ambition, and threats to legitimate authority.

The most conspicuous modern praetorians were found in nineteenth-century Latin America. Spanish praetorianism was the handiwork of disgruntled civilians and power-seeking, politically deprived politicians, all groping to dominate central political power. In seeking military support, however, they threatened the constitutional and political practices to which they as civilians were dedicated and on whose behalf they were recruiting the military. Furthermore, when army officers entered politics, they adopted civilian characteristics and expectations, and gradually lost their hold over the army.

In the twentieth century most of the new states find themselves in the

*M. D. Feld, "A Typology of Military Organization," *Public Policy* (1958).

early and middle stages of modernization and political mobilization. These unsettled social and political conditions are conducive to, or representative of, praetorianism.

SOCIAL CONDITIONS CONTRIBUTING TO PRAETORIANISM

Underdeveloped societies as a whole lack unifying orientations, and their social classes tend to be fragmented and incapable of mounting unified action even for the narrower benefits of a particular sector. These divisions exist in advanced societies, but they are especially acute in underdeveloped countries where social and economic change have been rapid and many stages of development have occurred simultaneously. In addition to the natural polarization between the wealthy few and the many poor in such countries, there are marked gradations and variations within all three social layers—bottom, middle, and top—which tend to conflict.

In a state with low social cohesion, personal desires and group aims frequently diverge; the formal structure of the state is not buttressed by an informal one; institutions do not develop readily or operate effectively; social control is ineffective; and channels of communication are few. These conditions indicate the lack of meaningful universal symbols that can bind the society together. The syndrome of disintegration of which these conditions are a party is typical in a state in which the traditional patterns of social cohesion have broken down and have not yet been replaced by new ones.*

In praetorian societies social groups and social institutions are highly politicized. Samuel P. Huntington has described this situation in underdeveloped societies:

In such societies, politics lacks autonomy, complexity, coherence, and adaptability. All sorts of social forces and groups become directly engaged in general politics.
    Studies of the military in modernizing countries naturally focus on its active political role which distinguishes it from the military in more advanced societies. Studies of labor unions highlight "political unionism" as the distinguishing feature of labor movements in modernizing societies. Studies of universities in modernizing countries stress the active political involvement of faculty and students. Studies of religious organizations stress the extent to which the separation of church and state remains a distant goal. . . . Clearly, such involvement

*Amos Perlmutter, "The Praetorian State and the Praetorian Army," *Comparative Politics* (April 1969): 385.

is not peculiar to the military or to any other social group, but rather is pervasive throughout the society.

In a praetorian system social forces confront each other nakedly; no political institutions, no corps of professional political leaders are recognized or accepted as the legitimate intermediaries to moderate group conflict. Equally important, no agreement exists among the groups as to the legitimate and authoritative methods for resolving conflicts.

In a praetorian society, however, not only are the actors varied, but so are the methods used to decide upon office and policy. Each group employs means which reflect its peculiar nature and capabilities. The wealthy bribe; students riot; workers strike; mobs demonstrate; and the military coup. The techniques of military intervention are simply more dramatic and effective than the others because, as Hobbes put it, "When nothing else is turned up, clubs are trumps."

In a praetorian society authority over the system as a whole is transitory, and the weakness of political institutions means that authority and office are easily acquired and easily lost. Consequently, no incentive exists for a leader or group to make significant concessions in the search for authority.

The changes which individuals make are thus imposed by the transfer of allegiance from one social group to another, rather than by a broadening of loyalty from a limited social group to a political institution embodying a multiplicity of interests.*

The existence of fratricidal social classes, coupled with an unconsolidated middle class, is frequently considered a precondition for praetorianism.

The top group is usually divided between traditionalists and modernists. The latter includes landowners who have adopted modern technology. The top-layer division between traditionalists and modernists is paralleled by a bottom-layer division. For example, large foreign-owned industrial enterprises may employ an urban worker elite. Because of the benefits this elite receives from the system, it is little inclined to suffer the deprivations that political action designed to benefit its less privileged brethren may entail. Yet, it is precisely these elite workers, concentrated in large enterprises, rather than the hundreds of thousands of domestics, shopkeepers' apprentices, and others, who technically could be "organized.". . .

The absence of a strong, cohesive, and articulate middle class is another condition for the establishment of a praetorian government. This absence is manifested in the polarization of the class structure—the gap between the few rich and the many poor.

*Samuel P. Huntington, *Political Order in Changing Societies* (New Haven: Yale University Press, 1968), pp. 194–97.

Cohesiveness is necessary for the development of political and ideological articulateness. Such articulateness, when combined with socioeconomic power, constitutes the foundation for the political influence of any class. A struggle for power
among the different strata of the middle class—the class which historically has
acted as the stabilizer of civilian government during modernization—creates
conditions beneficial to praetorianism.

The middle classes in most praetorian states are small, weak, ineffective, divided
and politically impotent.*

POLITICAL CONDITIONS CONTRIBUTING TO PRAETORIANISM

Weak and ineffective political parties and frequent civilian intervention in
the military contribute to praetorianism. Weak parties are a particularly
important sign of a praetorian state. Strong parties have often been the
most successful agents of comprehensive modernization and industrialization and of the resulting elimination of conditions that may result in praetorianism.

Military intervention into civilian affairs is usually not precipitated by military
groups. In most cases, civilians turn to the military for political support when
civilian political structures and institutions fail, when factionalism develops, and
when constitutional means for the conduct of political action are lacking. The
civilians, therefore, begin to indoctrinate the military with their political ideologies.†

THE PRAETORIAN ARMY

Political activity is contrary to the professional ethics and standards of the
modern military, and the code of the professional army dictates that promotions be determined by ability, expertise, and education. When army
affairs have become intertwined with politics, appointments and promotions are made on the basis of the political affiliations of the officer rather
than on his professional qualifications. In order to advance in the military
hierarchy, an officer is obliged to establish political alliances with civilian
superiors.

An army becomes praetorian when a small group of officers, a few key
activists, succeed in propelling the military into politics. The group is
never composed of more than five percent of the total officer corps.

*Perlmutter, "The Praetorian State and the Praetorian Army," pp. 386–87.
†Ibid., pp. 390–91.

Once in power, praetorian armies may be conceived of as being either of the arbitrator type or the ruler type.

The former tends to be more professionally oriented (with a greater emphasis on expertise) and has no independent political organization and little interest in manufacturing a political ideology. The latter has an independent political organization (an instrument for maintaining order) and, in most cases, a fairly coherent and elaborate political ideology.

The arbitrator-type army imposes a time limit on army rule and arranges to hand the government over to an "acceptable" civilian regime. The arbitrator-type army does not necessarily relinquish its political influence when it returns to the barracks; in fact, in many cases, it acts as guardian of civilian authority and political stability. Such is the essence of the Kemalist legacy in Turkey: the army serves as the guardian of the constitution.

An arbitrator army may eventually become a ruler army, if the conditions for the return of a civilian regime are not fulfilled. It is even possible for a ruler army to eventually turn the reins of power over to a civilian regime, if the conditions for the return of civilian rule are fulfilled. Although the arbitrator army is committed to a time limit, the ruler army is not. The arbitrator army expects an eventual return to the barracks; the ruler army makes no such provisions and, in most cases, does not even consider it.

The arbitrator-type tends to preserve military expertise; it is conservative and, on the whole, tends to maximize civilian power. The ruler-type, although it does not abandon expertise, sometimes subordinates it to political considerations, and may even support an already existing political ideology. It sacrifices professionalism to political expediency. In general, the ruler-type prefers to maximize an army ruler. It is imperative that he rule with the help of the army, and always at the expense of civilian rule and politicians.*

The arbitrator type of praetorian army is marked by eight distinguishing characteristics:

Acceptance of existing social order. In an underdeveloped country, acceptance of the existing order often implies antirevolutionary ideology. Thus, the arbitrator-type army may be the instrument of conservative and anti-liberal forces.

Willingness to return to the barracks after civilian disputes are settled. The officers of the arbitrator-type army are civilian-oriented. Even where the civilian groups are not organized enough to set up a government, and where officers occupy positions in the government, the officers obey the instructions of

*Ibid., pp. 392–93.

civilian political groups. They do not inject their own viewpoint. They desire to return to normality, which means that they accept the status quo.

No independent political organization and no attempt to maximize army rule.

Time limit for the rule of the army until an alternative and "acceptable" regime is established. The arbitrator-type army will return to the barracks if it is assured that corruption and other evils of the former regime have been eliminated. This type views prolonged army rule as detrimental to the professional integrity of the army. The arbitrator army encourages political groups which it considers capable of establishing order, preserving stability, and guaranteeing that the new government will not return to the practice of the old.

Concern with professionalism. In an arbitrator-type army, the officer corps, or important sectors of it, is strongly opposed to political involvement because involvement may destroy the professional norms of the military institution. Professional norms are valued because they provide security and predictability for the officers' career. The arbitrator type tends to defend the existing regime, lest its professional integrity be violated.

Tendency to operate from behind the scenes as a pressure group. Because of its fear of open involvement in politics, the arbitrator-type army tends to influence civilian governments to respond to popular demands, thereby making it unnecessary for the military to intervene openly. However, the refusal by the military to take open responsibility for its actors may increase instability.

Low level of national consciousness.

Fear of civilian retribution. The presence of organized civilian groups may produce fears in the military concerning the actions that civilian politicians might later take—such as the dismissal of officers, demotions, unprestigious appointments and assignments.

On the other hand, the ruler type of praetorian army has the following characteristics:

The officer corps rejects the existing order and challenges its legitimacy. The ruler type of praetorian army increasingly tends to abandon or convert existing institutions, ideologies, and procedures in favor of the newer institutions for modernization, industrialization, and political mobilization that are proposed by theories of rapid growth.

No confidence in civilian rule and no expectation of returning to the barracks. This attitude may be a consequence of the development by an important sector of the officer corps of an independent political orientation opposed to the ruling civilian groups. Alternatively, civilian disorganization may have reached the point where progressive elements are unable to put their programs into effect. Ruler-type officers distrust politicians to the extent that they themselves feel it necessary to occupy formal positions in the governmental structure.

Political organization and tendency to legitimize and maximize army rule. Taking advantage of the lack of political and social cohesion, the ruler-type army establishes an independent organization and strengthens its rule in order to manipulate unruly, disorganized forces. In order to achieve stability, it must legitimize itself by creating its own political party (or some type of corporate group) and an ideology to support its political organization.

Conviction that army rule is the only alternative to political disorder.

The politicization of professionalism. Where the army has—or dominates—an independent political organization, however minimal, the ruler type is common.

When the ruler-type army is committed to political action, it is forced to break with traditional concepts of the professional soldier. Political considerations take precedence over internal organization and career security. Politicization will, to some extent, destroy professional status and rank.

Operation in the open. The ruler-type army operates in the open because it wants to use the symbols attached to the military institutions to gain support for its programs and activities.

High level of national consciousness. In a praetorian country, the commitment to nationalism is more intense in the ruler-type army than in any other section of the population. Ideologically, nationalism is the most popular and most successful common denominator of praetorianism. In contrast to the arbitrator type, whose level of ideological commitment is lower, praetorians at one time or another have supported the whole spectrum of radical political ideologies.

Little fear of civilian retribution. By the time ruler-type praetorianism develops, the army tends to exercise so much power that it does not need to fear civilians.

A praetorian government is a type of military stewardship served on behalf of absentee executive and civilian political groups—a condition brought on more by the ineffectiveness of civilian political organization than by the political aptitude of the military interventionists. But professional military methods often prove to be poor substitutes for political skills. After entering the fragmented political arena, politically minded officers have frequently found it easier to deliver themselves of patriotic slogans and ideological pronunciamentos than to govern. Praetorianism is still government from turrets.

LATIN AMERICAN PRAETORIANISM

Civil-military relations in Latin America are characterized by (1) the highly developed and institutionalized politicization of the military organization; (2) the fulfillment of corporate ambition; and (3) the authoritarian nature of the military regimes.

The politics of oligarchy is at the heart of corporate praetorianism in Latin America. Regimes are oriented toward instituting autocratic oligarchic coalitional or oligarchic corporate arrangements.

Political mobilization procedures in Latin American praetorian systems are *relatively* institutionalized structures; the corporate coalition of military, church, labor unions, and the industrialists.

The postrevolutionary era, the era of the notorious *caudillos*, has been interpreted in several different manners.

Corporate praetorianism, Latin American style, is characterized by a military-civilian fusionist rule. Governmental authority, although founded in the military and politically unchecked, is a coalition of military and civilian governing with little or no external political control. The nature of the military tyranny is that the supreme ruler is exclusively a military officer. In the case of a military oligarchy, the chief executive is either a former military, now a civilian, or a civilian whose support comes exclusively from the military oligarchy.

No military oligarchy can survive politically without the support of the military establishment. A corporate military regime is almost exclusively composed of military, bureaucrats, managers, and technocrats, who elicit restrictive political support and restricted political mobilization. The authoritarian and corporate military executive could be composed of a majority of either military or civilians; the head of the executive does not necessarily come from the military, or, for that matter, possess military skills. However, the major source of support, as is the case with all military praetorianism, must come from the establishment. In the case of a military tyranny, electoral exercises are not even contemplated. On the other hand, military oligarchies spend considerable effort to create a facade of electoral support.

The corporate military regime seeks external (to the military) political support and is sincere in the exercise of restrictive elections, even if the choice is limited to the military supportive executive. However, this type of regime might tolerate other political institutions and structures on the national level (including parliaments, parties, and pressure groups) that are not necessarily oriented toward military rule and control. This type tolerates, on the whole, local government and regional authorities that are not directly dominated by or oriented toward the military.

Analyzing the military regime in Brazil in 1975, Juan Linz described military authoritarianism in the following manner: "Power basically remained with the armed forces, except for economic policy making, which is shared between the military, selected technocrats, and, to a lesser extent, businessmen. Institutions outside the armed forces have been created and disregarded constantly, leaving the military with ultimate power."

The inculcation of professional values into the Latin American military was fostered by Prussian, French, Italian, and British officers, who trained the military in the best traditions of European professionalism. While the Arab and the African military rejected the regimes of independence, the Latin American military, at the beginning of the nineteenth century, but especially during the rise of professionalism, became the clients *par excellence* of the state. The African and particularly the Arab military rejected the regimes, parties, procedures, and political structures of the regime of independence, and, instead, established surrogate executives of their own—for the purpose of achieving military autonomy and the freedom to take independent political actions.

In Latin America, the military, between 1890 and 1930, did not reject the state or the regimes. However, between 1930 and 1960 the Latin military overthrew those regimes whose political effectiveness was questionable. The Latin American army in that era supported presidential (executive) power. In retrospect, this period seems to represent the military's first phase of arbitrator praetorianism.

Since the 1960s, the era of mass praetorianism, the ruler type has emerged in Brazil, Argentina, Peru, and Chile. Now the military created executive structures for two purposes: for asserting their autonomy and for *directing* the modernization revolution through military cabinets.

Alfred Stepan sees a demarcation between the old and new professionalism in Latin America. Old professionalism, or the emphasis on external defense and the military as an instrument of foreign policy, was abandoned in favor of new professionalism. The new concern was with internal security and national development, which supplanted the concern with national security affairs.

The second generation in the Latin American military internalized the nationalist weltanschauung; their corporate ideology is one of the most sophisticated among modern militaries anywhere. The positive contribution of the Arab military was the radicalization of Arab nationalism, while the contributions of the Latin American military to the modern Latin American state are organization, ideology, and managerialism. The military in Latin America played, and still plays, a much greater and more durable role than the one in the Arab-African cases, even if in all three regions the military is imbued with praetorian interventionist orientations. However, the type of corporatist ideology that is espoused and disseminated by Latin American military elites is certainly different from those espoused by praetorians in different continents and in distant geographical areas.

The *caudillo* system was a traditional, patrimonial political system, lacking the elements of continuity, political sustenance, and hierarchical social organization. It perpetuated the Spanish imperial legacy of patron-client relationships and undermined the political authority of the center, the Republican power, which had replaced the old patrimonial state. Caudillo-guerrilla leaders exercised considerable local control and allied themselves with either royalists or republicans, as opportunity demanded. The caudillos, acting as "presidents" and "national leaders," worked against the institution of the modern state, being unable to renounce personalism, patrimonialism, and tradition for corporatism, rationality, and modernity. They particularly decimated military corporate professionalism by inflating ranks and commissions on the basis of personality and patrimonial relationships rather than on the basis of expertise and rationality. Thus, throughout the nineteenth century, the *libertadores* not only freed the Latin Americans from Spanish rule, but also "liberated" the Spanish military tradition in Latin America from its corporate orientation, replacing it with *mestizo* personalism and greed.

The caudillos went even further in destroying the municipal corporations and the Spanish *fuero* system. In Spain, the military fuero (law or jurisdiction), known as *fuero de guerra*, defined the military as an autonomous and privileged group. Before the revolution, this sort of organization had existed in New Spain, too; but it was decimated by the libertadores and caudillos. The fuero military system, a legacy left to the army by the viceroyal system, was abused by its possessors in promoting civil-military disputes and extending military privileges, and it "became a powerful element in promoting praetorian government in Mexico."

Eric Wolf and Edward Hansen interpret caudillos from a structural anthropological point of view. They see the caudillo system as marked by three characteristics: (1) the emergence of armed patron-client sets; (2) the failure of leaders to guarantee their tenure or to develop institutionalized means of succession; and (3) the use of violence in political competition. The caudillo system, they argue, depends upon a particular balance between the Spanish gentry, the Spanish-Indian unprivileged, and foreign interests. But by the 1870s, the caudillo system was giving way to more centralized dictatorship.

ERIC R. WOLF AND EDWARD C. HANSEN

Caudillo Politics: A Structural Analysis

The Latin-American Wars of Independence realized the long-standing hope of the *criollo**** gentry to rid themselves of Spanish limitations on their economic and political activities. From the beginning of the New World colonies, the Spanish rulers had labored diligently to check the aspirations of the colonial gentry by limiting their access to both land and status. Grants of *encomienda* had yielded up to the colonists use rights to Indian labor and produce, but not the ownership of land. At the same time, the Crown had curtailed the ability of *criollos* to obtain titles of nobility. These limitations had been supported by the prowess of Spanish arms, effective perhaps even more in keeping potential competitors at bay in Europe than in exercising viable military control in the New World. The failure of this ultimate means of control during the Napoleonic wars finally called into question also continued Spanish dominance over the American colonies.

In spite of the decline of Spanish power, however, the New World planter class proved too weak numerically and too lacking in cohesion to oust the Peninsular forces by its own unaided efforts. To gain their own independence they were therefore forced into political alliances with the numerically strong and highly mobile—yet at the same time economically, socially and politically disprivileged—social strata of the population which are designated collectively as *mestizos****. Not without trepidation, *criollo* leaders armed elements derived from these propertyless strata and sent them to do battle against the Spaniards. . . . Success in maintaining the continuing loyalties of these elements depended largely upon the ability of leaders in building personal ties of loyalty with their following and in leading them in ventures of successful pillage.

The emerging pattern had colonial prototypes. Landowners had long maintained armed retainers on their own estates. The creation of a colonial army had underwritten the creation of such localized militia. In Mexico, for instance, "the viceroy and the military authorities found it convenient that a militia be at one and the same time the landlord of the men who served under his command". . . . The Spanish government had thus contributed paradoxically to the diminution of its own power and to the formation of many local power centers. Yet the additional step of granting independent armament both to retainers and to other potential military elements in the population entailed further risks. Although the alliance of *criollos* and *mestizos* was

From Eric R. Wolf and Edward C. Hansen, "Caudillo Politics: A Structural Analysis," Comparative Studies in Society and History *9, no. 2 (1969): 168–71, 177–79, by permission of the authors.*

**Literally translated, *criollo* means a person of Spanish ancestry born in the New World.

**Literally translated, *mestizo* means a person of mixed Spanish and Indian ancestry.

instrumental in winning the Wars of Independence, granting arms to the *mestizo* elements freed these to create their own armed bands. The *mestizos* in turn were thus enabled to compete with the *criollos* for available wealth. The case of Venezuela, while unique in its extreme manifestations, nevertheless demonstrates this new and continent-wide ability of the *mestizos* to act on their own behalf. There the royalists were originally victorious by granting the *llanero* plainsmen, formerly *criollo* retainers, pillage rights against their own masters. Having eliminated their own masters, the *llaneros* then turned upon the royalists and massacred them in an effort to obtain additional loot. . . . In granting independent armament to the *mestizos*, therefore, the *criollo* gentry also sacrificed any chance it might have had to establish a monopoly of power.

The beneficiaries of this distribution of weaponry were the leaders on horseback, the *caudillos*,* the resultant political system, *caudillaje*. It came to be marked by four salient characteristics: (1) the repeated emergence of armed patron-client sets, cemented by personal ties of dominance and submission, and by a common desire to obtain wealth by force of arms; (2) the lack of institutionalized means for succession to offices; (3) the use of violence in political competition; and (4) the repeated failures of incumbent leaders to guarantee their tenures as chieftains. This paper is concerned with an analysis of this political sys-

tem, and with a search for its causes and consequences. It also wishes to suggest that this is best accomplished by an understanding of the system in Latin American terms, rather than in terms of concepts derived from events in Europe. The broad diffusion of military power among wide strata of the population differentiates the Latin American experience from what happened in Europe; *caudillaje*, as Richard M. Morse has aptly said, "deranges the predictable interplay of hierarchical class relations". . . .

THE CRIOLLO IN POLITICS: "ANARCHY" AND ALLIANCE

The desire to make use of European models in analyzing the Latin American experience has also obscured the role of the *criollos* during the "state of anarchy" which set in after Independence. Thus numerous historians appear to be speaking from the European point of view when they see the dominant political motif of this period in "the quest for stability". . . . The assumption implicit in such formulations seems to be that stability would fulfill the same role in commercial development in Latin America that it had fulfilled in Europe. It may be argued, on the contrary, that— far from being anathema to the *criollos*—anarchy was a natural condition of their existence.

We must not forget that *criollo* wealth was ultimately upon the hacienda:

Organized for commercial ends, the hacienda proved strangely hybrid in its characteristics. It combined in practice features which seem oddly contradictory

---

*Caudillo is best translated as chieftain. The term derived from the Latin *caput,* head. *Caudillaje* refers to the condition of caudillo competition and rule.

in theory. Geared to sell products in a market it yet aimed at having little to sell. Voracious for land, it deliberately made inefficient use of it. Operating with large numbers of workers, it nevertheless personalized the relations between worker and owner. Created to produce a profit, it consumed a large part of its substance in conspicuous and unproductive displays of wealth. Some writers have called the institution 'feudal', because it involved the rule of a dominant landowner over his dependent laborers. But it lacked the legal guarantees of security which compensated the feudal serf for his lack of liberty and self-determination. Others have called it 'capitalist', and so it was, but strangely different from the commercial establishments in agriculture with which we are familiar in the modern commercial and industrial world. Half 'feudal', half 'capitalist', caught between past and future, it exhibited characteristics of both ways of life, as well as their inherent contradictions.

The success of this hybrid institution in the period after Independence was in large measure due to its ability to flourish under anarchic commercial conditions. During this period all industries which had depended upon mercantilist protection were buried under the onslaught of the open market; even mining, the motor of the colonial economy, ground to a halt. Yet the hacienda survived and flourished. It could withstand the vagaries of supply and demand, because—in slack periods—it could return to self-sufficiency.

If the hacienda provided a bulwark of defense against the laissez-faire market, the hacienda system itself militated against the development of a cohesive political association of hacienda owners. Geared to a stagnant technology, yet under repeated pressures to expand production, the hacienda tended to "eat up" land, in order to control the population settled upon the land. The aim of each hacienda was ultimately to produce crops through the arithmetic addition of workers, each one of whom—laboring with his traditional tools—would contribute to increase the sum of produce at the disposal of the estate. While in some parts of Latin America, notably in the Andes and in Middle America, the expansionist tendencies of the hacienda could be directed against Indian communities, in areas without Indians a hacienda could expand only at the expense of neighboring hacienda. Not surprisingly, therefore, we find that blood feuds among hacienda owners are a notable feature of this period: each hacendado's bitterest enemy was potentially his closest neighbor. In this competition we must find the economic roots of *criollo* anarchy.

Such economic determinants of anarchy were reinforced further by social organizational factors. Competition and conflict on the economic plane could, to some extent, be compensated for through the workings of kinship. Arnold Strickon, writing about Argentina, . . . has noted that the *criollo* kinship system is radically different from that of other classes in Argentine society, in its tendency to build up extensive non-unilineal kindreds. He correctly ascribed this variation to the fact that the different classes have differential access to strategic resources. He notes, as others have done, . . . the growth of regional aristocratic families and their role in national politics. We do not yet possess adequate data on how such alliances were formed, how many people were involved, and how much territory they covered. Theoretical considerations, however, lead us to believe that the organizing power of such alliances must have been relatively weak. If we assume that hacienda owners favored the maintenance of large estates through inheritance by primogeniture; if we assume further that the chances are equal that the chief heir will be either male or female; and if we postulate that each hacienda owner strives to maximize the number of his alliances, then it seems unlikely that the number of strategic alliances based on landed property between a hacendado family of origin and other hacendado families of procreation will exceed three. The marriage of Father with Father's Wife creates one such alliance; the marriage of the first-born son with a woman of another family swells the number to two; and the marriage of the eldest daughter with the first son of a third family brings the number of strategic alliances to three. These considerations are intended to yield a measure of insight into the inability of the *criollo* gentry to form a wide-ranging network of strategic alliances for political purposes. [The authors now move to explain the transformation of the caudillo system in the twentieth century.]

CAUDILLAJE *AND MODERN LATIN AMERICA*

[The authors have explored] the causes underlying [the caudillo] political phenomenon. [They] have seen the reasons for its emergence in the inability of any socio-economic class to monopolize sufficiently both wealth and power in order to organize a centralized political apparatus. *Criollos*, while endowed with wealth, lacked the economic and social cohesion to develop the wide-mesh coalitions necessary to control government. The *mestizos*, on the other hand, lacked the permanent and replenishable sources of wealth necessary to support wide-ranging political activity. In the absence of a framework for institutional politics, Latin American politics became personalized.

In spite of its chaotic appearance, *caudillaje* was a true political system, an organized effort on the part of competing groups to determine who got what, when and where. For the *criollo caudillo*, possession of control often guaranteed a temporary position of preference in dealings with foreign trade interests; for the *mestizo* it meant access to a new arena in which to seek wealth. Given the terms of competition, violence constitutes a predictable aspect of the system. Leadership can be achieved only through violence; resources claimed only through violence; and the balance of power between *criollos*, *mestizos* and foreign traders only maintained by veto group violence against a *caudillo* who overstepped his bounds. While the endemic threat of violence rendered uncertain the tenure of any one *caudillo*, however, in the end it served to stabilize the system of *caudillaje* as a whole.

[The authors] have argued that the system depended upon a particular balance between *criollos*, *mestizos*, and foreign interests. [They] are thus arguing implicitly that the *caudillo* system could persist only as long as this balance of interests prevailed. [They] would thus take issue with investigators who continue to see in *caudillaje* the dominant political system in Latin America down to the present day. . . . While much of the code of *caudillo* behavior survives—in a continuing idiom of *machismo*, readiness to use violence, gift-giving, personalized loyalties—by the 1870's the *caudillo* system was giving way to a new political system, the dictatorships of "order and progress". While these dictatorships exhibited some *caudillo* features, the dictator functioned with an increasingly centralized governmental machinery, predicated upon a very different balance of social forces.

The cycle of change from *caudillaje* to these new dictatorships was triggered by the great European depression of 1873–86, which marked the onset of protectionism at home and of imperialist expansion abroad. Where overseas expansion before this time had been largely characterized by the simple extraction of goods from the dependent countries and the conversion of these goods into commodities on the home market, the new imperialists began to invest heavily in the transformation of certain sectors of production in the dependent areas. In Latin America, this signalled major changes in the production of cash crops; it also resulted in the growth of some light industry, primarily in urban areas. Most significantly, the hacienda—with its built-in defenses against the laissez-faire market—became a thing of the past. Large landed *criollo*-owned estates might remain intact, but they witnessed a wholesale transformation of their plant from labor-intensive hacienda to the mechanized and capital-intensive plantation, complete with railroad spur leading to the nearest port.

This transformation required the development of credit institutions, the stabilization of currencies, the improvement and widening of the network of transportation. In turn, these requirements demanded a modicum of political stability and an end to anarchic pillage. This need was met by the forging of alliances between foreign interests and native *criollo* oligarchies of landowners and merchants. The stability of such alliances for order and progress could be guaranteed by the use of foreign armed forces. The local representative of such an alliance was typically the new dictator, often a *caudillo* in origin, but no longer a *caudillo* in function. His recompense no longer derived from the systematic pillage of "free" resources; it was furnished by the alliance. In turn, he functioned as head of an alliance police force, neutralizing forcibly all threats to the alliance. The prototypical dictator of this type was Porfirio Díaz who ruled Mexico between 1876–1911. His expressive slogan *pan o palo* (bread or club) symbolizes the twin functions of his government: wealth (*pan*) to the beneficiaries of the alliance, the use of force (*palo*) against potential challengers. Thus while harbors were dredged, industry built, commerce expanded and foreign capital poured into the country, Mexico's prisons were filled to capacity.

The new balance of power represented by the alliances of order and progress spelled the end of the *caudillo* on horseback. On the national level, they produced dictatorships underwritten by foreign guarantees. At the same time, they drove the *mestizos*, deprived of resources which would have enabled them to participate in the alliance, to seek countervailing coalitions with groups not hitherto represented in the political process. They turned to the rural population of the hinterland. Everywhere they raised the slogans of land reform, popular education and mass participation in politics. In countries with strong Indian components, these countervailing alliances formed under the ideological banner of Indianism, a utopian ideology that envisaged a synthesis of the industrial age with the glorious Indian past; elsewhere they groped towards one form or another of populism. . . . Cast in the organizational form of mass parties like the Peruvian APRA, the Mexican PRM, or the Bolivian MPR, they substituted for the insurrectionary *caudillo* a very different type of leadership, skilled in the management of the "organizational weapon" employed to synchronize divergent group interests. Thus politics in modern Latin America is no longer *caudillo* politics; it is a many-sided conflict between alliances of order and progress ranged against populist coalitions.

For Robert Gilmore, caudillism is a prepraetorian institution that is distinguishable from militarism and that predates "militarization," i.e., the modern professionalization of the Latin American military. "Military men could become caudillos, but only at the sacrifice of their military character. Caudillos could become military men, but only at the price of professionalization."

ROBERT L. GILMORE

Caudillism and Militarism

THE PROBLEM OF DEFINITION

Analysis of Venezuelan society and its institutions in the nineteenth century demands a distinction between caudillism and militarism. . . . Cau-

From Robert L. Gilmore, Caudillism and Militarism in Venezuela, 1810–1910 (Athens, Ohio, 1964), pp. 3–8, by permission of Ohio University Press.

dillism was the preëminent trait of the political system of Venezuela from 1814 to 1935. Since 1935 Venezuela has rapidly acquired all the pressure groups of a modern industrializing society. As the only one of the pressure groups possessing an effective organization in 1935, the armed forces were inevitably involved in the turbulence of a rapidly changing society. Militarism has been, therefore, a recent problem for Venezuela.

Some consideration of the general character of militarism is a necessary backdrop against which to view the Venezuelan situation. Armed forces in the modern era have usually been defenders of the order in which they thrive. Only defeat has compelled them to accept revolutionary change; and revolutionary regimes throughout the world have formed new military forces which become conservative towards any effort to change the order which gave them being. Awareness of modern militarism arose a little over a century ago in Europe when it began to be a political issue "raised in the struggles of domestic politics as a reproach to parties and institutions which unduly furthered military desires." The Romantic Era with its "sentimentalism and conviction" knew modern militarism as an aspect of its reaction against the middle-class rationalism of the Enlightenment and against the shift of the locus of social power to the middle class.

The contribution of the Romantic Era to the formation of modern Western militarism was continued by the class and group imbalances of rapidly industrializing European societies whose vertiginously aggrandized rival interests constantly advanced the armed forces from the rear echelon of policy recourse nearer that of immediate selection. Concurrently, the increasing secularization of society constantly augmented and augments the role of the military in the rituals of the state. In contrast, the national guard or largely self-equipped militia was one of the means by which the bourgeoisie, even in Venezuela, defended its interests and advanced its role in society. Its origin was linked to the opening of what Robert Palmer has labelled the Age of Democratic Revolution. It ceased to be an effective, exclusively bourgeois institution about mid-nineteenth century. The victory —in some countries the defeat—of the middle classes in mid-century closed the Romantic Era, ended the role of the national guard as a class institution, and opened the age of the mass-based professionally-led army dependent on an industrial society. In industrial societies the managerial revolution, fraternal and veterans' associations, and totalitarian political movements have been assigned some influence in promoting militarism. It may be overemphasized.

Modern militarism has meant "the domination of the military man over the civilian, an undue preponderance of military demands, an emphasis on military considerations, spirit, ideals, and scales of values in the life of states. It has also meant the imposition of heavy burdens on a people for military purposes, to the neglect of welfare and culture and the waste of the nation's best manpower in unproductive army service."

Militarism as strength in terms of men and money is usually associated with imperialism, i.e., the extension of territorial holdings or of political controls. Among the Latin American nations, however, the manifestations of imperialism have been very limited. Thus in Latin America much greater emphasis and importance must be attached to the fact that the modern army sees but limited use, and in the long periods of noncombat duty militarism may flourish. Moreover, among the Latin American nations the secondary role of the armed forces of a major power, the maintenance of internal order, becomes in fact their primary role. Inevitably such a role involves them more intimately in the domestic political life of their nations. At the same time military people, like the members of any other profession, resent command by the masses and tend to cherish the ideal of the autonomous military institution free of civilian intervention despite the armed forces' dependence on the socioeconomic strength of society. A major element in the prolonged existence of militarism has been the civilian militarist in high public office who has used the armed forces to limit change, to assure group survival and security, or to control and discipline the governed. Somewhat less obvious has been the militarism of the lonely crowd seeking order and security in hierarchy and comradeship or finding in it an emotional compensation for economic and social disappointments.

Manifestations of militarism in a society have indicated that the established regime or the old order was passing, that significant middle and even proletarian groups were rising to economic and political power, and that the ruling groups of the old regime were casting about for some means to preserve their status. It has also meant that the wars for independence in Spanish America destroyed the old basis for the consent of the governed directed to the monarchy, which was the foundation and the

symbol of the rule of law, i.e., of civilian institutions. The restoration of a similar level of attachment to civilian institutions in republican Spanish America is still in process in most of the nations which emerged from the Spanish Empire.

The preceding generalizations constitute a standard against which to judge the existence of caudillism and militarism in nineteenth-century Venezuela. Caudillism is not in question, but the tendency to equate it with militarism in dealing with Venezuela is in question. The linking together of the two terms is based primarily on the fact that both are concerned with violence. The military institution is concerned with the management and use of controlled violence in the service of the state according to terms laid down by the state. When the military institution veers from this role to participate in or to influence other nonmilitary agencies and functions of the state, including its leadership, then militarism exists in greater or lesser degree. Caudillism is a political process in which violence is an essential element. It is anarchic, self-generating, instinctively aspirant to the vanished role of the monarchy. . . .

A related problem is the definition of a military man. The professional military man is easily identifiable, but there is a fairly common notion that any man who performs in the broader range of his occupational activities one or more military functions is, therefore, a military man. It is presumed, then, that a military function asserts a dominant influence over the outlook, conduct, and goals of an individual even though its performance be episodic, or when of frequent occurrence it is still ancillary to the vocation of the person. Such a view is unacceptable. Military men could become caudillos, but only at the sacrifice of their military character. Caudillos could become military men, but only at the price of professionalization, no matter how rudimentary. If the caudillo-become-military man desired to continue his political activity it would necessarily be through the military institution. The end result would be, if he succeeded, the formation of the Praetorian State. . . .

Description of corporate praetorianism in four Latin American states can assist in the understanding of the phenomenon. The monographic studies of Robert Potash on Argentina, Roy Allan Hansen on Chile, Alfred Stepan on Brazil, and Abraham Lowenthal on Peru are classic recent studies of authoritarian and corporate regimes.

Robert Potash's study of the June 1943 coup d'etat in Argentina shows that the army party, the Grupo Oficiales Unidos (GOU), was instrumental in the ouster of President Ramón Castillo. Two days after the coup, General Pedro Ramírez was appointed provisional president, and Colonel Juan Perón became head of the War Ministry Secretariat. Perón, one of the leaders of the GOU, used his position to further the power and influence of the GOU and to persuade nonpolitical officers to join the military group. The GOU split over the question of whether to break relations with the Axis powers, leading to the resignation of General Ramírez and his replacement by Perón's friend, General Farrell. At the same time, Perón built his personal support among labor leaders through his control of a newly formed secretariat for labor and welfare.

ROBERT POTASH

The Argentinian Army in Power, 1943–1944

[Between the promulgation of the Constitution of 1853 and the GOU coup of 1943, the Argentine military

Reprinted from The Army and Politics in Argentina, 1928–1945: Yrigoyen to Perón by Robert A. Potash, with the permission of the publishers, Stanford University Press. © 1969 by the Board of Trustees of the Leland Stanford Junior University.

intervened only once, in 1930. The coup of General Uriburu on the side of the Conservatives against President Yrigoyen was encouraged and promoted by the politicians. The Argentine officers mimicked the fascist notions of military exclusivity.]

The substitution of military for

civilian government in June 1943 took place under conditions quite distinct from those prevailing at the time of the first takeover thirteen years before. Missing was the atmosphere of public excitement that had preceded the Uriburu-led coup, an atmosphere deliberately fomented by Yrigoyen's opponents. The June uprisings, in contrast, came as a surprise to the general public and even to those politicians who were aware of the widespread discontent within the officer corps. The politicians were anticipating a move in September, not in June.

Still, it would be erroneous to claim that the military acted without regard for the civilian sector, or indeed without encouragement from it. The officers shared the universal concern over President Castillo's electoral plans even while they disagreed among themselves on the wisdom of his foreign policies. Moreover, the belief that it was their responsibility to take action was strengthened by their increasing contacts with political leaders, especially those of the Radical Party. Without this stimulus, it is questionable whether the liberal, pro-Allied sector of the Army would have risen, and without their participation the movement could not have succeeded. The inability of the nationalist sector to mount a successful coup by itself had been demonstrated time and time again in previous years.

In acting to oust the Castillo government, the military was responding to a harsh axiom of Argentine politics: that no constitutional authority is strong enough to prevent a determined President from imposing his will, even

if this involves violation of the laws and the constitution itself; and that only the withdrawal of military support can call a halt to such an administration. With his control over the Senate, Dr. Castillo could be unconcerned about impeachment proceedings; and he had shown by his continued extension of the state of siege his determination to ignore hostile opinion. The belief that it was up to the military to intervene was by no means limited to military circles; many civilians would have agreed with General Rawson when he told his comrades-in-arms: "When the Nation, as a result of bad rulers, is put into a situation where there are no constitutional solutions, [the military] has a duty to fulfill: to put the Nation in order." But here was the rub. Could an officer corps as deeply divided as that which existed in 1943 "put the Nation in order"? . . .

In this struggle, which was one of personalities as well as of policies, the contenders had to bear in mind the sources of their power. Victory or defeat would depend on the ability to gain or retain the loyalty of a large part, if not all, of the officer corps. It may be useful at this point, therefore, to review briefly the makeup of the Argentine officer corps in June 1943. Excluding reserve and retired officers, the regular Army officers, combat and service, numbered about 3,300. Of these, some eight hundred held the rank of major and above, the remainder being junior officers. At the top of the hierarchy were the *oficiales superiores*, the 37 generals and 121 colonels, followed by the *jefes*, the 233 lieutenant colonels and 371 majors.

Promotions had not come rapidly for these officers, as was evident in the ages and lengths of service represented in the upper grades: the lieutenant colonels ranged from 40 to 49, with upwards of 22 years of service since graduation from the Military Academy; the full colonels varied from 47 to 56 years in age, with the least experienced having had 27 years service; the generals ranged from 52 (a brigadier) to 62 (a major general), and could look back on 34 to 45 years of service.

Although these officers came from various geographic and social backgrounds, a substantial number now, as in the 1920's, were second-generation Argentines, immigrants' sons who had entered the Army in order to achieve status and respectability. . . .

As an instrument for maintaining discipline and reflecting the views of the officer corps, the regular chain of command suffered from serious disabilities after June 4. The revolution by its very success disrupted normal military relationships and made political criteria, i.e., support for the revolution or for particular leaders, the basis for military assignments, retirements, and promotions. The fact that the revolution was made by colonels and lieutenant colonels and that, with the exception of Rawson and Ramírez, Army generals took no part in it weakened the generals' ability either to impose control over the Army or to influence the course of public policy. The initiative for exercising such influence passed, therefore, to other groups and individuals, especially to the GOU [Grupo Oficiales Unidos]. . . .

An immediate demonstration of this shift was given in the behind-the-scenes struggle over the formation of the new government. The action of General Rawson on the afternoon of June 4 in calmly occupying Castillo's vacated office precipitated a split among the revolutionary leaders, several of whom expected either a three-man junta or General Ramírez himself to assume presidential authority. Nevertheless, there was a good chance Rawson might have been able to hold on had it not been for his unfortunate cabinet choices and his unwillingness to change them. For on the night of June 4, after dining with friends at the Jockey Club as was his custom on Fridays, Rawson offered portfolios to two of his dinner companions without any thought of the political implications. Perhaps it was fatigue from two days of continuous emotional tension, but more likely it was his lack of political experience that led him to invite two elderly conservatives, Dr. José María Rosa, an Axis sympathizer, and Dr. Horacio Calderón, who favored the Allies, to serve respectively as Ministers of Finance and Justice. These two men were identified with the same ruling conservative circles as the ousted Dr. Castillo, and their presence in the Casa Rosada produced a revulsion among all the military chiefs who had joined in the revolution. When General Rawson made known the names of his other cabinet choices, there was further consternation; again placing friendship above political wisdom, he invited Generals Domingo Martínez and Juan Pistarini to serve as Ministers of Foreign Affairs and Public Works respectively. Martínez had served until the previous day as Castillo's police chief, but what was more serious, both were well known for their German sympathies. In view of General Rawson's undisguised intention to break relations with the Axis, these appointments made little sense, confounding both foreign and domestic observers. . . .

The reactions of the revolutionary colonels and lieutenant colonels to Rawson's measures were far from uniform. The pro-Axis members of the GOU led by Lieut. Colonel González and Colonel Juan Perón were determined to oust Rawson. But GOU member Colonel Miguel Montes was equally determined to keep him, provided he would agree to cabinet changes. A similar position was taken by a group of pro-Allied Campo de Mayo chiefs led by the Garrison Commander, Colonel Anaya. For two days, beginning June 5 and lasting until late on the 6th, Rawson sat through a series of meetings in which these colonels pressured him to change his mind. Rawson's position was that he had given his word and would not go back on it. Colonel Anaya, however, who at first wanted Rawson to stay, used blunt measures to resolve the situation. When the civilians Rosa and Calderón appeared in the Casa Rosada, he had them escorted to an exit with the warning not to return; and together with Lieut. Colonel Imbert, he paid a visit to the foreign minister designate, General Martínez, and persuaded him to withdraw.

Despite these steps, which Anaya hoped would overcome Rawson's sense of obligation to his friends, the General still persisted in his original choices. In doing this, he finally alienated the Campo de Mayo chiefs led by Colonel Anaya, who now joined those GOU members, like González and Perón, who had been working from the first for his ouster. Unwittingly, Colonel Anaya himself served as the agent of the group's designs, when on the night of June 6 he entered Rawson's office to tell him, on behalf of the Campo de Mayo commanders, that he would have to go. Beyond expressing a pained "You, too!" General Rawson made no protest. After signing a resignation statement, he left the Casa Rosada alone, refusing the escort that was offered, while the colonels brought General Ramírez in triumph into the presidential office.

Years later General Rawson, in a letter to Dr. Ernesto Sammartino, explained his decision to resign in the following terms:

Intrigued against by the jefes, who courageously had accompanied me in the triumphant decision of the revolution—an intrigue planned from the very Ministry of War which General Pedro Ramírez directed and of which I, of course, was ignorant—they came led by General Elvio Anaya to put before me their disagreement on the cabinet I had designated. I found myself with this choice: either to move to a barracks, summon them, and once [they were] under arrest, to ship them to Martín García (or adopt an even more severe attitude), or to resign. I realized that the first course would discredit the revolution, which had been accepted frenetically by the public opinion of the country and justified even abroad. I believed it unavoidable to prevent this shame to a serious institution such as the Army. My resignation, on the other hand, could perhaps be a lesson in disinterestedness. I regretted the risk to the postulates and principles that inspired me, but I never thought of the significance it was to have. I had faith in the decorum of my comrades, AND I RESIGNED.

. . . The elevation of General Pedro Ramírez to the provisional presidency brought into that office a professional Army officer whose entire political experience was limited to the seven months he had served as Castillo's Minister of War. Distinguished by a taciturn manner, a slight frame—ever since his cadet days he had been known as "Palito" (Toothpick)—and an impassive face that might remind one of a deadpan comedian, Ramírez nonetheless possessed the leadership qualities that made for success in the military profession. Among his colleagues he was widely respected for his clear thinking, fairmindedness, and equanimity. To the general public, however, he was a relative unknown whose political views and capacities were a major mystery.

Certain civilian circles, nevertheless, viewed his assumption of the presidency with visible satisfaction. Some of the Radical leaders who had been conducting political talks with Ramírez before the revolution were reasonably optimistic about the prospects of reaching the goal they had been seeking since 1931—the guarantee of an honest presidential election. However, it was not the civilian politicians but the Army officers associated with the still secret GOU who were to become the immediate beneficiaries of General Ramírez's accession to the presidency.

The key that opened the first government door to GOU influence was undoubtedly the close relationship between General Ramírez and Lieut. Colonel González. On the night of June 6 "Gonzalito," together with his War Ministry colleague Lieut. Colonel Carlos Vélez and Campo de Mayo commander Colonel Anaya, met with General Ramírez to help him select his cabinet. Out of this small gathering came the decisions to install Perón's chief, General Farrell, in the crucial War Ministry post, with its control over all Army assignments, and give Colonel Alberto Gilbert, González's close friend, the politically sensitive post of Interior Minister. . . .

The allocation of posts can be viewed as an attempt to give the revolutionary colonels a direct voice in the government as well as to stengthen the government's naval support. In international orientation, however, the cabinet was sharply divided: Farrell, Mason, Gilbert, and Benito Sueyro held pro-Axis, or at least neutralist views, while Storni, Santamarina, Galíndez, and Anaya advocated closer relations with the Allies.

Offsetting this even division within the cabinet, however, was the assignment of major bureaucratic positions to members of the GOU. On June 7 President Ramírez designated "Gonzalito" to head the Presidential Secretariat, and the very next day General Farrell announced that Colonel Perón was to head the War Ministry Secretariat, a post equivalent to undersecretary. Moreover, the new Chief of

Police, as announced by the Interior Minister, was the Germanophile Colonel Emilio Ramírez. Within a matter of days, two other GOU leaders, Lieut. Colonel Domingo Mercante and Colonel Miguel A. Montes were assigned to the post of *oficial mayor* (equivalent to deputy undersecretary) in the War and Interior Ministries respectively. Meanwhile, command of vital troop units in the federal capital and at Campo de Mayo passed into the hands of other members of the logia. . . . By these means the GOU quickly constructed a power base from which to exert pressure on government decisions.

For the next four months the attention of many Army officers, as well as of the public-at-large, focused on two interrelated developments: the efforts of Colonel Juan Perón, from his post in the War Ministry, to build himself up into a major political force; and the bitter struggle taking place within the Ramírez administration between various men who sought to shape its domestic and international policies. The secrecy that prevailed at the time and the subsequent unwillingness of the principals to comment publicly about their experiences have long obscured the history of these developments. It is now possible, however, with the aid of interviews and foreign diplomatic records, to reconstruct the key events.

Almost at the moment Perón assumed the number two position in the War Ministry, he embarked on the complex task of achieving personal ascendancy over the officer corps. He was well aware that his ultimate weapon was General Farrell's total submissiveness to his wishes. Not overly endowed intellectually and given more to diversions than to his official duties, Farrell had learned to rely on the judgment of the hardworking subordinate who had served him consistently as chief of staff since March 1942. Perón, to be sure, was always careful at the War Ministry to preserve the fiction that it was General Farrell who made all decisions.

With the assurance that came from this support, Perón was willing to risk the hostility of certain officers as he worked to build up his prestige and power among the rest. Aiding him in this process were power-hungry nationalist intellectuals who saw in Perón a vehicle for fulfilling their own ambitions. Diego Luís Molinari and José Luís Torres were among those who offered him advice and supported him with articles in the sensationalist weekly magazine *Ahora,* a publication with wide circulation among military men. This magazine had been used in the past as a propaganda vehicle for the intellectuals' brand of nationalism. Now it served as a public relations medium for Perón, offering its readers such interesting fare as an illustrated interview with the colonel published on June 25 under the lead: "*Ahora* visits with the Chief of the Revolutionary General Staff of June 4." Those Campo de Mayo commanders who knew the truth about Perón's disappearance on that dangerous day must have had a few choice words to utter on reading this article. However, those among them who were sensitive to historical precedents might have reflected that Perón's hero, Benito Mussolini, led his "March on Rome" in 1922 from the safety of Milan, hundreds of miles to the rear, without hurting his subsequent political career.

It was not merely in a popular magazine the Perón worked to advance his own interests by rewriting the history of the revolution. The bulletins of the GOU also were used to spread a fictional account of the recent events. Anxious to expand the GOU's membership and aware that young officers would be more likely to join an organization if its image were one of broad support and accomplishment, Perón tried to create the impression that the GOU alone had been responsible for the coup. "The events that took place and which are of public knowledge," read the opening line of the GOU's *News Bulletin,* No. 5, issued late in June, "had in the GOU their gestation and execution." The bulletin continued in the same vein: "In spite of the precipitousness which found the GOU involved in the midst of recruitment, the majority of field-grade and junior officers already belonged to it, and this allowed it to carry out the revolutionary movement as the only patriotic solution to the grave situation created for the country."

To the original Campo de Mayo regimental commanders, most of whom had never even heard of the GOU, the preposterousness of these claims was self-evident, but the mass of officers now being solicited had no independent basis for judgment. From his War Ministry post, Perón was able to persuade hundreds of young officers that their affiliation with the GOU was the way to show support for the military government. Politically naïve and susceptible to appeals that stressed

corporate loyalty, they were ready to accept the proposition, especially since it emanated from the War Ministry itself, that "the GOU is the spirit of the Revolution of June 4; it is the memory of its past; it is the force of its present; and it is the hope for its continuation in the future." These new GOU members provided Perón with a significant weapon, for they were required not only to "defend the [Ramírez] regime, its ideas, works, and persons" but to inform on any officers who were opposed to its policies or the activities of the organization. This in effect created for Perón an internal espionage network for keeping tabs on the officer corps. The new affiliates, moreover, in accordance with GOU rules, provided guarantees of their own loyalty by voluntarily submitting undated but signed requests for retirement from active service.

Perón's flagrant use of his War Ministry post to promote the GOU, and with it his own prestige, did not fail to arouse opposition, especially among the jefes who had taken part in Castillo's ouster. Indeed, one month to the day after that event the Campo de Mayo commanders, smarting with resentment at Perón's activities, met in the home of the Director of the Cavalry School, Lieut. Colonel Ornstein, to consider a course of action. Present at this meeting were most of the regimental chiefs who had participated in the June 3 meeting. . . .

The decision reached by these unit commanders was to send a delegation to talk with President Ramírez about the necessity of getting rid of both Farrell and Perón. The next day Colonels Avalos and Mascaró, together with Lieut. Colonel Fernando P. Terrera, went on their mission. Perhaps it was at Terrera's suggestion that they first visited his former chief, Colonel Anaya, at the Ministry of Justice. As Anaya later recalled it, when he first saw this group of officers at the Ministry, he wondered whether they had come to demand his own resignation. But when he learned from Avalos, who acted as spokesman, that they wanted him to join them in calling on the President, Anaya urged them not to take this step. The revolutionary government, he pointed out, was only a month old, and it was necessary to preserve the appearance of stability. He promised, however, to speak to War Minister Farrell about curbing Perón.

The regimental chiefs went back to Campo de Mayo to await events. Anaya, as he had promised, did inform his cabinet colleague that night at a dinner that the Campo de Mayo chiefs were sick and tired of Perón's behavior. He did not tell Farrell that the chiefs also wanted to get rid of the War Minister. Through GOU channels, however, Perón learned of the details of their meeting and informed the War Minister of the threat to his own position. Faced with this common danger, they acted swiftly. An official investigation was launched, and in a matter of hours confidential War Ministry orders were issued relieving three of the commanders of their Campo de Mayo assignments. This was meant to be a lesson to the others. . . .

Aware that the Campo de Mayo base still had a potential for upsetting him, Perón now sought to protect this flank by winning over its commander, Colonel Avalos. What manner of persuasion was used is not known, but by mid-July Avalos became one of the hierarchs of the GOU, and by virtue of his seniority, presided over its weekly sessions in the War Ministry building. The relationship between Avalos and Perón, established at this time, was to be crucial in the coming months, and on more than one occasion it was Avalos's loyalty that would enable Perón to continue scaling the political heights.

Emboldened by his success in meeting the Campo de Mayo challenge, Perón undertook to spread his web into the Casa Rosada itself. To be sure, "Gonzalito" was there directing the presidential secretariat, but he could not be counted on to act as agent of Perón's personal aspirations. As one of the major figures of the GOU and as a close advisor to President Ramírez, González might well decide at some future point to influence the President against Perón. It was therefore necessary for Perón to have his own henchmen in the Casa Rosada so he could be kept constantly informed of possible dangers.

By mid-August Perón hit upon the solution to this problem. Serving in the Casa Rosada since the day after President Ramírez took the oath were four officers who had worked with him previously in the War Ministry. . . . If they could be persuaded voluntarily to accept other assignments, their places might be filled by Perón's agents. But what assignments could be more attractive than serving next to the President? There was only one that offered an overwhelming temptation in pay and perquisites: the post of military attaché in a foreign country. Perón found little difficulty in enticing three of the four officers, . . . with the attaché posts in Rome, Madrid, and Lima respectively. Only [one] refused the bait. Even so, Perón achieved much of his aim, for late in August it was announced that Lieut. Colonel Aristóbulo Mittelbach and Major Heraclio Ferrazano, charter members of the GOU executive, had taken over as Chief of the Military Household and presidential aide-de-camp, respectively. After this, there were few conversations in the presidential offices that did not come to Perón's attention.

In approving these changes—for the President's signature was required on every military appointment—General Ramírez rejected warnings that he was allowing himself to be surrounded by men he did not know and on whose loyalty he could not depend. Despite urgings from friends and relatives to stop Perón before it was too late, Ramírez refused to see any evil intent in the actions of the smiling colonel. And on those occasions when he was seemingly persuaded to remove Perón, the President invariably changed his mind. Indeed these reversals were so consistent that the President's wife, who often thought she had convinced him at home to act against Perón, wondered whether he was not being drugged through his coffee at the Casa Rosada.

This lack of firmness on the part of the President enabled Perón to surmount a series of challenges, the most serious of which took place in October in connection with a combined civilian-military effort to change the orientation of the government. President Ramírez, apparently convinced that the time had come to stop both Farrell and Perón, ordered General Santos V. Rossi, commander of the First Infantry Division, usually located in the Federal Capital but at that time about to return from maneuvers at Campo de Mayo, to bypass their barracks the next morning and seize the War Ministry in the center of the city. Farrell and Perón were to be arrested, and General Rossi was to become the new War Minister. Sometime between midafternoon, when the President gave Rossi his orders, and 2 A.M., the President changed his mind. An aide was sent to Campo de Mayo to tell Rossi the movement was off and ask him to report first thing in the morning to the President. When General Rossi reported as ordered, he was told by the President that the original directive had never been issued and that he was relieved of his command. Rossi swallowed this treatment, he said, as a sacrifice to the revolution.

It was in reality a sacrifice of the few remaining officers capable of opposing Perón and his nationalistic colleagues in the GOU. For Rossi's removal coincided with a much broader political and military shake-up that was the culmination of the struggle over administration policies that had been going since June.

The policy struggle, like the expansion of Perón's power, involved at critical moments a struggle to control the President's mind. For General Ramírez lacked firm ideas of his own and often reflected the views of the last person he spoke to. The vacillation that characterized his approach to policy-making was the inevitable result. He disliked controversy and preferred to postpone difficult decisions as long as possible. His critics, and they are many, have called him a man without character. A more generous view, perhaps, is that he had good intentions but lacked the strength to carry them out. As Presi-. dent he came under the influence of men far more clever and determined than himself, and as a consequence, became little more than the puppet of those around him.

The behind-the-scenes policy struggle within the Ramírez government revolved around two basic issues— one domestic, the other foreign. Was the military regime to seek the early restoration of civilian rule within the liberal constitutional traditions as those with centrist and moderate leftist views desired, or was it to make radical changes in institutional structure as clericalist and nationalist elements on the right urged? And in the international sphere, was Argentina at long last to join the rest of the hemisphere in opposing the Axis powers or to continue a neutralism that, whatever patriotic arguments could be made in its behalf, served the interests of the Axis?

From June to October President Ramírez's position on the basic domestic issue was close to that of the political parties. In his first press conference he insisted that the military had taken power not to make a revolution but to remedy the anguished situation of the people and to resolve the institutional crisis brought on by systematic fraud and corruption. A similar view was expressed a few weeks later by the Minister of Justice, Colonel Anaya, who stated at a dinner honoring Rawson and Ramírez that the military had not come to enthrone themselves in power. Even as late as his October 10 speech at Azul, President Ramírez emphasized the importance of political parties and praised the capacity of some of their leaders.

Yet other military men in public posts, especially those at the gubernatorial level, were taking an opposite view, arrogating to themselves a monopoly of civic virtue and administrative efficiency, and denouncing the political parties as the source of all evil. Not all the officers by any means reflected antiliberal views, but the appointment of notorious critics of the democratic process to serve in such major posts as *interventor* (governor) of Buenos Aires province and as *intendente* (mayor) of the Federal Capital was certainly disconcerting. Among liberal political elements, the original optimism about an early transition to civilian rule gave way to disillusionment as the evidence mounted that powerful nationalist elements were pushing the Ramírez government in the direction of prolonged dictatorial rule. The maintenance of the state of siege, the suspension of the September elections, the elimination of the word "provisional" from the official designation of the government, and the muzzling of the press were all indicative of such a trend, and this in turn seemed to lend credence to rumors of a secret plan to have the military rule for ten or twenty years, or as long as necessary to reform the character of the Argentines and their politics.

The internal debate over domestic orientation had its counterpart in the even more bitter controversy over foreign policy. For here, political and economic interests, ideological rivalries, and foreign pressures all converged around the issue of maintaining or abandoning Argentina's neutrality. On this vital issue Ramírez's position was, to say the least, ambivalent. As Minister of War under Castillo he had apparently associated himself with the General Staff's recommendation of February 1943 that Argentina move closer to the United States in order to obtain arms. Yet in a private conversation with Dr. Ernesto Sammartino ten days before the June 4 coup, he made plain his belief that Argentine honor was committed to the continuation of the neutrality policy.

As President he continued to follow an uncertain course, at times revealing an intention to move in the direction of breaking relations with the Axis but always abandoning it before consummation. . . .

The struggle between liberals and nationalists, between pro-Allied and pro-German factions, reached its climax early in October, when President Ramírez asked General Rossi to get rid of Farrell and Perón and then changed his mind a few hours later. Ramírez's vacillation emboldened the GOU leaders to push for complete control. Under circumstances that are still obscure, the President agreed to appoint General Farrell to the vacant post of Vice-President while allowing him to continue as War Minister, and to oust from the cabinet the remaining voices of moderation—Finance Minister Santamarina; General Anaya, the Minister of Justice and Public Instruction; and the Public Works Minister, Admiral (Ret.) Galíndez.

The political shake-up initiated on October 11 marked a new phase for the military government. Colonel Perón, whose friend Farrell in the vice-presidency was ready to move up should a vacancy occur, had obviously increased his power in the government. But in the cabinet reorganization the forces of reactionary nationalism also scored major gains. . . .

With these extremists in the cabinet, the Ramírez regime in the months following the October shake-up rapidly took on the form of a right-wing authoritarian dictatorship, somewhat on the Franco model. Repressive measures were employed not only against Communists, as had been the case ever since the military took power, but also against liberals who dared openly to criticize the regime. University professors and civil servants who signed a manifesto calling for a return to democratic practices and the honoring of the Rio Conference resolutions were summarily dismissed from their posts; students who protested found their organizations dissolved; and the press was subjected to various restrictions. The culmination of this process was the series of decrees signed on December 31 that dissolved all political parties, established compulsory religious education in the public schools, and created rigid controls over the gathering and dissemination of news.

The underlying philosophy guiding the nationalist cabinet ministers was set forth in the confidential instructions that General Perlinger, the Interior Minister, addressed to the provincial interventors sometime in November. In this document he called on them to go beyond the first stage of the revolution—the ouster of the previous authorities—to begin the second stage, that of forming a national conscience and achieving a "real integral unity of the Argentine people." In the language of the instructions:

The meaning of the revolution should reach as soon as possible all social, political, and economic orders. The social aspect should be conducted in such a form as to assure the most absolute justice and support for the weak. The people wish tranquility and justice. The political aspect should be characterized by an eminently Argentine orientation. No politician—whatever his affiliation—shall be summoned to collaborate with the government. Through education and energetic action the *régimen* must be broken. The mass of citizens should be disciplined. Minds should be transformed so that in the future they know how to be discerning and to find the path of truth and not be deceived by the words of demagogues. It is indispensable to define at once the problems and to find their solution in the shortest time. The political parties are not important now. All inhabitants should be directed in the same manner, with the sole exception of those who seek to disturb the government's actions. These shall be treated like enemies of the fatherland. The Communists and Communist sympathizers are enemies of the fatherland and as such should

be eradicated from the country. A special effort should be made to identify the principal leaders. No circumstance shall prevent the Communist, whatever his situation, from being treated as a declared enemy of the fatherland.

We don't want scandal. We only want [to achieve] purification, reorganization, improvement, and above all to govern with a future vision. The future vision should be directed toward the goals already stated: national sovereignty, well-being of the people. In the economic order, the aim is the total purification of the *régimen*.

That General Perlinger and his nationalist associates lacked a specific and imaginative program is evident from this document. Its clearest provisions were of the negative sort: the repression of enemies of the regime. But in place of concrete proposals for achieving their ideal society they fell back on vague, platitudinous concepts —purification, reorganization, improvement—and on the idea that the minds of the masses needed disciplining and guiding. Nothing was said about creating public support for the regime. The underlying assumption seems to have been that the military could remain in power indefinitely.

But while Perlinger, Martínez Zuviría, and their associates were busy with their antiliberal measures, Colonel Juan Perón began maneuvering on another level to win support, ostensibly for the regime, but actually for himself, in the ranks of the laboring masses. The social policies of the military government from June to October had combined paternalistic measures with strict controls over labor. Aware of the difficult conditions that confronted the lower classes, the government had imposed price controls and ordered a rollback in property rentals, but at the same time it moved to dissolve one of the two rival national labor centrals, to paralyze the activities of the other, and to require that trade unions obtain government approval before they could legally function.

The antilabor spirit that characterized the earliest official measures affecting the trade unions was altered after Colonel Perón had himself named, on October 27, to head the National Labor Department, a relatively ineffectual regulatory agency under the Interior Ministry, and proceeded a month later to have it transformed into the Secretariat of Labor and Welfare, directly dependent on the presidency. In his post as Secretary, which he assumed in addition to his War Ministry position, Perón began the process of winning over trade union leaders by offering them positions in the new agency. In time he would create a broad personal following among labor's rank and file as he placed the powers of the agency behind union demands for material benefits and fostered the unionization of the unskilled; and by treating labor grievances as legitimate concerns of the government he gave the ordinary worker a new sense of dignity.

The reactions of Army officers to Perón's increasing involvement with labor leaders varied, with junior- and middle-grade officers by and large taking a more sympathetic view than did their seniors. Undoubtedly a reason for the favorable attitude of some officers was their awareness of lower-class conditions (a result of their military assignments to provincial garrisons) and their experience in dealing each year with conscripts drawn from the poorer classes. A more decisive factor shaping their viewpoint, however, was probably their belief that Perón's methods were reducing the appeal of Communism to the Argentine worker. This indeed was the basis on which Perón sought to justify his activities to his fellow officers, whether through GOU channels or in direct discussions. A notable instance of his direct approach was his address to the entire graduating class of the Colegio Militar in December 1943 on the occasion of its unprecedented ceremonial visit to the Secretariat of Labor and Welfare.

Among GOU leaders, Lieut. Colonel Domingo Mercante was Perón's principal collaborator in promoting his labor activities. Mercante, who was the son of a member of La Fraternidad, the locomotive engineers' union, played a vital role in setting up the contacts that led union leaders to visit Perón in the War Ministry even before he assumed control of the National Labor Department. Mercante was later named government interventor in La Fraternidad and the Union Ferroviaria, the key railway unions, and worked closely with Perón in the newly created Secretariat of Labor and Welfare.

Not all GOU leaders, however, viewed Perón's activities with sympathy. As a result of an understanding arrived at by the members of the top echelon, control over the organization was supposed to be exercised by the "four colonels," Perón, González, Ramírez, and Avalos, all of whom had pledged not to seek public office. In the face of increasing evidence that Perón was seeking to convert the GOU into the instrument of his political ambitions, a cleavage developed between him and González, with Colonel Avalos remaining closer to Perón and Colonel Ramírez tending to side with González.

In his Casa Rosada post, which was given cabinet status late in October, Colonel González was in a strategic position to try to put a halt to Perón's maneuverings. Neither he nor President Ramírez had anticipated what Perón would be able to do with the labor secretariat. Ironically, the President had been happy to have Perón take over the agency in the belief that it would keep him too busy to conspire. Confronted now by Perón's efforts to create a personal following in labor ranks at the same time he was using the GOU to manipulate officer opinion, Colonel González attempted to check Perón's power through certain provisions of a new political party statute he was drafting. The dissolution of the traditional parties had placed a moratorium on civilian political activity, but under González's plan, Argentina would eventually return to party politics on the basis of reforms and safeguards written into law. Rejecting a suggestion from Perón, conveyed by an ex-Radical deputy, that he should consider running jointly with Perón on a future presidential ticket, Colonel González included in the draft statute a clause explicitly prohibiting military men from seeking office in the next election. It was apparently this move that convinced Perón to seek González's ouster from the government. The opportunity to achieve this, as it turned out, was furnished by the diplomatic crisis that broke out in January.

This crisis originated in the ambitious international policy that the Ramírez administration had embarked on after October, and specifically in two ventures that had unanticipated results. One was the Helmuth mission to secure German arms; the other was the attempt to create a pro-Argentine and, by implication, anti-U.S. bloc in South America by assisting revolutionary movements in neighboring states. In both cases documentary proof of covert Argentine activities fell into Allied hands.

Helmuth's mission, the security of which was compromised by squabbles among German agents, came to a sudden halt early in November, when British authorities at Trinidad detained him for questioning as he stepped off his Spanish ship. Word of his arrest was transmitted confidentially to Buenos Aires by the Argentine Minister at Caracas on November 5. The German intelligence agents in Buenos Aires learned of this development soon after from Colonels González and Perón. According to SD reports received in Berlin, the Argentine authorities decided against sending another agent to Europe, and instead dispatched a sealed envelope with instructions for their naval attaché in Berlin. Meanwhile they lodged an official protest with the British over Helmuth's arrest, and tried to secure his release and return to Buenos Aires.

German Foreign Ministry officials seem to have had a more realistic appreciation of the implications of Helmuth's arrest than did the Argentine authorities. In a farsighted memorandum dated November 17, Ambassador Otto Reinebeck of the Foreign Ministry pointed out that if the compromising letters and instructions Helmuth carried fell into Allied hands, or if a confession could be squeezed out of him, "the situation would be dangerous for the existence of the Ramírez government and therefore for the continuation of Argentina's policy of neutrality." Only in late December, after the British informed the Argentine government that Helmuth had confessed to being a German agent, did the Buenos Aires officials fully realize the seriousness of the situation.

But at this very moment they found themselves in an even more critical situation as a result of their second venture, the subversion of neighboring pro-Allied governments, which achieved its first success in the Bolivian coup of December 20. The overthrow of the Peñaranda regime not only alarmed the Uruguayan government, where extremist elements were also threatening to act, but convinced the United States that the time had come to take a tough line with the Ramírez government. While powerful units of the South Atlantic fleet moved into the River Plate, dropping anchor at Montevideo just across the estuary from Buenos Aires, and while the U.S. Treasury prepared to freeze Argentine funds on deposit in U.S. banks, the State Department let it be known that it was preparing for publication a memorandum that would give details of Argentine complicity in the Bolivian coup and intervention in the affairs of other South American countries.

Confronted by this situation, President Ramírez and Foreign Minister Gilbert decided to try to avert publication of the incriminatory material at all cost. On January 24, General Gilbert informed U.S. Ambassador Armour that, in view of the proof provided by the Helmuth case that Germany had broken its promise not to abuse Argentine hospitality by engaging in espionage or subversive activities, the Argentine government had definitely decided to break relations with Germany. It would require a few days to make the necessary arrangements. In the meantime he asked that the United States avoid any action that could be interpreted as applying pressure and, specifically, that the proposed U.S. condemnation of Argentina as the focal point for subversive activities against neighboring governments be stopped. In view of the promise to break relations, Washington went along with the Foreign Minister's request. On January 26 the Argentine government, in a decree signed only by Ramírez and Gilbert, broke diplomatic relations with Germany and Japan, giving as the reason the discovery of an extensive espionage network operating on Argentine soil. . . .

Indeed, the government's decision to break with the Axis came as a sudden and bewildering surprise to the hundreds of neutralist officers who comprised the rank and file of the GOU. Only two months before, a delegation estimated to number three hundred officers had called on the Foreign Minister to express full support for his declaration to a Chilean correspondent that Argentina's foreign policy was one of "complete and absolute neutrality" and that Argentina "did not wish to become the enemy of any country in the world." The only public inkling that something was amiss came on January 21, when the Foreign Ministry issued a statement mentioning for the first time the arrest of Argentine consul Helmuth by the British, and commenting that this had revealed the existence of an Axis espionage network in the country, which was now under investigation. Still, a GOU confidential bulletin dated the next day gave no indication of any change, and after referring to the Ramírez government's "wise and firm foreign policy and its sincere, loyal, and constructive domestic policy," it called on the members to close ranks behind the government and help promote an atmosphere of tranquillity.

The atmosphere was anything but tranquil, however, when scores of officers summoned by the GOU to a special meeting three nights later split into angry shouting factions on learning of the government's intention to break relations with the Axis. Many of those present at the tumultuous meeting in the City Council building rejected the Foreign Minister's statement that Axis espionage activities were the reason for the break, and attributed the decision to United States pressure. Unaware of the precise considerations that led President Ramírez and Foreign Minister Gilbert to decide on the step, they denounced it as an unwarranted abandonment of the neutrality policy with which the GOU had been identified and a shameful betrayal of national honor.

The cleavage at the meeting extended into the GOU executive body: Colonel Urbano de la Vega, Lieut. Colonel Julio Lagos, Lieut. Colonel Alfredo Baisi, and Major León Bengoa demanded the continuation of neutrality, while Colonels González, Avalos, Emilio Ramírez, and Alfredo Argüero Fragueiro supported the Foreign Minister in his insistence on the break. The role played by Colonel Perón was equivocal. Despite a request from Colonel González that he speak out vigorously in defense of the move, he limited himself to a statement that he had given his word to the Foreign Minister, and as a gentleman had to live up to it. Gilbert's announcement to the assembled officers that, with or without GOU approval, the break would be decreed that night put an end for the moment to the debate but not to the indignation.

Indeed, from that moment on the position of President Ramírez and his most intimate collaborators was severely weakened. The much-vaunted unity of the GOU proved illusory; and an atmosphere of uncertainty and confusion settled over the officer corps. From the ranks of the more doctrinaire nationalists, who now looked increasingly to the Interior Minister,

General Perlinger, for leadership, came pressure for a shake-up in the government. Although Perón himself was one of their main targets, he was able to exploit the situation to his own advantage, directing the discontent against Foreign Minister Gilbert and Colonel González.

The impetus for ousting Gilbert and González came from younger officers who were resentful at the recent break in relations and aroused by a false report that these officials were persuading President Ramírez to issue three decrees that would establish martial law, mobilize the armed forces, and declare war on the Axis. It seems fairly clear that Perón, using his persuasive talents and the mechanisms of the GOU to dissociate himself from the alleged moves, inspired the young officers' demand for the resignations. Although a Perón spokesman in a conversation with U.S. Embassy officials a few weeks later tried to place responsibility for agitating the officers on Perlinger's shoulders, González insists that it was Perón himself, accompanied by Colonel Avalos, who asked him for his resignation. Finding himself without strength to fight back, González complied, and his action was followed shortly by the resignation of Foreign Minister Gilbert. The GOU was now swallowing its own.

The political crisis precipitated by the suddenness of the break in relations did not end with these resignations, however. General Ramírez now found himself threatened from two different quarters: on the one hand, the anti-rupturists within the officer corps, some of them pro-German but

many of them genuinely isolationist, who were being pressured into action by civilian nationalists anxious to take control of the government; and on the other, the Perón-Farrell group of officers, moved less by ideological considerations than by the instinct for self-preservation, hoping to use the anger of others for their own political advantage. Once again President Ramírez revealed his indecision, his lack of firmness, and his dislike for confrontations, but this time he himself was the sacrificial victim.

Having allowed González and Gilbert to be pushed out of office on February 15 without protest on his part, Ramírez belatedly realized that his own position was at stake when the rumors that had led to their ouster continued to circulate. In the garrisons of the capital, at El Palomar, at Campo de Mayo, and even at La Plata, officers were repeating the story that the President had ready for signature or, in another version, had already signed the three decrees imposing martial law, declaring a state of war with Germany and Japan, and ordering general mobilization. Ramírez tried to scotch the rumors by addressing two large gatherings of officers at First Division headquarters at Palermo and at Campo de Mayo, but his categorical denials were not accepted. Apparently the source of the rumors was the War Ministry itself, and the officers preferred to believe Farrell and Perón over a President who had jolted their faith by his earlier action.

The crisis reached its peak on February 24, after a series of moves that set the stage for a confrontation.

Late the previous night Perón and his fellow GOU hierarchs, sensitive to military attitudes toward the pledged word, had looked for a means of escaping from the oaths that they, like all GOU members, had taken to support President Ramírez. They finally hit on the cynical device of dissolving the organization. They did this, they later claimed, because they thought "it might become an obstacle to the normal march of government." But more to the point was their statement to the rank and file that "even if General Ramírez should want to continue the work of the GOU, the members of the executive body were freed of the oaths and obligations they have contracted."

But General Ramírez, far from wanting to continue the GOU, was trying to get rid of its leaders and beneficiaries. According to the available evidence, his plan was to appoint his loyal advisors, Gilbert and González, to the cabinet, replacing Farrell and Perlinger in the crucial War and Interior Ministries respectively. He took the first step on the morning of the 24th when he asked Farrell to give up the War Ministry post. The Vice-President responded by summoning key commanders of the various garrisons to an emergency meeting at the War Ministry. It was in this situation that Navy Minister Sueyro (who was also serving as Acting Foreign Minister) urged the President to arrest both Farrell and Perón, and offered to support him with naval forces. Unwilling to accept the prospect of a military confrontation, Ramírez refused. That night Farrell and Perón at the War Ministry, supported by the

assembled chiefs, moved to take over the government by force. Ramírez's appointees were replaced at police and communications headquarters, while forces responding to the War Ministry surrounded the presidential residence at Olivos, making Ramírez a virtual prisoner.

Informed by a delegation of officers that the military chiefs of the several garrisons demanded his resignation, the President complied, but not without first placing a verbal booby trap in the text of his resignation. In this document, one copy of which was sent to the Supreme Court and another to the War Ministry, Ramírez stated:

To the People of the Republic. Since I have ceased to merit the confidence of the jefes and officers of the garrisons of the Federal Capital, Campo de Mayo, Palomar, and La Plata, according to what these chiefs have just expressed personally, and since I do not desire to compromise the fate of the country, I yield to the imposition of force and present my resignation from the post of President of the Nation.

Pedro P. Ramírez, Major General
Buenos Aires, February 24, 1944

The sense of satisfaction with which the resignation was initially received at the War Ministry was soon tempered when members of the cabinet, summoned at Farrell's request, pointed out that the terms of the resignation would create a problem of diplomatic recognition for Ramírez's successor. At the suggestion of the Justice Minister, it was decided to ask Ramírez not to resign but simply to delegate his powers. In the early morning hours of the 25th, General Farrell, accompanied by several cabinet members, paid a visit to Ramírez at Olivos and urged him to comply. Despite Admiral Sueyro's advice that he stand firm, Ramírez yielded and signed his name to a prepared statement. The War Ministry suppressed the publication of his original resignation, and in its place Colonel Perón turned over to the press the following text:

To the People of the Argentine Nation. Fatigued by the intense tasks of government which require that I take a rest, as of this date I delegate the post I am discharging to the person of His Excellency the Vice-President of the Nation, Brigadier General Edelmiro J. Farrell.

Pedro P. Ramírez, Major General
Buenos Aires, February 24, 1944

The coup d'etat that deprived President Ramírez of all but the title of his office converted him paradoxically into the object of an intense, if temporary, political courtship. Liberal opponents of the military regime, Radicals and Socialists, generals and admirals, now offered to support his return to office if he would agree to associate himself with a movement to restore constitutional rule. Ramírez at first seemed interested, and specifically encouraged the Radical leader Dr. Ernesto Sammartino, who visited him on March 4, to go ahead with the preparation of the movement. Five days later, without a word to its organizers, Ramírez threw in the political towel, resigning his post as President. Once again, but for the last time, this slender cavalry general, whom fate had placed in a position to influence his country's future, demonstrated that a soldier's uniform was no substitute for political courage.

General Farrell's tenure proved to be short-lived; he governed for less than two years. After the Allied victory, the officers determined to remove Perón from his position as vice-president, but union-led riots and demonstrations were responsible for securing his release from prison. Four months later, Perón, under the banner of the Partido Laborista, won the presidency of Argentina.

The challenge to corporate professionalism is best demonstrated in the case of Chile. The study of Roy Allan Hansen helps to explain the politics of military institutionalization in Chile and the challenges faced by the civil order. Hansen's analysis focuses on the reaction of the professional military to the decline in its functions. As the police assumed responsibility for internal order and the importance of national defense ebbed, conflict within the military grew. Some officers, on the one hand, sought to restructure the army's goals to involve the military in national development, while on the other, the more traditional officers, committed to a narrower definition of military professionalism, sought to encourage professional isolation.

Roy Allan Hansen

Military Cultures and Organizational Decline in Chile

THE SIGNIFICANCE OF CLASS DIFFERENCES IN PUBLIC ORIENTATIONS TOWARD THE MILITARY

The Chilean military, both traditionally and at the time of this study [1967], acted primarily on behalf of the established social order and, therefore, in the interests of the more privileged classes. . . .

[But:] (1) The lower class was more likely than the middle and upper classes to support and/or favor expansion of military activities.

(2) The lower class was more favorable to the political intervention of the military as a solution to socio-economic or political problems than were the middle and upper classes. The primary purpose of this chapter is to seek to account for this inverse relationship between class position and favorability toward the military.

Favorability to the military appears to rest upon three criteria of evaluation: (1) the nature of the issue involved, i.e., its importance and urgency; (2) satisfaction with existing institutional arrangements; and (3) perceived competence of the military in dealing with the issue. Basically we have argued that . . . the lower class were more dissatisfied with existing

From Roy Allan Hansen, "Military Cultures and Organizational Decline, A Study of the Chilean Army" (Ph.D. diss., UCLA, 1967), chapters 5 and 8, by permission of the author.

conditions and so were more likely to seek alternatives than were the middle and upper classes. . . .

CLASS DIFFERENCES IN IMAGE OF THE MILITARY

The greater favorability of the lower class to the military role in maintaining internal order derives in large part from their dissatisfaction with the police. The middle and upper class more critically evaluated this military function not because they were necessarily less concerned with problems of internal order, but because they were more satisfied with the status quo, i.e., with the performance of the Carabineros.

This same general argument may be applied with respect to their evaluation of other military functions. The lower class, due to their structural position in society, were more dissatisfied with existing institutional arrangements and so were more likely to favor alternatives to the status quo than were the middle and upper classes. The greater favorability of the lower class to increased participation of the military in national development, for example, undoubtedly derived in some measure from their dissatisfaction with current programs of socio-economic modernization.

We have previously shown that the lower class most readily sanctioned and accorded legitimacy to the political intervention of the military as a solution to socio-economic and political conflicts. In this section we seek to demonstrate the existence and to investigate the basis of class differences in conditions under which legitimacy was accorded military intervention and government. In investigating these differences, the following propositions are examined:

1. As a consequence of their positions in the class structure, relatively greater emphasis was placed by the lower class on problems revolving about administrative ineffectiveness while the middle and upper classes were centrally concerned with guarantees against the imposition of arbitrary authority.

2. Class differences in image of the military in relation to alternate governing elites reflected their divergent needs and expectations of the military role as constitutional guardians.

The middle and upper classes, although legitimizing temporary intervention by the military if necessary to prevent anarchy, rebellion, or civil war, primarily perceived them as guarantees against the imposition of arbitrary authority.

The concern of the middle and upper classes with the military role as constitutional guardians appeared to have a dual source. First, democratic norms and political institutions were intrinsically valued and deemed worthy of protection. A relatively high degree of economic and psychological security increased the utility of (and concern about) personal autonomy and political freedom. Their greater political sophistication and less authoritarian predispositions

made them less likely to perceive a dictatorial regime as a simple answer to complex problems. Secondly, the radical reform programs which have historically been advocated by popular demagogues tied the preservation of democratic political institutions to their class interests. They had a greater vested interest in democracy due to their success in attaining and/or maintaining a favorable social position within the system.

The lower class appeared less concerned with arbitrary authority than with ineffective administration, particularly with respect to socio-economic issues. . . .

The acceptance of the military as constitutional guardians has previously been shown to have rested upon a public image of personal integrity and political impartiality. We have further proposed that class differences in image of the military would reflect their divergent definitions of circumstances justifying intervention. Four major governmental groups (military, national police, civil servants, and politicians) were comparatively ranked by respondents with respect to a series of concepts. Class differences in evaluation of those characteristics bearing upon the relative capability of these governmental groups to effectively deal with internal crises lent support to this proposition. . . .

The military were perceived as both more efficient and more industrious than civilian governmental groups by all social classes. . . .

Class differences in evaluation of the remaining two characteristics, intelligent and capable leaders, were immense. The lower class perceived the military as both most intelligent and having the most capable leaders. The middle and upper classes, however, over-whelmingly evaluated politicians most favorably on these characteristics. . . .

The middle and upper class thus appeared to view the military as efficient and industrious but without the intelligence or capable leaders necessary to govern effectively. Should intervention be necessary, their mandate was limited to calling elections to reestablish civilian government as rapidly as possible. The lower class, however, not only viewed the military as even more efficient and industrious than did the middle and upper classes, but also defined them as more intelligent and capable leaders than politicians. Individuals of lower class status, therefore, might reasonably have been expected to more frequently look to military intervention as a solution to socio-economic and political problems and to legitimatize military government for extended periods following intervention. . . .

Lower class authoritarianism may have contributed to class differences in image of the military. With available data, its significance cannot be directly ascertained. However, the factors of primary importance appear to have been: (1) lower class dissatisfaction with current political institutions, i.e., with politicians and the civil service; and (2) a projection onto the military of those characteristics which would be necessary for them to effectively serve as an alternative to civilian government under those conditions where this intervention is

personally approved. Thus, the greater favorability of the lower class to political intervention by the military, like their more favorable evaluation of their roles in national development and internal order, reflected lower class dissatisfaction with the status quo and their search for alternatives.

SUMMARY

This chapter has sought to account for the inverse relationship that had previously been shown to exist between class position and favorability toward the military. In general, we have shown that these class differences derived from a complex interaction of psychological, sociological, and cultural factors generated by and responding to the socio-economic and political environment. . . . The lower class, due to their objective position in society, were more dissatisfied with existing institutional arrangements and so were more likely to favor alternatives. Favorability toward the military roles in maintaining order, development, and as constitutional guardian thus derived in part from lower class dissatisfaction with the police, current developmental programs, and civilian political institutions, respectively. . . .

In general, however, the socio-economic position and authoritarianism of the lower class lent urgency to a range of issues (defense, socio-economic change, political reform, etc.) relevant to the role of the military in society and made for dissatisfaction with existing institutional arrangements. A lack of knowledge of the military then allowed the lower class to project onto the military an image which portrayed them as an effective alternative institution.

ORGANIZATIONAL DECLINE AND CIVIL-MILITARY RELATIONS

Organizations decline when the social functions which they perform decrease in importance to their clientele. This can occur when either its specific functions decline in relative importance or when, although the functions remain important, another organization performs them more effectively. Both of the major traditional goals of the Chilean Army, i.e., national defense and internal order, were shown to have been declining in relative importance to the society. In addition, the Carabineros had assumed an increasingly greater responsibility for maintaining internal order. . . . The reaction of the military to this decline is of key significance to an understanding of emerging patterns of civil-military relations and ultimately to the democratic stability of the nation. A primary purpose of this and the following chapter is to investigate the response of the Chilean Army, as reflected in the professional military culture of the officer corps, to its declining status and to speculate concerning its implications for the future of civilmilitary relations in Chile.

Since organizations consist of persons who have strong investments in the fate of the system, organizational decline tends to produce some form of adaptive behavior. Potentially available to the military were at least three modes of adaptation: (1) decline may act as an incentive for active political intervention; (2) decline may lead to a redefinition and/or reorientation of military goals to increase their relevance to their clientele; or (3) decline may result in a retreat into professional isolation. Most frequently, accommodation might be expected to involve elements of all three modes in some proportion. In accordance with the open-systems theoretical perspective, the pattern which emerges is expected to be constrained both by internal organizational commitments and by the environment, namely the organization's clientele and other social institutions.

This chapter seeks to show how internal commitments and environmental factors had shaped the accommodation of the Chilean Army to its declining status. Briefly stated, we argue as follows. Military decline inevitably generates hostility and resentments, especially toward political institutions, and so acts as an incentive for political involvement. The means employed and the success of these efforts in dealing with organizational decline will depend upon factors such as the legitimacy and effectiveness of the nation's political institutions, the conditions, if any, which the citizens of the society perceive as justifying political intervention by the military, the coercive power of the military vis-à-vis other social institutions, the degree of homogeneity of attitude toward involvement among the military elite, and the significance of the military's functions to its clientele. Democratic development must set limits on the political influence of the military in the society. Hence, the particular pattern of adaptation is of crucial significance to the maintenance of a democratic system.

GOAL RE-ORIENTATION OR ISOLATION: TWO PATTERNS COMPARED

As the environment increasingly limits the effectiveness of direct political pressure, the choice of adaptation to decline is correspondingly restricted to either a redefinition and/or orientation of military goals or a retreat into professional isolation. This choice, as with most social trends, is only seldom a deliberately planned strategy. Rather, it represents a series of day-to-day decisions the implications of which are usually not clear even to those who make them.

A common response of civilian bureaucracies to organizational decline is to seek to undertake new and more viable functions and/or to change their clientele. Therefore, what we called a civilian bureaucratic mode of adaptation would require that the Chilean military redefine and broaden their professional role and/or reorient their goals around the interests of new social groups. However, this solution necessarily implies that two conditions obtain: (1) the socio-cultural environment must be receptive to and provide opportunity for this goal transformation, and (2) the military must demonstrate a willingness to recognize and accept social change within the society and seek to accommodate itself to their changing environment. The existence of these conditions should be reflected in a broad and flexible definition of what constitutes legitimate military functions, both in the military culture of society and the professional culture

of the officer corps.

We have previously shown that demands for economic development and the emergence of the lower class as increasingly effective participants in the political process appear to have provided respectively an alternate goal and a powerful new social group around whose interests military goals could be reoriented. However, for the military itself, a bureaucratic mode of adaptation entails significant costs to their self-image as military professionals and to their own evaluation of the meaning and worth of their careers. Not only does this path transform them from military professionals into engineers or teachers, but also it invites comparison and competition with civilian organizations and institutions specializing in these functions. In addition, a substantial modification is involved of what is for many a highly valued life-style.

An unwillingness or inability of the military to accommodate themselves to this process of greater involvement in the internal social problems of the society may lead to an alternative mode of adaptation, that is, to *professional isolation and the development of a distinctive professional military culture*. . . .

Isolation reduces the dissonance between their sub-culture and the military culture of society and so makes for an increasingly distinctive professional military culture. Taken together, professional isolation and the development of a supportive professional culture protects the self-image of the military and their own favorable perception of the meaning and worth of their careers. In addition, these measures facilitate the retention of the traditional life-style of the officer. We term this second mode of adaptation to organizational decline the "professional" strategy.

A professional mode of adaptation, like the civilian bureaucratic method, entails considerable costs. A retreat into professional isolation reduces the relevance of the military to society, which (all else equal) will result in further organizational decline. Reductions in the size and budget of the Armed Forces, in addition to damaging their personal interests, will be viewed as dangerous to the national security. Furthermore, the institution and profession may suffer serious loss of public prestige by appearing reluctant or refusing to assume those functions defined by society as legitimate and appropriate.

The civilian bureaucratic and professional modes of adaptation are not necessarily mutually exclusive, i.e., the military may still attempt to increase their relevance to society although already undergoing a process of professional isolation and the development of a distinctive professional military culture. However, they are essentially conflictive strategies since one requires a broad and the other a narrow definition of military professionalism. Needless to say, these two adaptations should appeal to different segments of the military elite.

ADAPTATION OF THE MILITARY TO DECLINE: KEY CIVIL-MILITARY DIFFERENCES

The decreasing relevance of the de-fense function to Chilean society and their demand for an expanded military role in national development had generated, at the time this study was conducted, the most controversial issue within the officer corps of the Chilean Army, i.e., a definition of the meaning and role of the organization. The crux of the controversy was the issue of the necessity, desirability, and practicality of the professional specialization of the military. Their role in maintaining internal order was largely uninvolved in this debate since there existed a widespread consensus that during periods of crises this was an essential and legitimate military function. In addition, the existence of an efficient national police force made the issue of their routine employment in police matters academic. On the other hand, the question of whether or not the military should continue expanding their role in national development was of an immediate practical concern both to the maintenance of the organization and to the self-identity of the officer.

MILITARY PARTICIPATION IN DEVELOPMENT PROGRAMS

The Chilean military did appear to understand and sympathize with public demands for socio-economic development. As military professionals, however, they viewed their primary responsibility as dedicated to national defense and few, if any, officers felt that a greater proportion of current resources, already perceived to be grossly inadequate, should be diverted into civic action programs. However, some officers would have accepted, and even actively sought, an expanded participation of the military in developmental programs provided that additional resources were made available for that purpose. But even given such resources, disagreement existed as to the appropriateness and/or desirability of such participation.

A complete lack of consensus best describes the attitude of the officer corps toward military participation in national development. . . .

The opposition of the officer corps to extensive military participation in developmental programs appears to derive in part from their higher evaluation of the probability of war and the importance of military deterrence. . . .

Many officers felt that even if additional funds were made available, developmental programs would impair their primary task of national defense, i.e., their combat effectiveness. . . .

A second and perhaps more important source of opposition to participation in national development lay in the officers' self-image as military professionals and in their attachment to the traditional role and life-style of the officer. . . . It may be suggested here that both international patterns of professional military culture and the traditional professional military sub-culture of Chile define an officer as a specialist in "the direction, operation, and control of a human organization whose primary function is the application of violence." To the extent to which initial predisposition or professional indoctrination internalize these norms within the officer corps,

pressures to broaden or redirect military goals will be resisted. . . .

POLITICAL PERSPECTIVES OF
OFFICERS AND ATTITUDES TOWARD
CIVIC ACTION PROGRAMS

In general, our data suggested a close connection between political views and an officer's orientation toward military participation in civic action programs. Officers who held leftist political sentiments were more favorable to civic action than rightists. Eighty-nine percent of those who identified themselves as "leftist" favored an increase in civic action programs as compared to 52% of "somewhat leftist" and 17% of "rightist" or "somewhat rightist." . . .

Irrespective of whether or not they personally supported an increase in civic action, officers believed that the government favored expansion of these programs. For example, only two of the thirty-eight retired generals interviewed perceived the government as unfavorable to this participation. Not surprisingly, the implications of this commonly-held opinion to different segments of the military elite depended upon their own attitude to an increase in civic action.

Officers favorable to an increase in civic action generally viewed the attitude of the government as providing an opportunity for the organization to increase these programs. For example:

General of Division: ". . . I believe that the government would receive it (expansion of civic action) with great pleasure for the reasons that I have said so many times, that is, as a very economical contribution to its plans."

General of Division: ". . . I think that after a conscientious study of what is required and of the possibilities that the Army has, the government will not be able to oppose itself to these activities."

Some fear was expressed that the government might not allow the military to assume as much responsibility for these programs as they themselves favored. In fact, both of those generals who perceived the government as opposed to military participation were themselves favorable.

General of Division: "Presently I believe that the civil leaders would oppose it since there are professional technicians specialized in order to do these things. They would believe that the job should be left to these professionals."

Brigadier General: "Well, the government has never looked upon us favorably. They do not believe that we have sufficient preparation to do this. This really is a pity since in the Army there are highly capable, instructed, and intelligent people."

Officers unfavorable to a military role in development feared that the government's attitude would necessitate participation regardless of personal preference.

Brigadier General: "The government cannot demand more from the Army than it is already doing. I do not believe the government would look favorably upon national security being neglected. In any case, the military authorities can influence the government so that it will not demand more of the institution."

Brigadier General: "For the government, it (civic action) is all honey and pastries, except if it is interested in the national defense."

Believing that the government does not understand (or care about) the military and/or problems of national defense, these officers generally resented, and advocated resistance to, government "interference."

We have previously shown that hostility toward the "ignorance" of civilian leaders with respect to defense issues was common. This hostility appeared to derive significantly from the consequences of civilian indifference to defense issues to the welfare of the organization. One mode of adaptation to the resulting organizational decline was through a reorientation of military goals, i.e., to an increase in civic action. A perceived favorability of the government to military participation in civic action might, therefore, be expected to reduce the hostility and resentment to the government of those officers favoring a civilian bureaucratic mode of adaptation. On the other hand, the hostility to the military policies of the government of officers opposing any change in military goals might be expected to increase.

Attitude toward the military policies of the government were probed as follows: "Frequently military and civilian authorities are not in agreement on matters of national security. To what do you attribute these disagreements?" Responses were classified in four categories, i.e., disagreements attributed primarily to: (1) mutually limited perspectives of officers and politicians; (2) inadequate institutional arrangements to assure adequate communication and understanding; (3) a lack of knowledge of defense issues by civilian authorities due to their training and their diverse responsibilities; and (4) civilian indifference, ignorance, and/or fear of the military. The first two categories are taken to indicate a low degree of hostility and resentment to civilian authority, the third an intermediate degree, and the fourth the highest level.

Officers favorable to an increase in civic action were less resentful and hostile to the government's military policies than were those opposed to these programs. Seventy-seven percent of officers "least hostile" to civilian authority favored an increase in civic action as compared to 50% of the "most hostile" category. . . . Simi-

larly, since a high correlation existed between political views and favorability to civic action, leftist officers might be expected to be least hostile to governmental military policies. As demonstrated in the table below, our findings generally confirm this relationship. Seventy-eight percent of leftist officers were classified as "least hostile" to civilian authority. No rightist officer was so classified. Again, although the number of cases is small, the differences are significant.

The degree of hostility within the officer corps to civilian authority was of crucial significance to the maintenance of democracy in Chile because of the fragility of Chile's democratic institutions. The military culture of Chile still viewed a military role as constitutional guardian as both legitimate and necessary. Officers also overwhelmingly viewed this function as an obligation incumbent upon their professional role.

POLITICAL IDENTIFICATION AND PERCEIVED CAUSE OF DISAGREEMENTS BETWEEN
MILITARY AND POLITICAL ELITES

| | Political Identification | | | | | |
| | Leftist | | Somewhat Leftist | | Rightist | |
	%	N	%	N	%	N
Mutually Limited Perspectives	44	4	5	1	0	0
Inadequate Institutional Arrangements	33	3	19	4	0	0
Civilians Lack Knowledge (Due to Training, Responsibilities, etc.)	0	0	19	4	0	0
Civilians Indifferent, Ignorant, or Fear Military	22	2	57	12	100	4
	99	9	100	21	100	4

General of Division: "The (role as constitutional guardian) is what we are for."

Brigadier General: "It is one of the obligations of the Army; it has to do this."

Officers more highly evaluated the importance of the role of the military as constitutional guardians than did middle and upper class civilians. . . . It should be noted, however, that the military was considerably less unanimous in its acceptance of this role than were lower class civilians. . . .

Our data generally indicate that no relationship existed between an officer's political views and his evaluation of the military's role as constitutional guardian. Two-thirds of the officers identifying themselves as leftist, somewhat leftist, and rightist in political sentiment "agreed strongly" with the statement: "The military is necessary for the country even if there is no war in order to act as a guardian of the constitution in case that a government tried to violate it." However, should a political or economic crisis have presented the military with an opportunity for political intervention, leftist officers, who under existing conditions were least resentful and hostile to civilian authority, might have been expected to least favor such intervention. A government fearful of military intervention may be reluctant to channel developmental funds through the military since these programs act to increase their popularity with the lower class and thus their interventionist capabilities. In this respect, a civilianist bureaucratic mode of adaptation to organizational decline rests upon the long-term goodwill of the civilian government. This acts as

an incentive for assuring the government of their acceptance, at least in practice, of the principle of military subordination to civilian authority. . . .

CONCLUDING COMMENTS

Chile's democratic development appeared to have reached a stage where, under normal conditions and in the absence of a clear threat to the national security, the political influence of the military was insufficient to intimidate the government. Under such circumstances, the Chilean Army had to seek alternative means of dealing with its declining status. Nevertheless, the fragility of Chile's democratic political institutions should not be overlooked. Under a variety of conditions, the public still accepted military intervention as legitimate and necessary. Thus, the attitude of the military toward intervention and the pattern of civil-military relations which emerges from their adaptation to their declining status were of crucial concern to the democratic stability of the society.

This chapter has sought to test a central hypothesis of the study which concerns the consequences for the society of the decline of the military. We hypothesized that this decline: (1) has led to internal dissension and conflict over the meaning and role of the military, and (2) has brought about a partial restructuring of military goals. We further proposed that these new goals would be primarily oriented around the interests of the lower class sectors of the society.

In accordance with the argument outlined above, we proposed that the availability of new goals related to socio-economic development and the greater favorability of the lower class to the military made for a civilian bureaucratic response to decline, that is, to a partial restructuring of military goals. However, commitment to a narrow definition of military professionalism and to the traditional role and life-style of the officer generated internal resistance to these changes and encouraged adaptation through professional isolation. The simultaneous occurrence of both patterns was symptomatic of internal dissension and conflict.

Orientations of the officer corps to military intervention in politics likewise reflected the impact of organizational decline. Decline may act as an incentive for political involvement and encourage a demand for military autonomy. Yet, a lack of political influence under normal circumstances means that the organization's welfare depends directly on the resources allocated to it by the civilian government. Under these circumstances, decline may act as an incentive for relinquishing autonomy and assuring the civilian government of the fundamental loyalty and professionalism of the military establishment. Resolution of this dilemma provided another potential source of internal dissonance and conflict in the officer corps. Furthermore, to the extent that the military seeks to maintain a degree of autonomy from the government, the emergence of the lower class as a major political force might be expected to motivate the military to secure popular support by reorienting their goals so as to gain political support from the lower class sectors of society. Hence, the very factors that were indicative of military political weakness will also function as potential sources of political power and strength.

To conclude, this analysis suggests that the military appeared to have adapted to organizational decline both through adopting civilian bureaucratic measures and by a partial retreat into professional isolation. Their simultaneous occurrence was reflected in the intra-organizational conflict between a broad and a narrow definition of military professionalism. Professional isolation appeared to be associated with a narrow definition of military professionalism which generated resistance to policies designed to deal with organizational decline by a partial restructuring of military goals. The lack of homogeneity among the military elite was seen as both a cause and a consequence of the decline.

[The Chilean army stood aside and tolerated the reforms of the government of President Frei, but in September 1973, they overthrew the leftist regime of Salvador Allende. The most professional of the officers intervened against the alliance of the civilian left and the military liberals.]

The story of the transformation from arbitrator to ruler praetorianism is found in Alfred Stepan's outstanding study of Brazilian civil-military relations. Stepan explains the manner in which the military establishment has legitimized itself, not as an arbiter, but as an autonomous and sophisticated political structure dominating Brazil's modern political arrangements and institutions. Since Stepan's book merits considerable attention, we shall divide the excerpts into the following categories: 1. The Institutional Background of the Military; 2. The Moderating Pattern of Civil-Military Relations; 3. The Emergence of Military Rule; 4. The Brazilian Military in Power.

ALFRED STEPAN

The Institutional Background of the Military in Brazil

MILITARY ORGANIZATIONAL UNITY AND NATIONAL ORIENTATION: HYPOTHESES AND QUALIFICATIONS

COMPARATIVE ANALYSIS

A classic criticism of the military has been that its codes, hierarchy, uniforms, and barracks set it dangerously apart physically and psychologically from civilian life. Recently, however, a new school of analysts, worried by the problems of national unity and nation-building in developing countries, has emphasized that the military can perform a constructive role in these areas precisely because its training, organization, and national recruitment mission help isolate it from subnational tribal, regional, or political pressures in the polity. . . .

As a group, this school of analysts has helped make political observers sensitive to the fact that under some

From Alfred Stepan, The Military in Politics: Changing Patterns in Brazil (Princeton, N. J., 1971), pp. 9-20, by permission of Princeton University Press. Copyright © 1971 by the Rand Corporation.

circumstances the military can make a contribution to development. Clearly, in a country such as Turkey the army has played an important role in nation-building and modernization. In comparison to other elites, the military is often less parochial and more national in orientation.

While recognizing this, I nevertheless feel that both the traditional liberal critics of the military and the modern "neorealists" often overestimate the unitary, self-encapsulated aspects of the military institution, and underemphasize the degree to which a military organization is permeated and shaped by outside political pressures. Obviously the situation will vary from country to country. However, if we examine the question of the military's contribution to national unity, much evidence exists that in many developing countries not only is the military not isolated from the tensions experienced by the general population and therefore not able to act as an integrating force, but the military is itself an element in the polity that may transform latent tensions into overt crises.

The armies of many of the new nations were originally created as instruments of imperial control. As such they were often deliberately constructed with extreme tribal, racial, and religious imbalances. This policy, coupled with the normal differential rates of recruitment based on education and inclination, makes these armies all too often both unrepresentative and explosive. Contrary to the national orientation and national integration hypotheses, the power to "socialize to national identity" of these armies has often been very weak. Primordial sentiments and loyalties frequently express themselves in violence. Three of the most costly civil wars in the newly independent nations had their immediate origins within the military. . . .

BRAZILIAN MILITARY: RECRUITMENT STRUCTURE

The Brazilian military outwardly appears to conform to a national and therefore integrating institution. Indeed, a motto is stamped on many of the army publications: "The Army— Agent of National Integration." Its proudest claim is that the army is, in the words of a minister of war:

. . . unquestionably a part of the people, perhaps the most representative of the people, because within its ranks the classes mix, the social standards become the same, the creeds and political parties are ignored, differentiation and inequality among men are forgotten. . . . The Army . . . has been since the beginning of the Nation the great armor which sustained the unity of the Homeland, preserving it from

threats of fragmentation, assuring the cohesion of that archipelago of provinces that tended to become isolated, each with its own peculiarities.

Undoubtedly, the army and the navy played a major role in suppressing the regional revolts that rocked Brazil between 1824 and 1848. Other undeniable contributions were the army's roles in linking the country by road-building and in establishing settlements in the previously almost unpopulated areas of the vast hinterland. But today how strong is the army's ability to inculcate a sense of national identification in its members? Is it exclusively a nationally oriented institution, or is it also strongly influenced by local factors? Does the ideal-type image obscure important aspects of the political behavior of the military?

To attempt to answer the question for Brazil, I have first analyzed the military draft structure. Evidence indicates that the claim to be a "melting pot," in which distinct regional and social characteristics disappear, is a gross oversimplification. The recruitment policy of the Brazilian army has traditionally been that of drafting men from an area *as close as possible to each garrison*, the vast majority of which are located in urban areas. In practice, this means that most of the draftees are urban and they serve in a unit less than ten miles from their homes and families. Additional factors inhibiting socialization to a national perspective or to army standards are that draftees are normally released after serving nine months of their year of obligated service and, while on active duty, normally return to their homes every weekend. Quite often, indeed, recruits eat lunch and spend their nights at their family's home during their period of service in the army.

These recruitment policies are formalized in army regulations. The major reason for local recruitment seems to be a desire to eliminate the considerable cost of transportation involved in taking a recruit from his home for a short stay in a different geographical area. Because Brazil has no organized reserve, local recruitment also increases the likelihood that a recruit will reside near the unit in which he formerly served, making it easy for the unit to call him up in an emergency. A third reason for the recruitment policy is a deliberate attempt to slow the rural exodus by not drafting rural recruits to serve in urban garrisons and thus risking the possibility that they would not return to the countryside upon completion of their military service.

What of the career-enlisted men and officers? Do they conform more closely to the image of the professional military man as encapsulated in a national institution without real links to his region of origin in what S. E. Finer termed the military's "systematized nomadism moving from one garrison town to another"?*

On the whole, one must answer in the negative. Family ties are still very important in Brazil. In addition, military pay scales are low. In order to avoid high costs for transportation

*The Man on Horseback. The Role of the Military in Politics (London: Pall Mall Press, 1962), p. 9.

to visit families and for other personal reasons, many officers, if they are not attending service schools or serving in army headquarters in Rio, prefer to be stationed close to their families. . . . Thus the national army of Brazil has some of the recruitment characteristics of a state militia, since it is largely manned by soldiers from the immediate area.

Another feature of the federal army also reduces its nation-building potential. Brazil, with a population of 90 million, has far more draftable men than it needs. Indeed, as in many developing countries, the problem quite often becomes one of establishing criteria for selecting draftees. As a result of excess supply, the army can afford to be very selective in recruiting draftees. Their choice lies between either emphasizing the nation-building role of the army by deliberately drafting a cross section of the population or satisfying army requirements for skilled and literate draftees who can rapidly develop some degree of technical military competence.

Official Brazilian publications often make allusions to massive numbers of illiterates who enter the army each year and are released only when they have become literate. The barracks are said to be "huge classrooms" within which the men of the countryside are given their first exposure to modernity. This is rarely the case. Analysis shows that faced with the choice between educating rural illiterates and drafting already trained men, the Brazilian army chooses the latter alternative. . . .

In Brazil, there is no centralized mechanism of recruitment. Each unit, in conjunction with a few local government officials, drafts its own recruits from its immediate geographical area. Whether to choose illiterates or not becomes a matter of the personal preference and professional needs of unit commanders. . . .

THE POLITICAL SIGNIFICANCE OF THE BRAZILIAN RECRUITMENT STRUCTURE

It is clear that an army organized on a local basis, with an exclusive system of recruitment that favors the literate over the illiterate, the urban over the rural, cannot bring ordinary soldiers from different geographical and educational sectors of Brazil into face-to-face cooperation in a nationally oriented institution. The hypothesis, therefore, that the recruitment structure of the military makes a major contribution to nation-building needs to be seriously qualified.

In fact, a locally recruited army in a federal system of politics has some serious political implications. Brazil has many political disputes which involve conflicts between individual states and the central government. In addition, many of the individual states have strong state military police forces, normally called militias even though they are full time. . . .

Since 1964, the successive military governments have attempted to tighten army control over the militias. Before 1964, these militias were largely commanded by the governors of the states. Equipment routinely includes rifles, machine guns, trucks, occasional armored personnel carriers and some light mortars. Judged by fire power alone, the state militias have

not been a match for the federal army since the 1930 revolution curtailed their equipment and autonomy. But since they were often the armed representatives of powerful state governors, at least until 1964, and since the federal army itself had a territorial recruitment base, the state militias nonetheless presented a periodic *political* and psychological threat to the national army. The local base of the national army, together with the fact that state politicians have been armed through state militias, has several times precipitated a crisis of loyalty that fragmented entire sections of the national army. In the conflicts of 1930, 1932, and 1961, armed civil war either occurred or seemed imminent.

In each case, a strong governor or state leader was initially in conflict with the national army. The state leaders were all backed by their state militias. In all three cases there was sustained "psychological warfare" in which appeals were made to local loyalties of federal troops, as against national loyalty to the federal army. . . .

Contrary to the suggestion that the national army is relatively immune to regional and local influences, these three cases reveal that in times of great political crisis, especially in a crisis involving regional claims, state leaders have been most successful in using state militias and the rhetoric of regionalism to win over or effectively neutralize whole segments of the national army. Clearly, the examples illustrate that to study the role of the Brazilian or any other army adequately, one cannot proceed from the proposition that the army, because of

its mission and organization, is exclusively a nationally oriented and
unified institution. Instead, as this
and the following chapter show, there

is a constant need to evaluate military
institutional characteristics within the
larger framework of the overall political system.

ALFRED STEPAN

The Moderating Pattern of Civil-Military Relations

THE MODERATOR MODEL OF
CIVIL-MILITARY RELATIONS

Before describing the specific characteristics of the model, it is useful to
sketch out some of the broad characteristics of the political culture within
which this pattern of civil-military
relations develops. Most Latin American countries are semielitist, semi-
mobilized, and semideveloped. Characteristically, no group or political party
has effectively harnessed political and
economic power to meet the demands
of development. Political demands are
high, but political capacity to convert
these demands into effective outputs
is low. The society is "praetorian" in
the sense that all institutions—the
church, labor, students—are highly
politicized. But at the same time, the
political institutions are weak.

In such a society the military is also
politicized, and all groups attempt to
co-opt the military to augment their
political power. This constant co-
option rules out professionalization
in Huntington's sense, even though

From *Alfred Stepan*, The Military in Politics:
Changing Patterns in Brazil *(Princeton, N. J.,
1971), pp. 62–81, by permission of Princeton
University Press. Copyright © 1971 by the Rand
Corporation.*

formal indicators of professionalism
may appear to be increasing. Thus in
the case of Peru, Brazil, and Argentina, hierarchical structure, internal
differentiation, and promotion patterns all indicate a fairly professional
military, yet at the same time the
military is highly politicized in each
of these countries. This pattern of
civil–military relations, in which all
political actors routinely attempt to
involve the military in politics, differentiates it from the liberal model
where the goal is an apolitical military.

These facts of military politicization
are often obscured, however, because
Latin American social and political
elites see themselves as part of Western
European culture. Part of their heritage is to view the parliamentary form
of government as an inherent part of
a civilized and developed polity. In
this view, military rule is thus ruled
out as a legitimate solution to the
problem of development. These aspirations coexist with a praetorian
society. This uneasy coexistence is
probably the key component of the
moderator model of civil–military
relations. It also sheds light on the
nature and limits of the military's role
in that society.

Typically, the parliamentary processes sought as an ideal form of government provide an ineffective mechanism for resolving political conflicts in a praetorian society. Political parties are often fragmented. Given the desire by the political elites to maintain internal order, to check the executive, and to control the political mobilization of new groups, and given also the absence of other institutions to carry out these tasks efficiently, political elites often find it expedient to grant the military a limited degree of legitimacy to perform these specific tasks under certain conditions. However, only a low legitimacy is given to the idea of government by the military itself.

In such a pattern of civil–military relations, the military is repeatedly called into politics to be the moderator of political activity, but is denied the right systematically to attempt to direct changes within the political system. Unlike the "nation-building" or "reform" military seen in some of the new nations, the military task in the moderator model is essentially the conservative task of systems maintenance. Military activity is usually restricted to the removal of the chief executive and the transference of political power to alternative civilian groups. Military acceptance of this role is contingent upon military acceptance of the legitimacy and feasibility of parliamentary political forms, and upon their assessment that in comparison to civilians they possess a relatively low capacity for ruling.

Like the aristocratic and professional models of civil-military relations, the moderator model does not rest upon a set of controls imposed by civilians, but on a set of norms both within and without the military. The norms encourage a highly political military whose political acts are nonetheless limited to certain boundaries. In this sense, the model assumes a military that is both controlled and yet highly politicized, and the nature of the control is very different from that found in the other models.

The key components in this pattern of civil–military relations may be summarized as follows:

1. All major political actors attempt to co-opt the military. A politicized military is the norm.

2. The military is politically heterogeneous but also seeks to maintain a degree of institutional unity.

3. The relevant political actors grant legitimacy to the military under certain circumstances to act as moderators of the political process and to check or overthrow the executive or to avoid the breakdown of the system, especially one involving massive mobilization of new groups previously excluded from participation in the political process.

4. Approval given by civilian elites to the politically heterogeneous military to overthrow the executive greatly facilitates the construction of a winning coup coalition. Denial by civilians that the overthrow of the executive by the military is a legitimate act conversely hinders the formation of a winning coup coalition.

5. There is a strong belief among civilian elites and military officers that while it is legitimate for the military to intervene in the political process and exercise temporary political power, it is illegitimate for the military to

assume the direction of the political system for long periods of time.

6. This rough value congruence is the result of civilian and military socialization via schools and literature. The military doctrine of development is also roughly congruent with that of parliamentary groups. The military officers' social and intellectual deference facilitates military co-option and continued civilian leadership.

Given the perspective of this pattern of civil-military relations, many somewhat paradoxical characteristics of Latin American politics fall into place. Whereas military intervention has traditionally been seen as representing the *decomposition* of the political system, in terms of the moderator model it may be seen as the normal method of *composition* in political life. What before have been viewed as rapid, secret, or unilateral coups d'etat by the military against civilian governments are now seen as slowly evolved, open, and dual responses of civilian and military elites to particular political crises, in which both civilians and the military look to the military for the resolution of the crisis. What has been called "pathological interventionism" in terms of the liberal model becomes the normal functioning of the political system in the moderator model, whereby civilians look to the military to perform a moderating role at certain times.

[We] examine Brazilian politics and civil–military relations as a paradigm case of the moderating pattern. The analysis deals with the period between 1945 and 1964, during which this pattern of civil–military relations was dominant and before it broke down in the revolution of 1964. Undoubtedly the parameters of the model were better established, the rules of the game more widely understood, and communications more sophisticated in Brazil than in other Latin American countries. Nonetheless, I believe that detailed research would reveal that some of the behavioral patterns and supportive attitudes that characterized the moderating pattern of civil–military relations in Brazil from 1945 to 1964 have been prominent at various times in many other countries of Latin America.

The questions raised by the model and which I attempt to answer . . . are these: Which civilians have wanted the military to play a political role, and why? What influences did civilian attitudes have on the propensity and capacity of the military institution to perform the highly political act of deposing a president? Under what conditions were coups likely to fail? [We] examine [here] the political reasons, historical development, and internal logic of this pattern of civil–military relations.

Two further introductory points can be raised at this point, one concerning the choice of the word "moderator" to describe the model, and the other concerning the definition of military legitimacy. According to the model described in the following chapters, the military in Brazil enjoyed the power to moderate the political system at times of crisis. The term "moderating power" does have a sense specific to Brazil, where, during the monarchy, the emperor had the constitutional function of intervening to resolve the political crisis at times of institutional deadlock on political conflict. This function was called *o poder moderador* ("the moderating power"). Many Brazilians have noted that since the fall of the monarchy in 1889, the military has both assumed and been delegated the traditional "moderating power" originally exercised by the emperor.

I have retained the Brazilian terminology to describe this model of civil–military relations, but I intend to use it in a broader generic sense to combine the meanings of the terms "arbiter" and "moderator." I prefer these to "guardian" because I do not mean to imply that the Brazilian military always exercised a benevolent, parental authority. The term "umpire" implies more formal rules than in fact existed, and does not carry the necessary connotation that the exercise of the arbiter-moderator function required a degree of *invitation* and *acceptance* to be effective. No analogy for the moderating function is perfect, however, and the full sense of the term will only emerge in my analysis of the dynamics of civil–military relations and military coups as they occurred in Brazil between 1945 and 1964.

The second point I wish to make concerns the legitimacy of the political role for the military. When we discuss the legitimacy of a government or the legitimacy of a political role for the military, we are largely concerned with what the participant civilian political groups considered appropriate political processes, given all the circumstances. My analysis indicates that the military was often felt to be the only available structure that could perform certain functions the partici-

pant elite felt had to be performed. Military performance of these functions—whether checking the executive or maintaining internal order—was thus granted some degree of legitimacy, even by many groups who on cultural grounds were deeply anti-militarist.

Thus when I argue in the following chapters that civilian groups "sanctioned" military intervention at certain times, my point is not to argue that I think such action was morally legitimate, just, or correct, but rather to illustrate how deeply embedded such activity was in the political system itself. I have thus attempted to develop systematically John J. Johnson's interesting insight that the phenomenon that exists in many countries of Latin America and that needs analysis is not "militarism" but "civil-militarism."*

CIVILIAN ASPECTS OF THE "MODERATING PATTERN"

INTRODUCTION

Historically, civilians who form the politically relevant strata of Brazilian society have always attempted to use the military to further their own political goals. Coupled with the diversity and openness of the Brazilian military institution, this has meant that military officers have always been highly politicized. A further consequence of the internal diversity of the military and persistent attempts by civilian

*John J. Johnson, *The Military and Society in Latin America* (Stanford: Stanford University Press, 1964), pp. 119–125.

groups to co-opt military officers into politics is that the military is never unified in its political beliefs and ideology, but is normally reflective to some degree of the broad range of civilian opinion.

To understand how this situation has arisen in Brazil, one can divide politically relevant civilians into three main groups, and examine each in turn. These elite groups are:

1. The president and his chief advisors, i.e., the government.

2. The antiregime civilians who oppose not only the government but the regime itself, and who wish to change the basic rules and authority structure.

3. The proregime civilians who, while supporting the basic rules of the regime, frequently disagree with the government and desire to check the executive by other than legislative or electoral methods.

Historically, proregime civilians were the most important group for determining the role of the military in the political system and the course of military coups in Brazil. Nonetheless, the other two groups have also played an important role.

POLITICIZATION OF THE MILITARY: THE EXECUTIVE

Brazilian presidents, for several reasons, have always tried to use the military officers as personal instruments of their government. In Brazil, as in many other developing countries, the relatively weak capacity to mobilize economic resources is matched by the government's relatively weak regulative, extractive, and distributive capability. The president often finds his reform proposals blocked by Congress, by powerful, entrenched elites, or by conflicting demands from his constituency.

In these circumstances, a classic manueuver has been for the president to attempt to gain military support for his proposals directly or indirectly, as a club against his opponents. Since the three military ministers and the commanders of the major territorial armies are appointed by him, the president can and has used these appointments as a means of gaining military support.

Examples of presidential co-option of the military exist in nearly every Brazilian government between 1937 and 1964 except Kubitschek's, whether they involve strong, semiauthoritarian presidents like Getúlio Vargas, or weak populist presidents, such as João Goulart. . . .

Brazil is not unique in Latin America in having presidents requiring active partnership from the armed forces, instead of professional neutrality or passivity. In Chile, the major period of military activism in politics between 1924 and 1931 was in part the result of President Alessandri's deliberate attempt to politicize the officers so that they would pressure a recalcitrant Congress to pass his reform legislation.

Another classic use of the military by presidents is as an extralegal force to repress political opponents. One of the first uses to which President Roca put the greatly strengthened federal army of Argentina in the 1880s, for example, was to curtail the powers of provincial governors. Later, after the first middle-class radical government came to power in 1916, the new president, Hipólito Yrigoyen, systematically attempted to transform the professional army into a personal political force to control provincial elections. In Brazil, the federal army was also often used in the period of the "Old Republic" for similar purposes. In the modern Brazilian period one of the more celebrated attempts by a president to use the army to eliminate a political opponent was President João Goulart's attempt to abduct his most vociferous critic, Governor Carlos Lacerda of Guanabara, using a paratrooper unit.

These examples indicate that presidential utilization of the military in politics occurs frequently in Brazil and Latin America, especially in cases where the president is faced with dissension among politically relevant groups. In this circumstance, presidents have traditionally attempted to increase their own power resources by using the armed forces as an instrument of political power.

POLITICIZATION OF THE MILITARY: ANTIREGIME FORCES

The same situation exists with antiregime civilians in Brazil. By antiregime civilians I mean those political actors attempting to change the basic rules of the entire political system and to alter the principles of authority and legitimacy. The most important groups who fall within this definition have also traditionally used the armed forces as an instrument of their political strategy, and have attempted to co-opt them ideologically.

This process began with the birth of the Brazilian Republic, when the Republicans systematically recruited military support in the overthrow of the monarchy. Similarly, the "Old Republic" came to an end in 1930 not so much because of the efforts of the young rebellious lieutenants within the army (the *tenentes*), but because of movements in the two major states of Minas Gerais and Rio Grande do Sul. Political leaders of these states waged a major campaign to win support or at least passivity from the army before the revolt. Several senior army officers were informed ahead of time that civilians would launch a revolution against the established regime. It was argued that given the nation's need to establish a new political order, it was the duty and obligation of the military not to resist. Officers and enlisted men of Rio Grande do Sul were bombarded with these and regional arguments long before the revolution was launched in the state.

Again in 1945 when the *Estado Nôvo* regime was overthrown, and in 1964, when democratic, competitive politics broke down, there were similar, systematic efforts by civilians and military men to co-opt the military to change the political regime. No more, indeed, than the presidents, have the antiregime forces in Brazil wanted a professional and apolitical military. Rather, antiregime groups have constantly employed the rhetoric that the military's special responsibility for the destiny of Brazil requires that they become active participants in creating a new political order. A study of other antiregime groups in Latin American countries reveals a similar process at work. . . .

THE MILITARY AND THE PROREGIME STRATA

The most interesting elite group within the political system in Brazil in terms of its attitude toward the military is what I have called the proregime civilians. In this group I include congressmen, governors, political party leaders, newspaper editors, and voters who generally accept the constitutional framework and support the existing regime, but who may or may not support the government at specific times.

It is this large group of people that have historically expected the military to play the key political role of checking the actions of the executive. In most political systems that have evolved beyond tribal chieftainships, or primitive, one-man dictatorships, one of the traditional goals of these civilians has been to control the executive within an accepted sphere of action. In strong party systems, whether of the British parliamentary type, or of the Communist type, the party itself performs this function. . . . The judiciary can also implement constraints on presidential authority by determining the constitutionality of executive decrees. In addition, and very importantly, elections themselves act as an important method of restraint by periodically subjecting the executive mandate to renewal.

In Brazil, however, as in many of the developing areas, the political institutions of the legislature and the judiciary are at times subject to complete executive control. Elections are often uncertain affairs or they are controlled outright by the executive. Many members of the polity have for these reasons felt little confidence in the efficacy of these institutions to check executive activity. Informally or formally, proregime civilian groups outside the government often tend to assign this task to the military.

The process leading to this state of affairs is clearly seen in congressional debates over the political role of the military in Brazilian society at the time of framing new constitutions. Congress is an important index of the opinion of proregime civilians in Brazil's federal system, since it is here that many of the most powerful groups within the political system publicly articulate their demands. The Brazilian Congress has been one of the strongest in Latin America in this century, and local and regional groups have traditionally received much of their financing via congressional legislation. Congress also passes or blocks such basic reforms as enfranchisement of illiterates or agrarian reform. It normally plays a part in the careers of the major national political leaders, who often move from the mayoralty of a large city to the Congress as a deputy, back to the state as a governor, and finally back to Congress as a senator, or on to the presidency.

The proregime civilians met collectively in 1892, 1934, and 1946 to draft new constitutions for Brazil. At these assemblies they expressed their ideas and opinions as to what they felt was the necessary and appropriate function of the military in the Brazilian political system. Their opinions, as expressed in the constituent assemblies, are an index of the *de facto* legitimacy accorded the military to perform a political role in checking the powers of the presidency and as such are extremely important in that legitimacy flows from operative attitudes. In addition, the final product of the constituent assemblies, the constitutions themselves, while not able to create a power that did not exist, could ratify an existing power and furnish it with the language and rationale necessary for its communication to the military and to other political actors.

The constitutions adopted in 1891, 1934, and 1946 were virtually identical in their two major conclusions in regard to the role of the military in Brazilian politics. This role was described in two key clauses. The first stated that the military was a permanent, national institution specifically charged with the task of maintaining law and order in the country and of guaranteeing the continued normal functioning of the three constitutional powers: the executive, the legislature, and the judiciary. The second clause made the military obedient to the executive, but significantly stated that they should only be obedient "within the limits of the law" (*dentro dos limites da lei*). This in effect authorized the military to give only discretionary obedience to the president, since obedience was dependent upon their decision regarding the legality of the presidential order.

The constitutional obligation of the military to ensure the proper functioning of and balance between the executive, legislature, and the judiciary has meant that in any clash between the president and the legislature, appeals have been made by civilians to the military to fulfill their constitutional obligation to defend the prerogatives of the Congress.

These constitutional provisions would be less significant if it could be shown that they were either unconsciously included in the constitutions, habitually so included, or were included due to imposition by the military themselves. But the evidence suggests that they were none of these. On the contrary, the role imposed constitutionally on the military, as expressed by the two clauses above, was consciously adopted in spite of the fact that certain members of the constituent assemblies brought forward specific amendments to abolish the two clauses because they gave too much power to the military within the political system. . . .

What were the arguments that were advanced and, after discussion, accepted by the majority of the proregime, politically relevant, strata over the years? The framer and principal advocate of the first constitution of the Republic, Ruy Barbosa, was known as a major spokesman against an overlarge role for the military in society. The theme of his presidential candidacy in 1910 was the need to contain military influence and ensure civilian control. Nonetheless, he still argued in 1892, and reiterated later, that the clause "within the limits of the law" was necessary because real obedience can only come if the superior of the military (i.e., the president) is obedient to the law. Thus, despite his antimilitarism, he expressed uncertainty in regard to the capacity of the civilian political system to produce and maintain presidents who would operate "within the law" without any military check. . . .

It is clear that many major actors in Brazilian politics have felt anxiety about the ability of civilian institutions to check the chief executive. They felt the need for a checking device, and before 1964 they consistently expressed the belief that the military was the appropriate institution for carrying out this role. In their informal attitudes they accorded legitimacy to the concept that the military was an integral part of the political system and they constitutionally sanctioned the view that the military had under certain conditions the obligation to intervene in the political process. To ensure that the military had the necessary autonomy to implement this function, they consistently made military obedience to the president not automatic, but discretionary. Thus *de facto* attitudinal legitimacy was supported and routinized by *de jure* constitutional legitimacy.

The fact that these attitudes had been incorporated in the Brazilian constitutions meant that an acceptable political formula existed, as well as a subtle but nonetheless widely understood language, for the politician and the public to use in appealing to the military to intervene in politics to check or even depose a president. . . . This was repeatedly used in the 1945–1964 period.

While Brazil is the paradigm case of this "moderating pattern" of civil–military relations, other Latin American countries have also given *de jure* legitimacy to the military performance of the role of checking the executive or

guaranteeing the constitution. For example, the 1965 constitution of Honduras states that the "armed forces are instituted in order to . . . maintain peace, the public order, and the rule of this constitution; and above all to see that the principles of free suffrage and noncontinuity of the presidency of the Republic are not violated." Thirteen other Latin American countries specifically charge the military with the role of protecting or guaranteeing the constitution.

The picture that emerges of the goals and strategies of major political actors in Brazil is one in which elite groups who are generally favorable to the regime ascribe legitimacy to the military for what one might call a "moderator role" in the political society. Neither of the two other political groups—the executive and his supporters, and the antiregime forces —consistently articulate the feeling that the military should be apolitical. As a result, the military has played a crucial role in politics in Brazil, with all groups trying to co-opt the military in times of political conflict, and with actual coups against the executive representing the *combined* efforts of both civilian and military groups.

The Moderating Pattern of Civil–Military Relations: Two Hypotheses Concerning Military Coups

A consideration of the ways in which civilians attempt to co-opt the military into politics in Brazil (and of the normal institutional inhibitions working against military intromission in politics in the form of an actual coup against the government) suggests the possibility that civilian attitudes toward the military may be as or even more important in determining the dynamics of coups than military ideology or military goals. This in turn suggests two hypotheses of civil–military relations, in which the normal picture of unilateral intervention is reversed and the military becomes more a dependent than an independent variable.

The first hypothesis correlates the propensity of the military to intervene with the cohesion of the relevant political strata, and argues that this propensity is high when civilian cohesion is low, and low when civilian cohesion is high. The second hypothesis relates the success of coups to the degree of public legitimacy ascribed to the executive and to the military. Military coups tend to be successful when, before the coup attempt, executive legitimacy is low and the legitimacy given by the relevant political strata to the military to intervene is high. According to this hypothesis, coups tend to be unsuccessful when executive legitimacy is high and the legitimacy given to the military to intervene is low.

I propose to examine the first of the hypotheses in this chapter. . . . The first of the hypotheses raises the question of the conditions that tend to increase or decrease the propensity of the military to attempt to intervene in the political process. What is suggested is that the propensity of the military to intervene in central political issues is increased when the executive and the proregime strata are sharply divided over political goals. At such times, a president tends to attempt to increase his own power resources by using the

military as an instrument. Conversely, significant elements of the proregime civilians tend to become antigovernment and to make appeals to the military to perform the moderating role of checking the executive. The stronger the proregime civilians' rejection of a president, the greater is the possibility of the formation of a strong coalition of civilians to encourage the military to exercise its traditional moderating role of checking the executive. Likewise, antiregime groups become most effective when major groups that were previously part of the proregime force join their ranks. Until some proregime groups join the antiregime group, the antiregime group remains relatively isolated and cannot make convincing appeals to the military to overthrow the regime.

This analysis suggests that, even if we assume (as I do) that at all times there are some military officers anxious to overthrow the government for personal reasons, either selfish or ideological, the attitudes of the proregime civilians are likely to be determining. My previous discussion of the bureaucratic norms of obedience and command, and of the normal internal differences over politics that exist within the military suggests that it is difficult for the military to put together a winning coalition for a coup unless there is a major split between the executive and the proregime strata and the latter begin to articulate the belief that in these circumstances the military should perform the moderating function.

The absence of such a split means that the president is less likely to risk tampering with the promotion or disciplinary structure of the military, the two acts most likely to create a temporary military consensus against the president on grounds that the military as an institution is threatened. In addition, without splits among civilians, military activists are also likely to be isolated, without strong civilian allies. This also makes it easier for the president to discipline minority elements within the military

plotting to overthrow him.

This analysis of political activities of civilians and military officers under normal political conditions strengthens the hypothesis that attempts by the military to intervene in the exercise of its moderating function will correlate inversely with the degree of cohesion between the proregime strata and the executive. . . .

Alfred Stepan

The Emergence of Military Rule

THE IMPACT OF POLITICAL AND ECONOMIC CRISES ON THE MILITARY: THE ESCOLA SUPERIOR DE GUERRA *AND THE DEVELOPMENT OF A NEW MILITARY IDEOLOGY*

A crucial supportive attitude for the moderator role of the Brazilian military, and especially for the maintenance of a limit to this role at the removal of the executive from office, was the widespread belief by the military officers that, in comparison to civilians, they had relatively low legitimacy to rule. In addition, as we have seen, the military officers did not have a high level of confidence that they were well endowed in terms of political or economic training to rule the nation. These two beliefs,

From *Alfred Stepan,* The Military in Politics: Changing Patterns in Brazil *(Princeton, N. J., 1971), pp. 172–83, by permission of Princeton University Press. Copyright © 1971 by the Rand Corporation.*

that the military lacked both capacity and legitimacy, were central to Castello Branco's arguments against military assumption of political office in 1955. They were instrumental in the return of power to civilians after the military had removed the presidents from office in 1945, 1954, and 1955. The crises of 1961–1964, however, in addition to eroding civilian confidence in the democratic framework of politics, also altered the military officers' previous image of their relative incapacity and illegitimacy to rule the country.

Brazil is the paradigm case of a military that felt it lacked the legitimacy to rule. However, such a belief has been an element in many military governments in Latin America, which, owing to their lack of political confidence, are only transitional or caretaker in form. Most cases of what appears to be long-term military rule turn out to be one-man, personalist dictatorships which manipulate and dominate rather than represent the military. Some military leaders in Latin America have, of course, experimented with directed social change with military support before the 1960s, such as General Ibáñez in Chile in the mid-1920s, General Cárdenas in Mexico in the 1930s, Colonels Toro and Busch and Major Villarroel in Bolivia in the late 1930s and mid-1940s, and Colonel Arbenz in Guatemala from 1950 to 1954.

The mid-1960s in Latin America, however, saw a change in the nature of military government; governments were more doctrinal, and initially more institutionally backed and self-confident in their attempts to direct and control social and economic change. Despite many dissimilarities, these characteristics were shared by the Brazilian military government that came to power in 1964, the Argentinian military government of 1966, and the Peruvian military government of 1968.

The emergence of this new pattern of military regimes was related to basic changes in the national and international environments of the late 1950s and early 1960s. The growth of doctrines of revolutionary warfare and, specifically, the rise of Castro engendered in military officers a complex set of responses: fear of Communism (especially because of its threat to the regular army), growth of counterinsurgency doctrines, and a conviction that basic change was necessary to avoid revolution. Because the strategy of revolutionary warfare was perceived to involve all phases of society, the military's concept of security began to encompass all aspects of social and political life. The military became concerned with civic action, with their role as a "nation-builder," and with global development plans. These responses involved a considerable expansion of the role of the military and a belief in the legitimacy of these new roles. These were all ideas advocated by the United States and taught in its schools for Latin American military officers. However, as the case of the Peruvian military government illustrates, these ideas did not always result in harmonious relations with the United States. To a significant degree, the idea of a more active political role for the military took root because the military institutions felt it was relevant and adaptable to their own countries' problems. Brazil, Argentina, and Peru all reshaped the idea to fit their own perception of their country's development and security problems.

The institutions contributing most to the reshaping and dissemination of the new concepts of national security and development, including a deepening military involvement in politics, were the Superior War Colleges of each country. In Peru it was the *Centro de Altos Estudios Militares* (CAEM), in Argentina the *Escuela Nacional de Guerra*, and in Brazil the *Escola Superior de Guerra* (ESG). It was largely because of the ESG that, as the general sense of crisis in Brazil deepened, significant numbers of officers began to feel that they had the most appropriate and realistic strategy to develop the country, and the most qualified technocrats to implement this strategy. The role of the ESG in the breakdown of the traditional pattern of civil-military relations in Brazil therefore deserves study. Because so little is known about it we must begin with the basic facts.

FOUNDING AND ORGANIZATION OF THE ESG

Brazil participated in World War II by sending a division, the *Fôrça Expedicionária Brasileira* (FEB) to fight in Italy. Weak coordination among the branches of the military itself and weak coordination of national strategy in all its military, industrial, and bureaucratic components spurred the desire after the war to formalize both a Joint Service General Staff and a National Security Council. Later the key organizers of the FEB, such as General Cesar Obino and the artillery commander, General Cordeiro de Farias, developed the idea of a special school to formulate a new doctrine of national security and development. Because the United States had a national war college, and because the FEB had been integrated with a U.S. army corps in Italy, the Brazilians requested a U.S. advisory mission to help in the formation of the school. This U.S. mission remained in Brazil from 1948 until 1960. Significantly, Peru's CAEM did not have U.S. officers of faculty rank, and unlike Brazil, Peru sent some of its military faculty to such civilian-run training programs on the problems of national development as those of the United Nations Economic Commission for Latin America and the Latin American Institute of Economic and Social Planning in Chile.

General Cordeiro de Farias was entrusted with the work of developing the subject matter and organization of the school in Brazil. After spending most of 1948 and part of 1949 on the task, he recommended a school patterned after the United States National War College, but different in two respects. The United States, he argued, was already a developed nation; so its main concern was the mobilization of existing resources for warfare. This task was carried out at the Industrial College of the Armed Forces. The main task of the United States National War College was that of foreign policy. General Cordeiro de Farias felt that in a developing country like Brazil, however, the question of a strong armed force could not be separated from the question of economic development, nor the question of national security from that of education, industry, or agriculture. He advocated that in the new Brazilian War College the functions of the U.S. Industrial College of the Armed Forces and the National War College be combined, and in addition that emphasis on internal aspects of development and security be greater than in the U.S. National War College.

The other Brazilian innovation was to make civilian participation a key aspect of the War College. In the United States, the National War College was mainly military, and the only civilians were those coming from the government agencies concerned with foreign affairs. But precisely because the Brazilian school was to be concerned with all phases of development and security, it was felt it needed civilians from areas such as education, industry, communications, and banking. The decision to include civilians as a central part of the ESG proved to be crucial for the development of the school. It brought military officers into systematic close contact with civilian leaders. This gave them civilian allies who shared many of their ideas on development and security, and also gave the military confidence to discuss problems on terms of equality with civilian specialists.

The military felt the participation of civilians in the ESG was so valuable that over time the ratio of civilian members to military increased. In the initial class of 1950, only 16 of the 62 graduates were drawn from civilian life, but 646 of the total 1,276 graduates in the overall period of 1950–1967 were civilians. The second commandant of the ESG, Marshal Juarez Távora, explained his thinking: "As commandant I wanted to increase the representation of civilians. I felt that the aim of the school was not only to train military men but also all those who would influence the government."

The *Escola Superior de Guerra* was formally established by presidential decree under Dutra on August 20, 1949. By 1963 its charter decreed its mission as preparing "civilians and military to perform executive and advisory functions especially in those organs responsible for the formulation, development, planning, and execution of the politics of national security." That national security was considered to comprise a wide range of affairs is indicated by the names of the seven academic divisions: (1) Political Affairs, (2) Psychological-Social Affairs, (3) Economic Affairs, (4) Military Affairs, (5) Logistical and Mobilization Affairs, (6) Intelligence and Counterintelligence, and (7) Doctrine and Coordination.

By 1966, the ESG had graduates from many of the key sectors of the political and economic power-structure: 599 were military officers, 224 were private businessmen, there were 200 civil servants from the major ministries and 97 from decentralized government agencies, 39 were federal Congressmen, 23 were federal and state judges, and 107 were various professionals—such as professors, economists, writers, medical doctors, and Catholic clergy. The requirement that civilians have the equivalent of a university education has meant virtually the total absence of representation from trade unions.

The graduates of the ESG were members of a very active alumni association, which served as a focus for intellectual and social contact with other graduates, with the ESG itself, and with society as a whole. Well-attended weekly luncheons with prominent speakers were held in Rio de Janeiro, and other major cities (especially São Paulo) had similar, although less frequent, meetings. There was an official liaison officer in each major government ministry. . . .

THE IDEOLOGY OF THE ESG

The intellectual focus of the ESG as it developed in the mid-fifties and early sixties was the interrelationship of national security and national development. The ESG doctrine strongly emphasized that modern warfare, whether conventional, as in World War II, or revolutionary, as in Indochina, involved the will, unity, and productive capacity of the entire nation. Thus those charged with the formulation and implementation of national security policies could no longer restrict their attention to frontier protection or other conventional uses of the army. National security for the ESG was seen to a great extent as a function of rationally maximizing the output of the economy and minimizing all sources of cleavage and disunity within the country. Consequently great stress was put on the need for strong government and planning. General Golbery, chief theoretician of the ESG and often called its father, stressed that in developing countries, such as Brazil "the planning of national security is an imperative of the hour in which we live . . . for us in the underdeveloped countries . . . planning assumes aspects of another order which puts everything else in relief."

Another key theme was that underdeveloped countries were under great internal pressures not only because of underdevelopment itself but also because of global ideological conflict, which had deep ramifications for the internal security of the country. From the beginning, the ESG was anti-Communist and committed in the cold war. Even before the emphasis in the cold war shifted in the United States from atomic to revolutionary warfare, the ESG became the center of ideological thought concerning counterrevolutionary strategy in Brazil. Since Communism was seen as the enemy, the United States, as the major anti-Communist country, was viewed as a natural ally. In early 1959, General Golbery argued that indirect warfare

was a much more realistic threat to Latin America than any direct attack from the exterior:

What is certain is that the greater probability today is limited warfare, localized conflict, and above all indirect Communist aggression, which capitalizes on local discontents, the frustrations of misery and hunger, and just nationalist anxieties . . . Latin America now faces threats more real than at any other time, threats which could result in insurrection, outbursts attempting (though not openly) to implant . . . a government favorable to the Communist ideology and constituting a grave and urgent danger to the unity and security of the Americans and the Western world.

In an intellectual formulation of the sort that would later be used to justify the progressive militarization of all phases of society when the military government assumed power in 1964, Golbery argued that when the security threat is great there is an urgent need for strong planning and control of a strategic nature because ". . . the area of politics is permeated . . . by adverse pressures, creating a form of universalization of the factors of security, enlarging the area of strategy [politics of national security] to the point where it almost absorbs all the national activities."

Given this view of the total managerial nature of the task of maintaining national security, the ESG went about the study of all phases of Brazilian political, economic, and social life. The high-level civilian technocrats, the colonels and the low-ranking generals studied inflation, agrarian reform, banking reform, voting systems, transportation, and education, as well as guerrilla warfare and conventional warfare. In many of their studies some of the fundamental aspects of Brazilian social and economic organizations were severely challenged as needing change if Brazil was to grow economically and maintain internal security. Initially these critiques seemed academic, and the influence of the ESG's doctrine was not pervasive within the military in the mid-1950s. But by the early 1960s, as the Brazilian crisis deepened, the ESG's emphasis on the need for a total development strategy to combat internal subversion found an increasingly receptive audience in the military. Much of its doctrine of internal warfare was incorporated at the General Staff School. For example, in the 1956 curriculum of the ECEME, there were no lectures given on counterguerrilla warfare, internal security, or Communism. Courses in all these subjects increased from 1961 on. . . . Almost all key Brazilian army officers received heavy exposure to the doctrines of internal war. . . .

The pervasive mood of the policy papers was a desire to perfect the Brazilian polity. Perfect democracy was always considered the ideal, yet political factors in the reform measures were either *ignored*, and only ideal policies discussed, or were treated as structural *obstacles* that had to be removed. Thus the policies suggested, while moderate and technocratic in terms of desired goals, were, in the context of actual Brazilian politics, quite sweeping, and in most cases incapable of being implemented democratically given the balance of political forces. . . .

Another common theme of the lectures and studies at the ESG was the need for greater centralization of power. At times this took the form of the reorganization of the borders of the states, both to weaken the power of old oligarchies and to allow greater economic rationality for development plans. But the main thrust of argument was that the executive had to be strengthened to protect the country from subversion. There was little praise for pluralism or participation and mobilization politics, while the cold-war necessity for hierarchy and control was a frequent theme. These arguments became a leitmotif of the military government when it came to power in 1964. . . .

Since the need for economic planning and mobilization of resources was seen as necessary for national security in times of great crisis, a central institution was required to perform this function of planning. An ESG lecturer on "economic mobilization" argued that the logical institutions for this purpose were the National Security Council and the General Staff of the armed forces.

Despite ESG emphasis on "statism," they argued that all possible resources, including private and foreign, should be used to develop Brazil. Leftist nationalists condemned this as *entreguismo* ("giving away"). The ESG countered by calling the left guilty of irrationality and "pseudo nationalism." The ESG desire for efficiency often resulted in their assuming a minority position in regard to nationalization of industries and services. The argument of Juarez Távora, the second commandant of the ESG, in regard to the state-owned coastal freight companies typifies the unemotional, efficiency-oriented approach that characterized the ESG. He argued that the state-owned coastal shipping companies, *Costeira* and *Loíde*, were inefficient. He said *Loíde* needed 12.6 employees per thousand tons of freight, and the other state firm, *Costeira*, needed 38.4 employees per thousand tons of freight. Whereas, he argued, the smaller private firm, *Navegação Mercantil*, needed only 1.3 employees per thousand tons. He maintained that this inefficiency threatened both national security and economic development because it created transportation bottlenecks and it contributed to inflation because it required government subsidies and its prices were too high. Later, as minister of transport in the Castello Branco government, Távora started proceedings to denationalize both *Costeira* and *Loíde*. . . .

ALFRED STEPAN

The Brazilian Military in Power

. . . The paramount importance a military institution gives to the maintenance of its own internal unity is sometimes seen as a political asset of military government. In fact it often becomes a characteristic liability. Fearful that criticism might erode its precarious unity, a military government does not easily tolerate the normal level of dissension and debate needed to build or maintain coalitions with civilians. This is an underlying reason why military governments so often become involved in a cycle in which criticism is repressed, so that in turn even sharper criticisms by civilians are provoked, which are then countered by the military with yet further repressions. Military concern

From *Alfred Stepan*, The Military in Politics: Changing Patterns in Brazil *(Princeton, N. J., 1971), pp. 263–66, by permission of Princeton University Press. Copyright © 1971 by the Rand Corporation.*

for unity and unanimity thus leads to progressive self-isolation.

This repression had reached such heights by 1969 that increasingly well-documented reports began reaching the Vatican and Europe that torture was being widely used at various levels of government in Brazil. Despite attempts by the military either to deny that torture had occurred, or to treat it as individual and unauthorized action by local units, there are indications that torture had in fact become an intrinsic part of the governing process, and that torture or the threat of torture was used to encourage compliance and discourage dissent. . . .

In the "succession" crisis of September–October 1969 caused by President Costa e Silva's illness, the senior officers were barely able to carry the day and install their candidate in the presidency. After the military's unconstitutional refusal to allow the civilian vice-president to assume the presidency, a bitter conflict developed within the military ranks, which took more than a month and a half to resolve. It involved intense political campaigning among officers, even polling of officer opinion down to the battalion level, and the issuance of numerous manifestos. Ranks were finally closed behind the choice of the senior generals, but only because of the specter of complete military fragmentation. Under these circumstances, the traditional military tendency to resolve conflicts on the basis of seniority prevailed, and General Emilio Garrastazú Medice, formerly chief of national intelligence (SNI) and a four-star general was elected. The possibility still remained, however, that if civilian political opposition to the military government intensified, and the high economic growth rate of 1968–1970 faltered, the Brazilian military could simultaneously find itself under a growing pressure for an authoritarian nationalist coup at one end of the ideological spectrum and, at the other, for an extrication coup aimed at holding elections and returning power to civilians.

Whatever the future outcome, it is clear that the attraction of military rule—its presumed stability, unity, and fixity of purpose—has been largely illusory. Even more importantly, the difficulties encountered by the highly professional army in Brazil, with its technocratic civilian allies, illustrate that there can be no apolitical solution to the problems of political development.

The experiences of the new pattern of civil-military relations as it has existed since 1964 lead one to ask what might be the consequences of a return to the older and traditional moderating pattern. Certainly, as internal divisions within the military proliferate and the alienation of civilian support increases, civilians and military men are beginning to advocate a return to the pre-1964 days. There can probably never be a complete return to the moderating pattern of civil–military relations, since the implicit trust between civilians and military that was an intrinsic part of that pattern has been destroyed. In the future, civilian elites will no longer automatically assume that if they encourage the military to overthrow a president, the military will refrain from assuming power themselves.

Nonetheless, it remains an intriguing idea to many civilians and military officers that the old style of civilian–military relations, in which the military periodically intervened to moderate the political system in times of crisis, should be conducive to peaceful and orderly political change. In retrospect, however, the consequences of the old moderating pattern were rather different. The constant participation of the military in the resolution of crises may well have had the long-term dysfunctional effect of preventing crises from forcing a change in the political system, thus forestalling the achievement of a new and more stable equilibrium between old and new political groups. It is possible that if power confrontations such as those in 1945 and 1964 had been able to run their course without the threat or possibility of the military intervention, new political groups seeking a voice in politics might have been incorporated into the political system, and traditional groups might have been more willing to come to terms with them as a tactic of political survival. Between 1945 and 1964, the military in Brazil clearly performed a short-term "crisis-limiting" function, but the long-term outcome of their intervention in politics was to leave most of the fundamental conflicts at the heart of the crises unresolved.

[Today, it can be argued that the Brazilian military has moved to the highest stage of corporatism, authoritarian corporatism. The modernization theorists failed to note that economic modernization without participation was as likely to result in an efficient, brutal authoritarianism as in political chaos.]

An analysis of a case of sophisticated and reformist military praetorianism is found in Abraham Lowenthal's study on modern Peru. Peru's military government has promoted substantial social and economic change in such areas as land tenure, water rights, education, multinational corporations, and labor-management relations. Although Peru's officers are clearly middle class in their social origins, they have caused distress and political alienation among the middle class.

After the coup, a specially created "all-military presidential staff" composed of the middle-level officers who plotted the 1968 intervention was formed. The *Comité de Asesoramiento de la Presidencia* (COAP) was charged with the responsibility for developing and coordinating legislation. COAP has been the arena in which the most politically oriented officers have made their influence felt, and has been responsible for shifting the government to the left when the first moderate reform efforts failed to have sufficient impact.

ABRAHAM F. LOWENTHAL

Peru's Ambiguous Revolution

Peru's "Revolutionary Government of the Armed Forces" has now completed its first six years in power,

From Abraham F. Lowenthal, The Peruvian Experiment: Continuity and Change Under Military Rule *(Princeton, N. J., 1975), pp. 3–6, 21–41, by permission of Princeton University Press.*

the equivalent of a presidential term under the country's constitution. Headed by General Juan Velasco Alvarado, the army's top-ranking officer when he led the October 1968 coup which toppled President Fernando Belaúnde Terry, the Peruvian regime has already attracted considerable attention. Military officers and civilian politicians in countries as different as Argentina and Ecuador, Bolivia and Brazil, Cuba and the Dominican Republic, Uruguay and Colombia, have expressed their interest in (and usually their admiration for) the Peruvian experiment. Fidel Castro has acclaimed the Peruvian undertaking; Juan Perón extolled it. *Peruanista* factions have been identified, and have sometimes identified themselves, in the armed forces of several South American countries.

The Peruvian regime is generally seen not as the typical Latin American *caudillo* government but rather as an essentially institutional effort. Although a government of force, it is widely regarded as relatively unrepressive. Although led by staunchly anti-Communist officers, many with considerable training in the United States, the Peruvian government has established friendly relations with several Communist nations as part of its campaign to escape external "domination," particularly by the United States.

Most important, although it is the nation's force for order, the Peruvian military has promoted substantial change. Through a burst of laws and decrees unprecedented in Peru, the military regime has set out to transform many basic areas of national life. Major structural reforms have affected land tenure and water rights, labor-management relations, the educational system, the state's role in the economy and in the communications media, the role of foreign enterprise in Peru's economy, and even

fundamental concepts of economic and political relationships. Particularly noteworthy has been the regime's announced determination to move steadily away from capitalist principles by creating a new "social property" economic sector (based on collective ownership of the means of production), destined to become the "predominant" mode of economic organization. And the Peruvian regime has emphasized its aim to promote a drastic change in national values, to create a "new Peruvian man," one dedicated to "solidarity, not individualism." . . .

Despite its international stature, the Peruvian regime finds itself almost bereft of conspicuous support at home. No group is likely soon to displace or even seriously challenge the military, but the government encounters concerted opposition within several important sectors: labor, business, peasants, students, and professionals. One politically meaningful election after another reflects antiregime sentiment; opposition candidates have won the recent polls held by sugar workers' and teachers' cooperatives as well as the lawyers', doctors', and engineers' associations, and militantly antiregime student groups hold sway in practically all Peruvian universities. Some backing, particularly among the urban poor and among highland peasants who have benefited from the agrarian reform, is demonstrated from time to time, especially through mass meetings, but contrary evidence is even more striking. General strikes in several provincial areas, including Arequipa, Cuzco, and Puno, forced the regime to suspend constitutional guarantees temporarily in mid-1973 and again later that year, and major antigovernment demonstrations have occurred on several other occasions.

The National System to Support Social Mobilization (SINAMOS) established in 1971 partly to organize support for the government, has instead been the object of intensifying attack from all sides, and even of some backbiting from within the regime. And though the army is surely Peru's preeminent middle-class institution, middle-class distress is increasingly perceptible. Housewives, bureaucrats, teachers, taxi drivers, secretaries: all are grumbling. . . .

BACKGROUND AND CONTEXT

How can one account for the adoption by Peru's military rulers of a genuinely reformist program, an occurrence so unexpected that, as Fidel Castro remarked, it is as if the "fire had started at the firehouse"? Why did the Peruvian army do the unexpected, or why were we not prepared to understand what they were doing?

There can be little doubt that most foreign (and even some Peruvian) assessments of the military regime have regarded it mainly in terms derived from the experiences of other countries, rather than from Peru's own past. Those who think primarily of other Latin American military regimes have understandably discounted the Peruvian government's professions of reform; they have consequently either been perplexed by what the regime seems actually to be doing or else quick to emphasize any evidence that it is doing less than it seems. Even those

who, recognizing that armies vary substantially in their political roles, frame their approach to different military regimes within a broader (often class-based) analysis, find themselves puzzled by the Peruvian case, for the army's program unquestionably outruns what most middle-class Peruvians support. . . .

In seeking to explain the Peruvian military's policies, one may profitably concentrate on understanding Peru before 1968, analyzing changes both within the Peruvian armed forces and in the larger society within which it operates.

Víctor Villanueva and Luigi Einaudi have focused on the Peruvian military's evolution. They advance several explanations for the army's recent course: the effects of recruiting and promoting middle-class officers, primarily of provincial origin; the impact of the army's extensive training program, particularly the course at the Centro de Altos Estudios Militares (CAEM), Peru's equivalent of the National War College, and the instruction at U.S. installations; the legacy of the army's past traumas and the officers' consequent distrust of civilians; and especially the experiences top-ranking officers suffered in putting down guerrilla uprisings in the mid-1960s. All these factors help account for the army's approach since 1968, clarifying in part why Peruvian officers reject the landed elite, favor planning and an expanded state role generally, oppose politics and politicians, and see reforms as essential for national security.

Comparative data suggest, however, that none of these factors by itself, nor even all together, can provide a sufficient explanation for the military's comprehensive reform program. Almost all officer corps in Latin American armies come predominantly from the provincial middle class, but few (if any) parallel the Peruvian army's current stance. The CAEM program is unusual among Latin American countries, but it is by no means unique. Most officers who have graduated from nearly equivalent institutions in Argentina and Brazil, for instance, have emerged with attitudes and policy preferences very different from those their Peruvian counterparts declare. Besides, not even the most ardent believers in the efficacy of education would claim that a nine-month course—or even shorter exposure to foreign training—could fundamentally affect the values and behavior of mature professionals. And other armies in Latin America and elsewhere have emerged from battles with guerrillas determined to repress them, not eager to foster structural change.

When one considers the civilian context in which Peru's armed forces has acted, however, the fact that Peru's officers came to power in 1968 with a reform program is much less surprising. What is remarkable, indeed, is that the goals and means the current military regime espouses took so long in Peru to become an implemented government program.

In 1968 Peru was poor—probably the least developed of the larger Latin American countries, not just in *per capita* income but in urbanization, literacy, mass media exposure, and other aspects of social development. . . .

Property and income distribution were exceptionally unequal. Less than 2 percent of Peru's agricultural estates (many of them owned by the same individuals or families) accounted for some 85 percent of the country's land, while 95 percent of properties took up but 10 percent of the land. One percent of Peru's population received about 31 percent of the nation's income; the top 10 percent obtained half the national total, and the bottom quarter got only 3 percent. This last group corresponded roughly to the residents of Peru's *"mancha india,"* the provinces of Ancash, Apurimac, Ayacucho, Huancavelica, Cuzco, and Puno. Eighty-seven percent of the persons over five years old in these six provinces spoke Quechua or Aymara at the time of the 1961 census, and more than half did not speak Spanish.

Industry, exports, and credit—like land—were controlled by small groups, members of a reduced number of Peruvian families or else foreigners, tied in with international firms. . . .

EVOLUTION OF THE "REVOLUTION"

It is not so difficult, then, to conclude that the Peruvian military regime is a genuinely reformist one and to explain why this should be so. But why have Peru's officers gone beyond their original program, as they seem to have done? Why have they deepened and extended the process of reform?

Available interpretations of the Peruvian military regime fit generally into two categories. The first and larger group takes the regime's decree laws and the speeches of key government officers as its primary, almost exclusive data. The analytical tasks adopted are principally to organize and explicate the regime's aims and assumptions, not always clearly stated, to deduce and define its "ideology," and then to relate these to already familiar cases. The Peruvian approach has been characterized variously as reformist, revolutionary, corporatist, populist, modernizing, authoritarian, Nasserist, Bismarckian, or something of the sort. Finally, speculation about the regime's future is derived from its supposed nature. . . .

The Peruvian regime proclaims itself and is generally accepted as an eminently institutional "government of the armed forces." Undoubtedly part of its strength, durability, and relative success does owe to its harnessing of military discipline and solidarity for political and administrative tasks. But it is important to note that the 1968 coup apparently resulted not from institutional deliberation and agreement among the services, but rather from a decision by selected army officials. When the new government was established on October 3, the ranking navy officer was not named minister but was retired instead. Both the top- and the second-ranking air force generals also resigned immediately, and five air force generals retired prematurely within the regime's first eight months. The ranking army generals with command of troops in the country's various geographic regions were made cabinet ministers, though there are indications that at least some of them knew nothing of the coup until it had

occurred. Several of the army's senior generals were excluded from the government from the start or were pushed aside in a series of internal changes during the regime's first year.

Of all the original cabinet members, only President Velasco himself retains the post he held at first. Most of the first cabinet members have long since retired: several prematurely, and at least some over policy or political differences. Their places and other key political and military posts have been taken by officers who were colonels in 1968. Of special importance is a group of men, most of whom have considerable background in army intelligence, whose alliance with General Velasco has catapulted them to predominant national influence. . . . Many of these officers reportedly worked on preparing the 1968 coup and the outlines of the eventual government program ("Plan Inca"). Most became members immediately after the coup of the Comité de Asesoramiento de la Presidencia (COAP), a specially created, all-military presidential staff, charged primarily with developing and coordinating legislation. . . .

The Peruvian regime, then, reflects the predominant influence of a minority army faction within the considerable constraints imposed by the perceived need to preserve the unity of the armed forces, that is, to secure acceptance of government policies by other army officers and by officials of the air force and navy. Policies are shaped, as well, by the conflicting advice of civilian officials, some of them with great influence in particular sectors.

Moreover, external pressure should by no means be discounted as an influence on the regime's evolving policies, however much the government denies that it can be moved from its course by unsanctioned protests or displays. Regime policy making has been characterized by an iterative process in which general goals are announced, a normative law is decreed, implementing regulations taking into account initial reactions to the law are released, and eventually the law is modified. In several fields the regime has amended its own laws in response to pressures and on the basis of experience; this was true regarding student participation in university governance, worker participation in the management of the sugar cooperatives, and the terms under which agricultural land is distributed or urban settlements authorized. Strikes and demonstrations on the sugar estates and at the Huando hacienda, the protests of small and medium landholders, the Pamplona urban land invasion: each produced a government response.

It should not be surprising, therefore, that actions taken by one ministry may not always be consistent with those taken by another, nor that decisions taken recently differ significantly from related choices in 1968 or 1969. Although some degree of consensus must have existed within the military hierarchy on the general aim of structural reform and perhaps on the main specific measures to be adopted (about which considerable accord existed outside the armed forces as well), the limits of that prior accord were undoubtedly reached early in the regime's tenure. Peruvian officers may have agreed, by and large, that improved national security would depend on growth and development, more equitable distribution, expanded education, greater participation in the national community by "marginal" populations, more nearly national control of economic and political decisions, and so on, but there was probably no clear agreement on how and with what relative priority to pursue these goals. From the beginning the Peruvian regime has been devising policies within a very broad framework, one which allows much scope for changing priorities and for reversals and contradictions.

Although the Peruvian military's course has been considerably less clearly defined than is generally recognized, the regime has tended to move beyond its originally announced program toward more extensive and fundamental reforms. The "revolution" has become radicalized, albeit within limits. Why?

One important cause has undoubtedly been the leadership of President Velasco. His skill in holding the military coalition together and assuring that discrepancies and divisions are kept internal is increasingly recognized, particularly after his sudden and severe illness early in 1973 removed him from the palace temporarily. What is not so generally perceived is Velasco's own tendency to push for more extensive reform. Velasco's commitment to sweeping agrarian reform has been demonstrated, for instance, by his unswerving support for officials (especially Benjamin Samanez Concha, the agrarian reform's director) whose handling of specific issues has drawn criticism— even from within the government— for being too extreme or rapid. Velasco's own desire to establish improved rapport with students (and to have something dramatic to say on the four hundredth anniversary of San Marcos University) is said to have precipitated the commitment to expanded student participation in university governance. Members of the Educational Reform Commission report that Velasco's personally expressed concern about the rural areas and about reaching the Quechua- and Aymara-speaking populations led to a revision of their draft proposal in order to give greater emphasis to bilingual education. Changes in the final draft of the social-property legislation, particularly those providing greater redistribution of benefits, are attributable to the president's initiatives. And at least some of the thrust in Peru's foreign policy may derive from the sense of indignation President Velasco himself has felt on account of foreign domination of Peru. Separating out General Velasco's personal impact on these or other questions is probably impossible on the basis of accessible information, but it seems likely that he has consciously led the armed forces toward policies most officers would have rejected in 1968 as too extreme.

A second important influence has been the COAP. COAP has clearly been central to the regime's development, though data about COAP's functions, its impact, and even its composition are hard to obtain. Enough has been learned, primarily from interviews with current or former COAP officers and other Peruvian government officials, to suggest that COAP furnishes important elements of policy coherence and continuity that might otherwise be lacking. COAP's role in initiating and staffing out reform measures, in helping to prepare presidential speeches, and especially in commenting on legislative drafts emanating from the various ministries provides a process by which differences among services or sectors may often be reconciled. . . .

COAP's effect has been to shift the government's center of policy-making gravity somewhat to the left: this may be because of its membership (first it was a haven for some of the colonels active in the coup who were too junior to take cabinet posts in this institutionally-organized regime, and more recently it has been an assignment for the most politically oriented officers), because it operates as the president's own staff and responds to his inclinations, or because its functions dispose or require COAP officers to see connections among problems that lead them to propose structural solutions— or for a combination of these and perhaps other reasons. (Experience in COAP seems to have had a similar effect on individual officers as well; officers like Ramón Meneses Arata, for instance, are said to have become much more radical during their tenure at COAP.) Part of the regime's general trend may be attributed to the unrivaled influence of COAP, together with that of Delgado, in formulating general strategy. COAP's influence on policy might well have been even greater had not COAP itself been subject to the military practice of rotating almost all officers; most COAP officials were transferred to other assignments in 1971 and 1973, and this led to a temporary decrease of the organization's effectiveness and influence. . . .

A third reason for the regime's evolution has surely been the officers' diminished confidence, based on experience, that the initial measures could by themselves produce the desired effects. At first, the military government seemed genuinely to believe that "prerevolutionary mentalities" would change and that conflict among Peruvians could consequently be avoided. That faith has been shaken. The various means used by businessmen to minimize or avoid the effects of the 1970 Industrial Law, for instance, apparently shocked those in the government who had expected rapid, if somewhat grudging, acceptance of the new arrangements. Reluctance by labor unions to have their prerogatives curtailed, even in cases where labor has in effect become owner, has also been revealing to the Peruvian leadership. The military's distrust of those whose interests are seen as obscuring or biasing their perceptions has been reinforced, so that critical response from affected sectors has largely been screened out. The exaggerated reaction of many businessmen to the regime's initiatives, on the other hand, has dampened the chances for improving the dialogue between business and government. The possibility that the military government might alter some policies in ways acceptable to the private sector has on several occasions been minimized by the private sector's own intransigence.

The influence of technocrats, not so easily understood as having interests of their own, has consequently increased. And the best-trained and most self-confident *técnicos* have tended to recommend that the reforms be carried further. The Planning Institute's impact, especially, has been to define the regime's approach in more comprehensive terms, to push for eliminating policy inconsistencies by generalizing the more radical of conflicting approaches. The regime has found itself both pushed and pulled to *profundizar la revolución.* . . .

Little has occurred so far, on the other hand, to cause the Peruvian government's leaders to consider abandoning their course. The reasonably good performance of Peru's economy (satisfactory growth with somewhat improved distribution and without startling inflation), plus the international reputation Peru has attained, have no doubt reinforced the convictions of Peru's officers that they are on the right track. That domestic support is clearly lacking has been understood by most government officials. But the absence of public enthusiasm is attributed largely to the continuing power of vested interests and to the regime's inability so far to provide many tangible benefits, or even a sense of genuine participation, to large numbers of Peruvians. Peru's rulers appear to believe sincerely that popular support will eventually be forthcoming, when the impacts of the reforms are more widely felt and when the structure for facilitating mass participation has been better established. Until then, apparently, opposition is to be conciliated whenever possible, but suppressed when necessary. So far, repression has not been required often enough to prompt the

self-questioning that more systematic measures might eventually induce within the armed forces. . . .

On the authoritarian nature of Latin American military regimes, the superb study, *Authoritarian Brazil*, edited by Alfred Stepan and including essays by several social scientists, led by Philippe Schmitter, Juan Linz, and others, represents an intellectual breakthrough. Stepan's essay on the "New Professionalism" is actually a case study of the most politically adroit modern military establishment—the Brazilian armed forces. Stepan puts forward a thesis on the relationship between military bureaucrat and modern professional. The military was highly professionalized in Brazil and Peru to deal with threats to internal security, hence, their "new" professionalism. The impact of the new professional socialization is to politicize the military and to foster military managerialism and role expansion. The new professional training emphasizes internal security rather than national defense policy and teaches skills that are extremely useful in the political and administrative arenas.

ALFRED STEPAN

The New Professionalism of Internal Warfare and Military Role Expansion

CONFLICTING PARADIGMS: NEW PROFESSIONALISM VS. OLD PROFESSIONALISM

In the 1960s, the political roles of the Brazilian and Peruvian military establishments underwent a great expansion. Yet, as measured by a number of indicators, these military establishments are probably the two

From Alfred Stepan, "*The New Professionalism of Internal Warfare and Military Role Expansion,*" in Authoritarian Brazil, ed. Alfred Stepan (New Haven, 1973), pp. 47–53, by permission of Yale University Press.

most professional in Latin America. They have relatively universalistic procedures for the recruitment and promotion of officers, highly structured military schooling programs that prepare officers for passage to the next stage of their careers, highly articulated and well-disseminated military doctrines and well-programmed military-unit training cycles, all coordinated by extensive general staff systems. If there is one central concept of modern civil-military relations, it is the concept of "professionalism." According to this concept, as the professionalism of a military establishment increases along the lines indicated above, the military tends to become less political in its activities. In the case of Brazil, however, professional standards coexisted with increasing politicization in the years leading up to 1964. Thus, either Brazil must be considered a deviant case, or one must suggest an alternative framework that is capable of incorporating Brazil, Peru (where a similar process of professionalization and politicization has been at work), and, I suspect, a number of other countries, such as Indonesia, as the predictable outcome of the new paradigm.

. . . the highly bureaucratized, highly schooled, and yet highly politicized armies of Brazil and Peru are best viewed not as lapses from the paradigm of the "old" professionalism, but as one of the logical consequences of the "new" professionalism. To clarify the theoretical and empirical aspects of this assertion, I briefly consider first the components of the old professionalism. Though many aspects of the argument are widely reproduced by writers who have not studied his work, the classic formulation of the argument about military professionalism and its relation to the political activity of the military is Samuel Huntington's. As quoted or paraphrased from his own writings,* his argument is as follows:

*Samuel P. Huntington, *The Soldier and the State: The Theory and Politics of Civil-Military Relations* (New York: Vintage Books, 1964); idem, "Civilian Control of the Military: A Theoretical Statement," in *Political Behavior: A Reader in Theory and Research,* ed. H. Eulau, S. Eldersveld, and M. Janowitz (New York: Free Press, 1956).

1. *On the nature of modern warfare and the requisite skills.* Modern warfare demands a highly specialized military; the military cannot master the new skills needed to carry out their tasks while at the same time "remaining competent in many other fields" as well. [*The Soldier,* p. 32.]

2. *On the impact of pursuit of professionalism.* As a result of this specialization, "the vocation of officership absorbs all their energies and furnishes them with all their occupational satisfactions. Officership, in short, is an exclusive role, incompatible with any other significant social or political roles." ["Civilian Control," p. 381.]

3. *On the relationship between political and military spheres.* The functional specialization needed for external defense means that "it became impossible to be an expert in the management of violence for external defense and at the same time to be skilled in either politics and statecraft or the use of force for the maintenance of internal order. The functions of the officer became distinct from those of the politician and policeman." [*The Soldier,* p. 32.]

4. *On the scope of military concern.* "At the broadest level of the relation of the military order to society, the military function is presumed to be a highly specialized one. . . . A clear distinction in role and function exists between military and civilian leaders." ["Civilian Control," pp. 380–81.]

5. *On the impact of professionalism on military attitudes to politics.* "Civilian control is thus achieved not because the military groups share in the social values and political ideologies of society, but because they are indif-

ferent to such values and ideologies."
["Civilian Control," p. 381.]

6. *On the impact of professionalism on civil-military relations.* "The one prime essential for any system of civilian control is the minimizing of military power. Objective civilian control achieves this reduction by professionalizing the military" and by "confining it to a restricted sphere and rendering it politically sterile and neutral on all issues outside that sphere." [*The Soldier*, p. 84; "Civilian Control," p. 381.]

This argument runs through a large part of American military writing and appears frequently in congressional discussions of the rationale for United States military assistance policies to developing countries. The argument that assistance policies should be given in order to professionalize the military has been rationalized on the grounds that in doing so the United States could help convert traditional, politicized armies into modern, apolitical ones. However, as the extensive quotations from Huntington illustrate, the professionalization thesis was rooted in the assumption that armies develop their professional skills for conventional warfare against foreign armies. In his later writing Huntington has stated that if the focus shifts from interstate conflict to domestic war it will encourage a different pattern of civil-military relations than that expounded in the passages quoted above. Since many later writers have failed to note this qualification, the concept of military professionalism is still widely misunderstood, and it is useful to

formulate explicitly the differences between the old professionalism of external warfare and the new professionalism of internal security and national development.

In reality, by the late 1950s and early 1960s, the success of revolutionary warfare techniques against conventional armies in China, Indochina, Algeria, and Cuba led the conventional armies in both the developed and underdeveloped world to turn more attention to devising military and political strategies to combat or prevent domestic revolutionary warfare. In fact, by 1961, the United States military assistance programs to Latin America were largely devoted to exporting doctrines concerned with the military's role in counterinsurgency, civic action and nation building. In Latin America the process by which the military came to define its mission primarily in terms of dealing with threats to internal security was accelerated by the defeat and destruction of the conventional army in Cuba by Castro's guerrilla force. In Brazil and Peru, where the military was highly institutionalized, the perception of the threat to the internal security of the nation and the security of the military itself led to a focusing of energies on the "professionalization" of their approach to internal security. The military institutions began to study such questions as the social and political conditions facilitating the growth of revolutionary protest and to develop doctrines and training techniques to prevent or crush insurgent movements. As a result, these highly professionalized armies became much more concerned with political problems.

Thus there was a dual process at work. Because of their preoccupation with subversion and internal security, many military establishments in Latin America attempted to undertake institutional professionalization and development and were given extensive United States military assistance in doing so. Yet, given the changed political climate, the formulators of United States military assistance programs and the chiefs of many Latin American military establishments now believed that professional military expertise was required in a broader range of fields. Instead of increasing functional specialization, the military began to train their officers to acquire expertise in internal security matters that were defined as embracing all aspects of social, economic, and political life. Instead of the gap between the military and political spheres widening, the new professionalism led to a belief that there was a fundamental interrelationship between the two spheres, with the military playing a key role in interpreting and dealing with domestic political problems owing to its greater technical and professional skills in handling internal security issues. The scope of military concern for, and study of, politics became unrestricted, so that the "new professional" military man was highly politicized.

The new professionalism of internal security and national development almost inevitably led to some degree of military role expansion. However,

CONTRASTING PARADIGMS: THE OLD PROFESSIONALISM OF EXTERNAL DEFENSE AND THE NEW PROFESSIONALISM OF INTERNAL SECURITY AND NATIONAL DEVELOPMENT

	Old Professionalism	*New Professionalism*
Function of military	External security	Internal security
Civilian attitudes toward government	Civilians accept legitimacy of government	Segments of society challenge government legitimacy
Military skills required	Highly specialized skills incompatible with political skills	Highly interrelated political and military skills
Scope of military professional action	Restricted	Unrestricted
Impact of professional socialization	Renders the military politically neutral	Politicizes the military
Impact on civil-military relations	Contributes to an apolitical military and civilian control	Contributes to military-political managerialism and role expansion

variables stemming from the larger political system in addition to those associated with the military subsystem affect the degree of this role expansion. The weaker the civilian government's own legitimacy and ability to supervise a "peaceful" process of development, the greater the tendency will be for the new professionals to assume control of the government to impose their own view of development on the state.

The old professionalism of external security and the new professionalism of internal security and national development share many external characteristics, especially those of highly developed military schooling systems and elaborate military doctrines. However, the *content* and *consequences* of the two forms of professionalism are quite distinct, as is shown schematically in the table above. It is useful to distinguish the two types of military professionalism for reasons of policy as well as theory. Since 1961, United States military policy toward Latin America has been to encourage the Latin American militaries to assume as their primary role counterinsurgency programs, civic-action and nation-building tasks. This policy has often been defended in the name of helping to create a professional army, and by implication, an apolitical force in the nation. However, in terms of the schema presented in the table, technical and professional specialization of the military in conjunction with doctrines and ideologies of internal security will tend to lead toward military role expansion and "managerialism" in the political sphere.

It also seems useful to point out for reasons of politics as well as theory that the new professionalism is not only a phenomenon of the developing countries. Some of the key ingredients of the new professionalism were observed in France in the 1950s and played a major role in the civil-military crises there in 1958 and 1961. Even in the United States, the military's development of the new professionalism in the fields of counterinsurgency and civic action has resulted in the development of skills that, though originally developed for export to the developing countries such as Brazil in the early 1960s, were by the late 1960s increasingly called upon within this country. Huntington's view of the old professionalism, where the military was functionally specific and unconcerned with domestic political events, is now less meaningful for this country. The United States Army has increasingly been used to quell riots and given the function of maintaining internal order. Once given this function, the internal logic of the new professionalism comes into play, and the military sets about in a "professional" way to train to perform this function. In the late 1960s, many units such as the crack 82nd Airborne Division spent an increasing amount of their time training how to occupy American cities in case of domestic riots. The next "new professional" question for the United States military was to inquire into the nature of the enemy. This involved the military in a surveillance and intelligence-gathering role within the United States. . . .

On the political future of the military and authoritarianism in Brazil, we find Juan Linz's essays interesting. Linz, a political sociologist, is the leading contemporary scholar on Spanish-Portuguese corporatism. In several essays on Spain, he developed an interesting theory on the role of modern corporate authoritarianism. Linz's effort to apply this model to Brazil is most instructive, even if it lacks a more complete analysis of the input of military corporatism into Brazilian authoritarianism. In our view, the intellectual linchpin between nationalism, syndicalism, and militarism is the Brazilian and Latin American model of corporate praetorianism. Linz's essay is nonetheless a valuable contribution to the literature on Latin American military praetorianism.

Linz argues that modern-day authoritarian regimes flounder about "because they lack an appealing ideological stance." Authoritarianism appeals neither to those who desire a competitive, democratic political system, nor to those committed to an ideological single-party model. In these authoritarian systems, decisions are made almost by default by the bureaucratic elite controlling the state apparatus.

JUAN J. LINZ

The Future of an Authoritarian Situation or the Institutionalization of an Authoritarian Regime: The Case of Brazil

. . . Brazilianists have made [use] of a model of authoritarianism that I developed originally for Spain. The work of the Brazilianists has helped refine my original model, as well as contribute to the important theoretical task of constructing a typology of authoritarian regimes. With some reservations, there seems to be a con-

From Juan J. Linz, "The Future of an Authoritarian Situation or the Institutionalization of an Authoritarian Regime: The Case of Brazil," in Authoritarian Brazil, ed. Alfred Stepan (New Haven, 1973), pp. 233–52, by permission of Yale University Press.

sensus among the contributors that in Brazil many aspects of the regime developed by Getúlio Vargas during the Estado Nôvo of 1937–45 persisted into the period of competitive politics from 1945 until the military assumed power in 1964. A more uneasy consensus seems to exist, as well, that no immediate return to competitive politics is in sight for Brazil. Concerning the degree and type of institutionalization achieved by Brazil's authoritarian regime and the capacity of the regime to become stable, consensus seems to falter. It is in regard to these latter points that I wish to raise some questions and offer some tentative answers.

The overthrow of a regime does not assure the consolidation, and even less the full institutionalization, of the successor regime. In Brazil, since many of the partisans of the 1964 coup viewed the subsequent military rule as only an interim process whose goal was to prepare the way quickly for a return to democracy, the entire question of creating new authoritarian political institutions was, in particular, fraught with ambiguity and contradictions. Nonetheless, some might argue that after eight years of rule by the military under three military presidents, the regime can be considered consolidated. This assessment gains further plausibility in view of the limited capacity of the old political classes to present any effective opposition, and the failure of the new Left to move from small-scale terrorism to large-scale insurrection. Indeed, those whose attention centers on the socioeconomic policies of the Brazilian military governments might even argue that the regime is already institutionalized because it has demonstrated staying power and the capacity to formulate and execute programs. Those who see the ideas of the Superior War College (Escola Superior de Guerra) as forming a coherent program, conceived even before the military assumed power, will tend to consider the regime even further down the road toward full institutionalization.

However, when we focus on the more strictly political actions of the successive military governments since 1964, such as the periodic issuance of drastic institutional acts, the making and breaking of constitutions, the constant changing of the rules of the game in regard to elections, and most importantly, the profound internal military struggles that marked the two succession crises, we sense a void in political institutionalization. It is true that, despite internal tensions, the military has been able to exercise power, but their hesitant efforts to "civilianize" their rule have had only limited success. Power has basically remained with the armed forces, except for economic policy making, which is shared between the military, selected technocrats, and, to a lesser extent, businessmen. Institutions outside of the armed forces have been created and disregarded constantly, leaving the military with ultimate power. Even those political figures selected by the military are thus dependent, almost day by day, on the internal consensus of the officer corps. When we examine the Brazilian national security doctrine, with its basically negative character and its ambivalent commitment to democracy, we must question its ultimate capacity to serve as the foundation for "legitimate" and stable authoritarian political institutions like those that have emerged in Spain under Franco.

All this leads me to suggest that the Brazilian case represents an authoritarian *situation* rather than an authoritarian *regime*. Furthermore, the nature of the regime that might eventually emerge is still largely undefined. That after eight years of rule there is an authoritarian situation, rather than an authoritarian regime, is evidence of the difficulties faced in the institutionalization of such regimes (difficulties compounded in the Brazilian case for reasons to be explored). It is also evidence that consolidation of power and even considerable success in specific policies do not in themselves ensure institutionalization and that the weakness of regimes is not determined only by the strength of the opposition. The Brazilian case in all these respects poses particularly interesting and important problems for the comparative study of the dynamics of authoritarian regimes.

In Brazil, even though fully competitive democracy (with freedom for all political actors and social groups) has now definitely been excluded through a variety of means, such as control of the press and the cancellation of the political rights of the most prominent politicians, the present government is still only in the constituent stage. What alternative models of authoritarian regimes are available to the present military leaders in Brazil, which ones have they considered, and what are the prospects of successful institutionalization of each of them? These are the basic questions.

Unfortunately, we are still far from an adequate typology of authoritarian regimes. For some answers to these questions we therefore have to turn to regimes found in certain countries, in order to see what parallels they suggest for Brazil. This explains the references in this volume to the "Mexicanization" or "Portugalization" of the Brazilian regime. In addition, since my original model of an authoritarian regime was developed largely by contraposition to both competitive democracies and strictly defined totalitarian systems, the inquiry into the prerequisites for stable authoritarian regimes still demands much work.

As a first (far from satisfactory) approximation, we may say that authoritarian regimes are likely to emerge wherever the conditions for stable democratic or totalitarian systems are absent. However, such a "residual" explanation does not tell us much about the conditions for their stable institutionalization and even less about the prerequisites for different types of authoritarian regimes.

In my original presentation of the model, I tried to distinguish between two main types of authoritarian regimes. The first type is characterized by the *controlled mobilization* of a population that by and large had not previously been mobilized and is thus reasonably available. The second type is one characterized by the *deliberate demobilization* of a population that had previously been mobilized within a more competitive political situation, but in which the political institutions did not possess the capacity either to satisfy the demands created by mobilization or to guarantee stable processes of political and social change. Using this frame of reference, the basic question the present rulers of Brazil have to face is whether they want and can create a mobilizational, authoritarian regime. If the answer to either part of this question is no, then the next question is whether a regime based on the demobilization of the population activated in the populist period before the 1964 coup is possible without excessive repression, and whether, if repression is necessary, it will assure stable rule.

I will now endeavor to examine in some detail the complex series of obstacles in Brazil to the institutionalization of either the mobilization-populist-fascist subtype of authoritarian regime, or the demobilization-bureaucratic-military subtype that Schmitter has in mind when he writes of the Portugalization of Brazil. In the comparative analysis of authoritarian regimes particular attention must be given to the immediate political circumstances surrounding the origin of the regime and the way in which these circumstances condition the evolution of the regime. Attention must also be paid to the way in which the country's social and political development, the international ideological climate of the time of the assumption of power, and the nature of the country's international links and dependencies combine to constrain or facilitate the legitimacy formulas and the political-party systems that are feasibly available to the builders of the authoritarian regime. It is in these areas that some clues must be sought for understanding the institutionalization of authoritarian structures.

THE FORMATIVE STAGE OF BRAZIL'S AUTHORITARIAN REGIME: BRAZIL'S AMBIVALENT LEGACY

Let us start with the circumstances surrounding the creation of the current Brazilian regime. In contrast to some of the most stable authoritarian regimes in the world today, whether left-authoritarian or right-authoritarian, the present Brazilian rulers did not come to power in the course of a bitter civil war nor after a serious national crisis accompanied by foreign threats, such as occurred with Atatürk in Turkey or Nasser in Egypt. Nor did Brazil experience a prolonged period of widespread terror, as did Spain and Yugoslavia, terror that helped assure the allegiance of those who participated in the formative stages of the regime, based on their fears and/or shared guilt, whatever their subsequent disillusionment. In Brazil, in contrast, despite the mobilization of some conservative middle- and upper-class groups, the active support of some Catholic conservative masses, and the collaboration of some leading politicians, the birth of the regime was fundamentally the result of a successful coup by the army.

There is another important contrast between Brazil and many of the fascist or semifascist regimes and even some of the leftist-nationalistic authoritarian regimes of the Third World. In Brazil, a civilian political party aspiring to fully noncompetitive rule did not exist before the beginning of authoritarian rule by the military. This obviously limits the possibility of creating a single party composed primarily of committed civilians who could link the current military-technocratic regime with a political movement of richer symbolic content or provide the military with a more widely recruited political cadre. In the absence of such a party, when the military felt the need of politicians to work with them, they have had to recruit these politicians from among the remaining members of the old political parties, particularly from the ranks of the União Democrática Nacional (UDN) and the Partido

Social Democrático (PSD). This situation creates a variety of problems for the regime's evolution. On the one hand, the bulk of the officers have a visceral dislike of the style and record of the old-school politicians. On the other hand, these politicians, though willing to cooperate in the official dominant party, Aliança Renovadora Nacional (ARENA), are more likely to feel at ease in a political system that is at least semicompetitive. They are not the kind of men that other authoritarian regimes have used to forge either a fairly disciplined bureaucratic-elitist cadre party, or a real or pseudo mass party.

Paradoxically, the relative ease and rapidity of the 1964 coup also created difficulties for the current rulers in Brazil. The fact that the coup was virtually unopposed makes the rationalization of "saving the country from communism and subversion" questionable. Samuel Huntington has noted that one of the characteristic forms of authoritarian rule is the "exclusionary one-party system" based on a clear identification of the "enemy."* The lack of a credible "enemy" in the Brazilian case makes such a basis for exclusion less clear. In any case, the destruction of much of the political class cannot be legitimated on the basis of their identification with the "subversive" government of ex-President Goulart. Many of the most prominent centrist or conservative politicians, such as Juscelino Kubitschek, Adhemar de Barros, and

*Samuel P. Huntington, "Social and Institutional Dynamics of One-Party Systems," in Huntington and Moore, *Authoritarian Politics in Modern Society*, p. 14.

Carlos Lacerda, all of whom later had their political rights taken away, were strong supporters of the coup against Goulart.

This raises the crucial question of symbols. Among the many important factors in the analysis of the formative stages of an authoritarian regime are the slogans, phrases, and symbols that accompany its birth. Whatever policies authoritarian regimes may later follow, it becomes difficult for them to overcome the image they have initially created. This image inevitably limits their freedom as they strive for political institutionalization at later stages. When the military assumed power in Brazil in 1964, some prominent officers articulated attachment to their "salvationist" mission to "clear up the mess" and restore democracy. Though many of the regime's later policies made carrying out such a mission increasingly unlikely, the constant restatement of the intention to restore competitive liberal democracy (whatever ambivalence these statements contained), was and still is a drawback for the legitimation of permanent authoritarian elitist rule. Only—and in this the hard-line wing of the military may be right—complete discontinuity with the initial leadership and ideas of 1964 and a displacement of the present ruling groups would open the door to an unabashed, self-confident authoritarian regime. However, such a reversal would undoubtedly be viewed by many officers as endangering the already perilous unity of the military institution. Furthermore, the negative component that justified 1964 would not be sufficient almost a decade later to justify such a step toward pure authoritarian rule. A large part of the population and even significant sectors of the military would legitimately ask why now, if not then. Only a greatly stepped-up campaign by urban guerrillas might rationalize permanent authoritarian rule.

There are thus contradictions and obstacles inhibiting the early establishment of a fully elaborated authoritarian regime. However, after the salvationist claims are finally renounced, as they are likely to be, the question then becomes what types of symbols or institutions might serve to rationalize permanent authoritarian rule. We will first examine the question of alternative legitimacy formulas, particularly charismatic or corporatist formulas, and then turn to the possible subtypes of authoritarian political-party systems available to the Brazilian military regime.

THE NEED FOR A LEGITIMACY FORMULA

As Alfred Stepan has noted, the Brazilian doctrine of national security, developed in the military milieu as an intellectual elaboration of responses to insurgency and as a result of the new professionalism, is too limited to provide a legitimacy formula because of its essentially negative character.* To say that the military espouses anticommunism tells us too little about the kind of society the rulers want to create and the kind of social and economic policies they want to implement. It tells us even less about

*See his *The Military in Politics: Changing Patterns in Brazil* (Princeton, N.J.: Princeton University Press, 1971), pp. 172–87.

the kind of political institutions and legitimacy formulas they want to use. Certainly, some repressive policies can be derived from an anticommunist stance. Some manipulation of interest conflicts by controlling and changing the leadership of labor and peasant groups and even some technocratic social reform and economic development policies can be justified by a doctrine of anticommunism. The success of such a combination of policies based on repression and development can assure some stability in periods of prosperity, but it can never satisfy those who ask questions about legitimacy, except perhaps in purely subject political cultures, with traditional rulers in the most narrow Weberian sense of the term. In any society that has developed beyond this stage, as Brazil clearly has, questions about legitimacy will inevitably be asked. They will be asked by intellectuals and those under their influence, by those concerned with religious values, and ultimately by some of those who have to use coercion, like judges or army officers confronted with subversion or public disorder. Only praetorian guards or the lowest ranks of a police force do not ask such questions. Anyone in a position of responsibility, one who must die or kill to defend a regime, must ultimately ask questions about why he should do so and whether he should obey in a crisis situation.

THE AVAILABILITY OF THE CHARISMATIC LEGITIMACY FORMULA

In the modern world, all legitimacy formulas refer in some way to the authority coming from the *demos*, the people. Who "the people" should be and how they should transfer their authority to the rulers are the great questions of politics. The number of answers is not unlimited, nor is it a matter of indifference which one is chosen. One "answer" that has had considerable psychological power to demand obedience is the establishment of an identity between the people and an extraordinary man who represents the people, who feels that he can speak for them, and who is accepted by the people as their leader in view of his unique quality. This is charismatic authority. Never mind that in many societies which are led by such a leader large minorities do not believe in the leader's charisma. The majority believe in his authority. More important, he too believes in his mission to lead.

Despite the widespread and often loose use of this term by social scientists, such authority appears rarely and only under very special circumstances. It cannot be produced "on order." The military organization, particularly (as in the Brazilian case) when bureaucratic seniority rules are adhered to and when achievement of the highest office requires corporate consensus of the officer corps, is not the best breeding ground for charismatic rule. Normally it is only after an international or civil war that something like charismatic authority appears within the regular channels of the army. Certainly, none of the presidents of post-1964 Brazil fit the role of charismatic leader, and probably none of them aspired to it. The officer corps, in fact, seems hostile to and fearful of the emergence of a "caudillo."

Even when charismatic authority cannot serve as a long-term and sufficient basis to institutionalize an authoritarian regime, it can serve to give it a lease on life and provide the leader with the opportunity to create an institutional framework out of other materials. This has probably been the role of Cárdenas in Mexico, and possibly that of Nasser in Egypt and Franco in Spain. Brazil, on the other hand, because of the circumstances surrounding the military's assumption of power and the bureaucratic nature of the military organization, has no charismatic leader in the making. Indeed, any officer with clear political skills and potential for populist charismatic appeal is vetoed by the military organization. Thus any use of the charismatic formula to help institutionalize and legitimate authoritarian rule is very unlikely in the Brazilian case.

THE CORPORATIST, NONPARTY LEGITIMACY FORMULA

Another option that might give a more democratic base to such an authoritarian regime is to reject "individualistic" democracy and substitute for it some form of corporatist organic representation. Organic democracy "in theory" offers a legitimate alternative to competitive-party democracy to assure the participation of people in their government. In practice, as Max Weber noted, it serves to exclude from political participation large numbers of people or whole sections of the society and to manipulate the composition of representative assemblies. This would be fully congruent with the idea of limited pluralism that is a key characteristic of the authoritarian-regime model and the realities of Brazilian politics since 1964. Furthermore, . . . Schmitter . . . demonstrate[s] corporatist institutions, ideologies, and policy-making processes have a certain tradition in Brazil.* If the current regime decided to go further in this corporatist direction, the Portugalization of Brazil would certainly be achieved with such a formula. As in Portugal, corporatist ideology and institutions would be combined with republican institutions like a directly elected national parliament. This formula would avoid the appearance of a complete break with Brazil's long history of commitment (despite lapses) to the form of direct and liberal democracy.

There are, however, some difficulties with this solution. The link established in the public mind between corporatism and fascism (whatever misunderstanding of many fascist regimes, particularly of the Nazi case, this involves), gives such a solution dubious attractiveness. It could, however, be argued that corporatism has been more important for Catholic conservative social doctrine than for fascism, and therefore would be congruent with the sentiments of those segments of Brazilian society identified with a conservative church. Certainly, if Brazil were to move in this direction, some of the ideologies of corporatist institutions would come from conservative clerical and lay groups. However, the traditional weakness of lay

*Also see Schmitter's *Interest Conflict and Political Change in Brazil.*

Catholicism in Brazil as well as the development since the late 1950s of progressive and even radical Catholic lay movements are obstacles to such a development. Even if these obstacles did not exist, international Catholicism has undergone significant changes since the late 1920s and 1930s, when corporatist authoritarian regimes of Europe were instituted as a new alternative to liberal, individualist democracies. The ideas of the early social encyclicals, quoted by Salazar in Portugal, Dollfuss in Austria, and important segments of the Franco regime, are still available, but their legitimacy within the Catholic tradition has been seriously weakened by Vatican II. Not only have large sections of Belgian, German, Dutch, and French Catholicism abandoned such ideas, but so have recent popes, whereas in the past many of the popes could be interpreted as preferring, if not prescribing, such a corporatist approach to politics. The Brazilian church is today divided over the position it should take concerning the authoritarian military regime. A militant minority would like to see the church systematically confront and oppose the regime, and they appeal to the "prophetic mission" of the church. On the opposite wing is a militant group of Catholic conservatives who actively urge the military to impose a corporatist state. A large part of the institutional church, however, is uneasily but passively acquiescing to the authoritarian regime—partly because of financial dependency, partly becausu of the church's historic caution in regard to major church-state conflicts.

In light of this political, ideological, and theological division within the contemporary Brazilian church, it seems reasonable to argue that the Brazilian military regime will not be able to persuade the church hierarchy to take an enthusiastic, unified, and active role in the construction of a corporatist state. Another limitation of a corporatist solution is its lack of appeal to intellectuals and even to those military officers who may feel that Brazil, as a potential world power, should be offering new political formulas. Corporatism, furthermore, would not provide Brazil with an appealing image abroad.

A further difficulty with a corporatist solution in Brazil is that it would be difficult (though not impossible) to harmonize it with the federal structure of the country or the traditional role of state governors. Over the long run, it might be useful to have some kind of party system for election of the state governors, and it might be too severe a break with tradition to have the governors elected by corporatist chambers. To have them permanently appointed by the central government would be an even greater break, although the centralizing tendencies and the weakening of the federal tradition have gone very far in recent years.

The combination of these national and international factors, plus the military's attachment to their "salvationist mission" to reestablish United States–style democracy, helps explain why the military rulers have not openly decided to use corporatist structures and ideologies to institutionalize the authoritarian regime or

to give it an ideological façade to date.

As we have argued before, the initial circumstances surrounding the founding of the regime influences the feasibility of subsequent steps. In the Brazilian case, the fact that the military governments have already created new electoral and political party laws, as well as a new constitution, means that the subsequent creation of corporatist institutions would entail a break with their own recent past and would alienate even more those who collaborated in experiments such as the creation of the government party, ARENA, and the half-controlled opposition parties such as the MDB.

ONE-PARTY ALTERNATIVES— FASCIST AND POPULIST

Thus the two nonparty legitimacy formulas—charismatic and corporatist—do not seem to be readily available to Brazil's current rulers. This section will explore the possible party-system solutions.

A single-party system at first impression would seem to be the simplest solution. It is important to repeat here that the present regime was not created by a coalition between the military and civilian political parties or politicians committed to the idea of a single party. In this, Brazil in 1964 was quite different from Spain in 1936. Obviously, many authoritarian regimes have used their power to create single parties even when such parties have been far from satisfactory for the long-run institutionalization of these regimes. In the Brazilian case the difficulties are compounded by a number of international and national circumstances.

The antirevolutionary, and largely antipopulist, initial thrust of the Revolution was supported by the upper and middle classes. Its appeal to symbols of order and tradition would inevitably tend to associate a resultant single party with fascism, an ideology and system of the past, viewed negatively by most people, probably even by many of the same people who support the regime on social or economic grounds. Single parties are far from being out of favor in the world, but a fascist single party is certainly not fashionable. The cultural acceptance of the United States' liberal political forms by many of the Brazilian elites also makes a single party that would inevitably be labeled as fascist undesirable.

What of the populist single-party option? In contrast to other military coups and regimes, whatever policies the Brazilians may pursue, they will have great difficulty avoiding the label "rightist." Military organizations that take power today in traditional societies, in which competitive or semicompetitive regimes are perceived as having failed by significant segments of society, have a chance to create a single party. But their rhetoric must be leftist; they must speak of socialism, of agrarian reform, sometimes of secularization, and above all, of nationalism, anti-imperialism, and (best of all) anti-Americanism. Some of these themes are not out of the question in Brazil. In fact, some members of the military might feel closer to them than corporatist formulas or to the defense of a dynamic

capitalism linked to the Western capitalist world economy.

A coup by some segment of the army attempting to turn the country toward such a left-authoritarian regime cannot be excluded, but it would have to overcome resistance both within and outside the military. Many within the military would fear it because it would risk dividing the military institution. Just as importantly, the economic policies of recent years, which many credit with contributing to the very high growth rates since 1968, would have to be abandoned. The successor policies would come into conflict with strong vested interests that would not tolerate such policy reversals passively. The recent success of Brazilian capitalism—national, mixed national, international, public and private—and the complexity of the financial, industrial, and commercial structure of São Paulo and Rio, as Stepan notes, is one among many factors accounting for the differences between the attitude of the Brazilian military and the more populist Peruvian officers toward the socioeconomic system. To reverse the ongoing Brazilian economic system would require a broader impetus than a faction of left-authoritarian officers in the army could provide.

A populist authoritarian regime with a single party created by the army in coalition with some intellectuals, searching for support among labor and seeking legitimacy by assuming an anti-United States stand in world affairs, with ties to the Soviet Union is not out of the question. Many factors would stand in the way of such a project, however. Not only the capitalist structure of Brazilian society, the conservative middle-class segments of Brazilian Catholicism, public and private pressures from the United States, but historical developments in recent years stand in the way. The fact that the populist appeal had already been made and to some degree organized prior to 1964 by politicians now in exile or deprived of their political rights, or dishonored and persecuted by the army, makes it difficult to shift to such an appeal without endangering very seriously the unity of the armed forces. In addition, it is doubtful that men who have experienced such defamation would collaborate with a segment of the army, even should some of the officers try to plot with them. After the last eight years it is very questionable whether the intellectuals, the students, and the Catholic Left would unite with a sector of the army in the building of an authoritarian regime with a left-oriented single party to which they would provide ideas but only a minority of leadership. Too many have undergone a process of radicalization and put their hopes in more revolutionary solutions, whatever the chances of success, or have become cynical if not outright hostile toward the military in general.

Populism is not a flag that the present rulers, or a segment of them, can appropriate easily, even though it is certain that they will do their best to appropriate some of its issues and some of its rhetoric in the coming years. The Brazilian military is far from institutionalizing the regime on the basis of a large-scale, manipulated single mass party like the one Nasser created in Egypt. The Peruvian military, on the other hand, given the anti-United States, antioligarchical "signs" under which their rule was born, and the social and economic structure of the country, as well as the more limited success of populist mobilization before the takeover, have some or perhaps many chances to do so. Their Brazilian peers have more limited and dangerous options. . . .

AUTHORITARIAN REGIMES IN THE CONTEMPORARY WORLD

Ultimately, authoritarian regimes, despite their pragmatism, their lack of ideological rigidity, the similarities across a wide spectrum of systems in terms of their institutionalization and uses of power, are very dependent on their symbolic identification when they face the problems of political institutionalization. Politics is not simply a question of policies and administration, but of appealing to politically interested segments of society. Millions of passive supporters and obedient citizens are insufficient, as are, also, numerous groups who see a coincidence of their interests with those of their rulers and are thus willing to abdicate political power for the sake of minding their own affairs— whether these affairs be business, personal social mobility, or welfare policies for certain groups. I agree with Philippe Schmitter's intriguing observation that in this respect the authoritarian-regime model is very similar to the Bonapartist model of Marx. Authoritarian regimes normally flounder about because they lack an appealing ideological stance. In the contemporary world large segments of society still believe, rightly or wrongly, in the desirability of an open, competitive, democratic political system or in the desirability of an ideologically driven, possibly totalitarian society whose elites provide some sense of historical mission to the nation, and thereby satisfy some of the more politically involved citizens. In this setting an authoritarian regime has serious weaknesses. Ultimately all authoritarian regimes face this legitimacy pull toward the polyarchical model, with political freedom for relatively full participation, or toward the committed, ideological single-party model. To resist those two pulls is possible de facto, but none of the authoritarian institutionalization attempts we find around the world have been fully satisfactory. The fact that the United States, Japan, England, the Soviet Union, and China are the models for those two polar alternatives and at the same time are the greatest powers of the day, makes the institutionalization of authoritarian regimes, notwithstanding the considerable achievements of some of these regimes, all the more difficult. There is ultimately no authoritarian regime in the world comparable in economic, technological, intellectual, or social weight to the major democratic countries or the major mobilizational one-party systems. The most important and successful authoritarian regimes, in the past Turkey, and now Mexico, Egypt, Spain, or Yugoslavia, are only imperfect models for those who want to bring their nation to the height of their times, to use Ortega's expression.

In essence, despite their variety, all the authoritarian solutions are dependent through symbiosis, mimicry, or transformation on the three basic great models of political systems—the liberal competitive democratic model, in any of its varieties; the communist, ideological single-party or hegemonic model; and the now defeated, but in the past appealing, fascist, nationalist pseudoconservative single-party rival. With great reservations, one might add the corporatist model. This fourth alternative has never been very appealing to intellectuals, and on a world scale has not succeeded to the same extent as the other three, perhaps because it is much more closely tied to the pragmatic bargaining or balancing of material interests rather than to ideas of a just and ideal society. As the group theory of politics has tried to show, largely successfully, elements of such corporatist politics are present in liberal, democratic systems and increasingly in complex communist single-party regimes, particularly Yugoslavia. In all of them, however, corporatism is, in reality, in conflict with the idea of some clearly perceived common good. Authoritarian-corporatist political regimes have a strong component of reality and pragmatism that makes them work, but the search for ultimate meaning, purpose, legitimacy, and justice demands something beyond the adjustment of interests conflicts through bargaining. That is the ultimate difference between systems with and without political parties. Parties, while representing interests, also stand for a certain type of social order, or at least make that claim.

In political systems which do not have either political parties that grow more or less spontaneously from the demands and aspirations of the people or a vanguard party that mobilizes the society the decisive actions will be taken by the bureaucratic elite controlling the state apparatus. This is so whether the bureaucratic elite is largely from a military, civil servant, technocratic, or managerial background. Almost by definition, such bureaucratic systems entail the rule of the state over the society. The state establishes the permissible limits of freedom and spontaneity in the society and attempts to control the ground rules by which groups can interact with the state. Such authoritarian rule works in many parts of the world. However, nowhere does it seem to have attained the degree of institutionalization achieved by systems characterized by competitive democratic parties or even by large-scale ideological mass parties. Ultimately, authoritarian regimes are condemned to constant experiments with other alternatives, to processes of institutionalization incorporating elements, symbols, and mechanisms, developed in those other political forms considered in line with modern historical development. The success in this process depends, as we have continuously stressed, on historical situations, on specific national constraining factors, on international situations, and on specific policies. All this leads to a strange combination between freedom of choice for the group wanting to institutionalize such a regime and constant limits to its choices. This situation introduces complex elements of unpredictability, uncertainty, ambivalence, and thereby lack of appeal. . . .

THE MILITARY THAT PATROLS SOCIETY: EVOLUTION AND STRUCTURAL CLEAVAGE IN AFRICAN AND ARAB MILITARY REGIMES

Arab and African military elites have not always been interventionist. In the pre-independence era in sub-Saharan Africa and in the Middle East in the period before the Second World War, the military elites were marked by satrapism, or the aping of a superior external culture.

Ruth First has noted the pro-French attitudes of the first officers in the francophone African armies:

Until independence, these armies were organized to meet French military needs, with a total disregard for territorial divisions between the colonies. . . . The concept of developing embryonic national armies was nonexistent; the only legitimate nation was France, with its overseas departments and territories, "une et indivisible." The African officer corps, no less than the army, was altogether oriented to France.

Then, with the onset of independence, national armies began to be constituted for the first time. African officers who had served in the French army were appointed chief-of-staff, military advisor to the head of state, or commander-in-chief. They were African army heads, but they differed from their professional counterparts in the French army proper only in the colour of their skin. Their commitment had been to France's army and wars, and their attitudes and experience had been suitably conditioned.

Colonel Jean-Bédel Bokassa, cousin to President Dacko of the Central African Republic, whom he toppled from power in the coup d'etat of 1964, served for twenty-three years with the French army. A communications expert, he received twelve decorations in Indo-China, and is passionately pro-French. . . . It was this first generation of officers, "anciens d'Indo-Chine," who, one after another, were seconded to their country's national armies when these were constituted at independence.

More than anything else, it was the Algerian war that groomed the next generation of officers.

At independence, of all those belonging to the Western-groomed élite, the military looked the least likely avenue to political influence; indeed, the army was not considered part of the equation of power in African states until other sections of the élite found themselves in crisis. Then it made up for lost time.*

There should be noted an important difference between the Arab and African external legacies: while the African officers were trained by and emulated colonial European professionals, Arabs were influenced by the legacy of the Ottoman Empire, with its sultanist, despotic, patrimonial orientations. Originating as an instrument of the Ottoman Empire, the Arab officer class was the first modern elite that did not belong to, or owe its emergence to, the historical medieval city.

Military intervention developed slowly. It is important to view intervention in terms of the politics of development and modernization and its impact on the military establishment. Intervention is propelled by organizational and collegial conflict within the army and exacerbated by the political struggle within the military establishment and between the military and the nationalist civilian regime. The major conflict—that between the military and the civilian bureaucracy—springs from the similar positions they occupy in the political structure.

THE IMPACT OF MODERNIZATION ON THE MILITARY

The modernizing elites which form the basis for the short-run coalitions of political-military or bureaucratic-military alliances in the Middle East and sub-Saharan Africa are composed of three functional groups—the politi-

*Ruth First, *Power in Africa* (New York: Pantheon, 1970), pp. 85–89.

cians, the military, and the intellectuals. Within each type, age is an important source of political cleavage, for each generational group prefers certain forms of institutional arrangements.

In the Middle East the founding fathers of the nationalist movements (1880–1919) were politicians trained in foreign schools or at home in foreign-acculturated schools.

Eliezer Be'eri describes the Arab officer politicians as the "intelligentsia in uniform." These modern intellectuals admit the supremacy of Western civilization, while struggling to preserve national independence. The officer corps is emotionally attached to the concept of modernism. As a result, revolutionary movements found their most effective supporters in the officer corps.

ELIEZER BE'ERI

The Self-Image of the Arab Officer Politician

The attempt to understand the motives behind the political activities of Arab army officers is not meant to be a psychological analysis of subjective motivations or a polemic over whether a certain officer who became president is a high-minded idealist, a soldier risking his life or a power-seeking schemer. In every political individual, from the purest to the corrupt, are to be found both the aspiration to be a leader of men and ideological motives, the desire to make a vision come true even when it is only a rationalized projection of hidden psychological drives.

Nor are we interested here in asking what is the nature of a leader—is it the "charisma" of Max Weber, that enigmatic quality of leadership, or the

From Eliezer Be'eri, Army Officers in Arab Politics and Society *(New York: Holt, Rinehart and Winston, Praeger, 1970), pp. 351–59, by permission of the publisher.*

glitter of success of some lucky adventurer? We shall try to clarify the diverse motives of the officers who are active in the Arab political sphere and their ideologies, beginning with some reflections on their self-image, or, as it has also been called, their auto-stereotype.

The appellations which the Arab officer politicians like to apply to themselves are of little use in analyzing the motives behind their activities. They are foremost among those whose self-image comprises various qualities characterized by such different epithets as "nationalistic". "revolutionary", and "socialistic". Formerly it would have been thought contradictory, like speaking of dry rain, if somebody were called a nationalist revolutionary or a revolutionary nationalist. Today this is the self-image of the adherents of many movements of Asians and Africans and American

Negroes as well. But it cannot help to explain their motivations.

The modern Arab officer class is sometimes called "the armed intelligentsia," and the officers themselves define their status in society as that of "intelligentsia in uniform." The interpretation implied by such names and definitions is a positive appreciation of both the intelligentsia and the officer corps as pioneers in the national awakening and in social and spiritual advancement.

This characterization of the officers as "intelligentsia in uniform" draws attention to a very significant fact, especially important as it projects the officers' self-image. But it is far too generalized. It is therefore desirable to clarify the terms and identify the phenomena referred to.

The expression *"muthaqqaf"* which means "intellectual" has become so common in modern Arabic that its original meaning has been blurred. Anyone who knows how to read and write and does not engage in physical labor, every teacher, clerk and official calls himself an intellectual, just as every pupils' riot is called a "students' demonstration." Before the singular noun *"muthaqqaf"* there appeared in modern Arabic usage the collective plural form *"al-muthaqqafūn,"* a translation of the French and English term "the intellectuals." As in western languages, this expression did not apply to all who had any erudition.

The western "intellectuals" were the modern rebel rationalists who burst the bonds of spiritual, in particular, religious, tradition. Opposition to the established intellectual and organizational authority of religion, militant anti-clericalism and agnosticism were fundamental parts of their outlook.

The term "intelligentsia" originated in Russia, and was coined apparently by Boborykin in the 1860's. His intelligentsia was a social group consisting of "that portion of the modern intellectual elite possessing an education equivalent to that of contemporary Western Europe which had no part in the government apparatus." Only later was the meaning of the term expanded to include all members of the free professions including teachers and some officials, but the intelligentsia as a social formation does not include either the disciples or the functionaries of religious tradition—shaykhs, imams, rabbis, religious sages, priests and monks. On the contrary, it embraces those with modern education and outlook of all kinds, so long as they are western-modern. At various times it was a source of ferment and revolution—in the eighteenth century in France, in the nineteenth in Russia and in the twentieth in Asia and Africa. It is "the social group which creates modern political ideas and provides the leadership for the revolutionary movements."

With the Arabs, like most other peoples, the first budding of the national movement took place among the intelligentsia. It was not by chance that the earlier proponents of the idea of the Arab awakening in the nineteenth century, beginning with the revival of culture, language and literature—at first without political aims—were Lebanese Christians, pupils of French and American missionaries.

For many Asian and African peoples, and especially for the Arabs, the rise of a modern intelligentsia represents something of a break in the history of their spiritual life. The essence of the beliefs and objectives of modernistic intellectuals was an admission of the supremacy of western civilization and, at the same time, a call to a struggle for the preservation or the restoration of national, spiritual and political independence, in opposition to the encroachment of those same western powers. The enemy and the model were one and the same. To hold their own against the west they had to westernize. The movement which aimed to ensure the survival and independence of the national culture was based on the negation of the national tradition. At the heart of the intelligentsia lies a deep-seated feeling of ambivalence: The intellectual is torn between the desire to learn and imitate the values and way of life of the foreigners and the will to protect himself against foreign principles and to reinforce his national values. This attraction-repulsion in respect of western culture gives rise to confusion and causes profound spiritual conflict. Whoever can see the synthesis of these contradictory forces, calling for acceptance of the west culturally but its rejection politically, may have solved the dilemma for himself and others who think as he does; but should he try to rouse the public at large, he will find that their reaction derives from tradition rather than from the new spirit. A call to enlightened nationalist feeling is always liable to be taken as a rallying cry for traditional Islamic zeal. This dilemma facing the Arab intelligentsia explains many of its reservations, its inconsistent thinking, its lack of self-confidence.

By "the west" we mean that philosophy, science, technology and civilization which is now conquering the whole world and which originated in Europe at the dawn of the modern era. To the west as thus defined belong both the USA and the USSR. In all the countries of Asia and Africa, new instruments of work, transport and warfare which have been developed in the west are being pressed into use, for these nations quite rightly see that local traditional tools and methods hold them back, and they know that the ability to produce a washing-machine themselves would be a great achievement. The same applies in matters far removed from tools and methods of work—to dress, for example, which although purely an external thing, nevertheless reflects the mentality of the wearer; Negroes in Africa, who used to go naked, and Eskimos in the far north adopt the universal mode of dress which is western, from head to toe. The same is true of the sciences and the humanities, in political science, in entertainment and in the arts. In most spheres the intelligentsia, through learning from others, pioneered the Arab awakening. In this may be seen a continuation of ancient Arab and Islamic tradition. Ever since the days of the prophet Muhammad, who based his new religion on knowledge and interpretation of the principles of Judaism and Christianity, the Muslim peoples—and particularly the Arabs and the Persians—have excelled in their readiness to receive the best of the heritage of other civilizations and their aptness in adapting it into a new entity for themselves. The present case is different, however. The westernizers in this new era, unlike the Muslims in the Middle Ages, did not learn from conquered peoples whose glory was past, but from rivals who excel them in the present, rivals who have overrun and subdued their pupils. "The intelligentsia of the early Abbassid period steeped itself in Hellenistic ways of thinking, took over Indian methods of medicine, adopted Iranian principles of administration, and in general delighted in widening its horizon and gratifying its curiosity about the world without feeling any (but occasional religious) hesitations about taking over elements of non-Arab and non-Muslim origin. The traditions from which influence would emanate were either politically dead, like Hellenism, or subjugated, like Iran, or irrelevant for the destiny of the empire, like India. The sense of the Muslims of being the master in their own house was in no way weakened by the knowledge that they were taking over the best the others had to offer . . . The completion of westernization during the last 150 years is totally different. It was the inadequacy of their power which first induced in some of the Muslim elites a readiness for reform . . . the removal of what was felt to be an inferiority . . . Can we ever become the political equals of the west unless we westernize completely."

The modernism of the new oriental intelligentsia had its origins in the feeling—and in the fact—of backwardness and it has evoked, as one would expect from its nature and from the character of the west of the period, not only a drawing-closer and attraction, but also repulsion and opposition. The relationship is basically ambivalent. The west has appeared not only in the guise of a shining example, but also as a trader and a jailer, as a conqueror of lands no less than as a conqueror of hearts. In the case of many members of this intelligentsia one can discern a feeling of inferiority, in more restrained form among the Turks and Persians, who have always managed to keep their national independence, and in more obvious form among the Arabs, who have been deprived of independence for many generations and who achieved it only after intense struggles. The Arab intelligentsia had undertaken to be the leader of the people in its spiritual and political war against the foreigner by acknowledging his superiority and studying his methods. The dilemma of the Arab intelligentsia in the twentieth century arises from the difficulty that it calls at one and the same time for a national struggle and for a kind of assimilation of the values and way of life of the enemy. It is not surprising that many of these intellectuals are left irresolute, hesitating in the middle of the road. Some of them are not ready to carry through to the end with the struggle for independence, fearing the rise to power of internal reactionary, conservative forces, who from time to time impress their characteristics on the nationalist movement as it becomes a popular mass movement, the native population being tied to tradition; some hold back from drawing all the indicated spiritual and cultural conclusions from westernization in their wish to enjoy the confidence and support of these masses. The intellectual who wishes to emerge from the seclusion of his ivory tower must take into consideration the mood prevailing among the public at large and try to adapt himself to it.

One result is the ideological and political differentiation within the intelligentsia itself.

This differentiation is also the result of the decisive fact that the intelligentsia is not an independent class. It plays a central role in the upward struggles of social classes; it is the group which has the courage and the ability to formulate their theories and provide them with their ideological weapons. No less than it serves itself, it serves the whole body politic. But it does not neglect its own group interests, quite often presenting them in the guise of the general national interest. Today members of the free professions, technicians and administrators of various kinds occupy key positions in the government, the army and all branches of economic activity and they are most active in collectively and aggressively bringing their own interests to the fore, even to the point of propagating ideologies such as James Burnham's doctrine of the "Managerial Revolution." But this is no proof of the intelligentsia's class-disinterestedness.

The French intelligentsia in the eighteenth century mostly ranged itself by the side of the rising revolutionary bourgeois class, as did the Russian in the nineteenth. The Arab intelligentsia in the twentieth century is much more split in its orientation. One reason is the great variety in its strata of origin. The French and Russian intellectuals of two hundred and one hundred years ago were in major part descendants of the bourgeoisie and the petty nobility. The Arab intellectuals of the last two generations come from various levels with conflicting interests —sons of the bourgeoisie and estate owners, sons of professional men, wealthy villagers and others. And despite the great importance of the intellectual born of the ruling class who goes over to the oppressed class and provides it with ideological ammunition, this is not the only image of the intellectual. Many intellectuals remain attached to their class of origin, serving it in their own manner, yet none the less faithfully and effectively. It would only be a mistake to regard all intellectuals or so-called intellectuals as automatically aligned with the forces of progress.

The intelligentsia as such is neither progressive nor reactionary. At times it serves as the all-important forum of ideas within every progressive movement and organizes its forces. But it fulfils the same functions in reactionary groups as well. It was the intellectuals who fashioned the ideological weapons of Marxism and Nazism, of internationalism and anti-Semitism, of the kibbutz movement and the Muslim Brethren. Karl Mannheim developed an entire theory of the "socially unattached intelligentsia (freischwebende Intelligenz)" using Alfred Weber's terminology, and the quest of these unattached intellectuals "for the fulfilment of their mission as the predestined advocate of the intellectual interests of the whole." But this is only an abstraction which incorrectly identifies the function of the intelligentsia in society with its own self-image and which converts a part of historical reality—disregarding the rest—into an historical and social law. There is no vacuum in society, and "the intellectual interests of the whole," like its other interests, have always been subjected to varying and contradictory interpretations, especially by the intellectuals of whatever stripe.

The officer corps has all along occupied a central position in the intelligentsia of Turkey, Egypt and the other Arab countries. By origins, customs and inclination the officers are kin to the civilian intellectuals and are indeed sometimes related to them. Their characterization as "intelligentsia in uniform" points to an important aspect of their social and psychological image.

This attachment on the part of the officer class to the intelligentsia and to modernism has its roots deep in history. Over a period of five hundred years, from the fifteenth to the nineteenth century, the military sphere was the main area of contact between the East and the West, their encounters being mainly on the field of battle, and it was in this sphere that western superiority stood out most strikingly and convincingly. It was undoubtedly from this specific area of contact that there arose the compulsion to learn the secrets of the new power.

Military science was, however, never the only, nor even the first, channel though which western civilization penetrated into the East. The Islamic armies were using firearms as far back as the Middle Ages, and the Turkish

science of artillery evolved as much from native sources as from European. The first innovation brought from the west was the printing press. The first books printed in a Muslim country by the revolutionary European method were Hebrew books, printed in Istanbul in 1493 or 1494. Refugees expelled from Spain in 1492, who found a haven in the Ottoman Empire, continued and renewed their spiritual and technical activities there. How revolutionary the introduction of printing was is shown by the fact that the printing of books in Arabic and Turkish, the languages of Islam and its holy books, was strictly prohibited up to the beginning of the eighteenth century. More than two hundred years passed between the setting up of the first Hebrew press in Istanbul and 1727, when the first Turkish press was allowed, but opposition to this act of heresy was so strong that the press had to close down again fifteen years later and was only reopened in 1784, when books began to be printed in steadily increasing numbers.

After the first printing works were established in Europe in the second half of the fifteenth century, the printed word spread rapidly in books, pamphlets and leaflets among a wide range of social strata. Many people could read and write. Democratization of learning began. If the number of books and the number of copies of each book in the Turkish language remained very small until the end of the eighteenth century, it must be remembered that the number who could read Turkish was very small. How much more tardy and slow, therefore, was the influence of civilization via the printed word in the case of the Arabs. On the other hand, the innovations in the military world quickly affected a very wide circle. Army officers were not the first to be touched by the winds of modernization, but the officer class was the first social group which, as an entire group and as a group of recognized social and political standing, was influenced by the new spirit of modernism.

Endless examples could be quoted of the introduction or penetration of western technical and spiritual innovations into the systems of work and thinking of the officers. It will perhaps suffice to give some examples from the nineteenth century alone:

European instructors in military schools were the first to have direct persistent influence over whole groups of native personnel. Egyptian army officers were the first to be sent to Europe for study. The Egyptian army was the first organization in a Muslim country to introduce, in the first half of the nineteenth century, European dress. Up to 1837 education was part of the task of the Egyptian Ministry for War. The army was also the first Egyptian institution to introduce compulsory education. In 1870, at the suggestion of Chief of Staff Stone, it was decided to establish a school in every battalion. It may be that in describing the results there was some exaggeration, but it was reported that by 1874 76 per cent of the army could read and write. Statistics on the subject of education which make no mention of the quality of the achievements are even today the most suspect of all statistics. Never-

theless, the attachment to learning, again found specifically in the army, is typical. Between 1865 and 1875 seven out of every ten graduates of the Egyptian civilian modern schools were taken into the army.

Revolutionary movements of the intelligentsia thus found their most active and effective supporters among the officers. The Egyptian movements were in this respect no exception, neither were they the first. The standard-bearers of the Decembrist Conspiracy in Russia in 1825 were officers. It was a great and at times decisive part that was played by the officers in the *Young Ottomans* movement in Turkey in 1865, in the *Young Turks* movement at the end of the last century and the beginning of this, in the movement for the introduction of a constitution in Egypt which ended in the 'Urābī rebellion of 1881, in the Arab national societies on the eve of World War I, and in other Arab groups of fighters for independence. Modern officer movements, from Bakr Ṣidqī and Sallāl, regard themselves as continuing the same tradition.

The intelligentsia was always an active element in political struggles. The intelligentsia in uniform continued political activity with greater intensity, sometimes to a point of one-sided politicization; by the nature of their profession they could not be as active or creative as the civilian intelligentsia in such fields as research, literature or education among the general public. This trend to greater politicization was strengthened by the relationship between the rulers and the intellectual officers. These rulers, whether governors of independent states like Sultan 'Abd al-Ḥamīd, Hashimite kings in Iraq and Jordan, or foreign governors in colonial or mandatory regimes, endeavored to keep officers away from politics. They feared the modernistic spirit and the nationalist zealotry of the officers—and so thrust them into the arms of the extremist underground opposition movements. Arab intellectuals, including the officer politicians, are unacquainted with Mannheim's theory of the "free intelligentsia" and its mission: had they been familiar with it, they might have found in it a faithful description of their self-image.

In a speech delivered in 1931 Atatürk described, in typically strong terms, the intelligentsia and the officer class as a social group who bear the standard of nationalist ideology and fulfil its aims. He said "Every time the Turkish nation wished to take a step forward, it cast its eyes on the army . . . When I speak of the army, I speak of the intelligentsia of the Turkish nation—the true masters of this country . . . The Turkish nation regards the army as the guardian of its ideals."

Already in 1931 the role of the officer class among the intelligentsia and the nationalist-conscious elements was overemphasized and exaggerated. Social and ideological developments among all Middle-Eastern peoples since then have broadened and diversified the ranks of the educated, and the officer class can no longer be claimed to have a monopoly of the characteristics of the intelligentsia.

However, the idealization of the officer class as the perfect and almost exclusive representative of the intelligentsia persists—and not only among those who are themselves in uniform. In a discussion among seventeen Soviet experts in 1964 on the subject of "Socialism, capitalism and the under-developed countries," G. Mirskiy said that in those countries the officers are "the best-educated section of the intelligentsia, always better equipped than others with progressive ideologies" and they "struggle for the modernization of their backward countries." This is not just a superficial and romantic generalization. G. Mirskiy himself was induced to revise his statement when he dealt, in 1967, with the problem of "the army and politics in the third world." There he wrote: "The ideological outlook of the military leaders is bourgeois in respect to its background and remains today the principal support of neo-colonialism. They (the military dictators in different countries of Asia, Africa and Latin America) have no taste for large-scale social changes. They also lack the necessary qualifications for leadership of a state."

Indeed, in the Arab countries, as elsewhere in Asia and Africa, there are other groups of intellectuals who are much superior to the officer class in the level of their education and more advanced in their political and social mentality and ideas. The officer class can now claim precedence with regard to power alone.

The Egyptian coup d'etat of July 1952, according to Gamal Abdel Nasser, was supposed to enable the Egyptians to govern themselves, but after the coup they were more concerned with revenge than with social revolution. Due to the backwardness of the masses and the selfishness of the old elite, Nasser believed that only the army could make Egypt "forget the past, while. . .restor[ing] the lost dignity of moral values."

GAMAL ABDEL NASSER

The Philosophy of the Revolution

Before proceeding with this discourse I would like to pause at the word "Philosophy." It looks big and sounds grand.

The truth is the Philosophy of the Revolution of July 23rd* should be treated by professors who should search deeply into it for the roots spreading at the very depth of our history. The stories of national struggles have no gaps that can be filled with nonsense. Neither have they the surprises that spring into existence without preludes.

I do not pretend to be a professor of history. This is the last thing my imagination may entertain. Nevertheless, if I were to attempt to study the story of our struggle like a schoolboy I would say, for instance, that the revolution of July 23rd is the realization of a hope that the people of Egypt, in modern times, have aspired to since they began to think of governing themselves and since they decided

*On this date in 1952, Colonel Nasser, General Neguib, and their followers in a bloodless revolution, seized the Government of Egypt and on July 26 forced King Farouk off his throne.

From Gamal Abdel Nasser, Egypt's Liberation: Philosophy of the Revolution (Washington, 1955), pp. 25-40, by permission of Public Affairs Press.

to be the masters of their fate.

One attempt failed to realize this hope when El Sayyed Omar Makram led the movement for appointing Mohamed Aly viceroy of Egypt in the name of its people. Another attempt failed to fulfil this aspiration when Arabi rose demanding a constitution. Other vain attempts followed during the intellectual fervour in the period between the revolt of Arabi and the Revolution of 1919. This latter was led by Saad Zaghloul who again failed to reach his goal.

It is not true that the revolution of July 23rd started on account of the results of the war in Palestine. Neither was it caused by defective arms, to which officers and men fell victims. It is still further from the truth to attribute it to the crisis of the elections of the Officers' Club. In my opinion its causes are deeper and farther. Had the officers endeavoured to avenge themselves because they were cheated in Palestine or because the defective arms strained their nerves and because they suffered an indignity in the elections of the Officers' Club, the whole affair would not have deserved to be called a revolution. A mere mutiny was the likely description even if it were attributed to causes fair and just in themselves. All these were incidental. Perhaps their greatest influence was that they urged us to march forward along the road to revolution; but without them we were marching just the same.

Today I am trying to recall all the events that passed and, after years have elapsed since we first thought of the revolution, to go back to the first day I discovered the seeds of revolt within me. That day lies farther back in my life than November 1951, which marked the beginning of the crisis of the Officers' Club elections. The organization of the Liberal Officers* was then existing and active. I do not exaggerate when I say that the crisis of the Officers' Club elections was caused, more than anything else, by the activities of the Liberal Officers. We were determined to fight then in order to test the strength of our mass formation and real organization.

That day lies again farther back in my life than May 16, 1944, which marked the start of my life in the Palestine War. As I trace the details of our experience in Palestine I feel a strange sensation. We were fighting in Palestine but our dreams were in Egypt. Our bullets were aimed at the enemy lurking in the trenches in front of us, but our hearts were hovering round our distant Mother Country, which was then a prey to the wolves that ravaged it. In Palestine, Liberal Officers' cells were meeting in trenches and posts studying and searching. And it was in Palestine that Salah Salem and Zakaria Mohyy-el-Din came to me after having penetrated the siege of Falouga; there we sat

*A secret movement organized in party cells.

besieged neither knowing what was to become of that siege nor when it would end. We spoke of nothing but our country and how to deliver it. It was in Palestine that Gamal-el-Din Hussein sat beside me one day and spoke as his eyes wandered and his thoughts dispersed; "Do you know what Ahmad Abdel Aziz had told me before he died?" he asked. "What did he say?" I asked in return. With a deep tone of voice and still deeper look he said, "Listen Gamal, Egypt is the field of our supreme war effort." . . .

The day I discovered the seeds of revolt within me was still further back than February 4, 1942 [when British tanks surrounded Abdin Palace seeking to force a change of government on King Farouk]. I wrote to a friend later saying, "What is to be done now that the catastrophe has befallen us, and after we have accepted it, surrendered to it and taken it submissively and meekly?

"I really believe," I continued, "that Imperialism is playing a one-card game in order to threaten only. If ever it knew that there were Egyptians ready to shed their blood and to meet force by force it would withdraw and recoil like a harlot. This, of course, is the state or habit of Imperialism everywhere."

Was it our duty, as an army, to do what we did on July 23, 1952?

I have just explained how the revolution of July 23rd was the realization of a hope that dangled before the eyes of the people of Egypt since they began, in modern times, to think of governing themselves and having the final word on their destiny. If this be so, and if what took place on July 23rd was only a military mutiny and not a popular revolt, why was the army then, apart from any other forces, destined to carry out this revolution?

Throughout my life I have had faith in militarism. The soldier's sole duty is to die on the frontiers of his country. Why then was our army compelled to act in the capital and not on the frontier? . . . "If the army does not move," we said to ourselves, "who else will?"

I confess that after July 23rd I suffered fits in which I accused myself, my colleagues and the rest of the army of rashness and folly we committed on July 23rd.

Prior to that date I imagined that the whole nation was on tip-toes and prepared for action, that it awaited the advance of the vanguard and the storming of the outside walls for it to pour down in a solid phalanx marching faithfully to the great goal. I thought we were only the pioneers and the commandoes, that we would only be in the front for a few hours, and that we would be soon followed by the solid masses marching to the goal. My imagination often carried me away. I felt I could hear the rattle of their solid, orderly rows as they marched onwards to the main front. My faith was such as to render everything I heard a concrete fact and not a mere vision.

After July 23rd I was shocked by the reality. The vanguard performed its task; it stormed the walls of the fort of tyranny; it forced Farouk to abdicate and stood by expecting the mass formations to arrive at their ultimate object. It waited and waited. Endless crowds showed up, but how different is the reality from the vision! The multitudes that arrived were dispersed followers and contrasted remnants. The holy march towards the great goal was interrupted. A dismal picture, horrible and threatening, then presented itself. I felt my heart charged with sorrow and dripping with bitterness. The mission of the vanguard had not ended. In fact it was just beginning at that very hour. We needed discipline but found chaos behind our lines. We needed unity but found dissensions. We needed action but found nothing but surrender and idleness. It was from this source and no other that the revolution derived its motto.

We did not expect this shock. We went to the men of ideas for counsel and to the men of experience for guidance, but unfortunately we did not find much of either.

Every leader we came to wanted to assassinate his rival. Every idea we found aimed at the destruction of another. If we were to carry out all that we heard, then there would not be one leader left alive. Not one idea would remain intact. We would cease to have a mission save to remain among the smashed bodies and the broken debris lamenting our misfortune and reproaching our ill-fate.

Complaints and petitions poured upon us in thousands. If these did refer to cases worthy of justice, or mentioned oppression that might be redressed, they would be understandable and logical. The majority of these were but persistent demands for revenge as if the revolution were meant to be a weapon for revenge and hatred.

If I were asked then what I required most my instant answer would be, "To hear but one Egyptian uttering one word of justice about another, to see but one Egyptian not devoting his time to criticize wilfully the ideas of another, to feel that there was but one Egyptian ready to open his heart for forgiveness, indulgence and loving his brother Egyptians." Personal and persistent selfishness was the rule of the day. The word "I" was on every tongue. It was the magic solution of every difficulty and the effective cure for every malady.

Often did I meet men, referred to in the press as "great men," of various tendencies and colours, from whom I sought the solution of a difficult problem. I could hear nothing from them save the word "I." He and only he was capable of understanding the problems of economics; the rest were but children creeping on all fours. He and only he was the expert statesman and the rest only learning their a & b and had not got to c. After interviewing any of these men I would go back to my colleagues bitterly exlaiming, "How utterly futile . . .! If we were to ask that man about a difficulty in fishing off the Islands of Hawaii his answer would only be 'I'."

I remember I once visited one of our universities and sat with professors endeavoring to profit by the experience of men of learning. Many spoke and spoke at length. Unfortunately not one of them presented a new idea. Every one introduced himself and listed his moral capacities which, in his view, could perform miracles.

Every one eyed me as if I were to him more precious that the treasures of earth or the blessings of eternity. I could not help but remark to them all, "Everyone in his place can perform miracles. The primary duty is to put all energy into it and if you, as university professors, ever thought of students and rendered them, as you should, your principal care, you would provide us with a tremendous force wherewith to build up our country. Let every one remain at his post and strive hard at it. Do not look up to us. Circumstances have compelled us to leave our posts to perform a sacred task. We sincerely wish the country has no further use for us save as professional soldiers in the army. There we would have remained."

I did not wish then to set before them the example of the members of the Revolution Council* who, before the crisis summoned them for the supreme task, were performing their duties in the army most diligently. I did not wish to tell them that most of the members of the Revolution Council were professors in the Staff-College . . . a clear proof of their distinction as professional soldiers.

Every nation on earth undergoes two revolutions: One is political, in which it recovers its right for self-government from an imposed despot, or an aggressive army occupying its territory without its consent. The second revolution is social, in which the classes of society would struggle against each other until justice for all

*The cabinet of Neguib and Nasser, consisting mainly of Army officers who were Nasser's associates in the Free Officers movement and in the Revolution of July 23, 1952.

countrymen has been gained and conditions have become stable.

Other nations have preceded us along the path of human progress and passed through the two revolutions but not simultaneously. Hundreds of years separated the one from the other. In the case of our nation, it is going through the two revolutions together and at the same time, a great experiment putting us to the test.

Political revolution demands, for its success, the unity of all national elements, their fusion and mutual support, as well as self-denial for the sake of the country as a whole.

One of the first signs of social revolution is that values are shaken and creeds are relaxed; fellow-countrymen struggle against each other, individuals and classes. Corruption, suspicion, hatred and selfishness dominate them. Between the anvil and the hammer we now live in two revolutions; one demanding that we should unite together, love one another and strain every nerve to reach our goal; the other forces us, in spite of ourselves, to disperse and give way to hatred, everyone thinking only of himself. . . .

I still believe until today that the revolution of July 23rd should retain its capacity for swift action and initiative in order that it may fulfill the miracle of proceeding with the two revolutions simultaneously, contradictory as our action may appear to be sometimes.

When a friend of mine came to me one day exclaiming, "You asked for unity to face the English and at the same time you permit the Graft Court to proceed with its work." I listened to him with the image of our big crisis in my mind: the crisis of being between two millstones. One revolution demanded that we should stand in one row and forget the past, while another revolution forced us to restore the lost dignity of moral values and not forget the past.

This was not my will; nor was it the will of those who took part in the revolution of July 23rd. It was the will of fate, of the history of our nation and of the stage it is passing through today.

Nasser established the first Middle Eastern oligarchical praetorianism. The RCC tried to solve all of Egypt's domestic and foreign problems, but failed in the end to successfully bring about land reform, to form a political party, or to lay the foundation of a modern army. "Traditional" Egypt triumphed over the "modern" command council.

But modernity was easier to preach than to effect. The history of the army in Syrian politics since 1949 bears witness to the inability of the praetorian soldier to bring about revolutionary change or modernization.

Amos Perlmutter shows how Syria's politics became a theater for ambitious army men. The first Syrian coup in 1949, like the intervention of the Egyptian Free Officers in 1952, was a result of the growth of nationalist sentiment among the officer corps. Shishakly, the leader of the first Syrian coup, stood for "militant nationalism and 'progressive' socioeconomic reforms." But instead of progress and reform, the Syrian army quickly became mired in "personal intrigues and fratricidal divisions." Nonetheless, Perlmutter concludes, the Syrian military has been able to keep its image of a new modernizing elite.

AMOS PERLMUTTER

From Obscurity to Rule: The Syrian Army and the Ba'th Party

Syria has had no stable civilian rule since 1949, the year of her first army coup; her politics have become a theater for ambitious army men. In the twenty-four years since Syria gained independence from the French, the country has had eight years of parliamentary rule (1945–49 and 1954–58) and five years of semi-parliamentary government (late 1961 to February 1966). Long periods of military intervention have alternated with shorter eras of parliamentary and semi-parliamentary rule, while the government has always stood under the shadow of military domination.

Since March 1949, Syria has experienced some sixteen army coups—nine of them successful. Only three times did the officers who achieved successful coups pass the reins of power to civilians and call for a retreat to the barracks. Since 1963 a pattern has developed in which civilians and the army have alternated in power, but

From Amos Perlmutter, "From Obscurity to Rule: The Syrian Army and the Ba'th Party," The Western Political Quarterly 22 (1969): 827–45, reprinted by permission of the University of Utah, copyright holder.

the army has never retreated to the barracks. . . .

THE BACKGROUND OF ARMY DOMINATION IN SYRIAN POLITICS

Syria is a product of Franco-British imperialist machinations, specifically of the hasty and thoughtless division of the Turkish Empire after World War I. The diminishment of Syria's territory after the Ottoman reign (1517–1918) brought political instability, economic insecurity and nationalist dreams of grandeur, the vision of Damascus as the center of a rising and progressive Arab Empire. Syria and Lebanon—and with them Iraq, Palestine, and Jordan, former Arab provinces of the Turkish Empire—emerged in 1918 as semi-independent countries governed, under a League of Nations mandate, by Britain and France. The Syrian Republic, created in 1920 under a French mandate, did not represent an integrated national entity.

Syria's economic power, since the days of the Turks, has lain in two middle-sized cities in its agricultural heartland, Hama and Homs, and their surrounding villages. Another vestige of Ottoman rule is the power concentrated in the hands of the few feudal families who dominate the two cities and the valley between Damascus and Aleppo—the 'Azm family rules Hama, the 'Atasi family rules Homs. These powerful local feudal forces, and religious, ethnic, and cultural differences, were Syria's inheritance when it became independent in 1945. Although the Suni-Moslem population in Syria comprises a majority of 72.2 percent of the total population, the significance of the ethno-religious division in Syria is political. Ethnic groups form consolidated political-ethnic entities, and the political support these ethnic groups derive from their group identity has since become Syria's most acute political problem. Ethnic identity in an age of Arab nationalism has produced a series of conflicts between a Suni-dominated central government (this before the military 'Alawi takeover in February 1966) and the politically isolated but consolidated ethnic groups, most notably the 'Alawi, Druze, and Isma-'ilis. Since 1966, these groups have gone beyond their "traditional" role as protest groups. Under the guise of the military the 'Alawi today rule Syria. . . .

The short experiment in constitutional politics (1945–49) set the form of Syria's parliamentarianism. The national executive increasingly lost power and influence, the political parties were reduced to cliques and alliances of ethnic, and local religious and cultural interests. The absence of political, social, and cultural cohesion and the deep antagonism between center and periphery doomed Syrian constitutional politics from the start. Corruption, nepotism, filial piety, kinship practices and related ills became the practice of parliamentary politics. A catalyst was necessary; it came threefold. First, there was an economic crisis and inflation which had been increasing since independence. Second, a parliamentary crisis developed, the result of the "cooking-fat" (*Samnah*) scandal when, during the 1949 Palestine campaign, the army had been supplied poor oil, implicating key political and military figures. The third and real catalyst, however, was the debacle in Palestine itself. This defeat brought an enormous burden to all Arab leaders, civilian, religious, and military. In its wake came the assassination of King Abdullah of Jordan 1951, and the Egyptian coup of 1952.

The Palestine debacle demonstrated the need for reform in the Arab world and provided the *coup de grace* for reactionary Arabs, ineffective politicians, and corrupt army leaders. Syria was politically one of the most sensitive eastern Arab countries—hence her first coup, led by Colonel Husni al-Za'im, the army's first chief of staff, came shortly after the Palestine war, in March 1949.

The Palestine war completely changed the nature of the Arab armies. Its effect added to other events that changed the politics of the army as well as Arab nationalism and politics—the decline of colonialism and the growth of nationalist activity elsewhere in the world, and the emergence of the Afro-Asian bloc in world politics. The Syrian coups indicated a dramatic change in the army's political role: the sudden intensification of army. officers' political consciousness and the rapid transformation of the Syrian army officers' corps into a political group.

The French policy had been to encourage non-Arabs or non-Muslims to join the army. The nationalist government after 1949, however, encouraged the majority of Suni Arab Moslems and Syria's rural population to serve in the army and go to the academy. The Homs and Hama academies are open to all, and, since 1954, rural and lower class groups have been encouraged to enter a military career; tuition is paid by the government. Homs' military college has become the home of Syria's new and rising army elite, a proud, nationalist, militant group. Serving in the army has become a national duty and a mobility factor for minority ethnic groups. After the Palestine war, nationalist groups attempted to enlarge the army, and to politicize, Arabize, and radicalize its officer corps.

The first three army coups in 1949 were still led by Ottoman- and French-trained officers: Za'im, Hinnawi, and Shishakly. The first two coups did not yet represent an emergent new army, but they served notice that the Syrian officer corps was a political force to be dealt with. Although civilian nationalist politicians rejected independent army rule, they favored the army's political activity and encouraged the officers' involvement in politics—not because they considered army rule good government but because they

felt that army officers would provide able, honest, decisive, and strong leadership. The fragile constitutional period and the strong tradition of provincial, ethnic, and kinship groups had prevented the emergence of political leaders with a national vision. It was hoped that the army group could produce such men.

THE SHISHAKLY ERA 1949–54

In the period after Shishakly's first coup—from the end of 1949 until November 1951—the army acted as arbitrator between civilian rivals and the officers; at this time the military was expected to return to the barracks. Shishakly's second coup in November 1951 initiated a new role for the politically minded army officers. Shishakly intended to "use" the army to weaken the traditional and conservative forces in Syria, and he soon interpreted the mandate given to him by the "progressives" as a mandate to establish a military dictatorship. He began with a reform of the army, promoting young officers, most of whom played prominent roles in his overthrow three years later and in the military coups in Syria since. The politicization of the army was combined with an intense program of Arabization of the officer corps and the rise to prominence of the provincial military academies, Hama and Homs. Politicization in the academies went hand in hand with the progressive ideology of the Hawrani-Socialist and Ba'th brand. In 1951, Shishakly established the first open political party in the Middle East that was dominated by the army—the Arab Liberation Movement (ALM)

(Nasser's clandestine Free Officer Club preceded it by two years). Like Nasser's Liberation Rally of 1953 (which must have been inspired by Shishakly), the new army-dominated party was to abolish the "corrupt" political system of parties and parliaments in Syria. The ALM preached militant nationalism and "progressive" socioeconomic reforms. Although it soon collapsed, its emulators have continued to flourish.

There were five primary reasons why the political party organized by the army under Shishakly collapsed: these are very significant for they set the pattern for subsequent civil-military relations in Syria.

(1) Lack of cohesion among the politically inclined officers, the division of the army into rival factions, and the personal struggles within the ALM organization. This fratricidal division between army commanders was responsible for the demise of Shishakly and of later military regimes.

(2) The antagonism of civilian progressives toward Shishakly's military dictatorship. Hawrani and Michel 'Aflaq, the leaders of the newly formed (1953) Arab Socialist Ba'th party, formerly Shishakly's protagonists, opposed his "unexpected" military dictatorship and ceased to support him.

(3) The old ills of Syria: its feudal and politico-geographical nature. The role of the politically semi-independent minorities, especially the Druze and 'Alawi, and the deep split between urban and rural groups (predominant among the latter).

(4) The ALM's failure to establish national authority in Damascus and to subdue outer and rural centers,

Hama, Homs, Jabal Druze. In fact, Shishakly "played cat and mouse with the People's Party" and was supported by Aleppo business groups.

(5) The role of inter-Arab intrigues. The Egyptian-Iraqi struggle over Syria. The active Egyptian support of Syrian progressives, and especially of the Ba'th party.

In February 1954, an army insurrection dominated by a Shishakly disciple, Captain (later Colonel) Mustafa Hamdun, and some Druze officers, and inspired by Hawrani, ended the reign of the military dictatorship and the political party of the army. But the way was open for future civil-military relations patterned after Shishakly's model. "Shishakly's rule made the Syrian army an unashamedly political instrument."

THE BA'TH PARTY AND THE SYRIAN ARMY 1954–58

The fall of Shishakly's reign in February 1954 restored constitutional order to Syria. The first free elections since 1947 brought new forces and ideologies to Syria's political arena. Although the old parties returned to power, the greatest beneficiary of the 1954 election and of Shishakly's fall was the newly emergent Arab Socialist Ba'th party. This party had been formed at the end of 1953 when Akram Hawrani's small Socialist party (actually Hama's anti-feudal group) joined the Ba'th (Renaissance) party, a small Damascus coterie of intellectuals and school teachers under Michel 'Aflaq and Salah al-Din Bitar. The latter group had been established in 1947 but had not participated in elections until 1949, when it secured one seat in parliament. In 1954, the Ba'th party received 15 percent of the vote and elected twenty-two representatives, although it won only a poor third place in the election. . . .

Most importantly, the Ba'th party added a socialist ideology to Syrian nationalist politics. Another new dimension, after Shishakly's fall, was the rise of Egyptian influence. International and inter-Arab politics had played an important role in Syria since 1949. Za'im, the instigator of Syria's first coup, had seen Syria in a wider Arab context and at first had negotiated with Iraq. However, when Za'im had begun flirting with the Egyptians (the Farouq regime), Hinnawi—with Iraqi support—staged his successful countercoup. When, in 1954, army rule in Egypt was consolidated under Gamal Abdel Nasser, and his group sought friends and influence in the Arab East, their most natural allies were the Syrian Ba'thists, especially in the army. Thus, the Egyptian army group was forging an alliance of great consequence for Syria and the Ba'th party.

The Ba'th was convinced that neither Arab unity nor security for Syria was possible without eventual union with Egypt. At that time, Soviet support of Syrian and Egyptian radical nationalists enhanced the position of the Ba'th (as well as that of the Kurdish-dominated Syrian Communist party led by Khalid Bakhdash, another resourceful Syrian politician). The rise of the Ba'th and its nationalist and socialist ideology, the projected union with Egypt, and Soviet military aid brought an expectation of unity to Syrian politics.

For a while, army rule and Syria's historic ills of divisiveness and particularism seemed things of the past. The new graduates of Hama-Homs academies and their leaders, veterans of the Palestine campaign, supported, and some even joined, the Ba'th. A new group of Suni-Moslem Arab officers emerged, dedicated to Arab nationalism and the aggrandizement of the army. . . . During the 1954–58 period, parliamentary politics gradually became paralyzed, while the forces of "resurrection" were rising. When the Egyptian-Syrian union, the U.A.R., was formed in 1958, politically oriented Ba'thists in the army and their civilian allies believed in a break with the past and that a new political order would begin in Syria. Expectations were high that the Ba'th, pursuing a progressive policy with Egyptian aid, would unite all Syrians. . . .

The nationalist awakening and the reform of the Syrian army since the Palestine war made the officers incline toward the Ba'th because the Ba'th ideology and aspirations fulfilled their nationalist desires. The army officers found in the Ba'th party a supporting political organization, although they sometimes clashed with the personalities of Ba'th leaders and politicians. Over the years, the Syrian Ba'th and the politically inclined army officers fluctuated between cooperation and recrimination, a process detrimental to both the Ba'th's and the army's political power and influence.

In 1949 the Ba'th was only a small coterie of a very few Damascus intellectuals ('Aflaq, Bitar, his cousin Dr. Midhat Bitar, Dr. Mu'nif al-Razaaz, and Dr. 'Ali Jabar from Beirut). At that time, the politically inclined officers were also few. The simultaneous emergence of the Ba'th and the politically oriented officers at the end of Shishakly's reign precipitated an eventual rivalry. Divisiveness and personalism within either group encouraged the ambitions of individual officers. Without group solidarity neither group could prevail.

In 1949, the infant Ba'th and the Socialist party and its leaders considered the political officers useful to further their ambitions. The politically minded officers, in turn, saw in the Ba'th their "natural" home and embraced 'Aflaq's ideology indiscriminately. Although few officers actually joined the Ba'th or became activists in the Ba'th during the middle 1950's, most pan-Arabist and Syrian nationalist officers embraced the Ba'th ideology.

From the beginning, Ba'th had difficulty attracting the masses and winning elections. Although 'Aflaq had served as Colonel Hinnawi's minister of national education in 1949, this did not increase the party's electoral strength. 'Aflaq resigned after three months and lost his seat in parliament during the November 1949 elections, the only Ba'th seat in parliament. In the October 1954 elections— the first free ones since the reign of Shishakly—the Ba'th received 15 percent of the popular vote and 22 out of a total of 142 parliamentary seats.

THE BA'TH, THE ARMY, AND THE U.A.R. 1958–61

The Ba'th and the Ba'th-oriented officers were instrumental in forging the Egyptian-Syrian alliance which culminated in the formation of an Arab progressive union, the U.A.R., in 1958. However ambiguous were the circumstances and rationale of the Egyptian-Syrian union, it emanated from a sincere desire on the part of all parties, especially the Ba'th, to advance the cause of Arab nationalism and its progressive wing. . . .

Unity with Egypt was sought as a cure for all ills: for the fratricide of the officer corps and the impotence of Ba'th at the polls.

The Ba'th was soon disenchanted with the U.A.R. The Egyptians were trying to weaken the party, and the Ba'th was torn asunder over the issue of support of the U.A.R. Instead of consolidating the party, the U.A.R. became a source of division which did not end even after its collapse in 1961. . . .

On the whole, the Suni-Moslem nationalist, and politically inclined, officers supported the U.A.R. The Syrian government during the last year of the U.A.R. (1960–61) was run chiefly by officers—Egyptians and Syrians. But, when the Ba'th clashed with the Egyptians, those Ba'thist officers and sympathizers who remained loyal to Ba'th were gradually removed and others joined the Egyptians. The Egyptians had encouraged, wherever possible, nonpolitical and non-Ba'thist officers. Loyal Nasser followers were elevated. The legacy of U.A.R. rule was not the unification of the officer corps that had been expected. On the contrary, the U.A.R. legacy to the Syrian army was a deepening and newly ideological split between unionists, and anti-unionists and gradualists.

The anti-U.A.R. coup was directed by nonpolitical officers who resented

Egyptian and Sarraj's rule over Syria. The coup of September 28, 1961, led by Colonels Kuzbari, Dahaman, and Nahlawi, brought an end to the U.A.R.

1961–1969—YEARS OF ASCENDANCY AND FRATRICIDE

After the U.A.R. debacle, the fact that the Ba'th never succeeded in becoming the most popular party in Syria is crucial to the understanding of its weakness and its search for "outside" help from the army and again from Egypt or, for that matter, from any Arab country willing to help. Even as recently as 1963, ten years after its formation, Ba'th received only one-fourth of the seats in parliament or 15 percent of the electorate. It is the party with the greatest potential among the Arabs, its leaders are revered, its ideology is espoused throughout the Arab world. It is the party of the new Arab intelligentsia, the party of the ambitious nationalists in the Syrian army, the only Arab nationalist party to penetrate the rest of the Arab world (having branches in all Arab countries, including secret ones in Egypt), and yet, for reasons that we shall discuss, it has never succeeded in getting a majority of votes and seats in its homeland. This failure left the party at the mercy of the Syrian army.

The period of constitutional government after the dissolution of the U.A.R. did not last long. Again no one party received a decisive majority in the elections to create a lasting coalition government and to end the fighting. The raucous Egyptian-Syrian denunciations only opened the

way for a new army intervention. At the end of March 1962, six months after the formation of a civilian government, the army revolted again. This time the rebels were the army leaders Nahlawi and Dehaman, anti-Egyptian officers in Damascus, who had led the anti-U.A.R. coup in 1961. Three days later pro-U.A.R. forces in Aleppo, led by Colonel Jasan 'Alwan, revolted against army pro-U.A.R. factions. Egypt did not come to the support of the Aleppo rebels who were soon subdued by Damascus. The army entered politics again and the supreme commander, General 'Abd al-Krim Zahar al-Din, became minister of defense in a government of civil servants and the army. Throughout the year 1962 coups and countercoups were successfully suppressed by General Zahar al-Din, a nonpolitical Druze officer. But unity did not last long. The fratricidal, divided officers had found a new opportunity to fulfill political and personal ambitions. This opportunity was sparked by the fall of General Qassem's regime in Iraq in February 1963, and the coming to power of the staunch pro-Nasser General 'Abd Salim 'Arif which changed Iraq from an avid anti-Nasser military regime into a close ally. These events were followed immediately (March 8, 1963) in Syria by a coup staged by General Ziad al-Hariri, Hawrani's brother-in-law and a frustrated pro-Ba'thist officer-seeker, in collaboration with Hama Ba'thists. The coup-makers launched a unity propaganda campaign but hardly mentioned Ba'th or socialism. As soon as the army overthrew Zahar al-Din, rival Ba'thist army officers claimed the coup as their own work. The Revolutionary Council was then headed by one of the conspirators, Colonel Luay al-'Atasi, a Ba'th sympathizer.

Out of twelve ministers in the new government seven were officers. General Hariri became chief of staff of the army. Thus, the Ba'th again was supported by the army but this time the army was no longer the Ba'th's instrument as it had been in 1954. The Ba'th cabinet was an uncomfortable coalition of Syrian progressive nationalists, socialists, and Unionists; nevertheless, the Ba'th hoped to be able to govern successfully.

There were three reasons why Ba'th-dominated rule was not sustained: (1) fratricide within the army; (2) the new unity negotiations with Egypt which started as soon as the Ba'th cabinet was formed in March-April 1963; and (3) the drift of the Ba'th leftward after its sixth national convention in October 1963.

The army's personal intrigues and fratricidal divisions soon were reflected in Ba'th-army rule. Hariri, who opposed Ba'th's demands for agrarian reform and Ba'th-inspired army appointments and removals, was dismissed by the Ba'th government while he was away. This could only have been done with the help of Hariri's chief rival, Colonel Amin al-Hafiz, a pro-Ba'thist army officer who soon became minister of defense and later was promoted to general. While Ba'th's rivals were defeated and went into opposition, the party itself was still divided and the army officers intended to dominate the Ba'th-army alliance in the government at the expense of coalition partners and the

Ba'th. Ba'th rule was further weakened by the collapse of Ba'th in Iraq six months later, in August 1963, and the strikes and revolts against the government in Damascus. General Amin al-Hafiz seized the opportunity to become the ruler of a Ba'th-army-dominated regime in Syria. Al-Hafiz secured a price for his support of Ba'th—the ouster of his rival, 'Alawi General Muhammad 'Umran, a devout Ba'thist himself. With the fall of 'Umran, another 'Alawi officer emerged, Air Force General Salah Jadid. The Ba'th party was left to face the challenge of its officers and followers in the army. . . .

Beginning in 1963, the top army command in Syria became more and more Ba'thist and the Ba'thist officers became progressive (or at least paid lip service to revolutionary slogans). The Ba'th officers were divided between leftists and moderates with the predominance of 'Alawis among the former. The radicalization of the army was sought through the formation of a national guard, the party's "ideological army" (an idea born at the sixth party convention), which was dominated by leftist Ba'thist officers. Among the left Ba'thists, 'Alawi and Druze officers (the "countryside boys") were predominant. The struggle for power in the party and within the Ba'thists in the army was resolved in favor of Jadid who prevailed over the national guard. Thus, while Hafiz was allied with the moderate (mainstream) faction in the Syrian Ba'th, Jadid and his allies in the army were supported by the Ba'th International Command, the left opposition in the

Syrian Ba'th, and the national guard. Finally, Jadid allied himself with Yousuf Zu'ayn, a leftist Ba'thist, and with the Druze officer Salim Hatum, and—backed by 'Alawi leftist officers —staged a successful coup on February 26, 1966.

The rise of the "countryside boys" in the army and in the Ba'th opened up a new era of erratic and radical politics in Syria. . . .

The net result of the "ideological army"—the left Ba'thist aspiration since 1963—is that now the Ba'thist officers can occupy the high army command and remove their anti-Ba'thist, "mainstream" and Suni, rivals, or for that matter, any other rival in the army. While the army was Ba'thized and radicalized, the Ba'th party was torn asunder between conflicting Ba'th-army officers and Ba'th-civilian factions. But it is interesting to note that while in Syria the army turned leftward, the leftist tendencies of Ba'th alienated the Iraqi army.

Thus, the Ba'th, in its third trial for power, once more—as in 1954 and 1958—became the victim of the "instruments" it chose to "educate" and abate. It fell prey to the strategy of infiltration and access of groups more powerful than itself. The mobilizing ideology of the Ba'th and its espousal of union with Egypt did not eradicate Syria's old ills—feudalism, parochialism, cultural and religious diversity. In fact, the failure of Ba'th created new tensions. The left Ba'thist stance brought more brutal frictions and antagonisms among Syria's new and emancipatory elites. . . .

The Syrian military prefer a prae-torian-patrimonial rule to parliamentary domination. Thus a nonconsolidated, newly mobilized rural elite rules by virtue of force, not by the expectation of political-parliamentary consensus. Legitimacy is sought in the doctrines of the permanent revolution, but the Syrian rulers do not have the commitment that this doctrine demands of it authors. Not unlike the second generation nationalists of the 1950's, the new Syrian elite is searching for new symbols of legitimacy for an organizational structure buttressed by a new ideology. But this search is pursued under military rule, if necessary by force. To overcome its fratricidal tendencies, this elite advocates domination by coercion using the military and the party as its chief instruments.

On the whole, this party has made more errors and had more failures than any other contemporary Arab nationalist party in the Middle East. Syria is not capable, physically or politically, of sustaining the most messianic Arab nationalist party in modern times. The burden of Ba'th ideology is too heavy for a country as poor and divided as Syria.

PROSPECTS OF THE ARMY

In two turbulent decades, the Syrian army has emerged from the role of a military force to become the political guardian of the country. The continuous civilian interference in army politics, and the politicization and radicalization of the army, increased the influence of military politicians. The army no longer acts as an arbitrator of nationalist and

THE IMPACT OF MODERNIZATION ON THE MILITARY

321

progressive forces. It has been persuaded of its unique historical destiny and special political role as the "savior" of society from the "corrupt" politician. It has assumed the "role of hero" and considers itself the key and the *only* hope for honest politics, stability, order, and progress. These expectations and aspirations, now claimed exclusively by the army, have been supported in the last two decades by the civilian politicians, by the progressive forces, by the intellectuals, and the modernizers. Because most of these groups have discredited themselves by one means or another, the Syrian army has remained the only political organization above the battle. But, interestingly enough, the army has not been consolidated since its political emergence. Nor did the officer corps become cohesive under the intense process of politicization. The politicization of the army encouraged independent army officers and cliques

to espouse a variety of rival political ideologies which only divided the officer corps. If civilian political groups had acted as the army now does, they would have been discredited. Yet, the army still increases its influence, and now actually dominates Syrian society despite its apparent fratricidal tendencies, the machinations of ambitious officers, and the espousal of rival political ideologies by different army officers. It still keeps its image as a new modernizing elite; of the honest rescuers of society; of the heroes and knights (*Fursan*) of Arabhood and of Syria. . . .

[In the end, the rise of the Alawi sect of the Ba'th party and General Assad made it possible for the army to maintain itself by leaving the society to the merchants and the agriculturalists, while building, with the help of the Alawi dominated Ba'th party, a strong military machine for international adventures.]

But the failure of the Arab military to modernize army society has not necessarily weakened the myth of the Arab national revolution led by the uniformed intellectuals. As late as 1969, the myth was still a strong motivating force in the Muslim world. Muammar Gadafi's coup d'etat in September 1969 was a testament to the endurance and appeal of the Nasserite vision of the brave new Arab world that inspired soldiers could help bring about. Gadafi modeled his life, his politics, and his army career on that of the late Egyptian leader. He insists that he has made a revolution, not a coup d'etat. Ruth First writes, "While Gadafi frequently talked of his urge to abandon politics for the army, he accepted Nasser's famous dictum that the army must permanently patrol society." But, she warns, the continued domination of the army, and the refusal to permit autonomous organization or initiative made Gadafi's intervention more a coup d'etat than a revolution.*

*First, *Power in Africa*, pp. 116–17.

PRAETORIANISM IN AFRICA

The central question concerning students of civil-military relations in sub-Saharan Africa has been, What is the impact of colonial training, education, and assistance on the African military? In the 1950s both scholars and European officers believed that the training of officers and men on the European pattern in European institutions would create carbon copies of the "apolitical" professional soldiers of France, England, Belgium, and the United States. Although there was already some experience with European-trained officers intervening in politics in the Sudan and Pakistan, hopes ran high for the implantation of Western-style multiparty representative government on the continent. But these hopes were to be dashed, first by the politicians who inherited power from the departing colonial authorities, and later by soldiers ousting the civilian leaders they had been trained to serve. The politicians-turned-rulers quickly restricted politics in general and opposition politics in particular. As opposition leaders were jailed or exiled in country after country, and as political parties languished and the scope of judicial authority was narrowed, Africa appeared to be becoming a continent of civilian authoritarianism. By the mid-sixties, however, a new pattern was emerging; chaotic multiparty systems and one-party autocracies alike were replaced by military men. By 1971, coups d'etat had occurred in such nations as Ghana, Nigeria, Zaire (the former Congo), Uganda, Sudan, Togo, Dahomey, Mali, Somalia, Sierra Leone, the Central African Republic, Congo-Brazzaville, and Niger. Africa had become the continent of praetorianism *par excellence*.

Scholars, plowing familiar terrain, asked themselves what had happened to cause these Western-trained soldiers to intervene. Upon reflection it seemed that training by the ex-colonial power had had very different consequences from those expected. Robert Price and Robin Luckham both addressed themselves to this issue, but came to somewhat different conclusions. Price argues from the Ghanaian case that when the organizational forms of European armies were transplanted to Africa, they underwent transformations in the process. Price poses an "emulation paradox" that produces military officer corps in new states that tend to be nonnationalistic and nonpuritanical. The lack of nationalist fervor results from a positive attachment to the former mother country and contempt for the former leaders of the anticolonial movement who became heads of government in the postindependence era. A final argument is advanced by Price: "reference-group identification with the British officer corps acted as a counterforce to the perquisites of political office, pushing or pulling the Ghanaian military officers to give up the power (in 1969) they had earlier seized."

Robert M. Price

A Theoretical Approach to Military Rule in New States: Reference Group Theory and the Ghanaian Case

[The Gold Coast was Britain's "model" colony in Africa, being the first colony on the continent to receive representative government, and, later, independence. Ghana began with a popular civilian government under Kwame Nkrumah, whose Convention Peoples' Party had won two successive parliamentary elections before independence. But Nkrumah succeeded in ruining his nation's economic health while curtailing his own popularity.]

NEW STATES AND ORGANIZATIONAL EMULATION

. . . [Military organizations in the developing areas, especially those in newly independent ex-colonial territories, have been formed along the lines of their Western counterparts. In The ex-colonial countries, the organizational structures are usually identical to those existing in the army of the metropole, often down to details of uniform, insignia, and rank. Training, especially that of senior officers, is usually undertaken by the army of the ex-colonial power.* But, however

*See William F. Gutteridge, *Military Institutions and Power in New States* (London 1964), passim.

From Robert M. Price, "A Theoretical Approach to Military Rule in New States: Reference Group Theory and the Ghanaian Case," World Politics 23 (1971): 401–27.

great the emulation of the Western military format, the consequences for the behavior of organization and officer corps cannot be inferred from the formal organizational model that has been emulated. For when the organizational forms of European armies are copied and transplanted to a "transitional" social and cultural environment they may undergo transformations in the process: transformations that may seriously alter the behavior of the organization and its members]. . . .

[In order to demonstrate and explain this weakness we shall concentrate on a number of propositions derived from the formal organizational model that relate to the ideology of military officers. A central proposition derived from this model is that the outlook and ideology of all military officers in the contemporary world will have certain similar components; that there are ideological "themes" that inhere in the military as a profession]. . . . [Among these common themes two are considered central and pervasive—nationalism and puritanism]. . . .

Although formal organizational analysis leads to such conclusions, an investigation of the process whereby ex-colonial armies seek to emulate the Western military format may call into question what otherwise would appear to be these almost self-evident conclusions. In the course of our discussion we will suggest that there occurs what might be called an "emulation paradox"—the very fact of emulation produces military officer corps in new states that tend in fact to be *non-nationalistic* and *non-puritanical*. To come to grips with this "emulation paradox" a scrutiny of the training process whereby the top officers in new states are professionally socialized is demanded.

In newly independent states the most promising officer material usually is sent for professional training to the elite military academy of the former mother country, the two most significant such academies being Britain's Sandhurst and France's St. Cyr. . . .

REFERENCE GROUPS AND OFFICER TRAINING

An individual's reference groups are those social groups to which he psychologically relates himself, with which he identifies. To become a member of a group in the psychological sense implies the internalization of its central norms and values—for to be a member implies certain modes of thought and behavior. . . .

The military training officers undergo can be viewed as a socialization process within which the recruit's identifications with his previous civilian reference groups are broken down and replaced by new ego-involved associations that are centered in the military organization. . . .

In the case of military officers from newly independent states, one likely consequence of this training process is the development of positive reference-group identifications with the officer corps of the excolonial power, for, as we noted earlier, the top officers in such states receive their training at European military schools. . . .

The powerful nature of the experience at an institution such as Sandhurst for a recruit from the "third world" and the positive manner in which this experience is viewed is illustrated well by a passage from a book written by a Sandhurst-trained member of the Ghana army:

I was thrilled by Sandhurst, the beauty of its countryside, and the calm Wish Stream which separated Sandhurst from the rest of the world. Sandhurst so far was the best part of my life—learning to be a soldier in a wonderful and mysterious institution with traditions going back to 1802. . . . It was a good, solid military school where one pulled one's self up as a man. I met many boys of my age for whom there was nothing sweeter than bearing arms in the service of their country, boys to whom Her Majesty's Army was a symbol of their very existence. . . .

Now I look back on Sandhurst with nostalgia. It is one of the greatest institutions in the world. Through its doors have passed famous generals, kings and rulers. . . .

I left Sandhurst, crossed the Wish Stream, looked back at my old school, and was filled with boundless gratitude.*

. . . To summarize our theoretical position, we are arguing that the training process undergone by the officer corps of many of the new states

*A. A. Afrifa, *The Ghana Coup* (London 1966), 51.

is such as to produce reference-group identifications with the officer corps of the ex-colonial power and concomitant commitments to its set of traditions, symbols, and values. Such identifications and commitments are seen to affect the behavior of these officers, both in their relations with civilian political authorities and in their capacity as governmental leaders should they accede to political power, in ways that are neither explicable nor predictable in terms of the formal organizational model.

In the remainder of this paper we shall offer some empirical validation for these theoretical observations through an analysis of one case of military rule, that of the National Liberation Council (NLC) of Ghana. Ghana is a former British colony that obtained its independence in 1957. As with most other ex-colonial countries Ghana moved to "Africanize" or "localize" its army's officer corps, replacing the British officers who were in command positions at the time of independence with Ghanaian nationals. By the time of the coup d'état in 1966 the officer corps was entirely Ghanaian. However, Ghana had followed the usual pattern of ex-colonial states in relying upon the former metropole for the training of the elite of her officer corps. The most promising cadets at the Ghanaian Military Academy are after six months transferred to the Royal Military Academy at Sandhurst, England, where they take the regular course. In addition, the best Ghanaian officers are periodically sent to England to attend British Army Staff College, Imperial Defense College, and Mons Officer Cadet School.

Military rule came to Ghana after an army-police coup against the regime of Kwame Nkrumah on February 24, 1966, and was exercised through a "junta" called the National Liberation Council (NLC). The NLC remained in power for three and a half years, after which they voluntarily returned governmental authority to civilians. . . .

In the discussion that follows, we shall make our assessment of the nationalist orientation of Ghana's military officers by reference to both their policy preferences and the affective mode within which they express these preferences. . . .

The analysis presented in the balance of this paper will rely heavily on two such recently published memoirs, those of Brigadier Afrifa and Major-General Ocran of the Ghana army, both of whom were leading participants in the coup that overthrew Kwame Nkrumah. Their books, *The Ghana Coup* and *A Myth is Broken** are attempts to explain the reasons behind the authors' participation in the military intervention. Brigadier Afrifa is thirty-three years old, a member of the large Ashanti tribe of central Ghana, and a graduate of the Royal Military Academy at Sandhurst. Prior to his entry into Sandhurst in 1958 he attended one of Ghana's leading secondary schools, after which he enlisted in the army, receiving officer training in Ghana and at Mons Officer Cadet School at Aldershot, England. In the military regime that followed the Ghana coup,

*A. K. Ocran, *A Myth is Broken; An Account of the Ghana Coup d'Etat* (London 1968).

Brigadier Afrifa was at first a member and later the Chairman of the ruling National Liberation Council. Following the return to civilian rule in the fall of 1969, he was Chairman of the transitional Presidential Commission.

Major-General Ocran is forty years old, and a member of the coastal Fanti tribe. He enlisted in the army in 1947 after completing his pre-secondary education. By 1954 he had risen through the ranks to be commissioned as a lieutenant. He has received officer training in the United Kingdom at Eaton Hall and Camberley. General Ocran participated in the coup of February, 1966, in his capacity as a commander of the strategically located southern brigade of the Ghana army, and was then made a member of the ruling army-police National Liberation Council. In May, 1967, he was, in addition, appointed Commander of the Ghana army, and then in November of 1968, made acting Chief of Defense Staff, head of the entire Ghanaian military establishment. In the period immediately following the return to civilian rule he was one of the members of Ghana's Presidential Commission. In social background, neither Brigadier Afrifa nor Major-General Ocran comes from a socially prominent family.

One aspect of the memoirs of both Generals Afrifa and Ocran is striking —the strength of their personal identification with Britain is such that it competes with their own nation as a reference group. This anomalous situation, in which a military officer holds a reference group identification that competes with that of his own nation, is succinctly expressed by Ocran in a single sentence. In a discussion of the history of the Ghanaian military he writes: "Its members fought and died as loyal soldiers who answered the call to defend the *Commonwealth, their country*, and *Africa's freedom*." Note, of course, that Ghana and Africa are placed after the Commonwealth in order of commitments. This allegiance to the British Commonwealth is something that recurs many times in the writings of both African officers. Take, for example, this passage from Afrifa's book: "One of the reasons for my bitterness against Kwame Nkrumah's rule was that he paid only lip-service to our membership of the Commonwealth of Nations and proceeded to undermine the bonds that bind us in this great union of people . . . ; so far as this Commonwealth is concerned, Ghana should not be different from Canada, Australia or New Zealand. For we have to learn to solve our problems like a family. Nkrumah made a mockery of this organization, and under the mask of African Unity and non-alignment proceeded to discredit the Commonwealth and to put difficulties in its way."

Along with an intense political allegiance to the Commonwealth, romantic descriptions of British traditions are found in the works of both Ghanaian officers. Afrifa, for example, at one point states: "This army has inherited wonderful traditions from the British, traditions of integrity, fair play and above all honour." . . .

In contrast the Ghanaian nationalist movement is depicted in extremely derogatory terms—its aims were "grandiose," its leader was a demagogue, and its rank and file were ignorant illiterates, whipped up to violence against both the British and those intelligent Ghanaians who wished to cooperate with them in working "step by step" toward independence.* Such a perception of the terminal colonial era is unexpected only to the extent that we are working within the framework of the formal organizational model, a major proposition of which is that an inherent characteristic of the ideology of military officers is intense nationalism and xenophobic patriotism. If, however, our analytic model is reference-group theory and we take account of training procedures for officers in the armies of the new states, then the discovery of this type of attitude is what we would predict.

FOREIGN REFERENCE GROUPS AND CIVIL-MILITARY RELATIONS

When the officer corps of a nation's military organization, its symbol of independence and sovereignty, identi-

*Objection may be raised here that Ocran and Afrifa are merely expressing their identification with one strand of Ghanaian nationalism—that represented by the "intelligentsia" who opposed Nkrumah and the CPP. It is true that such identification is expressed in these passages, but it would seem that what we find in these passages is more than comparison between two Ghanaian political traditions. Rather, the thrust of the argument is a comparison between the proper behavior of the colonial power and the illegitimate activity of the dominant anti-colonial forces in Ghana. To the extent that the political opposition to Nkrumah perceived and expressed its opposition in a pro-British mode, then the extent and intensity of its nationalism can also be called into question.

fies itself strongly with a political unit other than the one it officially serves, serious consequences for the stability of the state are likely to ensue. In the formerly colonial state, the officer corps not only is likely to share the disdain for politicians that is a component of the military ideology of the Army of the "mother" country, but also is likely to share its contempt for leaders of the anti-colonial movement, men who subsequently become the leaders of the governments under which these officers serve. Beyond this, there is an inherent source of tension in civil-military relations if the leaders of the new state are oriented toward nationalistic policies, since these policies are likely to conflict with the officers' psychological commitments to foreign reference groups. In the Ghanaian case this phenomenon played a crucial part in the breach between Nkrumah and his officer corps. In at least three instances Nkrumah undertook major policies that ran counter to the "extra-Ghanaian" political loyalties of his officers—in the Rhodesia and Congo situations and in the matter of acceptance of military aid from Communist countries. . . .

In addition to nationalism, the proponents of the formal organizational model view puritanism as a major theme of military ideology. This orientation, it is often argued in turn, will produce policies of austerity when armies intervene in the political process. Thus Samuel Huntington writes, "Like the Protestant entrepreneurs of western Europe, the soldier reformers in non-Western societies embody and promote a puritanism which . . . is a distinctive innovation in their societies." These propositions, as in the case of the alleged nationalism of military officers in new states, fail to take into consideration the reference-group identifications of military officers. The question of what is puritanical and ascetic is meaningful only in relation to a given standard. What is seen as puritanical living in one society may be defined as luxurious in another. This is the paradox surrounding military officers in new states. Although they hold a general ideological predisposition toward an austere style of living, the standards supplied by their European reference groups often lead them in practice to oppose austerity, especially when it affects the military. In short, they apply standards appropriate in the social and economic setting of an industrialized country to the situation in their own societies. If the political elite in their own country attempts to bring military organization more into line with conditions existing in a pre-industrial society they are likely to be opposed by the officer corps. . . .

FOREIGN REFERENCE GROUPS AND MILITARY RULE

If the "extra-national" reference-group identifications of army officers in new states can have significant consequences for the stability of post-independence civilian regimes, they have equally significant consequences when these officers seize political power. It is our contention that many of the policies and much of the quality and character of military rule in countries like Ghana are produced by, and therefore should be understood in terms of, the extra-national reference-group identifications of the officers in power. The three and a half years of military rule Ghana has just undergone provide many instances that can be used to illustrate this argument. . . .

Indeed, the absence of economic nationalism displayed by the policies of the ruling National Liberation Council became a major source of tension between the military and Ghana's civilian intelligentsia. The general policy of the NLC in regard to the economic quagmire it had inherited from the Nkrumah regime was to rely extensively of the managerial and financial capacities of European and North American governments and businesses. Symbolic of the extent of this reliance is the fact that even the job of cleaning the streets of the capital city was turned over to a foreign firm. The *Ghanaian Times*, under the banner headline "UK Firm to Clean Accra," noted that "a British company, Shelvoke and Drewry of Letchworth, South East England, has undertaken to clean up the present refuse problem facing Accra" and that "reliable sources said in Accra that the firm was confident to clear all the garbage in a matter of weeks."

The particular aspect of the general reliance on foreign economic and managerial assistance that was most resented within Ghana was the NLC's handling of the State Enterprises situation. The leaders of the coup had inherited from the Nkrumah regime fifty-four state-owned enterprises, most of which were running at a loss. There were three ways in which the NLC attempted to deal with this inheritance: by engaging private business organizations to purchase the state enterprise; by entering into joint state-private ownership agreements; or by leasing the enterprise to a private business concern for a period of years. Naturally, in the case of the more substantial state enterprises, the business firms in question were foreign since only they had the requisite capital. It should also be noted that this policy meant first, the "de-nationalization" of only the more profitable or potentially profitable enterprises, since these were the ones to which private entrepreneurs could be attracted; and second, the granting of important concessions to private firms so as to make up for the lack of financial attractiveness in the enterprises themselves. . . .

The absence of a nationalistic orientation in the economic sphere can also be observed in the NLC's handling of Ghana's foreign debt. At the time of the coup, Ghana had one of the worst foreign-debt servicing structures of any country in the world, with payment of over 51 percent of its external debt coming due within five years. The reason for this situation was the reliance of the Nkrumah regime on what are termed supplier credits to finance economic development. As his alternative sources of investment capital dried up, Nkrumah turned increasingly to the supplier-credit method of obtaining capital. . . . Under this system, private companies lend capital directly to the recipient government in order to finance a project that the company itself will carry out. Often

the loan is guaranteed by the government of the donor company. Such an arrangement lends itself naturally to "hard-sell" efforts by private businesses or capital-exporting countries attempting to increase their own profits or export earnings regardless of the economic implications for the borrower. . . . Thus Ghana found itself saddled with a huge debt, a good proportion of which was made up of supplier-credit high-interest/short-term loans for numerous economic ventures of dubious viability.

When Ghana's National Liberation Council assumed power it was faced with essentially two choices in regard to the country's foreign indebtedness. It could default on a good number of the debts, especially those involving supplier credits, or it could ask the lending businesses and their national governments to negotiate a rescheduling of the debt, to allow Ghana time to improve its foreign-reserve position before having to assume the major burden of the debt. The case for defaulting was a strong one and was favored by many Ghanaian civilians as well as by some foreign economists advising the NLC at the time. It was argued that many of the supplier-credit loans had been arranged under corrupt and deceitful conditions involving the bribing of Ghana government officials by foreign businesses and the submission of misleading feasibility studies. In addition, the political situation at the time of the coup appeared to preclude significant adverse reaction on the part of the Western governments who had guaranteed these loans, because they, and particularly the Americans, were hardly likely to turn on the avowedly pro-Western officers who had just over-thrown Kwame Nkrumah. The new military rulers, however, did not opt for this nationalistic alternative but instead decided to attempt to reschedule the debts. The reasoning behind this decision is not clear, although some informed sources in Ghana say that the major reason was the notion that "a gentleman pays his debts." . . .

Thus, in the case of two extremely important economic policies, the dispensation of state corporations and the handling of the external debt, the military government of Ghana behaved toward foreign businesses and governments in a manner uncharacteristic of intense nationalists. The openness and trust displayed toward foreign interests by the military regime appears anomalous within the framework of the formal organizational model, but is perfectly congruent with an approach informed by reference-group theory. The lack of a nationalist orientation on the part of the NLC is strikingly illuminated, not so much by contrasting it with its Nkrumaist predecessor, but by contrasting its orientation with that of the conservative Ghanaian "intelligentsia" who made up the main political opposition to Nkrumah. It was this latter group, which at first enthusiastically supported the NLC, that came in time to criticize it on nationalist grounds. . . .

FOREIGN REFERENCE GROUPS AND "THE RETURN TO THE BARRACKS"

There is one last aspect of military rule in Ghana that should be part of this discussion: the relinquishing of power to civilians by the National Liberation Council in the fall of 1969. To many people it appears surprising that a military group would, in the absence of a serious threat to its position, voluntarily turn over the reins of power to a civilian regime that had been chosen independent of military desires. For it is rightly assumed that the perquisites of political office, involving access to the very zenith of status and wealth, are not easily, or often voluntarily, relinquished by those who seized power by force in the first place. However, from the vantage point of reference-group theory, the behavior of the National Liberation Council is perfectly understandable and predictable. For it is a fundamental and centrally held tenet of British military ideology that the military and political spheres should be separate. . . .

The long preparation for civilian rule, then, and the eventual relinquishing of power to a civilian government should be seen as the bringing of behavior and belief into consonance. Reference-group identification with the British officer corps acted as a counterforce to the perquisites of political office, pushing or pulling the Ghanaian military officers to give up the power they had earlier seized. . . .

Robin Luckham concluded on the basis of his research on the Nigerian military that the British-trained Nigerian officers, due to their poor educational qualifications and low prestige among their elite reference groups, were led to emphasize the British notion that officers are gentlemen. Luck-ham contends that this notion serves a very different function in the British and Nigerian armies: in England it indicates that the officer has a par-ticular place in the class structure, whereas in Nigeria it is a device of collective military honor, affirming the professional identity of the indi-vidual officer and the corporate identity of the officer corps.

ROBIN LUCKHAM

Officers and Gentlemen: The Image of an Elite

[Nigeria was one of the few nations in Africa to maintain a multiparty sys-tem after independence. The country seemed too diverse, ethnically and religiously, for Nigerians to unite in a single party. But the Muslim North succeeded in controlling the central government in Lagos until January 1966, when Southern Ibo-dominated officers overthrew the civilian govern-ment. Six months later, however, the Northern officers regained control of the central government in the name of northern traditional leadership.]

. . . We are unable to describe in any detail the patterns of social recruit-ment of the military or the process of socialisation—the *manner* in which Nigerian officer cadets and officers were imbued with the rituals and skills of military life in foreign military schools and academies. We can, however, give some account of the *effects* of recruitment and socialisation on the cultural and professional image

From Robin Luckham, The Nigerian Military: A Sociological Analysis of Authority and Revolt, 1960–67 (Cambridge: Cambridge Uni-versity Press, 1971), pp. 109–30, by permission of the author.

of the officer corps, particularly those related to the notion that 'officers are gentlemen'. It will be shown that the poor educational qualifications of army officers and their consequent low prestige among their elite ref-erence groups tended to reinforce the gentlemen ethic and not to dilute it, as one might have expected. Low prestige led them to search for their own differentiated sphere of military honour with which to protect and validate their position in society. The definition of the situation which developed so very rapidly around the new role of the army officer after Independence was therefore such as to encrust in a new setting (with certain saving graces) a style of life that was already itself encrusted with the relics of the British rural past.

THE 'GENTLEMAN' OFFICER

The style of life of a Nigerian staff officer at HQ in Lagos is described by Lt Colonel (then Major) Akahan, the late Chief of Staff, in the following way, with tongue only half in cheek:

All Officers and Officer Cadets are traditionally referred to as gentlemen, but one cannot mistake the 'gentleman' Staff Officer when one meets him he is the most 'gentleman' of them all.

He is often seen arriving at the office at 07.55 hours; early enough to have five minutes to spare. He invariably arrives by boat or as a non-paying passenger in some other officer's car, depending on which part of Lagos he resides. He leaves the office at 15.00 hours prompt which, of course, is the closing time. As all soldiers are paid to work twenty-four hours a day, he is certainly going to do some work at home.

On weekdays all Officers are dressed alike; a near-white looking green uniform (unless he has a Quartermaster friend) a pair of brown shoes which should have been resoled last year, and a face cap . . . Saturday is the only day you can tell which branch of the Army HQ he belongs to. If he is in a Moss Brothers smart-looking suit, he certainly is from 'A' Branch—where the dress regulations are written; he must set the pace.

Gentlemen in the 'G' Branch are very nationalistic and so the gentleman Staff Officer from this section would probably turn up for work in an 'Agbada'. 'What is all this fuss about dressing up on Saturdays for work?' This remark is more likely to be heard from the gentleman in 'Q' Branch, and true enough he would turn up in a terylene shirt and a pair of skin-tight slacks. What could be more appropriate garb for counting rusty tins and 'compo hats' than that?

Invariably the contents of a Staff officer's briefcase are likely to be those files he took home but never had time to look at, a half filled flask of strong nescafe, a cheque-book he can only use on the first of every month, mess bills he should have paid last month, a 'Private and Confiden-

tial' letter from his Bank Manager about that overdraft, an equally 'Confidential' letter from the UDC Manager . . .

In the office he is a busy man. He reads newspapers during the first hour in order to keep abreast with world affairs, thereafter comes coffee time. The GOC's Conference followed by the COS's Conference come immediately after the coffee break in quick succession. He is back at his desk after these conferences only to make a short telephone call to that girl he met last night, a quick rude letter to the Brigadier copy to all units, A.C. paper—no that's for homework. Another Conference and oh! it's closing time already. How time flies.

The 'gentleman' Staff Officer loves games, but the facilities are only available Wednesdays. He looks forward to Officer Games days and starts off from his house every Wednesday all dressed up for a good game of volley-ball, but never quite arrives at the pitch . . .

He believes in maximum enjoyment, accepts invitations to all parties as long as there is to be free booze. He prefers 'Star Beer' to all those cocktails—it is more satisfying! He ensures that there is one Alka Seltzer with which to tranquilise the evening's debauchery. When there is no private party forthcoming he can always be sure of an equally exciting time at that 'Magic Nite Spot' the KKD.

We quote this at length because it illustrates in a pithy way three divergent themes in the elite image of the army officer. First, that he is a member of a social elite based on newly acquired skills, the values of which—like its patterns of conspicuous consumption based on the images of the Western world—he shares. Secondly, that these are fused into more indigenous and behavioural and cultural traits—like the wearing of an agbada—which are reinforced by an officer's access to social influence from below in an open elite structure. Thirdly, however, that officers have refined and developed differentiated conceptions of military behaviour and collective honour, enshrined in the slogan that officers are gentlemen.

SOCIAL BACKGROUND AND THE OPEN CLASS STRUCTURE

Nigeria's elite is an aristocracy of skills, for the most part acquired through the process of formal education. It is a recently created elite and therefore has been relatively 'open' in its pattern of recruitment from lower strata. Unfortunately, there are no systematic and comprehensive data either on the recruitment and social background of the elite in general, or the army in particular, on the basis of which one might generalise about patterns of occupational mobility, or compare the army with other elite groups. On the strength of an impressionistic acquaintance with the social backgrounds of officers, it is, however, possible to conjecture that the great majority of them have had relatively lowly origins. Farmer, clerk, - catechist, trader, primary school teacher, lower paid employee of the government or one of the large public corporations (like the Nigerian Railway Corporation) or noncommissioned officers in the army, are all fairly typical of the occupations of their fathers.

There are, however, one or two instances of distinguished families with soldier sons. For example, one large family of high traditional position in the North, which has produced a distinguished civil servant (formerly Permanent Secretary to the Ministry of Defence) and also three army officer sons (two through the cadet entry and one promoted from the ranks during the civil war). Or an Arabic scholar in one of the Northern Emirates who has produced two high-ranking civil servants (one at ambassadorial level) and a younger son in the army. . . . Or finally, Lt Colonel Ojukwu, son of a millionaire businessman, the late Sir Louis Ojukwu, who was connected closely by ties of friendship and political patronage with Dr Azikiwe, the former President, and his party, the NCNC. Such cases, however, are by no means typical. Good family connections have probably been an advantage, but not necessarily essential to a successful career, as is clear from the presence at the top of the hierarchy of many officers without such advantages. . . .

Indeed, it could be said that 'good' connections have been of less importance for career development in the Nigerian Army than in the British military elite. One essential ingredient of patronage and clientage in the British Army that is only weakly developed in Nigeria is the element of kinship between aspiring officers and top members of the military elite. If an officer has relatives of the older generation in the army—grandfathers, fathers and uncles—they are unlikely to be of much use to him in matters of military preferment, because they would all be NCOs rather than members of the officer corps (even though such men may have provided models for his original decision to enter the army). The only kinship links through which desire for preferment may be articulated are those between relatives within the same generation; and it is doubtful whether these are yet widely spread through the army.

One result of the openness of recruitment is the high accessibility of army officers (like other elites) to persons of non-elite background. On evenings and at the weekends, there is a constant stream of 'brothers', kinsmen, acquaintances from the same village or town-ward or the same ethnic group who come to pay their respects at an officer's house and to drink his beer and Fanta orange. They may be there for advice on recruitment into the army, to raise a contribution for a funeral or some other common function, to bring messages from family and friends, to pay homage, to listen to the radiogram or watch television, or merely to seek company. They may include private soldiers and NCOs in their off duty hours, as well as civilians: for it is impracticable to impose status barriers —as in the British Army—which cut across the accepted norms of sociability. Ease of access does not, however, free the more humble visitors of the obligation to make the suitable gestures of deference toward their host. Similarly, an officer, because of his high social position, will feel strongly obliged to demonstrate the appropriate hospitality, to keep an ever-open fridge, or to send his servant scurrying over to the mess for drinks, and in appropriate instances to expect his wife or manservant to produce a large supply of food for visitors.

Again, if he goes out, he may well stop on his way to visit a clerk who was a school-mate of his early days, or to pay respects to an important representative of his community in the urban area in which he resides. If he goes for entertainment in a public place, like a bingo hall or a night spot, there will be a stream of acquaintances pausing by his table to pay respects or to join him for a drink. As most of those at the table will insist on buying drinks for the whole party, the table will be covered from end to end with bottles of beer by the end of the evening, even if not all of them are consumed.

A degree of accessibility has its functions, both facilitating the maintenance of discipline on a consensual basis and making the military elite more responsive to changes in its social and political environment. On the other hand, the social linkages between NCOs and junior officers were used to exert pressure on the latter to revolt against authority in July 1966.

A high degree of access has also tended to make the officers corps more vulnerable to corruption and political pressure, though such pressures were not very strong in the period of civilian rule, and were on the whole successfully contained by professional and organisational controls. It is notable that, in the whole period up to 1966, there was no major scandal in the officers corps, merely two small affairs of lieutenants being cashiered for theft, and a senior officer being courtmartialled and reprimanded for appropriating government furniture from his house. On the other hand, the record of the military since it acquired power has not been as good. . . . A high-ranking officer anywhere in Nigeria is now constantly visited by persons seeking small favours and his goodwill sought with unsolicited gifts. Up to the civil war, one had the impression that outright attempts to bribe an officer on a *quid pro quo* basis were comparatively rare, because few army figures were then receptive to open invitations to corruption. Some, indeed, were still very sensitive as to the implications of accepting unsolicited gifts, and officers would reject crates of beer or bottles proffered at a night club because of suspicion as to the motive of those offering them. Others, however, were not averse to taking part in various business deals which are not strictly speaking proscribed by regulations, in the conclusion of which a military status is an advantage. The scope for such deals as well as for outright corruption was undoubtedly widened by the civil war and there were, it seems, instances of officers taking bribes, misappropriating stores and failing to declare casualties in order to collect the pay of the dead soldiers. Major General Gowon himself felt it necessary to call upon members of the armed forces to point out 'the bad eggs among you' in response to such accusations for 'honestly speaking, there is some justification in what these people say . . . some of us truly go below the level expected of good officers'.

The pattern of accessibility, it should be explained, is one that is normal among *all* persons in elite positions (it is probably less well developed in the officer corps than among other elites). It is predicated by the norms of hospitality and reciprocity in social relations that are common to the majority of West African societies. Even in the Hausa-Fulani Emirates the prominent members of the aristocracy keep up relatively little cultural differentiation from their inferiors and are normally very accessible to the latter at the appropriate times and places, in spite of the high degree of political and economic differentiation, a steep hierarchy of status and power and strongly marked patterns of deference between social superior and inferior. It would be a matter of surprise, indeed, if such traditions of access and sociability to kin and community were not preserved—outside, of course, the normal military lines of command and control and other such relationships which specifically exclude particularistic ties of friendship, clientage and kinship.

STYLE OF LIFE AND PATTERNS OF CULTURE

The officer's style of life contains a strong emphasis on material consumption and its symbols. A modern education and occupational role is sought after, mainly because it gives access to a high standard of living. In the occupational structure inherited from colonial rule, the 'plums' in terms of income and material perquisites go to the holders of 'senior service' posts formerly held by Europeans, like the lawyers, senior civil servants, business executives and army officers. Income differentials in favour of such posts are much greater than in the industrial nations and occupational aspirations influenced correspondingly. The flavour of these expectations is nicely conveyed by some lines from a beach prophet's prayer by a well-known Nigerian playwright:

Make you not forget those of us who dey struggle daily. Those who be clerk today, make them Chief Clerk tomorrow. Those who are Messenger today make them Senior Service tomorrow.

Those who are petty trader today, make them big contractor tomorrow. Those who dey sweep street today, give them their own bicycle tomorrow. Those who have bicycle today, they will ride their own car tomorrow.

I say those who dey push bicycle, give them big car tomorrow. Give them big car tomorrow. Give them big car tomorrow, give them big car tomorrow.

Education and occupational choice are manipulated in a highly utilitarian fashion by the individual to maximise the material and prestige benefits accruing to him. (And indirectly, therefore, to the kinsmen or community which financed his education.) When the military authorities sought to increase the numbers of Nigerians entering the officer corps rapidly in the late 1950s, they were forced to take these realities into account by raising officer salaries and introducing car allowances and car purchase loans comparable to those obtainable by civil servants.

Officers, unless they are exceedingly prudent, will normally buy the largest and most prestigious car their means and the financial limit on car purchase loans will allow. Most of them possess a large radiogram of German or Japanese manufacture, together with a stack of records for the entertainment of visitors, and usually one or two other conspicuous items of furniture, such as a television or an ornate table lamp or cocktail trolley. . . .* Their hospitality is generous, both at home and in the mess, where drinks are dispensed on a lavish scale. . . .

Standards of dress are meticulous. In leisure hours, an officer may wear European dress—with the appropriately conservative tie for more formal occasions, an open-necked shirt informally—or the indigenous agbada or similar costume, being equally at home with the cultural symbols of both styles of dress. At work and on mess occasions there will be an immaculate uniform, bright with brass buttons and shiny shoes, a swagger stick, and hat with the appropriate racy curvature. Public manners are tailored to the smartness of the uniform, a jump to the feet when ladies enter the mess, a snap of the heels as the Commanding Officer comes in, a brisk salute and 'sah!' when given an order. Officers who have received their training outside of the academies and cadet schools of Britain, India and Pakistan are sometimes a little less brisk in their habits than the others. American- and Canadian-trained officers, for instance, are less inclined towards spit and polish, even though they

*Most of the items of 'heavy' furniture, fridge, beds, chairs, tables, etc., being provided in their army housing for them, as is the practice in nearly all 'senior service' housing.

may be just as good soldiers in a professional sense. One American-trained officer of the writer's acquaintance developed an amusing sense of role-distance from the martinet image, wore a somewhat down-at-heel uniform, played drunk at parties when really sober, and used to mimic the military salute with a lank gesture like wiping the sweat off his forehead.

These specifically military traits apart, the characteristics of the officers' cultural image that have been described are shared in common with the majority of the other professional, Western-educated elites in Nigeria. The emphasis upon acquired cultural standards is perhaps stronger, however, among the officers than among other elite groups. In at least two garrison towns the writer has visited, the officers of the local military unit made considerably more use of the former European 'club' than any other comparable group, and in one of them at least the officers mess by custom purchased group membership of the club on behalf of the members. The maintenance of standards is viewed as a collective enterprise. Lapses in dress or misdemeanours in social behaviour are rebuked by Commanding Officers or made the subject of ridicule in the mess. The mess itself is full of tokens of continuity with the colonial past—silverware presented by 'twin' British regiments, photographs of regimental functions on the wall, relics such as captured flags or weapons from past campaigns in Burma, the Cameroons and the Congo, and hunting trophies protruding from the wall. Mess dinner nights are held to which other members of the elite—local and expatriate—may be formally invited. There are also early afternoon drinks on Saturdays in the mess of a number of the units, which every officer is expected to attend, to which they can bring friends of suitable elite status. (In contrast to the informal context of his house, an officer would *not* normally bring a humble friend or relative into the mess for drinks.) On such occasions, officers may arrange to partake in suitable games and field sports with their friends, like tennis or a shooting party, or to go out riding. The mess normally maintains a number of sporting facilities itself—tennis and squash courts, a swimming pool and sometimes riding stables. One of the Nigerian officer's role-images quite patently is the country gentleman posture of British officers, and hence the continuing emphasis on field sports and the like.

On the other hand, only the isolated officer (whom one does however occasionally meet) will go the whole hog, with cavalry twills, tweed jacket, moustache, tweed cap, shooting stick, field sports, polo and all. For most, such traits are mixed with and diluted by other images. Those who knew the colonial days say that protocol and style of life are less rigidly enforced now than they were then. Some of the older NCOs complain that the rituals and group life of the mess have fallen into disrepair and that officers are not what they used to be. It is not clear how far this represents a sentimentalisation of the past, or how far the fact that practices have changed: for instance, it is now usual for officers to have meals sent over from the mess to their houses rather than eating there, as it was in the past. Nor are commanding officers as rigid on matters of social behaviour as were some of the British. One commander, for instance, pointed out that one of his British predecessors used to keep the hedges and bushes clipped so that he could watch the entries and exits of his subordinates from his veranda (or so the Nigerians thought), and stated that he would not dream of imposing that much control over his officers' private lives. That daunting figure of British and American barracks, the commanding officer's wife, no longer controls standards of etiquette and entertainment: the wives of Nigerian officers for the most part lack a high level of education, spend most of their time on purely domestic matters and do not play a vital role in the social life of the unit.

In sum, the officers' style of life is strongly influenced by an ethos of conspicuous consumption, blending imported with indigenous images. This ethos might seem to be at odds with the image of austerity and self-discipline found in Western professional armies. The latter was for instance exemplified by the unwillingness of British military authorities to acquiesce in attempts to recruit Nigerian officer cadets by providing car allowances and increased salaries for them until the Nigerian forces were removed from control of the British War Office in 1958. Yet there is no evidence of any *necessary* inconsistency between a high consumption ethos and military values. Nigerian officers continue, as we will argue in the pages that follow, to subscribe to

notions of collective military honour; and indeed, as we have already begun to suggest above, certain of their conspicuous consumption traits serve to call attention to their distinctive identity as 'officers and gentlemen'.

SELF-IMAGE AND EXTERNAL REFERENCE GROUPS

A feature that is much apparent from his style of life is that the Nigerian army officer is a provincial in terms of his reference groups and his intellectual and cultural conventions. He borrows from the creative centres of Western culture, but has not himself a creative grasp of its traditions. It would be surprising, indeed, if he were not provincial, for colonial society was always peripheral to the intellectual currents of the metropolitan country and the new inheriting elites are not any closer. Nor, with the exception of one or two small circles of artists and writers and perhaps of social scientists in the universities, are they drawn towards vital intellectual and cultural centres of their own. Still less the military than other elites, for the educational standards imposed for entry into the officer corps and the intellectual stimulus provided during the process of military training are undoubtedly lower than those of all other Nigerian professional groups (except the police). The British officers of the Nigerian cadet's role model are themselves also very parochial in outlook. An impressionistic comparison of material in *Owl Pie* and *The Wish Stream*, the journals of the Staff College, Camberley and the Royal Military Academy, Sandhurst, with that in the *Nigerian Army Magazine* suggests that the former are no broader in their interests than the latter, nor any more sophisticated in their approach to social, political and military problems. The former devote more space to the trivia of social life—the sports, amateur dramatics, and foxhounds—and the latter more to matters of political and military concern. Many of the articles in the *Nigerian Army Magazine* are digests of military history taken out of the standard books on the subject, or generalisations about morale, personnel training and the like, picked up at the latest staff course abroad. . . .

People whose intellectual and social prestige horizons are at the periphery of a culture are in danger of acquiring a low or negative self-image. The American officer corps has had less prestige than other professions in the past, this being at least in part due to its lack of vital intellectual centres which might create and sustain its values. The result has been anti-intellectualism and an emphasis on collective honour, a retreat from the cultural standards by which it is evaluated so lowly. These reactions occur, too, in the British military, though they are somewhat muted by the fact that the British officer is more able to shore up his prestige by emphasising his social niche in the ranks of the minor gentry.

The Nigerian officer has no such refuge, and is furthermore at the periphery of an alien culture not his own: a culture which has very strong undertones of racialism and has frequently put forward stereotypes of Af-

ricans as primitives or worse. Many officers will have had to struggle with the conception that Europeans have a low opinion of Africans throughout the whole period of formal education in English; and many still continue to believe that this is so. Although some officers emphasise the multi-racial character of their training at Sandhurst, Mons and elsewhere, that they were treated as officers and gentlemen and not as members of particular nationalities and racial groups, others are more cagey about their experiences in England. At least one British ex-officer of the writer's acquaintance emphasises that although there was no *overt* discrimination against African officers as such, British cadets did not 'mix with the black chaps very much'. Relatively fewer African cadets were given responsible positions as platoon leaders in exercises or made under-officers; and the attitude towards them was often one of condescension.

The first few months at British training institutions and some of the hazing rituals (like the notorious kit parades at Sandhurst) they went through were sometimes traumatic. One officer of the writer's acquaintance, for example, said that in his first term at Sandhurst he was 'too busy to look for friends', practical jokes were played on him and 'I didn't understand their sense of humour and they didn't understand mine. I was accused of having an "inferiority complex" but it wasn't that at all'. He was always one of the last in the kit parade because he was not used to high collars and his fingers were always cold, and he refused to go to an English family for his first Christmas holidays because he was afraid of the social humiliations he might risk. He said, however, that he got on much better in his later terms and now looked back to his time at Sandhurst 'with pride'. Conformity to the military image was acquired by many officers at a high price: indeed, one suspects that the worse the humiliations endured the greater the attachment to the life of the officer and gentleman that was ultimately flaunted.

Beliefs about the perceptions and evaluations of oneself by others are intimately linked, both to self-conceptions and to reactions towards those others, in this case the white man. European friends may be made, or wives and girl friends acquired, but there is often an undercurrent of anxiety about their motivations, whether they approve of the Nigerian officer's behaviour, whether they are not ridiculing him behind his back, whether deep down they do not think him inferior. It is difficult to say other than in a highly impressionistic way how widespread such anxieties are or how deeply felt. The writer has friends who have shown no sign of them: and others who, while displaying stress and anxiety about their racial identities, seemed to have stable personalities in all other respects. It is possible that there are other aspects of Western education and professional socialisation which serve to integrate identities and nullify such anxieties. Yet disquiet about both national prestige and racial image seems overall to be a powerful theme in the officer's professional identity.

There are two kinds of reaction one

might expect under these circumstances, both of which many Nigerian Army officers seem to succeed in sustaining without noticing the apparent contradiction. The first is to knuckle under to the white man, to conform to the Sandhurst way of life, the polo, shooting and tweeds complex or the ritualisation of spit and polish in the mess. On the other hand, there may be reaction-formation, one form of which may be a recourse to national, Pan-African or racial images. This appears, for instance, in the earlier quoted cry of the January 1966 conspirators, that having done away with the corrupt old regime that brought Nigeria into disrepute abroad, 'you no longer need be ashamed of being Nigerians'. Or in the rage that the subject of white mercenaries in the Nigerian civil war can evoke not only, it should be said, among the soldiers; and the sensitivity to any hint of non-African interference in the war, whether from the American or European governments, or from charity organisations, portrayed very explicitly in Colonel Adekunle's statement that 'this war has shown the African not to trust anyone who is white'.

The themes of conformism and revolt are often combined, the conflict between them not resolved. The difficulties of reconciling the two are apparent in a retrospective article by Major Ifeajuna on 'The Nigerian Army after a hundred years' appearing in the issue of the *Nigerian Army Magazine* just before the January 1966 coup in which he took part. This suggests on the one hand that

if it is claimed that the British bestowed worthy traditions on the Nigerian army, the Congo was the place where it became very obvious . . . The army exists in the shape which our former imperial masters left it.

On the other hand,

with the passage of time it will change (or is changing) to conform to the social pattern of our people

for, during the colonial period

first all officers were white. This was not the main problem (sic). But then too there was the British NCO—that colonial institution of terrorism in the Lines. Claimed to be a vital link in the chain of command the British NCO was a veritable beast; treated like an officer, but behaving like a maniac. And yet, they had all the support, even when drawn against the earlier Nigerian Officers.

Such frustrations may help to account for the power of nationalism as a cultural motif among officers. On the other hand, the themes of humiliation, identity and self-assertion are the common stuff of nationalism among *all* groups in ex-colonial territories; and we have as yet given no reasons to suppose that the military is any different in these respects from other elites. If one looks more closely at the political beliefs of the officer corps differences in emphasis begin, however, to appear. Though it is difficult to be precise, one can say with some confidence that nationalism, distaste for corruption and mistrust of politics was greater in the military than in most groups outside it; and that each of these three themes was linked to specific conceptions of military doctrine and honour. . . .

What has been the source of emphasis on military values? This can be sought in strains generated upon the officers' self-image by their lack (until 1966 at least) of social prestige relative to other elites and the search for collective honour this encouraged. . . .

This ambivalence concerning prestige is perhaps the key to the search in the officer corps for differentiated conceptions of military honour. One officer, after discussing the 'sarcastic and jeering remarks' suffered after joining the army, illustrates this feeling well by saying that if the new officer had remained a civilian 'there would be no inspection or parades, frequent punishment and unnecessary "bull" . . . Nobody would chase him around . . . There would be no rigid discipline and little opportunity to test his leadership qualities . . . *He would only be subject to civil law and the question of being a gentleman would be at his discretion.*' For one very effective way of offsetting the dissonance between their own self-image and that held of them by other elites is to emphasise the special virtues that they must exemplify to civilian society, such as self-discipline, comradeship, purity from 'corruption and decadence', and nationalism.

This is why the idea that 'officers are gentlemen' is pivotal. The Nigerian Military Forces Act gives legal force to this conception when it states that 'every officer subject to law under the Ordnance who behaves in a scandalous manner, unbecoming the character of an officer and a gentleman, shall, on conviction of a court-martial, be cashiered'. To impugn the honour of an officer is also an offence, false statements and 'statements affecting the character of an officer' being punishable by imprisonment if considered serious enough. Nor is this just an anomaly, a hangover from colonial days or a ritualised excrescence of British military education. Officers are extremely sensitive to questions of honour, and there is a very strong reaction to any suggestion that they may not have acted as gentlemen in any given set of circumstances, to a point where it is not unknown for an officer to have threatened action against a superior under the act if he felt dishonoured by the latter.

The style of life in the mess is geared to the promotion of this image, and points of proper conduct and protocol are hotly disputed within it. . . .

Yet the notion that officers are gentlemen has a quite different function in the Nigerian military from that which it has in the British Army, in spite of the similarity in behaviour and style of life. Being a gentleman in England is a status that is independent of being an officer. The role and the patterns of action that go with it belong to a particular status niche in the structure of rural English society, even though they have also been adopted by a number of middle-class groups including the military. To emphasise that an officer is a gentleman, then, is to indicate that he has a particular place in the class structure. It dilutes the collective and corporate identity of the officer corps, and has served to secure its loyalty to the ruling political elite. In contrast, in Nigeria the gentleman notion is a device of collective military honour, being in this respect not unlike the

practice of duelling in the German officer corps. It affirms the professional identity of the individual officer and the corporate identity of the officer corps as a differentiated status group with its own system of values. There is no clearly defined status of gentleman outside the army, and no other elites make it part of their self-image in quite the same way as the officers.

To be a gentleman is therefore an effective way for the officers to provide honour for themselves on their own terms, to sustain a system of values that protects them from the shame and self-doubt inherent in the education-based status system operating among the elites. It also blends in with one of the standard military motivations for the production of honour, namely desire to remove and alleviate self-doubt in the face of the risk of death. One of the major grievances of Northern officers and men against the Ironsi regime was that it failed to acknowledge the death of senior officers in the January 1966 coup and thus to give them the proper military burial. . . .

Strain on prestige and insecurity about the prospect of death are not the only reasons for seeking to uphold military values. Some officers chose a military career because these values were sought as ends in themselves, saying, for instance, that the army offered an occupation that was free of the pressures for corruption in some civilian occupations, or because they 'would not have to worry about losing promotion from tribalism' as in other governmental structures, or simply that chivalric honour was sought after for its own sake. Lt Colonel Ejoor, for instance, claimed he joined up because he 'wanted to die honourably'. When he was in his final year at school, he had read about the impressive funeral given one of the first Nigerian officers, a Lieutenant Wellington, and decided he too would like such treatment when he died. Kinsmen who had served in the army gave many officers their first taste of chivalry. It is likely that the majority of Nigerian officers—and especially the Northerners—had relatives in the army. Many of them—including Ejoor and Gowon—mention the example of relatives as being one reason for enlisting. Some families, indeed, could definitely be called military families, like one Northern family with two brothers in the officer corps and a further three in the ranks as NCOs, and another containing three officer brothers; both families also contained relatives of the older generation who were NCOs during the period of colonial rule. And just as the system of collective honour is underpinned by role-models from the older generation, some officers seek also to project it into the future by wanting their sons to join the army, in order, as Colonel Adebayo put it, 'to retain my name in the army'.

By way of contrast to this corporative identification with the profession, let us provide an extract from an interview by a Nigerian journalist, Sad Sam, with Lt Colonel Ojukwu who, it will be recalled, differed from almost all of his colleagues in that his position in the elite owed very little to his membership of the officer corps. He had a degree from Oxford University, his father was a millionaire with very influential political connections, and he joined the army for political reasons as much as anything else. We find him rejecting the whole idea of military professionalism and by implication the conception of collective military honour.

OJUKWU: I would not like my son to be a professional. Let's leave it at that. I have never been a professional.

SAD SAM: You? Aren't you a professional soldier?

OJUKWU: I maintain my amateur status in all my approach. When you talk about professions, you talk about the specialist professions like lawyer, doctor, engineer and so on. I studied up to a point and left to become a soldier.

SAD SAM: Why did you become a soldier?

OJUKWU: Sam, I do not expect that from you.

To conclude, the latent consequence of the officer corps' low prestige, the insecurity of army officers in relation to their reference groups both in the ex-colonial metropolis and among the Nigerian elite, was a hardening and reinforcement of the corporate image and identity of the officer corps rather than its opposite. Officers were all the more gentlemen for being newcomers to the club. On the other hand, the short length of military careers, the fact that officers had had little time to internalise fully the pattern of expectations governing their life style and role, meant that this corporate image and identity was likely to be unstable, as in fact turned out to be the case. Being partly held in position, so to speak, by the prevailing definition of the situation, it was liable to change when that situation itself altered, as when the political events of 1966 suddenly shifted the distribution of power and values towards the soldiers themselves.

[A decade later, the military is still in control in Lagos, although the military has made and broken successive promises to return to the barracks. The latest plan for the return to civilian rule is an outgrowth of two countercoups which have split the army leadership.]

In the face of poorly institutionalized political systems, politically ambitious officers in both Ghana and Nigeria became praetorian, with little regard for the wishes of the British soldiers who had trained them. In Nigeria the military has held power since the first coup d'etat of January 1966. Although four different officers have served as head of state since 1966 (and two of them have been murdered), only in the last year has there been serious action toward returning Nigeria to civilian rule. In Ghana, by contrast, civilian government was restored in 1969 after only three years of military rule. But, as Valerie Plave Bennett shows, two years later the military again ousted the civilians. The Ghanaian economy had decayed under civilian leadership. While the military felt these economic privations strongly, they resented even more keenly the civilian efforts to ensure the loyalty of the army by interfering with promotions and postings. The second military government in Ghana displayed little of the pro-British, antinationalist behavior that had marked the earlier military regime. Kwame Nkrumah, the former president, was rehabilitated, British-held debts were repudiated, and a program of economic nationalism was undertaken.

VALERIE PLAVE BENNETT

The Motivation for Military Intervention: The Case of Ghana

. . . A study of the 1972 coup d'état in Ghana provides an excellent opportunity to examine in greater detail those factors that lead to self-interest intervention.

From Valerie Plave Bennett, "The Motivation for Military Intervention: The Case of Ghana," The Western Political Quarterly 27 (1974): 659–74, reprinted by permission of the University of Utah, copyright holder.

GHANA BETWEEN THE COUPS

The National Liberation Council formed by the officers responsible for the February 24, 1966, coup d'état in Ghana handed over the reigns of power to the Progress party led by Kofi Busia in October 1969. That this disengagement from politics was the most complete ever undertaken by a ruling military force is evidenced by the retirement of all the military members of the NLC once power was firmly in the hands of the Busia government. The Progress party leadership was "almost wholly merchant-professional middle class in composition." In ethnic terms, the supporters of the PP were primarily Akan—particularly those in Brong/Ahafo, Ashanti and Central regions. The opponents of the PP were mainly Ewe and non-Akans living in areas directly adjacent to the Akan.

The Busia government took office with the support of the civil servants, the students, the cocoa farmers, and the top military leaders. The only groups which may have viewed the accession to power of the new government with trepidation were the trade unionists and the urban unemployed, since it was the avowed aim of the PP to develop the rural areas which the party claimed (with some justification) had been ignored by the Convention Peoples' party (CPP) under the leadership of Kwame Nkrumah. At the time of the 1969 election 25 percent of the wage-labor force was unemployed.

Although Ghana's substantial external debt had not been paid in the intervening years, the time when Ghana would have to begin to make substantial payments on this debt was postponed as a result of the two rescheduling conferences which had been held in 1966 and again in 1968 and 1970. Adding to the Busia government's financial difficulties was

the fact that Ghana had no foreign exchange reserves in 1969. . . . Ghana's major earner of foreign exchange was cocoa; the price of that commodity had risen dramatically between 1966 and 1969. Consequently the outlook was more favorable for Ghana to bring her imports and exports into balance and to acquire enough hard currency to make the payments on the debt which would start falling due in 1970. However, none of these rosy economic predictions came to pass, leading to the erosion of support for the government as it was forced to retrench sharply to stem the tide of bankruptcy. . . .

ECONOMIC DECAY UNDER BUSIA

The Busia government continued to seek a resolution to the debt problem. The U.K. sponsored meetings of Ghana's major creditors in 1966, 1968 and again in 1970. At each of these meetings, attended also by representatives from the International Monetary Fund and the World Bank, the creditors were able to agree only that payments should be delayed for a year or two. In exchange for these delays a moratorium interest charge was added. The moratorium interest has added somewhere between $35 and 40 million to the original debt. As a result of the reschedulings, Ghana had been paying only about 10 percent of the amounts falling due on the medium term debts. . . . Even with these delays, however, Ghana still made $23.5 m. debt payments in the year 1970–71 and was scheduled to pay $36.3 million in 1971–72. The latter figure did not represent any increased ability to pay on the part of Ghana, but was simply the result of the formula used by the refinancing conferences. . . .

The Busia government, realizing the inability of the country to meet these payments, pressed for a composite refinancing loan which would have provided for a fifty-year repayment period, including a ten-year grace period with only a 2 percent moratorium interest charge. But the creditors would not accept this proposal.

In November 1971 the IMF again sent a team to Ghana, which probably recommended another delay in the repayment of the debt, in exchange for a display of action by the Busia government proving that it intended to deal realistically with its deficit in foreign trade through import restriction, devaluation, and increased exportation.

But the Nkrumah debts were not the basis for the financial crisis in the last months of the Busia government. That crisis was instead due to the size of Ghana's internal debt and her short-term debt that had ballooned under Busia. . . .

The really pressing debts, however, were short-term ones. Ghana owed Nc 200 m. in commercial credits (mostly 180-day credits) and Nc 60 m. in arrears on dividends and profits from foreign investment. (Much of the latter figure involves repatriation of assets by British firms.) The cost of short-term credit is very high; interest rates can be as high as 9 percent. Many of Ghana's commercial suppliers were insured under the U.K. Export Credit Guarantees Department. Under this plan creditors will be paid by the Department if the debtor does not repay after 120 days. Ghana had been

keeping precisely 120 days behind, not testing the principle; but to continue to do that would have involved borrowing more money. . . .

After the coup, Busia admitted that Ghana was "utterly bankrupt" and unable to buy imports from suppliers "who obviously cannot be paid from Ghana's own resources." In an attempt to solve the problem of the short-term debt, Busia, the Minister of Finance J. H. Mensah, and the Minister for Foreign Affairs William Ofori-Atta visited the U.S., the U.K. and Mexico; in addition, an IMF team came to Accra. Details of the arrangements worked out at the time are still sketchy, but they seem to have included a plan for Ghana to go on a cash basis in her foreign dealings. The plan involved borrowing between $170 and $270 million (two-thirds of it in the U.K., the rest in the U.S.); this loan would have enabled Ghana to transfer most of the short-term debt to medium-term debt at much more favorable interest rates (some as low as 1 percent). In return, Ghana was to devalue the cedi and permanently reduce the level of imports. The import deficit for 1970 was only –Nc 15 m, but this figure was artificially low and could not have been continued without greatly increasing the rate of smuggling. A year later the deficit had risen to –Nc 70 m.

BUSIA AND COCOA

Ghana's inability to pay her debts was compounded by problems experienced with her major export and foreign exchange earner, cocoa. Nkrumah encouraged increased cocoa production to increase foreign exchange. In 1964–65 Ghana experienced a record cocoa crop of 567,000 tons which gave her almost 40 percent of the world cocoa market. Since that date, Ghana's cocoa output has fluctuated between 325,000 and 415,000 tons. The over-supply of cocoa that resulted from the large 1964–65 crop pushed cocoa prices down from $840 per ton in 1958 to an all-time low of $204 in July 1965. . . .

At the same time that the Busia government was unable to increase cocoa production, the world price of cocoa has been falling. In 1970 the average price of cocoa was $790 a ton, in 1971 it was $470 a ton and the 1972 market fell as low as $360, as a result of the large crops in all of the major producing areas. It was the Ghanaian budget, rather than the Ghanaian cocoa farmers who suffered from the declining cocoa prices. The prices paid to the cocoa farmers were stable during the Busia regime. In 1969 Ghanaian cocoa farmers received 8 Nc per load for their cocoa (up from 7 Nc the previous year). Cocoa prices remained constant for the next two years, rising in 1972 to 10 Nc. The drop in cocoa prices was absorbed by the Cocoa Marketing Board.

Before the 1971 harvesting season a new cocoa purchasing scheme was introduced which led to delays in payments to the cocoa farmers. One month after the cocoa buying season opened, the Cabinet approved a sum of Nc 10 m. to pay for purchases in the Ashanti region which supplied most of the cocoa and the Progress party's supporters.

Declining cocoa prices worsened both Ghana's balance-of-payment difficulties and budget deficit. The decision to devalue the cedi by 44 percent in December 1971 was supposed to be an answer to these difficulties.

THE CAUSES OF INTERVENTION

Can it be said that the situation in Ghana at the end of 1971 evidenced the condition which has been described as political decay? With the exception of a strike in September 1971 by the port workers, protesting the introduction of a Development Levy and a new Trade Union Act, there are no incidents of violence, no riots, no student demonstrations, no open quarrels among the leading political figures, and no increased ethnic tensions. After the coup most commentators made the point that if elections had been held at the time of the January 1972 coup, Dr. Busia's government would most likely have been returned to power. Although such comments are obviously impressionistic, they do serve to point out that the Busia government was still functioning as well as it ever had and that the majority of the rural population still perceived the Progress party as a party concerned with their well-being.

The salient factor leading to the coup d'état appears to be the refusal of the government, in the face of the deepening economic crisis, to accede to the financial demands of the military.

THE MILITARY AND THE JULY BUDGET

The July 1971 Budget was meant to be an austerity budget, a signal to both the extravagant Ghanaian elite and the international financiers that the government was going to make an effort to deal realistically with Ghana's economic problems. The budget provided for a ban on all imports of autos, televisions, cigarettes, soda, aluminum sheeting, fruit, poultry, and crude rubber. There was also an increase in the petrol duty. Vehicle maintenance allowances for civil servants and army officers were to be abolished from the first of August, and the National Development Levy further reduced public officials' take-home pay.

In the July Budget the PP government further increased military resentment by attempting to cut military costs and to increase the productivity of the forces. The military suffered corporately under the new Budget because the expenditures of the Ministry of Defense were reduced from the Nc 45 m. in the 1970 budget (which was a reduction from the 1969 figure of 49.1 m.), to Nc 40.4 m. (Nc 31.4 m. for recurrent expenditure and Nc 9 m. for capital expenditure). When Finance Minister Mensah introduced the new budget he reminded the Assembly that the government had been faced "with the problem of what to do about a level of Defense expenditure which was clearly onerous for a small country such as ours." Mensah's statement was motivated as much by expediency as by budgetary realities. Reductions in defense expenditure would satisfy the demands of Ghana's major international creditors to effect selective cuts in government expenditures consistent with a program of economic development. The most severe cuts were experienced by the Air Force and Navy,

both bodies clearly superfluous to Ghana's limited defense requirements.

The Navy had not expanded for several years; its ships were in need of refitting but there was no money available for that purpose. The ships were reported to be in such poor shape that they could not be sailed to refitting. . . . The Air Force was not expanding either, no new planes had been bought for many years and very little flying time was logged on the planes already acquired because of the very high cost of fuel.

The army also had its share of cuts: the parachute battalion at Tamale was disbanded. It was later reformed as the Seventh Battalion at Takoradi to keep some airborne capability but, still too costly, the entire battalion was disbanded and the personnel absorbed into other units. There were also unconfirmed reports that the Seventh Battalion was suspected of plotting against the Busia government.

Under the new budget the military, like all other government importers, was expected to pay taxes on items ordered from overseas, making repair and replacement a great deal more expensive than previously.

The net result of cutting back the budget while maintaining the size of the establishment was that there was very little money for nonessentials such as exercises, training, and ammunition. Restriction on imports led to real supply and parts problems; as a result many vehicles were simply not locally repairable. One knowledgeable observer estimated in the Fall of 1971 that half of the total number of military vehicles were not road-worthy.

Another corporate problem faced by

the Ghana military was the question of the role of the forces. After almost fifteen years of independence the role of the military is still unclear. The army itself sees its main (and possibly sole) role as one of guarding the nation against its foreign enemies. To the Busia government this role appeared either insufficient or nonexistent. They found it difficult to justify enormous expenditures on an institution that contributed so little to the economic and social well-being of the nation. Consequently, they sought new ways to utilize the forces. Since April 1970 the military had been supporting the police in an anti-smuggling campaign on the borders. In addition, in September 1970 joint police-military operations against crime began. The army medical corps was active in the anti-cholera drive and the air force provided flood relief aid in the north. But despite these activities, Ghanaians were still left with the feeling that the military could be more useful. The National Union of Ghana Students suggested in the Summer of 1970 that the technical branch of the Ghana army should be used in agricultural and constructional work. The Minister of Defense, J. Kwesi Lamptey, said at that time that the Ghana army would only be used for defense purposes. But a year later, after the Ministry of Defense had changed hands, a Northerner, Alhaji B. K. Adama had become Defense Minister, and Ghana's financial conditions had worsened, the attitude toward reconstruction work changed. In the July budget Mensah was able to announce that ". . . it is possible to combine . . . training with substantial contributions to national development. Therefore during this financial year, it has been arranged that whenever units . . . go out on training exercises they will seek to leave behind them some positive development project . . . by way of roads or sanitary buildings."

But the corporate indignities of the new budget did not hurt the officers as much as the personal losses they experienced due to deprivation of income and perquisites. The Development Levy and the vehicle maintenance allowance have already been mentioned, but it is worth noting the impact of the vehicle maintenance allowance. A typical major who was taking home Nc 215 a month under the old budget would only receive Nc 125 under the new budget. The government had also eliminated or curtailed the free water and electricity that had been supplied to the officers. In addition, the telephone allowance was cut and the percentage of their salaries withheld by the government for rent payments was increased from 7.5 to 15 percent, previous to the introduction of the budget. In addition to the cuts in allowances, an actual cut in pay scales was also rumored. The final blow to the financial well-being of the Ghanaian elite came at the end of December when the Busia government dramatically announced that the cedi would be devalued by 44 percent. In terms of real income for those living in European style in Ghana, a 44 percent devaluation may have represented a loss of as much as 25 percent of an individual's purchasing power. The effect of the devaluation was immediate due to profiteering and hoarding.

The military's antagonism to a policy of retrenchment at their expense was sufficiently evident that after the coup Busia dismissed the event as "just an officers' amenities coup arising from their grievances at my efforts to save money."

The Busia government fully realized that the corporate and financial grievances of the officer corps were making it highly probable that the military would move against the government. In the words of Gamal Nasser, "a shabby army is a potentially disloyal army." To forestall the eventuality of a coup numerous shifts were made in top military appointments.

THE GOVERNMENT AND THE HIGH COMMAND

When the Busia government took over in 1969, the military's internal command and control capability was damaged, according to Jon Kraus, "and ambitions and further plotting nurtured, by the break in the chain of command and the arrest of senior officers at the time of the 1966 coup and during later attempts, and by the gradual elimination of many senior officers." The virtual decimation of the high command came in three stages. First was the retirement of the officers associated with the Nkrumah regime. . . . Retired at a later date were officers whose position at the time of the 1967 abortive counter-coup had been unclear. . . . The next group of retirements came when the National Liberation Council handed over power to the Busia government, and all the

military members of the NLC retired —Generals Afrifa, Ankrah and Ocran. Two top officers were killed in the two coups: General Barwah in the February coup and General Kotoka in that of April. The third group of officers lost to the army were those seconded to run other public bodies. . . . Colonel Quaye became head of the Navy, and four officers not in special favor with the government became Military Attachés abroad. . . . The result of all these shifts was that one-half of those who held ranks of lieutenant colonel, or above, at the time of the 1966 coup were not available in 1970. The command structure of the military was weak and inexperienced.

The retirement of the top officers meant rapid promotions for those officers who were in the middle ranks and in the good graces of the NLC or the Busia government. The colonels and brigadiers are typically young and inexperienced and as a result there were serious promotion blockages facing the junior officers, particularly because the military establishment had not been expanding. (The Ghana Military Academy which had intakes as large as 120 men in the early 1960s had cut back intakes to only 25 men a year.)

Scholars have long noted the fact that officers in developing countries have the administrative skills needed to promote modernization.* The as-

*Lucien Pye, "Armies in the Process of Political Modernization," in John Johnson, ed., The Role of the Military in Underdeveloped Countries (Princeton: Princeton University Press, 1962).

signment of a sizable portion of the officer corps to bureaucratic functions may have a disintegrative effect on the military institution that has not been previously examined.

Further changes in the top command came in the Fall of 1971. Lieutenant General Mike Otu had been appointed Chief of Defense Staff in March 1968; he still held that position in the Summer of 1971, at which time he strenuously objected to the cuts in the military budget. There were reports that he objected to the diminished budget to the extent that he was considering resigning in protest. This never came to pass; instead, Otu quietly retired and was rewarded with a new position by the Busia government. Major General D. K. Addo, the former Army Commander, was appointed acting Chief of Defense Staff; Brigadier J. R. K. Acquah, the former Director of Military Intelligence, became acting Army Commander; and Lieutenant Colonel E. M. Osei-Owusu, acting Commander of the Second Infantry Brigade. In mid-November another reorganization began; Brigadier Acquah was forced to resign after informing the government that he planned to retire early in 1972, to enter the building industry "while he was still young." Due to the earlier retirement date he lost many of his retirement benefits. He was replaced by Brigadier Twum-Barima, who had previously been head of the First Infantry Brigade in Accra. His position at First Infantry Brigade Headquarters was filled by Lieutenant Colonel Acheampong. This appointment proved to be a fatal mistake for the Busia government.

THE LOGISTICS OF INTERVENTION

At about 2 A.M. on January 13 troops of the First Brigade began to move on key installations in the capital: these included the radio station, the airport, external communications and the Castle. The logistics of the coup were relatively simple; all these installations were guarded by the Fifth Infantry Battalion which had been Acheampong's battalion command in 1970. What has come to light from subsequent interviews is that Acheampong had been thinking of engineering a coup in 1970; but only to the extent that he had begun to plan what he would do if he were ever in control of the First Infantry Brigade. His planning was interrupted when he was sent to Trinidad to serve on the court martial of officers who had mutinied against the government of Eric Williams. Suddenly, however, in November he found himself in control of the First Brigade. The period between November and January was sufficient for the short period of pre-coup conspiratorial activity characteristic of non-ideological coups. In intervention based on ideological motivation, on the other hand, "the actual coup itself is often preceded by years of discussion and preparation. The Thai Promoters of 1932 grew out of the organized discussions of civilian students and younger military officers in Paris in the 1920s. In Egypt the cadets at the military college organized discussions on 'The Social and Political Unrest' in 1938."

Up until this point, Acheampong's career had not been unusual. Born in Kumasi in September 1931, he earned the General Certificate of Education, "O" level, and later worked as a teacher, secretary, and school principal. In 1958, when he was 27, he joined the army. . . . Acheampong served as a Chairman of the Administrative Commission of the Western Region under the NLC. Before taking over the Fifth Battalion he had been commanding officer of the Sixth Battalion at Takoradi.

Acheampong belongs to a class of officers who were shut out of promotions because they were not affiliated with the group that brought off the 1966 coup. As Acheampong so plaintively explained, Afrifa had been a company commander of his, and now Afrifa was a retired Lieutenant General. Men such as Twum-Barima, who like Acheampong had been Lieutenant Colonels in 1967, were Brigadiers while the latter remained only a Colonel. Colonel Bernasko, one of the Regional Commissioners under the new military government, assured a group of Ghanaian students after the coup that "escalating promotions," which had characterized the NLC period, "is unlikely to be heard of this time."

Acheampong and the few majors who had served under him in previous postings—the only people he trusted with the plans for the coup—can best be described as the nonpoliticians of the army. These were the line rather than the staff officers. . . .

Busia was in London at the time of the coup. As Luttwak reminds us, coup makers often wait until the head of government is unavailable. His Cabinet Ministers were easily arrested, along with the President Akufo-Addo and Chief of Staff Addo, the Head of the Army, Twum-Barima, and the Head of Military Intelligence, Hamidu. The most pressing problem for the conspirators in the first hours after the coup was whether the Second Infantry Brigade Group in Kumasi (the center of Busia's support) would accept the coup. The Chief Regional Executive in Ashanti, Maxwell Owusu, went on radio saying that the coup had failed, but the third in command, Captain David Weir of the Fourth Battalion, later denounced Dr. Owusu's statement. The same day Lieutenant General Afrifa called on Acheampong to declare that the former supported the coup and considered himself a friend. But Afrifa was arrested on the morning of the fifteenth for plotting with Colonel Osei-Owusu, the head of the Second Brigade, to overthrow Acheampong by bringing troops down from Kumasi to challenge the troops in control of Accra. This plan was logistically similar to Afrifa's 1966 coup.

The remarkable thing about the small group of officers arrested in the first days of the coup (Generals Afrifa and Addo, Brigadiers Twum-Barima, Hamidu and Osei-Owusu) is that they are all Sandhurst men. Regardless of ethnicity or politics these men appear to have been loyal to the Busia government. For this loyalty they had been rewarded by rapid promotion. Osei-Owusu, for example, was a brigadier while his former peers were still colonels.

Acheampong was faced with the

difficulties inherent in naming a ruling council. The first broadcast gave the composition of the newly formed National Redemption Council (NRC) as: Colonel Acheampong, Major Kwame Baah, Commander Boham, Major Selormey, Lieutenant Colonel Barnor, Lieutenant Colonel Benn, and Mr. E. N. Moore (Attorney-General). . . .

At 6 A.M. on the thirteenth, Acheampong announced the reasons for the coup over the air. He first charged that the corruption, economic mismanagement, and other malpractices that had characterized the Nkrumah government had been equally in evidence in the Busia government. He then cited what were, in fact, the essential motivating factors:

The first people which Busia put his eyes on were the armed forces and police. Some army and police officers were dismissed under the pretext of retirement. Some officers were put in certain positions to suit the whims of Busia and his colleagues. Then he started taking from us the few amenities and facilities which we in the armed forces and the police enjoyed even under the Nkrumah regime. Having lowered morale in the armed forces and the police to the extent that officers could not exert any meaningful influence over their men, so that by this strategy coming together to overthrow his government was to him impossible, he turned his eyes on the civilians.

It was clear that Acheampong, as the leader of a coup motivated by the self-interest of the military had no real political objectives; he suggested no new policies or dramatic changes. He merely called for a review of the important decisions taken by the Busia government: the cocoa purchasing scheme; the Development Levy; the rural development program; the devaluation of the cedi; and the expulsion of the aliens. The only positive suggestion made dealt with the unemployment problem; he called for the reintroduction of the Worker's Brigade and the State Farms.

In a broadcast a few hours later, Acheampong stated that the Progress party had been banned along with all the opposition parties, Dr. Busia had been removed from office, and the leader of the opposition would also be dismissed. Since Acheampong had shared his secret with few people, new appointments had not been ironed out in secret before the coup; it was now that the jockeying for position began. The next few days saw incredible activity as army, naval and air force officers all attempted to gain positions on the NRC, ministerial portfolios, and the remaining military positions that were vacated by the successful claimants. The day after the coup the composition of the NRC was substantially changed; only Acheampong and the three majors remained from the first list. The new NRC was almost half Ewe, although the new list was meant to broaden the base of the NRC by including representatives from each of the services and the police. Two days later Lieutenant Colonel Benni was reinstated. On January 22, a fourth list added Major Felli of the Signals Regiment. On the thirtieth, Ministerial portfolios were assigned; only seven of the twelve members of the NRC received portfolios. Five new officers were added to the government. . . . The NRC found many collaborators among those officers whose careers had either languished or been permanently ended because of their association with the Nkrumah government. . . .

CONCLUSION

The recent coup in Ghana brings into question the validity of some of the current literature on the preconditions and motivation for military intervention in developing countries. Previous scholars have argued that political decay precedes military intervention; and, that officers intervene in politics either to change or to preserve the class or status stratification of society at large. Events in Ghana seem to show that economic crisis, in and by itself, may be the only precondition necessary for intervention. In addition, changes in the conditions of service and extent of military influence can cause the military to intervene although the level of politicization of the conspirators may be very low. Particularly, in new nations which suffer from the absence of political institutionalization, the motives for military intervention do not have to be acceptable to the public at large in order for the military to be able to bring down a civilian government. In countries whose governments are of low legitimacy, quarrels between the military and the government can lead to military intervention. In politics whose institutions enjoy wide legitimacy these clashes would be settled by interest group bargaining processes, not a coup d'état.

What then is the legacy of the colonial powers in Africa? Ruth First hypothesizes that it is the creation of military bureaucracies that in conjunction with the colonial-created civil service result in a "civil service–military axis in which armies have the physical power to conserve the regime, while the civil service wields effective executive power in the state."* In Zaire, as Jean-Claude Willame shows, it took a massive rebellion in 1964–65 and a coup d'etat against President Kasavubu and Prime Minister Tshombe to bring about a "caesarist bureaucracy." General Mobutu quickly sought to differentiate his leadership from the army and its high command. A year after the coup, military commissioners in the provinces were replaced by the former civil authorities. Mobutu even began to wear civilian dress. Governmental functions were placed in the hands of "experts," most of whom were depoliticized former university students. Willame notes a striking parallel with the former Belgian bureaucracy in which centralization, hierarchy, permanence, and expertise are the major structural features of the Mobutu government.

*First, *Power in Africa*, p. 432.

Jean-Claude Willame

Congo-Kinshasa: General Mobutu and Two Political Generations

[Zaire (the former Belgian Congo) is somewhat unique in Africa, never having experienced a period of stable civilian government in the post-nationalist era. Unlike the former French and British colonies, the Congo was not prepared for independence; rather, it had independence thrust upon it.]

For any observer of the Congolese political scene, significant changes seem to have taken place since General Joseph-Désiré Mobutu took over in November, 1965. A period of insecurity and uncertainty has been succeeded by a period of stability and reshaping the state apparatus; the previous institutional decentralization has been replaced by a unitary regime; after the generation of the professional politician has emerged that of the university student, the "young," and the "expert." This chapter analyzes these generational changes to illustrate continuities and discontinuities between the two periods. The two political generations of the Congo epitomize the impact of military rule upon tropical Africa's largest state.

From Jean-Claude Willame, "Congo-Kinshasa: General Mobutu and Two Political Generations," in Soldier and State in Africa, ed. Claude Welch (Evanston, Ill.: Northwestern University Press, 1970), pp. 125–51.

THE FIRST POLITICAL GENERATION: A PATRIMONIAL SYSTEM OF RULE

Literature dealing with the emerging nations emphasizes the "new elites" as main agents of modernization. Whoever they may be—university graduates, military officers, achievement-oriented bureaucrats, charismatic leaders—these elites are asserted to be in a strategic position. They must create new sociopolitical institutions to mobilize the nation, link all the people into a national communications network, and provide the symbols of national integration. The overwhelming majority of scholars have taken for granted that these elites wished to "modernize," or, as Edward Shils put it, to be "devoted to the public good, critical and yet sympathetic, interested in the immediate partisanship to constitute a corps of custodians of the public good in the present and the future."

Such assertions are now under attack. Aristide Zolberg, in his most recent book, asserted:

We have now reached an impasse. . . . We realize that, in spite of the huge growth of scholarly and popular literature, our information is grossly deficient. Much has been written about the thought of various leaders in the fields of international politics, about economic development, and about the one-party itself. We know what political organizations say their structures are like and what they say concerning their operations, but we have seldom gone beyond such declaratory statements.

Zolberg suggests substituting the concept of patrimonial elite for that of charismatic leadership. Although the charismatic aspects of legitimacy may have been most salient during the period of colonial rule and immediately after independence, the crucial process is similar to the one that Weber saw developing in patrimonial rule, namely, the appropriation of public offices and the establishment of relationships based on personal loyalties. Guenther Roth has even suggested that the treatment of almost all political leaders in the new states as charismatic has been completely misleading on at least two counts:

it has obscured the difference between charismatic authority and charismatic leadership, and it has taken at face value the international propaganda claims of some of the new leaders.

Roth goes further than Zolberg did by proposing two ideal types of patrimonial rule: the traditional patrimonial regime, exemplified by such a country as Ethiopia; and personal rulership based on loyalties "that do not require any belief in the ruler's unique personal qualification but are inextricably linked to material incentives and rewards." "In terms of traditional political theory," he concludes, "some of these new states may not be states at all but merely private governments of those powerful enough to rule."

In the Congolese case, the concept of patrimonial rule or personal leadership represents a useful starting point for examining the country's first political generation. Four aspects make the Congolese political elites similar to Max Weber's patrimonial rulers.

APPROPRIATION OF PUBLIC OFFICES

The political bourgeoisie takes over public offices that have become a major source of wealth and prestige. Let us recall how this phenomenon occurred in the Congo. Historically, the movement for independence had its roots in the growing pressures emanating from a relatively small group of evolués—mostly journalists, teachers, and clerks—upon the colonial bureaucracy. The bureaucracy in turn was increasingly unable to close the gap between its prime goal— the efficiency and profitability of the colonial economy—and the aspirations that this goal had created among "its" people. In other words, rising economic levels created the demand for greater prosperity.

Thomas Hodgkin described Belgian colonial policy as Platonic:

Platonism is implicit in the sharp distinction, social and legal, between Belgian philosopher-kings and the mass of African producers; in the conception of education as primarily concerned with the transmission of certain unquestioned and unquestionable moral values . . . in the belief that the thought and behaviour of the mass is plastic, and can be refashioned by a benevolent, wise and highly trained élite;

that the prime interest of the mass is in welfare and consumer goods . . . not liberty; and in the conviction that it is possible, by expert administration, to arrest social and political change.

The term "Platonism" is unfortunate, since the relationship between the philosopher-king and his subjects envisaged by Plato took place in a *homogeneous city* and in the realm of the *political*. These two basic points were missing in Belgian policy toward the Congo. On the one hand, the colonial situation entailed radical heterogeneity, a deep psychological and structural cleavage between a dominant foreign minority and a technically backward majority based on a dogmatically asserted racial superiority. On the other hand, the Belgian colonizers were willing to promote socioeconomic welfare and Christian civilization, even though they denied the colonials any share in decision-making.

The colonial situation brought an inescapable contradiction. The Belgian welfare policy produced a new type of human being—the colonized intelligentsia—whom the colonizer hated and fought. In the very beginning, this intelligentsia did not want to expel his benefactor, but to work with him. It sought, above all, to end its lack of status within the colonial structures and to solve the multiple wounds of racial discrimination. Its first grievances and demands were thus concerned with its "rights of expression," its "rights of association" . . . all demands that were expressed through such "liberal" oriented texts as the "Manifesto of African Con-

science," *Congo, My Country* by Patrice Lumumba, or through cultural organizations such as the "Association pour le Maintien de l'Unité et de la Langue Kikongo," later on ABAKO, party of Joseph Kasavubu.

The seizure of power by the former *evolués* broke down the unity of the mass and the new political leadership that, at the start of independence, joined both in the expectation of general prosperity. A political bourgeoisie emerged by securing or competing for public office. Two years after independence, about 163,000 persons were employed by the state in the administration, army, police and political institutions; their salaries represented 58 per cent of national expenses. As Hughes Leclercq stressed in 1961, this social stratum impoverished the whole country by inflation:

As a result of the credit drawn by the state on the Central Bank, an increased money supply was poured into the economy through salaries, wages and other compensations to the Army and the Civil Service. Raising the monetary income of some 150,000 privileged persons, the deficit financing exercised a strong pressure on demand and led consequently to a rise in the price level.

Inflated costs for manufactured goods did not further stimulate Congolese peasants to produce and sell their products to the internal or export markets but tended to drive them back to a self-subsistence level of economy. Inflation also abetted the formation of a parasitic network of foreign and native speculators with whom the political bourgeoisie closely associated in order to increase its revenue. Thus, the crucial process involved in the post-independence period was the appropriation of wealth through the control over the instruments of power—legislative assemblies, administration, government —by a social stratum whose homogeneity was rooted in its narrow association with the former colonizer. This group was not oriented toward production, invention, or construction. The dynamic and pioneering dimensions that one can find in any national bourgeoisie were completely lacking. . . .

PERSONAL LOYALTIES

The second central feature of patrimonialism rests, according to Weber, upon a relationship based on personal loyalties to the individual at the top. Weber describes these relations in the following way:

The organized group exercising authority is . . . primarily based on relations of personal loyalty, cultivated through a common process of education. The person exercising authority is not a "superior" but a personal "chief." His administrative staff does not consist primarily of officials but of personal retainers. Those subject to his authority are not members of an association but are either his traditional comrades or his subjects. What determines the relations of the administrative staff to the chief is not the impersonal obligations of office but personal loyalty to the chief.

In the Congo, a similar pattern of relationships has emerged from the tribalization or regionalization of the political life that has occurred since independence. A few words about tribalism are necessary. Many political scientists and African leaders have conceived of the relation between tribalism and nationalism as two ends of a continuum: "tradition–modernity." Tribalism is seen as corresponding to a state of backwardness, referring implicitly to the concept of tribe in its anthropological sense. There are, however, two basic differences between the old and the new "tribal" context. The "traditional" tribe is characterized by narrow and ill-defined ecological dimensions and by a set of kinship relations rigorously determined in terms of time and generation. Modern tribalism lacks these two connotations. It has been definitively affected by colonial policy aiming at fixing populations in well-bounded and larger administrative units (the *secteur*, the district, and the province). Moreover, modern tribalism involves a set of relations much more extensive than the previous network of kinship ties. The most striking Congolese illustration of this change in the nature of tribalism may be found among the Bangala, a name arbitrarily invented by Belgian officials to identify people living in an area extending from Coquilhatville (now Mbandaka) 400 miles upstream and running inland some 100 miles on each side of the Congo River. On the eve of independence, the Bakongo of Leopoldville referred to all non-Bakongo as Bangala and the term came to be accepted by the Kasaians, Mongo, and Kwango-Kwilu people. . . .

Thus, the contemporary form of tribalism is clearly a modern phenomenon. The ethnic rivalries that have developed must be understood as urban groups and communities competing against each other for modern objects. "Tribal nationalism" was the end product of socioeconomic differentiations originated by the process of colonization itself.

Decolonization in the Congo was accompanied by successive tribal awakenings, developing in a climate of intense politicization. Chronologically the first awakening came from the Bakongo, one of the most modernized ethnic groups of the country. Their political radicalism resulted from their fear of being outrun in the competition for power by the so-called Bangala, who had questioned the colonial regime by publishing their noteworthy "Manifesto of African Consciousness." Thereafter similar reactions came from the Kwilu elites. Afraid of possible Bakongo extension through their territory, they hastened to create their own political organization—the Parti Solidaire Africain (PSA). Later on, the same pattern prevailed in Kasai province among the Lulua and the Basonge, both increasingly aware of the privileged treatment provided by the colonial administration to their common enemy, the Baluba. On the eve of independence, the Congo was thus saturated with more than 150 parties or associations, each of them being constituted by a spontaneous reaction against "others." This phenomenon of dynamic and explosive ethnicity was eventually institutionalized by the division of the country into 21 new provinces between October, 1962, and April, 1963.

Yet the creation of these new entities was not the only result of ethnic awakening throughout the Congo. Their formation also illustrated the pre-eminence of political relations based on individual loyalties and allegiances developing not in the narrow framework of the family or household system, but in the larger context of ethnic and tribal identification defined above.

From January, 1961, onwards, the political center of gravity of the Congo did not rest on a single legitimate focus of authority. Instead, legitimacy rested upon powerful "suzerains," each of whom was influential and powerful in a specific region or within a particular tribe. Following the death of Patrice Lumumba, national political institutions either no longer functioned or survived in a comatose state. Political decisions were made by a series of "Round Tables" at which the most powerful politicians of the country gathered. These conferences legitimized the desire of these suzerains to transform their native territories into "provinces" or "states." . . . The central government had no legitimacy of its own; it was, in fact, a creation of United Nation officials, backed by a loose coalition of tribal leaders who had participated in the preceding Round Tables. From the beginning of 1962 onward, the process of partition took place within the National Assembly, the Senate, and the ministry of internal affairs.

Complex relationships developed between the center and the provinces as the new provincial governments were developed. Although the overall strategy of most of the national politicians was to control their constituencies through their personal supporters, this was by no means a general rule. Five types of relationship occurred: (1) Political activities in the provinces were clearly the direct consequence of those taking place in Leopoldville: Kwilu, Kwango, Lomani, Ubangi, Cuvette Centrale. (2) The national leader was chosen to act without intermediaries and to take the head of the government or the opposition in his native provinces: Lac Leopold II, Nord-Katanga, Sud-Kasai, Sankuru, Unité Kasaienne. (3) Conflicts arose between the "suzerain" and his "client," who, in turn, transferred his allegiance to another national leader: Moyen-Congo. (4) The center of political gravity was located at the provincial level, the national leader being merely a representative of regional interests of the province at Leopoldville: Nord-Kivu, Maniema. (5) Politics at the local level tended to be increasingly controlled by the central government: Maniema, Haut-Congo.

These five trends in the relationship between the national leader and his constituency clearly illustrate the instability of a patrimonial system of rule. As Weber pointed out, two prob lems recur in this type of domination. First, maximum control militates against an effective government over a large territory, since the cost involved readily exceeds the personal resources of even powerful rulers. Secondly, exclusive reliance upon personal instruments of force can jeopardize the ruler's authority, since it exposes him to the possibility of united action against himself by his dependents or those excluded from the share.

ROLE OF THE MILITARY

The third structural characteristic of patrimonialism is its large use of a coercive apparatus—military or paramilitary forces—for the ruler to extend or preserve his power over territories inside or outside his immediate domain.

Weber drew special attention to the social organization of the military force that enabled a patrimonial ruler to extend or preserve his power. He distinguished five types of military organizations: (1) an army composed of personal subordinates to whom the ruler has assigned rewards in return for services or payments in kind; (2) a force composed of people who are entirely divorced from society; (3) an army based on recruitment of alien mercenaries; (4) an army composed of alien people to whom the ruler has granted some rewards for their military service; (5) a personal military force recruited among the ruler's own subjects.

The National Congolese Army came from the second type, due to its roots in the former Force Publique. Government policies of isolating the military from its immediate milieu and sharing conscription among the main ethnic groups helped make the Force Publique the most integrated and most efficient repressive body during the colonial era. At the time of independence, however, the unity of the Force

Publique broke down. It could not avoid harassment by political leaders who attempted to find support among soldiers drawn from their own region.

Six months after independence, the National Congolese Army had broken up into four fragments: (1) The so-called South-Kasai State Constabulary organized by Mulopwe ("Emperor") Albert Kalonji and his prime minister, Joseph Ngalula. This army was almost exclusively composed of Baluba soldiers, and was not reintegrated into the NCA until October, 1962. (2) The army of the "Independent State of Katanga," created and organized by former Belgian officers and composed of three distinctive elements: a constabulary whose members were recruited among the Bayeke and Balunda tribes (the ethnic groups of Godefroid Munongo and Moise Tshombe); warriors depending on other Katangese paramount chiefs favorable to Moise Tshombe (e.g., Kasongo-Nyemlo); and a body of European mercenaries recruited among foreigners and the white population of Elisabethville. (3) The "National Congolese Army" of Stanleyville, directed by Congolese officers, most of whom were members of the Batetela and Bakusu tribes and, as such, favorable to the regime of Antoine Gizenga. (4) The National Congolese Army of Leopoldville, loyal to its commander-in-chief, Lieutenant Colonel Joseph Mobutu.

In addition to these four segments, numerous military units formed private bodyguards receiving their orders directly from the local ruler; this was the type (4) described by Weber. Finally, foreign mercenaries recruited

in South Africa, France, Portugal, and Belgium were also used by Congolese leaders, first at the regional level during the Katangese secession, and later at the national level during the 1964 rural uprising. It is certainly not exaggerated to say that without this small band of adventurers the Congo's political fate would have been completely different.

IDEOLOGICAL LEGITIMATION

Weber treated patrimonialism as a reality quite distinct from the two other variants of traditional domination: patriarchalism and feudalism. He considered patriarchalism a pure type of domination characterized by the arbitrary power of the master and the limitation of that power by sacred tradition. Feudalism, on the other hand, replaced the paternal relationship by contractually fixed fealty based on knightly militarism. Patrimonial rule was distinct from both by its use of *ideological* legitimation. As Bendix pointed out,

the ideology of patrimonialism differs from that of feudalism in all these respects. Feudalism is domination by the few who are skilled in war; patrimonialism is domination by one who requires officials for the exercise of his authority. A patrimonial ruler is in some measure dependent upon the good will of his subjects . . . feudalism can dispense with such good will. Patrimonialism appeals to the masses . . . not the warrior hero but the "good king," the "father of his people" are its prevailing ideal. That the patrimonial ruler sees the welfare of his subjects is the basis on which he legitimates his rule *in his own and their eyes.* The "welfare state" is the legend of patrimonialism in contrast to the feudal image of a free camaraderie of warriors pledged in loyalty to their leader.

The idea that the new rulers had to distribute wealth and welfare to their people was basic to the notion of independence. Immediate independence, slogan of Congolese nationalism in 1959–60, seemed to entail socioeconomic achievement for everybody. People expected no more taxes, no more cotton, no more census-takers, no more identity cards. The impression prevailed everywhere that the collapse of the colonial system would allow all social strata to enter the "golden age" with their rulers. Political parties and their leaders systematically encouraged utopian images through which the masses perceived independence. Four years later, the promise of an "indefinite social and economic prosperity," parallel to the theme of a "second independence," led to the uprising of the deprived peasants and the *Lumpenproletariat* of the cities. The language of the rebellion was similar to that previously used by the *evolués* of 1959–60: For the image of the colonizer was simply substituted the portrait of "the corrupt politician who had sold out the Congo to the Americans." The "Simba" were the "true successors of Lumumba," who were going, like him, "to liberate the Congo from those who had stolen its wealth."

How did the politician of the first generation try to legitimize his rule and his activities? Political leaders— national as well as local—used one of two approaches, according to their positions.

1. The *politician-executive*—governor, minister, head of civil service, territorial administrator, etc.—generally conceived of his role and function as being identical to those performed by former colonial administrators. His political programs remained based on the same welfare policies previously practiced by the Belgian territorial administrators or district commissioners. At both the provincial and central levels, there was a deep commitment to the basic colonial creed: Economic and social prosperity must be pursued through foreign corporations, external technical assistance, and Catholic missions—all backed by the political institutions. The decision-making process must go through the traditional hierarchy set up by the colonizer, from the central government down to the territorial administrator and the local chief, and back to the central government again. The government decides what is good for the people, who are occasionally referred to as "natives" (*indigènes*). Basic colonial institutions remain in operation, as well as the philanthropic organizations sponsored by the colonial government.

2. The *politician-representative*—assemblyman, senator, congressman— was a new person born with independence. More in touch with his constituents and thus more vulnerable to local pressures and criticisms, he was used to concealing inefficiency and lack of control over events behind emotive language and ritualistic activities. Members of this group called themselves "the highest authorities of the nation," the "keepers

of legality." These new political "priests" closed ranks as soon as the immunity of one was threatened. The process by which representative institutions worked was, above all, formalistic. Acts, gestures, and words were thought to be significant in themselves. The act of voting or the colorful political speech was believed to have magical efficacy.

THE BREAKING POINT: THE POPULAR UPRISING OF 1964–65

The rebellion of 1964–65 represents the turning point between the first and the second political generations in the Congo.

In a climate of intense socio-economic expectations as previously described, a patrimonial type of government had a fundamental weakness. Based on a generalized system of tribal and ethnic "patronage," it tended to create enclaves of prosperity or semiprosperity and to deepen the gap between elite and non-elite. In the Congo this cleavage was partly ecological, taking the form of growing opposition between the town and the countryside. During the colonial era a satisfactory equilibrium with respect to welfare and prosperity had been kept between the rural and urban areas. The Congo represented one of the most industrialized countries of Africa. In 1950, about 59 per cent of the male population was employed in commercialized production, contrasted with 41 per cent living from or in a subsistence economy. The gross domestic product in 1958 revealed no major distortion between the primary and secondary sectors

of the economy. At that time, agriculture, mining activities, and other industries represented, respectively, 44.6, 19.7, and 34.6 per cent of the total production of goods. Although information on agricultural production does not exist after 1960, export statistics indicate that the extent of peasant participation in the economy sharply declined. Production of manioc and bananas, the most common crops produced and consumed by Congolese villagers, fell from 50,000 to 3,000 tons, and from 30,000 to 13,000 tons, respectively, between 1959 and 1964. In many respects the rural areas were thus returned to self-subsistence. Bush schools, local hospitals, and welfare institutions ceased to function or were transferred into the towns.

At the same time, political frustrations grew. Between 1961 and 1964, the Congo was in fact ruled by a loose "one-party system" at the national as well as the local level. The so-called "moderates" systematically eliminated some political factions from public life, and there was a more general tendency on the part of any majority in power to disregard the rights and demands of political minorities. As a consequence, numerous nationalist leaders and local politicians, formerly followers of Patrice Lumumba, Antoine Gizenga, or Anicet Kashamura, were constantly harassed and eventually took refuge abroad, where they formed "governments of national liberation." The coalition of this "counter-elite" . . . with some rural leaders, unemployed youth, and the *Lumpenproletariat* of the cities allowed the rebellion to start. For a short time, it seemed that Fanon's prophecy would be realized. At the beginning of 1965, two-thirds of the Congo was in the hands of the insurgents. But neither they nor the professional politicians could subsequently gain a significant victory. Leaders of the rebellion, lacking leadership capacities and any revolutionary plans and perspective, lost their strength as soon as they began to expand, while the professional politicians, unable to understand that they were not the victims but the objects of the rebellion, continued to play the "game of politics." At the same time, changes were occurring within the Congolese military of immense—though little noticed— significance.

FROM THE FORCE PUBLIQUE TO THE NATIONAL CONGOLESE ARMY

Between the mutiny of the Force Publique and the military coup d'état of November 25, 1965, important transformations occurred within the Congolese army. The three most important were (1) the substitution of a trained army for a blind instrument of repression, (2) the birth of a military intelligentsia, and (3) the absorption of considerable technical resources by the army.

MILITARY RETRAINING

. . . Colonial forces were transformed into national armies by the training of an African career-officer cadre to replace European officers.

In the Congo, this process of conversion began, paradoxically, with the mutiny of the Force Publique in July, 1960. This revolt against their white officers brought about an immediate Africanization of the higher ranks—a striking contrast to most tropical states. Congolese soldiers dismissed their officers without warning and domocratically elected their own leaders. Recourse to an unusual procedure ran many risks, since the new officers derived authority from an unruly group of soldiers who could easily withdraw their support. In fact, only the semiautomatic reflex of obeying superior officers and the hesitation of the troops to utilize this newly acquired power prevented an era of anarchy. The soldiers chose officers according to the same criteria used by the Force Publique: training and rank. Command of the new army was taken over by former sergeants— the highest rank conferred on any Congolese during the colonial period— who succeeded in imposing authority upon the ranks without great difficulty.

As the institutional and political mechanisms under civilian control became ineffectual, the new army emerged as the sole force of relative unity. In this respect it benefited from Belgian policy which had, as a major objective, avoided introducing tribal differentiations into the Force Publique. It profited also from the excellent communications network built up by European officers which, ironically, had abetted the rapid progression of the mutiny across the country.

The unity of the army, however, was far from fully realized. Despite incessant propaganda of the army command attempting to isolate the military from politics, the Congolese national army could never escape external solicitations. From 1960 to 1962 it was cut into four rival groups, as previously noted: the Gizengist soldiers of Stanleyville, the Katangese gendarmes in Elisabethville, the pro-Kalonji militia in south Kasai, and the troops faithful to the central government stationed in Leopoldville and Equateur provinces. These divisions weighed heavily on the army's morale, particularly when the rebel troops were integrated at their former ranks when the various secessionist movements ended. To these horizontal differentiations were added vertical stratifications. Tensions resulted from the creation of an elite group within the army—the para-commandos, a sort of praetorian guard of General Mobutu. Further discontent occurred within the ranks after the massive promotion of officers and noncommissioned officers in June, 1964.

Despite these forces of disintegration, however, the Congolese national army demonstrated an *esprit de corps* that contrasted with the factionalism prevalent in politics. Among the soldiers, increased consciousness of their differences from the civilian sector grew. To quote the *Bulletin militaire*, the publication of the National Congolese Army:

The best remedy against subversion and corruption in the army is to isolate the military, while inciting within it a positive fanaticism in favor of both the honor of its work and the nobility of its ideal, to the great contempt of human masses deprived of any notion of discipline.

The military felt a profound scorn for politicians and civilians in general, who were considered directly responsible for political crises. The two groups spoke and lived a language with profound differences: the military spoke in terms of honor, discipline, sacrifice, and patriotism; the civilians propounded the concepts of justice, democracy, representation, and the rights of the population.

A NEW MILITARY ELITE

The second series of changes within the National Congolese Army resulted from the rise of a military intelligentsia. Immediately following the mutiny of the Force Publique, the soldiers elected as leaders a small group of sergeants who had been promoted to the rank of adjutant following a special training course in September, 1959. This group formed the nucleus of the high command of the Congolese army. In addition to this generation, who were imbued with the principles of the Force Publique, a new group of officers and noncommissioned officers progressively emerged. A large number of trainees was sent abroad, largely through the influence of General Mobutu and the massive assistance of international organizations and Western states. Considerable effort was devoted to training. In September, 1964, 664 officers and noncommissioned officers benefited from higher training in Belgian military schools. At the same time, 276 officers (compared with 183 in 1963) continued their training in Belgium. These figures are particularly significant when one realizes that the Congolese army included only 1308 officers and noncommissioned officers in 1964.

This new generation differed markedly from the preceding one. The older generation were practitioners of armed struggle, without extensive training; the new generation received training of significantly higher level in military academies. Tensions between these two generations have simmered outside general notice, and have greatly complicated the undertakings of the Mobutu government.

TECHNICAL CAPACITY

Finally, the Congolese army can be distinguished from the Force Publique on the level of technical capacity. Before independence, armaments were needed for the relatively small operations undertaken by the Force Publique. After crushing mutinies in 1895, 1897, 1900, and 1941, and stamping out various peasant uprisings as late as 1931, the Force Publique (like a simple force of gendarmes) carried out only small military expeditions within a limited area.

Even though it lacked men with conflict experience, the new army was equipped with some of the most modern armaments in Africa. The Congo benefited from considerable foreign aid. The United Nations command reorganized the Congolese army. Belgium, the United States, Israel, Canada, and Italy contributed to the new operational groups created within the Congolese army, including an air force, air transport, supplies, communications, river patrols, and the like. Foreign assistance also grew as a result of the campaigns against the Congolese rebels. . . .

Taking account of these different factors, the army lacked only the temptation to intervene in the political life of the country, despite the constant desire of its leaders to make of it a "great silent force." Its growing strength included, at the time of the coup d'état, a paratroop battalion, eight infantry battalions, three battalions of gendarmes, 11 commando groups of specialized volunteers, 20 companies of former Katangese gendarmes, a company of engineers, and a mobile machine gun squadron. The National Congolese Army included 26,400 soldiers, 900 noncommissioned officers, and 400 officers. . . .

These alterations helped transform the efficient but brutal Force Publique from a colonial army into a national army. Despite the shocks of the 1960–65 period—the collapse of government authority in many areas during the rebellion, the splitting and reamalgamation of the armed forces, the international repercussions of Congolese politics—the National Congolese Army emerged a far more powerful group. At the same time, many officers were confirmed in their scorn for politicians, whose machinations, self-enrichment, and concern with ethnic loyalties seemed to make them unfit for national office. The development of the National Congolese Army thus coincided with the breakdown of patrimonialism. The stage was set for the inauguration of a new regime, a new political generation.

THE SECOND POLITICAL GENERATION: RECENT TRENDS

Clearly, the 1965 coup d'état brought basic changes in the political stratification of the Congo. Although the National Congolese Army remains the central element of permanence and continuity, new strata have emerged whose political relevance was not meaningful before.

Describing the new regime is not an easy task. One thing is certain, however: military intervention by General Mobutu has *not* led to a military regime, in terms of a government directly controlled by the army. Since November, 1965, there has been no major shift in the goals, roles, and attitudes of the military vis-à-vis the society. . . .

To understand the significance of the 1965 coup d'état, we must compare it with Colonel Mobutu's first intervention in Congolese politics shortly after independence. In both cases, the army was threatened with division resulting from political and ethnic tensions; in both cases, the army had just painfully realized relative unity and stability after experiencing the 1960 mutiny and the 1964–65 rebellion. Both coups were self-protective reflexes on the part of a cohesive group.

The 1960 intervention occurred following a power struggle between President Joseph Kasavubu and Prime Minister Patrice Lumumba. The intervention must also be seen in the context of the mutiny of the former Force Publique, which had been steadily manipulated and corrupted through the interference of political factions.

On September 14, 1960, Colonel Mobutu decided to "neutralize" Lumumba and Kasavubu. Despite the interest he had shown for politics, Mobutu preferred the "techniques"

and "discipline" inculcated by seven years' service in the Force Publique. As a result of this preference, on September 19 he called upon university students and Congolese technicians (whether in the country or studying abroad) to aid him. This was the start of the "College des Commissaires Généraux," a transitional institution intended to fill the power vacuum before "national reconciliation" could be achieved. In reality, however, the unclear functions of the new College, the lack of cohesion among its members,* the large number of members (39 commissioners at the end of October) and the nearly complete absence of popular support, rapidly brought about its crumbling. As time passed, the political power which temporarily had been theirs escaped completely, and was divided among factions in Leopoldville: the followers of President Kasavubu, members of the Ileo government, the Sureté Nationale, the National Congolese Army, and politicians following their own leaders.

The coup d'état of November, 1965, occurred within a similar historical context: contention for control of power between the president and his prime minister, Moise Tshombe. On this occasion, however, the decision to intervene did not emanate directly from Mobutu. Although the exact circumstances surrounding the second

---

*Three divisions rapidly grew within the College: the technician-students, a politically neutral group; those who defended the intervention of Colonel Mobutu, a group composed of students already involved in political life (Ndele, Lihau, Mbeka, Cardoso, Mushiete); and political commissioners, such as Bomboko, Bolela, and Kazadi.

intervention remain unclear, it seems that the source of the coup was the army itself, whose higher officers deeply distrusted the men in the government. A political shift to the "left" by President Kasavubu following his return from the meeting of the Organization of African Unity in Accra (October, 1965), the menace that Kasavubu might dismiss the mercenaries who had given valuable support in the struggle against the rebels, a belief that the army had been the "savior of the Congolese nation," and fear of seeing the army manipulated by politicians again, were among the factors disquieting the higher echelons. A top-level meeting of officers the night before the coup indicated the collective army decision to intervene.

In the beginning, General Mobutu seemed to be and to act as the direct and personal emanation of a military junta, the high command of the NCA. In its name, he declared a five-year period of military rule. The influence of the junta appeared to be substantiated by three facts: (1) the nomination of military officers at the head of regions under constant political tensions (Luluabourg, Haut-Congo); (2) the use of special military courts of justice that had been previously settled to judge special military matters (e.g., desertion) for civilian purposes, such as the fight against corruption or political agitation; (3) the utilization of the army in some spectacular and symbolic operations of popular mobilization, such as the operation called "Retroussons les Manches" (Let's Roll up our Sleeves). It looked as if the military would be directly associated with the

executive and judiciary processes.

After a few months, however, General Mobutu appeared to stand apart from the army, particularly the high command. The principle of military noninvolvement in civil and political matters was reemphasized. Moveover, once the regime was firmly established, references to the high command as a "revolutionary instrument" disappeared. In October, 1966, Mobutu explicitly defined the role of the army as "an organism of execution operating in a strictly military context," not a "pressure group or a political assembly." In the provinces, the military commissioners were replaced by the former civil authorities. The special military courts of justice lost their meaning once the campaign against corruption was over. Finally, after a brief period of enthusiasm, the symbolic mobilization of the people by the army ended; probably tired, the soldiers returned to their garrisons. Mobutu himself began to wear civilian dress. The coup had occurred, the first ardor for change had passed. Mobutu sought to supplant the ineffectual patrimonial system by more efficient patterns of government.

A CAESARIST BUREAUCRACY

The current Congolese regime is best described as a "Caesarist" or "Napoleonic" bureaucracy. As such, it includes four basic features of the pure type of bureaucracy described by Weber: (1) Official business tends to be conducted more and more on a continuous basis. (2) It is conducted in relative secrecy by experts and in accordance with stipulated rational rules. (3) Officials' responsibilities and authority are part of a centralized hierarchy of authority. (4) Officials and other administrative employees do not own the resources necessary for the performance of their assigned functions.

In his analysis of rational legal authority, Weber was deeply concerned with the relationship between the struggle for power and the trend toward bureaucratization. He felt it indispensable to maintain some kind of equilibrium between them. Failure to achieve a balance meant that the bureaucracy had usurped political decision-making or, as Karl Mannheim put it, had turned "all problems of politics into problems of administration."

This trend toward "depoliticization" and the corollary emphasis on continuity of public office, hierarchy, and centralization are basic trends of the current Congolese regime. Not only has the politician been popularly designated as the source of all evil but politics itself has become the main evil to fight. The following decisions and events between 1965 and 1967 confirm these trends.

Declining Importance of Parliament

The definition of political goals and the choice of public officials are less and less entrusted to the changing and unstable representative institutions. One of the first public acts of President Mobutu was to limit the relative autonomy within which parliamentary institutions traditionally operated. Although the president kept parliament functioning and continued to formally recognize its prerogatives, he simultaneously decreed a five-year state of emergency applicable to the parliament and other institutions. It can be called upon to collaborate—it cannot decide any more. One of its most important privileges—the nomination and removal of cabinet members, a privilege which previously produced innumerable abuses—now is in the hands of the president.

Public debate has been discouraged. Political associations have been prohibited. The CVR (Corps des Volontaires de la République, an aggregate of youth associations backing Mobutu) has refused to define itself as a "political party" but rather as "the only flag of the new regime." CVR leaders do not emphasize elaboration of decisions or political education of the masses, but stress protection and surveillance. In brief, Mobutu has suspended politics—i.e., the development of regulative procedures, mechanisms and organizational patterns of communication, and setting up organs within which political struggle occurs. By stressing the elements of stability and permanence, he has shelved politics. Mobutu has failed to relate "tensional forces of society" to the political order.

Role of "Experts"

Governmental functions have increasingly been placed in the hands of "experts," acting in the shadow of the presidency and under its direct supervision. The progressive invasion of these experts, most of whom are depoliticized former university students, is illustrated by the decline of professional politicians in the cabinet between 1965 and 1967. In mid-1966, practically all ministerial portfolios were in the hands of professional politicians, many of whom belonged to the second wave of politicians elected in 1965. At the end of 1966, there were nine technicians and university students and 12 politicians in the government; at the end of 1967, there were 13 university and technical school graduates in the 22-member cabinet.

In November, 1966, President Mobutu created the presidential cabinet, intended in theory to assist and advise him on administrative affairs. In fact, its role goes further than that. It has become the compulsory channel for all communications between the ministries and the presidency, thereby making it an organism of decision rather than consultation. The presidential cabinet aims at "redefining the new civil order, rationalizing the institutional structures of the state and creating better standards of living for the population by an increase of the production and a more equal redistribution of the Gross National Product." It operates in complete secrecy, and is, in effect, a kind of private fortress which members of the government and parliament tried to penetrate in vain.

Centralization of Power

Parallel to the increasing importance played by the experts was an accelerating centralization of power. At the end of 1966, President Mobutu concentrated the functions of chief of state and head of the government in his hands. He could directly act upon mass media through a high commissariat of information, led by his personal friend, Jean-Jacques Kande. He kept the department of defense under his aegis and controlled the national security services through Colonel Singa and his agents in the provinces. In the realm of foreign policy, he created a system of personal representatives, resident ministers, and military attachés intimately acquainted with him. Finally, the president reduced the number of provinces and reimposed the authority of the central government upon them. This process was effected in two phases. In March, 1966, the president asked the parliament to prepare a bill aiming at "a valid administrative restructuring of our country." After a series of controversies among congressmen and senators, the number of provinces was reduced from 21 to 14, then to 12. Nine months later, due to the suspected participation of four governors in the mutiny of the Katangese troops at Kisangani (July–September, 1966), President Mobutu reduced the number to 8.

Role of Governors

At the same time, Mobutu took an unexpected measure. Provincial governors became state commissioners designated by the president of the republic during his term of office. No governor would work in his province of origin. This measure had the consequence of cutting the highest provincial authority from his popular and tribal basis. In Weberian terms, it meant that each governor, transferred to an alien territory, no longer owned the political resources previously necessary for maintaining himself in power; the executive office was now separated from the household and the private life of the ruler. This decision brought about one of the deepest changes in the institutional structures of the Congo. The provinces became mere administrative entities again. In the report accompanying the new law, the minister of internal affairs, Etienne Tshisekedi, concluded:

Thus, one paradoxically comes back again to the administrative structures existing before June 30, 1960, that is, a central and strong authority basing itself on decentralized provincial administrations which realize through district commissioners and territorial administrators all the options of economic and social progress.

Caesarism

The parallel with the former Belgian bureaucracy is tempting. Centralization, hierarchy, permanence, and expertise were major structural features of the colonial bureaucracy. Yet the setting in which the colonial administration operated was substantially different, owing to racial domination by a determined minority. The setting differed as well in the importance of personal attachments. As Weber noted, one of the main consequences of bureaucratic development in a modern environment is depersonalization.

When fully developed, bureaucracy stands in a specific sense under the principle of "sine ira ac studio." Its specific nature, which is welcomed by capitalism, develops

the more completely it succeeds in eliminating from official business love, hatred, and all purely *personal, irrational and emotional* elements which escape calculation. This is the specific nature of bureaucracy and it is appraised as its special virtue.

The Mobutu regime has not removed the personal and emotional elements cited by Weber. Although the president has made a serious effort to detribalize the society by administrative measures, his government is highly personalized. Personalization through patrimonial relationships is being transformed into personalization by attachment to the president. Mobutu has tried hard to introduce charismatic elements in his politics, especially by claiming to be the spiritual successor of Patrice Lumumba and by intimately associating his person to that of the Congolese people. "To deceive the people is to deceive me" is a favorite expression he uses in his speeches. The mass media, and especially the CVR, have echoed this policy by starting a campaign aiming at proclaiming the president "second national hero of the republic." Moreover, for the first time in the history of the Congo, the president traveled across the country many times to reinforce his popular image.

But it is primarily emotional and ideological commitments that best characterize the present regime. The dominant themes of the Mobutu government during 1966 and 1967 were highly moralizing and nationalistic. Initially, a generalized attack was launched against the professional politician whose image was associated with "corruption, treason, exploitation." When this campaign was over, the president used themes linked with the success of Lumumbism in the 1960's: complete decolonization, national dignity, and reduction of private foreign power in the Congo. From April, 1966, the theme of economic independence and Congolese control of the economy became predominant. This theme coincided with the givens of the Congolese sociopolitical setting: (1) mass expectations of a new independence; (2) pressures exercised by the upper strata of the population (middle classes, university students, bureaucrats) for full economic "congolization" to bring more rapid and deeper socioeconomic achievement; (3) the necessity for the power structure to counterattack the challenge launched by the 1964 popular uprising. Prestigious symbols, such as a new unit of currency (the "Zaire"), spectacular ceremonies, use of honorific titles, and deeper involvement in pan-Africanism, further indicated the national ends sought by the Mobutu government.

SOCIOPOLITICAL FORCES BACKING THE REGIME

Any political system—traditional, transitional, or modern—must secure some degree of internal support among several strata of the population in order to survive, let alone achieve political stability. In the Mobutu government, as in previous Congolese regimes, the army remains the central element of coercion. A second continuity appears in the ideological realm where, as previously mentioned, the shadow of Patrice Lumumba continues to determine the identifications of the ruling elite. Discontinuities appear in the diminished role played by a large segment of the political bourgeoisie and in the emergence of urban strata—the youth and the university student—who previously had not full shared the benefits of independence.

The Army

The Congolese regime, as previously mentioned, is not an out-and-out military government. Relations between President Mobutu and the NCA remain confused. Two examples demonstrate the ambiguous character of these relations: the "Pentecost plot" shows the Army as the most zealous watchdog of its unity and security; the "Mulamba affair" illustrates how President Mobutu is at times the prisoner of internal rivalries among the military rank and file.

On May 30, 1966, President Mobutu sent a personal message to the population:

Tonight, a plot against me and the new regime has been hatched by some irresponsible politicians. They have been arrested and will be indicted for high treason. This plot has been thwarted thanks to the vigilance and loyalty of the National Congolese Army.

Four persons were arrested: Evariste Kimba, who had been prime minister for three months in 1965; Jerome Anany, former minister of defense in 1964; Alexandre Mahamba, former minister of land from 1960 to 1961; and Emmanuel Bamba, former minister of finance and leader of a well-known Kimbanguist church. The "Pentecost plot," as it was later called, remains unreal for many observers. The four politicians allegedly involved had no popularity even in their regions of origin; no weapons or significant documents were ever seized; apparently the purported conspirators held very few meetings. On the other hand, the plotters reportedly came into contact with many military officers. According to official statements, one of them, Major Efomi, revealed the plot to both Colonel Bangala, governor of Kinshasa, and General Mobutu. A meeting of Colonel Bangala, other high-ranking officers, and the conspirators was arranged, at the end of which the four politicians were arrested. Although all the circumstances are not completely clear, the best explanation is that the plot was organized and dramatized by army officers to crush a very limited opposition coming from some politicians who had complained about the government's lack of regional representativeness. From a single political discontent, the army conjured up a conspiracy against the regime and its head.

The role of Mobutu as a prisoner of his army was made particularly clear when he dismissed Prime Minister Colonel Leonard Mulamba in October, 1966. During the rebellion, Mulamba had gained a reputation of bravery, even invincibility, among his troops. He stood in the front ranks to defend Bukavu against a heavy attack by the insurgents, while most of the NCA was in full flight. This was the first real battle won by the army without the help of white mercenaries. Mulamba naturally became one of the most popular figures in the Congo and was designated prime minister in November, 1965. The army was reluctant to support the rapid rise of this relatively young officer, however. Specific grievances openly expressed by the military high command concerned his attitude toward the Katangese mutiny. Mulamba was accused explicitly by Lieutenant Colonel Malila, chief of staff of the NCA, of having supported the rebels, or at least of having prevented the army from eliminating the mutineers by force. Mobutu tried to save his prime minister in vain. Even the ministry of defense was denied Mulamba by the military high command.

The Youth and the CVR

Since the military coup, Mobutu has received impressive support from youth organizations. In January, 1966, these groups joined to form the CVR. This movement has never tried to rally political support. Rather, it has served primarily as an organization of detection, parallel to the national security services controlled by military officers. During 1966 and 1967, the CVR served as a subsidiary instrument for the city police or as a primitive intelligence service to spy on foreigners and politicians suspected by the regime.

The spontaneous growth of the CVR and the eruption of youth into the political stage are rooted in the sociological role of youth and in the changing role of politicians. Both the frustrations and political awareness of youth have been rising. Nearly half of the population is less than 15 years old. Before independence, opportunities—education, employment—existed for them. After 1960, however, the situation deteriorated rapidly. The youngest found fewer schools waiting for them; the older ones found fewer jobs. Many of them found the only possible outlet in politics.

Since independence, local and national parties and, in some instances, the politicians themselves have recruited bodyguards among the urban youth. These young people, most of whom left school after primary education, played a limited role as a pressure group. They lived under the shadow of patrons, parties, or other political associations, and formed, in a sense, manpower available for electoral purposes. When parties were declared illegal, when the image of the politician became equated with corruption and dishonesty, and when it became clear that Mobutu would rule without permitting civil opposition, these unemployed young people spontaneously gathered together. . . .

TENTATIVE CONCLUSIONS

To conclude, I will rephrase the Congolese political process in terms of four concepts: power, authority, force, and influence. Power is a rela-

tion involving both a conflict of interests or values and the threat of sanctions, i.e., any promised reward or penalty by which a structure can maintain effective control over policy. Authority refers to both the source and the restraint upon the exercise of power or, in other words, to the legitimacy of political structures. Force, contrary to power, radically reduces the scope of decision-making since the subject has no choice as to course of action. Finally, influence like power has both rational and relational attributes; influence differs in that potential sanctions are not utilized.

The picture of Congolese politics drawn in this chapter shows that no autonomous structures of either power or authority have emerged. Instead, under the two political generations, decision-making has been carried out by force, violence, and influence. The patrimonial rulers initially monopolized public offices; contrary to traditional patrimonialism, however, they lacked authoritarian and centralized power of command. This group, torn by internal struggles, could not control events through meaningful sanctions. It failed to transfer the previous agreement on the need for independence to new, legitimized goals. Since the arrival of the second political generation, dominated by a Caesarist bureaucracy, the Congolese political process has shown increasing rationality and coherence. However, the legitimacy of the regime has been based on short-lived elements of emotions and personalization—in short, upon influence. Outside eco-

nomic and political agencies, partic- appeal among the rural masses, to
ularly major mining and financial create a new revolutionary leadership,
interests, the United Nations, and and to develop an ideology of political
powerful states linked to the Congo by and socioeconomic development; as
bilateral treaties continue to act in a result, its initial strength degenerated
the periphery of the sociopolitical into sheer violence.
realm; since they have no direct The Congo under President Mobutu
access to sanctions and legitimacy, thus continues to seek for a political
they rely upon influence and informal process based upon power and au-
pressures. Finally, the National Con- thority. Until the legitimacy of nation-
golese Army has remained an instru- al political structures is assured,
ment of coercion. The 1964–65 rebel- instability and uncertainty will con-
lion failed to rationalize its tremendous tinue to plague the country.

As the impact of Western values and traditions on the African military has
diminished over time, other observers have come to question the importance of the colonial experience in defining praetorianism in Africa. The
further into the past the colonial era recedes, the more to the fore come
traditional patterns of rulership. Ali Mazrui has asked:

What happens when a military establishment, based on Western organizational
concepts and conditioned by a Western approach to military professionalism,
seeks to operate in the culturally different conditions of African societies? Certainly, the military profession in its modern forms in African countries has overwhelmingly borne the stamp of the metropolitan power. In Uganda the organization of the armed forces was solidly patterned upon the British model. The
whole military ritual, including the pattern of drill, the categories and terminology of ranks, and the very music of the armed forces, all remained defiantly
British in tone and style.

The upholding of these rituals and British traditions could be seen as a form
of conservatism. But, clearly, in relation to the values of African societies, such
exercises in Anglocentric militarism are by definition a departure from the indigenous normative order, rather than an exercise in its conservation.

In a situation where the soldiers are recruited from among the least westernized
of former colonial subjects—at times directly from the narrow world of villagers
and their simple beliefs—this distinction between the military establishment as a
modern organization and the individual soldier as a traditionalist could have
considerable dialectical considerations.

. . . colonial recruiting officers [were] more inclined toward the least literate
of their subjects for use in the armed forces. . . . The less educated Africans
were in their general orientation and attitude more rural than the educated.

It is true that once the young rustic is in the army, he becomes subject to certain westernizing influences. After all, as I have indicated, the army is still substantially organized on the basis of a Western model, utilizes Western military technology, and is partly influenced by Western military values.

Many of the first wave of African rulers were in some sense products of the intellectualization of political culture in the colonies. A few of these leaders, including such figures as Kwame Nkrumah and Milton Obote, were basically intellectuals in their capacity to be fascinated by ideas and in their ability to handle some of those ideas effectively. Some of the soldiers who have replaced them bear a more modest impact of Western intellectualization than they did.

On balance, the level of political brutality and violent sanctions against offenders has been higher under military rule in countries like the Central African Republic, Uganda, and, in a special sense, even Nigeria. The invocation of physical force has tended to increase in such countries. It is, therefore, not clear why we should not regard it as a moral cost when men specialized in a profession of violence and combat assume supreme authority.

Many commentators on African behavior have too readily assumed that the reference point for African soldiers was always and inevitably the imperial model. But is the behavior of African privates in Nigeria or Uganda really like the behavior of British privates, or does it bear closer affinity to the behavior of traditional warriors? Is the soldier in Zaire more reminiscent of a Belgian soldier than of a precolonial Congo or Luba warrior?*

Michael Lofchie argues that the time has come to cease looking for explanations of the praetorian nature of African armies in the tribal or colonial past, and to begin examining the class basis of present African societies to discover the wellsprings of intervention. In Uganda, he tries to demonstrate, the military was a high-income group in a poor agricultural society. Its overriding *political interest* in preserving its economic privileges led it to oppose President Obote's "Move to the Left." From the standpoint of Uganda's military elite, the move to the left "represented a presidential decision to break the uneasy, but long-standing *quid pro quo* between the military and the state, a relationship in which the military had, in effect, been paid off not to assume full control of the society."

The prognosis then, in Africa, can only be for further military intervention and further evidence of the military's capacity merely to administer the state rather than truly to govern it.

*Ali Mazrui, "Soldiers as Traditionalizers: Military Rule and the Re-Africanization of Africa," *World Politics* (1976), pp. 250–65.

Michael F. Lofchie

The Uganda Coup—Class Action by the Military

[Unlike Zaire, Uganda appeared to have enjoyed six years of relatively stable one-party government before Idi Amin overthrew the government of Milton Obote in January 1971. The only instability occurred in 1966, when the Ugandan army invaded the Kingdom of Buganda and removed the leader (the Kabaka) in support of President Obote.]

There will undoubtedly be many interpretations of the Uganda coup. The purpose of this article is merely to suggest one and, on the basis of available, though admittedly incomplete evidence, to outline a case for its plausibility. The central argument is as follows. The Uganda army can be best understood as a kind of economic class, an élite stratum with a set of economic interests to protect. The coup of January 1971 was the army's political response to an increasingly socialist régime whose equalitarian domestic policies posed more and more of a threat to the military's economic privileges.

No other explanation accounts adequately for two paradoxical aspects of the coup. Why should an army whose officers and rank and file were drawn overwhelmingly from

From Michael F. Lofchie, "The Uganda Coup—Class Action by the Military," Journal of Modern African Studies 10 (1972): 19–35, by permission of Cambridge University Press.

sections of the society loyal to the régime, and which had in fact constituted one of the Governments' principal bases of support, turn against political authorities with whom it had been closely identified? Secondly, how is it possible to understand the new social basis of political power in Uganda?—a coalition which joins an officer corps, drawn almost entirely from the economically less-developed northern section of the country, with a civil servant and coffee-growing élite, drawn from the most wealthy region of Uganda, the districts of Buganda.

THE MILITARY AS A SOCIAL CLASS

The class character of the Uganda military helps to answer both questions. All three of these groups had one powerfu lcommon denominator— their high-income status in a generally poor agricultural society. Thus, they shared a common interest in opposing a government intent on equalitarian change. Their economic commonality has over-ridden regional and ethnic differences and, for the time being at least, created the basis for a stable political alliance.

The Uganda army was, of course, not an economic class in the strict sense of the term. For example, it had no readily identifiable position in the process of production. It neither owned nor controlled any important sector of the economy, nor, despite the fact that all soldiers were wage-earners, could it be considered an industrial or agricultural work-force. The class character of the Uganda army stemmed, rather, from the fact that, since the mutiny of January 1964, Uganda soldiers had come to constitute more and more of an economically privileged stratum, enjoying high salaries and lavish fringe benefits in a society where the average annual income *per capita* was less than $20. Its overriding political interest lay in preserving this position. Its power stemmed from its control of the means of violence.

Successive increases in salary scales, accompanied by a policy of rapid promotion, placed soldiers among the highest-paid ranks of Uganda society, on a par with civil servants. The officer corps, in particular, enjoyed a level of income directly comparable to that of the highest-ranking ministerial officials, such as permanent secretaries. As the military came to constitute a privileged element in the society, it became progressively more differentiated from the political loyalties and identifications of the various regions and ethnic groups from where the majority of its members had been recruited. Its economic stake in opposition to a socialist régime became identical to that of the well-to-do southern coffee planters, and to that of high-ranking Uganda civil servants, many of whom had close family ties with the coffee-growing élite. The common bond between these groups was largely a negative one: opposition to Uganda's 'Move To The Left'; a

set of presidentially articulated policies which had strong redistributive and social equalitarian implications. Each of the three principal groups which cooperate in the present Government —the military (particularly the officer corps), the civil servants, and the southern coffee farmers—stood to lose if a policy of egalitarianism was implemented.

The Uganda army's emergence as a privileged and politically powerful stratum in the society dates from the mutiny of January 1964. . . .

The principal feature of the Uganda Government's response to the 1964 mutiny was an apparent belief on the part of the political leaders that the only way to forestall the mutiny from turning into a full *coup d'état* was to give the army everything it wanted. Only a few of the mutineers were arrested for punishment and most of these were quickly released. Moreover, virtually all of their major demands were acceded to. One of these was for an immediate Africanisation of the officer corps. The British officers were transformed immediately into advisors and then, by August of that year, dismissed completely. Non-commissioned officers were promoted from the ranks, resulting in an officer corps of strikingly limited formal education. Partially as a result, Uganda officers have always been highly defensive of their position. The Uganda Government was chronically unsuccessful in leavening this rough-and-ready élite with professionally trained officers. In 1964 and 1965, the two years following the mutinies, Uganda sent only 16 officer cadets for training in Britain as contrasted with 89 from

Kenya and 59 from Tanzania. Moreover, due to the defensiveness of the officers just promoted from the ranks, very few of these were ever actually able to 'matriculate' into the army.

Perhaps most important, the Government acceded to the army's demand for immediate increases in salary and benefits, a situation which was to be repeated time and time again during the next seven years. . . . Certain military details are, of course, a state secret, but visual observations conveyed an unmistakable impression that, at its lowest ranks, the Uganda army had become an organisation of sergeants and privates There seems to have been a tendency for new recruits, enlisted at the rank of private, to be promoted quickly over the rank of corporal to that of sergeant. If correct, this interpretation suggests a special dimension to any analysis of the Uganda army as an economically differentiated stratum of the society. Not only is the overall salary scale for Uganda soldiers higher than that for other East African armies at the non-commissioned level, but vastly disproportionate numbers seem to have been clustered towards the upper reaches of the non-commissioned ranks. The Uganda army was not an organisation of relatively low-paid privates and corporals, but of quite well-paid sergeants and warrant officers. The salaries of even the lowest paid soldiers exceeded the average income *per capita* for other Africans in the country by a factor of between fifteen and thirty times.

In the context of a generally poor agricultural society, Uganda soldiers at all ranks were wealthy individuals.

If additional military benefits such as housing, food, medical treatment, uniforms, insurance and family allowances are taken into account, the material discrepancy between a Ugandan soldier and an average Ugandan citizen is little short of extraordinary. It amounts to a difference between opposed social classes: on the one hand, a professional military class receiving, by local standards, an enormously high income in cash and benefits; on the other, a society composed predominantly of small peasant farmers earning little, if anything, in the way of cash income, and enjoying few material income supplements.

There is nothing whatsoever surprising about the fact that an army in this situation should find itself in direct political antagonism to a political leader whose primary basis of social support lay among the poorer sections of the peasantry and who, reflecting the basic interests of his constituency, was increasingly committed to a more equalitarian distribution of the national wealth. The economic interests of the military in enhancing its income in salary and benefits were in direct contradiction to those of the majority of the society in economic redistribution and greater social equality.

THE ARMY BUDGET AND CORRUPTION

Two additional features of the army's economic position in Uganda reinforced its political characteristic as a corporate entity with interests that set it apart from the majority of the population: its annual budgetary allocation and its rampant corruption.

By 1968 the Ministry of Defence allocation was 10·2 per cent of the national budget, a figure that contrasts significantly with the 6·9 per cent of annual expenditures allocated to defence in Kenya, and even more so with the 3·8 per cent allocated to this purpose in Tanzania. Uganda spent more than £17 million on its military establishment in that year, an amount nearly equal to the combined military expenditures of Kenya and Tanzania. When linked with the inflated pay scales of the army, these figures indicate the extent to which the Uganda military had been able to establish an extortionary relationship to the state. Since the threat of mutiny, or worse, had not been dispelled by the Government's response to the 1964 insurrection, it remained an ever-present kind of 'mood music' in the background of Uganda politics. Its effect was to enable the military to make exhorbitant financial demands on the society and, in the context of a politically weak régime, to have these accepted.

The army's capacity to engage in financially irresponsible behaviour with impunity was nowhere so clearly evident as in the case of fiscal corruption within the military establishment. In his speech from Dar es Salaam immediately after the coup, Milton Obote placed the blame squarely on corruption:

There was a person very close to Major General Amin as the commander of the [Jinja] Depot; he ordered or is alleged to have ordered materials worth Shs 40,000,-000 [approximately $6 million]. There are no documents, no copies of the invoices, no copies of any delivery note . . . On the same day I left for Singapore, I asked General Amin, on my return, to give me a written report on how the Shs 40,000,000 was to be spent. I have no doubts at all that what is now developing in Uganda is another attempt to hide the loss of Shs 40,000,000 and an attempt to prevent me from getting back to the country and punish the culprits.

The post-regnum speech of a deposed President can, of course, easily be dismissed as an attempt to castigate the dubious morality of his successors and, by implication, to vindicate his own administration. If it were not for the availability of additional, more authoritative evidence of corruption, it might be necessary to disregard Obote's allegations as self-justifying. . . .

To sum up the economic argument to this point, the Uganda army had at least three economic interests to protect against a reform-minded President. First, it enjoyed an unusually high salary scale at the non-commissioned ranks, which, together with a policy of rapid promotion and considerable additional benefits, resulted in placing members of the army in the highest-paid strata of the society. Secondly, the military as a whole received a comparatively large share of the national budget. The more forward-looking officers could not have avoided the conclusion that a President intent on improving the level of national social services would, at some point, seek to cut into military funds as a means of doing so, Finally, there were obviously some officers, perhaps only a handful, who were engaged in illegal profiteering through the manipulation of military accounts. If it is true that President Obote had indicated his intention to take steps against corruption, this group would have an immediate interest in overturning the régime.

ADDITIONAL TENSIONS WITHIN THE ARMY

It is very rarely the case that any militarly coup stems from a single cause, and it is not the purpose of this analysis to stress a strictly economic argument. The economic interests of the military were not the sole reason for the seizure of power but, in the context of a régime moving rapidly to the left, they were primary. At least three additional factors operating within the military are also relevant.

The first of these might be called the precedent of the 1964 mutiny. Significant numbers of the highest officers were deeply aware that they owed their positions to a successful semi-insurrection against the state and, from their standpoint, the lesson was still valid: the Uganda Government was simply not strong enough to prevent a determined army from having its way. The 1964 officers were also naturally prone to a good deal of insecurity. Since they held their positions almost entirely as a result of the army's ability to hold the Government at bay, their status was in serious jeopardy if Obote should ever gain sufficient strength to introduce military reform. . . .

Even the army's occupation of Buganda was a source of irritation to military pride. This may at first seem paradoxical, given their defeat of the Buganda forces in late May 1966. Many Baganda, however, took the view that the battle at the Kabaka's Palace was not a defeat but a victory. In their view, the purpose for which the Kabaka's forces fought was to resist the Uganda army long enough to enable the Kabaka to escape, and only when this purpose had been achieved did they surrender. The widespread nature of this view among Baganda, and its persistence even after several years of military occupation, meant that the Uganda army found itself in the awkward position of exercising military rule among a people who refused to accept their own defeat. The one battle in which the army might have taken pride as a clear-cut victory was, instead, turned by popular mythology into a kind of defeat, and became an additional source of resentment and frustration. . . .

But military coups rarely take place for purely internal reasons. Elements of dissatisfaction within an army almost invariably combine with a reaction to some aspect of the broader political context. Thus the fundamental explanation of a military coup must lie in the rather imprecise chemistry of interaction between a military and the government of which it is a part.

UGANDA'S MOVE TO THE LEFT

The political climate of Uganda during the year or so preceding the coup was dominated by a dramatic change in ideological direction on the part of the régime. In late October 1969 President Obote issued the first of a series of five documents intended to lay the theoretical basis for a radicalisation of the society. Only 15 months elapsed between the publication of *The Common Man's Charter* and the military coup, and during this period little could actually be done to implement the society's leftward movement. . . .

The important feature of the 'Move To The Left' lay in what it represented to the military establishment. *The Common Man's Charter*, and the outpouring of documents which followed it, graphically symbolised the President's determination to eliminate the vast inequalities which had been inherited from the colonial and early independence periods, and to move the society in an equalitarian direction. This was to be accomplished through a major redistribution of wealth and services. Obote was known to have long considered himself a radical political figure and, in recent years, had developed a strong personal commitment to President Nyerere of Tanzania, and to the innovative social policies of the Tanzanian Government. From the standpoint of Uganda's military élite, the 'Move To The Left' had enormous significance as a portent of future change. It represented a presidential decision to break the uneasy, but long-standing, *quid pro quo* between the military and the state, a relationship in which the military had, in effect, been paid-off not to assume full control of the society.

The 'Move To The Left', then, placed the Government on an economic collision course with the army. To the extent that Obote's T.A.N.U. sympathies were suspected by the soldiers, the Tanzanian pattern of military policy was seen as an imminent possibility for Uganda. This too signified a substantial reduction in the army's material perquisites. It would also entail a drastic transformation in their political role from the heroics of border warfare (however frustrating to the army itself) to the rather more mundane tasks of self-help economics, such as road-building and school construction. If the 'Move To The Left' was allowed to continue, it spelt an end to the military's position as an economically privileged and politically inviolable corporate entity.

The Government's critical source of weakness lay in its institutional fragility. The U.P.C. had never been an effectively organised political movement and was, in fact, little more than a congeries of loosely associated and sometimes warring factions. Colin Leys has spoken of the U.P.C. as 'really a coalition of local organisations, or rather local political systems, each with its own political élite, including a small number of leaders operating at the national level.'* This condition prevailed even in the northern part of the country where the party was fairly popular. In meant that the U.P.C. was chronically unable to organise its popular support into an integrated political movement. Even in Lango, the home district of the President, there were in 1965 only about 2,000 paid-up party members out of a population of more than

*Colin Leys, *Politicians and Policies: an essay on politics in Acholi, Uganda*, 1962–65 (Nairobi, 1967), p. 10.

300,000. The internal factionalism and organisational immobility of the U.P.C. rendered it highly vulnerable to any attempted coup. Like the Government of which it was a part, the party was wholly unable to act decisively in the moment of crisis.

An impending reform of the party organisation may have figured prominently in the timing of the coup. For while it would have taken Obote a number of years to reorganise the class structure and income distribution patterns of Uganda, there was strong likelihood of a more immediate overhaul of the U.P.C., in an attempt to transform it into a genuinely national organisation. The purpose of a rather complicated set of electoral arrangements for a general election to be held during 1971 was to reduce the localised parochial basis of party leadership, and to lay the groundwork for the formation of a unified one-party state. The most significant feature of the electoral format was that each candidate for the National Assembly would be required to compete in four separate constituencies, one in each of the major regions of the country. A special method of calculating election results was devised to prevent a candidate from winning merely by compiling an overwhelming plurality in his home district. Since the implementation of these electoral plans was barely begun when the coup occurred, it is difficult to assess whether they would have accomplished the intended results.

The important point, however, is that the Government's plans for a general election placed the military, to some extent, in a now-or-never posi-tion. For, if a truly national election could be held, it would endow the regime with heightened legitimacy, and, for this reason, would have made it impossible for any coup staged after the election to claim overwhelming popular approval. The possibility of a military coup had been widely rumoured in Uganda for a number of years. Military men involved in discussing the feasibility of such a move would almost certainly have been aware of the need to execute a coup before the Government could gain an electoral consensus.

An additional source of institutional weakness for the Obote Government lay in the indifferent loyalty of the bureaucracy. The vast majority of higher civil servants in Uganda were from the southern districts of the country, where the President and the U.P.C. had never been especially popular. This situation grew worse after 1966 when the Government of the Kingdom of Buganda was dismantled and large numbers of Buganda civil servants were absorbed into the central Government. Many members of this group had suffered personal or family loss under the military occupation of Buganda, an experience which was often attributed to hostility on the part of Obote towards the Baganda. Large numbers of Baganda civil servants also had close family ties to the well-to-do coffee planters, a group which felt economically jeopardised by Obote's determination to redistribute more of the wealth of the country to the poorer northern regions. There was probably very little that the bureaucracy could have done to prevent a military coup, even if it had been politically sympathetic to the President. Its attitudes were significant, however, in explaining the ease with which the military was able to assume full and quick control of the government apparatus.

The overall picture of Uganda on the eve of the coup is that of a President virtually isolated from all the major political forces. Unable to depend upon a fragmented and desultory party organisation, unsupported by civil servants who were often critical of him and of his policies, and confronted with an overweening military establishment visibly hostile to his social equalitarianism, Obote's hold on political power was dependent almost solely on his own political dexterity. Out of the country, he was deprived of the opportunity to exercise even this means of political survival. . . .

[The results of the 1971 coup in Uganda are all too well known. General Amin proved to be brutal, cunning, and authoritarian. His forays into foreign policy with Israeli, Libyan, and Palestinian leaders pale in importance to the havoc that has been wrought within Uganda, where thousands have disappeared, been murdered, or hastened into exile. Although Uganda has returned to civilian rule, the Ugandan economy is not likely to recover from military extravagance and mismanagement for a long time.]

THE MILITARY AND POLITICS IN ASIA

There are several ways to classify Asian political systems. Geographically there is East Asia, comprised of Japan, China, Korea, and Formosa. Southeast Asia includes the states of Indonesia, Malaysia, Vietnam, Cambodia, Laos, Thailand, Burma, and the Philippines. South Asia is the Indian subcontinent: India, Pakistan, Bangladesh, Nepal, and Sri Lanka (formerly Ceylon). The only democratic regimes in Asia are Japan and India. Autocracy, authoritarianism, and praetorianism on the whole characterize the majority of Asian states. China, Vietnam, North Korea, Cambodia, and Laos are Communist authoritarian systems. Thailand, Burma, Indonesia, and Pakistan are ruled by praetorian regimes. The Philippines and Singapore are right-of-center authoritarian ruled regimes, while Sri Lanka is a leftist autocracy. The politics of Asia, especially of South and Southeast Asia, clearly mirror the multiracial composition of South Asian societies. Ethnicity, language groups, religion, and race influence the political behavior, arrangements, and procedures of these societies. Polyglot societies naturally produce different types of political order and arrangements of civil-military relations.

Japan, the most developed Asian society (like China, it is cohesive in race, religion, and language), did experience a considerable era of praetorian rule between 1931 and 1945. The displacement of Taisho democracy by nationalist and xenophobic regimes concerned with national defense, imperial conquest, and political-economic coprosperity lifted national security above diplomacy and politics. The unitary Meiji state and its successors reflected the cohesive homogenous nature of Japanese society and its politics. Yet the military intervened as it did elsewhere in homogenous societies whose modern political structure and leaders were not successful in providing a continuity and stability to civic political order (i.e., Germany and France, as analyzed earlier).

Amos Perlmutter

Japan: Soldiers Without a State

To Harold Lasswell, Japan of the 1930s was the epitome of military totalitarianism, the garrison state par excellence, the "state within the state" of the technician of violence. Yet most, if not all, of the recent studies of Japan's so-called fascist and militarist epoch conclusively demonstrate both the conceptual and the empirical fallacy of the garrison-state idea when deduced from or applied to Japan. The fact is that Lasswell mistakenly identified the technician of violence as the high priest of totalitarianism. A careful analysis reveals that the grand inquisitors and villains of the garrison state were actually the civilian ideologues and demagogues, the romantic primitivists of Japan (and of Nazi Germany, for that matter).

The history of modern Japan began with two fundamental transformations: the emergence of centralized

From Amos Perlmutter, The Military and Politics in Modern Times (New Haven, 1977), pp. 69–75, by permission of Yale University Press.

feudalism (the Tokugawa shogunate, 1600–1867) and the response to the challenge of foreign stimuli (the Meiji Restoration, 1868–1912).

Hideyoshi had begun to unify Japan in the late sixteenth century, and his efforts were continued by his adopted son Ieyasu, who founded the Tokugawa shogunate in 1600. The shogun ruled through a central administration, the Bakufu, a superfeudal state. During the Tokugawa period, which was one of prolonged peace, the military class, the samurai, developed new bureaucratic, administrative, and commercial talents. The rise of Bushido (swordsmanship) and Confucianism and the decline of Buddhism were contemporary with monetary and administrative reforms. Urbanization, the growth of a money economy, and the rise of "Dutch" and "Portuguese" schools—in other words, the stimuli of rationalism and the Western style of administrative organization—resulted in the Meiji Restoration of 1868. The Meiji Restoration represented the end of military feudalism and the beginning of the development of a centralized, modern nation-state.

Civil-military relations after the Meiji Restoration can be explained by two related factors: (1) the unsuccessful efforts of alienated and declining segments of the samurai to reestablish themselves as the leading political elite, and (2) the failure to create a strong and centralized state. As Meiji Japan moved away from feudalism, the military class became even more alienated. Although the bulk of the Meiji modernist elite was recruited from the samurai class, the samurai traditionalists were persistently antireformist. The friction between the founders and followers of the Meiji system and their radical, rural, and xenophobic opponents ended in the 1930s in an unholy alliance between the mystical nationalists and the alienated military class, a coalition that perpetrated the calamity of the China War of 1937 and the attack on Pearl Harbor. . . .

THE "IMPOTENCE" OF THE MEIJI STATE

When the emperor returned to power in 1968, the shogunate was theoretically required to relinquish its political power to him, because legitimacy resided in the imperial institution. However, the Meiji Restoration demonstrates instead the introduction of Weberian traditionalist legitimization for the purpose of organizing, developing, and enhancing a modern, rational, and bureaucratic order. "Surely there is no more amazing instance in world history of the use of traditionalist means to radical ends than when the leaders of early Meiji masked the political changes which they had made with the label of an 'imperial restoration.'" While the Tokugawa concept of the emperor had been one of limitation—a passive figure whose political symbolism masked his impotence—Meiji loyalists symbolically assigned political power to the emperor. The *exercise* of that power, however, was entrusted to other agencies, the Genro (senate), the cabinet, and the Meiji oligarchs.

To the Meiji oligarchs, harmony between the throne and government was a matter of natural law. The emperor's restoration settled the matter of legitimacy; clearly it rested with the throne. But "if the emperors of late nineteenth and early twentieth century Japan were not merely figureheads, neither were they the actual rulers of the country." The Meiji oligarchs left the question of who was to rule on behalf of imperial authority unanswered.

The Meiji's twentieth-century successors did not accept their organic concept of political behavior. Neither did extreme nationalists, rural radicals, and the alienated military establishment of the late nineteenth century. "The Imperial will then ceased to mean merely the ethical axioms of traditional Japanese society, but took on the new meaning of the expressed decisions of the emperor's government," and the nationalists, radicals, and the army dedicated themselves to restoring historical Japanese mores. Also, even if the orthodox Meiji group had wanted to relegate the emperor to symbolic authority, they would have had to contend with the twentieth-century nationalists. This group, bred in the 1920s, raising a challenge in the 1930s, and coming to power between 1937 and 1945 would insist upon one fundamental difference: they, not the Meiji oligarchs, should represent and defend the legitimacy of imperial rule.

Thus the contest for power between the Genro, cabinet, and Meiji successors, on the one hand, and the extreme nationalists, on the other, was essentially a debate over who represented legitimacy. The nationalistic military radicals and their cohorts challenged the government on behalf of the throne—the symbol of Japan, according to all Japanese theorists—seeking to defend it against the disloyal, and thus illegitimate, modernist state. Here the concept of clientship was clearly in question. The client of the military radical (who was a professional soldier) was the emperor as well as the defender of traditional Japan. The soldier could no longer defend the government and the state, because they were betraying Japanese values. The military, therefore, was prepared to overthrow the "Westernizers" on the emperor's behalf.

PROFESSIONAL SOLDIERS AS XENOPHOBES AND RADICALS

National security and the definition of national objectives became primary concerns of Japanese foreign policy in the 1930s. The dynamics of putting into operation a radical security policy gradually became the business of the military, which conceived of itself as the protector of Meiji legitimacy,

imperial grandeur, and national defense. To consolidate the empire, according to the army, was to pursue a "Chinese" policy, which involved gaining supremacy in northern China and Manchuria and instituting a planned economy at home. Thus would come into being a Japanese-dominated East Asian sphere of prosperity.

It was significant that the interests of Japanese national security converged with the cause of the alienated military class, for national security concerned the Meiji oligarchs only to the extent that it buttressed the Restoration regime. Certainly there were imperialistic oligarchs, but in their view it was not up to the military to define Japan's national security. The military, on the other hand, challenged the regime's attempt to dominate the army and to formulate foreign policy. This conflict took place after the decline of the traditional political elite and founding fathers' group, the Genro and the party leaders, when the professional officer class set out to become the new and legitimate heirs to state authority.

In the officers' view, their own concept of corporate responsibility did not violate the military professional rule of nonintervention. The officers did not challenge the Meiji doctrine that legitimacy symbolically resided in the emperor. On the contrary, the army's reason for intervention was to defeat the political forces that no longer "protected" the emperor. Intervention thus was actually seen as a corporate duty of patriotic military groups.

This attitude was not peculiar to the

military in the 1930s. Nationalists, romantics, bureaucrats, and politicians were also searching for a new definition of Japanese national security. In some ways the extreme nationalists among the civilians were more militant than the military in their desire to protect the legitimacy of the emperor against the politicians. The officers considered themselves to be restorers of imperial grandeur rather than insurrectionists. They saw themselves as the loyal servants of a legitimate and sustaining imperial order. The military (including the officers), however, fell into two groups; one supported a national security policy on behalf of legitimacy and the other challenged the political system because it was an alienated class.

Yet the insurrections of 1931, 1932, 1936, 1937, and 1941 succeeded not because the romantic anti-Meiji primitivists and the alienated class won out, but because they finally succeeded in challenging the political system and twisting the military idea of national security to coincide with the military concept of national security. The military triumphed also when the Genro, the cabinet, and especially the army came to be dominated by militant imperialists. It has been observed that the primacy of the war minister and the cabinet contributed to Taisho democracy, the era of party government in the 1920s. It could equally truthfully be said that when the war ministry and the cabinet were taken over by the military, the result was—an imperialist Japan.

The Japanese army, operating under a misguided concept of clientship, also violated another condition of professionalism—expertise. First, although admission to the academy in the 1880s was supposed to have been based on achievement and competitive exams, members of the traditionally military *hans* (tribes), the Choshu and the Satsuma, were given preference. Second, the ethics of the warrior, the cult of Bushido, was taught as a basic skill after cadres had been admitted on the basis of other value-oriented exams. Third, two different career patterns developed, one for the graduates of the academy and one for graduates of the war college, a small group composed primarily of Satsuma and Choshu officers destined for the high command.

It was not the traditional martial values that made the Japanese army powerful, however, but its militance. In the 1930s Japan's foreign and security policies were the outgrowth of three factors: (1) her changing diplomatic relations with the West; (2) factional conflict over the interpretation of national defense; and (3) struggles among the foreign, war, and naval ministries over the proper objectives of foreign policy. Because Japan's attempt at peaceful expansion, "economic diplomacy," had failed in the 1920s, the pursuit of co-prosperity goals had been turned over to the military. "Militarism triumphed not as a goal but as a means for obtaining the same ends which the diplomacy of the preceding era [the 1920s] had unsuccessfully sought." The degree of civilian control in the 1920s depended upon the extent of cabinet dominance over the political system. "The right of supreme command," promulgated by the cabinet in 1930 and mainly directed against militant nationalists, did preserve for a while civilian supremacy over the military.

The military violated yet another principle of military professionalism, corporate autonomy, in the 1930s. Political intrigues on the part of the field armies, especially the Kwantung army in northern China, succeeded in frustrating the efforts of the military in the foreign office to come to terms with Chiang Kai-shek. The violent struggles between agrarian radicals and other militants also blurred the line between the military and the civilian. The persistence of fascist and fundamentalist ideologues further politicized the army and was a necessary factor in propelling Japan along a militarist course.

Japan was brought to the brink of praetorianism when the state, the society, and the forces of ideology all converged in support of expansionism. The road to militarism was not paved by the army alone, even if it eventually did play a prominent role in subverting the civilian system. Military *pronunciamientos*, far from being autonomous military creations, resulted from the connivance of a number of groups under the influence of a militant weltanschauung.

The formulation of a militant national security policy could not end in the surrendering of political power to the military. Once the officers violated the professional dictum of civilian control, they, like their German counterparts, brought disaster on both their nation and on their own institution. Once again the demise of the cardinal principle of professionalism — nonintervention — coincided with the disastrous end of military corporatism. . . .

JAMES CROWLEY

Japan's Quest for Autonomy

HISTORICAL PROLOGUE TO THE 1930'S

In viewing the contours of modern Japanese history, one is reminded of a simile of Brooks Adams: history resembles the track of a comet, not the movements of planets. For a span of time a nation adheres to a steady course; then, as it rounds the sun, it dashes off

From *James Crowley*, Japan's Quest for Autonomy: National Security and Foreign Policy, 1930–1938 *(Princeton, N. J., 1966), pp. 3–15, by permission of Princeton University Press.*

in a new direction. Throughout the first two decades of this century, the foreign policies of Imperial Japan were fixed on a course of cooperation and accommodation with the Anglo-American maritime powers, only to become comet-like in the next decade, making a sudden thrust into a new path that led eventually to a fatal collision with these Western nations. One witnessed, in effect, the displacement of a diplomacy based upon patterns of collective security by a posture of autonomy, a national defense program that would assure immunization from attack or duress and an ability to pursue whatever political and economic policies were considered essential for the welfare of the Japanese empire. To understand the multiple causes of this transformation, the impetus behind the foreign and security policies of the 1930's, one must consider the bases of Japan's collective security policies in the preceding decades. Otherwise, it is difficult to discern many aspects of the configuration of political, diplomatic, and military problems which inspired the dream of national autonomy, the aspiration which sustained the imperialism and authoritarianism of the 1930's.

At the turn of the century, the diplomacy of East Asia was conditioned by a balance of power noticeably dissimilar from that which governed the European continent. Traditionally and theoretically, Asia had been dominated by one country; yet China, at this time, was militarily impotent, subject to economic, political, and geographical infringements by land and sea powers. In this anomalous situation, the chief roles in the power politics of East Asia were to be played by four actors—Japan, Britain, Russia, and the United States—and, in one fashion or another, their common object was the acquisition of privileged positions in China. When Japan became engaged in this imperialistic diplomacy, it did so with greater intensity than that displayed by the Occidental nations. Unlike the Western sea powers, whose continental aspirations and commitments were casually formed and easily realized,

Japan viewed Korea and South Manchuria as an area of prime strategic importance. In order to acquire political hegemony in this region, therefore, Japan fought two major wars; and, although the costs of these conflicts were high, both in material terms and in human lives, the victories in the field created a new pantheon of national heroes and a pervasive sense of nationalism. These accomplishments also sanctified Japanese rights and interests in Korea and Manchuria as matters of national honor. . . .

As a regional power whose influence in East Asia was a composite of its own armament and the friendship of Great Britain, Japan, in 1906, faced a tangle of diplomatic thickets. The battles of the Russo-Japanese War, symbolized by the bloody siege of Port Arthur and the swift but devastating engagement in the straits of Tsushima, had secured a foothold on the continent. Once this was obtained, the task became one of consolidation, the protection of Japan's position in Korea and South Manchuria. This assignment, reasoned Prince Yamagata, in an October 1906 memorial to the Throne, dictated the need for a comprehensive national defense policy, one that would clarify and confirm the basic strategic principles of Japan's foreign policy and designate the minimal force of strength essential for the realization of Japan's security needs. Acting upon this advice, the Emperor officially requested that a policy guide be prepared by the general staffs, in consultation with the ministers of state. By February 1907, this task was completed and the Saionji cabinet adopted a basic guide to national security. Here, the cardinal strategic concerns of the empire were articulated in a concise form, concerns which were to plague and condition national policies until the holocaust of the Pacific War effected a shattering resolution of the problems created by Japan's dual commitment as a continental and an insular empire.

As defined by both general staffs, the prime security missions of the services were to protect Japan's interests in Korea and South Manchuria and to ensure the safety of Japan's insular possessions, including the home islands. Essential to both aims, as Prince Yamagata had noted in his personal memorial, was the naval alliance with Great Britain; and, by 1907, this prerequisite seemed assured. The European diplomatic context had impelled the British government to prepare an Anglo-Japanese alliance in 1902; and, three years later, this alliance had been broadened to embrace a firm recognition of Japan's special sphere of influence in Korea and Manchuria. Although European problems, particularly the Anglo-German naval rivalry, were enforcing the viability of this security pact, both general staffs affirmed, and Japan's naval authorities emphasized, that the ability to wage war against Russia for control of the Liaotung Peninsula, as well as the safety of the home islands, had been derivatives of the Anglo-Japanese alliance. Hence, the key to national defense, to Japan's foreign and security policies, was the protective umbrella of the British fleet. Given this fundamental alliance,

the 1907 "National Defense Policy" postulated two distinct security conceptions, both of which were directed at the defense and enhancement of Japan's commercial and political interests in Korea, South Manchuria, and the treaty ports along the coast of China.

In the judgment of Japan's naval leaders, only one naval power posed serious problems. The recent acquisition of the Philippines had given the United States a major colonial possession in the Pacific. Potentially, if they were developed as a naval base, this would compromise the security of Taiwan. Secondly, the "open door" policy raised diplomatic dangers, especially if the United States were to invoke this doctrine as a means to challenge Japan's position in Manchuria and Korea. Aside from these worries, the festering Japanese immigration problem threatened to provoke political turmoil in both countries, thereby accentuating tension between them. Since these three points of conflict were real enough, it is understandable that, as Admiral Fukudome noted, Japan's 1907 naval policy designated "the United States as its sole imaginary enemy." With this axiom, the 1907 "National Defense Policy" advanced two key propositions: first, that Japan should maintain its naval parity with the American fleet; and, secondly, that Japan should construct two new battle fleets, each headed by eight capital warships. This latter stipulation was the well-known "eight-eight" plan and technically it called for the construction of eight battleships, eight heavy cruisers, 27 light cruisers, 177 destroyers, and 64 submarines. Lest the empire augment its fleet too rapidly and, in the process, stimulate fears in British naval circles, the 1907 plan judged that the government should, as its immediate goal, authorize twelve capital ships, the so-called "eight-four" program. . . .

In the early 1880's, the Meiji oligarchy had concluded that the security of the home islands was contingent on the "independence" of Korea. . . .

In harmony with this objective, the Japanese government, between 1885 and 1895, allocated approximately from 28 to 30 per cent of the yearly national budgets to augmenting the military and naval power of the country. The fruits of this expenditure were harvested in the Sino-Japanese War when Japan obtained its cardinal objective, control over the Liaotung Peninsula. As is well known, the 1896 Tripartite intervention of Germany, France, and Russia forced the return of this peninsula to China and shortly afterward Russia moved into Port Arthur. The Korean "security" problem was now no longer a Sino-Japanese affair, and Russia became the prime strategic concern. To counter this threat, the Meiji oligarchy, in 1898, decided to double the size of the Imperial army and navy. Six years later, the government secured a naval alliance with Britain; and, in June 1902, the general staff concluded that "for the long-range planning of our empire," it would be necessary to make "Korea part of the Japanese empire." Convinced of the paramount strategic importance of Korea to the security of the home islands and protected by the Anglo-Japanese alliance, the Imperial government, in 1903, decided to displace the Russians from Liaotung, a decision which precipitated the Russo-Japanese War.

Following this conflict, it is not surprising that Japan's army leaders deemed Korea and South Manchuria to be the basic strategic concern of the empire, or that they viewed the continental scene with a proprietary attitude. For twenty years the government had defined its foreign policy in terms of the "independence" of Korea; and Japan had fought two major wars in order to establish its control over Liaotung. Understandably, the general staff, in the 1905–1907 period, pressed for a formal annexation of Korea, a military government in South Manchuria, and the exclusion of American or European investments from both regions. Hence, when Foreign Minister Katō Kōmei, in February 1906, ventured to recommend that Japan should accept the "open door" policy, War Minister Terauchi's adamant opposition forced Katō's resignation after a brief three-month tenure as foreign minister. In addition, the army authorities were most reluctant to set aside the military government which had been established in Liaotung during the war; and it took a special Conference on the Manchurian Problem in March 1906 to end this form of government. Here, Prince Saionji, with the aid of the Genrō—Yamagata, Itō, Matsukata, and Inoue—managed to bring about several decisive administrative changes: the resident military governor (sō-

tokufu) in Liaotung was displaced by a governor general (*totoku*); the South Manchurian Railway was created under the presidency of Gotō Shūmpei; and a consulate general was located at Port Arthur, a post whose occupant was equal in rank to the highest-ranking army officer stationed in South Manchuria. Despite these changes, the first governor general, Field Marshal Ōyama, in November 1906, still argued that "the foreign policy of South Manchuria should be entrusted completely to the governor general." Although Ōyama's views were set aside by the Saionji cabinet, the army authorities obviously regarded South Manchuria as the army's special province; and the 1907 "National Defense Policy" drafted by the army general staff marked Tsarist Russia as the prime threat to the empire. Anticipating a "war of revenge" by the recently defeated enemy, the general staff calculated that it would be necessary to increase the standing army from 19 to 25 divisions, thereby assuring the empire of an immediate mobilization potential of 50 divisions.

The 1907 "National Defense Policy" had defined one comprehensive objective: the formation of a military establishment that would be capable of protecting Japan's rights and interests in Korea and South Manchuria. Within this postulate, each service had articulated a distinctive mission: the naval policy voiced the need for a fleet of twelve capital ships in order to retain Japan's superiority over the American fleet in the Western Pacific; the army policy claimed the necessity of a 25-division standing army in order

to protect Korea and South Manchuria. Both policies were predicated on an awareness of the paramount importance of the Anglo-Japanese alliance, on a recognition that the insular and continental possessions of the empire were ultimately protected by the British fleet. In 1907, however, neither service actually had the "minimal" strength to realize the desired strategic capabilities. The army stood at 19 divisions, not 25; and the navy possessed two new capital warships, not twelve.

1907–1913, NATIONAL DEFENSE AND THE CONSOLIDATION OF THE EMPIRE

The 1907 strategic calculations of the general staffs were not lacking in validity. The fear of a "war of revenge" by the Tsarist government could not be easily discounted; and the world tour of the American fleet of 1906–1907 was, from the viewpoint of Theodore Roosevelt, undertaken to impress upon the Japanese government the power and determination of the American government to exert its influence in Pacific affairs. Although the Japanese and American press promptly expressed belief in the imminence of a Japanese-American conflict, in strategic terms Roosevelt's "big stick" naval diplomacy was really a fragile reed. The Anglo-Japanese alliance precluded any Anglo-American accord against Japan; and the Imperial fleet was approximately equal to that of the United States. Given the cruising range of the warships of the period, this parity invested Japan with a commanding superiority in the

Western Pacific. Somewhat belatedly, Theodore Roosevelt realized the Philippines were an "Achilles' heel," indefensible against the power of the Japanese fleet. This perception soon reflected itself in a new style of American diplomacy, in the Root-Takahira and Taft-Katsura executive agreements which tacitly confirmed Japan's special position in Korea and South Manchuria. Parallel with this Japanese-American rapprochement, the Russian and Japanese governments negotiated in 1907 and 1909 an entente by which they recognized each other's position in North and South Manchuria. Finally, in 1910, Japan formally annexed Korea, without any objections or reservations on the part of the Western powers.

This favorable diplomatic context did not alter the strategic axioms of the Japanese general staffs. From their standpoint, the softened tone of Roosevelt's policy was the consequence of Japan's naval strength; and they believed Japan's standing army had forced the reluctant acquiescence of the Russian government. However well warranted these opinions may have been, the favorable diplomacy of the postwar period sharply reduced the willingness of the Japanese political parties to underwrite any major expansion of the services. In the past, in 1882 and 1896, the Genrō had only to formulate comprehensive armament programs and the necessary funds were allocated; but, between 1907 and 1911, neither the Diet nor the finance ministry was prepared to champion any significant increase in armament expenditures. This political context affected the services in strik-

ingly dissimilar ways. Since the navy was, after the Russo-Japanese War, literally building a fleet of new ships, it could, by scrapping outdated warships, realize its goal of twelve capital ships without enlarging its budget. The Imperial army, in contrast, could not augment the number of standing divisions unless the Diet authorized increased expenditures. Since this authorization failed to materialize, the army, between 1907 and 1911, remained at nineteen divisions, only one of which was stationed in Korea. To the army authorities this was intolerable, as it provided wholly inadequate forces on the mainland for the defense of Korea and South Manchuria. This frustrating situation bred a conviction in army circles that the government was not abiding by its moral and legal obligations to fulfill the estimates of forces sanctioned by the Throne in 1907, a sentiment which boiled over into a major political crisis. . . .

The political strategy of the army authorities, abetted by the covert influence of Yamagata, provoked a crisis of the highest order. Were the budget policies of the government, the legal prerogative of the Diet, to be dictated by a clique of army officers? Could the war minister impose his dictates on the other ministers of state? The challenges posed by the war minister's resignation alienated the political parties and the finance and naval ministers, a situation which temporarily at least forged a bond of political unity between two key ministries and the political parties. The results of this new political configuration were promptly displayed. When General Katsura set out to form his cabinet, he discovered the naval authorities were not prepared to provide a naval minister. This public stance revealed an intense resentment of the army's dictatorial methods and, more pointedly, it acted as a blunt warning that the naval authorities could also play the game of cabinet politics according to army rules. In contrast to Prince Saionji, General Katsura did not yield the point, preferring instead to invoke the aid of the Throne and obtain a memorial ordering the appointment of a naval minister. While this maneuver assured the formation of a cabinet, it also intensified the opposition of the majority party in the Diet. Consequently, the Katsura cabinet was unable to enact the desired two-division expansion of the army; and the transparent hostility between the naval ministry and the premier fostered a popular belief that a clique of Chōshū army officers, headed by Yamagata and Katsura, had engineered the downfall of the Saionji government as a means to receive its oligarchical control over governmental policies.

Motivated more by obstinacy than moderation, Katsura retained the premiership for fourteen months. In this interval, he made no serious overtures to ameliorate the conflict between the war ministry and the finance and naval ministries or to seek an accommodation with the Seiyūkai, the majority party in the Diet. As premier, he pressed for an enlarged army budget, only to see his recommendation vetoed by the Diet. Finally the impasse was vividly revealed in the public arena by Ozaki Yukio. On February 5, 1913, in one of Japan's

most memorable parliamentary addresses, often regarded as the symbol of the inception of Taishō democracy, Ozaki censured the Chōshū oligarchs for their wanton violation of responsible cabinet government and the vile technique of concealing partisan interests under the mantle of the Emperor: "They always mouth 'loyalty' and 'patriotism' but what they are actually doing is to hide themselves behind the Throne, and shoot at their political enemies from their secure ambush. The Throne is their rampart. Rescripts are their missiles." The vivid metaphor stirred the Seiyūkai to vote a formal censure of the government; and Katsura rashly retaliated with another Imperial rescript requesting the revocation of the censure. This crude stratagem proved his undoing. Defying the rescript, the Seiyūkai affirmed its lack of confidence in the premier; and, once Katsura's behavior had cast the sanctity of the Throne in jeopardy, Prince Yamagata added his powerful voice to the demand for a new government. The issue was decided. Katsura resigned and Yamagata asked Admiral Yamamoto to organize a cabinet in harmony with the expectations of the Seiyūkai. . . .

In one sense, the first bloom of Taishō democracy had been fostered by a profound conflict within the cabinet—namely, the army's strenuous efforts to impose its fiscal policies. From another perspective, the impasse between the army authorities and the Diet had been caused by two considerations: an international context which discounted the value of the army's estimate of its armament needs; and, within the confines of a fixed military budget, the inability of the service ministers to formulate a common national defense policy which would allocate the available funds according to a schedule of priorities, whether it be an enlargement of the army or a prompt realization of the "eight-four" building program. As war clouds gathered over the European continent, however, the domestic and foreign circumstances which had forestalled the two-division expansion of the army slowly dissipated. . . .

AKIRA IRIYE

The Failure of Military Expansionism

In the 1920's Japan tried peaceful expansionism and failed. If the nation was to continue to grow, military means must now be employed; the use of force would enable the nation to achieve ends which the "economic diplomacy" of the 1920's had not been able to obtain—such was the reasoning behind the militaristic adventures of the 1930's.

In discussing Japanese militarism after the Manchurian incident, it is useful to view it as the antithesis not of pacifism but of peaceful expansionism. Militarism triumphed not as a goal but as a means for obtaining the same ends which the diplomacy of the preceding era had unsuccessfully sought. By the early 1930's there was almost universal consensus that the peaceful, economic diplomacy of the 1920's had brought no benefits to Japan and that in fact it had been powerless even to safeguard the nation's existing rights and interests. The whole orientation of postwar Japanese policy could be at-

From Akira Iriye, "The Failure of Military Expansionism," in Dilemmas of Growth in Prewar Japan, ed. James W. Morley (Princeton, N. J.: Princeton University Press, 1974), pp. 107–15, 123–36, by permission of the publisher.

tacked and the fundamental assumptions underlying peaceful expansionism questioned. Without such questioning, it would be difficult to account for the general enthusiasm with which the bold military initiatives taken after 1931 were greeted. What united the military, the nationalistic groups, and the bulk of the intellectuals was the shared perception of the 1920's as a decade of futile attempts at peaceful expansion through international cooperation.

Certain images about the previous decade that were held by the proponents and defenders of the new order were central to their thinking. It is immaterial whether such images were accurate or realistic. What is important is that these perceptions defined a reality which the militaristic expansionists endeavored to overcome by means of their own strategy. The economic diplomacy of the 1920's had been based on a set of assumptions about the nature of the postwar world. What the men of the succeeding decade did was to challenge these assumptions and substitute for them their own ideas about the world.

Were the assumptions held during

the 1930's more accurate reflections of the realities of international relations than those common in the preceding decade? In the end both peaceful expansionism and military expansionism failed, and these failures constitute an important aspect of the story of the "dilemmas of growth" in modern Japan. The study of the ideology of military expansionism provides one way of examining changing attitudes toward growth in modern Japan and the relationship between domestic factors and forces external to the country.

Because the initiative to reorient foreign policy in the 1930's was undertaken by the military, and because military decisions were at the core of national politics, it will be meaningful to analyze military perceptions of the world in the decade preceding Pearl arbor. One way to do this is to examine memoranda, minutes of conferences, diaries, and other military writings to see how they tried to relate Japanese military action to the policies of other powers. Their writings almost invariably include "estimates of the international situation," "developments in foreign countries," and similar entries. By examining these writings it is possible to evaluate how the exponents of forceful expansionism visualized the world, sought to predict changes in international affairs, and called for corresponding responses by Japan.

It is, of course, doubtful that one can speak of the Japanese military as a generic collective term, any more than one can generalize about the civilian bureaucracies or business interests. Differences between the army and the navy, between service ministries and general staffs, and between sections

within each of these, were always of great significance, and some of them will be noted below. However, this essay is not a study in decision-making or in institutional history. Rather, it seeks to look at one aspect of the dilemmas of growth in prewar Japan by examining some of the ideas constituting the ideological structure of military expansionism. Since the failure of peaceful expansionism was fundamentally a failure to develop a realistic conceptual model of international relations, it is germane to ask if military expansionism was based on any more workable assumptions.

CONTINENTAL EXPANSION

The justification of the use of force was naturally the starting point of military expansionism. It was derived from the belief that, given such "objective" conditions as the disproportionately superior material strength of the Western countries, their exclusive trade and immigration policies, and Chinese nationalism, Japanese interest could not realistically be predicated upon the goodwill of these nations. If Japan was to grow, the necessity for which was never questioned, the nation must be prepared to use force. A Kwantung Army memo written just before the Mukden incident noted that the policy of gradualism in Manchuria had failed and that there could be no successful execution of a China policy without the resolution to use force. "If we win the war it should not matter what the world thinks of us." At a time when alien ideologies permeated Japanese society and when there were unprecedented economic difficulties, only a decisive blow in defense of national interests would enable the nation to attain its goals.

Force, however, must be used selectively. An indiscriminate resort to military measures would complicate strategic and diplomatic questions and defeat the very purpose for which force was employed. It was thus imperative to scrutinize carefully trends in the policies and strategies of other powers. The successful execution of military expansion depended upon an accurate analysis of these trends as well as a realistic evaluation of the probable responses to Japanese action that must be expected from foreign countries. It was particularly important to prevent an eventuality in which Japan was caught off guard and compelled to wage war against antagonists who were not of Japan's own choosing.

In 1931 a major decision was made—to use force in Manchuria—and the military judged correctly that war with other countries would not be involved. Yet they remained extremely sensitive to the possibilities of foreign intervention and actual conflict with third powers. Numerous memoranda, "judgments on current developments," and "evaluations of the international situation" written at the time give evidence of the intensity of this concern and the acute awareness of these possibilities. There was virtual unanimity in army writings during the period from 1931 to 1937 that the Manchurian incident would eventuate in hostilities with the Soviet Union. For instance, in the spring of 1932, Colonel Itagaki Seishirō wrote that "war with the Soviet Union in the future is unavoidable. . . . If the

Soviet Union should decisively intervene against our policy in Manchuria and Mongolia or persist in its communist propaganda despite our protests, we must be prepared to settle the Soviet question fundamentally." Much of the Japanese army's strategic planning at this time was based on the assumption that conflict with Russia was impending. This necessitated the avoidance of open hostilities with the Chinese government. Instead, it was considered desirable to persuade China to pool resources with Japan to prepare against the Soviet Union.

This is not to say that Russia was the army's sole concern. The General Staff conceded that in the event of hostilities with Russia there was a possibility of intervention by the United States, Britain, and China, either individually or jointly. An August 1936 memorandum from the second (operations) section noted that the opening of conflict with these powers would make the prosecution of the Russian war extremely difficult. Such a possibility, however, could not be ruled out. It was hoped that Japanese diplomacy would effectively check American and British intervention, but in the meantime the armed forces developed their strategic plans against them.

The army was in part indulging in a self-fulfilling prophecy when it visualized conflict with the Anglo-American nations. According to some Kwantung Army strategists, it was because of their belief in the inevitability of war with these countries that they had taken radical steps to expand forcefully into Manchuria. In Ishiwara Kanji's words, "the coming war with the Anglo-American nations will be mankind's last war, to be fought for the unification of world civilization." Japan was to prepare for the war by creating an "East Asian union" to liberate Asia from the West. The use of force was justified by the ends, but even so Japanese military action would be met by Western obstruction. "War will come," Ishiwara wrote in 1933, "when our national policy of establishing the East Asian union is obstructed by an enemy. Whether the enemy be America, Russia, or Britain, the war will be a protracted one." It is evident that pan-Asianism was both a justification for forceful expansion and a cause for anxiety when the military tried to relate their action in Manchuria to the attitudes of other powers. . . .

The outbreak of the Sino-Japanese War in 1937 did not alter such perceptions of international affairs. It is surprising that the war with China brought about little change in the army's view of Japan's relations with China, the Soviet Union, and the United States. Army Ministry, General Staff, and Kwantung Army memoranda continued to enunciate clichés about "cooperation and co-prosperity among Japan, Manchukuo, and China." They also visualized conflict with Russia as a distinct possibility, a sequel to or part of the Chinese war. The army remained hopeful that somehow the Chinese would recognize and appreciate the ideal of "harmony and cooperation" between Japan, Manchukuo, and China, so that the three could work together in a joint struggle against

communism. Toward the end of the year the General Staff reiterated that "our basic national defense plan is still directed toward the Soviet Union." Moreover, as the war in China dragged on, it came to be expected that open hostilities with Russia might come at any moment, before the settlement of the Chinese conflict. The war-direction section of the General Staff defined the goal for military planning during the period from 1938 to 1941 as national mobilization in preparation for simultaneous warfare against China and the Soviet Union. On November 18, 1938, the army supreme command adopted a strategic decision which stated, "We must carry on our war with China and at the same time strengthen our defense capabilities with a view to preparing the nation for war against both the Soviet Union and China."

Pan-Asianism, too, persisted after 1937. It became an instrument for the moral justification of the Sino-Japanese War, but its essentially self-fulfilling nature had not changed. The war was defined as aimed at "the construction of a morally oriented culture in East Asia." "The expulsion of Europe and America [from Asia]," exclaimed a November 1937 memorandum, "is a common concern of Japan and China." The two peoples had a joint mission to liberate themselves from Western influence, whether democratic or Communist. As earlier, pan-Asianism envisaged the establishment of imperial self-sufficiency. In a paper written in the early spring of 1938, General Staff officers defined "the national defense sphere" in terms of three areas: the core area (Japan,

Manchukuo, North China), the self-sufficiency area (Indochina, the Dutch East Indies), and the supplementary area (India, Australia). The core area was the "foundation of our national existence," and its security had to be the cardinal objective of all strategy. This necessitated preparedness against the Soviet Union. Japan should also undertake the defense of the self-sufficiency area, and this would require "adjustments" in Japanese relations with Britain and the United States.

Again as earlier, the army's view of the United States was cautiously optimistic. Pan-Asianist thoughts were essentially vague generalities that were not related to any kind of conflict with America in the near future. The above memorandum pointed out that the establishment of a new East Asian order would take thirty to fifty years, and at any event it was asserted as imperative that Japan first settle the war with China and then concern itself with the possible conflict with the Soviet Union, to be ultimately followed by probable changes in Japanese relations with the Anglo-American countries. . . .

SOUTHERN EXPANSION AND JAPANESE-AMERICAN RELATIONS

By the end of 1939, then, the Japanese picture of the international system was at variance with reality. Japan's continental expansionists envisaged a world which tolerated their action so long as they did not openly challenge the status quo outside of China. Changes in the international situation, far from altering the basic orientation of this thinking, served to reinforce the conviction that conditions were favorable to the speedy conclusion of the Chinese war. The inability to visualize Japanese-American relations in a state of crisis epitomized the illusion.

Even so, had the expansionists continued to confine their action to China, open conflict with the Anglo-American nations would have been postponed indefinitely. The war with China would have dragged on, but a simultaneous war with a group of Western powers would not have developed. That this was in fact what happened was due to a conscious decision to widen the sphere of Japanese expansion to include Southeast Asia. More fundamental than this decision, however, was the image of a world which tolerated such expansionism. This image was in turn related to the geopolitical notion of the world as divided into a few "pan-regions." The dream of pan-Asianism was to be put into effect, since the time seemed to be approaching when Asia would in fact be rid of Western influence and left to Asians under Japanese hegemony. Whereas the peaceful expansionists of the 1920's had envisaged an economically interdependent, open international society and failed to promote their goals, the military expansionists of the 1930's visualized a divided world, which they felt was emerging and which would best serve Japan's interests.

The trouble, of course, was that the Western nations, in particular Britain and the United States, did not accept such a definition of the situation. For them Asia was not synonymous with

Asians, but was an arena for a global struggle between freedom and dictatorship, the outcome of which was of the utmost importance for the future of mankind. These Western powers would not acquiesce in a Japanese hegemony any more than they would tolerate a German conquest of Europe. The United States would deepen its commitment to the maintenance of the status quo in Southeast Asia, and the status quo was based on the continued presence of Western rights and interests. Far from countenancing what the Japanese took to be the trend toward regional autonomy, America would keep Southeast Asia tied to the rest of the world, and the United States itself would become an Asian power to keep Japan from speaking for all Asians.

Some of this was well recognized by Japan's policy makers and military strategists, and the possibility of war with the United States kept them from undertaking expansion into southern Indochina until the summer of 1941. What is notable is the way in which considerations of southern expansion affected the course of war in China. It was a great tragedy that certain images about the Chinese war and the powers' responses to it had become fixed and that deliberations on policy toward Southeast Asia were therefore conducted with little regard to the Chinese situation. In other words, the view persisted that the powers would tolerate Japanese action in China. Because of this, the southern expansion tended to be considered on its own merit; Japan would undertake it as soon as international conditions were favorable, while the Chinese war

would settle itself sooner or later. This assumption was a fundamental flaw since China would have been part of the new Asian order the Japanese were trying to create, and if some Western powers opposed the scheme, there was no reason why they should not have disapproved of Japanese action in China itself. Through a process of feed-back, Western support of China increased the more the Japanese threatened to invade Southeast Asia. Thus in the final analysis, a failure to establish a clear conceptual connection between the war in China and the premeditated expansion southward was at the root of the failure of Japan's military expansionism.

In considering southern expansion, the military believed either that the war in China would somehow be settled before the thrust southward was undertaken, or that the invasion of Southeast Asia would not interfere with the prosecution of the Chinese war. The navy on the whole took the second position, while the army fluctuated between the two, but in either case complacency vis-à-vis China persisted until 1941.

It was the navy, of course, that had been most eager for southern expansion. Japan's basic naval strategy, as the Navy Ministry noted in 1935, was "to control the western Pacific, protect the lines of communication at sea that are necessary for national existence and expansion, and become the stabilizing force in East Asia." Such a policy dictated the primacy of a southern orientation in military strategy, with the implication that the United States and Great Britain, rather than China and the Soviet

Union, would be the likely enemies. In the mid-1930's, with the naval disarmament treaties abrogated and the army intent upon extending its sphere of influence into northern China, the navy began stressing the need for a southern advance and preparedness against the United States. It should be noted that the navy distinguished Japan's involvement on the continent of Asia from naval conflict in the South Seas and that war with the United States was postulated only in connection with this second eventuality. The Sino-Japanese War did not change this orientation. The navy, like the army, was convinced that the war could be terminated speedily.

It was in the spring of 1940, after the successful German offensive, that the navy came to visualize the southern advance as a strategic goal for the near future. The war in China was far from being over, but the navy showed a readiness to consider action which could lead to simultaneous wars with America and China. "The time for action has finally come," declared an exponent of southern expansionism. "Japan must once again become a maritime nation and expand its navy, not hesitating to go to war with England and America." The opportunity seemed to have arrived to seize Indochina and then other areas in Southeast Asia so as to establish Japanese hegemony in the area, which would give the nation strategic advantages in the anticipated conflict with the British and American navies. From this time on the navy became so preoccupied with Southeast Asia, Britain, and the United States

that one finds less and less reference to the question of China by naval spokesmen.

Army strategists kept China very much on their minds, but they, too, became infected with an urge to expand southward. Intelligence officers were dispatched to Southeast Asia in June 1940, and a southern section was created within the intelligence division of the General Staff. The problem of the relationship between continental and southern expansion remained, but generally speaking in 1940 and well into 1941 the army continued to believe that the southern advance would be undertaken after the Chinese war had been settled, or at least in such a way as to hasten that eventuality. In a famous decision, made on May 18, 1940, the General Staff and the War Ministry agreed that the war in China should be brought to a conclusion by the end of the year. The basic motive behind this decision was the increasing interest in expansion in the South Seas—the "long-term war" in the army's jargon. Germany's successful campaigns in May and June strengthened the conviction that Japan must quickly settle the Chinese war in order to expand southward. In July, in drafting the basic military policy for the new Konoe Cabinet, the army supreme command asserted that Japan "should quickly settle the China incident and then, improving conditions both domestic and external, seize an opportune moment to solve the southern question." When, around this time, the crucial "Basic Principles for Coping with the Changing International Situation" were drawn up, the army asserted time and again that it was "logical" first to finish the Chinese war and then strike southward. However, the southern advance might be undertaken even before the settlement of the war if a favorable opportunity presented itself, such as a German invasion of the British Isles. It was difficult to pass up what appeared to be an impending and spectacular opportunity for expansion southward. All the same, the army was hopeful that this would not cause prolongation and deterioration of the conflict with China. A strategic plan for Southeast Asia drafted by the operations section of the General Staff noted the desirability of at least maintaining the status quo in China as a precondition for launching military action in the south. At the very least, it was argued that Japanese control over French Indochina and the British colonies would cut off Chungking's only supply routes and serve to bring the latter more easily to its kness.

What is notable about these arguments is the army's continued optimism about settling the Sino-Japanese War without incurring the intervention of a third power. This can best be seen in the persisting belief that war with America was unlikely in the near future. The army insisted that in the event of a southern advance the initial attack should be upon the European colonies. As for the United States, "it was best not to provoke her at first . . . but expel her from East Asia after several years," according to an army memorandum written in the summer of 1940. It seemed possible to avoid war with America so long as Japan confined her assault to the European colonies. In a series of mem-

oranda written by General Koiso Kuniaki, who had just resigned as minister of colonial affairs, it was noted that the time had come to expand the Japanese-Manchukuo-Chinese block to embrace Southeast Asia, but that the United States would not resist such an attempt by force if Japan guaranteed the security of the Philippines. Such a view is remarkable for its extreme optimism which saw no open conflict with America as a result of the Sino-Japanese War even as late as 1940.

The navy, of course, was constantly aware of the possibility of war with the United States, but only as a corollary of the southern advance and not of the war in China. In a memorandum of August 1, 1940, the Navy General Staff warned that the Japanese occupation of French Indochina could bring about an American embargo on scrap iron and oil. Their supply was "a matter of life and death" for Japan. Whether Japan could prevent or overcome such an embargo was the crucial question which must be faced before the nation undertook southern expansion by force. As can be seen here, from the Japanese navy's point of view the timing of the southern advance depended ultimately on American behavior. A memorandum of August 27 pointed out that forceful action should be undertaken by Japan in one of three foreseeable circumstances: a total embargo by the United States, actual or anticipated cooperation between America and Britain to defend their mutual territories and interests in the Pacific, or steps taken by either of these countries to threaten the existence of the Japanese empire directly. These three possibilities dictated Japanese response regardless of whether or not Japan was ready. On the other hand, there was a chance that the European conflict would so tie Britain and America down that Japan would enjoy freedom of action in Southeast Asia. In such an event the nation should take the initiative to use force. This memorandum made it clear that in the Japanese navy's view the southern advance was synonymous with actual or premeditated hostilities with the United States. It is also evident that for the navy the question of China was not immediately relevant. The memorandum did not once raise the question of the relationship between the Chinese war and the anticipated war in Southeast Asia.

While both the army and navy supported the Axis alliance, concluded in September, and the expedition to northern Indochina, executed in the same month, their differences remained. The army supreme command viewed the southern advance favorably because no war with America was envisaged as a result and because it did not seem to inhibit the ending of the Sino-Japanese War. The navy was not concerned with terminating the Chinese war as a major goal, but it hesitated to undertake military action in Southeast Asia for fear of American retaliation. "Developments from now on," said the chief of the operations division of the Navy General Staff, "depend on when the United States completes its strategic mobilization in East Asia, and on whether or not at that point it carries out a total embargo *vis-à-vis* Japan." This embargo, it may be pointed out, was visualized

by the Japanese navy as an American weapon to restrain Japan's southern advance and otherwise prevent her naval expansion; the embargo was not something the United States was expected to resort to in retaliation against Japanese policy in China. Although the United States had already adopted a policy of limited economic sanctions in connection with the violation of American rights in China, the navy anticipated the embargo of the crucial item, fuel oil, only in the event of an actual or impending clash between Japan and America in the Pacific and the South Seas. For the navy, then, the primary concern was with the war against the European colonies and the United States, whereas the army was concerned with the war that was going on in China and another that might or might not develop as a result of an advance southward. The army leadership was still confident, at the end of 1940, that war with the United States could be avoided, since neither the Chinese war nor the premeditated thrust southward seemed a *causa belli,* so long as Japan refrained from attacking American territories and possessions. For the navy, on the contrary, the southward advance and war with America were aspects of the same situation: they expected either both or neither.

TWO ROADS TO PEARL HARBOR

Thus there were in fact two roads to Pearl Harbor. Without going into the details of decision-making in 1941, it may be pointed out that the Japanese navy's road to war with America was a much simpler one than the army's.

As early as 1940, the navy had postulated the possibility of conflict with the United States the moment the latter undertook severe economic sanctions, especially an embargo of oil, against Japan. Assuming that such a course of events was a logical possibility, the naval strategists of the section-chief level pushed ahead with specific mobilization and tactical planning. A long memorandum, which they wrote on June 5 and for which they subsequently obtained the approval of the navy minister and the chief of naval operations, asserted that Japan must immediately resolve on "war (including the United States)." This was not the same thing as an attack on American territory; rather, the writers urged military preparedness against the United States under the assumption that war was imminent. One of the specific steps recommended was the speedy occupation of Indochina and Thailand. This was particularly crucial since Japanese inaction might invite American and British advances into this area, a possibility which seemed likely in the event of America's forceful intervention in the European war. French Indochina and Thailand, the memorandum noted, "lie between the spheres of influence of Japan and the Anglo-American nations." In order to remove a threat to the Japanese empire, and as a first step toward building up a self-sufficient imperial bloc, the occupation of these countries seemed amply justified. This did not necessarily mean that there would be war between Japan and the United States—unless the latter embargoed the export of oil to Japan. The risk, however, was always there, and from

the navy's point of view Japan's decision to send troops into southern Indochina and America's immediate economic retaliation, in the summer of 1941, merely confirmed the logic of events.

As earlier, the navy's attitude toward the Chinese war was ambiguous and not related to strategy in Southeast Asia and Japanese-American relations. The above memorandum tried to argue that the occupation of southern Indochina and Thailand would help prosecute the Chinese war. It was also pointed out that the third powers' assistance to Chungking must be completely stopped and drastic measures, such as the declaration of war, must be taken to destroy China's will power decisively. At the same time, the memorandum supported the Hull-Nomura conversations only if they brought about a truce in China through American good offices. While the United States was recognized as an obstacle to the prosecution of the war in China, the navy did not envisage open hostilities with America on account of China. It continued to distinguish between the Sino-Japanese War and the southern advance and failed to time the latter in accordance with the progress of the former war. It was willing to consider the use of force in Southeast Asia irrespective of the course of the Hull-Nomura conversations.

The Japanese army's road to war against the United States was a much more tortuous one. Before 1941 it had not anticipated such a war as a result of either the southern advance or the Sino-Japanese War. By the spring of 1941, however, army planners had become persuaded that Japan's thrust southward might invite hostilities with the United States and that in the event of an American war Japan was quite unprepared militarily and materially. An Army Ministry study, completed on March 25, decisively concluded that Japan must avoid irritating Britain and the United States unnecessarily and should instead step up her preparedness by obtaining military resources from the Anglo-American bloc. This was tantamount to scrapping the 1940 decision to take advantage of the European war by advancing southward. Instead, the army confirmed its intention of giving top priority to a successful termination of the war in China. Ironically, it was then that the prospect of conflict with the United States began to loom large in connection with the Sino-Japanese War.

In the middle of May, Ishwara Kanji gave a series of lectures at Ritsumeikan University. He reiterated his decade-long conviction that a Japanese-American war would come when Japan completed "the union of East Asia." He predicted the imminence of a global war, which would prove to be the last war humanity would have to face since it would be a war between East and West. This war, however, would come *after* the Sino-Japanese War was concluded. Japan must first finish the Chinese war and establish a pan-Asian union and then take on the ultimate adversary, the United States. In such a view, typical of army thinking up to that point, no war with America was visualized as part of the war with China.

It was this optimism, coupled with pessimism about the possibility of terminating the Sino-Japanese War quickly, that finally reoriented the army's thinking. There was general agreement that the Chinese war must be settled first; in the meantime, friction with others, especially the United States, should be avoided. When such ideas were contrasted to the reality of a seemingly never-ending conflict on the Chinese mainland, it was natural that the Japanese army should have seriously entertained the possibility of settling the Chinese war through American good offices. If the United States could be induced to mediate between Japan and China, this would in fact be killing two birds with one stone. The long sought-after objective of terminating the Chinese war would be obtained, and the final showdown with the United States would be postponed while Japan reconstructed her preparedness program. At bottom, of course, was the by then long-established conviction that there was no basic conflict between Japan and America in China. It was believed that the United States would welcome the role of mediator if this would put an end to the East Asian crisis, even if it meant accepting certain Japanese terms for settlement, in particular the independence of Manchukuo. Thus emerged what Satō Kenryō has decried as the spirit of reliance upon America to settle the China incident, reflecting the inability of the Japanese army to do so by itself.

Because so much was expected of American mediation, the sense of disappointment and bitterness was profound when it became known that the United States had no interest in expediting the conclusion of the Sino-Japanese War on Japanese terms. Part of the Japanese-American difference was, of course, due to the stiff attitude of Foreign Minister Matsuoka Yōsuke, who went far beyond the army in presenting inflexible terms to the State Department. All the same, the tone and content of the American note of June 21, communicated in anticipation of the German invasion of Russia, were such as to shake the army from its short-lived delusion that peace could be restored in China through America's good offices. Moreover, for the first time, the United States began to appear as the obstacle in the way of terminating the Chinese war. Since the settlement of the war was still the army's chief concern, this new evaluation of the United States meant that Japan would have to be prepared either to fight against America in order to subjugate Chungking or to find some *modus vivendi* with the United States in China in order to avoid such an eventuality. Thus for the first time Japanese-Chinese relations and Japanese-American relations were related in army thinking. These two sets of relations would either simultaneously deteriorate or simultaneously improve. In the former instance, concurrent war against China and America had to be envisaged.

From the army's point of view, the decision to occupy southern Indochina was more an aspect of the Chinese war than the beginning of a southern advance. As Chief of Staff Sugiyama Gen stated at the crucial imperial conference of July 2: "It is extremely important at the present juncture to increase our direct pressure upon the Chungking regime and at the same time to advance southward in order to sever the link between the Chungking regime and Anglo-American power which is supporting it from behind and is instrumental in increasing Chungking's will to resist. The sending of troops to southern Indochina has been prompted by these considerations." It is revealing to contrast such an explanation with that given by Naval Chief of Staff Nagano Osami, who talked about the establishment of a self-sufficient imperial system as the reason for the decision. Neither army nor navy expected an immediate American reprisal; in their view the occupation of southern Indochina did not seem likely to provoke American retaliation so long as other areas in Southeast Asia were not touched. When, nevertheless, the United States responded by freezing Japanese assets and imposing an embargo on oil export, the navy took the logical step of preparing for war in the immediate future. The army agreed.

That war did not come until December was primarily due to the efforts of the nonmilitary, including Prime Minister Konoe Fumimaro and the emperor himself, to try to avoid an open clash with the United States. But it should also be noted that the army never lost sight of the war which was going on in China. It still preferred to settle that war somehow before another war began. Besides, after Hitler's invasion of the Soviet Union, the army once again had to consider possible action in the north. If negotiation with the United States could solve the Chinese question, the army would be able to reorient its strategy to cope with the developing international situation. By the same token, no temporary agreement with America was feasible which did not explicitly settle the question of China. This was why War Minister Tōjō Hideki balked at Konoe's effort at peace and why the Hull note of November 26 was considered a war message. The settlement of the Chinese war by Japan's complete evacuation not only from China proper but also from Manchuria was no settlement at all. Because the army had envisioned a more favorable outcome of the Chinese war, it felt it had no choice but to go to war with the United States. In the words of General Tōjō: "The stationing of troops in China is the heart of the matter. . . . To make concession after concession [to the United States] and to yield on this question is like piercing the heart and tantamount to surrender." If Japan accepted the American terms for peace, "the achievements of the China incident would be nullified, the existence of Manchukuo would be endangered, and our control over Korea would be shaken." Having started the Chinese war, the army was placed in a position where it was impossible not to fight against the United States.

CONCLUSION

"Lacking the resolution or capacity to choose," Raymond Aron has written, "Japan ultimately found herself in a war with China, which the Japanese

armies vainly attempted to occupy, and with the United States and Great Britain, maritime powers, protecting the islands."* While simplistic, the observation correctly refers to the fundamental predicament of Japanese military expansionism in 1941, an inability to concentrate on either continental or southern expansion. Yet it would be misleading to attribute the simultaneous war with China and with America and Britain to Japan's lack of resolution or the capacity to choose. The Japanese image of world affairs was such that, following the changes in the international situation in 1938–39, the time seemed opportune to create a pan-Asian sphere of autonomy, of which Japanese-controlled China would be a foundation.

The decision to go to war with the United States before the end of the Chinese war was made when the Japanese army and navy came to view an impending conflict with America as inevitable. This view in turn was derived from an emerging image of the United States as a power intent upon establishing its influence in China and in Southeast Asia, thereby obstructing Japan's paths of expansion. Having accepted this image, there seemed to be no alternative but to go to war. War against China and war against America were conceptually merged as a struggle for the establishment of a free Asia. . . .

*Raymond Aron, *Peace and War: A Theory of International Relations* (New York, 1966), p. 190.

The Indian subcontinent contains nearly a fifth of the world's population and is representative of the multiethnic, multiracial, multilingual states of

South and Southeast Asia. It is divided into thousands of castes, clans, and tribes, thirty language groups and several dialects, and is organized into social systems of varying complexity ranging from Hindu to Muslim civilizations. The Indian army, however, is a pure product of British rule, a true representative of the Raj.

STEPHEN P. COHEN

The Indian Army After Independence

The partition of British India into the states of India and Pakistan after independence in 1947, was accompanied by the division (some have said vivisection) of the British Indian Army into two national armies. Each of these armies shares the legacy of the British Indian Army, although that legacy seems to have been differently interpreted in the two successor states. What follows is not a history of the military in India and Pakistan since 1947, but an examination of the legacy and an interpretation of the organizational and ideological imperatives which have shaped and will continue to shape the two successor armies. Briefly, these imperatives were:

1) Under the British important decisions could be (and sometimes had to be) referred to London. Severe civilian-military disputes in India were decided by the Home government, which had the power to make its decision stick. In independent India and Pakistan new systems of

From Stephen P. Cohen, The Indian Army: Its Contribution to the Development of a Nation *(Berkeley, 1971), pp. 169–200. Copyright © 1971 by the Regents of the University of California; reprinted by permission of the University of California Press.*

decision-making had to be created, and the Indian elite had to learn how to operate in these systems.

2) The central position of the Indian Army in the British Raj was unacceptable in nationalist Pakistan, and especially India. The military was omnipresent in British India. It was particularly visible in its support of local police forces suppressing nationalist agitations. Presumably, independence meant a sharp reduction in the military's · internal security role, and a parallel reduction in the hostility between the military and Indian politicians, many of whom had their own images of the armies of a free India or Pakistan.

3) The organization of the British Indian Army was particularly subject to criticism during the preindependence years, and was regarded by many political leaders as hopelessly feudal, inequalitarian, and caste-bound. In particular the "martial races theory" and the selection of commissioned officers by social status were regarded as anachronistic, if not dangerous to the fledgling Indian democracy. The limited contact of politicians with the military before 1947 reinforced their suspicion of the motives and loyalties

of those who had voluntarily served under the British.

Had partition been followed by a long period of relative peace, the changes implicit in the nationalist criticism might have been speedily effected. However, partition also ushered in a period of permanent Indian-Pakistani hostility, complicated after 1959 by the presence of China as a major threat to Indian security. The effect of these hostilities was to postpone, rather than to precipitate, change, for the military resisted organizational changes in times when troops were needed for active defense. Civilians, overwhelmingly inexperienced in military affairs, were reluctant to press for change.

CIVILIAN-MILITARY RELATIONS AND THE HIGHER DIRECTION OF WAR

During most of the British rule strategic decisions were jointly made by India and Whitehall. The Indian Army had considerable autonomy in minor matters, but important decisions were made with the concurrence of the Viceroy, and often referred to London for further consideration by the British government and senior military leadership. Independence meant that decisions would be made in India and Pakistan, and that new personnel would be making these decisions.

In India civilian-military affairs quickly resolved themselves into a three-cornered relationship between young Indian officers, none of whom had served in a rank higher than brigadier during World War II, members of the civil service (very few of whom had served in the Defense Ministry or had been connected with military matters under the British), and the political leaders, who had even less defense experience. The administrative and organizational changes introduced after independence indicate a fairly effective alliance between the civil service and the politicians, an alliance created for the purpose of reducing the role of the military in the decision-making process.

A major blow to the autonomy and influence of the military—especially to the only substantial service, the army—was struck on Independence Day, August 15, 1947, when the position of Commander-in-Chief in India was abolished. India had always had a Commander-in-Chief, and he had hitherto been the single source of military advice for the Indian government. (The navy and air chiefs were his subordinates.) After this date the three chiefs were responsible to the Defense Minister, and were collectively the professional military advisers to the government. The ostensible reasons for this drastic reduction in the relative influence of the chief of the army were: to promote "balanced" growth among the three services, to provide better advice on technical navy and air force matters, and to follow all "modern" armed forces, which have each of the three services under an independent chief. There were also good unofficial reasons for this step. The only challenge to civilian authority could come from the numerically dominant army; reducing the authority of its chief to the point where he was not even first among equals made it easier to balance off the army with the other two services.

The strengthening of the civil-service dominated Ministry of Defense was a second critical organizational change. The military had always been under the close financial scrutiny of the Ministry of Finance. This scrutiny was not reduced, but it was complemented by the growth of the Defense Ministry's role in the decision-making process, quite often at a low level. Charged with the responsibility of providing expert advice to the minister or the Cabinet, the Defense Ministry expanded its capacity to control information and make decisions. It also assumed some of the former powers of the Commander-in-Chief, and it "became the responsibility of the Ministry to ensure that a uniform policy to the greatest extent possible was evolved and that decisions taken in respect of one Service did not produce repercussions on the other two Services." Information policy and—critically—responsibility for defense production were placed under the control of the Ministry of Defense.

These and other bureaucratic changes were accompanied by many adjustments in the status of the military in India. Some of these adjustments were symbolic, others were substantive. The adjustments made in the Warrant of Precedence during the postindependence years were of particular interest. A secretary in the government of India ranked lower than a lieutenant-general until 1947; afterwards he was made to rank with a full general. The Chief Secretary of a State formerly ranked with brigadiers;

after independence he was made to rank with a major-general. In 1948, the Chief of the Army Staff ranked with judges of the Supreme Court of India, but was senior to chief ministers outside their states or the Secretary General of the External Affairs Ministry. In 1951, Chief of the Army Staff became junior to the Supreme Court justices, and in 1963 he became junior to chief ministers outside their states, to the Cabinet Secretary, and to the Secretary General. Disparities in pay also developed. A deputy secretary in the government of India draws less pay than a brigadier, who may have ten years more service, but is equated with him in the Warrant of Precedence; even the relative status of the military in relation to the police has been downgraded, and officers deputed to quasi-military organizations such as the Border Security Force may find themselves under the command of police officers with less pay, less service, but a higher rank.

All these organizational changes had the effect of reducing the military's role in the decision-making process. The military was thoroughly indoctrinated with the principle of civilian control and never protested against the reduction of its own powers, or at least never protested to the point of resignation. Indian officers were relatively inexperienced and were reluctant to test their authority against that of the government. Unfortunately, neither civilian politicians nor civil servants developed the expertise and skills necessary to understand and meet the Chinese threat which emerged full-blown in 1959. Even today, the personnel of the Ministry of Defense is relatively inexperienced in defense affairs; out of fourteen officers of the rank of joint secretary and above, only four have risen from the rank of deputy secretary in the Ministry of Defense itself; the rest have entered directly at the level of joint secretary. The record of the political leadership of the Ministry of Defense is no better. Very few ministers of defense appointed since 1947 had any previous defense experience or recorded interest in defense affairs; many were not even politically influential. Krishna Menon (appointed in 1957) was an exception.

This paucity of talent reflected the small number of Indian politicians who were seriously interested in defense affairs. And, of these, many had been in non-Congress parties. The liberals as a political force had virtually vanished from India years before World War II, and their political descendents were able to mount only token opposition in Parliament. The slate of the Congress leaders was clean with regard to defense matters (they paid little attention to improving the military administration of the British, but did not attempt to subvert or infiltrate the military, either). Yet the Congress leaders decided early that defense was not a high priority as long as the only likely enemy was Pakistan. In effect, the decision was made over a period of years to keep military administration and defense matters out of the main stream of politics. An information policy was formulated which in many ways was more restrictive than that of the British, and continues to impair intelligent criticism of defense policy.

The Indian defense decision-making process is, as it was during the years of British rule, largely an administrative process, closed to outside scrutiny. If anything, the process has become more decentralized and more compartmentalized than the British Indian system. The military has sensed the difficulties of this arrangement and has frequently made proposals for the increased centralization of defense policy making, usually by the creation of a chief of the Joint Chiefs of Staff. They have not, however, gone beyond this proposal and presented a scheme for the thorough integration and reorganization of higher strategic decision-making which would take into account defense interests in several ministries. The present system is fragmented with several decision-making centers, none of which are adequately staffed or equipped to consider a broad range of security issues. For example, India has no single department or institution adequately equipped, either intellectually or politically, to make decisions or even to study such an important issue as nuclear weapons procurement.

Part of the difficulty of the government of India during the past twenty years in managing its security policy stems from an inadequate conception of civilian-military relations. The attitudes inherited from the British have turned out to be a crippling legacy, providing neither theoretical nor practical guidance.

Krishna Menon's formulation of the proper relationship is widely shared:

It is wrong for the army to try to make policy; their business is to be concerned with military tactics. Military planning and arrangements and things of that kind must remain in the hands of the Government, and even inside the Government these questions are largely conditioned by finance. I believe the statement that was made recently, that strategy was left with the army, was due to misuse of terms. The Government is not going to say that it wants one company here or two companies there, but the Government will certainly say, "we should attack Pakistan" or "we should not attack Pakistan" or "we should accept trainees from Indonesia and Malaysia," or things of that kind; these are all matters of policy. . . . Of course, military matters are merely questions of expertise; strategy includes considerations that are related to our political orientation.*

Except for the implications of the final sentence, even the military would agree to this statement. Yet, Menon's own actions as Defense Minister indicate the many gradations between military affairs and policy affairs, and, as in the Kitchener-Curzon dispute and other civilian-military clashes in British India, much depends on who defines precisely the meaning of "military" and "political." Menon found it difficult to adhere to a restrictive formula. During his tenure as Defense Minister he initiated many reforms in hitherto "purely" military affairs. He widened the base of recruitment of the officer corps, tried to make the military more aware of its social obligations, and greatly expanded the range of military items manufactured in India, laying the groundwork for relative self-sufficiency in the late 1960s.

But Menon's most significant departure from his own theory of civilian-

*Quoted in Michael Brecher, *India and World Politics* (London: Oxford University Press, 1968), p. 260.

military relations occurred during the prolonged confrontation with the Chinese along the Himalayan frontier. During the months before the outbreak of hostilities in late 1962, Menon and Jawaharlal Nehru directly supervised the placement of individual brigades, companies, and even platoons, as the Chinese and Indian forces engaged in mutual encirclement of isolated outposts. Neither Menon nor Nehru had any earlier military experience, and the Indian Army still harbors an extraordinary amount of bitterness at their use of troops as essentially political pawns. As far as the military was concerned, peace had turned into war and the politicians were still meddling.

The military's own approach to civilian-military matters is hardly more sophisticated than the civilians'. The British tradition of separate spheres of military and civilian activity has carried over. Even today Indian officers like to boast that politics and the military do not mix; that the two are immutably different and separate, and that the military is, and should forever be, outside (some say "above") politics. Junior officers in the Indian Army are taught to be political illiterates, and are content to remain so, concentrating on "purely professional" matters. Those few generals who have earned a reputation for political expertise (or at least familiarity with politicians), such as B. M. Kaul, have not been popular with their colleagues.

Yet, India's strategic environment, particularly her sensitive borders, makes it impossible for the military to avoid political questions in time of peace, let alone during hostilities. As officers are promoted beyond the rank of brigadier, they must demonstrate an understanding of politics. Whether politically sensitive officers tend to be promoted, or whether they are sensitized in their new roles is not clear. It is also difficult to tell the ratio of "fighting" generals to "political" generals. One must assume that the Indian government is concerned with the problem, for it has established an institution, the National Defense College, solely for the purpose of broadening the background of promising officers of brigadier or equivalent rank. The officers are exposed, for the first time in their service careers, to a wide range of political, economic, and strategic issues. The effectiveness of such training is uncertain, although Chinese-Indian politics can hardly be understood without it. Indian politicians and the military quickly grasped the motives and actions of the Pakistanis. The Indians and Pakistanis had common cultural and institutional origins, and frequently personal links. The rules were understood by both sides. The Indians discovered, however, that the Chinese challenge was different, both in substance and style, and the events of 1962 are remembered in the army with much bewilderment and bitterness. The legacy of the British was to keep the military politically neutral. The Indians learned, however, that it was necessary to equip the military with political understanding. . . .

RECRUITMENT AND REPRESENTATIVENESS

The organizational format of the British Indian Army had been particularly criticized by Indian politicians before independence, but was defended by those with close ties to the military. As we have seen, recruitment by class and caste was especially subject to attack, and World War II demonstrated clearly the irrelevance of much of the martial-races theory. Indianization of the officer corps had been another subject of hot debate, although the expansion of the army from 1939 to 1945 had led to the Indianization of most units. The role of the Indian officer was a related and still relevant question.

Few Indian politicians have articulated the deep, nonmilitary stakes behind the issue of recruitment, but many sense the importance of the question. The nature of recruitment is important to the whole issue of national identity and nation-building, especially in a democracy. Democratic states have always had difficulty in relating equalitarian, democratic values to the values of the military whose main purpose is to kill and destroy. Should this task be left to those who volunteer for it, or should it be one of the obligations of citizenship? The alternatives become more critical if the volunteers are an unrepresentative group, reflecting regional, class, or caste predispositions, or all three at the same time.

Representativeness is closely related to the spirit of a military organization. In any army individuals fight for several reasons—because of the pay, because of regimental or unit loyalty, because of personal loyalty to a civilian or military commander, and because of emotional identification with the larger political unit. Modern nationalism has emphasized the latter motivation—patriotism. Politicians who are trying to build or maintain a nation-state have always sensed the importance of using patriotism as a fighting motive. The spirit of patriotism increases political leverage over the military. It also increases national awareness in that part of society which is most likely to adopt purely professional, regional, or parochial bonds of loyalty. Politicians thus become concerned with the degree of equalitarianism within the military—the rank structure, officer-troop relations, pay, service conditions, and criteria for promotion. They also become interested in training and indoctrination programs having political content.*

After independence, Indian and Pakistani military and political elites turned to the problem of reshaping their military systems to reflect more closely their views of what an Indian or Pakistani army should look like. Both successor states are still—after more than twenty years—fundamentally reflections of the British Indian Army, although there has been considerable change since 1963.

THE OFFICER CORPS

Despite some desultory talk, neither army has changed the relationship of the officer to the other ranks, nor abolished the position of junior commissioned officer. Both armies still are class-bound in the sense that officers are generally drawn from higher strata of society. They must be

*Indian political leaders interested in developing an Indian nation were on firm ground in their criticisms of the Indian military system under the British. In the West, the rise of the modern nation-state was closely associated with the development of an equalitarian and representative military.

able to use English as their medium of communication, and aspire to a life style which clearly imitates the British Indian Army commissioned officer. Visitors to the subcontinent often conclude (as have many Indians and Pakistanis) that the military remains the last outpost of the British Raj. As in other former colonies the military is often regarded as the most "modern" sector of society. The military has a brusqueness of manner and a routinized method of problem-solving which often passes for development. Much of the recent optimism in Western intellectual circles (particularly American) concerning the great potential role the military might play in nation-building in the third world was based on this image of competence and efficiency.

Yet, behind the facade, even Indians and Pakistanis drawn from the most highly Westernized sectors of their societies have, as a group, transitional or intermediate personalities and outlooks. Individuals in the officer corps whose childhood and upbringing did not include a strong traditional component are rare. They have "honeycomb" personalities, and must shift rapidly from one role to another: from a purely technical encounter to a traditional home or personal life. They may present one face to a professional colleague,* another to a Western visitor, another to their

*Even in their professional life they may occupy a number of subroles and interact with a wide range of phenomena. An officer must learn to deal successfully with things—equipment, weapons, logistics problems—and with people. The latter will range from highly traditional *jawans* and camp followers to highly Westernized senior officers and civilians.

family, and still another in a nonprofessional indigenous context.

Two important trends are under way (especially in India) which make the contrast between traditional and modern modes of behavior even stronger in the officer corps: a changing base of recruitment, and a changing professional context.

For many years after independence it seemed as if nothing was being done to alter the composition of the officer corps in either India or Pakistan. A sampling of the cadets in the National Defense Academy (India) in the mid-1950s indicated a continuing preponderance of Punjabis, who comprised on the average a third of the cadet corps. Delhi, which is adjacent to the Punjab, supplied about 15 percent of the cadets during the 1954–1956 period, while Madya Pradesh, Madras, Mysore, and Kerala supplied less than 5 percent each. West Bengal and Andhra supplied less than 1 percent in some years. In Pakistan during this period virtually all army officers were recruited from the West Wing.

Yet, at least for India, these figures are not only obsolete, but they are misleading. They do not reflect important changes which have occurred in the social and geographical sources of the officer corps, and they do not reflect a rethinking of the problem of recruitment, especially after 1965.

Although precise data are unavailable, the status of the officer seems to have changed considerably, at least in India. Since 1939 the pay schedule of the lower ranks of the officer corps has remained the same while the value of the rupee has declined 80

percent. The attractiveness of officers in the marriage market (admittedly an indirect indicator!) has also suffered. Housing has become unusually difficult for the Indian officer corps, and since 1962 increased deployment in the Himalayas has led to a more rigorous pattern of life. The military has lost its attractiveness for the old elites of Indian society, and is becoming a more popular career for India's growing middle class.

The doubling of the Indian Army after 1962 (and large increase in the size of the air force and navy) has speeded up this process. The number of officers in technical and support branches has increased greatly, and these officers usually have an abbreviated professional military training. Some fighting officers are engineers or communications and logistics experts as well, and have dual professional loyalties. Unlike the infantry officers, they do not participate as intensely in the mystique of comradeship of arms based on ethnic or caste loyalties. Many officers, particularly the engineers, were not even interested in the military as a career, but were unable to find suitable jobs in civilian life. For them the military is a good, secure if somewhat arduous job, rather than a faith. These men are obviously more representative of Indian society than their pre-World War II predecessors, although there is no reason to doubt their quality as officers.

A second important modernizing trend has been the shift in the nature of the professional officer's purpose and function since independence. Although for many years after 1947 little changed in the Indian and

Pakistani military establishments, the Pakistan *coup* and the advent of V. K. Krishna Menon as Defense Minister in 1957 radically altered the traditional self-image of the officer corps. In the *coup*, the Pakistani military was thrust into the role of protector of the state. As for Menon, a powerful political figure initiated a series of reforms which stirred the political and social consciousness of some officers. The Indian military was further shaken by the advent of Communist China as a serious military threat.

These two trends—a gradual shift in the social base of the officer corps, and the rapid and increasing confrontation with a variety of new military tasks—produced a reexamination of the nature of the officer corps in India. The articles of the various professional Indian military journals—but especially the broad-gauged *Journal* of the United Service Institution of India—ask many of the same questions which were raised during the final years of British rule. "Officers for the Twenty-First Century" argues for a more scientifically trained officer candidate; "Our Military Tradition," savagely attacks all remnants of British customs in the Indian Army, and a letter rebuts it; "If Another Trial Comes" suggests the militarization of Indian society along Israeli lines; "Officer Like Qualities" describes the proper professional attitude of officers at each level of the hierarchy, and "Academic Recognition of Military Education" argues that military training and society have merged to the point where graduates of the various service academies should be given general societal recognition of their accomplishments.

Reconciliation between an increasingly middle-class officer corps, the proud, aristocratic traditions of the Indian military, and the growing military threat is the common theme of these articles. The problem is not simply to turn Indian youths into proper gentlemen, but also to turn them into effective officers. Considerable disagreement exists (especially between generations) about the degree to which a gentleman is automatically an effective officer. Thus, senior officers lament the radical changes that institutions such as the mess have undergone. This instrument of social indoctrination and professional control becomes increasingly irrelevant and ineffectual when young officers are already married, posted to distant operational units, or both. Conversely, younger officers are less enchanted with unit traditions of martial valor and are increasingly interested in the more mundane problems of service conditions, pensions, housing, and perquisites.

This extended and complex debate within the Indian military is a measure of the considerable—if belated—progress toward reconciliation of traditional, British, and contemporary modes of military and social organization. As the social composition of the officer corps continues to change, and as the military remains under external pressure, the debate will continue. The fact that it occurs at all—with considerable sophistication and apparently with no official approval or disapproval—is remarkable.

The officer corps of both successor states are examples of institutions whose members are successfully engaged in bridging the gap between past and present. Intellectuals in developing states are aware of the internal schisms in their society. Edward Shils notes that the alienation of the intellectuals in transitional societies is a state of being cut off from their indigenous culture: "the experience to which the allegation of being 'cut-off' refers is not to any serious extent a real result of the intellectuals' acceptance of the 'foreign,' modern culture. It rests rather on their own feeling of distance from the rest of their fellow nationals. . . ." Two paths are open to those whose aspirations and perceptions have been expanded through modern education: they may seek a "transcendence of concrete individuality," through communism, terror, and anti-authority movements, or they may adjust to a modern institutional role, become an individual within their own sphere of personal and private relationships. For an intellectual, this means becoming a gadfly of the existing social order without hostility for that order: criticism with affinity.

Military officers in India have been successful in following the second path of adjustment to their society. Although they may be deeply entangled in professional problems and debates, their commitment to the system which they criticize is firm. They do not display the symptoms of ambivalence and anxiety toward authority so often found in intellectuals although they criticize that authority. Probably no other group in South Asian society is so critical of politicians on particular issues, and yet is so strong in its support of the political system.

CASTE AND REGION IN THE RANKS

India and Pakistan have chosen to emphasize different components of their joint legacy, and recruitment to the two successor armies is based upon different principles. The Indian government made an early policy decision to terminate the creation of new single-caste regiments. The regiments which it raised were mixed, such as the Parachute Regiment. Since 1963, and the doubling in size of the army, an attempt has been made to broaden the base of recruitment of existing regiments. Although they bear the caste or class name of the older regiment, many are no longer single-caste or single-class. The Indian Army has, at present, three types of infantry battalions: "pure," "mixed company," and "totally mixed" heterogeneous units. The Gurkhas typify the pure unit; they are recruited primarily from Nepal, although some of their troops come from India (usually the relatives of former soldiers). Similarly, the Sikh Regiment recruits only Sikhs, and the Sikh Light Infantry Regiment recruits only scheduled caste Sikhs, who are segregated from higher-caste coreligionists. Some regiments, however, contain two or three "classes," and segregate them on the company level. The Punjab Regiment contains several classes organized in this way, as does the Rajputana Rifles, which has separate Jat Hindu and Muslim companies. The Rajput Regiment is composed primarily of Rajputs, but has several battalions of Bengalis who are enrolled as Rajputs in name only. Finally, and most interesting, is the third type of infantry battalion—that which is thoroughly mixed. The Madras Regiment recruits any eligible Indian from the southern states. It contains Christians, Hindus, Sikhs, and Muslims in the same section. They also mix Indians from all southern states in the same sections. The Parachute Regiment is similarly totally mixed, drawing from all of India. Some regiments bearing caste names draw, in fact, from all castes and classes in a particular region (for instance the Dogra Regiment, which recruits from Kangra and adjacent areas). Others bearing caste names have also expanded their base: the Mahar Regiment, which formerly recruited only untouchable Mahars, now takes in Indians of many castes, (but especially other scheduled [untouchable] caste groups seeking a place in the army.)

The Indian Army considers mixed-caste units as effective as pure units if they have been allowed to mature as a fighting force for a long period. Long-recruited classes have ready-made traditions and legends of martial valor. Newly recruited classes take some time to "settle down" and develop their own martial myths. One critical factor is the development of loyalty and affection between officer and soldier. Many officers have now come to regard mixed units with greater pride and respect than the old

pure martial units. They do, more truly, symbolize the Indian nation.*

The Indian government has annually found itself attacked from two directions with regard to the caste composition of the army. Every debate over Defense Ministry funds produces demands for new, single-class regiments. (The Chamars and Ahirs have been particularly vocal.) Other groups press for the total abolition of caste and class as principles of recruitment, in name and in fact. Since the government has not yet released any figures on the actual composition of individual regiments the debate is somewhat unreal, for it is impossible to calculate the actual rate of change in the composition of the military. The government is correct when it claims that any Indian citizen is free to join the army, but the critics are equally correct when they point out that certain regiments are reserved for certain classes.

These marginal but increasingly significant changes in the social composition of the military have been accompanied by the development of a new recruitment rationale. This rationale has had to serve several pur-

*Another factor which determines the stability of a unit (in terms of discipline and eagerness for combat, for example) is the attitude of the villages in the region in which the unit is recruited. Villages (or castes) with developed ties to the military serve as agents for recruitment and are important in maintaining discipline. To keep up their reputation they will return to duty any defectors, or informally punish soldiers whose actions might damage the group's reputation. Soldiering is not an anonymous profession for most Indian or Pakistani Army *jawans*.

poses. It had to be acceptable to the military and meet their manpower requirements, it had to take account of the democratic environment of the military, and it had to justify equal access to the military and equal obligation for all citizens. At the same time it had to account for the fact that the military was and is largely dominated by north Indian castes and classes.

This "secular theory of the martial races" was succinctly summarized by a recent Minister of Defense, Y. B. Chavan. He frequently declared, for example, that "we are all Ksatriyas now," and that when it comes to the defense of the Indian nation, all are equally martial, whatever caste or class label they may wear.

The consequence of this new theory is to stress the individual martial characteristics of each class. Thus, in a book recounting the martial traditions of the Indian Army (published under official auspices), the gallant traditions of the Bihari and Madrassi soldier were recounted along with those of the Rajputs, Sikhs, and Dogras. Its author advises the reader to pursue the study of the Indian Army in the works of such theoreticians of the martial races as Lieutenant-General Sir George McMunn, but provides an account of those martial races and martial heroes who had been ignored by the British. The source of fighting efficiency is seen in loyalty to the regiment and loyalty to the nation.

The secular martial-races theory attempts to combine aspects of the nationalist view and the martial-races theory. It is a melding of two popular views, and should grow in strength over the years with or without continued official patronage. Its attitude of compromise and its reconciliation of opposing theories of recruitment is strikingly similar to what Wilfred Cantwell Smith has termed the "Hindu view of secularism." Just as Hinduism permits a wide variety of beliefs and practices within its diffuse structure, the secular martial-races theory permits the continuance of strong martial traditions within a broad equalitarian framework. In both instances compromise is essential. Hinduism has had great difficulty absorbing a particularist, aggressive religion such as Islam. The secular martial-races theory has the same difficulty in dealing with a class or caste which insists on its superior status as a martial race. Some may want to be "more equal" than others. The various groups must compromise with face-saving devices for those not yet up to standard. Great care is taken to insure that minority communities are well represented in awards lists, and that the most favorable image is projected to the public.

The revised theory of the martial races is important to India because she is facing an opponent (Pakistan) who makes frequent and overt challenges to her secular underpinnings. To some extent, Pakistanis attempt to perpetuate the British image of an India composed of many discrete social bodies, destined to spin apart as a result of communal tensions. An expression of this image occurred during the height of the 1965 war when considerable Pakistani propaganda was directed at the Sikh community, supporting demands for a separate Sikh state.*

India has used the Chinese invasion and the conflicts with Pakistan to blunt external and internal efforts to divide her and to encourage national integration. During each recent conflict a systematic, deliberate attempt was made to point out the variety of the military, to list the communities of individual soldiers and units which have performed heroically, and to give special attention to members of minority communities or religions. This policy is a great change from British practice which tended to stress the fragility of the balance in the military, and the great danger of tampering with it. Contemporary Indian political leaders have not yet had serious conflict with their military, and can safely exploit for integrative and other political purposes the diversity that exists in the services. If the trend of the past few years is indicative, the stress on diversity will grow as an organizational doctrine.

Pakistan encompasses almost as diverse a social system as does India. Consequently, although Islamic doctrine is available as an organizing principle, Pakistan has as much, or more, tension in relating theory to practice as India. Pakistan was founded and survives because of two basic assumptions; one negative and one positive. Negatively, many thought that the Muslims of the subcontinent were culturally and socially backward, and were vulnerable to Hindu exploitation through the latter's

*A separate "Punjabi speaking state," a euphemism for a predominately Sikh state, was created shortly after the fighting ended.

greater numbers and Westernization. Positively, Islam provided a doctrine through which the Muslim community could identify and separate itself from the Hindus, thereby purifying and raising the community to a social and cultural level in which competition would be equal.* When Pakistan became a state, these assumptions were applied to the new nation's military organization.

The Islam religion in Pakistan overrides all cultural and historical differences:

The soldiers of the Pakistan Army . . . are drawn from many different tribes and people—from the Pathans of the North-West, from the Punjabis, Sindhis, and Baluchis and from the Bengalis of East Pakistan. All share a sense of pride in their past and a determination to serve Pakistan loyally and well in the future. Uniting them all is the bond of Islam with its straightforward belief in the one and only God and in the prophethood of Muhammad; a faith which transcends all barriers of geography and language.

Officially, all Muslims, because they are Muslims, are equally entitled to bear arms. This belief leads to the corollary that Muslim soldiers are more effective because for them reli-

*Because of the great diversity of Indian Muslims, Pakistan was first envisioned as constituting only the northwest portions of India, and perhaps adjacent portions of Afghanistan, a region bound together by cultural, historical, social and religious ties. When East Bengal was included, it became obvious that many of these ties were not really shared, and that even the call of Islam did not hold out the same attraction for millions of Muslims.

gion and state are united in purpose.

Theoretically, there should be no great imbalance in the composition of the Pakistani military, either in terms of numbers, or distribution among units. In fact, however, the Pakistani military (especially the army) is more unbalanced than the British Indian Army or the contemporary Indian Army. Two explanations present themselves. First, many Pakistani officers regard Bengalis as particularly unsuited for military life. They argue that a great deal of time, patience, and training will be necessary before a military tradition can be established in East Bengal. Second, and perhaps crucially: Can East Pakistanis be trusted to remain within Pakistan once a separation, already geographical, becomes militarily plausible and East Pakistanis can manage their own defense. Until the time comes when suitable recruits are available in adequate numbers, when political pressures for a more equalitarian recruiting system become greater, and when the integration of Pakistan has reached the point where the East can be fully trusted, it seems likely that the imbalance between the two wings will continue to be politically embarrassing to the military whose leadership is drawn almost entirely from the West. The military claims to be an all-Pakistani organization. However, East Pakistanis represent only 2 percent of the army, and racial, cultural, and political antagonisms have already produced separatist movements in the East. The official rationalization, that Pakistan is indivisible and the East should not mind being defended largely by units drawn from the Punjab and West Wing, does little to ease the concern and pride of East Bengalis. They have vivid memories of tough Pathan and Punjabi police and military units imported by the British for law enforcement and suppression of nationalist agitation. Continued inequality in the army keeps that memory fresh.

In summary, in both India and Pakistan, a considerable gap exists between equalitarian theories of recruitment and the actual composition of the military. If no effort is made to interfere with the system of recruitment already in operation (voluntary), then the armies of both nations tend to recruit from the classes, castes, and regions which already predominate. It is effective, cheaper, and coincides with the predispositions of many military men who believe in some variation of the martial-races theory. Since all Indians and Pakistanis now have the legal right to serve in the military, the military to that extent has come to reflect nationalist and equalitarian doctrine. But since recruitment to some units (especially the prestigious infantry units) is restricted to specific ethnic groups, the military has not abandoned its ties to traditional Indian and British patterns.

THE ARMY, ITS LEGACY, AND THE FUTURE OF INDIA

The legacy of the British Indian Army has been to limit the nonmilitary activities of the present Indian and Pakistani military. The present military plays no civic-action roles, and only limited "aid to the civil" roles, which are rapidly diminishing through the creation of paramilitary security forces. Although new tasks have been taken up by the two armies—road construction, weapons production, and, in the Himalayas, community-development projects—these are directed toward clear-cut military objectives. Indians have no interest in a "people's army," mass conscription, or use of the army for explicitly social-welfare ends. More surprisingly, there is no pressure from politicians, intellectuals, or the press for such an expansion of the military's role. The professional ethic of the old Indian Army dictated that the army's value stem from high standards of training and the unique mystique of the relationship of the officer to the other ranks. The standard of training remains high, and the mystique, though declining, is still present. To officers (in the Indian Army at least) profession comes first, and "politics" finds no place.

This relatively limited role was eminently compatible with the political system of India after independence. That system was dominated by a highly Westernized elite, intent upon establishing a parliamentary democracy based upon Western models. The military had no internal political role in their plans, and was to be confined to external defense activities.

However, even as this parliamentary democracy was being established, a mass political culture emerged, which took full advantage of the new political and technological innovations. The growth of this culture in India has been thoroughly documented. Modern technology has been introduced to local or regional groups which were previously isolated from the mainstream of political life. Paradoxically, regionalism and provincialism may grow proportionately faster than nationalism. The focus of public issues shifts from a nationalist orientation to the regional question of distribution of resources in a system of scarcity, especially such resources as jobs, profits, and status.

This vigorous growth of a mass political culture indicates that the revolution of modernity will not be led by the Westernized elites but by these newly powerful groups. Technology, and its frequent companions, democracy, are the keys to such groups. This postindependence development is probably the second phase of political change in many new nations. It is as important as the replacement of the Western colonial power by a Westernized indigenous civilian elite, or by a Westernized military elite.

What role will the military play in such a transformation? Given the continued growth of the scope and influence of the mass political culture, and no change in India's relationship to the great powers, three developments seem possible. They are not mutually exclusive and may occur simultaneously. In decreasing order of probability:

1) The military stands as a deterrent to regional fragmentation, separatism, or secession. Observers have often suggested that the intensification of provincial politics poses a threat to Indian unity. However, just as India's diversity acts as a deterrent to military designs on political power, a unified military acts as a deterrent to regional politicians eyeing separatism. Whether

the claim to independence of such politicians is based upon regional, linguistic, or ethnic distinctiveness, they will ultimately have to face the question of military viability. Presently, no region seems close to having the military resources to sustain its independence. To any politician contemplating separatism it should seem clear, after brief reflection, that military weakness is a powerful argument for remaining within, and supporting, the Indian Union.

2) The fact that the military of modern India recruits from all groups and has a national perspective, makes it especially sensitive to, and scornful of, political parochialism. As a group, the officer corps is critical of the disorder and unparliamentary behavior of groups newly "recruited" to the political system. The outlook of the officers remains that of the elite political culture, and they stress adherence to parliamentary procedures, in form as much as substance. The emerging mass political culture offends their sense of propriety and challenges their paternalist approach to social relations. The military could intervene in the political system as a result of their misperception of the significance of this growing mass political culture. Severe parliamentary instability in the center, or social and political instability particularly in several border states, would increase the military's disposition to intervene. Such intervention would probably come through the President and might simply demand a "cooling off" of political activity, or the elimination of particular groups from the political process. Without major social changes such reform

would hardly have anything but a marginal impact upon the increasing politicization of India, and might in fact hasten that politicization.

3) A final development might be the emergence of the military or of military symbols as a common denominator between the two political cultures. If, as it has been argued, the relationship between the growing mass political culture and the elite political culture of India becomes more tense in the next few years, a major elevation of the military as a model or as an object of veneration may well provide at least a temporary political solution on which both political cultures can compromise. The Westernized elite has often indicated its admiration for the way the military teaches western virtues such as self-sacrifice, loyalty, and discipline. Many of these same virtues are deeply embedded in Indian culture, which is laden with martial traditions and military heroes. If present military pressures continue, Indian society might be rallied around a quasi-militaristic ethic with a spirit drawn from traditional martial India and manipulative techniques drawn from the United States and the Soviet Union. This new ethic would justify the financial sacrifices necessary for economic development and the perpetuation of security measures necessary to meet political opposition.

Evidence indicates that this process has begun on a symbolic level. Political integration is ultimately a collective state of mind. It implies a group of people reacting together to common stimuli: a flag, a leader, a name, or—most relevant for our interests—a threat to a boundary. The military is a potent symbol because of its link to defense. Reaction to the military in times of crisis is a measure of national integration.

The military has always been a cathetic object to the classes, castes, and religions which have historically contributed heavily to its ranks. Since the military is closely related to the concept of a political unity (especially after its transformation from an imperial to a national froce) presumably there is some integrative by-product. This integration is of great concern to the military, which is preoccupied with the task of maintaining a stable and reliable recruiting base.

For the general population, and for many civilian elites with no earlier attachment to the military, the military can only serve as a symbol of what they would like the "new" India or Pakistan to be.

Through independence the leaders of the nationalist movement redefined the nature of the armed services and created a potential national symbol. Before 1962, Indians (for political reasons) had been reluctant to use the military as a symbol of nationhood, although the process began earlier in Pakistan. The first war over Kashmir, and the limited conflicts with neighbors kept the military alive as a minor symbol of nationhood, but its role was carefully circumscribed by Nehru. The Chinese invasion, the death of Nehru, second Pakistan war, the further shock of Lal Bahadur Shastri's death, and the apparent misdirection of economic priorities culminating in serious famine in 1966 have all contributed to a gradual shift in this role. Indians increasingly see existence as a matter of military might. A natural elevation of the military has occurred, and the employment of the military as a symbol of integration has been rapidly speeded up. Military symbolism is consciously and explicitly being taught to those hitherto unaware or unappreciative. Those most skilled in the dissemination of such doctrine—politicians, and communications elites—have undergone a cram course in military matters.

If the military develops new roles and new relationships with Indian society, important new differences between India and Pakistan may result. Not only will there be two different system types (assuming India retains a democratic government, a form perfectly compatible with a sophisticated or moderate militarism), but the relationship between army and society will be different. Pakistan may find its military more powerful politically but less powerful socially and ideologically. India will not find its military politically more powerful, but socially more pervasive.

The extent of the influence of the Indonesian army in politics in the last two decades has been considerable. From a passive, professional army in the years following the Second World War, it became in the next decade an alternative ladder to political success and eventually an alternative political organization to the Communist party. Once Sukarno's control weakened, and he tipped the balance of his influence toward the Indonesian communists in 1966, the army intervened and has since governed Indonesia.

HAROLD MAYNARD

Indonesian Military Elite Role Perceptions

[Since 1966 the Indonesian military has changed its role perception and expansion.]

INDONESIAN MILITARY ELITE ROLE PERCEPTIONS AS DERIVED FROM MILITARY WRITINGS

1. Role of a military born in revolution.
2. Role of the military as upholder of pledged norms.
3. Stewardship-leadership role of the military.
4. Role of the military in civil-military relations.
5. External defense role of the military.
6. Internal security role of the military.
7. Role of the military in national development.
8. Self-maintenance role of the military.

As with all inductively derived typologies, this one is tentative. It might be modified through analysis of

From Harold Maynard, "A Comparison of Military Elite Role Perceptions in Indonesia and the Philippines" (Ph.D. diss., The American University, 1976), pp. 170–76, 180–81, 184–91, by permission of the author.

additional documents. Certainly it will change over time as military roles and role perceptions evolve.

Noteworthy in this particular typology of role perceptions is the fact that it does not break neatly into the two roles specified by Indonesian military doctrine—namely, the "instrument of the state" role (the traditional Western concept of an apolitical professional organization directed primarily to defending the country from external aggression) and the "instrument of the revolution" role (the military as a functional group participating and leading in social, economic and political spheres).

Some individuals will argue that these role types can be divided between the two basic functions specified in the doctrine. And, to a certain extent, this is true. One might, for example, suggest that the internal security and external defense roles of the military fall within the scope of the first function while the role of the military as national leader and national developer clearly fall within the second function. At this point, however, the argument begins to break down, for each of the remaining roles is not clearly restricted to either the military or civilian functions. . . .

HISTORICAL ROLE: BORN OF REVOLUTION

First there is the legitimizing role of the military as born in revolution. This role perception is discussed by virtually all Indonesian officers who write about the role of the military. It serves as both the chronological and theoretical basis for the other role descriptions.

When one reads materials authored by Indonesian officers, one is immediately struck by the fact that they have developed a profound sense of history—history of their country and history of the military. For this reason the Indonesian military elite often refers to lessons learned from the past and honors the anniversary of the Republic (17 August) and anniversary of the founding of the Indonesian Armed Forces (5 October). On these days ceremonies are held, speeches made, and commemorative articles written. Such occasions are used to remind the military and the general public of the historical role of the military and, most particularly, the role that the military played during the struggle for independence.

On the twenty-fifth anniversary of the official founding of the Indonesian Armed Forces (ABRI), President Suharto underscored the military's revolutionary origins in an address to the Armed Forces. Suharto reminded military officers that the lofty ideals of the revolutionary army should be retained and strengthened. Specifically, he stressed that the origins of the military's dual function could be found in the revolutionary era. And, most importantly, he stated that the revolutionary experience meant that the military's civil role took *precedence* over its defense role. In his words:

The Armed Forces of the Republic of Indonesia was born in the midst of our struggle to uphold independence. Because of that a member of ABRI is first of all one who struggles, after that he is a soldier. It was the historical background of this birth that shaped the attitude of ABRI of sharing always the responsibility towards safeguarding the ideals of freedom and giving substance to this independence.

. . . The military is proud of the fact that the Indonesian Armed Forces were created by the Indonesian people, *not* by civilian politicians and *not* by the Dutch or the Japanese. The Indonesian military considers itself to be the embodiment of the armed fighting people. General Nasution, and military authors who have followed him, have discredited the idea that the army was actually an outgrowth of the Dutch Colonial Army (KNIL) or the World War II army built by the Japanese (PETA). Nasution labeled the KNIL as "simply a police army." It was, for him, a very small force made up of ethnic minority groups which became a caste apart from the people. The PETA, though composed of "true" Indonesians and nationalistic in spirit, was nonetheless a creation of the Japanese and was designed for Japanese purposes. In the end even PETA officers led rebellions against the Japanese overlords. Thus, it was not until after World War II that a truly Indonesian military was created. And, it was created not by government edit but by the spontaneous effort of the nation's youth to oppose the return of the Dutch. . . .

One can clearly see that it is on the basis of the revolutionary experience that the military justifies its civil function. In fact, in most cases after 1962 the military describes the two functions of the Armed Forces as consisting of the function of "instrument of the state" and "instrument of revolution." General Hartono claims that it is the second function which is much more important. He reasons that, disregarding adversity, the military must remain faithful to its original objectives. That is, "to be a progressive force, to be sons of the Indonesian Revolution, and to be the bearer of the ideals and aspirations of the people." . . .

ROLE AS UPHOLDER OF PLEDGED NORMS

Almost all Indonesian military authors emphasize that the Armed Forces are pledged to defend the Principles of the Panca Sila, the 1945 Constitution, the Sumpah Prajurit (Soldier's Oath) and the Sapta Marga (Seven Pledges). Other credos are occasionally referred to, but these four are of central importance.

The Panca Sila, which is the national philosophy, is expressed in the preamble of the 1945 Constitution as follows:

We believe in an all embracing God; in righteous and moral humanity, in the unity of Indonesia. We believe in democracy, wisely guided and led by close contact with the people through consultation so

that there shall result social justice for the whole Indonesian people.

The Panca Sila—belief in one God, humanitarianism, national unity, consultative democracy and social justice—are repeatedly invoked as criteria for judging the efficacy of particular programs or the danger posed by special social groups. Because it is the official national ideology, the Panca Sila frequently appears in the speeches of public officials and is often analyzed by Indonesian authors. The military, in particular, has found in the Panca Sila an unusually potent ideological weapon for use against religious fanatics, such as the Masjumi, and other political opponents, namely the PKI. The Panca Sila also seems to be sincerely respected by the officers, who like many other articulate Indonesians, invest it with considerable emotional-symbolic meaning. . . .

In late 1974 the Indonesian Defense Ministry joined with the Education and Culture Ministry to ensure that future generations of university graduates were properly indoctrinated in the values of the Panca Sila and 1945 Constitution. A pilot program was begun at three outlying universities which required all bachelor candidates to pass a sixty-four hour course designed to improve the military's image with the student community. Lecturers were provided by the Defense Ministry to instruct on the following subjects: the Panca Sila, the 1945 Constitution, National Resilience, National Integration, and Defense Policy and Organization. If nothing else, this mandatory training program points up the military's desire to enforce adherence to the Panca Sila and 1945 Constitution. Defense of the Panca Sila and 1945 Constitution are clearly seen as *active* roles for the military elite.

In addition to the Panca Sila and 1945 Constitution, military officers in Indonesia are specifically pledged to uphold two creeds—the Soldier's Oath (Sumpah Prajurit) and the Seven Pledges (Sapta Marga). These two pledges are internal military creeds not meant for application to the population at large. Though very few senior officers can actually recite these pledges, they nonetheless serve as a useful indicator of those social roles the military feels it legitimately fulfills. The Seven Pledges are:

I. We are citizens of the unitary Republic of Indonesia based on the Panca Sila.

II. We are Indonesian patriots, bearers and defenders of the state ideology, who are responsible and know of no surrender.

III. We are Indonesian knights, who are devoted to the One God, and who defend honesty, truth and justice.

IV. We are soldiers of the Indonesian Armed Forces, guardians of the Indonesian state and nation.

V. We soldiers of the Indonesian Armed Forces, uphold discipline, are obedient and observant to our leadership, and uphold the soldier's attitude and oath.

VI. We soldiers of the Indonesian Armed Forces, set ourselves to perform our task with courage, and are always ready to devote ourselves to the state and nation.

VII. We soldiers of the Indonesian Armed Forces, are loyal and keep our word and the Soldier's Oath. . . .

STEWARDSHIP-LEADERSHIP ROLE OF THE MILITARY

As both Indonesians and foreigners have noted, the Indonesian military is unique in several respects. Certainly it is unique in that it developed as a spontaneous institution without political guidance. Also one may argue that the *scope* of the role it plays in the country today is unique among the Armed Forces of the world.

In part, the military elite justifies its national leadership role as thrust upon it by the void of leadership talent available in other sectors of the government. General Hartono believes that, "As a body containing the greatest percentage of dynamic young leadership, the Armed Forces have to contribute in filling the shortages in other sectors of the government." Another military writer has claimed that:

The Armed Forces often had to patch up the muddle made by others every time those responsible could not surmount the muddle themselves.

Military officers justify their role not only by referring to the failings of the Indonesian bureaucracy, but also by pointing out the ineptitude of the country's political leaders. Because the military elite views political controversies as a threat to social progress, it has felt justified in stepping into the political sphere to prevent wastage of national resources.

At the same time the military elite feels that members of the Armed

Forces possess special attributes which qualify them for national leadership. Officers proudly point to the fact that the military is a well-functioning national organization, hierarchically organized from the capital to the remotest regions. They picture it as a relatively compact organization which has developed a firm esprit de corps. Furthermore, it is an organization peculiarly qualified to maintain political stability since it has both the intelligence and operations capabilities required to ensure law and order. . . .

The establishment of the New Order was accomplished according to the rule of law. Super Semar, the 11 March 1965 order which gave General Suharto full authority to establish political stability, was signed by President Sukarno himself and was confirmed by the MPRS on 21 June 1966. Furthermore, the restrictions placed on Sukarno's political activities and his ultimate replacement in office by General Suharto were determined by MPRS decision of 12 March 1967 and 27 March 1968. Since the MPRS stands clearly above the President, according to the 1945 Constitution, the military elite argues it came to power through legal means.

General Suharto is careful to note that the military's post-1966 expansion into traditionally non-military spheres was also accomplished legally. He has stated:

Everything done by ABRI is in conformity with the rules of procedure and the rules of the game we have decided together. ABRI is represented in the people's representative institutions, both in the Centre and in the Regions by virtue of the regulations in force. Members of ABRI have become civil servants with due observance of the requirements needed. Members of ABRI have become governors up to village heads based upon election. What is more, they accepted their assignment spurred by the idealism of struggle, not because they wished to occupy the post, not because they wanted to accumulate authority and power in the interest of ABRI.

The military also describes its leadership role as legal due to the July 1971 elections, which are seen as granting direct popular legitimacy to the predominantly military Suharto government. However, because of the highly fractious elections of 1955 and the ideologically divisive nature of Indonesian party politics, the Suharto government prepared for the 1971 elections carefully. Most importantly, it organized a political front called GOLKAR. This organization—designed to be a broad-based, pro-government party based on functional groups—eventually succeeded in capturing well over sixty percent of the popular vote.

GOLKAR became the political instrument of the military elite. General Ali Moertopo was actually assigned the task of ensuring a GOLKAR victory in the 1971 elections, and he accepted the task as the "greatest mission" and "greatest role" ever given him by the Army. One of the most important techniques he implemented to ensure GOLKAR election success was mobilization of the approximately two million government employees for campaigning and electioneering purposes. If in the past government employees had served the interests of diverse political parties,

after 1971 they became largely the political instrument of the government.
This led one Jakarta commentator to
remark that:

. . . in this pre-modern era the govern-

ment employees/government apparatus/
state instruments are synonymous with the
political public. Outside the bureaucracy,
outside ABRI/TNI, there is no more politics in Indonesia. . . .

The role of the military in Korea has been central since Korea's liberation
from Japanese occupation in 1945. Developed by Rhee, the military turned
eventually into a somewhat praetorian type and into one of the most
powerful contemporary military regimes.

JAE SOUK SOHN

The Role of the Military in the Republic of Korea

In the Republic of Korea, as in many
other new states in Asia and Africa,
the military has played an important
political role in the last few years.
On May 16, 1961, a Korean military
group assumed political control of
the civilian government after a period of ineffective civilian parliamentary leadership, climaxed by a series
of anti-government demonstrations
which precipitated a political crisis.
In December 1963 the military junta
formally transferred political power
to a civilian government chosen in
national elections. But the actual
control of the government remained
in the hands of junta core members
who had entered domestic politics as
"civilians" against their original revolutionary pledges. General Chung
Hee Park, Chief of the Military Junta,
became president for the four-year

From Jae Souk Sohn, "The Role of the Military
in the Republic of Korea," mimeographed (Paper
delivered at the 6th World Congress of Sociology
1966), pp. 1–12, by permission of the author.

term of the new civilian government,
and his Democratic-Republican Party,
which had been created during the
military rule, secured an absolute
majority in the National Assembly.
Furthermore, since the military coup,
many military officers have been
converted into high-ranking government officials, diplomats, and top
managers of public corporations. Thus
the military has emerged as a crucial
institution and power bloc, setting the
style of Korean politics in a new direction. It is the purpose of this paper
to trace the changing pattern of
civil-military relations, examine the
causes of the 1961 military coup from
the viewpoint of the internal social
organization of the military, and
evaluate the role of the military
in Korea's modernization process.

I

The South Korean armed forces were
first built up after liberation from

imperial Japan. During the thirty-six years of Japanese colonial rule, Korea's indigenous military institution was eliminated and displaced by the metropolitan power. This was because the Japanese exercised direct rule in order to assimilate the Korean territory into their imperial system. As a first step in the process of occupying Korea, the Japanese imposed a protectorate status in 1905, and two years later, they disbanded the Royal Army of the old Korean kingdom. For a long time after the formal annexation in 1910, Japanese rule rested on a form of military government, with the result that the military profession was not open to the indigenous people. After the Japanese seizure of Manchuria in 1931, however, this policy was modified; the Japanese trained a limited number of Korean officers for service in the Japanese armed forces as well as in the Japanese controlled Manchurian army, although they drafted hundreds of thousands of Korean youths during the protracted Sino-Japanese War and World War II. As a result, the withdrawal of Japanese colonial rule from Korea left behind no self-contained native army.

Immediately after national liberation in August 1945, there were formed several private military or paramilitary organizations, the common objective of which was to build up a unitary national army. These organizations were soon dissolved when the American military government in South Korea took steps to create a small-scale Korean constabulary as its subsidiary organ for the area's internal order and external defence. Toward

the end of 1945 the American military government set up a Military English School, predecessor of the Korean military academy, which was designed to train a professional cadre for the prospective Korean military establishment. When the South Korean Constabulary came into being in January 1946, it was officered by some one hundred graduates of this school, who had received American military language training for a few weeks. Since the Constabulary officer corps was almost entirely made up of personnel who had served under the Japanese, the Manchurians, or the Chinese, the different military backgrounds of corps members had a significant impact upon the new Korean military institution. Apart from being poorly armed, the South Korean Constabulary, which saw its steady expansion during the period of American rule, was a sort of forerunner in terms of personnel, organization, and training.

This rudimentary military establishment was transformed into the regular South Korean armed forces in August 1948, when the Republic of Korea proclaimed its independence. The withdrawal of the American occupation forces from South Korea was accompanied by positive measures to develop rapidly the three services of the Korean armed forces. But until the outbreak of the Korean War in June 1950, the national army was still a fragile structure composed of less than 100,000 men, whose functions were directed to the suppression of communist insurrections in the rear, as well as to the defence of the 38th parallel. It was during the

Korean War that the Korean army was built up with massive American military aid as the world's fourth largest anti-communfst force of nearly one million men. After the armistice of July 1953 the total manpower of the Korean armed forces was gradually reduced by 1960 to the present level of 600,000. Since they were established, the Armed Forces of the Republic of Korea have been heavily dependent upon American support for their maintenance and development.

In the midst of profound internal difficulties and continued external threats following the division of the Korean peninsula, the national army had a central place in the Republic, born as an anti-communist frontier country. From the first year of independence the constant problem of communist subversion forced the army to assume direct responsibilities for law and order in many districts, and during the Korean War army authority was expanded to cover the entire country. After the cease-fire some military men in the top echelons were frequently involved in domestic politics for the purpose of individual gain. As a matter of fact, the Korean military were a vital factor in the complex of political power even during the years preceding the military coup of 1961.

However, the military was an instrument rather than a master of the civilian government. This was largely due to the skill with which the Liberal Party government, and particularly President Syngman Rhee, handled military leaders. The founding father's authoritarian, personal control

enabled him to use the military to throttle political opposition and to manipulate elections. But after the Rhee regime fell, in the student uprising of April 19, 1960, the newly elected Democratic Party cabinet headed by John M. Chang was too weak to maintain civilian supremacy over the military, which had been accustomed to a charismatic control. As a result, in less than one year in power, the ineffective parliamentary government was overthrown by the military.

II

In the military coup of May 16, 1961, a group of military officers seized power when a stalemate developed in the struggle between two competing factions into which the ruling Democratic Party had split. For the justification of their action, they maintained that they were forced to take over by the failure of civilian government, and that they came to power with the purest of patriotic intentions to save the country from chaos, corruption, and communism. Although power went by default to the military officers, a number of considerations suggest that most of their drive for power came from the progressive crumbling of the military order since the armistice of the Korean War.

In Korea where the military profession suffers in social esteem largely due to the Confucian tradition, the military officers have been recruited from middle and lower classes and from rural areas. In its formative period before the Korean War, the military attracted young men from humble families who had had little formal education and who were seeking an avenue of upward social mobility. The military was accessible to these young men, and their social position and educational background did not constitute a hindrance to the expected career success. The three years of the Korean War led to the increased importance of the armed forces as the bulwarks of the state, larger defence budgets, and broadened internal functions of the military. Consequently, the prestige of the military as a profession had risen considerably and, in fact, the officer corps had become the most favored group in the country. In the postwar years, however, their relatively high prestige and advantageous status were declining, while the civilian politicians frequently interfered in the internal affairs of the armed forces and tried to use them in their political games. In addition, the professional officers were threatened by demobilization after the armistice of 1953. Thus the frustration and weakness of the officer corps as a dominant group contributed to their readiness to assume political power.

Since a purge of leftist mutiny agents from the army in 1948–49, the Korean military has been a relatively cohesive organization integrated by American-model uniform training and anti-communist combat experience, but with significant internal cleavages which have complicated its political intervention. One source of cleavage was the existence of various informal groups or factions which were formed around such elements as foreign military background, influential personality, regional origin, military academy class, etc. From the early years of the Korean army, factionalism was an important factor in the practice of patronage regarding promotion and assignment, so that unfair personnel management weakened discipline in the officer corps. At crucial moments of internal military politics, there occurred struggles among the three groups of foreign-trained senior officers previously mentioned and between two powerful groups of middle rank officers—graduates of the 5th class and the 8th class of the old Korean military academy, which provided a crash program of one to six-month career training in 1946–50. As in civilian society and government, the North Korean minority, who actually dominated the army throughout the whole precoup period, have maintained a most cohesive group so as to remain in an advantageous position to promote their interests. After the officers of South Korean origin came to dominate the military government, the North Korean minority repeatedly sought to launch counter-coups.

A more serious source of tension in the Korean military was the conflict between the generals and the colonels in the aftermath of the April 1960 student revolution. Korea's political and social turmoil had influence in the military, and the dramatic struggle that occurred between the old and the new and between the partisans of the traditional order and the supporters of the emerging forces in civilian society was clearly mirrored in the officer corps. In the midst of growing military disorder, young colonels initiated a "reorganization movement" for the army, which was destined to become a major political issue for the period of Chang's government. The movement called for the discharge of corrupt, politically-compromised generals so as to secure rapid promotions for the junior officers. In September 1960, a group of 16 army colonels armed with pistols, mostly drawn from the 8th academy class, broke in upon Chairman of the Joint Chiefs of Staff Lt. General Young Hee Choi and forced him to resign: "You are a lucky guy, General! You have now become chairman of the joint chiefs of staff through division commander, corps commander, field army commander, and army chief of staff. Like other generals, why don't you move out to a better post, such as minister of defence or foreign ambassador, and thereby open up the way for the latercomers." Less than one year after this revolt took place, the colonel group led a successful military coup under the direction of Major General Chung Hee Park.

Fundamentally, this cleavage resulted from a serious "promotional freeze" which began to emerge after the armistice of the Korean War. As described earlier, the Korean military was created from scratch and thereafter expanded rapidly in a short period of time. Hence the officer corps, particularly in the formative period 1946–50, was filled with men of roughly the same age, but they had unparalleled opportunities for promotion. Those first on the scene were catapulted into the rank of general in their twenties or early thirties and the later arrivals filled the junior ranks. Further, since all high posts in the military echelons had been occupied by young generals, the opportunity of promotion for lower ranking officers decreased continuously as demobilization proceeded in the postwar years. This introduced serious promotional problems and increased the possibility of frustration and intrigue in the junior ranks.

The young colonels with less seniority had fewer vested interests in the military system. And they were less involved in the social and political status quo and were more involved in contemporary political currents, with the result that they were inclined toward a more radical outlook. On the other hand, the long absence of war since the armistice had left them with time on their hands to pursue extra-military activities, including political ones. Probably recent developments abroad, such as a series of successful military coups in Burma, Pakistan, and Turkey, gave encouragement to their determination to take over. On May 16, 1961, they finally rode to power at the head of popular reform movements then active among student circles.

True, the military takeover was precipitated by the corruption and incompetence of the civilian government. Basically, however, the Korean military coup was the consequence of equal corruption and internal disorder in the military organization as well as the reaction of one power group—that is, the military, which had been swelled up as a result of United

States Far Eastern policy against communism—to another group—the civilian politicians, who had been trying to control a large standing military force.

III

The military coup of May 1961 brought to power the Supreme Council of National Reconstruction, composed of some thirty coup officers, including top military commanders. When the military officers first took over, they promised a speedy return to civilian government after they carried out a revolutionary program of political change, economic development, and social reformation. In addition to the usual procedure of blacklisting traditional and corrupt politicians, the military junta proceeded on a comprehensive basis and with radical measures. In the end, as will be examined later, it was unsuccessful in carrying out the revolutionary program for various reasons, the most important of which was the inherent limitations of military officers in political affairs, coupled with a fierce power struggle within the ruling junta.

The striking aspect of the Korean military junta was that it sought to conserve its political influence, in whatever form, after a return to civilian rule. As a result, in early 1962 the core members of the military junta, who had determined to participate in civilian politics, took steps to clandestinely organize a mass political party by dipping into the national treasury. After permitting civilian political activity as of January

1, 1963, and declaring elections for the restoration of civilian rule to be held later in 1963, they resigned from active duty to become the cadre of this new party, named the Democratic-Republican Party. Meanwhile, the military junta managed to effect a constitutional change on a popular vote, which was intended to establish a system for strong government—that is, a presidential form of government with a unicameral legislature. Therefore, it was not surprising when General Chung Hee Park, chairman of the SCNR, decided that, dishonoring his original promise, he would run for the October 1963 presidential election as a "civilian" under the sponsorship of the military-created political party. This prearranged program worked well to transform the military junta itself into a new civilian government, for General Park assumed a four-year-term presidency strengthened with the solid support of an almost two-thirds majority from his DRP in the National Assembly.

The majority of the military junta opposed any civilian party government as likely to cause the political situation to deteriorate after the transfer of power. In fact, they feared it might negate the validity of the "military revolution" and retaliate against them. However, the "designed" transfer of power to the new military-dominated civilian government in December 1963, through elections, did not create political stability. The internal political life of Korea has since been beset by conflicts between political parties and student demonstrations against government far more frequently and intensively than might normally be expected in a post-transfer period.

When we look into the character of Park's DRP regime, we find that it is a sort of military-civilian coalition, but with hegemony in the hands of military-turned-civilian politicians in both the party and the government. Since, in the process of transferring power, they recognized the need for a mass political base, they developed a system of alliance with old politicians, a considerable number of whom have been recruited from Syngman Rhee's former Liberal Party. Although on the surface it appears to be a relatively stable coalition, it should be noted that, because of such arrangements, tensions are bound to exist between former military officers and their civilian partners. Particularly, the influx of retired officers into key posts in the bureaucracy since the military coup has aroused a sense of insecurity among civilian officials and disturbed the discipline of the civil service. The problem is that new appointments in the government and public corporations tend to be made in the particular interests of the military class rather than on the basis of achievements and competence.

The political dominance of former military men, combined with unceasing reliance on police and espionage methods and with increasing corruption in the government, seems to be the fundamental cause of the civilian resistance which has continued since the restoration of constitutional rule. In general, the conflict is between the ruling party and the opposition, between the government,

on the one hand, and students, intellectuals, and journalists, on the other. Such confrontations have been intensified by outright disagreement on major foreign policy issues, such as the normalization of Korean-Japanese relations and the dispatch of Korean troops to South Vietnam. The basic attitude of oppositional parties can be found in the condemnation of the DRP regime as an extension of military rule dressed in constitutional garb. University student groups are centers of opposition, too, but their protest is motivated by aspirations for nationalism and social justice. Meanwhile, the government regards these oppositional forces as irresponsible and almost traitorous and meets them with repressive measures. Thus Korean politics is going on in a vicious cycle of mutual distrust.

Political developments in the past six years in Korea have changed considerably the functions of the military and their symbolic place in society, and have opened the way to a new pattern of civil-military relations. The forceful assumption of power by the military, and later the premeditated transfer of power to the military-dominated civilian government, divested the concept of authority of its constitutional cloak and plunged Korea into a period of group conflicts and power politics. The military coup led by a group of frustrated young officers in turn projected the military onto the national scene as an interest group. It no longer appears as the sole representative of the highest national ideals but as a group struggling for power with other civilian political groups. In this militaristic period, Korea's political future depends largely on the relationships of the military officers, whether in uniform or not, to the other civilianpolitici ans, particularly the emerging forces of younger generations.

IV

We have examined above the causes of military intervention mainly from the point of view of the internal social organization of the military, and also the changing pattern of civil-military relations since the military coup. Now let us turn to the role of the military in the modernization of Korea. There is a proposition often encountered that armies are powerful forces in the modernization process of the underdeveloped countries. Is this proposition supported by the Korean experience? What are the capacities of the Korean military to supply effective political leadership for rapid economic development and social modernization? What are the consequences that the Korean military's economic and social activities have for modernization? In seeking a realistic estimate of the role of the military in the modernization of the country it is necessary to examine non-military functions as they have been performed in Korean society.

When the Korean military officers came to power, whatever their actual motivation they were deeply committed to the goal of "rapid modernization of the fatherland." To achieve this goal they announced a revolutionary reform program reflecting popular demands, a program which was intended to eliminate unjust, corrupt practices from the government and society as well as to rebuild the national economy on a self-sustaining basis. In particular, their program aimed at changing the civilian political system, and involved planned industrialization and agrarian reforms. They also promised greater benefits to the down-trodden masses, proposing to curb the power of a few upper groups enriched through association with the government. Although the ambitious young officers displayed considerable ambition to lead a genuine social revolution, they failed to achieve its aims in the end.

Apparently the young officers had believed in 1961 that the country's problems could be solved if only the government displayed determination and a willingness to call for self-sacrifices. Viewing the spirit and the ethos of the civilian politicians as little more than uncontrolled cravings for corruption and compromise, they thought of themselves as enlightened members of a new, modern generation and as saviors of the nation facing a crisis. Within a few months the junta members came to realize that government was an extremely complicated and intractable business. The solutions were not quite so easy as they had assumed. Hence they began to compromise their original standards and take on some of the aspects of the politicians, whom they had held in contempt. Once in power, even the resolute military officers proved to be no supermen, for they were no more able than the

Korean politicians to rise above their cultural and historical heritage.

The fact was that military training did little to equip Korean officers with the skills necessary for running a country striving for rapid modernization. Because their professional careers isolated them from the main currents of society, their understanding of national problems was apt to be deficient. And as the Korean military was not highly developed in terms of armament technology and general staff work, so the transferability of their military skills to government administration was very limited. Therefore, the competence of military men for high political posts was open to serious question. The political deficiencies of the military government were further complicated by factionalism that developed within the junta. Conspiring officers, no longer united against a common foe, found the aftermath of a successful coup filled with conflicts between factions. As a result of power struggles, junta membership frequently shifted and seven members, including General Do Yung Chang, army chief of staff at the time of the military coup, were involved in two out of the ten counter-coups uncovered during the period of military rule.

As the junta members came to feel the strong attractions of power, the express aims of the revolutionary reform program began to be perverted. The Korean military regime was essentially a "caretaker government" because it promised a return to civilian rule. Nevertheless, it was not really oriented toward transferring power. In order to hold power

indefinitely, the revolutionary officers at last allied themselves with the blacklisted politicians, whom they had condemned as enemies of the people. This system of alliance in a military-created political party did not make any contribution to political change other than to bring the military class into political prominence. The organization and the conservative mentality of Korea's political parties were left almost intact. Furthermore, corruption came when the problem arose of conserving power through the establishment of a mass political party under the direction of trusted military officers. For this purpose funds were needed which were free from legal control. It was strongly hinted that the so-called four grave scandals under the military rule were connected with the creation of the Democratic-Republican Party. It was also discovered that some military officers used their government offices for purposes of illicit enrichment.

The Korean military government showed a great deal of initiative in dealing with national economic problems, appropriating the advice of civilian experts. Yet, as measured by over-all economic development, the experience of the military regime was hardly impressive. The outcome indicates that the military officers suffered from lack of experience in supplying central economic direction. They were particularly inclined toward ruinous financial policies, and their drive for rapid economic development led to overhasty industrialization programs. The First Five-Year Economic Plan launched by the military government was too ambitious to achieve its targets in the important initial period, and the failure of its ill-conceived currency reform aggravated the economic life of the common people. There was also little improvement in agricultural sectors in which the military government equally concentrated its efforts for a combination of economic and political reasons. Possibly, the acceptance of the legitimacy of economic motivation was a consequence of military rule. In fact, economic matters acquired top priority and resulted in freedom for occupational groups to seek economic advantages. However, the military government's economic policies led to the resurgence of corruption among big businessmen and opened the way to a wider gap between the few rich and the many poor.

The militaries of both Burma and Thailand, although structurally and ideologically opposites, nevertheless are characterized by role expansion; i.e., the penetration of the officer corps either as a collective or as individuals into various fields such as economic enterprises, education, and the training of civilian manpower. The officer corps have also served as administrative reservoirs for the bureaucracies of the two modernizing autocracies.

And finally, Moshe Lissak's comprehensive studies of the Burmese and Thai militaries demonstrate that military role expansion into social and economic spheres is attributable to the permeable structure of the Southeast Asian political system.

MOSHE LISSAK

Military Roles in Modernization: Thailand and Burma

THAILAND: THE CIVILIANIZED MILITARY

THE BEGINNINGS OF THE PROFESSIONAL ARMY AND ITS DEVELOPMENT

Despite Thailand's many wars, especially with Burma and Cambodia, and

From *Moshe Lissak*, Military Roles in Modernization *(Beverly Hills, Calif.: Sage Publications, 1976), pp. 91–107, 155–75, 227–39, 247–48.*

although the foundations of a professional standing army were laid in the second half of the nineteenth century, it was not until the 1920s that a more or less full-fledged army emerged. It started with the establishment, in the second half of the 1800s, of a military cadet school and later a naval cadet school. In 1894 the ministry of defense was formed and the armed forces were finally given a recognized and respected position within the government hierarchy.

In the spirit of absolute monarchy, the king and princes had full control over the armed forces. According to a law of 1904, the crown prince served as the commander in chief of the armed forces and the king headed the National Defense Council. This situation continued until the almost total eviction, following the 1932 coup, of the king and princes (although no nobles of middle and lower ranks) from senior positions within the armed forces. This dramatic act was followed by a change in the recruitment bases of the military elite. For example, during the absolute monarchy, officers from the royal family and nobility of high rank made up 87% of the military elite. Moreover, even among the rest, there was not a single commoner. In an unspecified period after the 1932 coup, commoners became the majority (52%) while the percentage of high nobles and princes diminished to 18%.

Nevertheless, the recruitment bases remained rather narrow. Military families became the most important single source for military officers. . . .

The quantitative and qualitative growth of the armed forces since 1932 reflects its crucial role in Thai political life. From 30,000 in 1920 they grew to 60,000 during World War II, with the most impressive growth occurring in the ranks of officers and generals. At the end of World War II, the armed forces were reduced to about 30,000 in the army, 3,000 in the air force, 10,000 in the navy, and about 25,000 men in the national police. However, with the return of General Phibun to the helm of government and especially with the inauguration of the United States' aid program, the expansion of the armed forces was once again resumed. Of the estimated 100,000 to 150,000 troops in the armed forces during the 1950–60 period, 80% belonged to the army; 25,000 both to the navy and air force, and an estimated 40,000 to 50,000 to the police. In addition to the regular armed forces and police, the various governments in Thailand established auxiliary services. One such service is the Volunteer's Defense Corps which, according to official statistics, was composed in the sixties of 120,000 troops. This force was established in 1954 and is under the control of the minister of the interior. On the whole, it is estimated that, from 1950 through the 1960s, the armed forces were composed of about 0.5% of the total population, and of about 0.9% of the population between the ages of 15 and 65. . . .

In Thailand there is compulsory military service. But only part of the entire eligible population is actually drafted. Those exempted are transferred directly to the reserves of the second category. Drafted service personnel who completed their term are transferred to the first category. Exempt from all military service are monks, career teachers, naturalized citizens, and any person whose father is an alien. These last two categories are directed mainly against the Chinese population. There is also a custom of exempting other ethnic minorities from military service. Thus the military establishment is in fact a monopoly of the Buddhist Thais.

Though very little is known about the criteria of promotion and the scope of annual turnover within the officer corps, we may assume that, at least during certain periods, the turnover was rather high. The various coups and countercoups in the 1950s and 1960s were followed, on the one hand, by purges of rival officers and, on the other hand, by the promotion of officers who supported the new leaders. Another source of personal mobility was the flow—although limited—between military and police positions and between military and civil bureaucratic positions. Some high officials in the civil service became generals without receiving any military training or without being promoted gradually through the military hierarchy. These generals usually filled administrative posts.

The Supreme Command Headquarters, which is subordinated to the minister of defense, is responsible for the operations of the three branches of the armed forces. In this context, two other bodies involved with defense should be mentioned. The first is the National Security Council. It is composed of nine members and headed by the prime minister. The second body is the Defense Council, composed of twenty-three members headed by the defense minister. Most of the members are senior commanders and deputies in the armed forces. While the National Security Council is the supreme political layer in the decision-making process, the Defense Council is the senior professional military layer.

The United States has done much to raise the professional level of the Thai armed forces since the end of World War II. Thailand was considered an anti-Communist strong-

hold and, starting in the 1950s, the United States sent military missions to aid in training Thai soldiers. The 1954 location in Bangkok of the general headquarters of SEATO was a clear indication of Thailand's importance for the United States. This importance has been translated into impressive investments by the United States in the development of the Thai army and economy. It has been estimated that, between 1946 and 1966, economic and military aid to Thailand reached the one-billion-dollar mark. . . .

Since the 1960s, subversive activities have been increasing in southeast and northeast Thailand. Generally, information about the extent of these activities and effectiveness of the response to them has been faulty, usually suffering from biases. After 1965, when a Peking-inspired union was established between the Patriotic Front of Thailand and the Thailand Independence Movement, the political situation worsened. The new body, the Patriotic Front, called for an armed revolt through a people's war. It is estimated that the union of these two bodies enabled them to mobilize about a thousand men. Their union also increased the scope of skirmishes and the number of casualties. Subversive activities, though on a slightly smaller scale, are to be found also in the southeast, on the frontier with Malaysia. In 1965–66 the number of guerrillas in the southeast was estimated at between five hundred to one thousand.

Regardless of the real threat—which, in any case, cannot be adequately estimated—the fact is that a rather large number of military and police units are engaged in the war against the guerrillas. Their measures include bombing of suspicious villages, the evacuation of village populations, and continual searches for guerrilla bases. Let us emphasize, however, that, in spite of the escalation of subversive activities in the period of our study, the "conventional" activities of the military were much more limited and marginal than those in the "nonconventional" areas—i.e., in the political, ideological, economic, and educational-cultural spheres.

THE COMPETITION FOR POLITICAL POWER

The unchallenged dominance of the military in politics in the period concerned has been rooted in the 1932 coup. The changes in the nature and style of political intervention by the military in the years following that coup have been conditioned by two major factors. Of these, the first involves changes in the international political constellation, such as World War II and the Vietnam war. The second involves internal changes within the military establishment itself. Our concern will be mainly with the second.

Intensive intervention by the army in politics is a clear indicator of the weakness of the civilian political elite. On the other hand, conflicts within the armed forces, coups and countercoups, reflect the weaknesses and inefficiency of the military high command's ability to provide military and political leadership for the state. . . . As may be recalled, the formal mechanisms of control have been embodied in the "civilian"-controlled National Security Council and in the military-controlled Defense Council. Officially, the main function of these two is to instruct and guide the Supreme Command on security matters. In fact, however, since both are at least partially staffed by the same personnel, the distinction between them is fictional. The importance of informal mechanisms of control is manifested in the simultaneous incumbency of key positions in the army and the civilian executive. In the early 1960s, General Sarit, then prime minister, was both the supreme commander of the armed forces and commander in chief of the army. General Thanom, his defense minister, served as first deputy supreme commander of the armed forces. The president of the constituent assembly also held the post of second deputy supreme commander. After Sarit's death in 1963, his successor, General (later Field Marshal) Thanom, served simultaneously as prime minister, defense minister, and supreme commander of the armed forces. The title "commander in chief of the army" was given to General Praphas who also served as minister of the interior. The minister of agriculture in this cabinet was nominated assistant supreme commander, and the air chief marshal became assistant defense minister.

To this phenomenon of multiple roles should be added the interchangeability between high-ranking officials of the civilian and military institutions. However, the importance of this practice should not be exaggerated. It is clear that the weight of the professional officers, especially of the army, is greater than that of officers coming from outside the military framework. The army's unduly heavy influence may be attributed mainly to the fact that they alone can ensure the loyalty of military units in cases of internal conflict between different cliques or branches of the army and police. At any rate, this concentration of authority in the hands of very few people not only underscores the dominant position of the military officers within the cabinet but makes it certain that the minister-officers do not lose contact with their political constituencies. Close operational relations with key units in the Bangkok area are not only a necessary condition for political mobility but also ensure the consolidation of power in the summit.

Legalization and institutionalization of coups. Military coups may or may not be followed by changes in the nature of the economic and political regime. However, they are almost always succeeded by intensive constitutional activities designed to provide ex post facto legitimacy for the military regime. The formulation of new constitutions and the calling of general elections may be viewed as typical examples. The Thai officers corps has distinguished itself in such legitimizing maneuvers no less than it has in the sphere of military coups. . . .

In short, coups and constitutions are Siamese twins in Thailand. The relatively large number of elections there reflects the variety of constitutions, whose purpose was to lend legality to at least part of the political manipulations connected with coups. Efforts to legitimize coups were encouraged by the Supreme Court of Appeal (*Di ka*) which extended a priori legality to a successful coup. The law states:

The overthrow of a previous government and the establishment of a new government by the use of force is perhaps illegal in the beginning until the people are willing to accept and respect it. When it is a government in fact, which means that people have been willing to accept it, any person who attempts by rebellion to overthrow the government violates the criminal law.

The number of coups (both unsuccessful and successful) have decreased in the fifties and sixties. This trend may be due chiefly to the consolidation of army and police rule in that period in Thailand. Though this consolidation was undermined for a short period after World War II, it was quickly restored through United States economic and military aid which provided, among other things, rapidly increasing rewards and benefits for the military. Along with personal and collective instrumental interests in the continuation of the aid from the United States, the political and military challenges presented both by the war in Vietnam and the underground subversive activities have further intensified the internal cohesion of the armed forces. In this situation, more subtle and surreptitious systems of competition have been preferred.

The occupation of power positions. The capture of the whole power basis of a society by the army depends largely on the army's operational capability. One condition for such comprehensive control is the expansion of the army itself—its budget must be increased and its officer corps enlarged. In Thailand, such changes in the balance of power between the armed forces and the civilian sector since 1932 are mirrored in the military budget. For instance, the budget rose from 19% of government expenditure in 1932 to some 27% in 1937, enabling the general staff to enlarge the officer class. The opportunity for a further increase came with the royal princes' ousting from the army after the 1932 coup. In 1939 the military budget consumed 32% of the national income. Its share increased still further during World War II, though between 1944 and 1947 it was reduced by the civilian regime. With the return of Phibun and the expansion of United States military aid, the military budget once again increased, although it never officially reached the level of World War II or even of the late thirties. The main reason is that the official military budget was supplemented by the huge U.S. military aid.

The proportion of officers to civilians in the cabinet. For obvious reasons, cabinet posts are among the most coveted rewards of coup promoters. Every cabinet since that of 1932 has included a number of military officers. . . .

Apart from cabinet posts, the senior positions in the civil service and its various extensions are the most important source for allocating power positions and prestige. There is no systematic information about the proportion of military and policy officers in the civil service. In general, it appears that there is no full-scale "exploitation" of the civil service as a source for positions for military and police officers. Such exploitative ac-

tivities are limited to senior positions. Membership in the National Assembly serves as another, though secondary, source for benefits. Indeed, among the officers nominated or elected to the National Assembly, there are many young ones, mostly captains and majors, and some lieutenants. The senior military officers in the National Assembly were largely retired or nearly retired.

The crucial role of the military and police officers is at least an indirect reflection of the rather *selective* and *limited* efforts of the ministers, many of whom are themselves military officers, to court public support through political organizations. This pattern was institutionalized immediately after the 1932 coup. The presence of a "party"—the People's Party established by the promoters—deducted nothing from the fact that the focus of rivalry was in the bureaucracy.

The need for public support gained urgency after World War II, when both the ruling circle and the opposition were dominated by civilians. Both sides established political parties which were supposed to run in the coming elections. The officers who, in this period, conducted subversive activities against the civilian regime also used the political party as an instrument. Such use of political parties lasted until the military's seizure of power and the subsequent banning of civilian political activities. The ban was removed because of internal conflicts which induced each military clique to become interested in broader public support. During this period, the generals became very active in party politics. This was the first time in the modern history of Thailand that high-ranking officers used the political party as an instrument of power. They exploited their power to eliminate competitors among the different military cliques and to resolve conflicts between the military as a whole and various political civilian bodies. Thus the role expansion of the armed forces —that, until this point, was either absent or very marginal—gained new momentum and dimension.

The ruling elite's instrument of party politics in that period was the Seri Manangkhasila Party. General Phao was the party's secretary general and strong man. All the promoters of the 1947 coup belonged to this party, which had at its disposal newspapers, radio stations, and legal as well as illegal economic resources. It had the support of more than half of the elected members of the National Assembly (eighty-three out of one hundred sixty) and of one hundred of its nominated members. Though General Phao's rivals publicly maintained their allegiance to the party, they clandestinely sought support beyond it. Thus General Sarit, for example, was active in the establishment of the national Democratic Party (the Unionists) and other political factions which collaborated with the main opposition party, the Democrats. Even Prime Minister Phibun was forced to follow this pattern. His name was associated with several lists put up for the election of 1957 (for example, the Labor Party, the Might Is Right Party, and the Hyde Park Movement Party). Phao was also connected with the establishment of "auxiliary parties," among which were the Free Democrats and

the Nationalist parties. The phenomenon of "auxiliary parties," through which patrons who belong to the same ruling circle and party fight each other by means of smaller parties, is one which, though found to some degree in other countries, is peculiar to Thailand. In Thailand, it may be viewed as one of the basic patterns which has dominated the power structure of the country since the earliest coups; namely, a *ruling circle* which meshes rival factions of patrons and clients, both of whom try to maximize ad hoc interests. . . .

The intensification of subversive activities in some of the districts of Thailand has added a new dimension to the army's political involvement. Historically, such involvement had been confined to the Bangkok area. However, the urgent need to ensure the peasants' loyalty in suspect areas necessitated new concepts and instruments of control. These centered primarily around so-called civic programs. The best example is the Mobile Development Units program (MDU). This project was controlled by the army but conducted with the cooperation of the civilian administration. The principal task of the MDU was to provide very selective and limited aid to the peasants in the form of road construction, public housing, public works, and health services.

The potential political repercussions of the MDU project are worth our attention. First, it should provide the armed forces with the opportunity of supervising the district officers more closely. Also, such bodies as the MDU were expected to open the way for new political bodies which could mediate between the peasants and the political center. A more balanced, two-way communication between the periphery and the center could thus emerge. Second, there were indications that the activities of the MDU could promote some economic and organizational initiative within local government—perhaps adding a new dimension of political power to that government. Third, MDU activities could promote more coordination between various government departments, especially on the local level. It is clear that the realization of the MDU's potentialities could provide the central government and the armed forces with a more efficient instrument for the social and political mobilization of the peasants. But there were some dangers involved as well. The chief danger was that new emerging local institutions, such as local councils and corporations, would become an ideal target for subversion by guerrillas. This can best be understood through considering the difficulties that both the guerrillas and the central government have had in gaining a foothold in the peripheral areas with a lack of clearly defined organizational frameworks through which to operate.

THE MILITARY AND ITS ACTIVITIES IN THE ECONOMIC ARENA

Except for the political, no other sphere can demonstrate so effectively as the economic one the scope of the symbiosis and the permeability of the boundaries between the civilian and the military segments of Thai society. Though this phenomenon is found in quite a few developing countries and in a number of developed ones, the degree of symbiosis in Thailand was perhaps greater than that prevalent elsewhere.

The activities of the armed forces in the economic sphere may be grouped under two major types. The first involves illegal activities as defined by the Thai criminal code itself—though not necessarily by the accepted social norms. The other involves those economic activities that do not particularly diverge from legal norms.

Another distinction is that between activities inititated by military men and policemen as individuals (or as tentative groups especially organized for the purpose) and those initiated by unit commanders, by one or another of the various branches of the armed forces, or by the supreme command itself. There is only a *partial* overlap between illegal activities and their individualistic character and between activities that are legal and institutionalized and those carried out in formal and collective frameworks (whether these be the various branches of the armed forces or the armed services as a whole). True, presently available data sometimes make it difficult to distinguish and to classify the various phenomena according to the simple categories just proposed. For instance, the fact that many army officers receive or have sometimes in the past received two kinds of payments does not facilitate a simplified classification of income sources. However, no difficulties arise in defining the nature of the income sources reported in the fifties and sixties. We refer here to the trade in opium, which at the time became a monopoly of the police, headed by General Phao.

The opium trade was perhaps the most important source of illegal income, though by no means the only one. Many observers report that police officials were partners in houses of prostitution, in illicit gambling, and in illegal trafficking in gold. Phao has even been accused by the Democratic Party of printing notes to the sum of 14 million baht. Nor were such activities confined to police officers. Army officers often outdid their police counterparts. For instance, the embezzlement of welfare funds by army officers in 1948 is well known. The best-known evidence is that uncovered after General Sarit's death. The officially estimated value of his known property amounted to $150 million. Of this total, about $30 million was defined as money taken in one way or another from the state treasury. Considering the enormous sums involved, we cannot be surprised to read, in one of the estimates of corruption in Thailand, that in 1954, about 12%(!) of the total national income flowed into the pockets of Phibun, Phao, Sarit, and their favorites. Since the Sarit scandal, a series of additional ones, though of minor proportions, have been uncovered.

With regard to economic activities whose legality is at least ambivalent—if impartially tested, those engaged in them would not be found guilty of criminal activity—the most typical examples are the business partnerships between Chinese businessmen and the Thai politicomilitary elite. The Chinese merchants enter these partnerships to seek political protection; for the Thai elite, they are lucrative. The two parties have taken measures to maximize the benefits they derive from these partnerships. The Chinese have offered people in the various cliques of the military-bureaucratic elite membership in the business boards of their firms, to secure maximum political support and prevent hazards emanating from possible changes in the internal balance of political power. And the members of the politicomilitary elite are only too glad to be appointed to membership on as many boards as possible, to increase their profits—and indirectly, their political power.

Another popular source for personal enrichment is membership on the boards of directors of those government enterprises controlled and managed by the various ministries. Economic enterprises either belonging to the Defense Ministry or being directly owned by diverse military units is a pure example of the nature and patterns of role expansion assumed by the Thai military establishment and hence differs from the type of activity pursued by the members of the elite as individuals or within the framework of small cliques. Further, this phenomenon possesses implications for the scope of permeability of the frontiers between the civilian and the military segments of the society. A review of these activities reveals the following:

1. In the last twenty years, a series of industrial enterprises and financial bodies have been set up within the framework of the Defense Ministry.

2. Patronage is not confined to members of the standing army but

also includes demobilized soldiers. The War Veterans Organization (WVO), founded in 1948, combines the roles of a holding company, a welfare organization, and a finance company for old soldiers. . . .

3. All the branches of the armed services of Thailand operate their own radio transmitters. Legally, all these stations are experimental; however, for all practical purposes they operate on a commercial basis. The military owners of radio and television stations are partners in the Thai Television Company, which owns and operates commercial radio and television in Thailand.

This domination by the military of the means of mass communication is yet another manifestation of absence of relatively autonomous centers of mass communication capable of controlling and supervising the various political and economic authorities. However, the control of the means of communication is by no means total, monolithic, and centralistic. On the contrary, what is peculiar is the quite unrestrained competition between the various government authorities and agencies over these communication media. . . .

SUMMARY AND CONCLUSIONS

Since the 1932 coup, the military-bureaucratic establishment has become an integral part of the political landscape. Until the late 1960s and the beginning of the 1970s, it was very difficult to envision the emergence of a significant and lasting opposition which could seriously challenge the regime. Any challenge from the remote periphery, and to a certain extent from the politically powerless groups on the margins of the center, was offset by the political support provided to the ruling groups by the bureaucracy. In other words, in spite of the internal turmoil and rivalry between the different cliques, the political center has been very homogeneous. The internal differentiation there during the period involved has not reached the point beyond which the emergence of sub-centers with wider prestige and reputation would be necessary. Operationally, the cabinet was still the backbone of political power and managed to apply rather successfully the somewhat fragile principles of reward allocation among the different cliques.

The scope and intensity of the ruling elite's exploitation of political power can be clearly and accurately understood in terms of a struggle over power · and prestige by groups of patrons and clients located within the military-bureaucratic elite. The conflict has been by and large between nominated or self-appointed officials rather than between groups of elected politicians with a wider social backing in the periphery. The prospects of partnership and collaboration among the members of opposing cliques hinge, among other things, on the differences or similarities in career channels within the military and civilian bureaucracies and, in some cases, on a parliamentary career. An ill-defined separation of career channels thus tends to create an intricate crisscrossing of these channels, giving Thailand a political system characterized by conflict rooted in interests of a corporate rather than a class nature. Conflict is largely focused on rewards derived from economic interest and control over sectors of the political and bureaucratic establishment. Rewards received in the form of bribery, gifts, and allowances further nourish the corporate interests of the chains of patrons and clients. The consolidation of these chains within certain political power positions eventually helped to establish an economic power base which in turn was exploited for further gains in the political sphere. Hence, since economic resources as such could not be easily converted into power resources, a major impediment to the achievement of political recognition by the Thai middle class. despite its possession of relatively abundant economic resources, was a lack of political power.

In contrast to the fairly high degree of institutionalization and modernization of the executive-administrative branch of the political system, the legislative branch was weak and unorganized. The egoistic and unrestrained employment of constitutions by the military oligarchy played a major role in undermining the organized and institutionalized basis of the legislature and the political organizations. Since the various constitutions did not succeed in promulgating universal rules of the political game, great tension has been generated between legal and informal rules. Nevertheless, it should not be forgotten that no regime up to the late sixties, even Sarit's, dared permanently to abolish the National Assembly. With all of its operational weaknesses and inability to impose sanctions, the National Assembly maintained an important potential for the legitimization of political processes in Thailand. The conditions under which the National Assembly could be converted into a more effective political instrument are difficult to determine. However, the qualitative and quantitative diversification of the politically conscious public and their rejection of apathetic compliance to the political decision-making process would be an important basic requisite. . . .

In Thailand, as in other southeast Asian societies, the new politically conscious public has polarized between the periphery and the political oligarchy at the center. Intermediate political groups, such as political parties, trade unions, and other voluntary organizations, which in other circumstances might act as mediators, are here ideologically, organizationally, and financially too weak. One ramification of this polarization is an increase in the intensity and scope of political activities that finds expression in violence. This violence is restrained not only by external factors but—even more significantly—by the fact that Thailand is not a one-party state or a totalitarian regime. Thailand is more accurately defined either as a bureaucratic polity or as an authoritarian regime. The authoritarian regime is, by and large, inefficient because it lacks the professional political apparatus typical of one-party regimes. Paradoxically, demands might be more easily articulated in a one-party regime, with its exclusive political channel, than in a bureaucratic polity such as Thailand, which substitutes a bureaucratic apparatus for clearly defined channels of articulating demands. In the period in question, the

Thai bureaucratic machine has been able to absorb some pressures from the loyal part of the periphery. However, the bureaucratic channels of communication between some groups like the students, and the non-Thai periphery and the center, have become so tenuous that their capacity to deal with political tensions has become greatly reduced. The more traditional intermediate groups, such as the district officers and the Chinese merchants, who have usually mediated the relations between the center and the periphery, are no longer capable of dealing either with the new demands or the means used to achieve them by the periphery. It should be remembered, however, that all these reservations refer to very specific areas of Thailand and that the core of the Thai Buddhist periphery is still loyal to the political center.

In all matters having to do with a distribution of labor between the military elite and the civilian sector, a policy of symbiosis between the two sectors and permeable or, at most, fragmented boundaries existed. This symbiosis occurred both on the personality and institutional levels. On the military elite level, it found expression in the occupancy by the army and police officers of high rungs in the focuses of military-political administrative and economic power. This phenomenon has been the primary source of personal enrichment and of the institutionalization of corruption that has spread into every stratus of the bureaucratic hierarchy. In the institutional sense, the military leadership personified the integration of most of the social, political, and economic elites of Thai society into a political core with great power and manipulative capability. This integration was one of the decisive factors in the high degree of stability of Thai society during the forty years discussed here. The unique position held by the armed forces in Thai society (a position attained by very few of the armed forces in countries with military regimes) has not served to foster a consciousness of reform and innovation.

The potentialities of the entrepreneurial traits of the military elite were brilliantly utilized in their entirety, mainly for personal ends. Though the army never rejected the self-image of a "modernizing agent," it took pains to impart to this image a most conservative and cautious character. This was demonstrated when the country's rulers publicly made the rare declarations aimed at formulating the basic premises of state policy. The rarity of these occasions indicates the relative irrelevance of ideological concepts and the absence of the kind of ambition in other military establishments which have striven for a respectable level of ideological articulation and sophistication. The symbiosis that marked the relations between the military and society in Thailand eventually left the initiative and the title "revolutionary" either to the country's most peripheral and marginal elements or to the intelligentsia, who had a much better access to the political center.

The intelligentsia have emerged as a serious challenge to the military, political, and economic elite complex. The challenge became real and eventually fatal in October 1973, when the students forced the ruling military elite to resign. There is no doubt that their sweeping victory surprised the students themselves. The students' willingness to fight the army and the army's reluctance to use all its force to crush the demonstration contributed.

We must note that the intelligentsia and the king—the two forces that opposed the regression from the level of competitive democracy that Thailand achieved in 1968—were part, although weak, of the national center. The change in the balance of power that has occurred in recent years *within* Thailand's political center has been one of the main reasons that Thanom and Praphas were unwilling to have a showdown with the students and the king—perhaps the most respected person in Thailand.

The military elite tried for a long time to win over the intelligentsia by a large-scale distribution of benefits, ranging from cash to scholarships to advisory posts. When these efforts and a limited use of force failed to neutralize the opposition, Thanom and Praphas preferred to withdraw and to go into exile. Another factor in the students' victory was the reluctance of some senior officers to continue the bloodshed. . . .

*BURMA: THE MILITARY—
INNOVATIONS AND
FRUSTRATIONS*

A SHORT HISTORY OF THE BURMESE MILITARY

The Burmese army originated in the Burma Independence Army (BIA) raised by General Aung San in 1941-

42 for a revolt against the British. Before independence, there had been only a few battalions. composed mainly of Karens, Kachins, Chins, and some Burmans. The nucleus of the BIA consisted of thirty men known as the "Thirty Comrades." Almost all of them were students who belonged to the movement founded by Aung San and U Nu that later became a part of the "Tankins," an anti-British, nationalistic, leftist political group. Under the Japanese authorities, the BIA was expanded to include between 20,000 and 30,000 men. It participated in some of the battles launched by the Japanese against the British. By 1944, the relations between the Burmese government established by the Japanese and the Japanese army had drastically deteriorated. The resistance movement, this time against the Japanese, was born, led again by Aung San, who was the defense minister in the Japanese-sponsored Burmese government.

However, at the end of World War II, Aung San's resistance movement was only one of many armed groups in Burma. There were also the Burmese forces which had returned from India with the British army and were mostly remnants of the colonial Burmese battalions. These two forces at first united. However, since many of the British Burmese forces were drawn from minority groups—especially Karens, who were opposed to Burmese nationalism—many deserted the new army and joined their tribesmen, who had already rebelled against the newborn state. In addition, there were two groups of Communist rebels—the

Red Flags and the White Flags—as well as the People's Volunteer Organization (PVO), a left-wing oriented militia organized immediately after independence, some of whose men refused to be disarmed.

Despite their brief existence under the Japanese, the BIA and the BNA not only laid the foundation for the post-independence Burmese army but also greatly molded the political structure and party setup of independent Burma.

A second factor which eventually had a tremendous impact on the political system was the vital need to establish a relatively large and strong army, because of the necessity of crushing the various insurgents who, in the first months of independence, controlled de facto almost all of Burma except Rangoon and its vicinity. In 1947, the Burmese army consisted of six regular battalions, fifteen military police battalions, and some thousands of irregulars. The strength of the armed forces has been increasing steadily since. By 1960, the army was up to 25,000; the navy, over 3,000; and the air force, activated in 1953, 3,000. In the late 1960s, the total number was 120,000. The army's combat experience, although limited in scope, was considerable. Some of the enlisted men and many officers had long experience in guerrilla warfare against the British and the Japanese. . . .

The degree and direction of professionalization of the Burmese army were determined by the type of enemy, their strength and tactics, and actual combat experience. They were, of course, also dependent on the kind of manpower put at the army's disposal. Unlike many other ex-colonies, Burma's army and political leader decided not to use foreign officers in command posts. The British officers were deposed immediately after independence, although a British military mission remained and Burmese officers continued to be sent to Britain for higher training after graduating from the Defence Services Academy. With the British officers deposed, wonderful opportunities opened to the Burmese noncommissioned officers and officers for promotion. However, this situation seems to some extent to have curbed the progress of professionalization. For example, in the first years after independence, a great shortage of officers and NCOs led the military to recruit many students who were actually politically nominated.

On 3 March 1959, the People's Militia Act was passed, prescribing compulsory military service for periods ranging from six to twenty-four months for every man between the ages of eighteen and forty-six; every woman between the ages of eighteen and thirty-six; and every doctor, engineer, or teacher between the ages of eighteen and fifty-six. In fact, this act was never implemented. The armed forces were maintained entirely on a volunteer basis, except for the conscription of a few needed doctors. Terms of enlistment ranged from four to six years, with a commitment to remain in inactive reserve status for a specified period on termination of enlistment. As there was no reserve organization or program, however, this stipulation did not entail any obligation.

Until 1937, the Burmese units were a part of the colonial Indian army and adopted its pattern of social and ethnic composition; that is, the regiments and companies were organized on an ethnic religious basis. The ethnic composition of the army at the outbreak of World War II was the following: Burmese, 12.3%; Karens, 27.8%; Chins, 22.6%; Kachins, 22.9%; and others, 4.3%. After the war, when Aung San asked to unite his BIA forces with the Burmese forces who had fought under British command, he insisted that the army should be organized on what was called the "class battalion basis"; in other words, on an ethnic principle. The object was to establish "pure" Burmese battalions—to counterbalance the battalions, composed mainly of minorities, which were considered disloyal to Burmese nationalism, and to assure the Burmazation of the officer corps. The army was reconstituted in 1949–50. The government's policy favored the acceptance of Burmans in increasing numbers. In 1967 a majority of the men in service were Burmans, although there were still many of other ethnic affiliations, principally Karens, Chins, and Kachins.

The top army leadership contrasts sharply with the bulk of the officer corps recruited in the 1950s and 1960s. Most of the senior officers were the cream of the resistance movement and its political counterpart before 1947. For example, twenty of the twenty-three colonels in key positions during the caretaker regime in 1958–60 had been engaged in politics in the pre-independence period and were nominated by the political elite to military roles.

One of the factors which contributed to the consolidation of the NCO and officer corps as a distinct status group was that the military has been, since independence, the most available channel of social mobility. The military has a considerable advantage, compared to other public institutions, in attracting the most qualified personnel in the country. One main reason for this is the prestige of the military profession. Although there is no direct evidence on this issue, it appears that the attitude of the Burmese people toward the military profession changed, from 1948 to 1962, from a negative to a much more positive one. The role played by the army on the battlefield apparently strengthened the soldier's status in Burmese society after independence. Another inducement was rewards—officers received a considerable salary in comparison to other groups dependent on the government and more or less equivalent in status.

One should also mention the opportunities, at the army's expense, to study and acquire a profession (such as medicine, engineering, or accounting) highly valued in civilian society and to which, in most cases, one could transfer. This greatly attracted the young to the military.

Many of the economic enterprises developed and controlled by the army were apparently viewed by the military as means for securing their own futures. Retirement, in the military services, comes early, and "the army is the promise of a vast reservoir of future well-paid jobs for military personnel, their relatives, and their friends." Political power became, after 1958, another inducement for those with aspirations for mobility. For the senior officers, this balance of rewards meant renewal of the "golden age" before and immediately after independence. The deposed Colonel Maung Maung, the number-three man in Ne Win's first administration, put it in this way:

After the Second World War was over and we had obtained our independence, the cream of the resistance movement stayed with the Burma army, and most of the rest became politicians. It was irksome to find that those who could not hold their own in the army came, in time, to be our political superiors.

Phases of Ideological Development in the Defense Services

In many ways, the Burmese army was an innovator in terms of the role of the military in developing countries. The redefinition of the army's role was certainly directly linked with the economic, political, and ideological crises of the first decade of Burma's independence. These crises troubled the politically conscious military elite no less than did their battle against insurgents. Moreover, the stalemate on the economic and political-ideological levels prevented, in a sense, any "final" victory on the battlefield. In this context, the propensity of the officer corps to expand and enlarge the "classic" roles of the armed forces becomes relevant to our discussion. In other words, one may ask whether the failure of the political elite to mobilize its resources and to "supply"

adequate "services" to its operational organs did not lead to the molding of a particular and unorthodox pattern of relations between the military and the civilian society? We shall consider this on two levels: (a) the ideological level; and (b) the application of ideology.

Prior to the 1962 coup, there were six phases of what the military elite itself defined as the "ideology of the defense services." The first two were preideological. The first phase involved BIA and BDA in 1941–43, when ideology was confined to the basic issues of independence and political freedom. The political and social character of the future independent state was a marginal concern. The second phase began with the establishment of a Japanese-sponsored Burmese government in 1944. Greater sophistication in ideological formulation was reflected by according priorities among goals—the most important ones being achieving political freedom, establishing a democratic state, realizing socialistic programs.

In the third and fourth phases, national ideology was rethought and reassessed. The third phase (1948–55) was defined by the military itself as a "period of ideological gestation"; and the fourth (1956–57) as a "period of thorough study and discussion of the ideology for the defense services." For this purpose, a special conference was called in 1956 to which all commanding officers were invited.

The last two phases were those in which a new version of an ideology was consolidated and the methods for its application spelled out. The army called the fifth the "first phase of ideological development." The sixth and last phase was that in which the specific role of the defense services was finally formulated.

At the Mehtila conference, it was stated that

Man's endeavour to build a society set free at last from anxieties over food, clothing, shelter, and the ability to enjoy life's spiritual satisfaction as well, fully convinced of the sanctity, dignity and essential goodness of life, must proceed from the premise of a faith only in a politico-economic system based on the eternal principles of justice, liberty and equality. This is our belief. We would rather give up life than give up this belief. In order to achieve the establishment of such a society, we have resolved to uphold this belief forever in this sovereign independent republic of the Union of Burma.

An outsider reading this document may be surprised that military leaders defined this period as the first phase of an autonomous ideological development. Even the participants at the conference emphasized that the declaration was in essence a repetition in "simple" language of three fundamental documents: (1) the Burmese Declaration of Independence; (2) the first address to parliament by the first president of the union; (3) the Constitution of the Union of Burma.

An answer may be found elsewhere in the document. Feeling that some more specific formulation of means and aims should be presented, its authors stated that "now the time has come to determine precisely and clearly the role and attitude of the

Defence Services in the second phase of ideological development." The reasoning behind this is both interesting and typical: "For the Defence Services simply to accept the National Ideology without giving thought to their role and defining this attitude is to develop a strategy without devising the tactics." What is implied here by "role" and "attitude"? The document assumes this question by presenting a clear order of priorities: "to restore peace and the rule of law— first. To implement democracy— second. To establish a socialist economy—third." These three objectives are viewed as interdependent:

To establish a socialist economy, democracy is a prerequisite: for democracy to flourish, law and order is essential. Without peace and the rule of law, no country can be a democratic one. In an undemocratic country, a socialist economy can never be established—a totalitarian government will impose only a rigid economic system which will deny the right of private property.

The definition of socialism is of great interest. In addition to the general and classic definition—"to build up a society in which there will be no exploitation of man by man" or to institute a "planned economy," the document states the ultimate problems of the Burmese economy:

The Union's economy is based on agriculture, but the methods of production are outmoded, and consequently our production capacity is limited. Small industry is not sufficiently developed to provide adequate consumer goods for all citizens. Therefore, the main feature of the national economic policy should be to modernize the basic agricultural economy, and secondly to develop local industries commensurate with the natural and human resources of the country. This will require deliberate and thoughtful planning. In the process of development this state-controlled economy may appear not to differ from state capitalism. But it should be noted, at the same time, that the state will continue to encourage those private enterprises which contribute to increased national productivity.

Two important items should be noted. First, the military before the coup felt it necessary to formulate its own ideology which, although based on the national ideology, was labelled the "Ideology of the Defence Services." Second, this ideology was all-embracing, including many areas of private and public activities. However, in the 1950s the focuses of cleavage between the military and the political elites became numerous and included many intellectual and practical fields.

In contrast to U Nu's strongly religious orientation, the military elite could almost be described as vigorously antitraditional, although not to the same extent antireligious. Ne Win did not hesitate to suspend, after the 1962 coup, the decree making Buddhism the state religion, despite the fact that U Nu considered this decree the most important development of the last decade in Burma. Ne Win also dissolved the executive and general council of the Buddha Sasana Council. The second military government also abolished the observance of the Buddhist sabbath enacted by the previous government. This had entailed the closing of all government offices on a different day each week, causing considerable confusion in the business community. In addition, the military regime abolished the ban on cattle slaughter, which is anathema to the Buddhist.

In spite of these extreme acts, in those days the military elite could by no means be defined, or its acts interpreted, as reflecting a militant antireligious attitude. The military's attitude could be more properly characterized as favoring an institutional separation between state and church and simultaneously encouraging a national culture based on a synthesis of the basic tenets of Buddhism and socialism.

Another source of antagonism between the military and civilians was the concept of government. Perhaps there is no other sphere in Burmese life with which the military leaders were more dissatisfied than the process and patterns of decision making at every level of government. They felt that inefficiency, corruption, and political considerations—instead of rational and professional criteria—characterized governmental operations, often with serious consequences for the nation. These were among the main charges in the military's opposition to the U Nu government. They are not really ideological in character but refer mainly to administrative practices which are means of achieving ideological ends. However, there is evidence that this extremely critical attitude was rooted in a basic disagreement about concepts and images of ideal government. For example, the army constantly tried to preserve and strengthen the authority of the central government apparatus against local political leaders who used to interfere in the activities of government officials. . . .

The issue of economic planning was a source of conflict as well. The official ideological declaration of the defense services refers very seriously to the problems of economic planning and to specific priorities in capital investment. Some clear indications of basic differences in this field between the attitudes of the military leaders and of the political leaders can be seen in the statement, made by Aung Gyi, after the coup d'etat in March 1962: "The economic program to be formulated gradually by the new regime will be cautious and more practical. We do not want to indulge in big dreams." . . .

The basic antagonisms were by no means confined to above mentioned areas. Another area where the policy of the government was opposed, and ostensibly, at least, provided the ultimate stimulus for the recent coup d'etat, was in the relationship between the constituent states and the central government. The last coup d'etat was justified by the contention that U Nu was inclined to give greater concessions to the constituent states, especially to the Shan state.

The preceding remarks may not allay all doubts about the military elite's sincerity in its ideological rationalization of the military's role in Burma. However, these doubts may well be eliminated by considering the actual events of 1958–60.

THE APPLICATION OF THE NATIONAL IDEOLOGY OF THE DEFENCE SERVICES: 1958–60

In retrospect, the efforts to elaborate a specific ideological identity for the defense services were apparently largely propelled by a desire for innovation—albeit a general, pragmatic one. In the early 1950s, Burma's military leaders had demonstrated those entrepreneurial qualities, which were to be so evident under Ne Win's first government, that greatly influenced the military's ideological development. They can be perceived in the economic, and to a much lesser degree in the political and educational, spheres.

The army's first steps into the realm of economic action were very modest. In 1950, the Ministry of Defence created the Defence Service Institute (DSI), a nonprofit association designed to supply consumer goods to soldiers through a department store— and to undermine the black market. All profit was to go toward promoting the welfare of the defense services' personnel. The next step, still very modest, was the establishment in 1951 of a book and stationery store, open to all, subsequently enlarged and then named Ava House. The Ava bookstore was a model for future, more widespread ventures into public enterprise, the development of which now accelerated. In 1953, the International Trading House was established to deal with government contracts. In 1956, the Burma Fisheries was formed. By 1957, 'the DSI had grown from a general store to a three-branch commercial agency which supplied goods to the armed forces and to the general public.

Economic activity was confined mainly to purchasing and selling consumers' goods without interfering with economic policy per se. . . .

In 1958, under the caretaker government, the DSI became the largest and most powerful business organization in Burma. Its subsidiary concerns dominated the vital fields of banking, shipping, construction, and fishing. Its holdings included Rangoon's largest department store, the largest automobile service station, a bus line, a radio assembly factory, a motor workshop, and a factory producing shoes and boots for the army. The DSI also became the nation's largest importer, controlling trade in coal and coke and holding agencies for the various automobile manufacturers. In addition, the DSI entered the world of tourism and hotels. All profits were reinvested in the expanding concerns. As a nonprofit organization, the institute received sizable tax exemptions not enjoyed by its competitors. Military enterprise as part of a nonprofit public corporation agreed with the economic objectives encouraged by U Nu's government of promoting cooperatives and nonprofit enterprises—which, until 1958, had received only lip service. The Burmese army thus revealed a capacity to apply abstract ideas systematically and comprehensively. Furthermore, its innovative spirit was expressed in its willingness to embark on new projects. In fact, most investment capital in this period was provided by the DSI.

Although the army maintained that it did not intend to compete with or displace private enterprises, private businessmen grew increasingly suspicious of the military's objectives. The majority of the Burmese mercantile community did not completely believe in the army's good faith. Even the cooperative movement felt it had been trumped. The new government headed by U Nu, reelected in 1960, also was apprehensive. To tighten civilian control over the military-economic sector, the legal status of the DSI was modified, and most DSI enterprises were taken over by the Burma Economic Development Corporation (BEDC). This newly established corporation was expected to help finance, coordinate, supervise, and assist all activities of the organized corporate bodies. The BEDC had seven members; the general managers of the Union Bank and ministerial secretaries were included ex officio. The corporation members and the chairmen were military men. Thus, although the military shared control of the corporation with civilians, the military's overall influence on economic policies was heightened owing to the broader fields now covered by the new corporation. The BEDC received new economic resources to promote economic development, but the military, through its strategic position in the corporation, could direct and regulate its course, and, no less important, it could provide jobs and economic rewards for its retired and active NCOs and officers.

While building the economic empire, the military elite by no means

overlooked the importance of accumulating popular support outside the
conventional channels of the political
parties. Political activities were not
unfamiliar to the senior officers; before
1948 many had belonged to the
young nationalist elite. Within the
framework of the BIA, the officers
played roles that were more political
than military.

Furthermore, in the first years after
independence, senior officers like Ne
Win and Aung San played clearly
political roles. A more definitely institutionalized division of labor existed in the urban political areas. In the
provinces, because of the long struggle against insurgents, regional commanders often assumed administrative
and political functions—which inevitably resulted in clashes between them
and party representatives.

In a period of severe political crises
—on the eve of the first Ne Win
government—the military unwillingly
was dragged into the arena of internal
political feuds where the chief political
factions were trying hard to win the
army's sympathies. . . . This conflict
ended with U Nu's resignation and
the military's creation of the caretaker government.

Just as it had in the economic field,
the military sought to pave new ways
in the political sphere. By declining
to identify with any political faction,
it hoped to gather support in another
form. It established a countrywide
movement called the National Solidarity Association (NSA or *Kyant
Khaing Ye Ahphwes*). Its official purpose
was to fight economic and armed
insurgence and to inculcate in the
people of Burma the values of law and
order and competitive democracy.
However, one of the undeclared aims
of the NSA movement. which appealed mainly to ex-servicemen, was
to encourage independent candidates
to run for parliament and to generate
popular support for them. The army
leaders apparently hoped that such
a body of independent professional
men—of the sort who served in various
capacities in the caretaker regime—
could be used to influence the outcome
of the legislative process. The NSA
was not dissolved after U Nu took over
the reins of government in April 1960,
but remained in army hands. The
army's original intention—that the
NSA be a mass movement—was
abandoned. With U Nu's return to
power, the organization became much
more elitist in character, an educating
rather than action oriented organization.

Until the March 1962 coup, the
educational and ideological training
of the Burmese army was of a limited
nature in comparison to its functions
in the country's economy and even
with its indirect influence on political
life. The army was mainly concerned
with agricultural training. It established an agricultural vocational training center, whose aim was to instruct
soldiers in agriculture, animal hus-
bandry, tractor driving, and maintenance. The army also provided
training for civil service personnel.
During Ne Win's first term, the man in
charge of military training conducted
a special school for public administration.

These two educational services indicate the range of nonmilitary education and training given by the military

to the wider Burmese society. Ideological indoctrination was apparently limited to the military itself and perhaps extended to the NSA as well.

One prominent result of these diversified activities was a considerable increase in the infiltration of officers into civilian posts. This was due less to a deliberate policy of posting officers and ex-officers to key positions within the civilian sector than to the expansion of military roles. The greatest opportunity arose, of course, under the caretaker government, when about 150 officers were shifted to civilian posts. A sizable proportion of these were drawn from the senior ranks. At U Nu's request, senior officers later remained in civilian posts. In addition, a number retained civilian posts at their own request and subsequently resigned from military service.

The army's pledge to return to the barracks after the election of February 1960 was duly honored. Since then, many hypotheses and speculations have been published about the reasons the army leaders kept their word despite their disappointment in U Nu's victory and internal pressure to disregard their pledge and to remain at the helm of the government. Some observers have attributed the military's retreat to disappointment. The military's great effort to restore law and authority had resulted in growing resentment and unpopularity within the population—who presumably preferred the permissiveness and tolerance of U Nu's regime to the brusqueness of army rule. Because of its inability or unwillingness to institute a new political organization affiliated with

it, the army was unable to maintain its close relationship with key groups in the population. This resulted in an ever expanding communication gap and growing unpopularity. The army may also have been reluctant to compete for popularity in the conventional political channels with the political parties. It did not want to abandon its professional image and adopt that of the politician whom it so despised. The fear of intensifying divisions within the army was also a factor that encouraged Ne Win to abide by his promise.

A further factor may be added. The military elite was not yet ready, psychologically or ideologically, to establish a prolonged military regime. It was willing to give the politicians another chance to prove the superiority of the democratic mechanism. In any event, the military's withdrawal must be seen as conditional; the democratic regime was on probation and was to improve and prove itself. The army did not completely abandon its power in the civilian sectors. Through the BEDC, it directly substantially controlled the Burmese economy and could eventually indirectly influence decision making in other spheres. Compared to other armies which managed to achieve what the Burmese army had, its return to the barracks was certainly an outstanding and unique act. Even in this respect the Burmese senior officers were innovators. However, the withdrawal was not unanimously accepted by all senior officers, and after U Nu's return to power the army was divided into three groups. The first, composed mostly of young officers, looked reluctantly at the army's retreat from politics and considered it a blatant error. The second group argued that the army should not interfere in politics in any way. The third group saw "the army performing limited, but still essential roles in national development."

The "probation period" for the civilian elite lasted two years. In March 1962, the officers finally concluded that the politicians had no intention—or ability—of changing themselves. The officers were disturbed by: (a) the concessions U Nu promised to the minorities—which the army considered to be the final step leading to the dissolution of the union; (b) the rapid succession of economic crises: (c) the proclamation of Buddhism as the state religion; (d) the inefficiency of the administration; and (e) the progressive disintegration of the ruling party.

THE MILITARY AS A POLITICAL ELITE AND THE CONSOLIDATION OF POWER

With the coup d'etat, the military elite entered a new phase of ideological deliberation, distinguished by a relatively higher degree of depth, articulation, and specification of the normative principles intended as guiding lines for Burmese society on its way toward progress. Army ideologists tried to define the "revolutionary philosophy" of Burmese socialism. Its uniqueness was established by contrasting the philosophy of the newly established *Lanzin* Party (Burma Socialist Programme Party—BSPP) with those of the Communist and of the Social Democratic parties. . . .

The alleged distinctiveness of this ideological formulation was achieved by oversimplifications and sweeping generalizations about the ideologies of the social democrats and the Communists, and hazy elaborations of the character of Burmese socialism. No wonder the translation of these vague slogans into concrete programs was confronted by serious obstacles and required great improvisational skill! Actually, built-in rationalization for such improvisations was provided by the very belief in a pragmatic and nondoctrinaire attitude.

If some of the general ideas were to be implemented, key groups within the population would have had to favor them and potential as well as real opposition groups would have had to be neutralized. The military revolution, however, resulted in a complete disintegration of the fragile balance of power within the old political center. The military had, therefore, to reconstruct a new political center and to redetermine the balance of power and the functions of various organizations. . . .

The new concept . . . called for total politicization of the army and its being molded into an instrument for the construction of a socialist state. In this task the auxiliary role was assigned to a civilian organization, whose main function was to enlist support from key civilian groups. This organization emerged in several phases, since a reorganization of the entire political order was necessary.

The first step was divulged about three months after the coup. On 4 July, the Revolutionary Council (RC) made it known that it proposed to constitute a new political organization or party. Before this, feverish negotiations had been held between the RC and the leaders of the old parties in order to find a common framework, but only the NUF would accept. As a result, the military leaders decided to go their own way and establish a cadre party without any foundation in the old parties. The various leading positions of the new party (the Burma Socialist Programme Party—BSPP) were allocated to members of the RC. For two years after the coup, the civilian parties continued to function (with some restrictions) alongside the BSPP. In March 1964, the RC promulgated the National Solidarity Protection Law, which immediately went into effect, dissolving all political organizations. This law further required all nonpolitical organizations, including religious associations, to be registered with the government. The *Lanzin* Party was initially planned, at least for a transitional period, to be a cadre party. The Revolutionary Council stated that "since the party is to be organized as a cadre party during the first stage it will be necessary to screen the candidate membership applications which had been submitted with diverse motivations." Obviously, the nucleus of the cadre was members of the armed forces.

Concomitant with establishing the BSPP, the RC was active in developing additional types of frameworks of political and administrative action among peasants and workers. In May 1964, the Security and Administrative Committees (SAC) were established, to replace the NSA. The SAC were composed of military personnel. The officers in charge were eventually to become full-fledged civil servants. A nucleus for a new type of bureaucracy was thereby created. The SAC were to form a link between the government and the people in the periphery, coordinating the roles of different government departments responsible both for keeping law and order and for properly distributing commercial goods, although a more specific function was to allocate loans to peasants. The next step was the proposed organization of peasants' councils to ensure political control in this sensitive sector.

These councils were supposed to be the first tier in a hierarchy of three proposed layers in the legislative process. Similar institutional frameworks were designed for the urban workers. In May 1964, the RC announced that it intended to set up the Burmese Way of Socialism Workers Units to establish a better system of organization for the workers. According to the declaration, under the new organization and system there would be effective control and utilization of manpower and labor and the elimination of exploitation—all conducive to greatly improved quality and productivity. Furthermore, the system would enable the units to be quickly converted into national defense units, defending the state in time of war and as effectively constructing it in times of peace. A full-scale campaign of political ideological indoctrination was also launched. The dissemination of the BSPP's ideological platform, "the system of correlation of man and environment," was primarily aimed at neutralizing hostile groups in the small middle class, civil service, students, and the sangha, and at re-socializing friendly elements among the army, workers, and peasants.

With the establishment of the Central People's Peasants Council (CPPC) and the Central People's Workers Council (CPWC), which were presented as the "bulwark of the Socialist Democratic State of Burma," the RC initiated political statements and programs whose aim was to reconcile the RC with various opposition groups. Thirty-two opposition leaders, including U Nu, were released from prison, where they had been since 1962. The RC then invited them to participate in the Internal Unity Advisory Board, to make suggestions about either amending the old constitution, which was in fact suspended at that moment, or drawing up a completely new one. The background to these dramatic gestures was the severe economic crisis and the failure to crush the subversive activities of the Communist and other minority groups. The political dialogue with opposition leaders failed, ending with U Nu's flight first to India and later to Thailand, where he allegedly tried to organize armed resistance to Ne Win's regime. . . .

In the political sphere, . . . the military was hostile to U Nu's religious policy and considered the proclamation of Buddhism as the state religion a serious error, since it caused the minorities to be more—and unnecessarily—alienated. "There was a strong feeling among the military that the country was in the hands of a religious obscurantist whose policies had the effect of disturbing national unity."

The RC was expected to modify U Nu's religious policy. Indeed, immediately after the coup, many laws enacted in the U Nu period were suspended but, by and large, the RC adopted a fairly cautious policy. The state religion provision became a dead letter without, however, being explicitly rejected. Ne Win was torn between the conviction that religion and politics should be separated and the feeling that the RC should occupy itself with religion to construct a new Burma according to the basic ideological outlines set forth in "Burma's Way to Socialism." . . .

The Communist underground, the students, and the sangha, all focal points of opposition, troubled the RC mainly because they were composed of people in elite social positions, although they did not endanger Burma's existence or its recognized borders and population composition. However, the ethnic minorities explicitly expressed their desire for more autonomy and in some cases even complete separation from the union. This, with its undercurrent of violence, was a real danger to the union. Until 1962, Burma's governments had continued the traditional policy pursued by the Burmese kings: the Burmazation of minorities and their absorption and assimilation into Buddhist-Burmese society. In the final stages of his rule, U Nu was compelled to respond to certain demands from the minorities about rights beyond those guaranteed by the constitution. The military cited these same concessions as a major reason for the coup—after which there was no doubt that the new government would nullify them and assume a tougher stance toward the minorities. In January 1964, the RC announced the decision to have one set of laws for all Burmese states in the union.

To the guerrilla warfare led by the Red and White Flags and the various minority groups, the army responded with severe countermeasures—but with only partial success. The situation in the beginning of the 1970s was substantially the same as in the early 1960s after the army took over.

Besides legal, administrative, and military measures to tighten control over ethnic and cultural minorities, the RC also explicitly encouraged the promotion of indigenous languages, folklore, literature, and religious beliefs. In this respect, the RC accomplished far more than the preceding governments.

Previous citations from "Burma's Way to Socialism" may have indicated the basic outlines of the RC's economic policy. Some illustrations from the economic field will help concretize them.

The main objectives of the RC's economic policy were to end all direct foreign investment; to nationalize all industries, particularly oil and rice; and to nationalize all trade and banks except for small retail stores. The rationale was provided by arguing that the coexistence of private and public enterprise was an economic and social evil in which the previous government indulged. It is interesting that, to legitimize its dramatic intentions, the RC resorted not only to secular-ideological arguments but also to Buddhist thinking.

Enactment of this extreme economic nationalism was slowed down by passive resistance from those primarily interested in maintaining an economic status quo and by insufficient professional manpower or adequate administrative infrastructure. Implementing the economic programs involved many compromises, and sometimes the RC was compelled to retract former announcements. Nevertheless, the basic outlines of the policy were carried through, despite severe internal disputes that ended in an internal purge of the RC. The immediate effects of the economic reforms were rather negative. Burma's gross domestic product (in constant prices) declined, both the volume and value of exports fell, and agricultural production was reduced. There were nevertheless a number of contingent achievements, such as an increase in foreign exchange resources resulting from curtailing . imports. Most of the economic activity during RC rule was concentrated in the industrial and commercial sectors. Relatively little was accomplished in the politically most sensitive sector—the rural—despite various programs of agrarian reform. Peasant frustration grew, centered around indebtedness, the need to improve markets, and rising prices.

SUMMARY AND CONCLUSIONS

Burma's structural features and political processes can be summarized in terms of the achievements and failures of the Burmese elite and its ability to maintain its organizational framework and the existing social-political arrangements while consolidating its authority—which was constantly challenged, particularly by various sectors of the country's heterogeneous periphery. The greatest obstacle to satisfactory integration of political action in the center with that at the local community was the government's inability to crush its most violent vocal opponents, whether Communist insurrectionists or minority groups. True, despite twenty years of armed struggle, the insurrectionists never succeeded in annihilating governmental administrative and political action in Burma's most important administrative and geographic centers. But in the more remote places, they occasionally disrupted the government's efforts to stabilize and pacify the population. Such regions were mostly populated by ethnic minorities who resented attempts to incorporate them fully into the Burmese national framework. In the eyes of these minority groups, the question of national sovereignty and autonomy within Burma had not yet been solved.

Thus, bespite being a Buddhist society—one that preaches against violence and killing—Burma became in actuality an extremely violent society. However, this must be viewed as a type of deviant subculture, for the intentions of the leaders were obviously quite different. The constitution was liberal in spirit and democratic in its recommendations. All parties—including the ruling party—were to be instruments by which the executive would seek to implement the government's plans and programs. This was the theoretical formulation, but the practice was quite different. Party organizations were very vague, especially for those in the middle and lower groups and on the local community level. In the rural sector, party organizations had almost no meaning at all. The parties' representatives deliberately used traditional communication channels to introduce new ideas, to safeguard political loyalty. Almost nowhere did a local party organization replace the traditional elite, for most of those nominated by the party or by a government representative already occupied a prominent position in the traditional rural structure. The government and the political elites endeavored to combine new ideas and organizational techniques within existing frameworks. Sometimes they established a substantial level of stability and cooperation between the government and the frustrated sectors in the periphery. The greatest weakness (excluding objective impediments) was that it was not part of a comprehensive and deliberate policy orienting the entire country toward a modern political setup within the traditional hierarchy of power. The dominant mood of the AFPFL, despite its desires, was that of an elite party rather than a mass movement, and the social composition of the political elite showed this mood. . . .

The army's desire to intervene in domestic affairs was tremendous. The army's ideological entrepreneurial orientation only intensified it. The stimulus was a direct result of the large gap between the prevailing civilian ideology (whose successful application would have required revolutionary change in the process of mobilization and allocation of rewards), the unstable political system, the lack of political solidarity, and inadequate psychological readiness to change. The military elite considered itself an "agent of modernization and nation building" and was therefore particularly sensitive to this discrepancy. Unable to give the military services adequate manpower, budgets, or political support, the political elite failed to provide and maintain a workable framework for mobilization. Thus the military gradually became involved in productive entrepreneurial activities of its own and wound up by finally taking over political power. Before the 1960 election, the military leaders were hesitant and lacked confidence in their ability to concretize a new basis for national consensus. They chose to abdicate. Later it appeared that the only possible means to transform the military rule into civilian rule would be by the civilianization of the military leaders themselves.

Finally, it seems that what the army is doing in Burma is more than a simple rebellion or even an ideological rebellion, since the military elite is not interested in reviving or reintroducing an idealized society. On the other hand, it is doubtful that the 1962 coup approached a total revolution or a revolution which intended to supplement the entire structure of values and recast the entire division of labor. At this stage in its evolution, the Burmese revolution may perhaps be most appropriately labeled, in spite of all innovations, a "simple revolution," a revolution with an ideology limited to the change of only a limited number of values. It affects the political order largely by its establishment of a one-party state. In the economic sphere,

no fundamental changes in policy are evident. The RC admitted that it was only implementing the principles formulated in the constitution of 1948. Nevertheless, in methods, rate, and temperament, some substantial changes have been made. This balance of achievements and failures in Burma is not unique. It is an example of the fundamental weakness of most military establishments. The army's unlimited ability to solve problems of the order of those with which the Burmese army is dealing is no more than a myth. And yet, the prospects of restoring civilian rule remain very remote. Equipped with its homemade brand of ideology, the military is convinced of its own diagnostic and therapeutic qualities.

A COMPARATIVE ANALYSIS AND SOME GENERAL CONCLUSIONS

THE MICROFACTORS AND MILITARY INTERVENTION

This chapter is devoted to a systematic comparative analysis of the civil-military relations in Burma and Thailand, with reference to the typologies and paradigms mentioned in the two introductory chapters. Their validity can thus be at least partially examined. The role expansion of the military with regard to the political, economic, administrative, and social spheres was the focus of both the analytical presentation and the historical description of Thailand and Burma. A military coup d'etat per se should be perceived as only one dimension of the possible variations of military role expansion. Some evidence of the existence of such variations is contained in the studies of Burma and Thailand. . . .

The main differences between Thailand and Burma will be considered later. Now, let us mention that the differences—either in terms of the intensity of the role expansion in different spheres stemming from a different range of priorities, or in terms of the scope of penetration and expansion—are the product of very different historical conditions.

We have distinguished between two groups of factors which were intended to explain the specific conditions for the execution of a coup, and the difference in the direction and the intensity of role expansion. We have referred to the internal factors exclusive to the military social system and to external factors. They may perhaps be defined as micro- and macrofactors. What was the weight of the microfactors in the circumstances brought about by the military coups in Thailand and Burma? And to what extent were they responsible for the different patterns of military regimes which subsequently emerged?

The two military establishments were similar in the instrumental dimension, i.e., the quantity and the quality of material and other resources necessary for implementing military rule. They were also similar in the logistic dimension, i.e., the dimension which can be measured by knowledge of the extent of mechanization, number of units, and degree of coordination between the different services.

Military experts can probably point out more specific differences with regard to logistic capacity in the light of the Burmese army's experience in warfare against various guerrilla movements. Nevertheless, one may reasonably say that those differences between the Burmese and the Thai armies had little if any impact on the patterns of the coups, much less on the types of the military regimes. However, the differential, internal cohesiveness and the different types of self-identity undoubtedly had a great effect on the number of the coups, on the scope and intensity of internal purges, and, of course, on the social and political features of the military regimes. In social cohesiveness, the Burmese army had a great advantage compared to the Thai army. Nevertheless, this did not prevent the Thai army from carrying out coups and from being, in its own way, consistent in economic and social policies. It was precisely the internal, personal conflicts within the Thai military elite in the 1950s and 1960s that strengthened the predisposition to solve conflicts by coups and countercoups. On the other hand, the stability of the military regime in Burma, and the fact that there was no countercoup up until 1973, can be explained by the relatively strong internal social cohesiveness of the Burmese military elite. This social cohesiveness must be described cautiously, since some internal purges occurred. However, they were limited in scope, and the measures taken against the deposed officers were very mild. This particular type of purge within the Burmese army can be attributed less to the social cohesiveness than to the ideological controversy which began in the 1950s and became more heated after the 1962 coup. The

Burmese army's internal social cohesiveness actually involves only those armed forces which were under the direct control of the general staff— not all the armed forces at the disposal, in one way or another, of the Burmese political elite. These include the various paramilitary units in the periphery and even the Union Military Police, under the control of the Ministry of Interior. For these units, internal rifts and conflicts were no less significant than in the Thai military. The strengthening of these paramilitary units and the danger of confrontation between them and the regular army was a major cause for the establishment of the caretaker government in 1958 and for the coup in 1962. The Thai military was spared such an unpleasant experience.

The more ruthless and resourceful officers of the Thai military expected to gain from the weak internal social cohesiveness. When there is relatively easy access to social and economic benefits and an absence of normative restrictions, there is a very high probability of personal conflicts and institutionalized corruption. It would be misleading to argue that personal corruption was a rare phenomenon in Burma during either civilian or military rule. However, although the Burmese military became almost the exclusive channel of mobility, the exploitation of power positions at the disposal of the officers for personal gain was very different in scope and intensity from that of Thailand. It would, perhaps, be naive to assume that the ideological approach of the Burmese military elite to public issues and social programs was what kept it from

this sort of moral deterioration. In any case, this ideological approach is a salient feature of the Burmese army; while in Thailand, the ideological approach is marginal and, in the opinion of some observers, even entirely absent.

Any explanation of the differences between the Thai and Burmese military officers in terms of personal histories would probably point out the socioeconomic backgrounds of the senior officers and their families, and the circumstances of political socialization, especially during the crucial adolescent period. The political education of the upper echelons of the Burmese military occurred in a particular political framework, i.e., the national independence movement or in the militant student organizations which eventually became the spearhead of the national movement. . . .

There is a great deal of selectivity in recruiting the officer corps. But in Burma, the selection is first and foremost on the basis of ideological commitment and through a political organization, i.e., the *Lanzin* Party; in Thailand, the selection is assured by informal mechanisms, for example, the encouragement of officers' sons to choose the military career. One may even say that in Thailand there is a consolidation of a military oligarchy in which the ascriptive criterion plays a very prominent role. However, in spite of this difference in selective criteria, class interest cannot be considered the dominant factor explaining the role expansion of the military establishments or their general attitudes toward social change and modernization. The distinction made by Finer between class interest and corporate interest is applicable here. The corporate interest, i.e., the demand for large budgets and other material privileges, does not play a smaller role than class interests and its presence, especially in Thailand, cannot be ignored.

THE MILITARY PROFESSION IN THAILAND AND BURMA

Since World War II, the Burmese and Thai armies substantially improved professional standards. The question is, however, whether one can confidently assert that these two military elites became full-fledged professionals. Any judgment in this respect is contingent on the definition of the concept of professionalism and especially on how the relationship between the different components of professionalism is perceived. From this point of view one can find many new clues to the professional character of the two countries. In Huntington's terminology, in the Thai army the corporate loyalty of the military professionals is more important than expertise or public responsibility. On the other hand, the Burmese military have made a great effort, with relative success, to reach an integrated and balanced conceptual relationship of the components. Is it possible that these nuances may explain the differences in the political militancy of the two military elites? At face value, it would seem that a more integrated approach to professionalism would restrain the inclination toward political activism. The qualifications mentioned earlier with regard to this thesis are rein-forced by the Burmese case. These qualifications stem from the fact that in many cases, and especially in societies undergoing rapid social and economic modernization, the professionalization of the army intensifies rather than reduces the feeling of mutual alienation between the civilian and the military sectors. Burma between 1958 and 1962 provides an excellent example. An accelerated process of professionalization of the military in developing countries like Burma, where political, economic, and cultural backwardness is prevalent, makes the officer corps stand out much more sharply as an elite group. The capacity to manipulate manpower and other resources goes hand in hand with the power and prestige of this group. The combination of prestige and the ability to manipulate administrative tools and material resources provides an ideal incubator for the growth of ideas about shaping the civilian society according to particular ideological doctrines. On the other hand, the slow rate of development of administrative and social systems sometimes creates the proper conditions for megalomaniac postures. The feeling of "historical mission" was used by the Burmese military elite as a justification for its political activism and role expansion.

In Thailand, as well, the pretensions of the military in the economic and political spheres are discernible— they stem from the sense of being a professional elite with a greater organizational capacity than any other social or political organization in Thailand. The gap between the rate of professionalization of the military and that of the civilian sector in Thailand brought with it a great deal of alienation and resistance by the military elite to any significant civilian control of the processes of decision making. Nevertheless, the Thai military regime is entirely different from its Burmese counterpart. The ideal of the Thai military regime is an apolitical society, namely, a society which allegedly releases the executive from harassing pressures by interest groups and permits a maximum avoidance of "compromise politics." The granting of optimal priority by the officer corps both to private interest and to corporate interest, at the expense of social responsibility and even specific professional qualities, may well explain the Thai military's inclination to depoliticize the society.

Thailand and Burma raise some additional questions about the circumstances which decrease the alienation and conflict between the military and civilian elites. These circumstances include, first and foremost, the necessity of a greater similarity between civilian and military practices. This similarity is due to the processes of bureaucratization, professionalization, and occupational differentiation in both sectors that increase mutual dependence and interaction. We have defined these processes as those of *militarization* of the civilian sector and *civilianization* of the military sector. However, this concept of civilianization does not apply to the specific civilianization patterns which characterize the Burmese and Thai military establishments. The civilianization processes in both are only partially a result of technological changes and

innovations within the military system. In Burma, the dominant factor is the desire to impose a specific doctrine of social change and to assume an exclusive monopoly of the techniques of modernization. In Thailand, the dominant factor is the desire to impose the corporate interest of the military on the civilian society as a whole. . . . Another proof of civilianization based on intensive role expansion in either the Thai or Burmese style is the fact that, simultaneously with the inclination to role expansion, in many cases the military has an inclination for autarky or autonomy in the socialization of manpower as well as in judicial processes. In other words, the crystallization of *permeable* boundaries between the two sectors does not contradict the establishment of more or less invisible barriers which prevent effective political, economic, and judicial control by the civilian elites over the military. On the contrary, the accumulation of resources within the internal barriers of the military establishment guarantees a more effective manipulation of the civilian social resources which are, for all practical purposes, available to the military elite as a result of role expansion.

THE POLITICAL AND SOCIAL STRUCTURE AND MILITARY INTERVENTION

The structural dissimilarities of the two military establishments, as well as their style of government, are, at least in part, a result of the original political characteristics of the Thai and Burmese societies which the military elites inherited and did not change to any great extent. Nevertheless, the two political cultures became vulnerable to military coups. . . .

The mere existence of several parties in Burma and not in Thailand—which for many political scientists is an important indicator of the potential vulnerability of Burma's political system—is not a significant variable in comparing the two countries. The emphasis on the importance of consensus about the rules of the political game does not contradict the fact that the absence of consensus is not confined to this sphere. It may spread to other spheres, for example, to ad hoc issues or to the ultimate and sacred values of the society. In Burma, and to a lesser extent in Thailand, examples can be found of a lack of consensus about specific ad hoc policies of the civilian elite.

All researchers who abide by the thesis which correlates the absence of an indigenous middle class to the frequencies of coups will find additional examples in Thailand and Burma. The importance of the middle class, according to these researchers, is primarily due to the fact that its existence allows a real alternative for social mobility and for another access to prestige and political and economic power. In the absence of a middle class, the civilian and, especially, the military bureaucracies are for all practical purposes the exclusive substitute for what the classical and modern middle class could offer. The conclusion applies to both Burma and Thailand. Moreover, in both the civilian and the military bureaucracies were forced to compete with an alien middle class which

had accumulated extensive economic power. True, in Burma another option was open, namely, the political sphere. But the low level of institutionalization of this sphere, the large extent of oligarchization, nonconsistency, and corruption damaged the image of political activities as a suitable mobility channel.

The fact that the middle class had limited scope because it was mainly composed of aliens and the dubious character of the political channels for social mobility contributed to the imbalance between the rates of upward and of downward social mobility. Reliable quantitative data are absent, but this gap is reflected in the relatively great amount of upward social mobility compared with the low rates of downward mobility. This state of affairs is likely to produce frustration which can influence the predisposition of the officer corps to become an active partner, if not the sole participant, in policy making, especially with regard to the criteria which permit access to the political center, in order to reshape the patterns of mobility. Is it possible to say that reshaping these patterns by the officer corps means modernization of the system of stratification? If this is the case, the officer corps fulfills a very similar function, at least in this respect, as the middle class in Europe fulfilled in struggling for a redefinition of the criteria of social stratification and especially for access to the center.

One crucial indicator of modernization of stratification is the emergence of specific status groups within a socially and culturally pluralistic society which, owing to their particular entrepreneurial qualities, function as meeting points among various strata. They thus facilitate the upward and downward flow of persons who become released from various ascriptive and particularistic frameworks. Analysis of social stratification in Thailand and Burma indicates the development of a limited number of objective conditions which enable their officer corps to serve as intermediaries or brokers among the various sectors and elites. However, the differences between the two countries are reflected in the officers' willingness to exploit these conditions and to cooperate with other elites or status groups in fulfilling such functions. The Burmese officer corps expressed the desire to fulfill them, although it advocated total monopolization of the interactions with the various associational groups via an exclusive political organization. The Thai military elite, however, expressed indifference to this issue. It was ready, by and large, to cooperate with the royal court, the civilian bureaucracy, the intelligentsia, and even with other political organizations—as long as this cooperation did not endanger its own corporate interest. These differences between the two countries explains, from another point of view, the differences in the scope of role expansion, its intensity, and the list of priorities of their military elites.

THAILAND AND BURMA AS PROTOTYPES OF CIVIL-MILITARY RELATIONS

Intermediation between the different sectors in a pluralistic society is in a sense only a particular case of a broader issue: that is, intermediation between the political and cultural center, which is basically urban and Westernized, and the periphery, which is basically, although not exclusively, rural and traditional. The function of intermediation among the various sectors of the elites is not confined to intermediation per se. It is also related to the mobilization capacity of the elite of both traditional and modernized status groups. The greater the differentiation and political activism of the periphery, the greater is the challenge confronting the ruling elites. Often the demands of the different groups conflict with each other. Thus it is much more difficult for the political elite to respond to these demands, either because of the absence of various facilities and social services or because of basic political principles.

We have made two assumptions about the various prototypes of action between the center and periphery. The first is that the extent of stimulation and temptation the military has for extending its conventional roles differs according to a specific prototype. The second is that the military's ability to make a new, enlarged definition of its role varies from one prototype to another according to the military's character, magnitude, and power. Thailand may be classified as prototype C, where the strengths of the center are relatively unchallenged because of the periphery's apathy and the lack of mobilization. Such a situation is not static. There were certainly periods when the center reflected weakness, for example, in the late 1940s, the middle 1950s, and the beginning of the 1970s. Some changes occurred in the periphery as well. However, except in the northeast and the southeast, the major part of the Buddhist periphery was distinguished by its extreme passivity, at least until the late 1960s, in comparison not only to Burma but to all other countries of southeast Asia. Thailand lacked the conditions which elsewhere allowed for the politicization of the society as a whole. . . .

1. Thailand was never a colony. A colonial regime generally serves as a catalyst for political and social development. Colonialization effects the crystallization of militant political elites which are the products of the colonial regime's educational system and demand social and political reforms. The more radical frequently advanced their cause by mobilizing the urban and rural periphery. The degree to which Thailand was exposed to colonial influence only strengthened the ruling elite, compared to the periphery, by improving the military's warfare capacity and introducing administrative reforms, etc.

2. Thailand was not involved in large-scale wars with its neighbors or the big powers. This saved her from the humiliation of defeat which, in other countries, usually causes social and political ferment among the counterelites.

3. The government was uninterrupted, whereas in ex-colonies there was the transfer from colonial rule to political sovereignty. Thailand was thus ensured a relatively high level of physical and economic security and a minimum level of social services both in the center and at the periphery.

4. Thailand had no key groups (excluding the Chinese minority and recently the intelligentsia) which suffered from severe frustrations and made excessive demands that the political center was unwilling to fulfill.

In addition, the specific cultural characteristics of the Thai Buddhist society also had a great impact on political behavior—the deference to authority, the unquestioning acceptance of existing rules of conduct, and the belief that an individual's position in life is the result of good deeds and good luck. These factors made it much easier for the royal court, until 1932, and for the various military cliques, after 1932, to handle the relatively moderate demands from the margins of the center or from the periphery itself. The channels connecting the periphery to the center were largely one way, used for the transmission of instructions and demands from the elites to the periphery. The best examples of these channels are the bureaucracy, the parliamentary framework, and the Buddhist church. Other frameworks, for example, the trade unions, student organizations, and the intelligentsia, were organizationally and economically too weak to be institutionalized, enduring channels for transmitting demands.

In sum, the Thai elite was not compelled to develop political frameworks which could be used as "institutional means of bridging the rural urban gap." In the period concerned in this study, the passivity of the periphery enabled roughly the same pattern of military bureaucratic regime that had emerged in 1932 to continue. Nevertheless, in those cases where frustrated groups, especially among the officers, emerged, "the looseness of allegiance and the flexibility of standards of status have permitted the groups which circulated around the center of power to absorb new elements without difficulty."

Burma belongs to a very different kind of prototype, namely, prototype B—a society where the power of the center is inferior. In other words, it is a center which cannot cope with the demands and pressures from the accelerating process of differentiation, formation, and consolidation of new groups within the periphery. Historically, conditions in Burma were conducive for the political activization of the periphery and of various groups within the center—a phenomenon relatively absent in Thailand. The long-lived colonial government completely destroyed the monarchy and, more important, prevented the emergence of any alternative power, either local or national. This was accomplished by the system of direct rule, which was an exceptional principle with regard to the general imperial policy and was applied mainly in Burma. British economic policy brought about the disintegration of the periphery as well, by not taking any measures to prevent peasants from being evicted from their land and becoming rural and urban proletariat. The side effects of this disintegration were extremely high rates of physical and economic insecurity, increased by the destruction of the Burmese economy during World War II. The large number of minorities and the military power of the various underground groups added to the general administrative and economic chaos and encouraged the more militant political socialization of peasants, students, and monks. Thus the leaders of the national movement were confronted, immediately after independence, with a full spectrum of political groups. However, in Burma this broad basis for political recruitment—in other words, this political and social "catching area" of the various political parties—was actually responsible for the almost total collapse of the political system in the early 1950s.

We have seen the differences between the Burmese and the Thai officer corps in terms of the stimulus and impetus to intervene. But, as suggested earlier, it would be worthwhile to refer to two more variables, although only the first is really relevant to our discussion—namely, the propensity and the predisposition to intervene, and the real and effective power of the military. We have suggested, in regard to the former, the willingness or unwillingness of the officer corps to maintain a balance between group cohesiveness or ideological exclusiveness, and promotion of professional standards, especially in technology, logistics, and warfare strategy. A distinction between the two officer corps from this point of view is more difficult to make than from the point of view of the stimulus to intervene. However, the Burmese officer corps can be classified as one which is typical of prototype C, namely, a military system in which integrative and pattern maintenance are overemphasized at the expense of logistic and technical performance. This general characterization of the

Burmese officer corps describes the situation which began in the middle of the 1950s, on the eve of the establishment of the first Ne Win government. The senior officer corps then started to devote more and more attention to more general policy issues, followed by their exclusive and different political stand toward the civilian political elites. This process reached a climax in the first years after the 1962 coup, when a great part of the officer corps' activities were devoted to indoctrination and political resocialization of officers and rank and file.

This trend in the Burmese officer corps indicates very clearly the propensity to intervene in the decision-making processes within political and other important spheres. The Thai military officer corps was, at least until the middle 1960s, very close to prototype D, namely, to an officer corps characterized by relatively low achievement in the logistic, technical, and cohesive ideological spheres. This sort of "negative" balance does not necessarily decrease the basic propensity for intervention. Sometimes it does the opposite. However, the general trends of intervention after the seizure of power and the general quality of the political regime will be very different from the case where the officer corps belongs to the opposite prototype, as in the Burmese example.

Some of the most important differences between the two armies, in the essence if not the magnitude of military propensity to intervene, are reflected in the entrepreneurial qualities and the ideological articula-tion accompanying role expansion. It would be very easy to perceive the Burmese army as an almost classic illustration of prototype A, which distinguishes itself both by a high level of entrepreneurial activities and by ideological articulation. Typical are the far-reaching economic reforms, on the one hand, and the great extent of "productivity" in the ideological sphere, manifested by the publication and the declaration of a series of political, economic, and social programs, on the other. Thailand may also be classified, without much hesitation, in the fourth prototype, namely, as a military in which the principal motive of the army or its powerful cliques is the consumption of economic and political benefits and rewards. There is hardly any incentive to create new economic and social institutions and to toy with abstract ideologies. The distribution of private and collective, legal and nonlegal, corruption, the extent of symbiosis between the senior officers and the economic elite—these fit very well into this schematic description.

There is still another dimension for distinguishing between the two armies: their relative power vis-à-vis the underground or subversive groups. Undoubtedly the relative power of the Burmese army is less than that of the Thai army, because Burma's enemy forces are bigger and better trained. However, the relative power of the Thai army is decreasing as the underground organizations grow stronger. But it seems unlikely that the Thai army will come close to the kind of military standoff as occurred in Burma.

Coups, Rebellions, and
Revolutions in Thailand and Burma

In the period involved in our study, the Burmese military executed one and a "half" coups, while the Thai military executed about half a dozen successful or nonsuccessful coups. Were all these coups of the same order or quality? The answer is obviously negative. It is possible to say that Ne Win's coup d'etat was basically . . . a *simple revolution*—i.e, a case where the revolutionary ideology was restricted to more or less fundamental changes of only a *few* values. In Burma, there were changes in the political rules of the game from a multiparty, parliamentary system to a one-party system. There was also an almost total nationalization of the means of production. We can include in this category the 1932 coup in Thailand, since it eliminated the principle of absolute monarchy. It would be more questionable to include the 1947 coup against Pridi, although it removed the short-lived parliamentary regime. Nevertheless, all other coups that occurred in Thailand may be defined without any hesitation as *simple rebellions*—violent action or the threat of using violence against the ruling elite that was not motivated by new, ideological motives or by a desire for the rehabilitation of ancient norms. Instead, they were motivated first and foremost by the urge to use the existing rules of the game to become a more active partner in the decision-making process and to be able to distribute the rewards.

The difference between the two types of coups is also reflected in the patterns of role expansion before and, especially, after the coup. This may be examined from three aspects: (1) from the order of priorities of the aims of role expansion; (2) from the point of view of the intensity of role expansion; and (3) from the point of view of the simultaneity of role expansion. The Burmese military is distinguished in its desire to monopolize control both of the political and of the economic spheres. Previous to the 1962 coup, clear priority was given to economic development. After 1962, equal weight was apparently given to both, although the activities in education and indoctrination lagged behind slightly. The intensity of activity was very high, as measured by the willingness and actual use of power. Between 1962 and 1972, the Burmese army engaged not only in intensive role expansion but also in attempting to achieve simultaneously a variety of economic and social aims. All of this was done without neglecting routine military activities against insurgents.

The order of priorities of the various Thai military cliques between 1932 and 1972 was rather different. Excluding the seizure of power per se, role expansion was largely in the economic sphere. But this was accomplished mainly through competition between military cliques and not through collective endeavor by the military as a whole. The penetration of the Thai army into the civilian economy was less than that in Burma. The training of manpower within autonomous frameworks was very high on the Thai list of priorities. In the political sphere, however, there were only bursts of activities—for example, the party political activity in 1955 to 1957 and on the eve of the election in 1969. The intensity of the role expansion was fairly moderate, as the military elite did not show de facto a clear intention to monopolize resources and services in the sphere of their action. This moderation may also stem from the fact that the military was not inclined to act simultaneously in many spheres and did not try to set unrealistic goals that could not be achieved with a reasonable investment of resources and within a reasonable period of time. . . .

Toward the end of the 1960s, Burma and Thailand were ruled by officers who served simultaneously as cabinet ministers, commanders in the armed forces, and leaders of political parties. Nevertheless, the similarity between the two officer corps, at least in participation in executive positions of political parties, is only formal. There is almost no common denominator between the United Thai People's Party in Thailand and the *Lanzin* Party in Burma. That is particularly true of their basic aims. Although the *Lanzin* is essentially an elitist party, its objective is optimal mobilization of the Burmese population and resources, working either within the party framework itself or within the various affiliated organizations. This mobilization is aimed at achieving total control and regulation of the economy and society. The *Seri Manangkhasila* Party during Phibun's rule and the UTPP in the late 1960s were, in a sense, elitist political organizations as well. However, for all practical purposes, they were not more than popular cliques aimed at

participation in the political parliamentary game according to the rules established by the military elite.

These and other characteristics previously discussed may also help explain some of the different alternatives of civilianization of the military regimes in the two countries. The Burmese military elite, which evolved as an entrepreneurial and ideologically articulated elite, preferred to civilianize itself at least partly and to find a proper ideological justification for doing so. The military elite's main argument was that there was no place for any alternative social doctrine or for any other competing social and economic organization. On the other hand, the Thai military elite, which is basically nonentrepreneurial and not ideologically oriented, did not show an inclination to civilianize. However, it was ready to make some gestures in order to become involved in party politics during election campaigns. Moreover, when it faced the danger of a fullscale showdown with important social and political forces, the Thai military elite preferred, at least temporarily, to withdraw—as it actually did in October 1973.

THE MILITARY AS A PSEUDO-MODERNIZER

. . . The armed forces have been considered modern social systems possessing the institutional and personal qualifications for leading and directing social change and modernization in developing countries. Some of the most popular arguments in this respect are based on a belief in military superiority in technology and administration over civilian managerial units, and the military's application in, for example, maritime and land transport or engineering services. Although this issue was never examined in a comparative, systematic way, it seems that, at least in Burma, where one can compare the situations before and after 1958, the argument for the superiority of the military was corroborated, especially with regard to brief and short-range operations—for example, cleaning the streets of Rangoon, taking measures against black marketeers and money changers, and assisting victims of natural disasters. On the other hand, when more administrative, routine work extending over a long period of time was involved—like the problem of food marketing, etc.—the efficiency of the military administration decreased over time. The accusations against it were not different from those raised against the civilian regime.

Such a comparison for Thailand is much more difficult, because there has been no true civilian government since 1932. It is thus possible only to compare different periods of the history of modern administration in Thailand and to evaluate the degree of improvement. In this respect, it would be difficult to say that the initiative and ideas for greater rationalization and improvement of the civil bureaucracy came particularly from the military elite. The various administrative reforms in the nineteenth and early twentieth centuries were initiated by the royal court through foreign experts. After World War II, foreign experts played a very important role in planning reforms in the bureauc-

racy. Although the military supported these reforms, officers as individuals or as a collective did not serve directly as agents of change and modernization.

Another type of evidence about the military establishment as an agent of modernization has been that the military more than any other organization combines traditional structural features with a division of labor based on universalistic principles. Thus the military establishment may be considered as one of the most adequate frameworks for absorbing new and innovative concepts by people raised in and accustomed to a traditional background. . . .

With regard to the alleged advantage of the military as an organization capable of assuring law and order to the population, the evidence is quite conclusive. The success of the two military establishments, especially the Burmese one, in imposing law and order has been partial and limited. The military power and managerial qualities could not serve as a substitute for adequate political leadership able to solve the problem of subversion and guerrilla warfare.

It seems that, of all the alleged positive qualities attributed to the army, one is undebatable: More than any other social organization, except the royal court in Thailand, the army served in the period involved as a focus of solidarity and an embodiment of the respected and sacred symbols of society. However, this status does not necessarily go along with the political capabilities of negotiation, bargaining, brokerage, and appeasement between ethnic minorities and the dominant segments of the population. In Burma, the officers succeeded from time to time in destroying the social networks vital to a two-way political interaction. We may refer here to the contacts with legal oppositional groups, such as students and the different national minorities. In Thailand, one can also discern failures in interaction with minorities and opposition groups, but it seems that while in Burma the failure stems mainly from *overpoliticization* of the society at large, in Thailand it is related to the officer corps' adherence to a specific model, namely, a *nonpolitical* model of power relationships. This model is based more on imposed cohesion than on comprehensive social consensus. . . .

PART III

The Revolutionary Professional Soldier

UNLIKE the professional soldier, who attempts to protect his professional orientations by a retreat to corporatism and exclusivity, and unlike the praetorian soldier, who ignores all boundaries between the civil and the military, the revolutionary professional soldier is neither corporate nor anticivilian in his orientations. Ideally, the satisfactions for the revolutionary professional soldier derive from his importance in "making" the revolution rather than from promotion, budget increases, and perquisites. His achievements are tangible and recognized by both the civilian revolutionary leadership and the wider society. Without the military, the revolution would have failed in those countries such as China, Vietnam, and Israel, in which a political party allied with an ideologically committed military cadre fought to bring about the new order. The esteem accorded the professional revolutionary soldier is of a much higher order than that granted the professional soldier in postindustrial society.

The professional revolutionary soldier, because he has a place in the making of and maintenance of the societal ethos, is not prone to praetorianism. His political involvement is perceived as legitimate by civilian elites, while he admits the preeminence of the revolutionary party in decision making.

The symbiotic relationship between the party and the army precludes efforts by the military to preempt and replace the civilian leadership. The orientation of the professional revolutionary soldier is to maintain the revolution and to protect the independence of the revolutionary state. While this represents an idealized description of the professional revolutionary soldier's self-image and of his interaction with the civilian leadership, there are tensions that develop in the postrevolutionary period both within the military and between soldiers and civilians.

Within the military, there are strains between those officers who value the revolution more than the army and those who place the army above the revolution. James Jordan describes the change in the Chinese Communist military forces after 1949. The veteran guerrilla leaders had been selected without regard to educational standards; the main criterion was their willingness to commit themselves to the revolution. After 1949, officers were selected and trained primarily to run a complex military establishment rather than to pursue revolutionary goals.

In Israel, as Amos Perlmutter shows, the tensions grew out of differing perceptions of the revolution. In the 1930s, Zionist military forces split between militants who advocated terrorist tactics (grouped in the Irgun Zvai Leumi) and the socialist-oriented Haganah with its commando force, the Palmach.

In the postindependence era, conflicts between the civil and the military authorities have been resolved in favor of the civilians. This balance clearly sets the professional revolutionary apart from the praetorian soldier.

JAMES D. JORDAN

The Maoist vs. The Professional Vision of a People's Army

A fundamental factor that has influenced the orientation of the People's Liberation Army since its 1927 origins has been Mao Tse-tung's interpretation of sinified Marxist-Leninist ideology as it applies to military ethic and style. Basically, that interpretation has visualized a primarily domestic role for the PLA in applying two general principles: the employment of the "mass line" in all enterprises, and the struggle to eliminate class differences in Chinese Communist society.

Depending upon whether or not the views and style of Chinese generals accurately reflected the Maoist vision, they have been labeled either "prole-

From James D. Jordan, "The Maoist vs. The Professional Vision of a People's Army," in Military and Political Power in China in the 1970's: Organization, Leadership, Political Strategy, *ed. William W. Whitson (New York: Irvington Publishers, 1972).*

tarian" or "bourgeois". Ideally, a proletarian army is an army of the people in which the people identify themselves as part of the military system, and soldiers regard themselves as members of the masses. A proletarian army is one that is politically active and attempts to be responsive to the party of the proletariat. A bourgeois army is, by contrast, a force divorced from the people. It is an instrument of the state and is described by Samuel Huntington as a "professional" army. Ideally, a professional army, according to Huntington, is politically sterile.

Although the terms "proletarian army" and "bourgeois army" are not entirely synonymous with "revolutionary army" and "professional army," historically the Chinese PLA has certainly been proletarian in the sense of being of the masses and relying on the masses for support. As early as the 1946–50 civil war, however, and especially after the ending of the Korean War in 1953, the PLA has tended to adopt the values and goals of a professional army. By the nature of its requirements for sophisticated tactics, techniques, and equipment, the PLA has had a tendency to become increasingly differentiated and isolated from the civilian masses.

THE MAOIST VISION

The fundamentals of Marxism-Leninism from which the Chinese Communists have developed their ideology have been strongly influenced in China by Chinese thought and culture. In recognition of the need for sinification of Marxism, Mao Tse-tung wrote in 1938:

Hence to apply Marxism concretely in China so that its every manifestation has an indubitably Chinese character, i.e., to apply Marxism in the light of Chinese specific characteristics, becomes a problem which it is urgent for the whole party to understand and solve.

One Marxist-Leninist military principle adopted by the Chinese Communists has been an emphasis on the concept of "mass" and an "army of the people." In Chinese Communist ideology, the "mass line" is a basic principle not only in military doctrine, but in all other activities as well. The mass line is characterized by Ralph Powell as a "mystical belief in the capabilities of the mobilized and indoctrinated masses." A firm belief in the "mass line" by China's leadership

should foster certain fundamental military policy premises: the superiority of men over weapons, protracted war, and, most important, "politics should take command."

A second fundamental ideological principle is that of the single class. Communist belief holds that all social ills (including war) are the result of class struggle, and the way to end the problem of constant class struggle is to eliminate class distinctions. Society may eliminate these distinctions by establishing a dictatorship of the proletariat. The military implication of this principle would be the creation of a proletarian-class army. Such an army could not have class differences within itself, nor could it form a class separate from the rest of society. In a truly single-class society, as envisioned by Peking's leaders, all people are to be simultaneously producers and fighters.

Before 1946, the role of the military in Mao's China seemed to conform to the principles outlined above. The pre-civil war revolutionary army had been basically a decentralized semi-professional army in which maneuver elements were relatively small, weapons and equipment unsophisticated, and all supported by a rather rudimentary logistical system. Despite its semi-professional characteristics, however, its essential focus on domestic roles imparted and reflected qualities that Mao considered essential even in a modern military force. It was an army of the people, an army controlled by the Party, and an army deeply involved in the creation of a new China. According to Chairman Mao, the army was responsible for the creation of Party organizations, of cadres, of schools, of culture, and of the mass movements so essential to Chinese Communism. Thus, the army was indispensable to the creation and survival of the Communist system in China. Indeed, after 1936 and the end of the Long March, it had been responsible for Communist success in Shensi: "Everything in Yenan has been created by having guns," Mao explains.

With the formation of the new Communist state in 1949, Mao continued to perceive the army not only as the primary work force, but also as the principal instrument of power to ensure Party control. In Mao's words: "Every Communist must grasp the truth. Political power grows from the barrel of a gun. Our principle is that the Party controls the gun, and the gun must never be allowed to command the Party."

THE PROFESSIONAL VISION

Planning for the modernized army commenced simultaneously with the establishment of the People's Republic of China (PRC). The Common Program adopted by the Chinese People's Political Consultive Conference (CPPCC) in September, 1949, stated the intention to build a "unified army" with a "unified system, unified organization, and unified discipline." It further provided for modernization of the land force and the establishment of an air force and navy. The Korean War was probably instrumental in speeding up the modernization of the Chinese army, but modernization was not undertaken in anticipation of Chinese involvement in Korea. . . .

Clear evidence of the Chinese adoption of the Soviet model was the publishing of the "Regulations on the Service of Officers of the Chinese People's Liberation Army" in February, 1955. This document classified and assigned officers in fields of specialization and provided for distinctive uniforms and rank insignia. A regular pay scale replaced the previous system, which relied primarily on allowances. A conscription law based on that of the Soviet Union was introduced, replacing the traditional volunteer system of the Communist army and specifying periods of service in the various armed services of the PLA.

Almost at once, with the inception of modernization, a professional vision began to emerge in opposition to both the principles of the mass line and class struggle. Modernization along the lines of the Soviet model and professionalization of the Chinese officer corps challenged the continued relevance of Mao Tse-tung's principle of the army as a work force as well as a fighting force. The continued employment of the army as a work force evoked professional officers' opposition to such a diversion of military resources and time on nonmilitary tasks, a diversion that might adversely affect the efficiency of a modern military establishment. In addition, the creation of a professional officer corps brought a new sense of military eliteness, a sense of class consciousness and an estrangement between officers and men.

One of the early casualties resulting from burgeoning professionalism in the PLA was the People's Militia.

Article 23 of the Common Program states:

The Chinese People's Republic shall enforce the system of people's militia to maintain local order, lay the foundation for national mobilization and prepare for the enforcement of an obligatory military service system at the appropriate moment.

According to James Garvey, the Chinese military system had tended to be unique in its affection for the generalized militia concept as part of the mass line—"The people armed and militant."

Early in Mao's revolutionary experience, during the 1927 Autumn Harvest Uprisings, he formulated his theory of the role of the peasant militia. Here, Mao developed his principle that "without the poor peasants there can be no revolution. To reject them is to reject the revolution." The Autumn Harvest Uprisings, which sought to arouse the peasants, were a failure because the masses were not sufficiently organized and indoctrinated to take part in the insurrection. Mao was criticized by the Party, which asserted that armed insurrection meant insurrection by the workers and peasants themselves, who should have been secretly trained and armed. They should, the Party claimed, suddenly rise up to overthrow the government and seize power. In the vanguard of the peasant army would march a highly disciplined and politically concious Red Army, but the "people" should make up the main force. Failure to maintain a militia meant failure to use the mass line.

Since 1949, sporadic attempts to revive the militia have met with limited success. Even the massive "Everyone a Soldier" campaign of 1958 (which claimed an enrollment of 200 million people in the militia) fell far short of its objective. Published militia figures, like many of the statistics of the Great Leap Forward period, must be regarded with caution. Powell states, "The hastily enlarged militia suffered from a 'degree of formalism'—a Marxian euphemism for a paper organization." In referring to militia problems, the official army journal wrote in 1958:

For a certain time after our country was liberated, the glorious tradition of unity of labor and army was neglected by people and lost. Some comrades mistakenly believed that in the modernized war against imperialism the usefulness of the militia was no longer very great. Therefore, in practical work, they allowed their leadership of the militia to lapse, with the result that the work of the peoples armed forces was weakened and the militia's organization became dissipated.

Three years later, however, military units were still being told that "the militia must be put in the hands of reliable people" and "the militia activities this year must take hold at the primary level."

The development of professional officers in place of the traditional guerrilla-type officers created the greatest change in the relationship between military commanders and the political officers of units of the PLA. This change reinforced a dichotomy within the army that hampered its ability to act as a unified force. During and prior to the Korean War, there was minimal friction resulting from the dual political and military leadership of army units. The majority of both military and political officers had had considerable battle experience. Military commanders were capable in the political field, and most political officers were experienced combat soldiers. In theory, they were co-leaders, and neither had superiority over the other. Since the political officer was also secretary of the "Party" element of the military unit, however, the dictum that the "Party will always command the gun" threw the balance of authority to the political officer.

With the growth of professionalism in the army, however, young political officers had little experience other than the political training they had received; junior military commanders were technically qualified but not sufficiently politically educated. The younger, school-trained officers were no doubt strongly influenced by their Soviet advisers and leaned toward the Soviet model, in which the political arm played a less dominant day-by-day role. By 1961, the deterioration of the influence of the political officer had become especially significant in the lower echelons of the PLA, where it was reported that 7,000 companies, or roughly one third of the PLA, had failed to establish Party branch committees. Some of the remaining companies, having established committees, failed to allow the committees to carry out their functions of recruiting Party members.

The second major ideological principle to be violated through professionalization was that of a "single-classed" society. Modernization was creating a gulf between officers and men and difficulties in army/civilian relationships. A salaried officer corps provided the means by which officers could bring their families to remote stations and live on a much higher scale than did the enlisted men and the peasants in the locality. The availability of salary allowed some officers to dabble in the black market and other bourgeois activities. The creation of rank in the army brought complaints of "big bossism, of harsh disciplinary measures, and of arrogations of privilege by officers. Furthermore, some officers were found to be avoiding physical labor and exhibiting a superior attitude toward those who labored. In particular, the newly emerged professional officer was accused of adopting an overbearing attitude toward subordinates and of failing to appreciate the primacy of politics over all phases of the Communist system. Finally, he was blamed for being indifferent to the well-being of the local civilian population.

The Maoists were thus threatened by the emergence of a military class that was becoming alienated from the civilians. Some military leaders were accused of adopting an arrogant attitude and committing highhanded actions in commandeering school buildings, restricting scenic spots, and seducing village girls and women. In the construction of camps, barracks, and drill fields, a great deal of arable land was usurped and the peasants evicted. Probably many of the PLA members felt that, since the revolutionary war was over and the conscription system provided a regular input into the army, good relations with the people were no longer important. Therefore, conformance to the traditional Communist three main rules of discipline and eight major points of attention, which regulated soldier behavior with civilians, was no longer necessary.

THE CRISIS OF 1959

The deterioration of political influence in the PLA was obviously inimical to the stated doctrine of Mao Tse-tung on military affairs and to the traditions of the PLA. To Mao, political awareness was as necessary an ingredient of the military system as it was among the masses. Expertise should be gained through modernization, but not at the expense of a lapse in political ideology. Political motivation was credited with providing the one resource in which the Chinese army had an acknowledged superiority—esprit. One had to be "Red *and* expert," and, if a contradiction developed, then "redness" was more important than "expertness." Redness emphasized the ideological factor of the mass line.

By 1959, the Maoists believed that they had discovered a solution to the emergence of class distinctions within the PLA. In an attempt to instill appreciation for the democratic values of the old Red Army officer-enlistee camaraderie, they initiated the Officers to the Ranks (*hsia-lien tang-ping*) movement. This movement was the result of a September 28, 1958, directive by the GPD of the PLA. It required every officer to spend thirty days each year performing the duties of an ordinary soldier. By February,

1959, over 150,000 officers, including 160 generals, had "returned to the ranks" and had performed such menial tasks as mess duty, cleaning spittoons, and sweeping out barracks. Eventually, the extreme measures of the movement were abandoned, but the practice and encouragement of officers to return to the ranks continued at least until 1966.

Despite these preliminary countermeasures against adverse manifestations of professionalism in the PLA, a polarization developed between professional military leaders and Maoist ideologues. It is difficult to isolate the purely ideological factors in the reaction that began in 1958. Contributing factors certainly included the Chinese disillusionment with the USSR and certain failures in the Great Leap Forward programs. Maoist perspectives and military policies were reflected in at least six visible spheres: (1) the "men versus weapons" theme; (2) the rejection of the Soviet military model; (3) the democratization of the army with the Officers to the Ranks movement; (4) the massive Everyone a Soldier militia campaign; (5) the struggle for ideological control within the army; and (6) the diversion of military resources of men and material into the Great Leap Forward programs.

The question of a professional army as opposed to a revolutionary army became a basic one. Representing professionalism was Marshal P'eng Teh-huai, Minister of Defense, a soldier with a long and distinguished military record. Directly opposed to P'eng was Mao Tse-tung, an ideologue who believed in the military superiority of the politically indoctrinated masses over a professional army. Probably the main factor in P'eng's complaint was the diversion of PLA resources into nonmilitary production. In 1959, P'eng's GPD wrote:

There is a definite conflict between participation in national construction and training in their respective demands for time . . . Needless to say, as the army is an armed combat organization, it must carry out its task as a "work force" in such a way that its task as a "combat force" is not affected . . . It is obviously wrong to think that, as no war is going on at present, the army should exert itself mainly in the direction of production construction, or set too high requirements concerning the army's participation in construction and labor production. Anything that may weaken war preparations and training tasks is impermissible.

Since the Common Program (see above) provided that the PLA was to be a "work force" when not training or operating as a "combat force," the disagreement was one of degree, with considerable support for both sides. The debate reached a climax at the meeting of the Eighth Plenum of the Central Committee at Lushan (August 2–16, 1959) with Mao's attempt to take control of the army from P'eng Teh-huai. According to David A. Charles:

At one stage there was an emotional scene when Mao, in reply to a suggestion that the disgrace of P'eng might be a signal for a revolt by the armed forces due to his popularity with them in the country, declared with tears in his eyes that, if this happened, he would go back to the villages and recruit another army.

Mao eventually prevailed at the conference and P'eng was shortly dismissed from his position as Minister of Defense. The primary cause, as given by the Chinese, was P'eng's espousal of a "bourgeois military line" against the Party's "proletarian military line."

The showdown at the Lushan conference brought a close-fought victory to Mao Tse-tung in the ousting of of P'eng Teh-huai and some advocates of a professional army, but at the expense of Mao's resignation from the post of Chairman of the People's Republic. Surrender of the government post was probably also influenced by the failures of the majority of the programs of the Great Leap Forward. In any case, it allowed Mao to avoid the responsibility for the three difficult years that were to follow.

One may conjecture that a compromise was reached that allowed Mao to retain his position as Chairman of the Party and of the Politburo, while relinquishing control of the government bureaucracy. It is too simplistic to state merely that Mao was "forced to resign." He retained his positions in the Party and controlled the army through the appointment of his trusted marshal, Lin Piao, who was named Minister of Defense and head of the powerful Military Affairs Committee (MAC). As to Mao himself, some analysts believe that Mao's power and influence actually increased after his retirement from the post of Chairman of the People's Republic.

IDEOLOGICAL RESTRUCTURING OF THE PLA

Almost immediately after Lin Piao became Minister of Defense and, more important, *de facto* chief of MAC, he launched the rebuilding of the army according to the thought of Mao Tse-tung. Under Mao's guidance, Lin Piao commenced to restore Party leadership in the army. Within a year, a detailed program for political and ideological work in the army was clearly spelled out in a resolution at the October, 1960, meeting of MAC.

The endorsement by the central authorities states that the resolution "pointed out the direction of ideological work in the army in the *new historical period* that has begun. . . ." It is apparent that reemphasis on political and ideological work in the army was a first step toward renewed political and ideological conciousness among professional military leaders. The endorsement stated further that the program should be distributed to the local committee level and above for use in "Party organizations, government organs, schools, and enterprises at various levels . . ." It is also clear that the central authorities on December 21, 1960, when they ratified the resolution, were themselves aware that Mao's thought was being sanctified. The first page of the resolution contains the statement that "Mao Tse-tung's Thought, whether in the past, at present or in the future, serves always as the guide for building up of our army . . ."

The immediate effect of emphasis on politics in the PLA was the res-

toration of political leadership at the company level and below. Political officers and platoon representatives were assigned to lower-level military units, and recruiting for Party membership was stepped up. It has been reported that 78,000 cadres were transferred from other duties to the company level, and 229,000 new Party members were recruited by the PLA during 1960. All companies that had lacked Party committees (or in which Party committees had been inactive) now established them. Eighty percent of the platoons of the PLA organized Party cells, and 50 percent of the squads had at least one Party member. Of all the elements that make up Chinese society, the soldiers of the PLA became probably the most politically motivated, if not politically conscious. Military commissars sought to imbue them with the utopian aspects of Mao's vision of Communist China and the mass line.

By 1964, central leaders evidently felt that the army had been remolded sufficiently to serve as an example for the rest of society. Mao undertook to revive the army's mass-line domestic role. A massive campaign called for the whole country to "learn from the PLA." The campaign stressed the unity of the army and the people and the need to apply the principle of "putting politics in command." The *People's Daily* editorial asserted:

In learning from the PLA, comrades on each front should raise even higher the Red Banner of Mao Tse-tung's thinking, and resolutely use it as a guiding principle to constantly examine their own ideology, work and behavior and to study and sum up their own work experience.

The use of the PLA example to instill ideological rebirth and political control in industry and agriculture was summed up by Chou En-lai at the Third National People's Congress in December, 1964. Chou said: "All our Party and government organs and the broad mass of our cadres should learn from the thoroughly revolutionary spirit and style of work of the Liberation Army . . . and advance along the road of revolution."

The emergence of class distinctions was another matter and still had to be dealt with. Theoretically, in a revolutionary army, no particular deference should be paid to rank; officers and men should live together, eat the same food, dress alike, and be financially and socially equal. In the modernized army, however, troops had become differentiated according to rank and branch of service, and officers, by virtue of the graduated pay system, lived better than enlisted men. The new system of discipline in the professional army had encouraged officers to adopt perquisites and demand privileges according to their rank. A new class had thus been created within the hitherto single-class army and even the Officers to the Ranks movement had been insufficient to regain unity.

In 1965, the Standing Committee of the National People's Congress announced the abolition of the system of rank in the PLA. While the order was signed by Liu Shao-ch'i, as Chairman of the PRC, it is apparent from the wording of the order that the decision was initiated by Mao Tse-tung, as Chairman of the Party, and that the army was an instrument of the Party rather than the state.

The state adopted the following decision . . . so that the revolutionary spirit and glorious tradition of the PLA—a great army led by the great CCP and guided by the great Mao Tse-tung's thinking—should have full expression and so there should be identity between the three services and between officers and men . . .

The order went on to say that the cap insignia, epaulettes and collar insignia, and the insignia denoting various services, arms, and branches should be abolished. The *Liberation Army Daily* editorial on the democratization measure stated:

Our army had no system of military rank during the protracted revolutionary wars in the past. This system [rank, different uniforms, and so on] came into effect in 1955, after victory throughout the country. Ten years of practice has proved that it is not in conformity with our army's glorious tradition with the close relation between officers and men, between the higher and lower levels, and between the army and the people . . .

While stating that in general the system of rank was not in conformity with the army's glorious traditions, the editorial went on to specify benefits to be derived from abolition of rank differentiations

The abolition of the open expression of gradations in military rank will help eliminate certain objective factors contributing to breeding rank conciousness and ideas to gain fame and wealth; it will also help us more consciously to place ourselves in the position of ordinary soldiers and ordinary workers, *remold ourselves ideologically*, and go further in establishing the idea of whole hearted service to the people.

The editorial concluded that the effect of the order would promote the revolutionization of the army, and, under the leadership of Mao Tse-tung, make it "an extremely proletarian and militant army."

THE ATTEMPTED USE OF THE ARMY IN THE CULTURAL REVOLUTION

Politicization and democratization of the army had apparently brought it more into line with Mao Tse-tung's ideology. The influence of political officers and Party representatives had increased greatly in the PLA, and now Mao was prepared to use the army in the ideological indoctrination and reformation of the masses. As early as 1964, Chou En-lai foretold the coming storm of the Cultural Revolution. As he summed up the campaign to "learn from the PLA" at the Third National People's Congress, he warned that constant vigilance was necessary to attain and retain a uni-class society. He stated:

New bourgeois elements, new bourgeois intellectuals and other new exploiters will be ceaselessly generated in society, in Party and government organs, in economic organizations, and in cultural and education departments. These new bourgeois ele-

ments and other exploiters will invariably try to find their protectors and agents in the higher leading organizations.

Chou went on to warn that a great debate was taking place on a series of questions of principle, involving philosophy, political economy, history, education, culture, and art. He specified, "In the Cultural Revolution building of the new comes only after, or side by side with the destruction of the old."

The Cultural Revolution finally exploded in August, 1966, and heralded two turbulent years of struggle to reform the Chinese people as the PLA had been reformed. On August 8, the Central Committee of the Chinese Communist Party issued its sixteen-point decision aimed at crushing "those persons in authority taking the capitalist road." It was apparent that Mao felt that the ideological indoctrination of the PLA needed little additional guidance. In the twelve columns of type in which the decision was printed, only six lines were devoted to the PLA. These read:

In the armed forces, the Cultural Revolution and the socialist education movement should be carried out in accordance with the instructions of the Military Commission of the Central Committee and the General Political Department of the People's Liberation Army.

The decision to use the army to take sides and support the "side of the left," was probably not anticipated, but the use of the army to indoctrinate the masses was certainly planned. As early as 1966, it was reported that members of the PLA were transferred to teaching positions in schools while remaining full-time members of the army.

Ideologically reliable and politically indoctrinated teams of soldiers were formed to propagate the "thought of Mao Tse-tung" throughout the countryside. *CNA* reports in June, 1968:

Some troops in North China organized 100,000 persons for the propaganda of the Thoughts; the troops in Lanchow sent 15,000 military Party members in 500 Mao Thought Propaganda Teams to the villages of 110 counties. Mukden and Tsinan troops each sent 100,000 of their men to the villages; the troops stationed on Hainan Island went to the hamlets of the national minorities of Li and Miao tribes.

Fifteen thousand troops organized into 500 teams would mean teams of 30 soldiers each. If the same organization were used by the North China troops, this would amount to 3,300 teams of 30 soldiers each in that part of North China alone. There are only slightly more than 2,000 counties (*hsien*) in the whole of China. If the function of propaganda teams was carried out in all military regions on the same scale, it seems a reasonable calculation that a majority of the people were reached by the PLA Mao-Thought teams.

Not only was the PLA used in ideological indoctrination, but it was also instrumental in the formation of Revolutionary Committees through which China has been governed since the Cultural Revolution. (Party Committees on the provincial, *hsien*, and municipal level are still being formed

and will presumably take over some of the responsibilities of the Revolutionary Committees. The PLA is also substantially represented on these.)

Since the Cultural Revolution, the army has been lauded as "a pillar of proletarian dictatorship," and a great deal of care has been taken to ensure that the soldier and civilian population do not become alienated from each other—that the army and the people are one and the same. It is through identification of the people with the army that the leaders of Communist China retain control over the military.

There still remains, however, the issue of civil (Party) control over the army to ensure that the gun does not control the Party. As the aim of objective control of a professional army is to render it "politically sterile," subjective control over military forces is attained by "denial of an independent military sphere, and maximum participation by the military in politics." Mao Tse-tung and Minister of Defense Lin Piao have repeatedly attempted to avoid identification of the army as distinct from the people. To accomplish this, numerous campaigns have been organized to "serve the People" and "learn from the PLA," culminating in the movement to Support the Armed Forces and Love the People. This latter movement was originated in 1956, but received a great deal of attention as a result of army involvement in the Cultural Revolution. Lin Piao clearly stated the position of the PLA in his report to the Ninth Party Congress:

The People's Liberation Army is the

mighty pillar of the dictatorship of the proletariat. Chairman Mao has pointed out many times. [*sic*] From the Marxist point of view the main component of the state is the army. The Chinese People's Liberation Army personally founded and led by Chairman Mao is an army of the workers and peasants, an army of the proletariat . . . We must carry forward the glorious tradition of "supporting the government and cherishing the people," strengthen the unity between the army and the people, strengthen the building of the militia and of national defense and do a still better job in all our work.

Thus, the dual ideological principles of the mass line and class conciousness continue to govern the orientation and style of the PLA. The PLA depends on the active support of the politically indoctrinated and aroused people. The PLA itself is a politically active and highly indoctrinated element of Chinese society.

Second, the revolutionary army is identified synonymously with the "people" and hence does not represent a military class distinct from the people. Its role, however, must remain that of a servant of the people and never the master. In this respect, the *People's Daily* states: "An army above class is non-existent in this world and an army without the leadership of the 'Party' is non-existent. . . ."

If in the 1970s the PLA continues to adhere to the principles of the mass line and a single class in practice, it will be unique among the armies of the world. Certainly, its strength will lie in the active support of the masses and in its identification as an army of the Party of the proletariat. While organizationally the PLA may remain an element of the state government, in practice it will probably be the army of the new Chinese Communist Party.

Amos Perlmutter

The Israeli Army in Politics: The Persistence of the Civilian Over the Military

The 1967 lightning victory of Zahal, the Israel Defense Forces, was the result of a philosophy that had considered military effort as an instrument of nation-building from the very beginning of the Zionist movement in

From Amos Perlmutter, "*The Israeli Army in Politics: The Persistence of the Civilian Over the Military*," World Politics 20 (1968): 606–43, by permission of the editors.

Palestine. In 1948, the Israeli War of Liberation thrust the army into prominence, and from then on army leaders have been influential in the governmental and economic elites committed to rapid modernization. The Sinai victory in 1956 and the third military success in Sinai, Jordan, and Syria in 1967 further enhanced Zahal's reputation. Although Israel's standing army is no larger than 80,000 men, one-seventh of the country's total Jewish population of 2.5 million is on active military reserve. Given these conditions, it is natural to wonder what impact the army has had on the political life of Israel.

This study turns its attention to the persistence of the civilian over the military in Israel despite the extraordinary role played by Zahal. . . .

In this review of civil-military relations in Israel and their accompanying tradition and its stresses, we shall focus on (1) the expectations and role of the military elite before and after the formation of Israel in 1948; (2) the ideology and role-expansion of the Israeli military; and (3) the great influence the military has wielded in foreign affairs and security policies ever since David Ben Gurion became Defense Minister in 1948. We shall also challenge a number of hypotheses that have been advanced concerning patterns and types of civil-military relations. Our analysis of civil-military relations in Israel challenges (1) Andreski's contention that a high Military Proportion Ratio—"the proportion of militarily utilized individuals in the total population"—enhances the supremacy of the army; (2) Huntington's contention that the combination of a pro-military ideology, high military political power, and high military professionalism produces military political supremacy; and (3) the rigid preconception—advanced by General Von der Goltz—that the "nation-in-arms" enhances militarism.

Israel demonstrates exactly the contrary of each of these three hypotheses:

the role-expansion of the Israeli army —a concept that will be explained later in detail—in a nation-in-arms has played a major role in creating a predominantly civic culture. None of the hypotheses applies to civil-military relations in Israel, although the types advanced by Huntington and Andreski suggest that Israel should fit the model of civil-military relations in which the military achieves ascendance over the civilian. We shall also demonstrate that Israel has not fulfilled Mosca's prognosis that "the military predominance of the West may revert to other races, other civilizations, that have had, or will have had, different development from the European"—which has proved true in numerous developing polities.

Because there is so little material in English on the subject of recent Israeli history, we have combined our analysis with some historical narrative, thus placing the discussion of the Israeli army in the wider context of Israeli politics.

THE PRE-INDEPENDENCE DEFENSE UNITS AND THEIR POLITICAL EXPECTATIONS, 1909-1948

THE MILITARY AS AN INSTRUMENT OF NATION-BUILDING

Much of this analysis depends on an interpretation of the circumstances under which the Israeli military structures were formed and eventually consolidated. Israeli society, its political and social structures, can be explained only in terms of a constellation of factors. No single factor can explain the creation of a new social system in Israel or the development of its political structures and its army.

The modern army of Israel has its roots in the security structures of the pre-independence pioneer movement of the Jews in Palestine. These defense units were created by the Socialist-Zionists, the most significant, powerful, and mobilizing elements of Jewish colonization. Socialist-Zionism—the House of Labor (HOL)—embraced a wide range of men, ideas, and organizations in both the Diaspora and Palestine, but only in Palestine was it forged into a movement of great consequence. There it came to represent the interplay between socialist ideological commitments and the pragmatic considerations that modified them. The result was the gradual transformation of a colonization effort into a program for national liberation. The Socialist-Zionist movement became the chief instrument of nation-building, the mobilizer of the pioneer revolution, the creator of a new society, and the founder of the Israeli army.

The pioneer Zionists had a genius for organization which enabled them to develop very elaborate institutional frameworks prior to nationhood. To create a new society, the HOL groups consolidated an immigrant-settler movement with one of national liberation, based on a socialist and egalitarian ideology. To carry out this task they established three separate but complementary mobilization systems: the first organized workers into an elaborate institutional structure, the Histadrut, established in 1920. The second was the kibbutz movement to support the agricultural settlement

system. The third structure was made up of the political parties of the HOL led by Mapai, which was created to represent Socialist-Zionist interests and institutions within the Yishuv (the Jewish community in Palestine) and in dealings with the British Mandatory Administration. These three systems were to become the most powerful organizations in Israel. The HOL fused the Socialist-Zionist ideology with its political parties, its trade union, and its kibbutz movement; and it spread this ideology throughout the Yishuv. Thus the HOL created the first comprehensive social, political, and economic structure of the Jewish community in Palestine, independent of both the Mandatory and the Palestinian Arab community.

It was within this framework that the HOL created what eventually became the Israeli army. HOL leaders were especially instrumental in developing military structures, with other Zionist groups firmly implanting in the Israeli army the HOL ideology of "revolutionary constructivism"—the gradual accumulation of functions and powers for an eventual independent Jewish socialist state. This ideology of nation-building was well inculcated in the army. Fraternity, cohesiveness, egalitarianism, leadership training, and subservience to national and civil authorities are the legacy of Socialist-Zionism to Zahal, now the leading bearer of national identity and pride.

THE FIRST SECURITY UNITS

Jewish defense units were organized in Eastern Europe in the late nineteenth century by the Poale Zion (Workers of Zion) party, the first Socialist-Zionist party, and functioned temporarily as guard units during pogroms. Under the aegis of the Poale Zion party, the first defense groups were also formed in Palestine. The defense society called Hashomer (The Watchman) was organized in Palestine in 1909. Originally composed of Socialist-Zionists from Poland, Russia, and Lithuania, it soon was joined by Russian Jewish Marxists, who brought to it the sort of militance that the Iskra group had introduced into the Russian Social Democratic Labor party. Hashomer did not merely protect Jewish villages from Arab assaults, but also sought to integrate the revolutionary ideology of Socialist-Zionism with a military organization. After trials and tribulations with the HOL, it was finally dissolved in 1925. But not its legacy—defense as an instrument of nation-building.

The next effort to form defense units was the Jewish Legions. Early in World War I, Zionist leaders decided that a Jewish armed force serving with the Allies in the Middle East could prove useful in political bargaining with England for the creation of an independent Jewish national home in Palestine. The Zionist leaders also felt that such a force's war experience would create a "new Jewish soldier type," a useful instrument in an activist nationalist movement. Two legions were created, composed of Jewish volunteers from the United States, Great Britain, and Palestine. The legions also formed a political structure and a base of operation for

the competing factions of Zionism. Jabotinsky, a right-wing Zionist, saw the legions as the future base for a Jewish army in Palestine, but Trumpeldor, a left-wing Zionist, advocated transferring the legions into the political arena of HOL settlement in Palestine. At the war's end, despite the effort of Jabotinsky to influence the Mandatory to keep the legions as the army of occupation in Palestine, which would have given them control of the Mandatory's defense function, the legions were dissolved.

FORMATION OF AN ARMED NUCLEUS

Beginning in 1920, the catalytic forces for maintaining an independent Jewish defense organization in Palestine were Arab nationalism, the reluctance of British occupation forces to protect Jewish settlements, the kibbutz movement, and the rise of a militant Zionist movement founded by Jabotinsky. From the beginning of Zionist settlement in Palestine, the local Arabs were opposed to Zionism. Anti-Jewish Arab activity began in northern Galilee late in 1919, when the settlement of Tel-Hai was attacked but successfully defended by Hashomer and the demobilized legions led by Trumpeldor. The Arab riots in Jerusalem and Tel-Aviv in the 1920's indicated that the Jewish community in Palestine, especially in the cities, was not ready to defend itself; without the support of veterans of the legions the cities would have been prey to Arab riots and abuse. But these veterans hardly represented a permanent defense organization. By contrast, Hashomer had successfully defended Tel-Hai and the Galilean agrarian settlements.

In their drive to consolidate and institutionalize the organizational structures of the House of Labor, the leadership of the HOL had overlooked the importance of security. Only the militants in the kibbutzim recognized the necessity for maintaining a permanent defense organization. While the attack on Tel-Hai awakened the HOL to the significance of a defense capability, the leadership was slow to assume this responsibility, and its efforts to wrest control of this function from the leftists were sporadic. Eventually, however, the leadership of the Histadrut accepted the recommendation of its committee for defense that it organize the Haganah, the first Jewish underground in Palestine. Thus it could be said that the Haganah, as an organization, came into being on June 25, 1925.

For the Jews in Palestine, the years 1925–1929 were relatively peaceful and prosperous. With large-scale Zionist immigration and negligible Arab nationalist activity, the Haganah had little need to grow. The situation took a turn in 1929, however, when the Arabs attacked Jewish communities in Hebron and Safad and Jewish businesses in Jerusalem and Tel-Aviv. The Mandatory was caught unprepared and the Haganah was not sufficiently developed to defend the Jews effectively. This set of circumstances brought the Haganah into the spotlight of Zionist politics. As David Ben Gurion has reminisced, "I told Dr. Weizmann

[in 1929] that the Jerusalem riots of April 1920 and the Jaffa massacre of 1921 would be as nothing compared to what we would face in the future." Ben Gurion adds that Dr. Chaim Arlozoroff (then head of the political department of the Jewish Agency, a quasi-governmental body representing the Yishuv advising and cooperating with the Mandatory) said, "In view of the present circumstances [1930], there is no way to fulfill Zionism without a transition period in which the Jewish minority takes over control of Palestine as an organized revolutionary elite."

The issuance by the Mandatory of the Passfield White Paper, in 1930, marked the end of the period of relative tranquillity and prosperity in Palestine. The Mandatory became more precise regarding its attitude toward the emergence of a Jewish national home and recommended stricter land transfer and immigration controls. This was interpreted by the more militant Jewish leaders, especially Jabotinsky and his followers, as reneging on the Balfour Declaration, Britain's earlier declaration of sympathy with Zionist aspirations. This change in the Mandatory's attitude came at the same time that the Arab nationalist movement in Palestine picked up momentum as it was radicalized by the fundamentalist and extremist al-Hajj Muhammad Amin al-Husayni, the Mufti of Jerusalem. Both developments constituted a formidable challenge to the Yishuv's aspirations to nationhood.

The turn toward extremists and desperadoes by the Arab nationalist movement in Palestine can be attributed to several factors: the feudal and transitional nature of the Arab community, the growth and success of the Jewish community, and, above all, the Arab opposition to the Mandatory. The Arab revolt (1936–1939) began with a general strike that quickly collapsed, continued with riots and terrorism directed against Jewish settlements, and ended as a furious but futile revolt against Great Britain. This first large-scale all-Arab nationalist insurrection ended in despair because of fratricidal rivalries among several Arab nationalist leaders. Its failure must particularly be laid to the Mufti, whose personal ambition to dominate the Arab community in Palestine entangled this fragile Arab nationalist movement in a hopeless struggle against the powerful resources of the Mandatory.

Although these were years of growing strength for the economic, social, and political efforts of the Yishuv, the Arab revolt and the concurrent British withdrawal of support for the principles of the Balfour Declaration divided the Yishuv on the issue of self-defense. The problem was twofold: what form of resistance should the Jews adopt against the Mandatory and what type of war should they wage against the Arabs?

For the duration of the Arab revolt, the biggest bloc within the Yishuv— the HOL, led by David Ben Gurion— pursued a policy of restraint (havlagah) toward both the Arabs and the Mandatory. Realizing the futility of the Arab revolt, the Jews sought to turn it to their advantage. The Jewish leadership knew that if they adopted the same strategy as the Arabs against the Mandatory the effort would end in catastrophe, for once the Mandatory was overthrown they would be left alone to face the Arabs, which at that time would have been disastrous. Thus they followed a course of moderation which dictated cooperation with the Mandatory and defense against the Arabs. The reaction to the policy of restraint exercised by leaders of the Yishuv was the formation of another camp, not as politically powerful, represented by members of the younger generation, especially those born in Palestine, who advocated active resistance (maavak). These young rebels were found in the Haganah, in the kibbutz movement, within the Socialist-Zionist youth movement, and within Jabotinsky's youth movement.

For the Yishuv, the Arab revolt worked as a catalyst. The advocates of a permanent defense organization now had more of a case to convince the Yishuv's highest authorities and the leaders of the World Zionist Organization of the need for a Jewish army, independent of the Mandatory and ready to meet the Arab challenge. While conditions favored the development of a strong Jewish defense force, they left the Arab community impotent and unprepared to meet the double challenge it had set for itself, the ouster of the British and the surrender of the Jewish community in Palestine.

The fruits of a policy of restraint eventually matured. But the policy created a division within the Haganah. The first break with the official policy came when a militant group, called Haganah B, was formed in the early 1930's. Its leadership did not want to support any political party, but could not maintain a neutral position in such politically explosive matters. Its leaders were inclined toward Jabotinsky's Revisionist Zionist party (a militant splinter of the World Zionist Organization formed in 1925). After a series of schisms and splits, Haganah B and Jabotinsky's youth movement united into a terrorist organization called the Irgun Zvai Leumi (National Military Organization—NMO), led by David Raziel. By 1940 an independent Revisionist and the leader of Jabotinsky's youth movement, the poet-intellectual Avraham Stern, took over the NMO. Under his leadership the organization adopted the doctrine of total military struggle with the Mandatory. Within the House of Labor, the advocates of an independent Jewish military force came from the Palestinian-born members of socialist youth movements. Here the United Kibbutz movement (Ha-Kibbutz ha-Meuchad), which had been formed in 1927, played a key role. It gave protection, guided, and supported the advocates of resistance, who were to become the next generation of Haganah leaders and the elite of the Israel Defense Forces.

If the years 1937–1939 in Palestine formed a period of incubation for Jewish efforts to create an independent Jewish military force, the year 1939 brought to an end the policy of limited cooperation between the Haganah and the Mandatory. The White Paper issued by the Mandatory in the middle of 1939 seemed to go a long way toward recognizing the basic claims of Arab nationalists. This was the end of active cooperation between the Jewish community and the Mandatory, and the Colonial Office turned openly against the Jewish community's military preparedness. This trend, like most policies of that fateful year, lasted only until the British-French declaration of war against Germany on September 1, 1939. On September 3, 1939, President Chaim Weizmann announced the support of the Jewish people of Palestine for the war effort. This move opened another fruitful era for the Jewish defense forces. Ben Gurion and the Jewish Agency called upon Jews to enlist in the British army, and eventually more than 30,000 volunteered to serve with the Allied forces. The United Kibbutz movement and its rebel leadership, however, were concerned lest the Arabs take advantage of the war to improve their position in Palestine. General Yigal Allon argued: "A force protecting the Jewish community in Palestine is necessary. The Jewish community's best men are fighting on a variety of fronts far from home, and protection of the Yishuv may not be forthcoming since the Mandatory has not relinquished its White Paper policy."

In May 1941, the Haganah created a commando force, the Palmach. This new group, which was dominated by the United Kibbutz movement, set for itself the task proclaimed by Allon: the formation of an independent Jewish military force. The Palmach was the first full-time, professional, elite military unit of the Haganah, which, except for its General Staff, had been composed of part-time volunteers. The importance of the Palmach as the intellectual and organizational training ground for the future elite of the Israeli army can be seen in the later careers of its members.

The war years, especially 1941–1945, transformed the Haganah from a decentralized, voluntary, and part-time organization into a structure with a permanent headquarters, a general staff headed by a chief of staff, centers for officer training, an organized clandestine supply and purchasing operation (Rechesh), a far-flung and efficient network for gathering intelligence and information (Shay), an organization for clandestine immigration (Ha-Apala), and, of course, the Palmach.

THE FORMATION OF THE ISRAELI ARMY

THE FRAMEWORK OF ZAHAL

The single most important development in civil-military relations in the new state of Israel was Ben Gurion's takeover of the defense structure. "With the end of the Second World War," writes Ben Gurion, "it became clear to us that Britain would not and could not uphold the mandate, and that it could not participate in the creation of a Jewish state, even in that part of the country allotted to the Yishuv under partition." This meant that political solutions to the Palestine problem were to go hand in hand with military preparedness and that, to create a unified military command, Ben Gurion found it necessary to bring all military structures under the direction of one political headquarters, the Jewish Agency for Palestine. The

years 1945–1947, preceding the establishment of the state of Israel, were thus crucial for the future of the armed forces and their role in the campaign for independence. The Haganah headquarters was assailed by an intensified conflict over the destiny of the military structures and their relationships to society and politics. While some Palmach leaders foresaw the Palmach as the cadres that would produce Israel's people's army, the NMO advocated the formation of independent military and terrorist organizations to end British rule in Palestine.

Left-wing Socialist-Zionists and right-wing Revisionist Zionists clashed at this time, with the aid of the military structures at their disposal. The United Kibbutz movement, which controlled the Palmach General Staff, considered the struggle against the Mandatory imperative. However, despite its militant and ideological inclinations, the Palmach demonstrated an unusual discipline by accepting the leadership of the Haganah and the Yishuv as final arbiters of the policy toward the Mandatory. But it relentlessly opposed the partition of Palestine, cooperation with the Mandatory, and, above all, cooperation with British Intelligence in its campaign to annihilate the "terrorist organizations."

Ben Gurion had by then come to believe that in the struggle for statehood, which meant struggle against the White Paper policy and against Arab political opposition, the role of the military would be decisive. The army would become the "mailed fist" of the Jewish state. Thus, by October 1947, a month before the United Nations proposed a partition of Palestine that the Arabs rejected, Ben Gurion was ready with an armed Jewish force.

On May 15, 1948, when the mandate expired, the Jewish forces met the invading forces of five Arab states. The Palmach, numbering just over 4,000 men (including reserves), absorbed the first Arab offensive in northern Galilee and in Jerusalem. Palmach units participated on all fronts (it had three battalions in Galilee and three in Jerusalem) and led the major counteroffensive of the liberation campaign, which began in the south in late June 1948. The forces on the southern front were led by Palmach's chief, General Allon, and the main thrust of the Negev campaign, which repulsed the Egyptian army (the largest organized Arab force), was made almost entirely by Palmach divisions. By January 1949, the Palmach was in Egyptian territory, and in March the new Israel Defense Forces, led by the Palmach, conquered the southernmost tip of Palestine and the port of Eilat. By that time, the political struggle for control of the army had become inevitable.

Already, in late June of 1948, Ben Gurion had ordered a Palmach battalion stationed in Tev-Aviv to destroy the "Altalena," a ship commanded by the NMO, which was attempting to distribute arms to its independent troops waiting on the shores of Natanya on the Mediterranean coast between Haifa and Tel-Aviv. After this showdown, the NMO was dissolved. Further, after taking steps to bring military policy under the control of a unified political leadership, on October 29, 1948, the Chief

of Staff, General Ya'aqov Dori, had issued an order that Palmach headquarters also be dissolved and that General Allon serve only as commander of the southern front.

The framework for the transformation of voluntary military forces into compulsory military structures was set by Ben Gurion during the debate on the Defense Service Bill in the first Knesset (parliament) in 1949 after his successful nationalization of Zahal. He proposed that the army should be small and professional, with a large reserve system, and that it should adopt the most recent scientific and technological innovations, inculcate the spirit of the Haganah and the Palmach in the new conscripts, act as a citizen-maker and aid in the integration and Israelization of the new immigrants, pay close attention to agriculture and participate in agricultural settlement efforts, serve as a model of fraternity, and associate itself with the youth movement. In short, a nation-in-arms must mobilize the public to civic action. These functions of Zahal were conceived after much heated debate in the Knesset and within Zahal's high command. Only when General Dayan assumed the post of Chief of Staff in November 1953 did Zahal combine the traditions of the Haganah and Palmach with the demands of a highly professional force.

FORMALIZATION, PROFESSIONALIZATION, AND DEPOLITICIZATION

The Haganah, as one of the major Jewish national institutions in Palestine, reflected the patterns of a community that was politically very active but, because of the conditions of the mandate, had no formal state structure to formalize practices (although formal Jewish national institutions—such as the National Committee, the Jewish Agency, and the World Zionist Organization—did exist). The most significant change in political institutions and practices in the new state was the growing formalization and bureaucratization: voluntary civil action gave way to formal compulsory units.

The formalization and professionalization of the Israeli army reflect the fact that the practices, institutions, and behavior of this colonizing political community were being transformed into a formal political system. The creation of Zahal out of the Haganah illustrates this basic change that turned a colonizing movement and a society of social mission—predominantly maintained within primary, nonformalized groups—into formal bureaucratic structures. . . .

THE ISRAELI SOLUTION OF THE CIVILIAN-MILITARY CONFLICT

It would be pointless to pretend that Zahal's elite is in any simple sense a political group. It has no political aspirations as a group. But we hope to have marshalled enough evidence to have demonstrated that in defense and foreign affairs, Zahal's elite wields an enormous influence. The very fact of this influence is dictated by Israel's situation as a garrison state, struggling for its physical survival for the last two decades in a fiercely hostile environment; it is due as well

to Ben Gurion's legacy of dominating defense and the army. Now, it may be tempting to advance the argument a step further and contend that at times, especially during General Dayan's tenure as Chief of Staff, Zahal's elite has attempted to dominate Israel's foreign and defense policies. But the real truth of the matter lies in precisely the opposite direction: Ben Gurion, as Defense Minister, chose his chief aides from among those he could count on as devotees of his own conception of Israel's defense posture. He especially chose those he could trust to operationalize his security concepts successfully. Also this very Defense Minister did not hesitate to "retire" before their time some of Israel's most capable senior officers, including three chiefs of staff—Yadin, Makleff, and Laskov—when they sought greater independence for the military in security matters.

General Dayan certainly proved to be one of Israel's most loyal officers—which is to say, most dedicated to his civilian chief. And now, surely no one intimately acquainted with the policies of Zahal will propose that General Rabin or his successor would remain long in his position if he manifested any serious opposition to Dayan in his new civilian role as Defense Minister. To argue that Dayan represents the so-called "military clique" is no more true than to claim that Ben Gurion or Eshkol—or Eisenhower, as President of the United States—represents the same; the "hard line" of Ben Gurion and Dayan does not reflect the will of any behind-the-scenes defense establishment, but rather the realities of Israel's predicament as a garrison state, as well as the sentiment of the Israeli electorate. An awareness of these distinctions, coupled with all the varied evidence we have brought forward in the course of this article, leaves no grounds for the argument that Zahal's elite seeks domination of the government or that the army dictates the political, economic, and social destiny of Israel, as is the case in numerous new countries. For Zahal to be able to distribute political offices and welfare, it would have to have achieved the following: the formulation and promotion of an alternative to the national ideology; domination over economic policies; control of the process of modernization; demonstration of its legitimacy through some type of an autonomous political organization.

Typically, in new nations, the army moves to power because it has lost its confidence in the "corrupt politicians." That is, of course, conspicuously not the case in Israel, where Zahal's high command and officer corps are loyal to civilian authorities. We know of no instance in which Zahal's elite has demonstrated lack of confidence in the Israeli political system, although as bureaucrats and citizens, Zahal officers may doubt the political vision of some of Israel's civilian leaders. The power of those who have control over Israel's army does not derive from that control, but rather from their dominant positions in the HOL and Mapai. Thus, despite Ben Gurion's extraordinary influence over Zahal, when he formed the splinter Rafi party in 1965 he lost control over defense and the army. Levi Eshkol, as incoming Defense

Minister, assumed full and *firm* control over Zahal, even though some officers' private opinions of his capabilities as Defense Minister were not high. General Dayan was appointed Defense Minister in the crisis of June 1967 not because he had control over Zahal but because of the wishes of Israel's electorate.

Any contest between military and civilian authorities thus has been resolved in favor of the civilian. In fact, conflict clearly has not been based on a civilian-military rivalry for political supremacy. The underlying factors in the rivalry have been a consequence of the asymmetry between voluntary and compulsory institutions, structures, practices, and procedures in Israel's political transformation. . . .

Formalization and bureaucratization have brought along changes in structure and activities of elites and in the formation of nonpolitical elites, a rare phenomenon in the pre-independence era. Zahal is such a group. The political consciousness of Zahal junior officers is rather low. The whole spectrum of ideological intensification and pressure has diminished and in some areas has been eliminated. We would venture the hypothesis that the political consciousness and ideological inclinations of Israel's junior officers (with the exception of those who come from the left-oriented kibbutzim) are much lower than those of civil servants, legislators, and students.

The political ambitions of the senior officers are also restricted. Only a few senior army officers have joined a political party (in fact, most of those who have joined were affiliated with a party before Zahal was established) or have become active political figures, manipulating their war exploits and their charismatic appeal. Among these few are Generals Dayan, Allon, and Carmel (the Minister of Transportation).

Zahal's elite veterans do play a key role in the industrial and bureaucratic complex in Israel. Many have become prominent in the Israeli civil service, especially in the foreign service, and have important positions in Israel's foreign aid system in Africa and Latin America. This "smooth" integration of the Zahal elite is crucial for civilian-military relations in Israel. On the whole, because of the diverse needs of the Israeli economic and bureaucratic structures, the absorptive capacity of the society has been adequate and the integration of Zahal veterans has been satisfactory.

Israel, in contrast to the other states in the Middle East—and, in fact, to most newly emergent countries—is not a praetorian state. . . .

Among the political conditions contributing to praetorianism are these:

1. An ineffective and army-sustained civic culture. In Israel, the civic culture has been long established, and the persistence of the civilian over the military has been successfully pursued both before and after independence. Civilian supremacy has not been challenged since 1948—despite twenty years of security and border tensions, constant military preparedness, and three major wars.

2. A low level of political institutionalization and a lack of sustained support for political structures.* Israel is one of the most politically complex and institutionally well-established of the developing or newly developed states, demonstrating a high level of political institutionalization and sustained support.

3. Weak and ineffective political parties. In Israel, highly cohesive stratified classes, groups, and political parties prevent the predominance of one political section. Mapai and the Histadrut are themselves confederations of interests, sections, political cleavages, and persons.

4. A lack of common purpose and of ideological consolidation. In Israel, practically no gap exists between the ideology of Zahal and that of the state or its major political forces. The universality and identity of values between civilian and military sectors make a common effort inevitable. The army's role-expansion is no more threatening to civilian supremacy over politics than is that of the Histadrut or settlement systems. This does not mean absence of constraints, but, since the formation of the Yishuv, the history of Israel has involved role-expansion—the accumulation of many functions to establish an independent Jewish state. Of course, role-expansion also means that each group naturally will take political advantage of its power, position, and influence.

5. A lack or decline of professionalism because political considerations win out over those of internal organi-

*See Samuel P. Huntington, "Political Development and Political Decay," *World Politics*, XVII (April 1965), 394.

zation and career concerns. In Israel, professionalism and depoliticization have been on the rise. Depoliticization does not, of course, mean that the army elite has no political influence or that the army could not serve as an avenue for attaining political leadership, but only that the army's functions are not to be determined by the internal and parochial politics of labor or any other political organization. The officer corps could not become an ally of one political faction or another, as occurred in the Egyptian army before 1952. . . . The policy of depoliticization restrains the Israeli army and its officer corps from becoming a vehicle for political power.

The maturity of Israeli political structures, especially the highly complex and institutionalized political parties, the kibbutzim, and the Histadrut, would present a formidable challenge to the army if it were to choose to play independent politics. The identification of the most powerful and popular party, Mapai, and the kibbutz movement with the state leaves no room for army officers' maneuvers of the type that can occur in praetorian states. The army could not claim that the politicians had "betrayed" the nation. No civilian politicians, either as individuals or as organized groups, have meddled in the politics of the army since the dissolution of the Palmach and the NMO in 1948–1949. If some former military men, such as Generals Dayan and Allon, play a key role in Israeli politics today, it is only because they have resigned from the army and

sought power through civilian political parties. The reputations they gained in the army may have enhanced the political chances of these prominent army commanders, but did not guarantee their political success. An attempt on their part to influence politics while in uniform would have been crushed with little effort. In fact, if army officers desire to become successful in politics they *must* channel these ambitions through civilian political procedures. . . . On the whole, the social isolation (not to be confused with a societal isolation) of today's professional officers—their tendency to keep to themselves and their apolitical attitude—has been greater than that found among the Haganah-Palmach and 1948–1950 Zahal officer corps. In fact, this type of corporate and professional separation has become the mark of the professional soldier. Because Zahal has been a people's army and a reserve organization, its barracks life is short, its officers are permanently integrated with society, and the chances of the officers' becoming ideologically or professionally independent of the society are meager. A long military career in Israel is unlikely because the officer corps is being continuously rotated by putting an age limit on service in the army.

Under present conditions in Israel, a highly professionalized army dependent on a reserve system, with an unusually rapid turnover of officers and men, acts by virtue of its formal status and is harnessed to civilian control, as are the armies of the United States and Western Europe.

The chances for military coups, therefore, are nonexistent; the chances for political support for the army from the powerful political parties and the effective kibbutz and Histadrut systems are nil. The officer corps as a professional group is removed from politics. Officers are prohibited from actively participating in politics and so far have shown little interest in politics after retirement. This again does not prevent army elite veterans from actively pressing for and seeking managerial, economic, and administrative positions. Neither the size of the Israeli army nor the enormous defense budget. . . . dictates the political and attitudinal behavior of the Israeli army and its high command. Size and budget of armies are determining factors in praetorian states. In nonpraetorian states, the size of the army and the defense budget affects the economic structure, which in turn may bring about structural changes in society and politics but will not lift the army into the most prominent position as the political ruling group, as is the case in praetorian states. Nor does Israel fit the thesis that in a garrison state the army is prone to forgo the principle of professionalism or political nonintervention, as was the case with the Prussian army from Bismarck to Hitler. The values and the ideology of Zahal stem from the permanent Arab threat, and Zahal is committed to the nationalism espoused by most Israelis. The army elite is differentiated from the social structure in a manner not unlike that of other elites; it is not a politically privileged group.

Thus, the absorptive capacity of the economy, the rapid turnover of officers, the successful integration of Zahal veterans, the army's dependence upon the reserve system, the identity of military and national political goals, and Zahal's professionalism preclude the army's active intervention in politics. In addition, the institutionalized legitimacy of independent civilian political structures furnishes an effective guarantee of civilian control. However, the military in Israel—as a pressure group similar to those in other nonpraetorian states in which the civilian authority is formally and informally supreme—will continue to challenge the civilian, especially in the realm of defense and foreign affairs.